LIBERATION SUMMER

THE MOMENT THAT CHANGED THE WOMEN'S MOVEMENT AND THE FUTURE OF AMERICAN POLITICS

MICKI McELYA

AVID READER PRESS

NEW YORK AMSTERDAM/ANTWERP LONDON
TORONTO SYDNEY/MELBOURNE NEW DELHI

Avid Reader Press
An Imprint of Simon & Schuster, LLC
1230 Avenue of the Americas
New York, NY 10020

First Avid Reader Press hardcover edition July 2026

Interior design by Ruth Lee-Mui

Manufactured in the United States of America

1 3 5 7 9 10 8 6 4 2

Library of Congress Control Number: 2026930812

ISBN 978-1-9821-6676-2
ISBN 978-1-9821-6678-6 (ebook)

For Alexis,

a study in all that is beautiful

Every day in a woman's life is a walking Miss America Contest.

—Ros Baxandall (1968)

CONTENTS

SELECTED CAST OF CHARACTERS

Part of what makes this history so compelling are the complex journeys of self-discovery and political outlook of its actors. These also make categorizing them difficult; most individuals represented here could be included under multiple headings. For the sake of clarity, this list of characters locates the book's principal figures by their primary affiliations in the late 1960s; those with more than one significant affiliation at that time are repeated.

THE FEMINISTS

National Woman's Party (NWP)

Alice Paul
Marguerite Rawalt

National Organization for Women (NOW)

Delores Alexander
Ti-Grace Atkinson
Cindy Cisler
Anselma Dell'Olio
Muriel Fox
Betty Friedan
Florynce "Flo" Kennedy
Kate Millet
Marguerite Rawalt

Jeannette Rankin Brigade (JRB)

Donna Allen
Florynce "Flo" Kennedy
Coretta Scott King
Jeannette Rankin

WOMEN'S LIBERATION

New York Radical Women (NYRW)

(Chude) Pamela Allen
Kathie Amatniek (Sarachild)
Rosalyn "Ros" Baxandall
Cindy Cisler
Anselma Dell'Olio
Peggy Dobbins
Judith Duffett
Shulamith "Shulie" Firestone
Anne Forer
Bev Grant
Florynce "Flo" Kennedy
Anne Koedt
Carol Hanisch
Kate Millet
Robin Morgan
Florika Remetier
Alix Kates Shulman

Washington D.C. Women's Liberation

Charlotte Bunch
Marilyn Salzman Webb

West Side Group (Chicago)

Jo Freeman
Shulamith Firestone
Fran Rominski
Marilyn Salzman Webb

Boston Women's Revolutionary Liberation Front (BWRLF, renamed to Cell 16)

Dana Densmore
Roxanne Dunbar (Ortiz)

Gainesville Women's Liberation (Florida)

Judith "Judy" Brown
Carol Giardina
Beverly "Bev" Jones

THE BLACK FREEDOM MOVEMENT

NAACP

Daisy Bates
Gloster Current
Edgar Harris
Henry Moon
Phillip H. Savage
Roy Wilkins

Southern Christian Leadership Conference (SCLC)

Ralph Abernathy
Coretta Scott King

Student Non-Violent Coordinating Committee (SNCC)

Julian Bond
Stokely Carmichael (Kwame Toure)
Casey Cason (Hayden)
James Chaney
Andrew Goodman
Mary King
John Lewis
Diane Nash
Michael Schwerner
Ruby Doris Smith Robinson

Black Power

Stokely Carmichael (Kwame Toure)
Florynce "Flo" Kennedy
Ruby Doris Smith Robinson

THE NEW LEFT

National Mobilization Committee to End the War in Vietnam (MOBE)

David "Dave" Dellinger

Students for a Democratic Society (SDS)

Casey Cason (Hayden)
Tom Hayden
Marilyn Salzman Webb
Cathy Wilkerson

Youth International Party (Yippies)

Abbie Hoffman
Paul Krassner
Robin Morgan
Jerry Rubin

THE PAGEANTS

Miss America Pageant Organization

Elizabeth B. Alton
Irene Bryant
Albert "Al" Marks Jr.
Bess Myerson
Bert Parks
Adrian Phillips
Lenora Slaughter

Miss America Winners and Finalists

Norma Smallwood, Miss America 1926
Bess Myerson, Miss America 1945
Yun Tau Chee, Miss Hawai'i 1948
Erma Vasquez, Miss Puerto Rico 1948
BeBé Shopp, Miss America 1948
Yolande Betbeze, Miss America 1951

Anita Bryant, Miss Oklahoma 1958
Betty Buckley, Miss Fort Worth 1966
Deborah Bryant, Miss America 1966
Debra "Debbie" Dene Barnes, Miss America 1968
Judith "Judi" Ford, Miss America 1969
Cheryl Browne, Miss Iowa 1970
Terry Anne Meeuwsen, Miss America 1973
Vanessa Williams, Miss America 1984
Suzette Charles, Miss America 1984
Gretchen Carlson, Miss America 1989

Miss Black America Pageant Organization

J. Morris Anderson
Phillip H. Savage

Miss Black America Winners and Finalists

Theresa Claytor, Miss NAACP, Washington D.C. 1968
Vivian Whitted, Miss Harlem 1968
Saundra Williams, Miss Black America 1968
Gloria O. Smith, Miss Black America 1969
Stephanie Clark, Miss Black America 1970
Oprah Winfrey, Miss Black Tennessee 1971
Claire Ford, Miss Black America 1977

Native American Pageant Queens

Jesse Jim, Princess America II, 1926
Luzenia Ann "Lucy" Yellowmule, Sheridan WYO Rodeo Queen, 1951
Thomasine Hill, Miss Indian America 1968

ACTIVIST CONSERVATIVE WOMEN

Mary Brooks
Anita Bryant
Gretchen Carlson
Terry Anne Meeuwsen
Phyllis Schlafly

THE JOURNALISTS

Delores Alexander
Marylin Bender
Gretchen Carlson
Steve Conn
Charlotte Curtis
Clifton Daniel
Betty Friedan
Phyllis George
Judy Klemesrud
Bill Price
Nan Robertson
Gloria Steinem
Lindsy Van Gelder

PROLOGUE

BOARDWALK REVOLUTIONS

SEPTEMBER 7, 1968

Perched atop the backseat of a moving convertible, Saundra Williams focused on looking graceful and keeping the wrinkles out of her evening gown as the motorcade made a slow cruise along the Atlantic City boardwalk. Four other women sat across the top of the backseat alongside her, their dresses tucked neatly between them. Williams had made her white gown herself, hand-sewing hundreds of individual white paillettes across the bodice and over the shoulder straps. The large sequins fluttered in the breeze. Tonight, they would sparkle under the stage lights. The effect would be subtle and elegant, but right now she was roasting under the midday sun.

Another Pageant Week in Atlantic City was nearing its spectacular close. The small resort community had been packed with pageant fans for days, all of them eager to see contestants posing swimsuited for photographers, waving in evening gowns from parade floats on the boardwalk, or simply out at local spots in carefully chosen ensembles of the latest fashions. No contestant would be caught dead in public looking anything less than immaculate—a judge or pageant official could always be near, watching and wondering, *Will she be the next Miss America?*

But this afternoon, celebrants and the curious had gathered on either side of the boardwalk from the corner of Iowa Avenue, down past the Million Dollar Pier to get a look at the finalists, including Williams, for another contest in town: the Miss Black America Pageant. More people joined the crowd as motorcycle police carved out a corridor for the short line of convertibles, observers hemming in behind the last car. The spectators were close enough that Williams could have reached out and touched them if she hadn't been seated in the middle of the row of women in her car. She could hear scattered cheers and applause amid the motorcycles' sirens and the drumming of the bongo players wearing African textiles, who marched with the motorcade.

It was going to be a long day. The Miss Black America finals weren't set to begin until midnight, after Miss America—the white one—was crowned by a panel of white judges in front of more than ten thousand live audience members in Convention Hall and millions of viewers at home. That night, the next Miss America would bawl her eyes out, having burst into tears when the first runner up was named, signaling her victory, and thousands of white people in the audience would applaud. Then, a very tan white man would sing, "There she is, Miss America! There she is, your ideal." *Not my ideal, Bert Parks,* Williams thought, waving to the crowd on the boardwalk. Once Miss White America was done, all the reporters in town would be free to cover them just a few blocks away, at the Ritz-Carlton. Then the Miss Black America Pageant would show the country that Black women were beautiful and talented, too.

At the semifinals the night before, Williams had performed her own poem, "Awareness," as spoken word set to music. The poem was about a little girl ashamed of her hair, her lips, and her dark skin, convinced that she is ugly and always will be. In the course of the poem, she learns that she is beautiful; by the end, she is proud to say, "I Am Black!"

It was a message Williams had needed to learn herself. She had stopped straightening her own hair a few months earlier. She hadn't been trying to imitate white women before—not consciously anyway; like everyone else she knew, Saundra had grown up understanding the difference between "good hair" and "bad hair." Straight and smooth meant pretty and presentable, and could make a real difference in a Black woman's life. Now her short Afro said: *I refuse to imitate white women. I am Black, and I am beautiful.*

The procession of convertibles creeped down the center of the boardwalk toward Convention Hall, the massive Beaux Arts building where Miss America would be crowned. Peering around the women beside her, Williams could see the promised women's liberation demonstration—the day's other counter-event to the Miss America Pageant—just getting underway. The protesters were penned in by a colonnade facing the beach and police barricades along the wide expanse of boardwalk. They marched and sang, hoisting hand-lettered signs like: "ALL Women are Beautiful," "Can Make-Up Cover the Wounds of Our Oppression?," and "Women Not Things." Onlookers were beginning to press against the wooden barriers set up to divide them from the protesters and the protesters from the building's entrance. City police were stationed around the area, billy clubs and sidearms prominent at their hips. Tensions mounted, reminiscent of the moments before mayhem erupted outside the Democratic National Convention in Chicago just a week before.

Nothing about the women's liberation action, from the white women who populated it to their songs and slogans, called to Saundra. The distance between it and her own experience and political concerns was far wider than the expanse of boardwalk that separated them. "They're expressing freedom, I guess," Williams would tell a reporter. "To each his own."

When the motorcade turned off the boardwalk and onto Kentucky Avenue, the heart of Atlantic City's Black business and entertainment district, Williams could see the crowd change from predominantly white to almost entirely Black. She and the other contestants continued to wave as they made their way past the famed Club Harlem and headed toward the city's all-Black Northside neighborhoods. *This is who I'm doing this for,* Williams thought.

The Miss Black America motorcade had long since passed the women's liberation demonstration when three women appeared at the police barricades with their own signs reading, "Miss America is Still Our Ideal" and "There's Only One Thing Wrong with Miss America. She's Beautiful." In town from Wisconsin to attend the pageant finals, the women had come to the protest to defend Miss America and the national ideals and patriotism they believed she embodied, and to defend women like themselves from feminist radicals. One member of the threesome was a recent Miss Green Bay; she displayed a prominent "Nixon for President" badge along with her sign. Performing exactly the kind of feminine poise and refinement they thought the protesters were attacking—and sorely lacking—the women stood out in a crowd that had grown bigger, louder, and seemed to vibrate with hostility, as some jeered the women's liberationists, hurling insults at them and mugging for others who laughed and egged them on. "You're too ugly to be in the Miss America Pageant," and several variations on that theme rang across the boardwalk. "Go back to Russia, you ugly, lezzie, commie whores!"

INTRODUCTION

Labor Day 1968 was in the rearview mirror, but summer was never really over until the country crowned a new Miss America. That year, the pageant brought not one, but three groups of protesting women to the Atlantic City boardwalk on that first Saturday in September. Each was driven there by ambition, political fervor, and activism that drew on idealized notions of female beauty and competing visions of the world they wished to live in—and that they had come to Atlantic City to build. The revolutionary upheavals, violence, partisan contests, and activist struggles of the summer of 1968 were already being referenced in a shorthand of key locations of their events: Paris, Prague, Chicago. The bloody confrontations in Chicago had not only torn a gaping wound in the Democratic Party coalition but it had also rocked the very foundations of American politics and national self-conception. Now, a week later, another city was poised to join that list; Atlantic City would show the country where it was headed and the diverse groups of women who were going to take it there.

But Atlantic City did not take a place on that list of locations-turned-icons of those radical transformations of 1968. Instead, the fundamental political changes set into motion there have been reduced to a self-explanatory notch in every timeline or activist chronology of 1968, pinned to the history with a burnt bra. That pin marks—incorrectly—the start of the women's liberation movement in the United States as part of feminism's second wave. Then the general narrative moves on (or returns to the main stage, as it were) to the prosecutions of the radical men of the Chicago 8 who were charged with causing the violent disruptions at the Democratic Party convention.

• • •

So much has been lost through the dramatic narrowing of the lens on this history, not least of which is the development of a new politics of beauty that coalesced around the Miss America Pageant and its critics in 1968, and has threaded through American political culture ever since. This book tells the story of this powerful beauty politics and of the women who created it.

Readers will be well familiar with some of the prominent characters here, although in the pages that follow they may encounter these women in a new way. Women like Betty Friedan, who was born about six months after ratification of the 19th Amendment granted the vote to women and six months before the first Miss America pageant was held in Atlantic City. Hers was the first generation of Americans born into this new version of women's citizenship and its limitations, which Friedan would go on to name as the author of *The Feminine Mystique* and would seek to change as the founding president of the National Organization for Women (NOW).

Friedan would spend many of those years going head-to-head with civil rights attorney and activist Florynce "Flo" Kennedy, who pushed NOW to be more expansive and intersectional in its conceptualizations of what constituted women's issues. At the same time, Kennedy worked to amplify the voices of Black women and feminism in the agendas of the Black Power movement and helped forge a new Black feminist organizing path when all those agendas were found wanting.

Kennedy created a vast network of activists, organizations, and allies through her relational politics that put her at the center of many key events in the radical 1960s and 1970s, including the women's liberation protest of the Miss America Pageant in 1968. It would also see her partnered on feminist speaking tours with Gloria Steinem, whose role in this book is more limited than readers might anticipate. Steinem enters the story later, not as an activist at first but, rather, as a journalist with a reputation for being as beautiful as she is smart and talented.

Events at the 1968 Miss America Pageant put the former Miss America finalist and future evangelical anti-gay crusader Anita Bryant on a collision course with the conservative Republican activist Phyllis Schlafly. In the 1970s, Schlafly became instrumental in the defeat of the Equal Rights Amendment through her promotion of the "Power of the Positive Woman" as feminism's alternative, a concept that overlapped with the popular ethos of the Miss America organization.

Other figures in this book will be new to many readers, perhaps surprisingly so, like Carol Hanisch, the women's liberation activist who came up with the idea to protest Miss America, along with popularizing the phrase, "The personal is political." Or Miss America 1951, Yolande Betbeze, whose refusal to make appearances wearing only a swimsuit would be the first of many acts of resistance from the former Miss Alabama, who later protested in support of the sit-ins and lent her voice to women's liberation. And then there is the incomparable Charlotte Curtis, society reporter and editor of Women's News for the *New York Times*, who would go on in 1974 to be the first woman ever to appear on the masthead of "the paper of record."

These are just some of the women whose stories drive the action of this history—a moment that shaped American politics, feminism, and the making of contemporary life; a moment driven by women. Some of these women were exceptional, others deeply ordinary, but all confronted a world that measured their worth, ability, and authority by their looks.

As an ideal, as a set of practices, and as daily labors, *beauty* could be a public platform, a safe harbor, a prison, or a seemingly impossible achievement, but it was fundamentally always about power. Common to all involved in the story of the 1968 Miss America Pageant and its legacies was an investment in claiming the power to define beauty—and to harness its liberating possibilities.

PART I

FINDING LIBERATION

1

NEW FEMINIST EYES

JUNE 4–6, 1968

Another man was explaining the revolution to Roxanne Dunbar. Sitting in a tile-covered eighteenth-century palace turned café at the heart of Mexico City's Centro Histórico, she tried to focus on the centuries of history that surrounded her. Pancho Villa and the Zapatistas had once occupied the palace during the Mexican Revolution; now, on an afternoon in early June 1968, they gazed at her from old photos lining the café's walls. *It was all so beautiful and inspiring,* she thought. She could not say the same for the conversation.

Nearly two months into her stay in Mexico, Dunbar was feeling restless. She was supposed to have been in Cuba by now. That, at least, had been the plan when she and her boyfriend, Jean-Louis, left Berkeley, California, to stay with his family in Mexico while making the necessary travel arrangements. Like many young radicals in America, they wanted to help build a truly socialist society on the island so that one day, they would know how to do the same in the United States. The couple were both graduate students, she in history and he in French, but Dunbar mainly thought of herself as an activist, while Louis, as she called him, had grown more enmeshed in the counterculture. The difference in perspective—making a revolution versus rejecting mainstream society in pursuit of new ways of being and expression—had troubled their already stormy relationship. While Jean-Louis had grown up in Mexico, he and his family were French; nationals from both countries were free to travel to Cuba uninhibited. As an American, Dunbar's trip to the communist nation had been more difficult to arrange. Cuba had been under embargo since 1962 and was effectively closed to U.S. citizens. Passage through Mexico was the best option, but it wasn't an easy or fast one. Hoping to speed things along with a new passport, Dunbar had married Jean-Louis in Mexico City, a decision she soon regretted as she watched him slide so easily into the comforts and racial hierarchies of his family's wealth and status in Mexico. *So much for radicalism,* she thought. When he had announced a new plan to move to France, Dunbar had been more angry than surprised. He was free to go, she had said, but she was moving to Cuba—as soon as her papers came through.

Now, Jean-Louis sat beside her in the café, arm draped around her shoulders in a maddening if mundane assertion of possession. The man across from them continued talking, drumming a rolled-up newspaper against the palm of his hand for emphasis. It was only when he paused to unfurl the paper and jab at an article to prove some point that she saw it: "Super Woman-Power Advocate Shoots Andy Warhol."

She grabbed the paper and devoured the slim facts of the story. The artist and another man had been shot the day before in New York City, and the woman who shot them, Valerie Solanas, had surrendered to police a few hours later. Both men had survived, but Warhol remained in critical condition. Solanas, according to the report, was the author of a manifesto for a group called the Society for Cutting Up Men, or SCUM.

Super Woman-Power Advocate.

Woman Power.

Dunbar gripped the paper, oblivious to the world around her and hungry for more information. *Could it be true that women were finally rising up?*

What if she stuck to her plan of going to Cuba to learn from their revolution and missed her own at home?

Solanas had changed everything; Roxanne Dunbar would not be going to Cuba after all.

Two thousand miles away, Andy Warhol's condition at a Manhattan hospital was still critical when Robert F. Kennedy was shot in Los Angeles at the Ambassador Hotel, shortly after winning the California Democratic presidential primary. The next morning, June 6, Bobby Kennedy was declared dead.

Upon hearing the news, Bev Grant, an activist, musician, and photographer, walked out of her apartment with her camera and into the early summer air on New York City's Lower East Side. She set out on a familiar path uptown, past favorite diners and university buildings along NYU's creeping eastern border. A sickening feeling of déjà vu had fallen over Grant—she had been twenty-one when the country was plunged into horrified mourning over the death of Robert Kennedy's brother five years earlier; more recently, a woman had interrupted an activist meeting she'd been attending with the news that Dr. Martin Luther King Jr. had been murdered in Memphis. As she weaved her way through familiar streets, Grant took in her adopted city as it took in the news of Kennedy's death. Everyone looked as stunned as she felt. She headed toward Union Square and the small stretch of Broadway between 14th and 17th Streets that had become so much a part of her daily routine. There, she hopped on an uptown subway to 42nd Street and Times Square, where she found the headline zipper at One Times Square had not been updated: "KENNEDY STILL UNCONSCIOUS" ran in all-capital letters around the low belly of the building.

Originally from Oregon, Grant had married young and moved to New York so her husband could pursue his career as a jazz musician. The couple divorced not long after, but as one relationship ended, another blossomed. New York City was Grant's new love, encouraging her evolution as an artist and activist. In 1964, she read Simone de Beauvoir's *The Second Sex*, an experience that stuck with her less for the text and more for the fact her boyfriend at the time had grabbed the book and thrown it out when she tried to discuss it with him. Three years later, while attending a Students for a Democratic Society (SDS) meeting at Princeton University in New Jersey, she saw a notice for a lunchtime workshop for women organized by Shulamith Firestone and Pam Allen. "It was a life-changing experience for me," Grant explained later. "I began to understand that my life was an example of a social problem shared by women, something we were capable of changing."

Bev Grant wasn't the only woman to leave that workshop transformed and eager to make change. Several of the women in attendance, including Grant, formed the original core of New York's first women's liberation group that would in 1967 become New York Radical Women (NYRW). It had been during one of the group's weekly Thursday meetings that she and the others first learned of King's assassination. Now, two months later, another Thursday brought yet another assassination, and the women would be meeting that night.

Temperatures in the city climbed as that sad, strange Thursday wore on, making it feel more like August than early June. New York was enveloped in a heat wave thanks to Hurricane Abby, which was making a slow churn up the coast. The first officially dangerous storm of the season had a woman's name, as always, taken from the alphabetical list of all-female-coded names published annually by the National Hurricane Center. Abby would be followed by Brenda and Candy.

It was a blessing that attendance was smaller than usual for a NYRW meeting. The roughly twenty women didn't have to sit shoulder to hot, clammy shoulder on the low-slung couch, in the limited chairs, on tops of desks, or on the black-and-white checkerboard linoleum floor. It also meant that late arrivals weren't stuck in the alcove near the door, which always made them feel a little out of the action and more like spectators. The space belonged to Carol Hanisch's employer, the Southern Conference Educational Fund (SCEF), a civil rights organization run by married activist legends Anne and Carl Braden, in Kentucky. For the last two years, she'd managed their New York office; for the last several months, the Bradens had allowed Hanisch to use the space after hours for women's liberation meetings.

SCEF, as the women called it (pronounced "Skeff"), was on the fourth floor of a nineteenth-century building on Broadway, at the corner of 11th Street. Shadowed by the Gothic Revival grandeur of Grace Church, across the street, it had been designed as a hotel by the same architect to complement the historic religious institution. The St. Denis Hotel became host to the likes of Mark Twain, Sarah Bernhardt, and Ulysses S. Grant; in 1877, Alexander Graham Bell chose it for the first public demonstration in New York of his latest invention, the telephone. After changing hands in the early twentieth century and failing under the new owners, it had been stripped of its ornamentation and eventually converted to an unremarkable six-story office building.

With its assortment of mismatched furniture and propped-up bulletin boards covered in schedules and flyers, room 412 appeared the epitome of an activist organization office put together on the cheap, just like many others on the fourth floor and scattered throughout the building. Wide metal bookshelves designed to be sturdy and useful rather than decorative were pushed up against one wall, housing a hodgepodge of messy stacks of paper, coffee mugs, boxes of printed materials, and a bottle of dish soap, while several metal filing cabinets lined another wall. The space wasn't large, but it was a much better option than rotating among the organizers' cramped tenement apartments as word spread and more women showed up each week.

Hanisch wasn't surprised by the low turnout for the meeting that night. Rosalyn Baxandall was on Cape Cod with her husband and young toddler; Shulamith Firestone and "the Annes" (Anne Forer and Anne Koedt) were all in France. Kathie Amatniek*—probably the person Hanisch missed the most—was in San Francisco trying to make it work with her boyfriend while bringing NYRW's methods of consciousness raising (CR) to the two women's liberation groups she'd found out there. Hanisch would be leaving soon herself to join other regional SCEF representatives for several weeks of work with the Bradens in Louisville, Kentucky.

Like Amatniek, Hanisch believed CR was the key to making women's liberation a mass movement—that bringing women together to share individual experiences of the same situations would allow them to see that the problems and limitations they faced were common ones, not just isolated personal issues or cases of maladjustment. The sessions bonded the women while making them aware of their collective structural oppression—raising their consciousness—and thus creating the basis for organizing and change. Amatniek had always been the more assertive of the pair. If she had been there that night, rather than in San Francisco with her boyfriend, Ted, they might be starting the CR session Hanisch had wanted.

Instead, a woman lugged in a 16-mm film projector and the group prepared to watch an avant-garde film Hanisch had never heard of. Given the office's spare furnishings and minimal decoration, the setup was easy. When someone hit the lights, the projector's beam caught the cigarette smoke that hung thickly in the still, hot air. Its mechanical whir blended with the sounds of Broadway's traffic coming through the open windows from four stories below.

* In the summer of 1968, Kathie Amatniek had not yet changed her name to Kathie Sarachild.

Dracula music—Bach's Toccata and Fugue in D minor, for organ—sliced through the noise as the black-and-white film began. It cut from jumpy shots of a wooded landscape to a woman's silhouetted head and shoulders, as thin swirls of paint came together to make the film's title: *Schmeerguntz.*

The ominous, if somewhat ridiculous, music continued over a new image of what appeared to be flesh, soon revealed to be an extreme close-up of an enormously pregnant stomach, skin straining, belly button popped out. A small figure cut from a magazine moved around the stomach like a little astronaut in jittery orbit. Then the stomach became the moon and more little astronauts skittered into and then out of the scene.

Hanisch had been irritated already, and nothing about this film was changing her mood. *What is the point of this,* she thought, as the jumpy cuts and collaged images continued—magazine advertisements and fashion shoots featuring pretty young white women; makeup, shampoos, trendy clothes, toothy smiles, and pouting lips interspersed with scenes of the pregnant woman in various rooms of a cluttered house. In one, she soaked in a shallow tub, soap suds bobbing around her painfully large belly, breasts, and knees that poked high above the waterline; in another, she rested on an unmade bed; she folded laundry; she shaved her armpit; she considered a sink full of dirty dishes; she vomited into an already filthy-looking toilet basin; she got dressed while awkwardly negotiating her own body. At one point, Bach's organ piece was replaced by a series of audio clips of disembodied male voices narrating snippets of romantic scenes, including the moment in the film *Sleeping Beauty* when the princess is finally awakened by the prince's kiss. Jangling calliope music played over a manipulated photo of a group of nineteenth-century European theology students, all men, ice skating and frolicking like boys; next appeared a Clorox advertisement featuring a group of women of various ages in smocks and maid's uniforms.

Hanisch stewed as the vomit swirling around a flushed toilet dissipated into women gliding around a roller rink as a man sang a song about the USA and apple pie. Then, the scene turned to a long shot of a beauty queen's crown and scepter resting on a plush, tufted pillow. The pageant theme song continued, and the film cut back to the roller derby. Women in skates and knee pads hit and jostled for supremacy while the crowd cheered and male referees jumped in to break it up. The scene shifted again to historic beauty pageant footage before cutting to recent pageant telecast footage. Miss Illinois and Miss Georgia introduced themselves.

And then it happened.

Hanisch watched as beauty contestants paraded across a stage in swimsuits, heels, and sashes. With smiles plastered across their faces and hair teased and sprayed into immobility, the women presented themselves for judgment by those on the scene and to viewers at home. The shot included the edge of the television screen being filmed—a reminder of the cameras, ever-expectant audiences, and the film viewer's own spectatorship.*

The images transported Hanisch back to the living room of her childhood home in Havelock, Iowa, where her family had gathered every year to watch the Miss America Pageant. She thought about that scene replicated in the homes of her neighbors and schoolmates, how she and her friends had celebrated each new Miss Iowa, identified with them, and fantasized about one day being crowned Miss America.

Now, seeing the pageant with what she called her "new feminist eyes," Hanisch was rocked by the monstrous, oppressive spectacle of it all. *Oh my God,* she thought, staring at the women. There was no glamour here, nothing to celebrate— just fake smiles, empty accolades, and coercive beauty standards.

Later that night, Hanisch moved around the SCEF office performing her Thursday night ritual search for forgotten cups turned makeshift ashtrays; if New York women's liberation had a signature scent, it was the stale smell of cigarettes and old coffee. She returned chairs to their desks, swept the floor, and closed the windows, all the while still thinking about the pageant. She hadn't said anything to the others, but now that she had seen Miss America with new eyes, Carol Hanisch couldn't let it go; or, Miss America wouldn't let go of her.

* Everyone from the filmmakers and members of NYRW to later historians has misidentified these clips as depicting the 1965 Miss America Pageant. They appear to come from its competitor, the Miss USA Pageant, which was nationally televised from California for the first time that year. Notably, a Black contestant appears briefly in the swimsuit competition; no Black finalist would walk the Miss America stage until 1970.

2

WOMEN'S NEWS

JUNE 8, 1968

Charlotte Curtis raced through Washington, D.C.'s Union Station, trying to get to a pay phone before they were all taken. Her *New York Times* colleague, Russell Baker, kept pace beside her—aided, no doubt, by the fact that he was wearing neither heels nor a funeral dress. It had been a long day. After covering Robert F. Kennedy's funeral mass at New York's St. Patrick's Cathedral earlier that day, she had joined her fellow reporters (as well as Kennedy's family, friends, and a cohort of select politicians and celebrities) on a twenty-one-car funeral train carrying the senator's body to Arlington National Cemetery, where he would soon rest alongside his late brother. Now, she had a story to file.

The somber journey had been set to last about four hours, but the train's creep along tracks and station platforms lined with well over a million mourners and curious onlookers had nearly doubled the time frame; it was after nine o'clock at night when the train finally arrived in Washington. Every reporter aboard had spent the evening scribbling their stories in jostling notepads, each becoming increasingly agitated as the threat loomed of missing deadlines to file for the next morning's papers. When the doors to the train opened, the crowd all but tumbled out, desperate to locate a way to call their newsrooms.

As Curtis wove her way wildly through the station, dodging civilians and the U.S. Marine Band, which was playing a stirring rendition of the "Battle

Hymn of the Republic," she heard a man's voice call her name. Looking around, she saw that it belonged to Steve Conn, a young reporter who'd recently left the *Times* to work for the late candidate's communications team. Curtis had been his editor and mentor at the paper. A long letter from Conn, written on Kennedy's Senate stationery, had been waiting for her a few days earlier. Conn seemed unhappy in his new role, but he had characteristically made a joke of it: "Use of this stationery for commercial, personal or any other reason is not to be construed as an endorsement of the product advertised in any way, shape or form." Now, he was standing in front of her, newly unemployed.

"Where's the goddamn telephone?" she yelled over to him.

Conn grabbed her hand and pulled. "Come with me!"

Running ahead, he clapped his hand onto a booth's handle at the exact moment another man grabbed for it. Charlotte jogged up to find them glaring at one another, refusing to let go. She laughed, the sound deep and throaty.

"Steve, this is Bill McWhirter from *Time-Life*. He's an old friend." Curtis smiled at the men. She and McWhirter had shared a brief, if lopsided, flirtation that McWhirter had tried to keep going during his stint at the magazine's Saigon Bureau in 1966. As he and Conn held their positions, Curtis explained to the men that both had claimed the same phone for the same woman. Then she brushed past them, entering the booth and closing the door firmly behind her to call the *Times*.

From the moment she had been offered the position of reporter at the *New York Times* in 1961, Charlotte Curtis had been told in no uncertain terms that she would not be covering politics or any other subjects beyond the purview of "women's news." Those beats, everyone knew, were the men's games, but Curtis was undeterred. She didn't plan to wither in misery covering home furnishings and fashion when her recent assignments at the *Columbus Citizen-Journal* had included dispatches from the South Pacific and the Ohio campaign trails of John F. Kennedy and Richard Nixon. No, she would be in the action, no matter what it took.

Born in 1928 to a well-off family, Charlotte Curtis had come to her ambitions honestly. Her mother, Lucile Atcherson, was a suffrage activist in Ohio, and the first woman in U.S. history to sit for the Foreign Service exam—and pass it. In 1922, Atcherson was nominated by President Warren G. Harding for an overseas diplomatic appointment, the first woman to be presented for confirmation in such a role. When the Senate rejected the nomination on the grounds that it was inappropriate for an unmarried, twenty-eight-year-old woman to travel and represent the country abroad, she instead took a post at the State Department in Washington, D.C. This led to a flood of protests from across the country, largely from women's rights groups fresh off their 19th Amendment victory. As a result, the Senate Foreign Relations Committee was forced to reconsider the case and ultimately recommended acceptance. In 1923, she was sent to Bern, Switzerland, where she met Dr. George Morris Curtis, a medical research fellow from the University of Chicago. The couple married in January 1928, settled in Chicago where Curtis was a professor of surgery, and started a family; Charlotte was born that first year, and her sister Mary followed in 1930. When George got a faculty appointment in the medical school at Ohio State University, the Curtises resettled in the tony Columbus suburb of Bexley.

After attending the same private girls' school as her mother, Curtis matriculated to Vassar College in 1946. During the summer after her freshman year, on a lark she applied for a job at one of the local newspapers, then called the *Columbus Citizen*. The girl from the wealthy part of town, just home for the school break, seemed an odd fit—a fact her co-workers never let her forget that first summer, nicknaming her "Vassar"—but Curtis became hooked on reporting and the world of newsprint, and she never looked back. She returned to college that fall with plans to go back to the paper the following summer, and with a recommendation from the features editor that helped her get jobs during the school year as a stringer with *College Digest*, Tobe College Fashion Board, and *Mademoiselle*. Curtis's "performance rating was exceptionally commendable on women's features which varied greatly in subject matter," the editor wrote. "Her consistently attractive appearance, and the ease with which she contacts people, made her a valuable asset to this paper."

Like her mother before her, Curtis's talent and ambitions ran against what was—and was not—appropriate behavior and aspirations for a privileged, white, college-educated woman. She was an attractive, fashionable, clever young woman with all the right manners who was good with people; the most anyone in her position hoped for her was an interesting, if not intimidating, job that would be replaced swiftly by marriage and the roles of wife and mother. Rather than defy those expectations head on, Curtis worked with and through them, stretching their boundaries where possible but otherwise acknowledging and accommodating the limits before her. In her second summer at the *Citizen* in 1948, she took on everything she could, from fashion stories and covering for the section's editor while the woman was on vacation to reporting from the Ohio state Republican Convention alongside a political correspondent from *Life* magazine. She also, for a time, lived with the Ringling Brothers Circus to write what she described as "a story on the women of the big top." Thanks in part to Vassar's proximity to New York City, the *Citizen* hired Charlotte during the next academic year to cover one of the biggest stories of 1949: the start of the Smith Act trials, in which eleven leaders of the Communist Party of the United States were brought before a federal court for advocating the violent overthrow of the government, based only on the fact of their roles within the party.

During her senior year, Curtis and her boyfriend, Dwight "Butch" Fullerton Jr., a Yale student in pre-law from Circleville, Ohio, got engaged and then married right after their graduations in 1950. Much to Curtis's parents' delight, they made their home in Bexley. Fullerton began law school at Ohio State University, and in October, Curtis began a full-time position at the paper. To all appearances, they were the model of mid-century newlywed life for college-educated couples; she would use her education to support them while he earned his law degree, and once Fullerton's career was launched, Curtis would leave her job for full-time homemaking and motherhood.

Appearances, however, could be deceiving.

Charlotte Curtis embarked upon married adulthood and her career as the postwar baby boom was hitting its stride, and the United States was mobilizing in Korea for its first major military engagement of the Cold War. Traditional gender roles, idealized domesticity, and the primacy of family were taking center stage in U.S. policy and popular culture as keys to national character and security—and as unique spots of vulnerability for the country. The G.I. Bill and downstream effects of defense spending were facilitating the mass movement of mostly white Americans to suburban developments and technology-filled single-family homes, as well as to the dramatic expansion of access to college educations and professional degrees for non-elite men.

Overall employment numbers for single and married women continued to grow, however, confirming that the oft cited postwar retreat of white, middle-class women from the workforce was less about women's presence in waged labor generally and more about the loss of access for some of them to high-earning jobs that had been reserved for men before the war and were reclaimed when it was over. Access to the professions remained largely limited to men, but the pool of qualified male candidates with appropriate degrees and credentials was expanding significantly. By 1950, a majority of all employed female workers were secretaries, bookkeepers, cashiers, telephone operators, typists, or those performing other office tasks, which led to their definition as *women's* jobs—and in the case of clerical work, mostly to *white women's* jobs. Intensified occupational segregation by sex also intersected with ongoing racial segregation in the labor sector, supported by both law and custom. This was reflected in the data: in 1890, 92 percent of all employed Black women were in agriculture or service (domestic work, food service, custodial, and industrial cleaning); in 1930, that figure was still at 90 percent. The first significant change occurred after the war, but it remained slow: in 1970, the number of Black employed women still clustered in the two sectors was 70 percent.

Charlotte Curtis was far from alone in feeling trapped by marriage and the versions of gender and domesticity it required, yet even popular outlets for expressing one's desire for autonomy, personal satisfaction, and sexual freedom—and freedom from the responsibilities of family and home ownership—seemed limited to men. They could literally and imaginatively follow beatniks to downtown clubs or out "on the road," or subscribe to *Playboy* magazine, which had become a cultural mainstay after its debut in 1953. Hugh Hefner built a brand empire on pictures of nude women, clubs worked by scantily clad waitress "bunnies," and the heterosexual male fantasy of freewheeling, cosmopolitan bachelordom, filled with stylish urban apartments, abundant sex, perfectly mixed cocktails, and the latest in surround-sound stereo equipment.

While she struggled to carry on in her marriage, Curtis thrived at work. Her first beat at the *Citizen* was covering church news, and after just two months she was made the subject editor. But even if Curtis had been inclined to forget how a "proper woman" should act, reminders of constant scrutiny and judgment were never far away. Not long after the promotion, she received an anonymous postcard, most likely from a parishioner or church staff member: "Just because Emily Post says it is alright to smoke don't make it so. She or anyone who does is no Christian—you know it is a bad habit. Looks awful." Curtis kept the postcard and kept right on smoking, and the promotions kept coming. In early 1951, she was named Society Editor. Two years later, she took an enormous leap from the paths of propriety and divorced Butch Fullerton. "He assumed I'd be Mrs. Lawyer and do the canapes," she latter offered by way of explanation for the separation. "I wasn't deceiving him, that was my assumption, too, but I turned out to like newspapering more."

Once freed from her marriage, Curtis immediately began looking for other jobs; she did not intend to stay at the *Citizen* or in Ohio for long. It took seven years of searching before she got the chance to convince Elizabeth Howkins, Women's News Editor at the *New York Times* (at the time, the section was called "Food, Fashion, Family, Furnishings," or "the 4F's"), to hire her. There, she became a beloved, but feared, society reporter known for blending coverage of the

Charlotte Curtis, June 1965

nation's elite with piercing social and political insights and wry humor. She often described her work as a kind of "sociology," showing how the mighty wielded power by revealing how they lived, who they partied with, what they bought, and where they went. Along the way, Curtis also highlighted their vulnerabilities and inadequacies, often by simply allowing her subjects' own words to lead to the conclusions she wanted drawn. When Howkins retired four years later, in 1965, no one was surprised when Curtis was named her successor.

Equipped with a rare kind of power, Curtis seized the opportunity to stretch the limits of what could define "women's news." Since the 1890s, the women's pages had been a regular feature of mass-circulation newspapers. Aimed at building and sustaining large female readerships, women's news sections were designed to make their papers more attractive to advertisers who recognized women's enormous purchasing power as the primary shoppers, if not the breadwinners, of their households in an increasingly consumer-driven U.S. economy. The pages were filled with recipes, tips for mothers and housewives, and stories about fashion, home décor, and news of local society, schools, and volunteer organizations. Everything else in the paper, it was implied, was of little consequence or interest to women.

The sex segregation of American newspapers was also mirrored in their staffs. Unlike many large-circulation women's magazines at the time, such as *Ladies Home Journal*, women's news in the newspapers was mostly reported and edited by women, who found themselves marooned on an island of the 4F's. For decades at the *New York Times*, the section's staff was sequestered on the ninth floor of the building, far from the male-dominated news floors.

After World War II, a small number of women began to make the section to which they were inevitably first assigned a point of departure rather than their last stop. When Betsy Wade was hired by the *Times* in 1957, she became the paper's first ever female copyreader. To get ready for her new job, she cut her long hair short and went shopping for the most conservative professional wear she could find. How, she quipped later, does one ask a saleswoman in a department store for "a suit in which I can sit in the middle of an ocean of men and not be noticed?" Wade described her male colleagues at the city news copy desk on the third floor as falling into one of three categories:

> The first mumbled, just loud enough to be heard, "Damn, hell, nonsense, place is getting to be a bloody tea party, not like the old days." The second group was too kind. She could not struggle twenty seconds with a headline before someone would present her with his version. . . . The third [type of male colleague] just toiled away and ignored her.

Pulitzer Prize–winning journalist Nan Robertson wrote of her own journey at the *Times*, from starting in women's news in 1955 to the city desk downstairs, where she was working when Charlotte Curtis started at the paper. In 1963, Robertson was promoted to covering politics in the Washington Bureau. At the time, women were not allowed membership in the National Press Club, which was central to the job of political reporting in D.C. Any female reporter attending an event or press conference held at the club's building was allowed entrance only to the second-floor balcony, and they were not allowed to ask questions. Robertson described the comradery born of collective humiliation she shared with the other "girls in the balcony," noting that their experience was "a metaphor for what working women everywhere faced" in the 1960s. Indeed, women were not admitted as members of the National Press Club—and thus allowed on the main floor—until 1971.

This was the landscape of women's journalism that Charlotte Curtis wanted to change—and she had support from her mentor and friend, Clifton Daniel, who had himself recently ascended to the powerful role of *Times*'s Managing Editor. "If you could forget that the page has an FFFF masthead and could write any story you wanted to for a women's news page," Curtis queried her reporters in the summer of 1966, "what stories would you suggest?" By 1968, articles about women and the Vietnam War, law, politics, and feminism were peppered liberally among the section's usual fare. Some of these were written by Curtis herself, who never stopped reporting after her promotion to Women's News editor, and would write some of her most celebrated work while in the position.

Charlotte Curtis was not without detractors, and there were many who found it curious that the 4F's section and its editor should garner so much attention and authority. In *The Kingdom and the Power*, Gay Talese's best-selling exposé of the *Times*, he described her as a "five-foot fast-stepping Vassar alumna" sitting in editorial meetings wearing a Pucci dress, left leg tucked under her right, "letting a high-heeled shoe dangle from her tiny toes under the table." Talese reprinted portions of a letter from his colleague, David Halberstam, in which the 1964 Pulitzer Prize winner for reporting from Vietnam called Charlotte Curtis "one of the most powerful men on the paper, since Daniel values her opinion on everything and reads mostly her section." It was a gendered dig at them both, concerning her outsized power and questioning Clifton Daniel's masculinity for allowing it. Nevertheless, Halberstam concluded, you had to give it to Curtis, she was a "[b]right, tough little broad." Talese echoed Halberstam's comments elsewhere in the book. "Miss Curtis is rarely flattering to her subjects, many of them lack the wit to realize it—but what is more important about Miss Curtis's work is that Clifton Daniel likes to read it."

As Curtis made the transition from comrade in the 4F's trenches to boss, she could not ignore the structural inequities her reporters faced. Just months into her tenure as editor, she received a hastily typed, two-page letter from one of her reporters, Marylin Bender. Addressed to "Charlotte Chere," it was full of crossed-out phrases and words inserted by hand, and was signed with a frowny face surrounded by radiating jagged lines and the initials MB. Do not be alarmed by the "angry words leaping from the page," the letter opened. "It's just that neither of us has time right now for mid-afternoon, face to face rehashing of personal matters. I just want to go on record as being absolutely bugged about the money situation."

Compensation had always been an issue for women at the *Times*, and for Bender in particular—her pay was not commensurate with male colleagues' and had not kept pace with the salaries of newer hires, male or female, despite her record of performance and reliability. In recent months she had watched prima donnas and squeaky wheels get raises, only to have her own request denied. This time, though, was different for her, because the person denying the request was Curtis, who maintained that any pay increase would be based on future production.

Bender had expected a different and perhaps more understanding response: "Now comes a new order in which I told you I would do anything to support you—and I still mean this willingly and joyously," but "[i]n the last month, I have incurred about $75 in extra babysitting fees while I tried to do my share here." The whole thing, she concluded, was "damned unfair" and "I'm mad as hell."

Bender's assumption, to some extent, was that Curtis would understand her predicament because they were women of the same generation. But Curtis's life outside of work—to the extent that she had one—was very different from Bender's. She was divorced and had no children. She hosted potluck brunches on the weekends for a rotating group of friends and young reporters new to the city. She dated other journalists, stayed friendly with ex-boyfriends, and generally appeared not to have any relationships that competed with her career for time or attention. While she had some resources from her family, Curtis had struggled to survive on her low salary at the paper when she first moved to New York, but instead of arguing with her bosses, she had sought to supplement her income by writing a book about one of her former classmates at Vassar to make extra money: *First Lady: The Glowing Up-to-the-Minute Story of Jacqueline Kennedy's Life in the White House* was published in 1962. From then on, her skill and growing public profile as a *Times* society reporter had afforded her steady promotions and raises, with which she needed to support only herself.

The dynamic between Curtis and Bender was reflective of a growing tension within the workforce, and within the female experience at large, as the gulf between married and unmarried women, and those with and without children, began to widen. The same year that Curtis published *First Lady,* Helen Gurley Brown published *Sex and the Single Girl,* a frank and humorous guide for women that urged them not to jump right into marriage, despite overwhelming cultural pressure to do so. In Brown's view, there was greater fulfillment and fun in staying single longer, cultivating one's own home, building a career, and pursuing men and sexual pleasure. Often understood as the female counterpart to Hefner's "playboy," the "single girl" recognized that the popularly celebrated roles of marriage were stifling, but with one key caveat. While Brown advocated for the freedom of women, she was careful to clarify that women should not altogether reject becoming wives. In fact, the behaviors of the "single girl" weren't only for personal development; they were for romantic development as well—the more interesting and experienced the woman, the more she would attract potential husbands. "I think marriage is insurance for the *worst* parts of your life," she wrote. "During your best years you don't need a husband. You do need a man of course every step of the way, and they are often cheaper emotionally and a lot more fun by the dozen." The book was a massive bestseller and helped ignite a national conversation on female behavior and sexual freedom. It would be another decade before all single American women gained unfettered access to the birth control pill, which had been approved by the FDA in 1960. Nevertheless, Brown's book was part of the rapid cultural transformation already underway, fueled by the possibility for women to control contraception and thus their own reproduction.

Sex and the Single Girl also urged women to embrace the notion that beauty could be made, rather than born. With hard work, perseverance, and the right tools (Brown was a copy writer for an advertising agency before becoming an author), the appearance of beauty could be crafted and performed successfully—again, largely for the benefit of men. "To get into a position to sink *into* a man you must at least create the illusion of beauty by *acting* beautiful," she explained. "You must love yourself enough to employ every device—voice, words, clothes, figure, make-up—to become beautiful."

There were hard limits to the possible, though, and there were some standards that only certain women possessed. The "fabulous face," as Brown called it, that was "even featured . . . meltingly, gaspingly beautiful" couldn't be achieved with "make-up, prayer, incantations or sending your face back to the factory." Listed among the traits of such a face, subtly but pointedly, was "alabaster skin."

At age thirty-four, Charlotte Curtis was hardly a girl, yet in many ways she epitomized the glamorous, interesting, self-sufficient, successful "single girl." She was conventionally pretty, thin, ever fashionable, smart, and funny. She could hold her own in any environment or situation, never acting precious or hesitant, but also never posing as one of the guys. Her looks—and ability to project refined beauty and femininity in a male-dominated profession—were a big part of her success and remained so throughout her career. Fan mail and kudos from colleagues at the *Times* and in the wider industry often noted her style and attractiveness. "You're intelligent as well as beautiful," a sportswriter at the *Times*, ten years Curtis's junior, wrote to her in praise of a story in 1967; two years later, a CBS news executive closed his letter of congratulations for winning an award and getting a good notice in *Newsweek* magazine with a reassurance that Curtis was "as lovely as I remember you, and younger still." (Such compliments were never found in the many cards and letters Curtis saved from female colleagues, like famed political reporter Helen Thomas, historian and essayist Barbara Tuchman, or *Washington Post* owner Kathryn Graham.)*

In May 1968, Curtis covered a press conference held in a private apartment at the Dakota, the storied residential building on Central Park West, by its owner Betty Friedan, founding president of the National Organization for Women (NOW) and author of *The Feminine Mystique*. Upon its release in 1963, the book had been a smash hit; where *Sex and the Single Girl* had championed young working women who delayed marriage and motherhood, *The Feminine Mystique* examined what happened to those who didn't. It exposed the plight of suburban housewives and the systemic gender inequality—rather than the personal inadequacies or mental illnesses of the women themselves—that created it.

To Curtis and the other reporters gathered in her living room, Friedan explained that while she had planned to announce NOW's endorsements for presidential candidates, she would be unable to do so, given that only two of six had responded to the questionnaire about their positions on women's issues. The "delinquents," Curtis reported, were Vice President Hubert Humphrey, New York State Governor Nelson Rockefeller, former Vice President Richard Nixon, and the still-undeclared-but-obviously-running California Governor Ronald Reagan (the organization had not queried former Alabama Governor George Wallace). This "left the women with 'generally unsatisfactory' statements from Senator Eugene McCarthy and Senator Robert F. Kennedy, neither of whom would come out for repeal of existing anti-abortion laws." Betty Friedan, Curtis added, "wore a purple satin minidress with white stockings and a 'Freedom for Women' button," and said the laws were a "crime" because "every woman should have the right to control her reproductive life."

* The same year Curtis was promoted to Women's News editor, Helen Gurley Brown was named editor-in-chief of *Cosmopolitan* magazine. From the post, which she held until 1997, Brown would build a cultural phenomenon, trendsetter, and tastemaker for sexually expressive young women. She and Curtis moved in the same cultural and professional circles in New York, both giants in different parts of a gendered-information media landscape. Brown wrote some fan letters of her own to Curtis: "Dear Charlotte: You are such a good writer! I loved the Palm Springs piece . . . fabulous! All my best wishes, Helen B" (Brown to Curtis, March 17, 1970, box 7, folder 10, Charlotte Curtis Papers).

When she read Curtis's coverage in the *New York Times* the next day, Friedan was horrified and immediately fired off a long letter of complaint, demanding corrections. Her most pressing concern was the syntactical implication that NOW found McCarthy's and Kennedy's responses to their questionnaire equally disengaged and lackluster, when Friedan had said so only of the latter. As co-chair of Women for McCarthy, she feared personally that the anti-war Democratic candidate would question her support and reconsider her high-profile role in his campaign. Friedan also took issue with the article's tone, which she read as dismissive and sneering, and she charged Curtis with making a mockery of feminism and NOW—and by extension, of Friedan herself. More than this, she resented the story's appearance in the 4F's section, writing that it "should have been treated as serious news and not a humorous feature for the women's page."

Betty Friedan wasn't the only McCarthy supporter worried about her candidate's prospects in early May 1968. It had been six weeks since Lyndon Johnson's announcement that he was not seeking reelection and a little over a month since the assassination of Martin Luther King Jr. Now, Bobby Kennedy was surging in the polls; he won the Indiana Democratic Party primary on the same day Curtis's story appeared in the *Times*. McCarthy came in a disappointing third.

How different the picture would be just one month later. McCarthy's victory in Oregon on May 28th would lift the campaign and the candidate's hopes as they charged into California, only to be quashed once more. And then, before the next day's papers could report his victory, Bobby Kennedy would be shot and the Democrats' path to choosing a presidential candidate rocked—again. Charlotte Curtis would find this story in the disconnected scenes of irrepressible politicking aboard Kennedy's funeral train and in the thousands of stricken faces lining the tracks as the train carried his body to Washington.

3

TRULY EQUAL PARTNERSHIP

Thrust onto the public stage at the age of forty-two as an expert and then advocate for American women, Betty Friedan found that she thrived there. By 1968, she was a household name, synonymous with the American women's movement and recognized leader of a resurgent feminism that some were just starting to call a "second wave."

It was not a path Bettye Naomi Goldstein imagined for herself while growing up in Peoria, Illinois. Smart and driven, as a teenager she had settled into a lonely bookishness, holding fast to her ambitions despite feeling constantly admonished or dismissed for being too argumentative, unladylike, too loud, too Jewish, and too ugly.

Smith College gave Bettye Goldstein new interests and opportunities—including her decision to drop the "e" from Betty—but not much reprieve from the sense of unrelenting judgment. She excelled on campus, where she was drawn to psychology and journalism, she acted in student theater productions, and she explored radical labor organizing and leftist politics (putting her on the FBI's radar in its sweeping hunt for subversives). After graduation, she began a PhD program in psychology at Berkeley, but she decided to leave after a year and move to New York City to work as a journalist for union and labor newspapers.

Three years later, in 1946, she met Carl Friedan on a blind date set up by one of her colleagues. He was managing an Off-Broadway theater and worked for a summer company in New Jersey. The couple married in 1947 and had their first child, Daniel, in 1948. Having outgrown Betty's tiny studio apartment on West 86th Street, the Friedans moved farther uptown and then to Queens, where they had two more children, Jonathan in 1952 and Emily in 1956. Throughout this time Friedan continued to work, still writing under her maiden name before adopting a series of pseudonyms as McCarthyism intensified, while Carl tried to find success in the theater world. Their marriage, which had its ups and downs from the start, became increasingly rocky as Betty's income became more stable and substantial. In 1957, the family moved to the Long Island suburbs, and Carl began a new career in advertising, commuting to work in the city. While the Friedans appeared to slide into a relatively conventional, suburban life, neither adult was happy. Betty freelanced, and after completing a project for her fifteenth college reunion that sparked the idea, began work on the book that would change the lives of millions of women, including her own.

The Feminine Mystique was based on survey data Friedan collected from fellow Smith College class of 1942 graduates about their lives, families, and work. In aggregate, they created a devastating picture of dissatisfaction, suburban isolation, boredom, and torment from feelings of failure; being wives and mothers, they had realized, wasn't enough. *How had American women ended up here after the Second World War,* Friedan wondered, *where a* "woman's world was confined to her own body and beauty, the charming of man, the bearing of babies, and the physical care and serving of husband, children, and home"? Friedan pointed to consumer capitalism, advertising, women's magazines, and mainstream psychology as the culprits—all were actively contributing to and propagating the message that women's natural roles were to be wives and mothers in single-family homes and then blaming them if they could not find complete fulfillment and happiness in these lives. Friedan's book convinced millions of women that there was nothing wrong with them, that the problem was the "feminine mystique," which was not natural or timeless, and that they were not alone in their suffering.

Friedan included little in the book about her own background, leftist politics, or career in journalism, but instead chose to address her readers as if she were simply one of the women she was writing about (and for): a struggling suburban housewife suddenly awakened to the truth of her situation, to the existence of the feminine mystique. Her expertise came from shared experience, and her mission for change was that of an insider. From this perspective, Friedan wrote in the language of universals, never dwelling on the fact that her "housewife heroines" were all white, college-educated, and middle-class or elite women living in the suburbs.

If aspects of Betty Friedan's life distanced her from the women she wrote about, as many critics have noted over the years, much of it was painfully familiar. This was especially true of the impact of dominant beauty standards, pushed on women from all directions, she wrote, in ways that were not only damaging to their senses of self and limiting to their potentials but also keeping them feeding the profits of lucrative industries in cosmetics, fashion, diet foods, exercise, and new medical interventions, which in turn fueled the advertising revenues of the publishing, television, and radio industries.

Betty Friedan, June 8, 1965

The same fame and authority that was so heady and thrilling to Friedan came with intense scrutiny, particularly for women whose looks, demeanor, clothing, and style were assessed and judged incessantly. Betty Friedan was found wanting in just about every respect and she knew it. As the invitations grew to give public lectures and do television talk shows, Friedan became even more concerned with her appearance. She decided to dye her hair blond, but went with red at a stylist's insistence (the change didn't last long; within days of her arrival at the family's summer rental on Fire Island, her new dye job turned green); she wore trendy new clothes that some considered "too young" for her, and she started taking diet pills that made her (more) moody. It didn't help that the more famous Betty Friedan became, the more her marriage with Carl deteriorated. He enjoyed leaving the suburbs for an apartment in the Dakota, in New York City, and a summer house on Fire Island, but he resented that it was her success that paid for it all.

The founding of the National Organization for Women (NOW) was deeply rooted in women's activism, collective organizing, and ranging advocacy that not only continued uninterrupted after the achievements of women's suffrage but also were boosted and proliferated by them. This was the case in the quest for passage of an Equal Rights Amendment (ERA), the growth of professional women's associations, increased representation in organized labor, and the work of Progressives and New Dealers in federal, state, and local government agencies dedicated to policymaking for women and children. As was true with the "first wave," this was never a unified movement; rather, it represented a broad range of philosophies and aims, many of which were contradictory.

This was perhaps never truer than in the case of the Equal Rights Amendment, first proposed by Alice Paul and her National Woman's Party (NWP) in the near aftermath of the 19th Amendment's ratification. At the most radical edge of the early-twentieth-century women's suffrage fight, the NWP next turned its formidable energy toward gaining a constitutional mandate for unequivocal equality of the sexes, for which they were able to get legislation introduced in Congress in 1923. The wording was short and direct: "Men and women shall have equal rights throughout the United States and every place subject to its jurisdiction." Should the amendment be proposed by Congress and achieve ratification by the states, its impact would be swift and monumental: any law discriminating against women or treating them differently from men would be unconstitutional. For those in organized labor and government, particularly the new Women's Bureau of the U.S. Department of Labor, however, it meant a dismantling of hard-won protective labor laws that regulated the hours and working conditions of American women.

As various women's organizations and activists split over the issue of the ERA, the seeds were sown for a debate about the meanings of equality that would endure for decades: Should women and men be understood as the same in their humanity and thus equal in all things? Or were the sexes fundamentally different but unequally valued for their distinct contributions?

For years, the NWP worked to get the amendment through every successive Congress. In the context of the mass mobilizations of women and men during World War II, interest in the ERA was sparked and its prospects seemed brighter; in 1946, the Senate passed the amendment but failed to achieve the necessary two-thirds majority. At the same time, ERA opponents worked for an equal pay law that would address an essential gender disparity while leaving extant protections intact.

Elected in 1960, John F. Kennedy never came around to supporting the ERA. Some of this was due to a degree of deference to organized labor and its essential role in the Democratic Party coalition that had elected him by a narrow margin over Richard Nixon; but more significant may have been the influence of Esther Peterson, Kennedy's new assistant secretary of labor and director of the Women's Bureau. Peterson came from organized labor and was adamantly opposed to the amendment. In June 1961, she suggested that the president appoint a commission on the status of women to generate new policy recommendations and to direct focus away from ERA proponents and their "present troublesome and futile agitation." By the end of the year, the President's Commission on the Status of Women (PCSW) had been established by executive order, with Eleanor Roosevelt as its chairperson (a position she held until her death the following year). Nearly all twenty-six members were on record as opposing the ERA. Marguerite Rawalt, eleven years Eleanor Roosevelt's junior and a long-time attorney in the chief counsel's office of the Internal Revenue Service, was the only vocal advocate for the ERA appointed to the commission.

Like the former first lady, she'd spent decades in the women's movement. A member of the National Woman's Party (NWP), she had served as president of the National Federation of Business and Professional Women's Clubs and the National Association of Women Lawyers, and, in 1943, had been the first woman elected president of the Federal Bar Association.

Ultimately, the PCSW became an essential vehicle for various wings of the women's movement, its importance and usefulness far exceeding its original aims. Chiefly, the commission established a network of state commissions and provided resources, structure, and contacts that facilitated connections among otherwise dispersed groups of women. State commissions remained under the aegis of the Women's Bureau until the 1970s, when they established their own nongovernmental organization; today, the National Association of Commissions for Women continues to support state and local commissions around the country and acts as a public policy advocate on the national level.

When Black college students began to sit in at segregated department-store lunch counters in February 1960, they catalyzed a new stage of the Southern civil rights movement and set into motion the ideas and conditions from which the U.S. women's liberation movement would emerge eight years later. Practicing nonviolent direct action, the students, who had come of age in the immediate wake of the *Brown v. Board of Education* ruling against school segregation, literally put their bodies on the color line and invigorated a generation of young activists through the Student Non-Violent Coordinating Committee, or SNCC (pronounced "Snick"). By compelling active enforcement of segregation laws, the sit-ins not only highlighted the quotidian brutalities of segregation in the South but also invited white supremacists to show their true faces in all their vicious contradictions and bloodthirst. Over and over, the country and world watched as clean-cut young Black people in their Sunday best remained seated and stoic as white men, women, boys, and girls taunted them, smeared them with ketchup and mustard, dumped hot coffee and soup over their heads, pulled at their clothes, beat them, and threw them to the floor before white police stepped in to break it up; if arrests were made, it was the sit-in activists who went to jail for disturbing the peace and defying segregation laws. By the end of the year, an estimated seventy thousand people had participated in a sit-in, and more than three thousand of them had been arrested for it.

The actions also threw glaring light on the violent complicity of the bystander, whether she was standing near the lunch counter or sitting in their family room in Wichita, watching the evening news. Growing numbers of supporters outside the region began to amplify SNCC's work through sympathetic boycotts and picket lines at local outlets of the national Woolworth's and Kress chains, which profited from segregated stores in the South (profits made from the purchases of Black shoppers, for whom it was illegal to sit at a counter for a cup of coffee or a hamburger).

Cultivating this kind of national support and publicity was a crucial part of SNCC's strategy from the beginning. During the summer of 1960, the organization sent a delegation to the annual convention of the National Student Association (NSA) in Minneapolis, Minnesota, seeking its endorsement. At the time, the NSA was the largest national group of college students in the country drawn from members of student governments.* Sensing resistance to such a move from the majority of delegates present, the convention organizers called a special session and gave the stage to a panel of four Southern students—all white—to respond to SNCC. The first three speakers argued against the endorsement on grounds that the NSA should not support breaking state laws. Then, the fourth and last panelist—from the University of Texas, Sandra "Casey" Cason—began to speak. After challenging the necessity of upholding discriminatory state laws that violated the U.S. Constitution, Cason turned to her own experience with the sit-in movement in Austin. Like many white Southerners in the civil rights movement of this period, Cason had come to work for racial justice through her Christian faith and campus ministries. As she gave her testimony on that stage in Minneapolis, the energy in the room shifted. The NSA endorsed the sit-ins. The next morning's *Minneapolis Tribune* reported the events under the headline "White Coed Backs Sit Ins, Gets Ovation." The story to follow made clear how important Cason's body and its appearance had been to the power of her argument, leading with "A beautiful University of Texas coed with honey blond hair

* In 1967, *Ramparts* magazine reported that the National Student Association, founded in 1947, was funded in significant part by the CIA, and had been since at least 1950.

and a southern voice so soft it wouldn't startle a boll weevil made a statement of ethical principles on the Negro sit-in movement Thursday."

The speech—and the woman who gave it—made an impact on Al Haber, the president of a new student organization called Students for a Democratic Society (SDS). Filled with emotion, he'd rushed to Cason after her remarks and pulled her into an enormous, congratulatory hug. With him was another man, Tom Hayden, editor of the student newspaper at the University of Michigan. Haber urged Cason to join SDS, and she became for the group an early conduit to the Southern Black Freedom movement. She also became Hayden's wife in 1961. Her perspective helped him come into his own political values and activism; he followed her into SDS and to civil rights work in the South, where SNCC's direct-action tactics were expanded to include the Freedom Rides and voter registration campaigns. These experiences led to the vision of "participatory democracy" Hayden would outline later in SDS's 1962 manifesto.

After mobilizing the National Guard in Tuscaloosa on June 11, 1963, to enforce the desegregation of the University of Alabama—during which the state's governor, George Wallace, made his now infamous "stand in the schoolhouse door" in a show of resistance—President John F. Kennedy went on national television to address the country and call upon Congress to enact civil rights legislation. "We face," he said, "a moral crisis as a country and as a people," and it was time—past time—for Congress to act.

In the weeks and months to follow, the legislation took a tumultuous journey, with passage constantly in doubt. After the president's assassination in November 1963, the bill regained momentum as his successor, Lyndon Baines Johnson, vowed to memorialize him through its passage. But his attempts were met with a slew of amendments from Southern Democrats and other anti-statist conservatives, all designed to limit the legislation's scope—if not kill it outright. The most notorious of these attempts came from Virginia Democrat Howard W. Smith, who offered an amendment to add the word "sex" to every reference to Title VII prohibitions against employment discrimination based on race, color, religion, or national origin. At eighty years old and in his thirty-third year in Congress, this vocal opponent of the civil rights legislation insisted he'd offered the amendment as a joke—and indeed, it drew rounds of uproarious laughter from fellow congressmen when it was presented on the floor. The idea of women as a protected class was preposterous to them—so much so, opponents hoped, that it would sink the bill. Instead, the term—and the workplace protections for women it generated—was part of the Civil Rights Act of 1964 that Johnson signed into law in July of that same year.

That is how the story usually goes of how the qualifier "sex" ended up in the Civil Rights Act. But that satisfying narrative of unintended consequences and comeuppance leaves out a key detail: Were it not for the legislative savvy of Michigan Democrat Martha Griffiths, who maneuvered the amendment to passage by capitalizing on Smith's stunt, it is unlikely Title VII would have become the tool for addressing workplace gender discrimination that it did. Were it not for Equal Rights Amendment advocates from the National Woman's Party seeding the idea with Smith before that move, he might never have proposed the amendment at all, depriving Griffiths of the opportunity to promote it.

Ultimately, the inclusion of the "sex" category in Title VII protections created a mechanism for remedy, but it provided little guidance on workplace requirements or enforcement. As the Equal Employment Opportunity Commission (EEOC) moved forward on cases related to workplace racial discrimination throughout the 1960s, those concerning sex discrimination were left unattended. Shortly after the law's passage, a national flight attendants' union filed a Title VII case challenging the industry's weight requirements and the forced retirements of women when they reached thirty years old or got married. The cases languished.

Through interpretive rulings, commissioners sought to maintain the status quo. This was the case with a November 1965 interpretive guideline stating that employers could still place ads in sex-segregated classifieds sections—"Help Wanted–Male" and "Help Wanted–Female"—which the commission found were "not intended to exclude or discourage applications from persons of the other sex" but were simply separated for the "convenience of readers." It was inconceivable to most at the EEOC—and to many across the political spectrum—that women faced structural inequities and oppression simply *as women*. Some jobs, like office supervisor, construction worker, or pilot, were obviously only for men, while the positions of secretary, maid, and stewardess were the sole purview of women. To suggest otherwise, went the conventional wisdom, flew in the face of nature and reality.

It was clear that only outside pressure from an NAACP-style organization for women could compel the feds to act on the sex-discrimination clause of Title VII. At the third national conference of State Commissions on the Status of Women, Friedan and others started sketching organizational aims and parameters via notes on napkins passed among the tables during a luncheon. By the time they got to coffee, twenty-seven women had signed on and committed $5 each to get the organizing and letters of invitation started. The National Organization for Women (NOW) was born.

NOW held its first national conference in October, where Friedan was elected president. Constituted as an organization "for" and not "of" women, its membership included men from the start. "The purpose of NOW," explained its founding document, was "to take action to bring women into full participation in the mainstream of American society now, exercising all the privileges and responsibilities thereof in truly equal partnership with men." It was a perfectly concise statement of liberal feminism, grounded in the idea that the systems of mainstream America provided the best conditions for freedom and individual thriving, but failed certain populations by excluding them. Aileen Hernandez, a Black labor leader and former deputy chief of the California Division of Fair Employment Practices, was elected as vice president. She had been the only woman appointed in 1964 to serve as an EEOC commissioner.

In January 1967, less than three months after its founding, NOW petitioned the EEOC to change its ruling on sex-segregated classified ads. It was the group's first major action as a civil rights organization for women.

4

FREEDOM SUMMER

The SNCC communications office in the organization's Atlanta headquarters was just big enough to squeeze in two desks, topped with identical typewriters. One belonged to the communications director and founding member, Julian Bond; the other was Mary King's. When Freedom Summer officially got underway on Sunday, June 21, 1964, with the arrival of the first volunteers in Mississippi, Bond was still in Oxford, Ohio, leading orientation. This meant King was alone when the phone call came, cutting through the early evening quiet and her already ragged nerves.

Instigated by SNCC, Mississippi's Congress of Federated Organizations (COFO) had spent months planning the monumental summer project to bring nearly a thousand mostly white college students to work on its voter registration campaign and companion initiatives in the state, including education and community empowerment work. Critically, their presence would also draw national attention to what was happening in Mississippi and generate publicity going into the party conventions and presidential election that fall. Everyone expected violence that summer and they worried for the safety of volunteers; much of the training was devoted to security.

Mary King had started the day by tracing the progress of the two southbound buses carrying the first group of volunteers. They had left Ohio late the previous afternoon to ensure that their travel through the state of Mississippi would occur under the cloak of darkness, in early morning. By noon on Sunday, King had been able to confirm by phone that all had been safely deposited at one of seven project sites around the state, where they had been met with no violence and only minor harassment by police in the towns of Ruleville and Clarksdale. Most of the new arrivals had spent the morning at church, getting their first introductions to the Black communities they would be living in and working with for the next six weeks. Other than periods when WATS lines* had been suspiciously unavailable, cutting off communication between project sites and headquarters, the rest of the day had seemed largely uneventful, which had only amplified King's tension. But when she picked up the phone and heard Louise Hermey's anxious voice on the line from Meridian, she knew that something terrible had happened.

When Michael Schwerner, James Chaney, and Andrew Goodman had failed to return to the COFO office in Meridian by the agreed-upon time of 4:00 p.m., Hermey notified the local directors and King. The men had left at 9:00 that morning to investigate the burning of the Mount Zion AME Church and the beating of three Black residents in the town of Philadelphia, which was about forty miles away.

Like Andrew Goodman, Hermey was a new volunteer from New York City; both had been in Mississippi for mere hours when the three men headed to Philadelphia, leaving the new communications person to manage the office and notify project directors if they failed to return by 4 p.m.

On the phone with Hermey later, King realized that she and anyone else at the field office must be hungry. Had they eaten anything since lunch? King called a local minister, who showed up at the office with a box of hamburgers and a shotgun. He posted himself outside the entrance while the volunteers ate and continued their phoning in search of the men.

In Atlanta, Mary King began making her own calls to county sheriffs and others in the area where they were last known to be. She pretended to be a journalist—a

* Bell Telephone Company introduced Wide Area Telephone Service (WATS) in 1961. Their allowance of flat-rate purchases and ability to handle lots of traffic were a lifeline for SNCC. WATS would be the foundation for the first 1-800 numbers, introduced a few years later.

ruse that had worked in the past—to get better information and lend some safety to those in the field. The jailer who had Chaney, Goodman, and Schwerner in custody was one of the first she called; he denied knowing anything about them. Hermey had phoned and been lied to by the same man earlier.

Late that night—early in the next morning, really—King called the U.S. Department of Justice and asked for the FBI to investigate. Then she began contacting the loved ones of the missing, starting with Andrew Goodman's parents in New York.

When the men's burnt-out car was found two days later, they were presumed dead. They would not be the only civil rights workers, or Black residents claiming their voting rights, to die in Mississippi that summer, but the disappearance of the three men, two of whom were white, and the subsequent search for their bodies made national headlines and cast a heavy shadow across the project.

Exactly two years after the founding of SNCC, Mary King spent her Easter break from Ohio Wesleyan University traveling to Nashville and Atlanta, and to Tuskegee, Alabama, on a "study tour" led by one of her professors. They were studying Southern segregation and the work of student civil rights activists. It was a life-altering trip for King, who would go on to work for SNCC in their Atlanta headquarters after graduation, a path set for her by a serendipitous meeting with Casey Hayden (formerly Cason). She "fascinated me," wrote King of that first meeting twenty-five years later. Hayden "was unselfconsciously beautiful, slender, blonde with translucent skin and a low-voiced throaty laugh," she explained, with "symmetrical features [that] were arranged with appealing fragility." The juxtaposition of her beauty and style ("the epitome of Southern propriety") with her passionate commitment to SNCC, integration, and racial justice electrified and inspired King.

Hayden and other SNCC activists, including John Lewis, who met with the Ohio Wesleyan students in Nashville, spoke to them of the "Beloved Community" their nonviolent direct action would make possible. Inspired by the early-twentieth-century theological foundations of the Fellowship of Reconciliation, a still-extant Christian anti-war organization founded in 1914, Martin Luther King Jr. used the term to describe the society to come after integration and meaningful reckoning with the injustices of the past and reconciliation. "The aftermath of nonviolence is the creation of the Beloved Community," he argued, "so when the battle's over, a new relationship comes into being between the oppressed and the oppressor." This resonated deeply with students like John Lewis, Casey Hayden, and Mary King—devout Christians whose social justice values and activism seemed obvious outgrowths of their faith. The Beloved Community represented a hopeful future, worth the sacrifices of the present, for non-believers and non-Christians as well.

Those present sacrifices often included romantic relationships, friendships, and family ties strained to breaking point by the demands of living lives in activism. After about two years of marriage, Casey and Tom Hayden separated around the time that Mary King began working for SNCC. Hayden returned to Atlanta to heal, work, and rebuild, and she found a home and lasting friendship as King's roommate. The women grew together as feminists, spending evenings in their apartment reading, discussing, and rereading *The Second Sex*, the book "underlined, creased, marked up and finally coverless from our study of it." They also read *The Feminine Mystique* when it was published in 1963, but found alienating Friedan's lack of engagement with the Black civil rights movement—making the book seem, said King, "irrelevant and marginal to us."

As a central organizer for the summer project, Casey Hayden's spring of 1964 was spent recruiting on campuses in the Midwest and Northeast, managing applications, creating training materials, and developing curriculum for the Freedom Schools in which many volunteers would teach. She trained volunteers in Ohio alongside Julian Bond, before returning to COFO headquarters in Jackson for the project's duration. In addition to the day-to-day work of managing county field offices, one of Hayden's primary responsibilities was developing a challenge to the seating of the all-white Mississippi delegation headed to the Democratic National Convention in August.

Forty-four days after the murder of Chaney, Goodman, and Schwerner, President Lyndon Johnson got word from his assistant director of the FBI that their bodies had been found just after 8 p.m. on August 4th. That same night, the White House was in a fever of activity responding to events in the Gulf of Tonkin. A few hours later, shortly before midnight, the president interrupted regular television programing to inform the nation of what he described as two unprovoked attacks on U.S. naval vessels by North Vietnamese forces and the subsequent response. On August 7th, Congress passed the Gulf of Tonkin Resolution, escalating U.S. involvement in the Vietnam War.

At the Democratic National Convention in Atlantic City a few weeks later, the credentials committee, following Johnson's directives, refused to seat the racially representative delegation from the Mississippi Freedom Democratic Party. It was a destabilizing and eye-opening blow to SNCC's Black membership. The Democrats' capitulation to the party's Southern segregationist wing—again—made clear the limited efficacy of Black votes in the absence of profound systemic change, and it highlighted the folly of continuing to trust white officials, and white so-called allies generally. The massive influx of young white men and women to the work in Mississippi had literally changed the complexion of the movement, and issues that had dogged the interracial organization from the start were made acute by numbers and regional differences. The Beloved Community was starting to look more like an Edenic sanctuary for those in flight from guilt-laded white supremacy and privilege, rather than a means for actual transformation or a sustainable communal outcome. Black self-determination increasingly seemed incongruous with interracial organizing and the quest for integration.

In November 1964, SNCC held a retreat in Waveland, Mississippi, to address the summer project's revelations and aftermath, and to chart a way forward. One of the workshops was on "Women in the Movement," prompted by a position paper submitted anonymously. Its authors were Casey Hayden and Mary King. Hayden later explained that they did not include their names on the paper because they hoped people would think some men were among the authors and therefore be less inclined to reject it outright; perhaps, too, they had hoped people would think some Black women had written it. Whatever the case, Hayden and King's authorship was identified almost immediately, and the conversation did not go well.

Hayden and King opened their argument with a series of examples of discrimination against SNCC women that had occurred during the prior summer. These ranged from exclusion from leadership roles, and expectations that those who were in positions of authority would defer to men, to tasking seasoned activists from the field with all the clerical work—only ever asking the women to take notes in meetings. They also included examples of qualifying the work of women in ways that diminished them, as in a report on personnel that listed the number of people at each post but, for the town of Laurel, listed "not the number of persons but 'three girls.'" Next, Hayden and King laid out the paper's animating racial analogy, including comparing the SNCC men's chauvinism to the unconscious behaviors of white people steeped in white supremacy: "the average white person doesn't realize that he assumes he is superior. . . . So too the average SNCC worker finds it difficult to discuss the woman problem because of the assumption of male superiority." Their point was that men were not bad actors, just unaware; and now that the issue had been brought into the light, SNCC men could change—that they would want to change. Not only did this not happen, but also the workshop's vast majority rejected the picture altogether, including many Black women.

Hayden and King were exposing conversations that Black and white women had been having for months. In early July, an informant for the Mississippi State Sovereignty Commission (a state agency tasked with preserving segregation) reported that he had overheard "strong females" in COFO headquarters, Hayden among them, promoting a "revolution" that would include "the women's fight for equality with men." While white members were prominent in these conversations, Black women had been a part of them, too. Nevertheless, most Black women in Waveland did not see their experiences reflected in Hayden and King's paper—or if they did, they saw white women's privilege and expectation of leadership shining through the document much more strongly. Many at the retreat, male and female, resented the imposition of an issue they believed secondary to and potentially undermining the critical Black freedom struggle at hand.

Hayden and King were demoralized but not defeated by their paper's reception, which they saw largely through the prism of the growing divisions between Black and white SNCC workers. As both moved into their next roles—Hayden to Chicago "on loan" from SNCC to work on an SDS Economic Research and Action Project (ERAP) with poor white migrants from Appalachia; and King to field work in Mississippi—they continued engaging with other members on women's issues in the movement. In a turn devastating to both women, neither Hayden nor King would be on SNCC's payroll or be members of the organization by August 1965.

Broke and heartbroken, King retreated to her family's cabin, tucked in the backwoods of Spotsylvania County in Virginia, to grieve SNCC and her lost Beloved Community. Hayden joined her there in November to channel their sorrow into writing and circulating "A Kind of Memo," addressed to about forty Black and white movement women. For a short time, they were roommates again, struggling together and mapping feminist possibilities. Hayden would come to associate the memo with the smell of wood smoke from the cabin's chimney, as they walked and talked through their ideas and memories in the "quiet isolation of the forest."

"A Kind of Memo" echoed Hayden and King's paper from the Waveland retreat, but it was more directed. This time, they weren't trying to open men's eyes but, instead, were calling the women to a dialogue. Hayden and King were expressly pessimistic that "we could start a movement based on anything as distant to general American thought as a sex-caste system," and seemed resigned to the hierarchy of concerns already leveled at them: "most of us will probably want to work full time on problems such as war, poverty, and race." But their letter struck a chord. That winter, *Liberation*, a magazine popular with the New Left, approached Hayden and King with a request for permission to publish the memo, which later appeared in April 1966 under the title "Sex and Caste."

What had begun as an appeal to a specific group now read as a call to every woman who came across it in the magazine. The racial analogy from the original Waveland paper became the basis for an argument that women in the United States constituted a "caste."

> The caste system perspective dictates the roles assigned to women in the movement, and certainly even more to women outside the movement. Within the movement, questions arise in situations ranging from relationships of women organizers to men in the community, to who cleans the freedom house, to who holds leadership positions, to who does secretarial work, and who acts as spokesman for groups.

The conflicts among women that had emerged in Waveland were incorporated into the memo and framed as a twofold issue: not all women see a problem of sexism or feel "held back" in their work, and "there are problems with relationships between white women and black women." The adapted material had a much larger and longer lasting impact than its initial iteration: the original memo had been addressed to specific Black and white women listed in the document itself, making the recipients known to one another and thus generating the presumption of an interracial group to discuss the "problems with relationships" among them. In the absence of this limited context, the published memo read more as descriptive of a problem than as generative of solutions or alternatives, and it highlighted the white perspective of its authors and imagined audience.

Two months later, Stokely Carmichael electrified a SNCC rally in Mississippi by calling for "Black Power," his first public use of the phrase. SNCC members then elected Carmichael to replace John Lewis as chairman and Ruby Doris Smith Robinson to replace James Foreman as executive secretary, signaling a true end to earlier commitments to interracial organizing, nonviolence, and the Beloved Community. Julian Bond resigned soon thereafter. The remaining white members and allies were asked to redirect their activism toward fighting white supremacy and inequality within white communities—a charge that was experienced by many, including Casey Hayden and Mary King, who had already been ousted, as a clear purge. They carried their pain and frustration from this time into other organizing and into the nascent women's liberation movement.

Armed with Congress's Gulf of Tonkin Resolution and the mandate of a landslide victory, President Johnson directed the massive escalation of the war with air campaigns and the deployment of the first combat divisions to Vietnam, despite his campaign promises of peace in Southeast Asia. By the end of 1965, 184,000 American troops were in the country, more than 230,000 young men had been drafted, and the New Left turned its attention to campus anti-war organizing and draft resistance. Tens of thousands marched on Washington that summer, demonstrating against the war for the first time.

Since Freedom Summer, SDS had shifted its focus to draft resistance, which brought significant growth to its national membership and new tensions to the organization's already fraught gender dynamics. Women's military service was not insignificant in Vietnam, nor did it equate to uniform support for U.S. policy, but it was always by choice, not as part of the draft. The only obvious role available to women in a movement dedicated to fighting conscription and ending the war was to facilitate and support the actions of men; they could encourage and adore those who burned their draft cards, but they had no cards of their own or similar actions to take. The attendant atmosphere of male posturing, combined with new expectations of the "sexual revolution" and emergent counterculture, led to an increase in the overt sexual objectification of women. This was clear in the ubiquitous draft resistance motto: "Girls Say Yes to Boys Who Say No."

Things came to a head within SDS in June 1967, at the annual convention in Ann Arbor, Michigan. For the first time, a meeting for radical women was held among the strategy sessions and working groups that would produce resolutions to be heard for a vote at the convention's plenary. The schedule published in the special convention issue of *New Left Notes* titled the session (in very Old Left fashion): the "Woman Question." Those who attended called it the "Women's Liberation Workshop."

Before any of the women at the convention had a chance to meet and discuss their place in SDS and the wider revolution, *New Left Notes* made clear what they were up against, running an advertisement for the book *Containment and Change: Two Views of American Society and Foreign Policy in the New Revolutionary Age,* co-authored by former SDS President Carl Oglesby and Richard Shaull, a theologian and Presbyterian missionary. Blocked off from the surrounding text with a thick black border, the ad's copy dropped the authors' subtitle description of the book's subject matter in favor of text that read: "[T]here is a certain kind of woman who reads NLN [*New Left Notes*] and threatens draft boards. For that certain kind of woman, there is a certain book . . . CONTAINMENT AND CHANGE." The single illustration in the ad is a photo of a young woman on her knees in a sleeveless minidress that rides high on her bare thighs, her arms cinched tight with rope at her wrists, hands pushed between her legs. The woman looks into the camera through a curtain of long, blond hair, with an expression somewhere between seduction and submission.

In this atmosphere, members of the Women's Liberation Workshop drafted a resolution on the "liberation of women," with a call "for programs which will free women from their traditional roles in order that we may participate with all of our resources and energies in meaningful and creative activity." On a broader scale, this meant re-imagining the domestic responsibilities of men and women, including childrearing, and access to birth control and legal abortions. In the case of the movement and SDS, it meant ensuring that women and men share the work of all things, "whether licking stamps to assuming leadership positions," and recognizing that "people who identify with the movement and feel that their own lives are part of the base to bring about radical social change must recognize the necessity for the liberation of women." This could not happen, the resolution continued, until "our brothers" recognize "that because they were brought up in the United States they cannot be free of the burden of male chauvinism."

Expecting to be challenged on the fundamental premise of women's oppression in their personal relationships and in their work in SDS, as well as in the world at large, the Women's Liberation Workshop added to their resolution a section on "analysis" to develop their case. Well-steeped in the theories and histories of socialism and communism, and the "woman question," they similarly sought to underscore their assertion that liberation for women would not come after and because of a successful revolution; rather, the revolution could never be successful without women's liberation at its heart. Their analysis drew analogies between their oppression as women in the United States and the anti-capitalist, anti-colonial struggles of the "Third World" (the heart of SDS's position against the Vietnam War), Black Power, and the organization's commitment to creating radical socialism in the United States. Because of this "colonial relationship to men," the women argued, they had no choice but to fight for their own independence. Only that would "lead to the growth and development of the revolutionary movement in this country. Only the independent woman can be truly effective in the larger revolutionary struggle."

The Women's Liberation Workshop also expected the men at the convention to resist acknowledging their own privileges and roles in oppressing women in their personal relationships, in their activism, and in society at large. "We seek the liberation of all human beings," their resolution continued. "The struggle for liberation of women must be part of the larger fight for human freedom. We recognize the difficulty our brothers will have in dealing with male chauvinism and we will assume our full responsibility in helping to resolve the contradictions. Freedom now! We love you!"

When the resolution was introduced at the plenary, vast proportions of the men in attendance decried the analysis and the resolution; they demanded to be allowed to make amendments, and when they were reminded that amendments would not be heard—that the resolution was to be voted up or down as is—they complained that their right to "participatory democracy" was being denied. The crowd yelled and jeered the women and those running the session. Although the resolution was passed, the scene of its hearing was ugly and deeply disheartening.

In an account of the convention published in *New Left Notes* at the end of the summer, SDS member and a past assistant national secretary of the organization, Donald McKelvey, wrote: "The most disturbing session was the plenary on 'the liberation of women' question. The men distinguished themselves by an extraordinarily clear manifestation of their insecurity." If one needed evidence "of the existence of a really deep-seated sexual caste system," he concluded, they had it in the "very disturbing spectacle" they'd witnessed. "Disturbing . . . but hardly unexpected."

When the post-convention issue of *New Left Notes* was published in July, it reprinted the resolutions that had been passed. Unlike for those on the war and poverty, the editors added a cartoon alongside the women's liberation resolution. It depicted a young white woman in a baby doll outfit, holding a sign that read "We want our Rights & We want them NOW!" The demand is signed "WLF," or Women's Liberation Front, a reference to the North Vietnamese National Liberation Front (NLF). Here, the cartoon seemed to say, is your American "Third World" woman revolutionary. She is ridiculous and cute, hardly radical in her appearance or even a fully mature person, but nevertheless adorable in playing at revolution. When asked what drew them to the women's liberation movement, most SDS women included their utter fury at seeing that cartoon—at seeing themselves reflected in their "brothers'" eyes.

5

WE NEVER TOOK ANY SHIT

The first organizing meeting for the New York City chapter of NOW took place in early February 1967. The city was in a deep freeze, but that was no match for the frosty looks Flo Kennedy felt from Betty Friedan and the meeting's host, Muriel Fox, that night. Kennedy had not been invited to the well-appointed Upper East Side townhouse; she had been brought to the meeting by a fellow attorney, who had received an invitation via letter. She was far from being the only person there to have come with an invited friend, but Kennedy was a Black woman in a mostly white crowd. She knew she stood out; the tenor of the room made her feel it.

Over the course of the next hour, every suggestion Kennedy made for the work of the new organization was shot down. When she urged that they take a stand against the Vietnam War, it was rejected, as were her suggestions for mobilizing consumer boycotts against militarism and calling out misrepresentations in the media and advertising. When Kennedy got to her argument that "NOW should be for Black Power," Betty Friedan erupted.

"We are not here to talk about the war," or Black Power, she said. They were there to talk about *women's* issues, which to Friedan, Fox, and many others in the room meant a narrow version of equality between the sexes, in work and in public life. They were unpersuaded by Kennedy's position that the war and white supremacy were, in fact, women's issues, not just because women were involved in and affected by them but also because, like patriarchy, they were part of the same system of structural inequality and exploitation.

From that first meeting, Kennedy knew that NOW "was no place for [her] to spend much time," but that it was worth some of her energy. "I saw the importance of a feminist movement," she later explained, "and stayed in there because I wanted to do anything I could to keep it alive."

Florynce "Flo" Kennedy was born to Wiley and Zella Kennedy in 1916, the second of what would eventually number five daughters, in Kansas City, Missouri. The city of her youth was in many ways just as segregated as cities in Alabama, where her father, Wiley, was from. Her mother, Zella, had also been born in Kansas City to parents who had migrated there from Kentucky. (All four of Kennedy's grandparents had been enslaved in those states.) Flo's maternal grandfather, William H. Jackman, served with a Kentucky regiment of the United States Colored Troops in the Civil War, and he met his wife, Lucy, in Kansas City when both were still recent arrivals. Together, they raised a family and worked their way into the city's Black middle class. Maintaining that status and respectability was paramount for Flo Kennedy's grandmother, especially when, after twenty years of marriage, her husband left her around the time Wiley Kennedy began courting their daughter. She discouraged Zella from forming a relationship with the dark-skinned man from Alabama, believing he could only drag her daughter and any future grandchildren down the scale of color that permeated the hierarchies of Black status.

Lucy prided herself on her own fair complexion, and she was "very snobbish about color, and hated my daddy because he was black," wrote Flo Kennedy later in her 1976 memoir, *Color Me Flo: My Life and Good Times*. It is one of the first things Kennedy explains about her family background in that book, after describing her witnessing as a young child her father's armed resistance to Klansmen who were trying to force the family (including her grandmother, who lived with them) out of their home in a majority white neighborhood. What follows is a long discussion of colorism in Black communities, particularly as it affected the girls and women in Kennedy's family. "Black people always described a person by their color and their hair," she explained, presumably for what she knew would be the large white readership of her memoir who did not live with these aesthetic conditions. "The first thing you noticed—before shape or legs or anything—was dark brown skin or yellow skin—'real light,' you might say—with bad hair or good hair, 'good' meaning you didn't have to straighten it. Bad hair was of course like Black people's hair." Her grandmother's hair had not required straightening, but because she herself had married a "dark man," their daughter had had to constantly work to straighten her own "bad" hair. Zella's "hair was longer and thicker than ours, and she had a long, straight nose and lighter skin, so that meant she was prettier than we were. We thought she was beautiful," writes Kennedy. Zella began straightening her daughters' hair when they still sat in highchairs.

Flo Kennedy's immediate family was not involved with Black organizations or in reform movements, nor were they active in a church, but she credited her parents with teaching her to be an activist: "We were political in the sense that we never took any shit."

She also credited her parents with teaching her about patriarchy and its costs to women, however indirectly. Zella was smart and college educated, but was thwarted in her ambitions, first by her husband, who did not want her working outside the home, and then by limited options when the economic hardships of the Great Depression drove her into the workforce. When Flo was eleven, her parents separated and her mother moved her and her two sisters to Los Angeles. Kennedy would later say that move marked the beginning of her understanding that while marriage and motherhood could be death to a woman's ambitions, the security they represented, no matter how tenuous, had a gravitational pull that was hard to resist. Her parents reunited after two years.

In 1942, Kennedy moved to New York City with her sister Grayce, who was getting married to a soldier there. Flo was committed to remaining unmarried herself, and at twenty-nine, she enrolled at Columbia University as an undergraduate in the University Extension School. She majored in pre-law because all the attorneys she knew of "were better off than others," and it seemed the best path toward independence and financial security. Colleges across the country changed dramatically after the war, with the enrollments of veterans using GI Bill benefits, a trend that transformed Columbia's classrooms before Kennedy had completed her degree. She became known on campus as a vocal critic of racism and gender inequality, as well as the limitations of marriage for women. In January 1946, Kennedy wrote a paper for her sociology class on "A Comparative Study Accentuating the Similarities of the Societal Position of Women and Negroes," which became a touchstone in the development of her Black feminism, and she reprinted a long excerpt from it thirty years later in *Color Me Flo*.

Kennedy graduated from Columbia Law School in 1951 as one of eight women and the only Black person in her cohort. After passing the bar the following year, she struggled to find a job, did clerical work for a large Manhattan law firm, and eventually opened her own practice in 1954, specializing in copyright and entertainment law. She became known for her work in helping Black musical artists—including Billie Holiday and the widow of Charlie Parker—resist industry exploitation and gain compensation for past work.

The latter 1950s were exhilarating times for Kennedy. She grew her firm, bringing on a partner, Donald E. Wilkes, with his own entertainment law clients and connections, and she fell in love with a white science-fiction writer originally from the West Coast named Charles Dye, known to all as Charlie. With Dye, she found a partner who did not threaten her independence or ambition, and in 1957, Kennedy did what she'd vowed to herself and others that she would never do: she married Dye. Their relationship flouted convention from the start, even outside the racial difference: Charlie was nine years younger, and they kept a circle of Bohemian musician and writer friends. Their marriage was no different. Kennedy kept her last name and maintained her own apartment in Midtown Manhattan, while the couple's life together was based largely in and around Dye's place downtown. Yet their relationship grew increasingly tumultuous owing to Dye's alcoholism and bouts of liquor-fueled violent rages. Kennedy's biographer, Sherie Randolph, characterizes the relationship as "collapsing" in 1959, when her law partner embezzled the firm's cash reserves and disappeared. Wilkes's actions threatened the survival of her law firm in the short term and threw Kennedy into a cycle of debt not of her own making. Her husband tried to stay sober and support Kennedy through the damage, but he resumed drinking and demanded back wages for the work he'd done. The pair separated, and Kennedy began pursuing a divorce, which was difficult, expensive, and time-consuming under New York State law; Charlie died of alcohol-related liver disease while the process was still ongoing. It was a terrible time for Kennedy. "The white men she trusted most, professionally and personally, had more power to hinder her independence and success than she calculated," writes Randolph, and had "threatened her security and livelihood." Kennedy would remain more circumspect and careful in relationships long after she'd rebuilt what the two men had taken. She never again married or took on another law partner.

In 1964, Kennedy began writing a regular column in the Black-owned newspaper *Queens Voice* about the entertainment industry and its demeaning representations of Black people in the popular media. She also joined Wednesdays in Mississippi (WIM), an interracial organization of women in their forties and fifties who worked to support Freedom Summer. Her entwined networks from legal work, community journalism, and civil rights activism expanded when she began hosting a Sunday evening radio show called *Opinions*, which focused on Black issues and politics, and which featured ranging interviews with city politicians, activists, and community organizers.

On an otherwise unremarkable late afternoon in August 1965, Kennedy's life changed forever. Walking home from a doctor's appointment, she arrived at a police barricade on Madison Avenue, where police were detouring people around several blocks, owing to a gas main explosion. Her apartment was inside the cordoned-off area, but she wasn't concerned, as she'd just watched a patrolman usher three white men past the barricade so they could get to Grand Central Station. Kennedy, who was forty-nine at the time and wearing the conservative attire of a courtroom attorney, approached the same officer to request passage. He refused her, not believing that the middle-aged Black woman before him could live in such a nice Midtown neighborhood. While Kennedy produced identification as proof of her address, she watched at least fifteen men walk through without hassle from police; all the men were white. Still, the officer blocked her way, ignoring evidence of her address, and ordered her to walk away. By this time, bus traffic appeared to be resuming through the area and the officer moved to leave, so Kennedy fell in with the next group of pedestrians to pass through.

That was when the "police pounced on her," reported the *Amsterdam News*, "and arrested Miss Kennedy" for disorderly conduct—for "getting loud," she explained—and resisting arrest. After hauling her first to the 17th Precinct, the police moved Kennedy to the 14th Precinct, where a female officer was on duty. The woman ordered Kennedy to strip naked and then squat for a cavity search.

Two days later, on the other side of the country, the Watts uprising erupted in Los Angeles, in response to police harassment and the daily humiliations of segregation in that city. After six days, 4,000 California National Guard troops had been deployed, thirty-four people were dead, and more than $40 million in property damage was reported. The Watts uprising broadcast to the country and the world what Flo Kennedy and most other Black people had known all along: state violence and structural racism were not just Southern but also national facts of life in the United States.

"Flo was different after the arrest," her sister would later tell her biographer. Something had been taken from her in that precinct station, but the arrest had also fueled the urgency of her politics and cemented her commitments to emergent Black Power. In 1966, she was one of a hundred people invited to the planning meeting for the first National Black Power Conference. Later that summer she founded the Media Workshop to address racism in advertising and popular

Florynce Kennedy, October 4, 1979

media, and to promote the empowerment of Black consumers. When Flo Kennedy became active in NOW-NYC, the reactions from chapter leadership ranged from discomfiture to outright dislike, but her principled presence was undeniable. In some of the younger, more radical-leaning members, Kennedy found an opportunity to educate and expand their visions of what constituted freedom for women, encouraging them to protest the war and to learn about Black Power, treating NOW-NYC as a kind of activist mission field. (None was more affected by this than Ti-Grace Atkinson, a graduate student and art critic who hailed originally from Louisiana.) Entering a new era in her role in the movement, Kennedy hung up her uniform of suits and began to sport what would become known as her iconic loud fashion.

6

MOVE ON, LITTLE GIRL

Convened over Labor Day Weekend in 1967, the National Conference for New Politics (NCNP) sought to forge an anti-war, pro-civil rights coalition from a spectrum of the American left, ranging from Reform Democrats and Old Left labor and peace groups to the New Left and Black Power movements. With President Johnson and the Democratic Party establishment committed to an ever-expanding war in Southeast Asia, and little hope for an anti-war ticket from the Republicans in 1968, the NCNP called a convention in Chicago with the aim of creating a viable third-party challenge. About three thousand people representing around two hundred different organizations attended.

Donna Allen was one of only a few women on the NCNP's board of directors. She was a leader of Women Strike for Peace (WSP), which had been founded in 1961 to protest nuclear proliferation and federal investigations into subversive activities among private citizens, public employees, and industries. As the U.S. military's "advising" role escalated into full-scale war in Vietnam, WSP became a central feature of center-left opposition and often was the lone women's group represented in coalitions. This was true again at the NCNP convention.

When Allen protested the Chicago program's initial failure to include a single female speaker, the rest of the board responded, "Fine, you do it then," which was how she became the only woman among the scheduled speakers. "If you want to know how I got in the women's movement," Allen later said, "it was working with these men's groups [her description of the NCNP] and seeing how little interested they were in the women's point of view." The weekend also included a scheduled Women's Workshop, led by another member of the WSP, to generate a resolution for discussion during the main sessions.

The workshop's WSP conveners expected to produce a women's resolution against the war, whereas many who attended, including some who had been at the SDS convention earlier in the summer, expected to create a far more expansive statement of liberation and feminism. These latter women were frustrated by the WSP-focused resolution that resulted from the meeting. A few negotiated a little time to create an amended resolution, with a "minority report" attached. They were given twenty-four hours before the plenary session scheduled for the next day. Notably, the women's workshop reflected the unwieldy collection of interests at the NCNP with one crucial exception: by the time it met, most Black women and men, including Flo Kennedy, were assembling in a separate Black Caucus. She and Ti-Grace Atkinson traveled to Chicago together and shared a hotel room; Atkinson attended the women's workshop.

Two women in their early twenties, Jo Freeman and Shulamith Firestone, set about drafting the more radical amendment. Both lived in Chicago, although they had just met for the first time at the workshop. As a political science major at Berkeley, Freeman had been radicalized by that campus's Free Speech Movement; she wrote for the student newspaper and participated in Freedom Summer. After graduating in 1965, she went to work for Martin Luther King Jr.'s Southern Christian Leadership Conference (SCLC), and she moved to Chicago the following year on a short-lived SCLC project. When the project "faded out," she went to work for a community paper to gain more experience and then began looking for jobs at city newspapers. Freeman was rejected everywhere she applied, not because she wasn't a good enough journalist, her interviewers made clear, but because they "already had a woman working at the paper" and couldn't "send a woman to cover a riot." Pushed to think about women's conditions generally, Freeman began seeking out others who felt similarly, and she took a summer course on women, taught at the University of Chicago's Free School by two women from SDS.

Her new compatriot, Shulamith "Shulie" Firestone, was born in Canada, with the last name of Feuerstein, to strict Orthodox Jewish parents. When she was still a child, her family moved to St. Louis, Missouri, and they changed the spelling of the name to "Firestone." As Firestone grew up, her relationship with her parents grew increasingly volatile, especially with her father, as she bristled at the gender expectations of her family and their faith. After attending Washington University in St. Louis, she graduated in 1967 from the Art Institute of Chicago with a degree in painting.

After working all night to create a "minority report" amendment to the resolution, including cutting a mimeograph stencil for the text, the two women managed to distribute 2,000 copies at the plenary. NCNP organizer William Pepper knew an amendment was coming that day, and he saw Freeman and Firestone ready at the mic, but he failed to introduce them. Despite protests coming from those in the auditorium, including from some WSP members, Pepper called the vote and the original resolution passed as it was.

Outraged, Freeman and Firestone approached Pepper and continued arguing for the amendment to be heard and voted on. Instead, he recognized the person who was next on the agenda. As that young man elbowed his way toward the mic, past the still arguing women, Freeman recalled Pepper's patting Firestone on the head and saying, "Move on, little girl; we have more important issues to talk about here than women's liberation."

"That was the genesis of the Women's Liberation Movement," Freeman said. "We had a meeting the next week with women in Chicago."

7

DOING WOMEN'S LIBERATION

Carol Hanisch was introduced to women's liberation by Shulamith Firestone, who was introduced to Hanisch by a middle-aged journalist named Bill Price. "I met this wonderful woman in Chicago," he'd told Hanisch, "and I want you to meet her."

Firestone had moved to New York City in the fall of 1967, with plans to pursue her painting career and to start another women's liberation group. The meeting in Chicago, dubbed the West Side Group in reference to the neighborhood where they convened, was thriving. Firestone arrived on the East Coast with a list of contacts that included Pamela "Pam" Allen,* who had attended a collective in Chicago while staying with a friend who was also in the West Side Group. With Allen's help, word quickly spread through the radical circles in New York City.

Hanisch had known Bill Price since her days with a civil rights information service in Mississippi. In 1956, the World War II veteran had been famously fired by the *New York Daily News* for defying a U.S. Senate committee that was hunting for communists in the press industry. By the time of Price's hearing

* Pamela Allen later changed her name to Chude Pamela Allen, as she is known today.

on contempt charges, the Montgomery Bus Boycott was going into its second month, and the country was just getting to know Martin Luther King Jr., the twenty-six-year-old Baptist minister leading the boycott. After being convicted and serving three months in prison, Price headed south to report on the civil rights movement as a freelancer; by 1968, he was covering politics and radical movements for *The Guardian*, a historic alternative newspaper in New York City.* From there, the fifty-two-year-old journalist moved through every corner of the movement and seemed to know nearly all the players. He'd thought to connect Hanisch and Firestone, after speaking with both Carol Hanisch and Kathie Amatniek about the need for a women's movement at a party earlier that year—a need he'd witnessed firsthand in Chicago while covering the National Conference for New Politics (NCNP)—where he had met Firestone.

Hanisch liked Firestone immediately, admiring her temper and frank way of criticizing the behaviors of New Left men, and finding her "very energetic, forceful and wonderfully up about what she was doing." Firestone was "very angry about what had happened in Chicago and not afraid to show her anger," said Hanisch. "She was livid, she had been so insulted." Before that conversation, it never would have occurred to Hanisch to criticize movement men so directly or to be so assertive with her anger; she found it all "very refreshing." Firestone said that she and some others were getting a meeting together, but didn't have a time yet. "Let me know," said Hanisch, handing over her contact information.

Carol Hanisch was born in 1942, in Havelock, Iowa, an agricultural community that listed 326 residents in the 1940 census. Like most of her peers, she grew up on a small family farm that relied on the labor of everyone, male and female, young and old. Later, she would realize that her first awareness of men and women being treated differently had been at home, where she and her mother shared double domestic duties; once the day's farm work was done or even before it started, they still had cooking and cleaning to do—and her father always

* Until February 1967, the paper had been called the *National Guardian*. Founded in the 1920s, the journalistic standard-bearer of the Old Left had become an important voice for the New Left, which was reflected in its new name, *The Guardian*.

Carol Hanisch (second row, fourth from left), pictured in her Drake University yearbook, *The Quax*, 1964, as one of 19 students selected for Who's Who Among Students in American Colleges and Universities

controlled the money. At the consolidated high school in the neighboring town of Fenton, Hanisch was active in band, choir, theater, speech, and cheerleading. She played softball and basketball, served as editor of the school paper, and was a member of 4-H. Her club's February 1960 program, covered in the local paper, made clear the gendered expectations that ruled the community's rural ideal. At the meeting, "Carol Hanisch demonstrated how to make and use pressing equipment," while other girls did presentations on patching and caring for sewing machines.

Moving to Iowa's capital city and attending Drake University transformed Hanisch's political perspective. In a class on "Democracy and Its Enemies," she read Marx for the first time (assigned as an "enemy") and recognized her own family's struggles in the pages. As a woman on campus, she was required to wear dresses or skirts to class, no matter the conditions (the only exception being for during below-zero temperatures) and was held to a strict curfew. One night, Hanisch attended a lecture by her future employer, Carl Braden, about the House Un-American Activities Committee (HUAC) and red baiting of civil rights organizations. His talk had been electrifying, at once infuriating and inspiring, before it was suddenly halted for every woman in the auditorium—who were all forced to leave before the Q&A in order to make curfew.

With the threat of student loan payments looming, Hanisch was forced to abandon her dream of volunteering for Freedom Summer after graduation, and she instead landed a position with the UPI news service in Des Moines, Iowa, hoping to cover politics at the Iowa Statehouse. She was assigned to Women's News, writing articles like: "Let Children Assist with the Decorations" and "For Your Party Favors: Popcorn Christmas Trees." Was the sum total of her contribution to the world to be found in edible crafts for the holiday table? Her disappointment calcified into regret with every new assignment on homemakers' tips.

Hanisch quit the UPI in 1965 to take a job in Mississippi with the Freedom Information Service (FIS), a new Delta Ministry* initiative for the various civil rights organizations active across the state. Distinct from the syndicated news provided by Hanisch's former employer, the FIS's aim was not only, or even primarily, to facilitate information sharing among organizations but also to close the "large information gap between Movement leadership and followers" by providing local, Black community members with "meaningful access to the information and experiences to write a new story" of their own liberated futures. After a year of work there, when SNCC called for white activists to fight racism and segregation by organizing within white communities, Hanisch left to do just that—through her new job with the Southern Conference Educational Fund (SCEF) in New York. Hanisch was unfamiliar with the city, and she had visited only once before in the previous year to attend a fund-raiser for the work in Mississippi. It was there that she had met Kathie Amatniek.

Amatniek could not have been more different from Carol Hanisch. A New Yorker born in the Bronx, she had been raised in young childhood by her divorced, single mother, Sara, who was an artist and teacher. When Kathie was five years old, Sara remarried Ernest Amatniek (mother and daughter both took

* The Delta Ministry was established in Mississippi by the National Council of Churches in 1964 as Freedom Summer concluded, and it remained active in the state until the 1970s.

his last name), who worked as a labor organizer and who spoke proudly of his time as a volunteer in the Spanish Civil War, fighting Franco with the famed Abraham Lincoln Brigade. At home, the Amatnieks created a world full of art, books, and leftist politics, and they were happy to demonstrate how women and men could be equal in all things; Kathie's friends often encountered Ernest doing housework when they came to play. When Kathie was in the seventh grade, she and her mom protested her school's curriculum for not allowing girls to take shop classes or for boys to take home economics—and they won.

Kathie's feminist awakening came at age fourteen, after reading Simone de Beauvoir's *The Second Sex*. When she'd first spied the title among her mother's books, Kathie had picked it up, assuming it was a dirty book about sex. It wasn't, of course, at least not in the titillating way that young Kathie had imagined, but she kept on reading, having already discovered something else exciting in its pages. Like most teenagers, she worried constantly about how she looked; reading Beauvoir put those anxieties in a new light, not to mention giving an awareness of their astronomical costs in time, money, and self-esteem. Gendered inequalities, she realized as she turned each successive page, were systemic, not the natural order of things. Her parents had already taught her that people could change bad systems—so why couldn't she be a part of doing the same?

In 1960, Amatniek arrived at Radcliffe College as an outspoken, intellectually self-assured student who rarely shied away from a debate or failed to act when confronted with injustice. She grew into one of just two anti-war voices on the editorial board of the university's student newspaper, *The Harvard Crimson*, and she joined other women demonstrating against Radcliffe's mandatory curfew and its policing through dormitory sign-ins. (Never imposed on male students, the sign-in system was common across institutions of higher education in the United States. Many women's liberationists shared the formative experience of collectively resisting these institutional curfews.) Amatniek departed shortly after graduation, for training and a post in Mississippi for Freedom Summer.*

* Now living outside the city, in Westchester County, the Amatnieks joined a local network of parents who lobbied elected officials for federal protection for the activists and raised money for legal defense funds.

Kathie Amatniek (fifth from left) with Batesville Staff, Freedom Summer, July 1964

A week after the disappearance of civil rights activists Chaney, Schwerner, and Goodman, Amatniek and several others from the Batesville field office were similarly harassed by police. After a church meeting in another part of the county, the group squeezed into a single car, with Amatniek tucked in the middle of the backseat. By the time they got close to Batesville, it was pitch-dark but for the beams of their headlights. The road was empty, until a police cruiser appeared and began riding their bumper. The patrolman eventually pulled the car over for a moving violation. *Had something like this happened to the three men before they went missing?* they all wondered, petrified. The officer finally let the activists go, but only after ticketing the driver.

After that summer, Amatniek moved back to New York City and worked as a film editor, making a short piece for anti-war organizing that was advertised in *New Left Notes* and a documentary about the summer project. When Hanisch moved to the city, the women's friendship grew through common activism and backgrounds organizing in the South.

In the end, it was Bill Price who also connected Amatniek to women's liberation. "These two women are starting up a group," he'd told her. Not long after that, Amatniek found herself squeezed into Pam Allen's tiny apartment on East Third Street, listening as Shulie Firestone led a group of women all about her age in an animated discussion. As she sat there, Amatniek was flooded with emotion—chief among them, relief. *This is me*, she thought. She "disagreed with practically everything that was getting said," but she "was so grateful to them all for being there," so happy and loving "the spirit" of the women's planning, that Amatniek didn't feel like arguing with anyone.

In the fall of 1967, it seemed to Anne Forer that every woman she knew or met in New York City was, as one told her, "Doing women's liberation these days." A child of leftists from Queens, Forer thought of herself as a "red diaper baby," born to her idealism and radical socialist politics. She was a recent graduate of City College, living in the East Village, working as a kindergarten teacher, and active in the New Left. Twenty-two and single, she was also, by her own account, "always looking to meet boys." If you were "a radical and you want[ed] to meet boys," she told an interviewer later, you would "go to meetings and groups." (Forer made the point twice, urging, "You have to get a true picture here.") That fall, whenever she asked friends in the movement what they were doing and what meetings they were attending, they all replied with something about women's liberation. *Not a great place for meeting men*, thought Forer. But she went anyway; luckily, it turned out the group was meeting right around the corner from her apartment.

> I showed up and that's when it was instant love. I fell totally in love with women's liberation. It all happened in one meeting. Everything that women's liberation offered me. My biggest problem was the competition, that I saw women as competition. . . . I walked into that meeting and it was a different relationship. It was that we saw our interests as one.

Sitting in a little apartment, nary a man in sight, listening to everyone talk and plan, Forer was ecstatic. It was like she was seeing other women for the first time, past all her usual comparisons and judgments, in a place with potential for true friendship and alignment, "and it was the most wonderful thing that ever, ever, ever, ever happened in my whole life."

And then, suddenly, Forer grew anxious. She loved what these women were saying, but she wasn't sure she was quite able to identify with it. "I have no idea how we are oppressed," she blurted out during one conversation. "I don't know how I'm oppressed. How are we oppressed as women?" Then, pulling from the radical history she knew well, Forer made a suggestion.

"If everyone could give an example from their own life [about] how they experienced oppression as a woman," she said, "maybe it would help to raise my own consciousness." It was like "Marxism where we said the workers don't realize that they're oppressed," she explained, "we have to raise their consciousness."

Kathie Amatniek, sitting just behind her in that crowded room, was struck by Forer's suggestion and the reasoning behind it. She suspected that every woman there needed to have her consciousness raised.

8

DON'T CRY, RESIST

Inspired by Jeannette Rankin's urging for ten thousand women to come together in protest against what at that point were the ten thousand American soldiers killed in Vietnam, the Women Strike for Peace (WSP) called for women from all over the country to converge on Washington, D.C., on January 15, 1968—opening day of Congress—to demand that lawmakers end the war. By the time Rankin's "brigade" arrived in Washington seven months later, the number of American troops that had been killed had more than doubled, to 20,500.

At the age of eighty-seven, Jeannette Rankin brought fiery energy and tradition to the anti-war movement. In 1916, the Montanan had been the first woman in history to be elected to Congress, where she introduced the resolution that became the 19th Amendment, extending the vote to women in 1920. A pacifist active in the Women's International League for Peace and Freedom, she had voted against declaring war on Germany in 1917, and after winning election again in 1940, was the only member of the House or Senate to vote against declaring war on Japan after Pearl Harbor. To some she was a pariah and to others a hero, but in any case, by 1968, she was a legend.

The WSP's leadership had seized upon the opportunity of Rankin's remarks and stature to bring a mass demonstration of "woman power" to the Capitol. Calling themselves the "Jeannette Rankin Brigade" (JRB), the women would petition lawmakers to make their first act of the new session a resolution to end the war and immediately withdraw all U.S. troops. In addition to the Brigade's namesake, marquee sponsors included Coretta Scott King (officially referred to in publicity materials only as "Mrs. Martin Luther King, Jr."), folksinger Judy Collins, author Susan Sontag, actress Ruby Dee, and various wives and daughters of national leaders in religion, politics, and the arts, such as "Mrs. Benjamin Spock" and "Mrs. Harry Belafonte."

Women "have a special power," Coretta Scott King asserted from her seat beside Rankin at the announcement event, and the moral obligation to use it. "Women are fortunate in having the responsibility of bringing life into the world," she continued, and "it is their sacred task to preserve this life."

One syndicated news service described the women at the press conference as "sweet-faced, gentle-voiced, and in dead earnest," while the *New York Daily News* dubbed their plan a "Waltz on Washington." Capitol Police were unpersuaded by the supposed sweetness and gentility of it all, and they moved quickly to thwart the JRB by invoking a rarely used 1882 law forbidding demonstrations on Capitol grounds. This effectively barred the women from standing outside or entering the building, prompting Rankin to scoff, "[T]here is no reason why old ladies shouldn't be allowed to go into the Capitol." Organizers challenged the police order in court, but set about making alternative plans.

More than an inch of fresh snow had blanketed the capital on the morning of the protest, and even for January it was bitterly cold. With the JRB's case against the police still tied up in federal court, the demonstration would now be a short march to Union Plaza for a rally, near but not at the Capitol. Afterward, chartered buses would take all who wished to go to the Omni Shoreham Hotel for a Women's Congress. Everything about the plan was designed to project an image of respectability, civic responsibility, and gendered moral authority. The JRB had come to petition their representatives (almost all men) as mothers, wives, and daughters. This attitude was echoed in the women's neat dress, subtle makeup, and generally conservative style, signaling the feminine propriety resting at the foundation of their "woman power."

Organizers had been adamant that the Brigade would follow the law, no matter how unjust, and they monitored participants throughout to quell possible infractions. Handmade signs were forbidden; the women marched behind a single, long banner urging, "End the War in Vietnam and Social Crisis at Home!" and beneath another that read, "Welcome to the Jeannette Rankin Peace Parade." Despite the cold and snow turned into slush beneath their feet, every woman with the honor of leading the protest wore a skirt or dress and heeled boots.

As the marchers gathered in Union Plaza, young women in noticeably different attire moved among them, handing out folded flyers with thick black borders:

YOU ARE JOYFULLY INVITED
TO ATTEND THE BURIAL

of

WEEPING WOMANHOOD

who passed

with

a

sigh

to her Great Reward

this year of the Lord

1968

after 3000 years of

bolstering the edges of the

warmakers

and

aiding the cause of war . . .

Inside was a direct appeal to the JRB: "Don't bring flowers. Do be prepared to sacrifice your traditional female roles."

"Now you must resist approaching Congress playing these same roles that are synonymous with powerlessness," it warned, and it invited them to celebrate the death of "Woman Power," which was hardly any power at all. "If you are really sincere about ending this war, join us tonight and in the future." The back of the invitation identified its organizers as the Radical Women's Group, and provided contact information for two people, one from New York and the other from Chicago.

The appearance of the Radical Women's Group was a surprise to the Jeannette Rankin Brigade, and to most of its leaders and members an unwelcome one—but not to all. As they distributed their invitations, Bev Grant and a few other women from New York found Flo Kennedy, who had played a significant role in organizing the JRB demonstration and served as one of its national sponsors. She was happy to see them. Both Flo Kennedy and Donna Allen had witnessed that patronizing pat on Shulamith Firestone's head in Chicago a few months earlier.

Allen felt "just as much with [the Radical Women's Group] as with anybody else." Despite being a founder of Women Strike for Peace (WSP), and thus nominally an organizer of the JRB, she shared the conviction that "woman power" could not "afford to be sedate" but, rather, had "to be radical"—which, she believed, could happen only if women were no longer limited by dominant gender expectations and the systemic inequalities they reproduced. *The Radical Women should have a spot at the post-demonstration Women's Congress,* she thought, and she negotiated a place for them on the speakers' program.

The Radical Women's Group arrived en masse at the hotel ballroom, where hundreds of Brigade members were convening from all over the country. Among the things they carried were a coffin bier hung with streamers and representative objects of women's oppression, such as hair curlers, garters, and sheets of S&H green stamps (part of a popular national shoppers' loyalty program). On this bier rested a "larger-than-life dummy" of traditional womanhood, as explained Firestone, that was "complete with feminine getup, blank face, blonde curls, and a candle."

The group paraded down the room's central aisle in a mock funeral cortège to a dirge performed on kazoos, and they sang songs composed by Bev Grant for the occasion. Some carried a large banner chastising the ballroom's occupants, "Don't Cry: Resist!," while others handed out more flyers.

"ARE AMERICAN WOMEN TRULY BEAUTIFUL?" queried one. Not yet, it replied, because when "we" consider attractiveness or beauty, "we think of turning ourselves into the 'Glamour'-puss sex symbol sponsored by the American Capitalist ruling class." Beauty would be found only in the personal strength that came from "feeling ourselves as truly growing developing human beings." Another flyer, written by Kathie Amatniek, elaborated on a series of all-caps proclamations:

TRADITIONAL WOMANHOOD IS DEAD!

TRADITIONAL WOMEN WERE BEAUTIFUL . . .
BUT REALLY POWERLESS!

"UPPITY" WOMEN EVEN MORE BEAUTIFUL . . .
BUT STILL POWERLESS . . .

SISTERHOOD IS POWERFUL!

HUMANHOOD IS THE ULTIMATE!

They had come to Washington to challenge activist women to let go of the traditional foundation of their power: the female reproductive body and the qualities of nurturing, sacrifice, and moral authority said to flow from it. It is no surprise that Amatniek and others looked to that other special provenance of women—beauty—to make their case. The flyers' appeals challenged the dominant standard of beauty that constrained women by making its cultivation the necessary means of their acting upon the world. This kind of beauty was a flawed and unnatural thing, and it should be consigned to the grave with the rest of traditional women's roles, they urged—but beauty itself was not flawed. Beauty remained central to their understandings of what womanhood, unfettered from the requirements of patriarchy, might become.

Amatniek had been appointed the group's representative speaker. Now, she took the stage to deliver "A Funeral Oration for the Burial of Traditional Womanhood." Elaborating on points from their flyers, Amatniek ended by calling for those in the room to get up and walk across the hall for a "counter-caucus" to the JRB's Women's Congress.

In the silence that followed, the air crackled with anticipation and anxiety. Women looked around the room and at one another, some in horror, and others with a question, *Should we?* And then women began to rise from their seats.

As the mock funeral cortège reversed course and left the ballroom, about two hundred people followed their banner out of the JRB's Women's Congress. Though Allen was adamantly opposed to the decision to separate the groups and form a counter-caucus—she wanted the activist women to work out their differences together so they could build something bigger, more effective, and in no way sedate—she still believed that the arrival of women's liberation was a very good thing. When her oldest child, Dana Densmore, answered her telephone in Cambridge, Massachusetts, she heard her mother exclaim, "Women's Liberation! It's happening!"

From the moment she'd seen the women enter the room, Rosalyn "Ros" Baxandall knew she wanted to be part of the Radical Women's Group. Born Rosalyn Fraad in Manhattan in 1939, Ros was the oldest of what would ultimately be three daughters to radical parents who were both members of the Communist Party. The Fraad sisters' early childhoods were shaped by their parents' leftist politics and the close-knit radical communities and summer camps that dotted the Northeast. That was until the twin devastations of the Cold War and McCarthyism tore these supports away, leaving the girls to negotiate a household fraught with ambiguities, secrets, fear, and grief. The family was relatively affluent—their father, Lewis M. Fraad, would eventually be named chief of pediatrics at Albert Einstein College of Medicine—and before she had children, their mother, Irma (née London), had been an attorney with her family's radical law firm. Law wasn't Irma's first choice of career path, but leaving it behind to become a full-time mother and wife gnawed at the woman, and her relationships with her daughters suffered. In a short essay about growing up

"Red Sisters of the Bourgeoisie," Ros and her sister Harriet* described the costs when their "mother found herself trapped at home. Too guilty to continue a career that took her away from serving Dad and managing an elegant home, she was also too angry to enjoy her children. Mom was a frustrated housewife who didn't admit that she was miserable." Irma might not have admitted it, but her misery was evident and painful to her children. It was also instructive. In high school, Ros turned to Simone de Beauvoir's *The Second Sex* as a book of advice and sustenance: "I read and reread every wilted page," she said, describing the French feminist as "my Ann Landers."†

Ros Fraad graduated from the University of Wisconsin in 1961, returned to New York, and married Lee Baxandall six months later. They had a son in 1967, making Baxandall one of the few mothers in her circle of radical women. That same year, while working as a community organizer and welfare rights advocate, Baxandall helped start the Liberation Nursery in a run-down storefront in the East Village, between Avenues C and D: the city's first feminist daycare center.

Sitting in that ballroom with the Jeannette Rankin Brigade, witnessing the righteous sabotage of the funeral for "Traditional Womanhood," Kathie Amatniek's oration resonated deeply with Baxandall, as did the sheer spectacle of it all. Baxandall jumped from her seat without hesitation to join them. Falling into line next to Amatniek, whom she already knew a little through a shared friend in New York, Baxandall asked, "What are you doing next?"

* Two years younger than Ros, Harriet Fraad was active in New Haven Women's Liberation and became a feminist psychotherapist.

† "Ann Landers" was the pen name of Esther Pauline "Eppie" Lederer, who wrote the enormously popular, nationally syndicated weekly advice column, "Ask Ann Landers," from 1955 until her death in 2002.

9

THE MINISKIRT CAUCUS

The postcard that arrived at Ros Baxandall's apartment about a month after the JRB action invited her to "Come to the first city-wide meeting of Radical Women" at the Free University of New York (FUNY) on 14th Street, overlooking Union Square. Founded in 1965, FUNY was a New Left experiment in education, staffed by a radical faculty, many of whom had been fired from their university teaching positions for protesting the war, being outspoken socialists, or both. Ros knew it well; her husband had lectured there on Marxism and the arts during the school's inaugural year.

Shulie Firestone and Pam Allen had come home from Washington, D.C., with contact information for women from around the country who'd expressed interest in women's liberation. The list had been divvied up by region: West Coast, Midwest, and East Coast. Given that more than half of those on the list lived on the East Coast, that part was subdivided into North, coordinated by Pam Allen and another woman, and South, to be managed by Marilyn Salzman Webb. In this case, "South" meant only the states bordering the Mason-Dixon Line: southern Pennsylvania, Maryland, and Washington, D.C., where Webb lived. It was hardly the entire South, by any definition; the regional spread of where the women were living in January 1968 was notably tilted toward college towns and New York City. But this was less about where they came from and more about where their educations, jobs, and marriages had subsequently taken them. What had been obvious at their counter-caucus remained true of the list of women who became the seeds of the movement—they were almost entirely white.

Marilyn Webb was emblematic of the group. At twenty-five, she was a recent transplant to the nation's capital. Originally from New York City, she went to college in Chicago, where she joined SDS. She was part of the Women's Caucus that had outlined its vision for women's liberation in the New Left at the 1967 SDS convention, before assuring the men in the audience, "We love you!" Later that year, she became a founding member of the West Side Group. After leaving the University of Chicago's doctoral program in educational psychology, following several incidents of sexual harassment by faculty members, Webb went on to run a number of preschools for poor children, including one for Saul Alinsky's community organizing project.* Her husband, Lee Webb, former national secretary of SDS and then co-director of the anti-war Vietnam Summer project, moved them to Washington so he could take a position with the Institute for Policy Study, a progressive think tank. Marilyn also took a job at the Institute, where she battled a new arena of New Left male chauvinism, and attempted with little success to get family issues and women's concerns onto the agenda.

As the postcards went out, the newest issue of *Ramparts,* a New Left–leaning mass-circulation glossy magazine, hit the newsstands. The cover story was devoted to the Jeannette Rankin Brigade (JRB) march and surrounding events, including the counterprotest, as a window onto the resurgent feminism in the United States. Written by brother and sister Warren and Marianne Hinckle, "A History of the Rise of the Unusual Movement for Women Power in the United States, 1961–1968" recounted developments in women's activism and the emergence of a new movement. It credited Marilyn Webb with a reporting role for the story, and along with being quoted several times, she was featured prominently in one of its accompanying photos, posing in a miniskirt alongside Anne Scheer, wife of the magazine's managing editor and a New Left

* In 2018, Marilyn Webb petitioned the University of Chicago for recognition of the past harassment, compelling the university to review her case. She completed the necessary requirements and earned her doctorate in education in 2019. The University issued a statement that it regretted the inappropriate behavior that contributed to the long delay in completing her degree (Jack Wang, "Marilyn Webb Comes Full Circle to Complete PhD Degree," *UChicago News*, May 13, 2019).

activist in her own right. The Hinckles' timeline included the publication of Betty Friedan's *The Feminine Mystique* in 1963; the founding of the National Organization for Women (NOW) in 1966, with Friedan at the helm; and the more recent insurgence of a radical "Women's Liberation Front," which the authors mostly referred to as the "Miniskirt Caucus." Despite Webb's role, the radical women's critique of JRB-style "woman power" was minimized in the article, which kept discussion of the activists' distinguishing features mostly to points of fashion, attractiveness, and age. "You won't mind twisting your neck to look at the girls on the very left of the Brigade, since they are the prettiest," the Hinckles wrote. "They are the stylish ladies who graduated from college with majors in the civil rights fights and campus free speech revolutions of the early 60s." In addition to their being mostly in their twenties, white, and middle class, the authors described the activists as generally "articulate and confident if not aggressive; they are usually attractive, most are liberated sexually, and the majority dress in miniskirts, high boots and bright colors."

Amid the article's deluge of snarky vitriol for feminists of the nineteenth century and modern day, and the patronizing "Miniskirt Caucus" moniker, perhaps nothing was so infuriating as the magazine's cover. It featured a photograph of a headless, buxom white woman wearing a large "Jeannette Rankin for President" button pinned onto her right breast. It drew the eye to the cover's central feature: the plunging neckline and exposed cleavage. Labeled simply "Women Power," the cover image literally framed activist women as jokes—all tits and no brains.

Mention of the *Ramparts* cover and article came up at nearly every radical women's event and meeting in the weeks that followed. The magazine—which was faced out on newsstands and magazine racks across the country—stared at the viewer in a way the headless woman it depicted could not. It appeared in subscribers' mailboxes or as well-thumbed copies in the stacks of newspapers, magazines, and flyers in coffeehouses and college dormitory common rooms; it was scattered across the tables and it littered the bathroom floors of homes women visited and lived in—yet another reminder of what women were, should, or could ever hope to be in 1968 America. It was a lesson in what was valuable and possible for women, a lesson that assumed desirability and beauty came only in young, white packages.

But there was great power in this outrage. The *Ramparts* cover story became a tipping point for many women, catalyzing the nascent movement for women's liberation and growing its numbers. Writing from Chicago, Jo Freeman captured this in a tongue-in-cheek letter to the *Ramparts* editor, published the following month. She asked if the magazine could send her the names and addresses "of the radical women, and other interested people who write to you to protest" the piece, so she could send them a copy of *Voice of the Women's Liberation Movement.* Jeannette Rankin weighed in, too, writing that she "loved" the cover, "though one really needed a magnifying glass to see whose picture that was on the button."

Freeman edited the *Voice of the Women's Liberation Movement,* which was the newsletter established in Chicago as part of the next steps post-JRB protest. While its title made claim to being the singular voice of the new movement, it was clear from the first issue that the newsletter represented one side of an emergent conflict about the fundamental aims of women's liberation.

Its contributors wrote from the general position that all forms of oppression and systemic inequality, including sexism and male chauvinism, were at base the products of capitalism and, by extension, the political liberalism that facilitated it. Men were not the "enemy," they explained, but similarly were constrained by dominant gender roles and the hollow individualism that was promised by American democratic institutions and consumerism. While they argued that men and women were both oppressed by this system—if, admittedly, in very different ways—no one was letting radical men off the hook. Rather, their central focus was the stark gendered inequality so evident within the movement itself, in the roles and expectations that dogged every New Left woman. To them, the successful liberation of women had to start with a dismantling of the New Left's endemic sexism and the creation of opportunities for radical women to realize their individual potentials and assume meaningful leadership in movement efforts to end the Vietnam War and tackle racism and poverty—with the understanding that all were rooted in the entwined problems of capitalism and liberalism.

On the other side of the argument were the women, many of whom were clustered in New York, who sought to build a completely autonomous movement devoted to raising the consciousness of all women and challenging the specificities of their oppression. They identified that oppression's causes as patriarchy, male chauvinism, and the privileges enjoyed—and jealously guarded—by all men, including but hardly limited to those of the New Left.

Early on, these philosophical differences took on an easy shorthand of geographic opposition: Chicago vs. New York City. Like all binary pairings, this view obscured more than it illuminated by flattening what was a far more complex and shifting terrain. In the case of New York Radical Women (NYRW), for instance, both poles—notably flipped from their cities of origin—were represented by co-founders Pam Allen (Chicago) and Shulamith Firestone (New York). Other than Marilyn Webb, who had just moved to Washington, D.C., Pam Allen was the only contributor to the newsletter who wasn't actually living in Chicago. She'd put the group's stamp on the JRB counterprotest immediately afterward, with a letter to the *Guardian* that was published as a January 27, 1968, opinion piece under the headline "Beyond a . . . Feminist Stance." In it, Allen wrote that most of the radical women at the counter-caucus "had moved beyond a mere feminist stance to a position of seeing that women's liberation is intimately bound up with the movement for radical change in the United States." Webb elaborated on this argument in the first issue of the *Voice of the Women's Liberation Movement*: "Our enemy is not men, but an oppressive system that pits group against group, denying each [men and women] self-control and self-confidence."

By the summer of 1968, the oppositional stances of women's liberation would be known by new labels: the "Politicos" vs. "Feminists," the former a common term to distinguish movement activists from the counterculture and "hippies" that they saw as apolitical and checked out.

Webb didn't reject or distance herself publicly from the representation of women's liberation in *Ramparts,* but she tried in her own writing to reframe the magazine's emphasis on looks and sex appeal so as to focus on radical women's agency and their choices in fashion as emblematic of their politics. "We have developed our own femininity and enjoy being women who love men and do not see them as the enemy," she wrote in a June issue of *New Left Notes.* In this way, Webb drew a stark contrast to the New York City feminists: "We are not the cold, gray-suited women of the Twenties, nor the 'masculinized' ones of the present. Staid suits have been replaced by the colorful dress of a turned-on generation of women who are asserting themselves as females as well as intellectual politicos."

10

WHAT ARE YOU DOING NEXT?

Ros Baxandall's question to Kathie Amatniek at the JRB protest in January—"What are you doing next?"—echoed through NYRW meetings in the months to follow, as the group attempted to settle on a focus for their activism and theories of women's liberation. Three factions came together, vying to set the agenda. One faction thought the women should meet primarily as a reading and study group to better understand the sources of their oppression and build the theoretical foundations for liberation; another faction urged focusing mostly on direct-action protests; and the third faction, which included Kathie Amatniek and Carol Hanisch, argued that the foundations for liberation would be found only through consciousness raising (CR), which should be the core of the group's work. Ultimately, their "faction . . . won out," explained Hanisch, but "not without ongoing dissention." From that point on, the group's weekly Thursday night meetings were usually dedicated to CR.

Inspired by the Cultural Revolution in China, and "speaking bitterness" as it was depicted in William H. Hinton's popular 1966 book, *Fanshen: A Documentary of Revolution in a Chinese Village,* as well as their experiences working for the civil rights movement in Mississippi, Amatniek and Hanisch honed their process and worked to identify the most effective methods for facilitating sessions. Much of the time, the group would go around the room, each woman responding to the same question or prompt from her own perspective. In the spring of 1968, the topics included: Woman as Child; Woman as Adolescent; Woman as Student; Woman as Single Woman; Woman as Worker; Woman as Head of Household; Woman as Wife; Woman as Mother; Woman as Aged; Woman in Male Power Structure; Woman in Capitalism; Woman in Socialism; Woman in Revolution.

Before each session began, Amatniek would hang a poster she'd made:

SPEAK PAINS TO RECALL PAINS
—THE CHINESE REVOLUTION
TELL IT LIKE IT IS
—THE BLACK REVOLUTION
BITCH, SISTERS, BITCH
—THE FINAL REVOLUTION

The CR was meant to be a supportive process, but not a comfortable or easy one. It "packed an intellectual and an emotional punch," said one participant, but it provided for her "relief from a tension I had always had, between who I was and who and what I was supposed to be."

"Early consciousness-raising groups were combative," recalled Ros Baxandall. She explained:

> We talked as honestly as we knew how about sex, school, street hassles, our childhood, the men in our lives. Discussion was intense because we were speaking about subjects formerly whispered or entirely suppressed. Orgasms: do we fake them? What gives us pleasure? Housework: who does the dishes and laundry? Who vacuums? Who takes out the garbage? Some spoke animatedly for ten minutes, others whispered a few sentences. We would challenge one another, often too roughly, but this harshness actually helped us learn from each other. We interrupted each other when someone said something that didn't sound authentic, or was antiwoman, racist, or elitist.

The meetings could be tense because the stakes were so high and personal, but they were also deeply satisfying and joyful in ways that none of the participants had known before or found elsewhere. "We were, we believed, poised on the trembling edge of transformation," described Baxandall. "All the walls and boundaries inside and outside us might be knocked down. There was a yeastiness in the air that made us cocky and strong. Sure, there were splits and backbiting among us, but there was also fun and great times."

Meetings were cramped, with anywhere from twenty to thirty women showing up on Thursdays as word got out around the city. Beyond a feeling of basic unwieldiness, the congested conditions facilitated the creation of smaller groups of the like-minded. Carol Hanisch provided a solution to the space problem when she got use of the SCEF office, making effective large meetings possible. Some groups continued meeting on their own, but that was in addition to coming every Thursday for the general NYRW meeting, rather than instead of it. Without the common space, NYRW might well have fractured into several smaller collectives before the summer of 1968.

Consciousness raising was not an end in itself but, rather, part of a process to develop the collective knowledge, anger, and bonds to challenge and transform the structures of inequality and women's oppression that were identified through the sessions. While some would never think the group had taken enough action—that they'd stayed too often in the SCEF office talking when they should have been out organizing and protesting in the streets—nevertheless, NYRW participated in various demonstrations around the city during this period, especially those held in favor of decriminalizing abortion and in expanding access to birth control. Though the action was initially dominated by professional men—doctors, lawyers, state officials, journalists, and those seeking to reform religious institutions—feminists were seizing the initiative by 1967.

NOW's second annual convention, held in Washington, D.C., in November of that year, was contentious on the issues of whether to endorse the Equal Rights Amendment (ERA) and to commit the organization to the legalization of abortion. Supporting the ERA troubled the group's relationships with organized labor, while the issue of abortion threatened significant splits within the membership. While the abortion resolution vote itself looked overwhelmingly in the affirmative, with 57 in favor and 14 against, nearly a third of the delegates abstained. A group from Ohio walked out in protest after the vote, arguing that their constituencies would never approve of such a thing. Within a year, they had started a new organization seeking similar general aims, but refusing to take a position on reproductive rights.

The inclusion of official support for the ERA was similarly, if not quite so spectacularly, a problem for many members from organized labor, whose unions were expressly against the amendment, as well as some who felt the time was not right for putting the organization's name behind the version of the amendment before Congress in 1967. The matter also unsettled for many at the convention the difficult balance they saw between one's personal opinions and those that should be endorsed by NOW in order to advance its mission and support its growth. The health of the organization was on the line, argued Dorothy Haener during debate on the resolution. "This is not an opportune time to give NOW support to the resolution supporting the Equal Rights Amendment," she urged. "The UAW [United Auto Workers], which I officially represent, supplies NOW with supplies and services such as free paper, printing, mailing, etc. If this resolution is passed, since the UAW is against it [because it would negate decades of hard-won protections for female workers], then the services will no longer be supplied." Starting and running a national civil rights organization was expensive, which not only made growing membership and collecting annual dues crucial but also necessitated grants and donations to cover the significant shortfall. "We need support from organizations," Haener said, "and although I am personally in support of the resolution [to endorse the ERA], I do not see how the support of the amendment will accomplish much at this time." Ultimately, and after much debate, the resolution passed with 82 in favor, 3 against, and 12 abstentions.

In the late spring, Shulamith Firestone proposed creating the journal that would become *Notes from the First Year*, a collection of materials documenting the women's movement in the 1960s and 1970s. By Carol Hanisch's account, Firestone believed "it was time" for the group to "get some of our ideas down on paper for distribution to other women." The driving force and primary coordinator of *Notes*, if never identified as the editor, Firestone was anxious to produce the journal quickly, so she could take a copy with her to Paris in June to present

Anne Koedt and Carol Hanisch (in sunglasses) carry "Don't Cry: Resist!" banner at a demonstration to legalize abortion, Times Square, New York City, March 1968

to the woman whose work had been so important to the movement: Simone de Beauvoir.

Notes opened with a question from Firestone: "What does the word 'feminism' bring to mind?" Perhaps, she suggested, one thought of "a granite-faced spinster obsessed with the vote? Or a George Sand in cigar and bloomers, a woman against nature?" Whatever the word conjured, Firestone concluded, chances were high that the associations were negative. The word "feminism" had become so tarnished "that a young woman intellectual, often radical in every other area, will deny vehemently that she is a feminist, will be ashamed to identify in any way with the early women's movement, calling it a cop-out or reformist or demeaning it politically without knowing even the little that is circulated about it."

Firestone urged the embrace of a "new view" of feminism and of the nineteenth- and early-twentieth-century women's movement in the United States that focused on its "dynamic radical potential." If that dynamism had died on the vine of suffrage, it was not a cause for wholesale rejection of this past but, rather, a chance for learning what wisdom it held for contemporary women's liberation. "There are several important lessons to be learned this time around if we don't want to be subtly subverted again," concluded Firestone: "never compromise basic principles for political expediency"; "agitation for specific freedoms is worthless without the preliminary raising of consciousness necessary to utilize these freedoms fully"; "put your own interests first, then proceed to make alliances with other oppressed groups."

Notes from the First Year did not just offer an alternative view of the past and its meanings; it also staked a claim to history itself and to future accounts of the women's liberation movement. The rest of the journal was a carefully presented archive of key documents, speeches, and ideas generated by NYRW, starting with the Jeannette Rankin Brigade protest and the first New York City radical women's meeting that followed, as well as a rally in March of that year for the legalization of abortion and greater access to birth control. It included two articles crafted from consciousness-raising sessions, to "give the reader some sense of what a typical discussion is like at the weekly Thursday night meetings," as well as the first publication of Anne Koedt's foundational (and infamous) essay, "The Myth of the Vaginal Orgasm." The journal was capped by "Roz's [*sic*] Page," a textual collage of quotations, lists of the condemned ("Males who continue to say 'Chick' after being told to stop") and the supported ("Linda Le Clair: Barnard martyr for equal cohabitation rights"), and superlatives like "Aunt Tom of the Month: Helen Gurley Brown," and "Most Chauvinist Publication: *Ramparts*."

Notably, although *Notes* was published under the general authorship of NYRW, it hardly represented universally held perspectives. Among its contributors were none of the group's more outspoken politicos weighing in on the fundamental problem of capitalism, or questioning the importance of feminists of the past to liberationists in the present as anything other than cautionary liberal tales. In this, the journal was also a record of the conflicts and factionalism that characterized NYRW's development after the JRB protest.

Roxanne Dunbar had left Mexico City for the United States shortly after learning about Valerie Solanas after her arrest for shooting Andy Warhol. With no intention of returning to California, she decided to move to Boston because of its long connection with nineteenth-century feminism and abolition. She found an affordable apartment in a racially diverse, predominantly working-class neighborhood across the Charles River in Cambridge, tucked between the campus environs of Harvard University and that of MIT.

Dunbar found the Cambridge-Boston activist communities "very open," and she immediately volunteered with the Boston Draft Resistance Group (BDRG), where she advertised a women's history class that centered on Solanas. She still wrote to her husband Louis regularly, debating revolution, explaining her commitment to Solanas, and trying to enlist him in the cause of feminism. "I think you are wrong to focus on Valerie Solanas's 'insanity,'" she wrote in one letter. "Perhaps you fear the consciousness in her statements. Sure, she was 'crazy' to shoot Andy Warhol. The kind of oppression we experience as women does make us kind of crazy one way or another. I think compulsive shopping and plastic surgery are acts of madness."

On the hunt for her "Super Woman-Power" uprising, Dunbar placed an ad in the BDRG newsletter, *Resist*, inviting women to a meeting about feminism. The only person to respond was Dana Densmore. When she arrived, they connected immediately: Dunbar had found a soulmate.

At the time, Densmore was working at the MIT Instrumentation Laboratory as part of the team that created guidance systems and software for NASA's *Apollo* program. She was a control supervisor for the lunar landing software that helped put the first astronauts on the moon in 1969; she also volunteered as a draft counselor, was active in the anti-war movement, and had been on her own search for others interested in women's liberation. She had read the first issues of the *Voice of the Women's Liberation Movement*, prompting some correspondence with Jo Freeman, and like Dunbar, Densmore was excited about and inspired by Valerie Solanas. It was Densmore who introduced Dunbar to the term "women's liberation," explaining that she'd first heard it used by her mother, Donna Allen, in January.

The pair decided to place another ad in a wider circulation alternative weekly, inviting women to an organizing meeting for the "Female Liberation Front for Human Liberation." Their goals, they listed, were "personal-social, surely inseparable," including questioning "all phallic social structures in existence" and the "historic-psychological role of females," while demanding unfettered access to free birth control and abortion, the "communal raising of children by both sexes and by people of all ages," and an end to "man's exploitation of human, animal, and natural resources."

In late June, Dunbar went to New York City looking for copies of Solanas's *S.C.U.M. Manifesto* and hoping to connect with other women's liberationists. She met Ros Baxandall, who invited her to a small gathering of NYRW members and gave Dunbar a copy of *Notes*. Dunbar sent Baxandall a postcard when she got back to Cambridge: "I hope I did not disrupt your meeting too much. I felt I had to find out so much, since I was leaving the next day. . . . I felt more optimistic than I have in years meeting women like those in your group. I read the *Notes*, and it was like reading my own mind. Can I get more to distribute up here?"

Few of the primary contributors to *Notes* had been in New York when Dunbar visited. Carol Hanisch had left for Kentucky not long after the meeting showing the *Schmeerguntz* film, and Kathie Amatniek was still in California. As planned, Shulamith Firestone had gone to France with a copy of the inaugural issue for Simone de Beauvoir. In Paris, she met up with Anne Koedt, and together the women went to the philosopher's house unannounced to present the journal. They were disappointed to learn that Beauvoir was out of town and would be for several more weeks. (Koedt had gotten the address in a telegram from her friend, Ti-Grace Atkinson.) By the time she jotted off a postcard to Ros Baxandall in July about Paris, seeing "both Annes" and missing Beauvoir, Firestone was in London and was disappointed to find little in the way of women's liberation in the UK; "nothing at all is happening here," she complained.

The other Anne—Anne Forer—also wrote to Baxandall about being in Paris in May, where she'd witnessed firsthand the student strikes and national uprising of workers. Squeezing as much as she could on the front and back of a piece of thin, blue air mail stationery, she told her friend about standing at the student barricades near the Sorbonne and suddenly realizing how much she missed New York City. "It is strange that I should miss most of all our group," she wrote. "When I would have phantasies about staying in Paris or London the main thing that made me want to return to New York was our group." NYRW was her "real roots" in the city, and the "only people I belong to and feel committed to." In the long tradition of American women marveling at the distinctive, easy style of French women, Anne noted to Ros later in her letter, "French girls, too, have real style. They dress in perfect taste and have an extremely attractive look about them no matter what they look like." All of this attention to style, looks, and women's bodies clearly made Forer self-conscious. At the end of her letter, she jotted an addendum, "p.s.: I'm getting plump on French bread and ice cream," illustrated with a charming doodle of a female figure with a round protruding belly putting something in her mouth, labeled, "me eating." Beneath it, Forer wrote a final message in large block letters: "MY LOVE TO THE GROUP," jokingly comparing NYRW and its conflicts to Mary McCarthy's 1963 best-selling novel *The Group*, about the post-graduation struggles of eight female friends from Vassar.

Being away from New York City made Kathie Amatniek similarly lonely for NYRW. "I really miss you and the group," she wrote to Carol Hanisch from California. "Only the memory of the hot, sooty air of New York and the screeching of subways is keeping me from heading straight back to my little apartment." Amatniek had located two women's liberation groups in the Bay Area, one in San Francisco and one in Berkeley, and she was regularly attending the meetings of both. She was facilitating CR sessions with them, but didn't feel like it was working—the women kept identifying their issues as being with themselves, and hence requiring individual changes as opposed to systemic. "All in all, I don't think there's anyone in either the Berkeley or 'Frisco groups that I am as close to politically as I feel toward you, or even Shulie or the two Anne's. But if the New York group is breaking up for the summer, I guess there's no real reason for me to return right away. Still, I don't know, I really miss you all . . . and even dirty old New York."

11

A BUNCH OF MAN-HATING NUTS

JUNE 13, 1968

Six months into her tenure as chapter president and a week after Bobby Kennedy's death, Ti-Grace Atkinson took a seat inside the imposing New York County Supreme Court Building in Lower Manhattan to await the start of a habeas corpus hearing for Valerie Solanas. She was excited for the opportunity to watch her friend, mentor, and fellow NOW member, Flo Kennedy, argue the case on Solanas's behalf. The hearing, however, was getting off to an unusual start.

Before he would allow Kennedy to begin her opening statements, Justice Thomas Dickens chastised the attorney for what she was wearing, describing it as inappropriate attire for a female lawyer in his courtroom. It was hard to know what made Dickens angrier: Kennedy's trousers, her hat with a prominent "Freedom for Women" button attached to it, or his expectation that another successful Black professional like himself would always maintain exceptional decorum as a representative of their race. For her part, whether it was Dickens's performative patriarchal rebuke, his uptight respectability politics, or both, Kennedy was having none of it. She drew laughter from the courtroom and stoked the justice's fury with her retort: "Well, your honor, you are there in a dress. How can you question me?"

Atkinson was wearing the same "Freedom for Women" button. While the intra-racial contest of the moment appears to have been lost on her, she thrilled at Kennedy's quick wit and the eloquence of her statements. It was a feeling and moment she would recall decades later as one of Kennedy's finest, emblematic of the oratorical fireworks and humor she brought to courtrooms and rallies alike.

Kennedy and Atkinson had been surprised to run into one another at Solanas's arraignment the week before, which each woman had felt compelled to attend for her own reasons. Kennedy, who had most recently been part of the defense team for Black Panther leader H. Rap Brown, had gone to witness the arraignment, believing that Solanas had little hope of getting a fair hearing. Atkinson had followed an urge to show support for Solanas after reading her quoted in the press, saying she shot Warhol because "he had too much control over my life." It resonated with Atkinson as being part of a larger swelling anger of women, and she recalled thinking that "finally some woman had done something that was appropriate to the feelings we were having."

That first hearing had taken two days, during which Valerie Solanas rejected court-appointed defense lawyers and then refused private attorneys hired by Maurice Girodias, the publisher of her book, *S.C.U.M. Manifesto*. When the judge denied Solanas's request to defend herself and remanded her to the psychiatric ward of a hospital in Queens for evaluation, she asked Flo Kennedy to help her. The attorney agreed without hesitation and promptly filed for a writ of habeas corpus seeking Solanas's release from the hospital, which had led to the hearing in Thomas Dickens's courtroom a week later.

When Justice Dickens finally allowed Kennedy to proceed, she argued that Valerie Solanas was being detained unlawfully and treated prejudicially because she was a woman. She described Solanas as "one of the most important spokeswomen of the feminist movement," and called her actions politically motivated. "She has been called a female Genet," Kennedy said, likening Solanas to the French playwright and political activist who composed much of his work from prison, "but she has not been taken seriously." She should be heard in court, Kennedy insisted, and be allowed to speak for herself—and for all women—rather than be locked away and silenced. Unmoved by Kennedy's appeal, Justice Dickens denied the motion; Solanas would remain at the hospital and continue to undergo psychological testing.

The Warhol shooting remained a sensational story that filled not only New York City tabloids but also the wire services and newspapers around the country. Fueled by celebrity and the voyeuristic appeal of Warhol's risqué Factory art scene, it was about to take on new significance as offering a glimpse into the supposed world of radical feminists. Marylin Bender, who covered the day's hearing for the *New York Times*, played a significant role in this new framing. In that evening's city edition of the paper, and again the next day in the "Food, Fashion, Family, Furnishings" section, Bender explained how Solanas "was cast yesterday in the role of a heroine of a revitalized feminist movement," and described Kennedy and Atkinson as "representatives of NOW (National Organization for Women), which seeks 'true equality for women,'" who had appeared in court on behalf of "Miss Solanis [*sic*]." Atkinson was so delighted by Bender's article she was prompted to write a letter telling her so. "Beautiful!" she exclaimed. "That's the straightest piece the Movement's had. I <u>like</u> feminism in the Women's Section—very Black Power."

Friedan wasn't as pleased, and nor were many other members of NOW. "I was most disturbed to read the account of Ti-Grace's and Flo Kennedy's support of Valeria Solanis [*sic*] in the TIMES," wrote a NOW-NYC member to Friedan the same night Bender's story first appeared in the early city edition. "Backing this woman and her alleged movement 'to cut up men' subverts the serious endeavors of NOW by making the organization seem like a bunch of man-hating nuts."

And there it was, in a nutshell. From the time she had been taken into police custody and throughout the two days of her first arraignment, journalists had had significant access to Valerie Solanas. After describing Solanas as a "mannishly dressed brunette who crusades for a one-sex world free of men," the *New York Daily News* had summarized her mission as one to "eliminate through sabotage all aspects of society not relevant to women (everything), bring about the complete female takeover, eliminate the male sex and begin to create a swinging, groovy, out-of-sight female world." The picture of Solanas that emerged was that of a murderous, man-hating lesbian who wasn't appropriately feminine or pretty; instead, she was a jealous, unsuccessful playwright and actress who was sometimes homeless, a sex worker, and obsessed with Warhol and the Factory. Any association with her case, NOW members felt, could destroy the legitimacy the organization had built in its first two years, especially so soon after the Kennedy and King assassinations.

Friedan's cohort immediately went into damage-control mode, beginning with a telegram to Flo Kennedy. It demanded she "DESIST IMMEDIATELY FROM LINKING" Solanas's case to NOW, adding that her actions and S.C.U.M. were "ENTIRELY IRRELEVANT" to the organization's aims.

Next, Friedan was set to handle Ti-Grace Atkinson. In addition to their shared membership in the New York chapter, Friedan knew the younger woman through Atkinson's work as chair of the Finance Committee and member of the national board of directors. Friedan herself had recruited Atkinson to run for president of the New York chapter; she was pretty, had a Southern accent, was serious but clever, and as a doctoral student in philosophy at Columbia University, obviously was smart. Friedan had thought Atkinson to be the type of woman who would appeal to potential members of NOW, as well as to the press covering the organization and the governmental and corporate entities NOW sought to persuade to the cause of women's equality.

Delores Alexander, a founding member of NOW-NYC who was at the time a reporter for *Newsday,* could still picture many years later the moment she first saw Atkinson in a "dramatic" fur coat at a meeting; she "was always a beautiful woman." Alexander bristled at the notion that Friedan had chosen Atkinson to be chapter president—"it's an elected post"—and described many members' notable concerns with appearances, amplified by their location in New York's national media market. She believed that the first president of the chapter, Jean Faust, had also been elected partially because of her looks. According to Alexander, Faust "was a fabulously good-looking woman and also because . . . she was married—she presented the right image—and she looked good and she sounded good, too, on television."

Perhaps more important than appearances, however, was a united, consistent message. And, as of late, Atkinson had not quite been playing the game. Starting in early 1968, she had begun to use the chapter's profile and platform to spotlight her own ideas, like an instance in March when the *New York Times Sunday Magazine* published a landmark article on resurgent feminism by Martha Weinman Lear. The article was a sweeping long-form portrait of the new feminist foment that centered NOW-NYC as representative of national trends and popularized the term "second wave." Lear framed her story as a picture of the real feminists behind the caricatures, noting that she'd gone into the project with some of those stereotypes in mind herself: "When I prepared to do an article on this new tide," she wrote, "I prepared also to be entertained; it is the feminist burden that theirs is the only civil-rights movement in history which has been put down, consistently, by the cruelest weapon of them all—ridicule."

This ridicule, Lear showed, had weighed on her subjects, dragging them down as they attempted to pursue educations and careers. Jean Faust, whom Lear described as "37, married, attractive," told her, "I managed to get to college. I would try to express my ideas, and the men would laugh. They'd say, 'That's funny; you don't *look* like a feminist.' You know—if you're a feminist, you're not feminine." Faust went on to describe working her way into an executive role at a cosmetics firm and learning that two men who worked for her were making more money than she did. When she complained and asked for a raise, her boss told her, "You're a married woman. You don't need a raise. Your husband will support you." So, she quit, and "joined NOW as soon as I heard of it."

Within the organization, Lear also wrote, she had identified the existence of a "small group called [New York] Radical Women—young, bright-eyed, cheerfully militant—which recently splintered off from Students for a Democratic Society." Some had joined NOW-NYC, she continued, which had created some tension within the chapter. "Their thesis," Lear said of the younger radicals, "is that true equality for women can come only with profound social revolution. Their *haute* thinker, and thus the key to their spirit and style, is Ti-Grace Atkinson (in the *patois* of Louisiana, where she was born, 'Ti' designates a namesake), president of the New York chapter." She went on to describe Atkinson as "29, unmarried, good-looking (in the *Times*, she has been described as 'softly sexy,' which is not *necessarily* a compliment to a feminist). She is an analytical philosopher, working for her doctorate at Columbia." The rest of the long article gave most of its space to Atkinson's story and her radical ideas, particularly on marriage and the family, as well as her criticisms of NOW's liberalism. "I'm afraid the women's movement in this country is still pretty low-class, intellectually," she told Lear. "Practically all we talk about is equal rights in employment. That's not opportunity; it's *opportunism*." Atkinson professed being "a little bored with the abortion issue," because what she really wanted to talk about was the "demise of marriage."

> To say that you can be both a career woman and a wife and mother, and that the institutions won't change and won't be threatened—that's a cop-out. Any real change in the status of women would be a fundamental assault on marriage and the family. People would be tied together by love, not legal contraptions. Children would be raised communally; it's just not honest to talk about freedom for women unless you get the child-rearing off their backs.

Atkinson described joining NOW in its early days—famously because Simone de Beauvoir suggested she look up Friedan—and how she was first put to fund-raising. "Her social connections were good," Lear wrote before adding, "it may have occurred to some NOW officials that her appearance might dissipate the traditional image of the feminist as a castrating crow in bloomers."

Atkinson got the most column inches, but Lear gave Betty Friedan the last word. In her interview, Friedan made her own perspective clear: her central worry was not aligning with so many advanced ideas of feminism but instead alienating mainstream American women before they could see how much NOW's work would help and resonate with them. Friedan agreed that NOW might have a role to play in raising larger, structural questions, adding that she had grown more critical of the institutions of marriage and family herself, but "as an individual, not as a member of NOW." The organization had to "work with the realities of American life."

"In reality," she said, "our job now is to make it possible for women to integrate their roles at home and in society."

The next chapter meeting after the publication of Lear's article was disorganized and fractious, according to the accounts of several members who later complained to Friedan. Atkinson also wrote to Friedan to explain her perspective on the meeting. In the envelope, she included a new Freedom for Women button, and wrote in one of her characteristic postscripts, "I wanted to give you one of these buttons. You looked great in that pink dress!" Atkinson's offerings of a button and a compliment could have been friendly, tactical, or both. Friedan wore the button, but her relationship with Atkinson only continued to deteriorate.

For many in NOW-NYC, including Friedan, Valerie Solanas was the last straw. Atkinson "would just go and do whatever she wanted to do, you know?" explained Delores Alexander. "I mean, firsthand on the Valerie Solanas thing . . . on the Women's Page of the *Times*—and we were all outraged because it was hard enough in those days to call yourself a feminist or a member of NOW, and here's . . . Ti-Grace saying that Valerie Solanas is a near murderer and, you know, the Joan of Arc of the Women's Movement—shit—we were really upset at that."

12

A NEW WOMAN POWER

"Mrs. Richard M. Nixon still has what in the 1952, 1956, and 1960 presidential campaigns were known as respectable Republican cloth coats," noted Charlotte Curtis in the opening lines of her July 1968 story about Pat Nixon, on the campaign trail for her husband in Texas. "But there's been a mink coat in and out of her closet since 1964, and mink, as virtually everybody knows, is one of the marks of achievement in American society." In two sentences, Curtis encapsulated not only Richard Nixon's political career and the wealth he'd accumulated as a partner with a white-shoe Manhattan law firm after declaring himself finished with politics in 1962—"You don't have Nixon to kick around anymore, because, gentlemen, this is my last press conference"—but also everything that he demanded from his wife, especially now that he'd decided to run for president again.

The "Republican cloth coat" reference brought readers back to the 1952 presidential election, when a campaign finance scandal accusing him of accepting large personal gifts from donors and using earmarked money for private expenses threatened the future president's place on the ticket as Dwight Eisenhower's running mate. In a last-ditch effort to save his candidacy, Nixon took his case directly to voters in a prime-time television address. Sitting at a simple desk, he read a prepared statement denying any personal use of campaign funds and gave a detailed accounting of his family's income and debts. Twice the camera focused on Pat Nixon, primly perched at the front edge of an upholstered chair and watching her husband, the camera making a slow pan over her somber face while he itemized their finances in front of the entire nation. "Well, that's about it," he said at the end of the segment. "That's what we have and that's what we owe. It isn't very much but Pat and I have the satisfaction that every dime that we've got is honestly ours. I should say this—that Pat doesn't have a mink coat. But she does have a respectable Republican cloth coat. And I always tell her that she'd look good in anything!"

The address was an enormous success; it saved Nixon's spot on the ticket and became legend among campaign professionals and political commentators. It is known today as the "Checkers Speech" for a reference to the black-and-white cocker spaniel gifted to the Nixons by a donor. "Our little girl Tricia, the six-year-old, named it 'Checkers,'" Nixon explained, "and you know, the kids, like all kids, love the dog, and I just want to say this, right now, that regardless of what they say about it, we're gonna keep it."

Over the years, Pat Nixon had gone from silent, supportive wife to savvy advocate for her husband and formidable campaigner in her own right. She described herself to Curtis as "a volunteer for Nixon—his eyes and ears with the women voters," filling "him in on what the women think." Curtis detailed the grueling schedule of a candidate's wife, describing Pat's meetings with local Republican leaders and journalists, luncheons, public speeches, and participation in an awards ceremony for women, at which she said, "Woman power is unbeatable; I've seen it all over this country."

"This year, as in 22 of her 56 years, Mrs. Nixon is out again on the campaign trail," wrote Curtis, clearly admiring of Pat Nixon's political abilities and perseverance. Her story drew energy from the implied question: What did it mean to love Richard Nixon through his political highs and lows, to interact with "well-scrubbed young girls in hats banded with 'Nixon's the One' stickers," as the older version of the young woman who'd once looked at Richard Nixon and decided that he was "the one" for her?

Curtis's story was a 4F's tour de force, deftly blending coverage of each of the section's eponymous subjects with an analysis of their political impacts and the gendered authority of political wives. Not only did the story underscore how thin the line was between "Women's News" and "News," but it also made clear the fundamentally political natures of fashion, food, furnishings, and family. When the *Chicago Tribune* reprinted the story a couple of days later, they ran it with the headline: "Pat Nixon's Rewards: A Mink, Woman Power."

If the Pat Nixon story highlighted the inherently political aspects of women's news, it was Curtis's subsequent story about Arkansas Senator J. William Fulbright that proved her political chops among colleagues in and beyond the *New York Times*.

As chairman of the Senate Foreign Relations Committee, Fulbright was an uncommon anti-war voice in the Democratic leadership, a rare internationalist in the party's Southern wing, and a longtime thorn in Lyndon Johnson's side. A month before Johnson announced that he would not seek reelection, Fulbright's committee began hearings on the administration's response to the Gulf of Tonkin incident and on whether Johnson had misled Congress in seeking the resolution that made escalation possible in the absence of a war declaration. With a history of fighting McCarthyism in the 1950s and his Oxford-educated intellectualism, globalist values, and anti-war stance, Fulbright could seem an odd duck in mostly rural, conservative Arkansas (despite his days as a University of Arkansas football star). In 1968, a hawkish, vehemently anti-communist, conservative segregationist threw this into stark relief with a primary challenge.

This was where Curtis entered, covering a Fulbright campaign stop at a fair in Bradford, Arkansas, where the economy was struggling and political temperaments ran far closer to his primary opponent's. A small timber and agricultural community along the White River, Bradford's rich soils produced the area's famous strawberries but it was under constant threat of flooding. The people wanted better resources and work from the Army Corps of Engineers for greater flood management. "The only thing holding up development here is the war in Vietnam," Fulbright told the locals. "We've spent almost as much on the war as has been spent on all our efforts in Arkansas for the last 30 years." For *Times* readers well familiar with the common anti-war argument that resources needed at home were instead being poured into a misguided war in Southeast Asia, Curtis offered a different perspective on its conservative resonances. She showed that Fulbright was not the Arkansas oddity many believed him to be, a reputation he often banked on in the Senate. While his primary challenger,

James D. Johnson, a former associate justice of the Arkansas Supreme Court, "is frankly against civil rights," in a state where 23 percent of the population was Black, "Mr. Fulbright says virtually nothing on the subject, speaks at what amounts to segregated audiences and consistently votes against civil rights legislation in Congress."

The day after Curtis's story ran, the editor of the *New York Times*'s Sunday edition reached out to see if she had enough material left from her "very fine piece in Monday's paper on Fulbright" to give him 500 to 700 words for Sunday. Not long after, Frank Trippett, associate editor of *Newsweek* magazine, felt moved to write to the *Times*'s new executive editor (and recent Washington Bureau chief) James Reston about Curtis: "I write to pay her a compliment on a superior piece of political reporting." Beyond a winking suggestion that Curtis be given a raise retroactive to the Arkansas primary, Trippett wrote, "I invite you to wonder with me why so much of our political reportage—and I include us all—falls so short of her standards." Reston forwarded a copy of the letter to Curtis, with a note scrawled in blue ink across the top: "A new beau."

Everyone was talking about the Arkansas story. Right before she left for Miami Beach, Curtis received a letter from Steve Conn, her former *Times* colleague who had been hustling with no success for a freelance gig to cover the conventions. "I assume that by now you've been made an honorary citizen of Arkansas (that was great stuff) and recent reports list you as the dark horse in Miami." He was looking forward to Curtis's coverage of the convention, he wrote, the next best thing to being there himself.

Recently separated from Carl, and with two kids still at home, Betty Friedan's concerns were heightened that summer. She devoted the better part of July to preparing to testify at the conventions, urging the Republicans and Democrats to include the "Bill of Rights for Women" in their platforms. Much of that time was spent hustling for freelance assignments to cover the costs of going to the Republican National Convention in Miami Beach, Florida, and then the Democratic National Convention in Chicago, Illinois. With just a week before her scheduled testimony in Miami Beach, Friedan finally secured an assignment from *Mademoiselle* to write a piece about women at both conventions.

Friedan had sounded "a battle cry for the election year ahead," announced

NOW's press release. They would pull women and men into the "'New Woman' power block"—Friedan's synonym for "sexual equality power," as she deemed the term "woman power" as excluding men. NOW's "Bill of Rights for Women" was the key. It would "be presented to all political parties and candidates in the coming election year," and candidates would be assessed by their commitment to its proposals. In addition, NOW "called for the abolition of the women's divisions of the major political parties and [for] their integration into the parties' main structures," and urged women to "refrain from merely doing the traditional menial work of sealing envelopes, ringing doorbells, raising pin money and holding koffee klatches unless they are also admitted to the policy-making mainstream of the political parties." The organization declared its dedication to nonpartisanship and urged women to cross party lines to support any candidate who would work for "equality for women, and to defeat its enemies."

13

TARGET: REPUBLICAN WOMEN

JULY 29, 1968 - AUGUST 4, 1968

The official, nationally televised opening of the Republican Convention wouldn't happen until Monday, August 5, but the small island-city of Miami Beach was already crammed with party operatives, delegates, campaign workers, vendors, journalists, and television crews. There were forty-nine people in town from the *New York Times* alone, Charlotte Curtis the only female reporter among them.

Miami Beach had a lot invested in hosting Florida's first-ever national political convention (and the first convention held in the Deep South of the former Confederacy for more than a century). In its less than seven square miles of total land mass, the city expected a hundred thousand visitors, which would double its population and then some. Florida's new Republican governor, Claude R. Kirk Jr., the first of his party in the state executive role since Reconstruction, was equally determined to make the event a success. The city spent at least five million dollars on improvements and additional services, four million of which went toward a massive addition to the Miami Beach Convention Hall. It was all to showcase that South Florida wasn't just the nation's "Winter Playground" but now also a year-round tourist destination (thanks to air-conditioning and municipal mosquito control) that would give "America's Favorite Playground," Atlantic City, a run for its summer season money.

This meant all hands were on deck to make visitors from the GOP and the press feel welcome. Miami Beach residents were "being urged to smile as much as contestants in a Miss America Pageant," quipped one reporter, as were members of the Miami Beach Police Department, whose preparation for the convention included "a special crowd control training session that taught them to keep smiling" as they enforced temporary new traffic patterns and heightened security measures. (It was a barbed observation, given that by the 1960s, the "Miss America smile" was synonymous with the notion of a practiced, inauthentic expression designed to sell, rather than to relay genuine feeling.)

Beneath the smiles and polish, however, lay officials' deep-seated anxieties about safety. The assassination of Bobby Kennedy two months earlier had transformed the tenor of campaign season. All major candidates and their families—except for third-party challenger George Wallace—had been immediately assigned Secret Service protection. In South Florida, local cops were just one part of a thick web of state and federal police powers blanketing the region, which included the police departments of Miami Beach and the city of Miami, the Dade County Public Safety Department, Florida state troopers, the Secret Service, and a private security company out of Chicago that managed access to the convention hall. Curtis described these local security plans in one of her many pages of typed notes and observations, labeled "ODDS AND ENDS: Flak jackets, sniper rifles and a 6-foot fence hidden by a flowering hedge will surround the convention hall. Police Chief Rocky Pomerance said his problem was 'a peculiar dichotomy, maximum security with low visibility policing.' Also 40 shot guns, 20 combat flak jackets, three .30-06 Remington rifles with telescopic sights described as sniper rifles and 50 smoke grenades."

More than stopping a potential assassin, however, the immediate security concern was containing and thwarting any possible disruptions by the public. Biscayne Bay separates Miami Beach from mainland Florida and the city of Miami, making it accessible to vehicular traffic only by a series of causeways equipped with drawbridges. One news report described the "nine-mile-long sandbar" of Miami Beach as having "one advantage above all others" as a convention location: "it is remote," making it "easy for Republicans to avoid the danger of large militant demonstrations." Local boosters did what they could to limit organized protest, and they assured Republican conventioneers and tourists that Miami was different from other cities in the Deep South—more liberal. They claimed the city was home to more contented Black and Latinx residents who hadn't participated in local uprisings while other American cities erupted in violence, downplaying the significant history of and contemporaneous civil rights activism in South Florida. Efforts were also made to convince the Democrats to shift the location of their convention, scheduled for Chicago later in the month, to Miami Beach, so as to avoid a city wrenched by "riots," ongoing labor strikes, and the disruptions already promised from SDS and the Youth International Party (better known as the Yippies), which looked to merge antiwar activism, direct action, and the Free Speech Movement (FSM) with the counterculture, expressed mostly through guerilla theater and spectacles of the ridiculous. But Johnson stepped in, and the convention remained in Chicago.

The Republican Party, too, had a lot riding on the convention's success. Lyndon Johnson's landslide defeat of Barry Goldwater for the presidency in 1964 had been a devastating and consequential blow, especially after the conservative Republican's nomination had exposed significant conflict among and between the Republican rank-and-file and establishment leaders. Since the start of the Cold War, a hard-right coalition—energized by shared alarm at the continued expansion of the welfare state, federal civil rights intervention, the Supreme Court, and what they saw as a retreat from firm anti-communism and necessary military preparedness—was gaining strength in the party. Emboldened by the support of defecting Southern Democrats, this coalition had been strong enough to sway the nomination to Goldwater but it proved to be out of step with the electorate at large.

This convention was designed to show voters that those cleavages were behind them. It would be a tightly choreographed, prime-time pageant of party unity and reasoned moderation in the face of a culture driven to dangerous and violent extremes. It would showcase a modern Republican Party offering greater opportunities for women and racial minorities that would also return the nation to traditional values, order, and respect for authority.

A key part of this strategy was making visible the GOP's diversity (for what it was). Opening night would introduce Edward W. Brooke, the former governor and now senator from Massachusetts—and most prominent Black Republican politician in the country—as the "temporary" convention chairman. It would also feature a prime-time speech from Mary Brooks, the associate chair of the Republican National Committee (RNC) and state senator from Idaho, one of the most powerful women in the party.

Striking a balance between reform and tradition—claiming to be a new party without rejecting much if any of the old—was tricky for the RNC. The work of easing that contradiction fell in large part to women as political actors and symbols in the convention spectacle, as the RNC tempered "liberal" claims to diversity through insistent, performative compliance with traditional gender roles and patriarchal authority.

Mary Brooks was one of the people most responsible for managing this balance. Born in 1907, she was raised on her family's ranch in central southern Idaho. In addition to being a rancher, her father had been a banker and U.S. senator. In 1929, Mary graduated with a degree in economics from the University of Idaho, where she met her first husband, Arthur J. Peavey Jr. After spending two years in Salt Lake City, Utah, the young couple returned to Idaho, where Arthur assumed a management role with her family's ranch and Mary resumed frequent notice in the state's society news; a son and daughter soon followed. Tragedy struck when Arthur Peavey was killed in a hunting accident in 1941, a week before the attack on Pearl Harbor brought the United States formally into World War II. Now widowed with two young children, Mary joined her parents in Washington, D.C. In 1946, she remarried, this time to her father's colleague, C. Wayland "Curly" Brooks, a Republican senator from Illinois, and took quickly to the role of political wife. She became active in the Federation of Republican Women and a respected, involved partner to her husband as he moved from the Senate to a leadership position in the RNC.

Brooks's role was made official just months after being widowed again in 1957, when she was named Illinois's Republican National Committee member. "I have been related to politics all my life," she shared with a reporter at the time, "but I always wanted to be in it on my own." With a smile and nod toward a clutch of "jabbering females" (as the reporter put it), Brooks continued, "I have a theory that American women can be made to see that politics is fun. And that the fun party is the Republican party." Rather than trivialities and gossip, why couldn't women get together to "discuss the issues of the day?" Women could "satisfy their desire for club life in political clubs; in political study and discussion groups. They [could] sponsor political picnics for the whole family." In 1960, Brooks was elected vice chairman of the RNC. She left the position and Washington, D.C., three years later, and returned to Idaho to run her family's ranch, but within a year she was back in public life, when she was elected to the Idaho State Senate, a seat she still held in 1968.

In the aftermath of Goldwater's defeat, Brooks was named assistant chairman of the RNC as part of the party's wider realignment project. She spearheaded several initiatives aimed at drawing a new generation of young married women from the suburbs into the GOP, with an eye toward their mobilization for the next presidential campaign. In the spring of 1967, she announced four regional meetings to be held during the summer, in Denver, Little Rock, Chicago, and Boston, that would serve as women's "strategy sessions" for the 1968 elections—the first time in the fifteen-year existence of these meetings that they would occur outside of Washington, D.C. More women could get to a regional meeting than to the nation's capital, she argued—especially those with young children. Most of Brooks's work for the party was geared toward energizing and growing a reliable part of the Republican base—suburban women—who performed most of the local, on-the-ground campaigning, handled the mailings, hosted events, and knocked on doors. The importance of these women would only grow, Brooks believed, as candidates scaled back their own ground games and relied more on television to reach voters, leaving the women to be the personal, locally familiar faces of national political campaigns.

Brooks spent the months leading up to the 1968 convention traveling around the country to encourage more women to volunteer, promoting a suburban-focused "10-Point Program for VICTORY '68," and issuing a steady stream of press releases about the convention. These press releases detailed the history and contemporary picture of women in the party, and they outlined a heavy schedule for delegates' wives and daughters in Miami Beach, as well as the women in town as delegates or alternates themselves. That number of women delegates or alternates had gotten smaller since 1964; only 224 of the 1,333 delegates and 335 of the equal number of alternates in Miami Beach would be women. Nevertheless, Brooks promised that this election would be the "Year of the Women," and she issued an RNC press release that tried to spin the overall reduction of women delegates: "Eighteen States Increase Number of Women Delegates to GOP Convention."

Image was everything. "Brunches, lunches, fashion shows, sightseeing tours and parties were announced July 16 in Washington," jotted Charlotte Curtis during a press briefing. The RNC "advised women delegates and participants to wear clothes with 'emphasis on keeping cool,' and reminded them that 'all the convention sessions will be televised in color.' Shorts and slacks were approved for recreation 'but never for convention business.'" Curtis also noted Brooks's admonition to "Just remember while you are in Miami Beach the world is watching."

In the weeks before Miami Beach, Brooks collated the responses to questionnaires she had sent to female delegates and alternates. She used her findings to create a composite picture of the average GOP woman active at the convention level, whom she dubbed "Mrs. Delegate." This woman "now holds, or has held, public office; is active in public service programs in her community; attended college; is under 45 years of age; has children whose ages range from 10 to 25 years; is employed or has a professional background; and has actively worked as a volunteer for her party on the state and local level." Like Pat Nixon, Mary Brooks celebrated the party's "woman power" as part and parcel of its commitment to traditional gender roles and family. A piece run in the "women's news" section of the *Miami Herald* detailing Brooks's conclusions demonstrated how effective but also how tenuous this projection of GOP women was. Alongside the article's headline, "Average Woman Delegate Is . . . ," the paper ran a picture of two white women grinning at one another over a platter of home-baked cupcakes festooned with tiny American flags on toothpicks.

Mary Brooks's insistence that 1968 would be the "Year of the Women" for Republicans was as much an effort to rebrand "woman power" within the GOP as it was an appeal to voters at large. In the aftermath of Goldwater's epic defeat, much of the responsibility—the blame—was laid squarely at the feet of women in the party, including those of the National Federation of Republican Women (NFRW). Shortly before Richard Nixon announced his return to presidential politics (a comeback trail paved by his own contributions to the work of party unity and moderating the GOP's messaging after 1964), he told the *Saturday Evening Post* that women had been a central source of party rancor. They were "great workers, but they're idealists and emotionalists," he said. Republican women were "the real haters," Nixon explained. He continued:

> Any Machiavellian scheme, they go for. They die hard. They tell me, 'You didn't hit them hard enough. Why don't you give them hell like Truman?' I explain I not only have to appeal to partisan Republicans but also have to get Democrats to cross over. But the women don't understand that. Occasionally I say a good word for Johnson or Humphrey. It's a device, of course, to show I'm fair-minded, but the women don't see that. That's why the women liked Barry [Goldwater] so. He didn't give a damn about Democrats. But to win, you have to.

This was true of the women in his own family, Nixon said later in the piece, describing how Pat and their daughters, Tricia and Julie, found it difficult to let go of slights against him. "Families never take it very well when their man is criticized. . . . A wife and children are extremely sensitive—overly sensitive." This was the "New Nixon," no longer grousing about unfair treatment by the press or stewing in the past, but instead confident and reasonable, forward-looking, and ready to reach across the aisle if that's what it took to better the country—and his newness was most visible in contrast to the "overly sensitive," emotional women in his family and the Republican Party.*

Beyond blaming women generally for the GOP's embarrassment in 1964, much of the responsibility for Goldwater's nomination was attributed to one Republican woman in particular: Phyllis Schlafly. When she burst onto the national political scene with her book, *A Choice, Not an Echo*, Schlafly was already a prominent figure among conservative Catholics and Republicans in the Midwest. She had first run for Congress in 1952 and was subsequently elected as a delegate to

* Patrick J. Buchanan, New Right conservative commentator and two-time Republican presidential candidate, described dealing with the repercussions of Nixon's statements about GOP women while serving as a campaign aide in his 2014 book, *The Greatest Comeback: How Richard Nixon Rose from Defeat to Create the New Majority*. From the vantage of the twenty-first century, Buchanan noted, "Though impolitic, Nixon had a point about women in politics and political wives" (Buchanan, *Greatest Comeback* [Crown Forum, 2014], 112).

three Republican National Conventions. As president of the Illinois Federation of Republican Women (IFRW), she advocated for more women to enter politics as officeholders, rather than just ground workers, arguing that they would bring the same inherent moral authority they held in the home to policymaking and elected office. "For many years," she explained, "women have been carrying the major burden of the precinct work and doorbell pushing which win elections," but they are "becoming more important in their own right, and not merely as the mirrored reflection of their masculine counterparts." A month later in her report to the Illinois Federation, entitled "Each Member a Leader," she repeated, "The time is past when the women of the Republican Party are merely doorbell pushers. We have earned our right to participate in the making of policies at the top which spell the difference between defeat and victory."

Schlafly's arguments were notably like those made by Betty Friedan when she urged NOW to mobilize for the 1968 elections and to create a "Bill of Rights for Women." In some ways, the two women were quite similar. While Friedan was a student at Smith College, Schlafly went to Washington University, where she majored in political science and worked the night shift at the St. Louis Ordnance Plant, making and testing ammunition for American troops in World War II. After graduation, Schlafly headed to Cambridge, Massachusetts, to earn a master's degree in political science from Radcliffe College. While Friedan was working as a journalist for union and labor newspapers, some with Communist Party affiliations, Schlafly headed to Washington, D.C., in 1945, to start her life's work as a hawkish, conservative Republican, beginning with a year-long research position at the newly established think tank, the American Enterprise Association (today's American Enterprise Institute). Friedan and Schlafly each got married within two years of one another, in 1947 and 1949, respectively, and continued in their public roles while starting families. Friedan, who would have three children to Schlafly's six, became a national figure in 1963; Schlafly quickly followed a year later.

Schlafly's book, *A Choice, Not an Echo,* took its title from a popular line in Goldwater's book, *The Conscience of a Conservative,* and it endorsed the senator through a frontal attack on the Republican establishment, outlining a conspiracy of elitist, Eastern "kingmakers" who rigged conventions, trampled the rights of individual voters, and colluded with Democrats. The solution to these problems, she concluded, was a knowing and vigilant rank-and-file led by Barry

Goldwater. Yet while the book promoted Goldwater's candidacy, it was simultaneously and perhaps more obviously selling Schlafly. After all, the only image on the simple red-and-white cover is a professional black-and-white headshot of Schlafly, coiffed and smiling, wearing a double string of pearls and scooped-neck top, her lipstick pronounced, but not garish.

Just a few months shy of her fortieth birthday, Schlafly's good looks, classic fashion, and charm had long been the subjects of consistent commentary among fellow activists and in press, and was especially notable in the coverage of her successful primary challenge and ultimate loss in the 1952 congressional race. Schlafly's hometown newspaper, the *Alton Evening Telegraph*, declared her obvious "edge on [her male opponent] for looks," and described her appearance at a community meeting alongside him, noting she was, "an attractive, neat woman who wore a gray business suit, black high heel pumps, pearl earrings, and who offset the distracting influence of her femininity" through fine public speaking, showing conviction, and exhibiting charts and maps to support her points. The effect was intentional on Schlafly's part; she always dressed her intelligence and policy positions in desirable femininity and the tone of a concerned housewife. Compared to other state leaders within the NFRW, Schlafly was quite young; she was a mother of six children in her mid-thirties when she assumed the presidency of the Illinois federation in 1960. Promoting her visit to a suburban Republican women's club in 1963, the group's president described Schlafly to a political columnist for the *Chicago Tribune*, "This lady has everything: youth, beauty, a Phi Betta Kappa key, and a house full of little Republicans."

Goldwater's landslide defeat by Lyndon Johnson threatened to take much of this away. With voters' apparent rejection of Goldwater's extreme conservativism, the Republican Party sought to limit the power and visibility of his supporters in its leadership. Consequently, the presidential race for the NFRW that followed in 1966–67 became a struggle to push "extremists" out. As vice president of the NFRW, Schlafly had been widely presumed its next president. When the organization's nominating committee did not select her, choosing more moderate members as candidates, she made an insurgent run with significant membership support. Introducing the undeclared candidate at an event in Southern California, a GOP national committeewoman said the federation needed a leader like Schlafly, describing her as a woman of "youth, beauty, and grace," who had doubled the membership of the Illinois Federation of Republican Women as its president. But her opponents took aim at her ambition, arguing that choosing a woman with six children for the presidency was tantamount to the federation's endorsing "child neglect," and suggesting that her beauty and put-together look were mere artifice concealing a tactical mind and cold heart. One federation member in Louisiana shuddered at what she described as Schlafly's ability to turn her "charm and graciousness on and off at will," implying that these were not authentic qualities but, rather, all surface and calculation.

When Schlafly lost her bid for the presidency at the federation's national convention in 1967, her supporters were devastated; one recalled a room full of sad, wrung-out women waiting late into the night to hear her concession speech. "Finally, Phyllis appeared, poised and gracious," she said. How she "could even be on her feet, let alone smile, was beyond us." Soon after, Schlafly announced her plans to form a new organization for Republican women to promote a "strong pro-American viewpoint, and advocate for morality in government, constitutional government, a strong national defense, and free enterprise." She promised "to build an army of dedicated women wearing eagles as the symbol of American freedom." In August 1967, she distributed her first issue of the *Phyllis Schlafly Report* and her fourth book, *Safe, Not Sorry,* not long after that—a "handbook on current political issues" to guide readers in the coming election that included a chapter detailing her version of the post-1964 attempt to "purge" Goldwater Republicans, attributing it to a conspiracy of "liberals and their allies" who would doom the Republican Party and the country if they weren't stopped. There had also been, she alleged, a "long series of secret meetings held by the get-Phyllis cabal" to deny her the NFRW presidency in a section called "Target: Republican Women."

Miami Beach was Schlafly's third convention as an elected delegate, this time for Nixon. She hadn't looked forward to the fashion shows or ladies' luncheons but planned to devote her time and energy to keeping moderate Republicans off the presidential ticket. This included giving testimony on Monday, July 29, before the Republican Platform Subcommittee on Foreign Policy and National Defense. "Mrs. Phyllis Schlafly" was the only woman on the day's schedule, appearing in the early evening between the president of the Polish American Congress and the day's last speaker, Major General Dale O. Smith.

Phyllis Schlafly's entire family went to Miami Beach. She and her husband, Fred, overspilled their accommodations with the rest of the Illinois delegation in the Marco Polo Hotel, and resorted to settling their youngest, four-year-old Ann, in a makeshift bed in the closet. While Phyllis was the formidable power in the GOP and an elected delegate, Fred worked the convention alongside her; they were a political team, though Fred was often in the background. Together, certain that Nixon was set to pick a liberal running mate who would appeal to moderate Republican voters and disaffected Democrats, they spent the rest of the week trying to rustle pledges from different state delegations to follow Phyllis in declaring for Ronald Reagan if Nixon wouldn't commit to a conservative for the VP. They were unsuccessful; the delegates loved Reagan, but he was not officially in the race for the nomination, and most were holding the line for Nixon.

NOW was assigned to the Subcommittee on Equal Opportunity in an Urban Society, which met for three days. The subcommittee's purview was large and ranging, covering everything from the American Library Association and U.S. Catholic Conference on parochial education, to the American Civil Liberties Union (ACLU), National League of Cities, and the Conference of Concerned Afro-American Republicans. Several Black civil rights organizations were represented, including the NAACP, Southern Christian Leadership Conference, and the Congress of Racial Equality (CORE), as were a number of women's advocacy groups in addition to NOW, including the League of Women Voters, National Woman's Party, and the National Council of Jewish Women (whose representative was scheduled to speak after the man from the American Jewish Committee). The subcommittee's implied designation of all "minority" communities and their advocates as limited to "urban society" reinforced the notion, promoted by Mary Brooks and others, that the heart of the Republican base was suburban and small-town white America. It also signaled the growing primacy of the party's "law and order" reaction to urban uprisings, student radicalism, and claims of Black Power.

Friedan arrived for her hearing on Wednesday afternoon, July 31, with three, legal-sized pages of remarks, typed and single-spaced, that outlined her argument for adopting the Bill of Rights for Women. After identifying herself and NOW, Friedan began her appeal to the subcommittee.

> I ask with some urgency that you give more than token attention in your national platform to the unfinished revolution of the 51% of the American people who happen to be women, who will no longer tolerate their exclusion from full participation in the mainstream of American society. The alienation of millions of women suffering today in inner city poverty is merely an extreme case of the alienation of those millions of other discriminated-against women, meekly bitter in their office anonymity; and millions of suburban housewives also alienated, in the midst of their material affluence, by their lack of participation in the major decisions of their time.

Changing this, she added, would address the discontent and radicalism of the young: "Children brought up by people impotent to affect the conditions of their own lives may well resort to violence." With characteristic bombast, Friedan rolled with her analogy of families in crisis to urban "riots" and violent demonstrations. "Like other subject people, women have for generations turned the kind of violence negroes [*sic*] and students are showing now in the streets, inward against themselves . . . and inadvertently on their husbands and children." And while she wasn't suggesting that women would be "rioting now in the streets" or "burning down their suburban dream-houses" in 1968, they very well might in the future without the Bill of Rights for Women. She continued:

> Men are not the enemies of women's unfinished revolution, but fellow victims, along with children, of the suppressed violence bred by sexual inequality. But if the real problems dividing the sexes are not faced, if the urgent demand for some real voice and power for women in the mainstream of our society is not met, this presently suppressed violence could also burst into an Armageddon between the sexes that could make the riots in Newark and Detroit, and the torn up paving stones of Paris, seem like child's play.

Recounting her testimony to Carolyn Jay, a reporter from the *Miami News*, Friedan remarked with obvious satisfaction, "Everyone looked so shocked." She hoped she'd jarred them into incorporating the Bill of Rights into the platform.

Everything about Friedan seemed a little shocking to Carolyn Jay—delightfully and refreshingly so. "I'm in my mid-40s, I feel younger than when

I was in my mid-30s," Friedan declared to the reporter. "There is a new zest in my life. I am a new woman." Through feminism she had been reborn, or at least powerfully renewed, and Friedan urged, NOW could bring this to all American women. She spoke to the fears and misconceptions she imagined were held by readers of the *Miami News*'s women's page: "The old feminist had to fight a terrible battle for just her legal rights. The very term 'feminist' had a connotation of some asexual, man-hating woman. But the new woman is not man-hating, is usually attractive and has husbands, lovers, or boyfriends as well as male colleagues."

The interview took place in Friedan's hotel room, where, in a short, tropical-print dress with a deep, ruffled scooped neck, she sometimes "sprawled across" the bed to reach the phone, and was a confident, formidable whirlwind of action and ideas. During the interview, Friedan fielded calls and organized an impromptu meeting for South Floridians interested in joining NOW by convincing two local members to host a coffee over the weekend (the article included the time and location).

"All I've got to say," said one of the women Friedan had just persuaded to host an open meeting for strangers with less than two days to plan, "is that she should be running for president."

"Not president," Friedan quipped, "but maybe the Senate."

All of Charlotte Curtis's notebooks were the same: 7.25 by 5 inches with a kraft cover, "Eye-Ease" off-white, lined paper, and a left-side spiral, rather than the top-spiraled, narrow notebook so commonly associated with her profession. In Miami Beach, she opened a fresh one, writing her name and work address at the *New York Times* near the bottom of the front cover and its contents across the top: "Republican National Convention '68." Curtis tucked her deep orange News Media Work Areas pass for the Fontainebleau Hotel inside the notebook, and she began her convention work there on Saturday morning, August 3, with a *New York Times* staff meeting. That was followed by a press briefing about Sunday night's gala in the hotel's grand ballroom. From there, Curtis headed to a much smaller meeting room to attend Mary Brooks's scheduled briefing.

Speaking to a group of predominantly female journalists and flanked by several women in national or local Republican leadership positions, Brooks seemed more at ease. Her initial statement was mostly focused on her upcoming, historic opening-night speech. It wasn't quite finished, but would be "very simple," she explained, "and short because men hate it when women talk too long." (Curtis underlined this in red ink.)

Before closing, Brooks turned to her regular theme of women's importance to Republican victory in 1968, which she described as "a very unique year" (also underlined by Curtis). "Women are so much involved emotionally," she said, more now "than perhaps any time in history," chalking up the change to three key issues, which would also be the central points of her speech. Curtis jotted them down: "1. safety in the streets 2. cost of living 3. and women hate war—they've always hated war through the centuries."

When the floor was opened for questions, Brooks offered characteristically little by way of policy details or her own positions. On Vietnam, she said she didn't know if the "war should be stopped or fought more aggressively," only that whatever the Democrats were doing wasn't working. To a question about legalizing abortion, she demurred, replying simply, "I wouldn't want to get into that." She said that she didn't understand hippies, calling them "youngsters" in "revolt," and drew a distinction between a nostalgic, notably male version of cheeky student rebels past, who "used to swallow goldfish and panty raid" to the student radicalism she saw around her, which had created "something else again, a sort of hopelessness." Even so, though, she expected plenty of young people to stand with Republicans in 1968, particularly women, who were now "more—I hate the word "militant" [quotes added]—maybe more determined to win this year. So many more want to help." The response was limited to the experiences of women who, like herself and most of the journalists she was speaking to, worked in male-dominated professions, but she argued that it applied to the Republicans' primary female constituency and volunteer pool, as well.

Betty Friedan was among the journalists gathered in the small meeting room, but Curtis didn't note if she was the one who brought up discrimination against women. Brooks was unequivocal in her response and tacitly recognized the necessity of militants (among whom she would certainly have included Friedan). There was "no doubt that women have been discriminated against," she replied. "A militant pushes and we go a little faster." Was Brooks looking at Betty Friedan when she said this?

14

WHO IS THE ENEMY?

JULY 29, 1968 - AUGUST 4, 1968

Back in early June, Ros Baxandall had received a letter from Marilyn Webb about a meeting at the end of the summer. "Some of us in Radical Women's Groups in several cities felt the need for us to get together and talk about what we mean by working to build a Women's Liberation Movement," wrote Webb. It would be an opportunity to dig in together about priorities, tactics, and strategies for building new groups and reaching different kinds of women. Webb explained that the group needed to be small—no more than twenty people, which was the maximum number they could fit into the house in Hershey, Pennsylvania, where they would hold the meeting. "We would like it if one person could represent the views of all the groups" from their city, "but I understand that there are real ideological differences between groups not only in New York but all over . . . so you may need to send more than one person."

Now the meeting was upon them, and Marilyn Webb's conference list was a mess. Her neatly typed original was full of edits and additions between the lines and along the margins—the layers of black, red, and blue ink forming a record of how often Webb had returned to it, grabbing whatever pen was handy. Several crossed-out names denoted women unable to attend, like Baxandall, as well as those who had refused the invitation, like SDS's Bernardine Dohrn, who'd accused Webb and other women's liberation organizers of dividing the movement at a crucial moment, undermining not only pressing work against the Vietnam

War but also revolutionary change in general. The rejection stung, but the list of women who believed in the necessity of organizing women for their own liberation (and good of the movement) was longer.

The list had grown long enough that Webb and the other organizers from Washington, D.C., and Baltimore had been forced to locate a larger venue. Now, they would be meeting at the Sandy Spring Friends School, in Montgomery County, Maryland, about a forty-five-minute drive from the capital. It would be hot, warned Webb, in her last letter to attendees containing meeting logistics and recommendations for what to bring. They would be staying in dormitory-style rooms and have access to a common kitchen attached to their meeting space. Each person needed to send or bring $12 to cover lodging, food, and the costs of the printing, postage, long-distance phone bills, and other organizing miscellany for the weekend. Any position papers the attendees wished to circulate should be copied (on their own dimes) before they came.

"This meeting should not be seen as one which comes out with a set program or structure of any sort," Webb explained. "It is just a beginning attempt to build those things in the future if people think that is necessary. So, we shouldn't get uptight about making sure all we need to talk about is thoroughly covered and/or solved, 'cause it won't and can't be now. Hopefully we can come away with an idea of where we're at and where we have to begin moving towards, and with a closer relationship to each other as people."

The Tentative Agenda outlined an ambitious schedule from the afternoon of Friday, August 2, to Sunday, August 4, at 1:00 p.m., when they were required to check out. The first evening would be devoted to introductions and a conversation to identify some common threads connecting the groups, and to discuss the "goals and priorities in building a women's Movement." Saturday was to be their only full day, with an agenda running from 9:00 in the morning to 10:00 that night, with a couple of breaks for meals. The major questions were: Who are their constituents? Who is the enemy? What issues and ideologies are important? What points of collaboration might they find among the groups? And how should they relate to "the rest of the movement"? Their final session was reserved for early planning on a National Women's Liberation Conference for late fall, which one of the Chicago women had suggested. In an uncharacteristic appeal to feminist history, Webb noted in her agenda, "We might call it Senaca

Falls II [*sic*] since it commemorates the 120th anniversary of the first Senaca Falls [*sic*] convention held in 1848. That was the conference which marked the beginning of the women's suffrage movement!"

It was hot and steamy in Sandy Spring when the women arrived on Friday, just as Webb had warned. The school was new, but was attached to one of the oldest, continuously active Quaker communities in the United States, dating to 1753 and the Maryland Colony. Reaching back centuries before the Quaker settlement on the unceded land of the Piscataway People, the largest tribe of Algonquian-speaking Indians between the Chesapeake Bay and Potomac River, the area was a dense historical terrain of conflict, faith, and activism to which the women's liberationists would be a fitting addition. Men and women of the Sandy Spring Quaker Meeting had been spearheads in anti-slavery work and women's rights, including several women who would go on to be leaders of the suffrage movement in Maryland. In more recent decades, the historic village had become popular with Washington's political classes as an idyllic retreat from the capital city's political intrigues and social fishbowl. Dean Acheson, secretary of state under President Truman, key architect of early Cold War foreign policy, and advisor to many presidents after his retirement, including Lyndon Johnson, had a house there, less than a mile from where the radical women's liberationists were gathering.

In the end, about twenty women (and one baby) attended the meeting in Sandy Spring. Most hailed from New York, Chicago, and the D.C. area, but some came from as far away as Florida and North Carolina. The list of attendees had grown over the summer as word had spread, but there had never been an open announcement; it remained largely an invites-only affair. The result, intended or not, was that several women who'd requested to attend (and who mostly identified as feminists) arrived on Friday feeling less than welcome.

Jo Freeman, there from Chicago, had only found out about the meeting when she got a phone call from another West Side Group member who was soliciting money to cover airfare for the two women chosen to attend. Already feeling alienated from the group she'd helped to found as a feminist critical of politicos, the call still came as a surprise to Freeman.

"Oh," she stuttered, before responding, "I want to go."

The caller replied that the group already had their representatives, and now just needed to raise the funds to get them to Maryland. Freeman, angry and undeterred, went to the meeting anyway. Unable to bankroll the trip on her own, she'd hitchhiked the nearly seven hundred miles from Chicago to Sandy Spring.

Several women from New York attended the meeting, including Kathie Amatniek and Carol Hanisch, neither of whom were on the original invitation list. Amatniek, who heard about the meeting from Ros Baxandall, believed that Webb's failure to invite "the *Notes* people" was purposeful, designed to minimize the feminist voices in the room. Both arrived in Maryland concerned about how they would be received.

As the day's turn toward evening was heralded by the rising whine of cicadas and the first lightning bugs bobbing above the greenscape, the women gathered in the common room to begin. When it was time for the women from New York to speak, no one referred to themselves or their collective as New York Radical Women (NYRW), but they described a history of division leading to the development of two groups currently active in New York. In a summary of the meeting constructed afterward from an audio recording and from memory, the unidentified writer described their introduction this way: "The first of the Lower East Side groups had two factions which eventually split. One felt that organizing radical women was a first priority. Others felt that we should immediately go for a mass base [for women's liberation] which meant figuring out an ideology." Kathie Amatniek spoke for the group seeking a mass base for women's liberation—*feminists,* in the common binary appellation—and described their process of consciousness raising.

Amatniek and Hanisch had arrived in Sandy Spring feeling isolated in their position but righteously assured they were on the right path and would have to convince others to see it as well. The only way to do this, they agreed, was to get the leftist politicos to recognize where the true enemy of women's liberation lay—in their own beds.

Florika Remetier spoke after Amatniek on behalf of what the summary author referred to simply as the "Other NY Group." She didn't dispute the picture of division and opposition drawn by Amatniek, but she suggested that positions were more fluid than she had made them sound. "Our group did not know: one, who the enemy was; two, we were not at all clear about what women would, should, or could do." She devoted most of her introduction to describing a recent action against Revlon cosmetics, seeking to tie their corporate activities and profits to the war in Vietnam.

The next morning, Marilyn Webb started recording on a reel-to-reel tape machine to preserve the weekend's conversations. The recorder sat on one side of the large meeting room, which meant its single microphone would capture an imperfect copy of the meeting. That is, the voices of those sitting nearer the machine or who spoke loudly would come through clearly, while others would only barely register. Long periods of conversation would be consumed irrecoverably—maddeningly—in scratchy static.

The first session started with Beverly "Bev" Jones and Judith "Judy" Brown giving presentations that went deeper into the ideas they'd offered in a coauthored paper published at the start of the summer, "Toward a Female Liberation Movement." Soon known commonly as the "Florida Paper," it had hit the movement hard, energizing a great deal of conversation especially among those who identified themselves primarily as feminists. Carol Hanisch first encountered the Florida Paper in Kentucky while working at the main SCEF office, and she was so excited by the paper that she wrote to Brown to not only tell her how much she liked it but also to discuss the points of confluence in their understandings and visions for liberation—which they did in a phone call later that summer. It was Brown who first told Hanisch about the meeting in Sandy Spring.

"Toward a Female Liberation Movement" was constructed around the central premise that radical women could never find their own liberation, much less forge a mass movement while trying to organize from within the New Left. Revolutionary change would be achieved only through an independent women's liberation movement modeled after the Black Power movement. Presented in two parts that were each individually authored by Jones and Brown, the article's structure animated their differences in age, status, and perspective while also demonstrating the unifying possibilities of their argument. When they began the project, Jones and Brown were both part of the interracial community of civil rights activists in and around the University of Florida. Brown was a graduate student and Jones was the wife of a faculty member who also had a graduate degree in psychology and clinical practice. When the women met, Jones already knew she would be moving to Pennsylvania soon, where her husband was taking a new job. Their collaboration thus continued by telephone, which was how they finished the paper.

In her address to the group, Jones spoke of the problem of media and representation. "I am just so convinced that the consensus is carried and hammered in daily at a very early age through that television set and it makes it all seem impossible for an individual parent or an individual group to overcome," she said. She worried for her daughter, who was already learning that "she's got to play out a role."

"I think that we've got to get into the media and insist that they start presenting women as we feel women should be presented," she said. "I suggest that we go over to a TV show and pick the most horrible one we can find where the woman is being the biggest slob and we can sit in and yell and hand out pamphlets and make press releases you know, get clobbered by the men and the cops and stuff—and keep it up."

The questions and long discussion that followed centered largely on the fundamental points of contention Kathie Amatniek had outlined the night before: Who was their enemy, men or capitalist liberalism? And, was "culture" just as important an arena for organizing and change as the economy? These were versions of the contests they'd been having from the start, but in the closed and saturated environment of the Sandy Spring meeting, they became a set of full-throated arguments, made face to face. At one point, Amatniek jotted a note to herself during Jones's and Brown's presentations, "No one's going to understand what I think is our 'cultural revolution' analysis."

The tension amped up throughout the day. For hours, they struggled over fundamental aims, as well as the concrete methods for organizing, including the question of who their target audience was. Should they form as a vanguard to eventually lead other women to liberation, or should they organize as a mass movement from the start?

Roxanne Dunbar and Dana Densmore showed up late, in the midst of this conversation. The pair had spent the morning in Washington, D.C., with Densmore's mother, Donna Allen, who was the reason they attended the meeting in Sandy Spring—as the original invitee, Donna Allen had declined and had encouraged Marilyn Webb to ask her daughter, Dana, who was working in Boston's women's liberation movement. Inviting Densmore meant inviting Dunbar, too. They showed up at Sandy Spring with a copy of Solanas's *S.C.U.M. Manifesto*; they were costumed in miniskirts and combat boots, and were heavily made up with teased hair, ready to confront SDS women and enact Solanas-esque creative disruption.

No one would forget their entrance or subsequent contributions, including Dunbar herself, who cringed at some of their antics when describing them later. But at the time, she'd been struck by how prim the room seemed. "These SDS women. I had never met so straight-laced people in years, since I had left Oklahoma."

When the conversation resumed, it wasn't long before Dunbar interrupted Bev Jones. "You said that none of us is economically exploited," she stated.

"None of us here," replied Jones.

"As a non-middle-class person and as a woman," Dunbar disagreed. "I had to figure out where my oppression lay as a half Indian, poor white, and woman," she said. Dunbar had often felt despised and out of place as the child of sharecroppers, as well as the darkest skinned of her siblings. Getting married at a young age had been her ticket out of poverty, but being a wife and mother in California had become its own alienating confinement. Radical politics helped her question her shame and emerge as a rare voice for the poor among the more privileged and educated of her movement circles.

Like many conversations at Sandy Spring that weekend, this one came to no satisfying resolution.

At one point, the room grew loud as several women started talking over one another in attempts to redirect the conversation, prompting one woman near the reel-to-reel recorder to moan, "Just when it gets interesting everyone talks."

"We're talking about who is the enemy," one of the voices from the loud din responded, "and if we're going to try to clarify who is the enemy, then we've got to have the discussion about what the power structure is."

"Men! That's good enough, isn't it? Men." To which a chorus of women yelled, "No!"

"When I say men are the enemy, I include radical men, you know, in that. I think we're going to have to recognize that the men we are married to, with whom we live, and so on, share a lot of these identifications. I'm not suggesting we fuck up the New Left." But that is exactly what it sounded like to Marilyn Webb, who argued that what the feminists were talking about would slow the revolutionary work of the New Left—of men like her husband. She was interrupted by a woman who said, "A lot of people keep coming up saying they're starved."

Maybe the interjection was intended to cool down the room more than it was aimed at silencing Webb. In any case, kitchen duty and lunch preparation were given primacy over continuing the conversation. Some balked at the interruption and similarly directed their complaints to Webb.

"Why don't we bring the peanut butter out here," Webb asked, her irritation rising, "and make the sandwiches while we're sitting around the table?"

Another woman made a crack about whether Webb envisioned a communal lunch production or individuals taking care of themselves. Too agitated to even offer a polite laugh, Webb responded with total seriousness that it would, of course, be communal.

If people were hoping that a lunch break would drain some of the conflict from the meeting, they were wrong. This was clear even before Roxanne Dunbar began a largely unwelcome reading of passages from Valerie Solanas's manifesto. Kathie Amatniek and Carol Hanisch watched the clock as the minutes clicked by until Hanisch could no longer contain herself. "We've been waiting for nearly an hour" to make their presentation about consciousness raising, she protested.

Once they had the floor, Amatniek began with a direct statement of where they stood. "We fall into the man-is-the-enemy camp, you know, in terms of our analysis," she said, laughing slightly. This meant, she clarified later, that "male chauvinism—men—and the institutions that institutionalize their privilege should be our enemy. And that's what we should fight until the bitter end because everything will go in its way."

"Not when the enemy, that final enemy, is also the enemy of those men," interjected Fran Rominski, one of the women chosen by the West Side Group to represent Chicago at the meeting.

Amatniek fired back before Rominski could finish, "Which is your final enemy?"

To which Rominski burst, "Capitalism!"

"That's not our final enemy. That's not our final enemy," Amatniek countered in a near chant. Listening to the recording more than fifty years later, one can almost hear the rueful shaking of her head.

The long back and forth that followed between Amatniek and Rominski was a verbal spar punctuated by staggering rhetorical jabs. Both women refused to budge from deep-seated and seemingly irreconcilable positions, illustrated neatly in a moment when Rominski believed she'd won the argument, catching Amatniek in a contradiction. "You just said you can't have women's liberation in a capitalist society," she stated triumphally, only to be met with Amatniek's swift retort, "I know, but you just said you can't have male chauvinism in a socialist society"—a position she found unrealistic and illogical.

Threaded through this fundamental disagreement about what or whom was the real "enemy" of women's liberation was the creeping worry that history was about to repeat itself, that all the radical potential of women's liberation was poised to be co-opted by liberal feminists, just as the radicalism of the "first wave" had been cut down by the single-minded quest for white women's suffrage.

"I guess the thing that concerns me," said Rominski, "is that what you begin to build a movement upon is very essential and that a movement operates and flows on a dynamic rather than a theoretical artifice." The dynamic that begins their movement, she explained, "has to be very explicit about those connections and about the enemies that we see even though they overlap." As she spoke, Rominski's voice grew louder and more urgent, and then she began to pound the table. "I believe that there are enough variations of Betty Friedan and the NOW people in this country to completely . . . [at this point, the sound of her hand slamming the table covers the word on the recording] every kind of antagonism, women against men, and co-opt it into a reformist movement which will not [another pound of her hand] accomplish female liberation and which would reinforce. . . ."

Amatniek, who had been muttering the entire time, finally interjected, "You don't think very much of other women, then."

"I think women are very oppressed and they don't understand their oppression," replied Rominski.

Without missing a beat, Amatniek fired back, "Well, you're just as oppressed as they are, I can assure you."

"I know that," conceded Rominski, "but that's exactly what I'm trying to deal with."

Amatniek, nearly yelling now, continued as if the other woman had said nothing. "You don't have to worry about the masses of women—I mean, if they really get turned on to women's liberation, I think they're gonna be so much more conscious of capitalism than you are!"

There was a gasp, and then everyone fell silent. Amatniek had apparently found the line and barreled across it. The group erupted in angst-filled murmuring, complete with pained exclamations of "Whoa, whoa!" and "Oh, no!" Someone turned to Amatniek and asked, "Do you really think that's true?" She sounded both appalled and devastated.

While anger still crackled between Amatniek and Rominski, several women who up to that point had not spoken then offered their perspectives, which shifted the focus away from the two women's argument for a time. Then someone asked Rominski if she could explain what she'd meant by her comment about NOW and Betty Friedan.

"What I am most concerned about," she replied, "is that we are not the only people who are, who want to speak to those women. There are many other people who want to speak to those women . . . [and] Friedan, as much as we may hate her, she's stirring things up."

To which Amatniek charged back in, "We hate Friedan; do we hate Friedan?"

"I don't hate her," offered Cindy Cisler. "She's extremely interested in what we're doing—we can maybe co-opt her!"

Someone else wondered, "Do you think she [Friedan] has the proper woman consciousness?"

"We can argue about Friedan some other time," sighed Rominski, trying to steer the discussion back to her point. "There is going to be a movement in this country of women for women's rights. What the nature of that movement is, what it identifies as the enemy, what kind of changes it demands, how it defines women's liberation is going to be determined by somebody," and she certainly didn't want that to be Betty Friedan and the National Organization for Women.

One thing everyone could agree upon was that the day had been hard, draining, and upsetting, no matter where you fell in the debates. The participants were also becoming acutely aware of how little time they had left together—just the Saturday night and Sunday morning remained—and how little had been accomplished, in a concrete sense. So, it was decided to shift focus for the night and share with one another how they came to women's liberation, to focus on the women themselves and their relationships to family, community, activism, and one another, rather than on the big issues and on the political philosophies that had ruled the day. It would be a reset of sorts, some hoped, so they could go into their last session on Sunday with less conflict, address original agenda items, and leave with a clear sense of their next collective steps—namely, to plan a larger conference.

In the end, it seemed to work, although some felt that they had spent too long discussing their personal stories. On Sunday morning, one woman remarked, "What happened yesterday is that we got ourselves into a box of really going at each other and we wouldn't have gotten out of that unless we had seen each other as people." It was important, certainly, but how much time should be devoted to these topics at future meetings? Should they do something like it at their larger conference?

They turned to making plans and setting tasks for a national conference on women's liberation during the Thanksgiving holiday. At this point, someone raised the issue of Black women's absence at their present meeting and the urgent need to remedy that in the future, suggesting that women from the Black Panthers be invited to help plan the conference.

The conversation that followed included frank and direct statements from white radical women about their connections—or lack of them—to Black radical women that are rare in the archives of feminism. It has since become legend among the first women's liberationists, for the generations of radicals who followed them, and in the histories of the movement—and it became notorious in its own time, from the minute it started. (About twenty-five years later, Chude

Pamela Allen would quip in a letter to an interviewer, "I'm glad I don't have that discussion about including black women in my history!")

The discussion as it was represented in the partial transcript, which did not identify the speakers, went in several directions at once. Some rejected the idea of extending invitations to any Black activists at all, while others debated whether they should be made to women from the Black Panthers or from among the small number of Black women already involved in or at least known to the women's liberation groups represented at Sandy Spring. Someone recommended asking Flo Kennedy for suggestions, adding that she assumed Kennedy wouldn't want to come herself. This presumption that any Black woman asked to attend the conference would almost surely decline was a common refrain. Often sounding preemptively aggrieved by rejection, the white women's comments tended to carry the unspoken question: *So why invite them at all?* At least one person felt that membership in the Black Panthers made any woman suspect where feminism was concerned, because the leadership was "fantastically chauvinistic."

"I know," replied another, "but I still think we should give black women the option." She elaborated:

> Either way it matters. This question of how we work out how we are oppressed, I don't think we are going to be able to work that out without the experience of black women in the room. If we are going to find out what is common in our oppression versus what's different in our oppression, we can't do that with just a white women's group. It's absolutely essential for our ideology that we have militant black power women in on the formation of our ideology. It's for our own good that we need it.

Several white women expressed concerns that if Black women were included, they would direct all conversations toward issues of racial oppression and away from women's liberation. "The reason she said you're opening a can of worms [if you start inviting Black radical women] is that they are going to want to discuss different things, have different concerns. We're going to get so involved with them that we are not going to talk about female liberation," said one woman.

Remarks like these highlighted the fundamental premise driving most of these arguments: the two issues—women's liberation and Black Power—were distinct, and Black women were always necessarily Black before they were women.

Describing herself as "really upset about the direction of the discussion," one woman offered a long explication of the major differences between Black oppression and women's oppression. She urged her compatriots to recall the discussions they had already had that weekend about the difference. The woman continued:

> We are not as oppressed as the blacks. The oppression is different. We don't really understand our racism at all, our own oppression, or our relationship to ourselves, let alone blacks. . . . My understanding from talking with a woman from Black Student Union that their women's liberation groups are into very different things. That's good because they are defining it in terms of their own oppression.

She pushed the other white women at Sandy Spring to follow the lead of Black radical women and determine the specificity of their oppression. "I suspect that if we say if you define women's liberation the way we define it, that's a very white racist thing to do," she continued. "That's not where we should be at. At this point, we should be defining what we think about our racism and our oppression and that we should not pass judgment on their liberation movement at all." They should use this meeting to more fully understand their own oppression, "to see if there is a common bond of where we should build" and then move to create coalitions.

So, the woman concluded, they should not invite Black women to the conference in November.

At a different point in the conversation, someone noted that extending invitations to Black women was not going to solve the racial exclusions already baked into the women's liberation project as it had been undertaken at Sandy Spring. "If the thing is that black women can come to the conference if they are interested, then that's not sufficient because we've excluded them in the planning session," acknowledged one woman. "If you know of black women who are feminists, our problem is really getting black women on the planning session. Then why don't we put that woman who we already know is a feminist on the planning session? That takes care of the problem."

"The problem with that is tokenism," came a derisive reply. "It is worse to do that than not do anything." The comment was telling; the speaker identified the problem while using the point to bypass the issue of racial exclusion altogether—*best not to address it at all.* Best for whom?

"That's not another problem if we are talking about building a women's liberation movement in this country. It's very much our problem and it's our problem because we are the racists," said a woman [the transcript makes it impossible to know if this comment came from the woman who'd advocated for inviting Black women to participate in the conference planning]. Others chimed in with support, agreeing that the burden to remedy exclusion fell to white women, and that demanded urgency.

"I have a feeling that there are a few black women who are thinking along the lines that we are, and I think we ought to make an effort to dig them out."

Another offered, "We have one such woman in our group; she is very militant on both the woman thing and the black power thing."

"It's up to us to make that effort. If they say no, my feelings won't be hurt a bit."

And there it was. Someone had said the quiet part out loud. Sort of. The potential for hurt feelings, for guilt, and for the incredible discomfort of being put on the spot as the individual object of a Black woman's anger, of being made responsible for that woman's oppression and the benefits of white privilege, was more than many of the women at Sandy Spring thought they could bear. Those who wanted to discuss these underlying factors directly met knee-jerk resistance and seemed to make little headway.

"I think that the reason we don't want to do this is that we are afraid to deal with black women," offered one woman.

"I think that statement is really unfair and baiting," someone rejoined.

"No," she replied, attempting to salve the sting of perceived accusation, "I'm saying that of myself." This move seems to have been unsuccessful, as far as the record of the last session goes, in prompting a deeper discussion of fear as a motivating factor of the women's decision making.

That didn't mean that those fears weren't still on clear display.

"If you get black women there, who have by and large worked a hell of a lot harder, and been oppressed a hell of a lot more, and here we, or at least I, have been talking about the oppression of the middle-class wealthy housewife, I think what you get are snickers and sneers," said one woman. "In great measure we are talking about the shitty jobs you can get . . . only $70/week. Well, for some of these women, that's damn good. Do you think it would interrupt real interchange among white women?"

Another woman described her experience working with Black women in welfare rights organizing as an example of what would transpire if they invited Black women to the conference. She added:

> I know that black militant women rule the day. They set the tone and they managed to completely cow the white women in welfare organizations. I've seen it time and time again. I understand the problem. But they hold the cards on oppression, they hold the cards on being shot down in every single way and they let white women know that. I don't want to go to a conference to hear black, militant women tell me she is more oppressed and what am I going to do about it.

The final session of the meeting ended when the group had to check out and vacate the facilities of the Sandy Spring Friends School. It had been a hard way to conclude, sending the women on their separate ways worn out and absolutely furious. They had come to no resolution or agreed-upon steps forward where the issues of race and racism were concerned, which in itself became a kind of decision to continue on as they already had been. This was perhaps best summed up in the report author's description: "The question of bringing black women to the conference now muddies up the issue. That what we have to do is have our own meeting and if we are really concerned with black women's liberation and how it relates to us, we have to wait to some future time to set that meeting up. But right now, we have to concentrate on our own oppression."

While it would be easy—and not at all wrong—to zero in on this moment at Sandy Spring as a clear benchmark in the white supremacist genealogy of Western feminism generally, and in U.S. feminism in particular, it would be a mistake to stop there. This argument about whether or when to include Black women in developing women's liberation provides uncommon access to activist white women speaking with little inhibition about their understandings of race and gender oppression, and their own roles within it.

Hanisch, Amatniek, and Cisler rehashed the weekend on their drive back to New York after the meeting's fractious conclusion. They were exhausted, raw, and at once angry and inspired. Perhaps it was Bev Jones's suggestion that they occupy a television station and demand truthful representations of women, or even Florika's fight against Revlon, but at some point Hanisch had begun to think about Miss America again. Its connections to the conversations raging around her seemed everywhere: beauty standards and the role of the media, the need for consciousness raising and the desire to reach the widest possible swath of American women, the racism. When she thought about aspects of women's oppression that clearly affected them all, across lines of race, class, and education, she landed on *beauty*. Arguably, every woman experienced judgment and the constraining effects of dominant beauty standards—if not in the same way, at base they shared the same problem. And what better encapsulation of that problem and its reach than the Miss America Pageant?

Hanisch was at the wheel, fighting the vehicle's broken power steering, when she announced: "We should protest the Miss America Pageant."

PART II

PAGEANT HISTORIES

15

THERE SHE IS

An estimated 100,000 visitors jammed into Atlantic City for the fall pageant and beauty contest right after Labor Day, in 1921. To Margaret Gorman, the first Miss America in history, it felt like she'd shaken the hands of most of them. From the moment she and her fellow title-seekers set foot in the resort community, they were presented at events and parties, and paraded up and down the city's boardwalk and pleasure piers, always thronged by crowds jostling for closer looks and quick hand clasps, sometimes offering small gifts of taffy, chocolates, or flowers. Everywhere the group went, the sixteen-year-old Gorman—who wore a sash that read "Miss Washington, DC" and bore a notable likeness to silent film star Mary Pickford—drew the loudest cheers.

The multi-day event officially got underway in the late morning on Wednesday, September 7, when King Neptune (portrayed by 68-year-old Hudson Maxim, the inventor of smokeless gunpowder) arrived at the Million Dollar Pier on a barge decorated with large shells and young women clad in mermaid costumes. He was greeted by the mayor of Atlantic City and other local leaders, presented with the beauty pageant contestants, and transferred to his rolling shell throne pulled along by costumed "slaves" portrayed by the only Black people on the scene. With Neptune in ceremonial command, the beach censors were officially off duty until midnight the following day, until which time women were allowed to wear more form-fitting bathing costumes and to show their bare legs above the knee. The beauty contestants weren't the only girls and women whose bodies and looks were on display.

Some of the last hands Margaret Gorman shook before leaving Atlantic City were those of the president of the United States, Warren G. Harding, and the first lady, Florence Mabel Harding, who arrived from Washington, D.C., not long before Gorman was set to return. The *Washington Herald*, which had run the contest that Gorman won to represent her hometown at the pageant, reported that the president had taken her hand in front of a crowd of 10,000 to announce how well-deserved she was of the "tremendous honors . . . heaped upon her while she was at the shore," followed by Mrs. Harding, who gave Gorman a flower and remarked that the lovely pictures run in the *Herald* had "not done the little beauty justice."

The inaugural Miss America pageant was held a little over a year to the day after the 19th Amendment to the U.S. Constitution, granting the right to vote to women, was ratified. Originally, it had been called the "Inter-City Beauty Contest," one part of a multi-day Atlantic City Fall Pageant created by a local organization of hotel managers, who hoped to lure tourists to the resort community beyond the Labor Day weekend. The pageant, which began as a swimwear competition, built on the popularity of newspaper-based beauty contests for women, girls, and babies: entrants were mostly from urban areas in the Mid-Atlantic and were selected from contests sponsored by local papers like the *Herald*, in which they were judged by their photographs. While the finalists hailed from cities in the East, papers across the country reported the events in Atlantic City and ran Margaret Gorman's picture after she was named "the most beautiful girl in the United States." Samuel Gompers, the leader of the American Federation of Labor (AFL), later gushed to a journalist that Gorman represented just "the type of womanhood America needs—strong, red-blooded, able to shoulder the responsibilities of homemaking and motherhood," concluding that it was "in her type that the hope of the country resides."

While Gompers focused on the contest's display of the domestic strengths of ideal American womanhood, the crowds were most drawn to seeing—and assessing—the women's bodies and looks, particularly when they were dressed in bathing costumes that, for the period, were quite revealing. In its breathless account of the inaugural fall festival, the *New York Times* returned repeatedly to this aspect of the event, highlighting in its headline the "1,000 Bathing Girls on View in Pageant," followed by a note that many of the women in Atlantic City had worn "one-piece suits," thanks to the fact that the ban on exposed knees and tight bathing suits had been suspended city-wide for the pageant festival. Of the contest itself, the newspaper reported that "spectators gasped as they applauded the girls, who were judged on their shapeliness and carriage, as well as beauty of face." When Gorman won, she was named "the most beautiful bathing girl in America." (The title "Miss America" would not become common until a few years later.)

Over the next decade, the early-fall affair got bigger, longer, and incorporated more events and participants. By 1925, the festivities had gone from spanning two days to five, boasting a ranging itinerary. The pageant itself—always the heart of the lineup and the primary draw—similarly evolved. In 1921, judges were asked to assess eight Inter-City Beauties; the next year, contestants numbered fifty-seven. By 1927, there were seventy-five entrants from all over the country vying to be crowned with the new official title of "Miss America."

Beyond geographical diversity, however, little set the contestants apart. As a statement of national values, self-conception, and ideal female beauty, the pageant winners in the 1920s were commonly celebrated for being, as one judge described Miss America 1923, "typically American, an altogether ideal type. Her forebears for ten generations have been American born." Conceived amid the post–World War I rise of anti-radicalism and the anti-immigrant politics of "100% Americanism" (which in turn had led to the ascendance of the Second Ku Klux Klan as a mainstream, national movement of white Protestants), Miss America steadily mirrored the dominant racial attitudes and fears of the period, shaping and promoting certain versions of whiteness as the national ideal.

The first pageant was staged within months of the passage of the Emergency Quota Act of 1921, which introduced a system designed to radically limit immigration by restricting the number of people allowed entry from countries (not already excluded altogether via the Asiatic Barred Zone) to 3 percent of their populations in the United States, as represented in the 1910 census. The racial, ethnic, and religious contours of immigration restriction were made even more clear with the passage of the Immigration Act of 1924, which changed the quota calculus to 2 percent of populations in the 1890 census, aimed at severely constricting entrance of people from southern and eastern Europe who were largely Jewish and Catholic. A year later, Fay Lanphier's Miss America victory was attributed to "the difference that comes with generations of American-born ancestry behind a girl," making the pageant a micro-example of the popularization of eugenic science in the early-twentieth century.

The beauty of women has always been very serious politics in the United States. From the start, denoting who possessed it and who beheld it was a central facet of the American democratic experiment. And like everything else about the origins of the United States, it was inseparable from slavery and definitions of Blackness.

The importance of female beauty for setting the contours of citizenship and for belonging in the new republic was made clear by one of its most eloquent architects, Thomas Jefferson. In *Notes on the State of Virginia,* first published in 1785 while he was minister to France, Jefferson argued that Black and white people could never live together in equal freedom for many reasons, including the terrible wrongs of slavery, and the "ten thousand recollections, by the blacks, of the injuries they have sustained." Chief among Jefferson's reasons, however, was race, which he described as a "difference fixed in nature." From this point, what had begun as an argument against the continuation of chattel slavery in Virginia, and by extension the republic, became a rationalization for it that was grounded in assertions that Black people were not human in the ways that white people were. His first case in point: beauty. "And is this difference of no importance?" Jefferson queried. "Is it not the foundation of a greater or less share of beauty in the two races?" What follows remains one of the most notorious passages in Jefferson's many writings on race and slavery, in which he argued that beauty was made impossible by an "immovable veil of black." They did not have "flowing hair" or share a "more elegant symmetry of form," but perhaps, most telling, reported Jefferson, was "their own judgement in favor of whites, declared by their preference of them, as uniformly as is the preference of the Oranootan [*sic*] for the black women over those of his own species. The circumstances of superior beauty is thought worthy [of] attention in the propagation of our horses, dogs, and other domestic animals; why not in that of man?"

A widower when he left for Paris, Jefferson was joined there two years later by his young daughter and her enslaved traveling companion, Sally Hemings, who was herself just a teenager. Hemings was the very light-skinned, Black half-sister of Jefferson's deceased wife. Historians generally believe that the sexual relationship between Jefferson and Hemings began in France. In the context of later political fights when Jefferson was president, Hemings would appear in the press as "Beautiful Sally" and "Black Sal." Her beauty stemmed from her proximity to whiteness, her enslavement from her mother's Blackness.

Jefferson and other Enlightenment thinkers believed that female beauty was not only a pleasure but also fundamentally necessary to civilization and the rational individualism of men. His English contemporary, Mary Wollstonecraft, devoted much of her work *A Vindication of the Rights of Women*, published in 1792 and considered a foundation of Western feminism, to refuting these claims and their attendant assumptions about the supposed nature of women. Educated to their inferiority, women were "made to assume an artificial character before their faculties" of rational intelligence could be developed, an absence that was in turn offered as proof of their inherent lack. "Taught from their infancy that beauty is woman's sceptre, the mind shapes itself to the body, and, roaming round its gilt cage, only seeks to adorn its prison." That those consigned—and enthralled—to the bondage of beauty were necessarily white and elite was presumed by Wollstonecraft, cemented in the similarly specious teachings of empire, extraction, and slavery.

Teachings like the display of Sara Baartman, a Khoisan woman from South Africa who was exhibited as the "Hottentot Venus" in England and France between 1810 and 1815 as a physical oddity and the antithesis of (white) female beauty. It framed the Black woman's body as other, the opposite of beautiful, and available for examination and consumption by whites in spaces of entertainment, sex, and science.

When Baartman died in Paris in 1815, her corpse was made a specimen and continued to be exhibited as the opposite of classical beauty. Her skeleton and a cast of her body were displayed in the Muséum d' Histoire Naturelle until 1937, when it was moved to the new Musée de l'Homme, where it remained on view for the Parisian public and tourists alike until the mid-1970s. That bears repeating: *the mid-1970s*. Despite official requests for the repatriation of Baartman's remains beginning in the 1940s, they were not returned to South Africa until 2002.

Sara Baartman's story is very much a part of the beauty pageant's racialized history, with its elements of display, spectacle, and judgment. Mary Wollstonecraft echoed through the arguments of women's liberation and other feminists in the 1960s, but those arguments were also haunted by the restless ghost of Sara Baartman and the compound legacies of the violations committed against her. One did not have to grasp at the deep reaches of the past for these connections. Baartman's body was still on exhibit in a museum when Shulamith Firestone traveled to Paris in 1968, in hopes of meeting Simone de Beauvoir and sharing a copy of NYRW's *Notes From the First Year*.

By the time the first Miss America title was granted to Margaret Gorman, the NAACP's magazine, *The Crisis*, which had been established in 1910 and was edited by W. E. B. Du Bois, had for years been regularly featuring the daughters of Black elites and professionals on its covers—a significant achievement not only for the model but also for her entire family. Yet the registers of Black beauty were still largely gauged through proximity to whiteness. This meant not only light skin and soft, straight hair but also economic status, education and professional training, conformity to heterosexual norms and gender roles, and unimpeachable respectability. These elements of beauty both signaled and reinforced the social qualities of Black female refinement, which extended to family and community. While *The Crisis* avoided ads for products promising to whiten dark skin, most Black-owned publications in these years were full of ads for lightening creams, hair-softening solutions, and hot combs and presses. The social and material consequences of colorism's punishing politics were profound, dictating everything from access to education, social standing, and earning potential to whomever one could befriend or love.

Resistance to these standards came in various forms, including from within the Black beauty industry itself. During the summer of 1921, as contestants for Atlantic City's first Inter-City Beauty contest were being selected from the winners of newspaper beauty contests, *Half-Century Magazine* announced its own contest to decide, "Who is the Prettiest Colored Girl in the United States?" Created by Black beauty mogul Anthony Overton to advertise his cosmetics, *Half-Century Magazine* began encouraging its predominantly female readership to submit photos of any Black woman over the age of sixteen for a contest targeted explicitly at white supremacist versions of beauty. "Many white people are under the impression that there are no pretty Colored women," explained the call for photo submissions. "We want to show them that there are many Colored beauties of varying types." With a pageant in its pages, the magazine would "show them that all beautiful hair is not straight, that all beautiful skin is not white, that all the pretty profiles do not belong to the white race." Photos published in subsequent issues for the contest featured a range of women with varying skin tones.

As the segregated Miss America Pageant gained in popularity and cultural profile, so, too, did alternative beauty contests staged by Black organizations and commercial interests. In 1926, the Harlem Savoy Ballroom held a bathing-beauty contest in New York City, explicitly designed to look like Miss America, with a beach-resort theme and a stage resembling Atlantic City. Similar to its white counterpart, its contestants were chosen via contests held by Black papers and the entire process was covered in detail, as was the final pageant in New York.

While Black people were acutely aware of the exclusions of the dominant culture and paid significant attention to the Miss America Pageant and its meanings, the acknowledgment was not mutual or reciprocated. The creators of the Miss America Pageant and its contestants were likely unaware of the Black worlds and the communities represented in the Black press, and so Black and white beauty pageant worlds developed in tandem in this period—but rarely intersected.

Native American women were the complex exception to this racial exclusivity in the earlier years of the pageant. In 1924, the same Congress that intensified immigration restrictions also passed the Indian Citizenship Act, which gave citizenship to all indigenous people born within the territorial limits of the United States. From the 1920s through the 1950s, Indian "princesses" or "Miss Indian Americas" were featured periodically as special guests of the pageant, wearing sashes of identification and ensembles of buckskin, beads, and feathered headbands. The women's involvement as guests—never contestants—signaled their embodiment of the histories of conquest and empire, as well as a kind of nostalgic patriotism. The ideal modern American woman remained white.

A staged photograph taken at the crowning of Miss America 1926 demonstrates the power of these associations. Flanked by the pageant directors and ceremonial hostess Miss Atlantic City, King Neptune holds the crown just over the head of Norma Smallwood of Oklahoma. The outgoing Miss America, Fay Lanphier, smiles beside her, scepter in hand and body draped in a large, white-trimmed cloak. Standing on a lower step of the dais, partially obscured by Lanphier's dramatically arranged train, is another young woman wearing a beauty queen's sash over buckskin and beads. Jesse Jim, a member of the Syilx Okanagan Nation, had been named "Princess America II" at the second annual Northwest Indian Congress, in Spokane, Washington, earlier that summer. Created the year before as part of local non-Native business leaders' initiatives to draw tourist dollars to Spokane, the congress enjoyed a close relationship with federal authorities and agents from area reservations; Jim was crowned by Major General Hugh L. Scott of the U.S. Army.* A local paper described her as "exemplifying the highest type of Indian beauty," and described the processions that followed her crowning as "vividly depicting the days of the old west. . . . Indians in all their tribal regalia, painted for the war path, trappers, soldiers—a string of characters that made history in the valley of the Columbia [River]—fascinated the great crowd lining the streets," including older Native American men "whose names in the early days were names to conjure with." Jim and the other contestants, all referred to as "princesses," rode on a special float. "Some gazed without smiling," wrote the reporter, while "others appeared as aware of their importance as any group of white girls. It was a great day for the princesses and many an admiring glance was cast their way."

* Scott was himself a living embodiment of U.S. empire building and global military power. After West Point, he was commissioned as an officer in the 7th Cavalry in 1876, and was sent to fight in the "Indian Wars" of westward expansion. After twenty years stationed at various frontier posts, where he became known within the army and among civilian leaders as a negotiator and expert on Native American cultures, Scott was dispatched to Cuba and the Philippines to fill a similar role during the Spanish-American War, as well as having participated in negotiations with Pancho Villa during the Mexican Revolution. After being part of the Wilson administration's 1917 delegation to Russia, Scott retired. He spent many of the following years on the Board of Indian Commissioners, during which he participated in the events in Spokane (Army Historical Foundation, "Major General Hugh Lenox Scott," Army History website, https://armyhistory.org/major-general-hugh-lenox-scott/).

Whereas Atlantic City offered the beach, nightclubs, and entertainments of its famous boardwalk, Spokane promoted "living" history and patriotic celebrations of Manifest Destiny, embodied in the faces and forms of young women like Jim. Her visit as an "honored guest" of Miss America was nationally reported and commemorated with the gift of a silver loving cup. Subsequently, similar trips and appearances were offered to newly crowned American Princesses as part of their winnings.

While newspaper accounts of Norma Smallwood's victory dwelled on how different she seemed from the other contestants, no one identified her as Native American at the time, nor does it appear she ever self-identified publicly. (Wider knowledge of Smallwood's ancestry became public only well after her crowning, in the wake of a scandalous divorce and child-custody battle with well-known Oklahoma oilman Thomas Gilcrease. Himself of Creek descent and raised in the Creek Nation of the Indian Territory, Gilcrease had become enormously wealthy when his 160-acre Dawes Act allotment was discovered to be sitting amid Oklahoma's famed Glenn Pool oil field.) Instead, the press focused on the style and color of her long, dark—not blonde!—hair, which Norma parted down the middle and coiled into buns over each ear (similar to Princess Leia's iconic look from *Star Wars*, which was itself copied after a Native American style).

Beyond remarking on her hair, reporters strained to specify what it was that so distinguished the winner, sometimes brushing against but never speculating overtly about her heritage. "With a seriousness, strangely attractive in the girl who is the cynosure of the eyes of the Nation," the *Boston Globe* reported, Smallwood had "told of her childhood out in the land of the oil wells and Indian Reservations." When the judges selected her by an 8 to 7 vote, they said it was Smallwood's enigmatic quality that appealed to them. "She has mystery, and intrigues the imagination just as the Mona Lisa does," explained one jury member. "In other words, she is different."

Miss America was never unilaterally disavowed by non-white people, nor was the contest entirely accepted by the women it worked to exalt. In fact, protests against the pageant by white women's groups and religious organizations, among others, are almost as old as the event itself, arguing that the pageant was degrading to national ideals and was an assault on the morals of participants and viewers alike.

In 1922, members of the Florence Crittenton League, an organization devoted to the rescue and reform of sex workers and unwed mothers, argued that modesty had been "thrown to the wind" by the contest's bathing-suit parade, and could lead to greater sexual promiscuity and the victimization of women. Two years later, the New Jersey State Federation of Women's Clubs took this criticism a step further by introducing a resolution denouncing the pageant at their annual conference and urging the women of the United States "to wage a concerted campaign against the promiscuous display of beauty." One editorialist for the international edition of the *New York Herald* appeared to support this opinion, proclaiming, "The young woman who deliberately exhibits her charm of person to a gaping crowd descends into the sphere of the vulgar, if she is not already there. . . . The contests for the 'Miss America' crown have never truly represented young American girlhood or womanhood." Others decried the creeping of market forces and profit motives onto the bodies and souls of young, white women. In 1923, Reverend James E. Lake, who served an evangelical community in Ocean City, New Jersey, only twenty miles from Atlantic City, condemned "the willingness of a few businessmen to profiteer on the virtues" of contestants; a few years later, a Catholic bishop from Maryland called the pageant "an exploitation of feminine charm by money-mad men."

Criticisms intensified again in 1927, particularly from the American Federation of Women's Clubs, which worried that "American women are sleeping while American girlhood is being degraded." State federation meetings from Los Angeles to Philadelphia adopted resolutions of protest, asserting the pageant's "exploitation of young women," and lobbied the Atlantic City Chamber of Commerce to end it. The Chamber of Commerce dismissed the complaints, but some of the controversy must have made an impact: the Atlantic City fall pageant was not held again until 1937, after owners and managers of the large beachfront resorts turned against the pageant, suggesting that it had "outlived its usefulness" and was driving middle-class customers away who thought it—and the people drawn to it—vulgar and immoral.

The hotel interests were ultimately too persuasive to counter, but once the Great Depression hit, those same businesses turned again to the pageant in hopes of generating more visitors to the now struggling resort community. The revival was a significantly scaled down affair, focused almost entirely on the beauty pageant, with no extra events or entertainment. The field of contestants was smaller, too—thirty women from twenty-eight states who were each sponsored by carnivals and amusement parks. The pageant was generally less well organized and less successful than its predecessors in the 1920s. Many contestants were required to participate in a seven-week vaudeville tour before arriving by train together on the "Beauty Express," so they were exhausted, and the concluding event was so chaotic that the winner, fifteen-year-old Miss Connecticut, Marian Bergeron (the youngest Miss America ever), had no idea she had been selected as Miss America until a program assistant placed the banner across her shoulder.

After the fizzle of the 1933 pageant, there was no event in 1934, but it came roaring back in 1935, thanks to the organizing power and vision of the indomitable Lenora S. Slaughter, who had been dispatched to Atlantic City "on loan" from her position with the Festival of States parade in St. Petersburg, Florida, and would later become the executive director of the organization.

Upon her arrival in Atlantic City, Slaughter set about transforming the look, feel, and aims of the pageant, with an emphasis on making it a spectacle of refinement and idealized bourgeois femininity. This meant reducing the associations with public sexuality (i.e., the bathing suits) and popular entertainment, although the traveling vaudeville show appearances continued as a good source of post-pageant revenue and publicity. While the swimsuit competition wouldn't be dislodged from the pageant for nearly eight more decades, Slaughter sought to temper its primacy in the judging by amplifying the evening-wear portion of the contest and adding a talent segment, an interview, and the award of Miss Congeniality. One Miss America who reigned under the early leadership of Slaughter later remarked, "She picked up the pageant by its bathing suit straps and put it in an evening gown."

Slaughter also added several new rules to and imposed structural changes on the competition, including a mandate that it was limited to women between eighteen and twenty-eight years-of-age who were not—or ever had been—married. She removed contestants sponsored by businesses to focus only on geographical representation—which increasingly meant states and territories rather than individual cities—and expanded the preliminary competitions to build an even larger national network of local volunteers and organization-sponsored pageants that fed "qualified" winners to the national title.

Slaughter was also responsible for the addition of Miss America's infamous Rule No. 7, making official what had been a common understanding since the very first pageant in 1921: "Contestant must be in good health and of the white race." As a Southerner, the resort community's enforcement of racially segregated public spaces, beaches, accommodations, neighborhoods, and jobs in Atlantic City had been familiar and comfortable. The desire to preserve white women's innocence was infused into every regulation Slaughter instituted: those who came to Atlantic City to compete for the title of Miss America were heavily chaperoned, strictly monitored, and threatened with elimination should they break any of the rules, which now included curfews; no drinking, smoking, or nightclubs; and no keeping company with any man, family relation or otherwise. (Pageant lore is rife with tales of young women unable to see their fathers during competition week, for fear of disqualification.) All this was managed by Slaughter's new system of hostesses and official personal chaperones, who were all elite, older women. Families, local communities, and the nation could rest assured that their national beauties—and their morality and reputations—would be protected.

As with much of America, it was the Second World War and military contracts that ultimately pulled the resort community from the Depression's brink. Europe had been at war for a year with Nazi Germany, which had occupied France that June. The United States was preparing for the involvement many thought inevitable. With the institution of the country's first peacetime draft in the fall of 1940, Atlantic City became a military installation, its many hotels ready-made to house large quantities of recruits, while the cavernous enormity of Convention Hall was perfect for processing thousands of men at a time. A *Saturday Evening Post* article about Atlantic City's transformation denoted the prominence of its national associations with the pageant, explaining that now "the boardwalk witnesses daily a Mr. America parade of singing men marching."

The year 1940 was also when the competition was incorporated as a nonprofit organization and was officially called the Miss America Pageant, although the title had been common since 1925. The pageant was held in Convention Hall for the first time that year, but it promptly lost that iconic venue to the War Department. Lenora Slaughter negotiated a new space in a local theater and put the pageant and its contestants in the service of selling war bonds. It was the beginning of Miss America's long association with the American military, particularly in times of war.

The pageant's famed scholarship program came to exist through this effort to promote war bonds. In 1943, Slaughter chaperoned that year's Miss America and several finalists (the beauty queen's "court") on a national tour of college sorority chapters. "I was *delighted* to talk with [the sororities] because I was trying to reach the nicest girls in the country," she explained, "and I knew that through them I would get to the nicest girls."

During the trip, someone remarked that young women really needed help with college tuition; upon return to Atlantic City, Slaughter set about raising funds from sponsors and making the pageant one of the first organizations to offer significant scholarship assistance to women. "I never went to college," Slaughter said. "I wanted to go to college more than anything in the world, but I didn't have the money. Now I wanted my girls to have a scholarship, something *constructive*. I knew the shine of a girl's hair wasn't going to make her a success in life."

At first, providing academic scholarships to the winners of the Miss America crown did not seem to be of obvious value to the pageant's board of directors. Slaughter convinced them in November 1944 with a six-page memo outlining her assessment of the pageant and her vision for its future.

Finding ideal women required some cultivation, Slaughter argued to her board. The Miss America crown needed to appeal to ambitious, talented, smart—and, yes, also beautiful—young women. The prospective contestant had to "envy Miss America," to *want the title*, and believe that happiness, satisfied ambitions, and life-long honor would come with the crown. "We must give Miss America the advantages which will bring to our contest the type of girl most capable of selling the Pageant for us."

This would take strategic planning. "We must plant in the minds of every girl at the age of 16, a keen interest in the title Miss America, because of the opportunities it offers. By the time she reaches 18 she must be sufficiently sold on this title to equip herself to compete," Slaughter wrote. The emphasis on education and ambition wouldn't take contestants too far from their roles in the family and society, Slaughter assured the board. "The average young American girl has two primary ambitions by the time she reaches the age of 18. The first is a happy and successful marriage. The second is proper education to develop whatever talents she might possess. The second ambition will certainly better equip her to attain the first ambition."

Two things were standing in the way of this goal, she explained to the "gentlemen" of the 1944 board: unreliable sponsorship of the local events required to feed contestants into the national contest; and the unreliable quality of those contestants or, as Slaughter put it, the need for a "better disposition of Miss America after she is selected." The bottom line, she argued, was that fixing the latter problem would solve the first, while taking immediate steps to address the sponsorship issue would make it easier to improve contestant quality.

Slaughter invited the Junior Chambers of Commerce, or "Jaycees," of North Carolina and Texas to sponsor their state pageants in 1944. They had sent, by Slaughter's measure, excellent contestants to Atlantic City—Miss North Carolina and Miss Texas had been "properly wardrobed," had "good talent," and were generally "typical and representative American girls." Furthermore, she had made a point to meet with both young women's mothers, whom she deemed "charming, agreeable, and excellent Pageant boosters." This, along with the fact that the first and third thank-you notes to arrive from contestants after the pageant were from Miss North Carolina and Miss Texas, respectively (Miss Atlanta sent the second), led Slaughter to conclude: "Good breeding should certainly be a requisite for the typical American girl," and could be assured by reaching out to the Jaycees in more states. Thus began the Miss America Pageant's long relationship with the Jaycees to support state pageant systems, which grew as membership in the men's civic group swelled after World War II and became a central feature of Cold War suburban culture. Slaughter was said to have quipped of the Jaycees' growing prominence in the pageant's operations, "What better than to have the ideal man of America run a pageant for the ideal woman?"

Slaughter was determined to get the scholarship award in place as soon as possible so it could be a part of promotions (and the acquisition of new sponsorships) for the 1945 pageant. Raising money during a multi-front global war to fund a $5,000 prize for a beauty queen's education was no easy matter, but Slaughter managed it, securing $1,000 donations from five different companies. The Joseph Bancroft and Sons Company, a Delaware-based textiles manufacturer, was the first to commit funds to the new program, beginning what would become one of the pageant's longest relationships with a national corporate sponsor. This was followed by commitments from another key sponsor, Catalina Swimsuits, as well as a grocery chain, a national hair-care brand, and a watch company.

Lenora Slaughter believed that every typical American girl would want to become Miss America by the time she was sixteen, but that only a select few had the substance and ability to achieve it. That exclusive group could never include Black women, in her estimation, and the system she convinced the board to support would help ensure that. Mid-century civic associations and public and private institutions of higher education, particularly "Greek Life," were largely segregated, by design and daily practice. Slaughter did not visit the campuses of Historically Black Colleges and Universities (HBCUs) or reach out to chapters of national Black sororities to promote the Miss America Pageant—even though Black women's colleges like Dillard, Spelman, and Bennett offered "deportment" classes, in which students trained their appearance and manners in the name of racial progress—nor did she consider Black businessmen's organizations to be appropriate pageant sponsors.

The same year the Miss America Pageant began its scholarship program, the United Negro College Fund (UNCF) was founded to provide scholarships for men and women to attend HBCUs. Its annual Miss United Negro College Fund beauty contest was a key fund-raising tool from the early days of the organization; there was no companion competition for a Mr. UNCF. Unlike the Miss America Scholarship program, Black women competed to raise money for scholarships for others, not necessarily competing for their own educations. The program lasted more than two decades. In December 1963, the student paper of Stillman College in Tuscaloosa, Alabama, wrote about how excited everyone was for the Miss UNCF contest, saying they looked forward to an event that would have "as much splendor and excitement as if it had been the Miss America Pageant."

• • •

Despite the reinforced racial exclusions of Slaughter's new system and the persistence of Rule No. 7, the Miss America Pageant did become more diverse in some ways after the Second World War. Most famously, Miss New York City, Bess Myerson, became the first Jewish woman to win the title when she was crowned in 1945, a week after the formal surrender of Japan. Her victory generated intense pride among American Jews, as well as many others who saw in her success a testament to national values of freedom, equality, and the American promise.

Myerson was also the first Miss America to win a scholarship along with the crown. She had been an early favorite among contestants headed to Atlantic City, and Slaughter had hardly concealed her own preference for her. The pageant's program said it all: in the section of contestant photos, Myerson was pictured in the center of the page wearing her college graduation regalia in a yearbook-style head shot. She was surrounded by images of three other contestants, all in full-body poses, two wearing swimsuits and the other, Miss Birmingham, Alabama, in a revealing "Native American" costume of fringed shorts, cropped vest, and large, feathered headdress. The stark contrast with Myerson's mortarboard—and its implications—is impossible to miss.

Bess Myerson, September 8, 1945

But even Slaughter's support and the postwar flush of victory, relief, and patriotism, coupled with increasing understandings of the horrific scope of the Holocaust, could not shield Myerson's faith and ethnicity from being a point of focused concern. Sponsors failed to use her in national advertising to the same extent as they had previous winners, and her public bookings suffered by comparison. The pressure of being the first "minority" Miss America and constant confrontations with antisemitism weighed on her.

At a booking for a country-club event in the South, Myerson recalled being enchanted by the plantation ambiance and its liveried (undoubtedly Black) workers, Southern manners, and décor. After changing in an upstairs room into the enormous hooped gown she would wear for her appearance, Myerson came to the top of a grand staircase and paused. "I felt like Scarlett O'Hara," she later said. But as she started her glide down, a woman from the club came running into the foyer to stop her. There had been a mistake, she explained. Jews were not allowed in their restricted club, and Myerson would have to leave immediately. Myerson was stunned. For decades, the humiliation of that moment endured. "As I sit here, I remember the pain," she told her biographer. "I felt as though I had walked into a stone wall. I went upstairs, took off the ball gown, and stopped pretending to be Scarlett O'Hara."

It was not as if Myerson had no experience with antisemitism, but the Miss America crown could be like a magnifying glass in sunlight, condensing the hateful scrutiny and rejection to a blistering point. She recounted an uncomfortable conversation with Lenora Slaughter around the time she was to be crowned Miss New York and would be on her way to the national competition, during which Slaughter suggested that Myerson change her name to something more "attractive" and generically "American" (read: Protestant). Myerson refused—a decision she knew had been the right one as the importance of her presence as a Jewish beauty queen became clear.

To the frustration of Slaughter and the entire pageant organization, she took the reins of her own publicity and began to work for the Anti-Defamation League of B'nai B'rith, touring schools and college campuses around the country, speaking against antisemitism and racism as antithetical to democracy and American values, all under the banner of her new motto: "You can't be Beautiful and Hate!"

"Hate is a corroding disease," Myerson explained to a reporter in March 1946, "affecting everything you do and distorting your appearance and your personality." The campaign was designed to educate and inspire change, she said, born of "a need for mutual respect and understanding among young people regardless of race, color, or creed; it is up to the young people to create" it. Bess Myerson's activities vexed Slaughter, who called them "political events" inappropriate for a Miss America and she suggested that Myerson was being manipulated as a "tool of the racial minorities." But Myerson's public authority, charisma, and blooming television career were impossible for the pageant director to reject.

This was the first in a growing stream of protests involving the Miss America Pageant from within the organization itself. Whereas past controversies had emerged from external critics, the voices were now coming from inside the proverbial house, turning the crown into an argument for multicultural democracy and freedom, rather than a paean to white supremacy. Slaughter's system had been designed to centralize her aesthetic and values, but now diverse communities from the vast sprawl of the country and its territories were pushing back on the national pageant, saying they could not—or simply would not—hold the color line in a new postwar world of shifting national ideologies.

The first major challenge to the systemic racism of the Pageant came in 1948 from Eva Nichols, a member of the Yankton Sioux Tribe and president of the Black Hills Council of American Indians in Rapid City, South Dakota. She protested Rule No. 7 in a letter to Lenora Slaughter, parts of which were published in the *Rapid City Daily Journal*, after learning that the city's local pageant was required to operate by the whites-only regulation dictated out of Atlantic City. The newspaper reported Nichols's charge that it was "one of the most un-American forms of discrimination this western part of the country has seen in all its history of contests," and noted her promise: "Our Indian population is rising up in arms against this kind of discrimination. It is our aim to fight this, not only locally, but nationally as well." Inspired by Nichols's protest, the local chapter of the American Federation of Musicians, who were sponsoring the "Miss Rapid City" pageant, made their own announcement the next day: their union was "a staunch advocate of racial equality and always has combatted discrimination and segregation in every form." So the chapter's board had decided unanimously to eliminate "any restriction as to color or race from the Rapid City beauty pageant," and pledged to support the winner as she moved on to the state contest, no matter her race. This, in turn, led to a similar pledge from the sponsors of the Miss South Dakota Pageant, the winner of which would go on to compete in Atlantic City.

The escalating protest forced a swift response from Slaughter, who offered the most detailed, public account she would ever make of the reasoning behind the Miss America Pageant's whites-only rule. In a written response to Nichols that was similarly quoted in the *Rapid City Daily Journal*, Slaughter assured South Dakota's civic leaders that the pageant did not intend to restrict participation from "the Indian race" at the finals in Atlantic City and that Miss America would "be proud and happy to accept a candidate with Indian blood." Rule No. 7, she explained, was really aimed at excluding the participation of Black women. "We have eliminated the negro [*sic*] from this contest due to the fact that it is absolutely impossible to judge fairly the beauty of the negro [*sic*] race in comparison with the white race," quoted the newspaper. Besides, Slaughter reportedly added, "there is a Miss Sepia America contest conducted in this country which is open only to the negro [*sic*] race." The Miss America organization had "assisted the people running this contest" and "they understand fully our position."

Founded four years earlier, the Miss Sepia America Pageant was still forming when Slaughter pointed to the contest as justification for her segregationist rationale (and placed the Miss America organization in the paternalist role of "assisting" it). The NAACP's July 1944 issue of *The Crisis*—by that time under the editorship of Roy Wilkins, future executive director of the entire organization—had featured contestants from the nascent Black pageant, including putting one of the women on the cover, in swimsuit, identified only as "Tan Tidbit—Summer Style." Priscilla Williams, the "tan tidbit," who appeared to be the darkest skinned among the five women included in the magazine, was still noticeably light complected, with long, straight hair that had been curled, pinned up at the sides, and decorated in the signature style of Billie Holiday, with a large white flower at her temple. The cover photo was taken from below, looking up at Williams as she stood on the ladder-like rigging of a ship, in a white swimsuit with a skirt riding high on her thighs; her crossed, fully exposed legs were the only thing concealing a full view up the skirt. Williams joined four other contestants in a one-page photo spread inside the magazine entitled, "Lovely Lassies in the Sepia Miss America Contest." There was little information about the contestants other than their names and the fact that they all hailed from the Greater Boston area. One of them, it was mentioned, had a scholarship to a screen actors' workshop in Hollywood. The photo's caption noted, "the Sepia Miss America Committee of Boston, Mass., has launched plans for a nationwide series of contests to select the outstanding Negro beauty in the country and crown her Miss Sepia America."

The creation of the Miss Sepia America contest did not support the racial exclusivity of the Miss America Pageant, as Slaughter and her pageant board had hoped. While the deep traditions of independent Black pageantry would persist, albeit in complex and increasingly contested ways, individual Black women began to seek the Miss America crown for themselves in the postwar period, marshaling their beauty, bodies, and talents against the color line by competing in local pageants that allowed interracial competition and fed into the state contests that created the group of finalists bound for Atlantic City each year. These early, semi-inclusive contests occurred in large urban areas, like Washington, D.C., and Philadelphia, or on the campuses of integrated colleges and universities—but never in the South. Whatever the region, Black women were rarely greeted with open arms or clear invitations to compete; they faced hostility, dirty tricks like "misplacing" applications, or painful and pointed indifference.

While Slaughter and others attempted to draw a hard line between Black and white beauty, the year 1948 presented two diversity milestones for the pageant in the form of women representing insular territories and U.S. empire. In September, the finalist from the territory of Hawai'i, Yun Tau Chee, became the first Asian woman to appear in the national competition; that year also saw a guest appearance at the pageant by Miss Puerto Rico, Erma Vasquez. So, Rule No. 7 was quietly dropped from Miss America contestant forms in 1949, but the racial exclusion it dictated remained very much in force.

Black Americans followed these developments closely, seeing both hypocrisy and opportunity in the Miss America Pageant's equivocation on their whites-only rule. This tension between the pageant's steps toward greater diversity, paired with the insistent exclusion of Black women, was emblematic of the wider transition in American political culture toward racial liberalism after World War II, between the spectacle of equal opportunity and integration as fundamental democratic values and the hallmarks of the American promise and fierce commitment to maintaining white supremacy. While Bess Myerson's win in 1945 was very much a part of this developing liberal story, her move to seize the narrative to attack those exclusions ("You can't be Beautiful and Hate!") served to highlight the contradiction rather than ameliorate it.

If Bess Myerson was the perfect "Good War" Miss America, Yolande Betbeze, Miss Alabama 1951, was the Cold War embodiment of idealized national beauty. When she was crowned on September 9, 1950, U.S. combat troops had been on the ground in Korea since July. The pageant created a new calendar for itself by postdating the winner's reigning year—there is no Miss America 1950 because Betbeze was crowned Miss America 1951. From that point onward, the pageant would always in some ways be looking ahead, toward the future. In the context of Cold War American culture, this national future seemed preordained, vastly affluent and powerful, technologically advanced, and absolutely terrifying. Fears of nuclear annihilation; the Soviet Union and spread of global communism; internal subversion by political radicals, African Americans, gays and lesbians, juvenile delinquents, overbearing mothers, and more—the list of enemies and potential threats seemed limitless and intersecting. The Miss America Pageant became for some a bulwark against these dangers, an annual inoculation of patriotism, gender normativity and beauty, commercialism, and hopeful anticipation.

What Leonora Slaughter and other pageant management may not have anticipated was Yolande Betbeze's persistent deviation from the Miss America ethos of conformity and idealism. She is best known today as the first Miss America to refuse to make public appearances in a swimsuit after winning the crown, arguing that she should be celebrated instead for her talent as an opera singer and her academic successes. Slaughter supported Betbeze in what she believed to be an impulse toward respectability—the demand conformed, after all, to the image of the pageant Slaughter had been building for years—but the decision cost the Miss America organization financially when Catalina Swimsuits discontinued their sponsorship and started a competitor contest in California—the Miss USA Pageant.*

Betbeze's activism did not end there. After her year as Miss America, Betbeze moved to New York City, where she attended the New School for Social Research, and eventually became active in a number of causes, including work with the NAACP and the Congress of Racial Equality (CORE). In 1953, she would sit vigil at Sing-Sing prison to protest the executions of Ethel and Julius Rosenberg; Slaughter, suffice to say, was far less supportive of these activities.

In 1952, Betbeze joined Bess Myerson and BeBe Shopp (Miss America 1948) in making public calls for a racially integrated pageant after Native American organizations declared a boycott of the Miss South Dakota Pageant, charging the state-wide contest with discrimination against indigenous women, thus ensuring they could not appear at the national finals in Atlantic City. The *Baltimore Afro-American*'s coverage of the controversy centered on the stated support for integration from Betbeze, Myerson, and Shopp under the headline, "'Miss America' Calls for End of Color Line." Referencing her earlier campaign against antisemitism and racism, Myerson argued, "Naturally a contest like this should be the epitome of democracy."

Though the Miss America Pageant "cleared themselves of any responsibility" for actions taken by state organizations, reported the *Afro-American*, stating that at the national level there were "absolutely no qualifications of race, creed, or color so far as the finalists in the contest were concerned," the pageant's spokesperson had to concede to past discrimination. "It's true that we had a white race restriction until three years ago but it's not there now," he said.

When a Miss Indian America Pageant was introduced in 1953 as part of a new annual event in Sheridan, Wyoming, called All-American Indian Days, the Miss America organization sought a relationship with the organization not unlike the one they'd forged with the Miss Sepia contest. The following year, a

* Donald Trump owned the Miss USA Pageant (along with Miss Teen USA and Miss Universe) from 1996 to 2015.

trip to Atlantic City to appear at the Miss America finals as a special guest was offered to the winner, among her other prizes.

The impetus for the new pageant had been the selection in 1951 of the first Native American queen of the Sheridan WYO Rodeo, a sixteen-year-old barrel racer from the Crow Nation, Luzenia Ann "Lucy" Yellowmule. She was not the first indigenous rodeo queen of the twentieth century, but she was the first to be chosen by the popular mandate of cheering from the stands (measured by a sponsoring radio station's applause meters), rather than a panel of judges at a major rodeo. Centrally located near the northern border with Montana, just south of the Little Bighorn Battlefield National Monument and Crow Indian Reservation, where Yellowmule's hometown of Wyola was located, and about halfway between Yellowstone National Park and Mount Rushmore, Sheridan, Wyoming, was a commercial center and regional tourist hub that swelled with visitors every summer for the large, multi-day rodeo. Heralded as a sign of progress in local and regional "race relations" (read: an unusual instance of white embrace of an indigenous person and celebration of her community's contributions), Yellowmule's selection was seized upon by Sheridan's Chamber of Commerce and a local public relations consultant, Francis Howard Sinclair, as an opportunity to sell the Western city as a good place to do business and encourage commitments to anti-discrimination.

Thanks to Sinclair and Yellowmule's willingness to act as the face of the campaign, Sheridan garnered significant national publicity and accolades over the next two years. The idea for a Miss Indian America Pageant emerged in this context, for, asked Sinclair, "How could anyone ever feel prejudice toward a girl so beautiful, gracious, and accomplished?" A delegation of business leaders from Sheridan and Billings, Montana, including Sinclair, accompanied Yellowmule and her "court" of four other young Crow women on a trip to Washington, D.C., in March 1953, to receive a Silver Anvil Award from the American Public Relations Association for "outstanding achievement in human relations." It was presented by the new Eisenhower Administration's secretary of the interior, Douglas McKay, whose agency included the Bureau of Indian Affairs (BIA). U.S. Congressman for Wyoming William Henry Harrison celebrated the award in a newspaper editorial, remarking that "Miss Yellow Mule [*sic*] will stop plenty of traffic in Washington, when she appears in her white buckskin, beaded costume." He also made special mention of the cooperation of the BIA Area Director in Montana who facilitated her excused absence from the Flandreau Indian School in South Dakota so she could make the trip to the capital. While the delegation was not able to meet with President Eisenhower during their visit to the White House, Yellowmule left him a gift of a "peace pipe." She also made an internationally broadcast greeting on *Voice of America* radio, a cornerstone of U.S. Cold War cultural diplomacy in the fight against communism.

Sinclair and the city of Sheridan were also awarded a George Washington Medal from the Freedoms Foundation at Valley Forge for "outstanding achievement in preserving the American way of life by promoting better understanding between American Indians and white races, and the elimination of racial discrimination." Founded in 1948, the Freedoms Foundation was an early Cold War collaboration of leaders in American business, Christianity, and conservative politics to bolster that "way of life," and the "American free enterprise system" it relied upon, against threats from within and abroad through popular education campaigns and awards. Future President Dwight Eisenhower and former President Herbert Hoover penned the foundation's charter and its "Credo of the American Way of Life," first published in *Reader's Digest* in 1949, which illustrated the political and economic rights of American democracy as a towering monument resting on the base of "Fundamental Belief in God."

The notion that one was what they consumed—and the transformation of wants into needs through advertising—was not novel, but it was newly invested with national triumphalism and a global political mission in the Cold War era. The culture was defined by a consumer-driven economy spurred on by the expansion of credit, the development of teen culture and the youth market, suburbanization supported in part by the creation of the national highway system and the automobile industry, and the spread of television. Freedom was expressed as the freedom to consume. General Motors, Buick, Chrysler, and Oldsmobile were major sponsors of Miss America; consequently, their cars featured in the boardwalk parade and pageant print ads, and the reigning Miss America frequented dealerships and car shows during her year with the crown.

The Miss America organization and national pageant became increasingly suburban and small town, as contestants mostly represented their states rather than specific cities or metropolitan areas. By 1949, the only cities still allowed to send their own contestants were New York, Chicago, Philadelphia, and Washington, D.C.; by 1961, Washington, a unique entity, was the only remaining urban center, now likened to a state. The very structure of the preliminary pageant system, with its reliance on volunteers from the Jaycees or other civic organizations that proliferated in new suburbs, rather than on business sponsorship, reinforced this transformation. This was a far cry from the Inter-City Beauties pageant of the 1920s and '30s. Where Miss America began as an urban phenomenon, few city-based contestants remained by the 1950s, its whiteness and version of national beauty mapped "white flight" and reflected the changing demographics of American cities. By the 1960s, "inner city" and "urban" were synonymous in the popular imagination and domestic policy with crisis and the non-white, impoverished, and criminal.

The opening moments of the first national telecast of the Miss America Pageant were in many ways disappointing and jarring to viewers. On September 11, 1954, at 10:30 p.m. on the East Coast, 130 ABC affiliates around the country began airing the contest finals live from Atlantic City, in spite of the fact that the pageant had started two hours earlier. Television viewers joined the show in the middle of the talent competition, having missed the acts of the first two contestants, a greeting from Miss Indian America—Mary Louise Defender of the Yanktonai Dakota Nation—and the evening gown and swimsuit competitions in their entirety, as well as the presentation of the boardwalk parade awards and Miss Congeniality, leaving them without much context or appreciation for the event at large and the women participating in it.

And yet, it captured their attention. Across the country, exhilarated viewers tuned in to witness the announcement of the five finalists as it happened, rather than only hearing it on the radio, reading descriptions of the women's reactions in the next day's papers, or witnessing it after the fact in a newsreel at a movie theater. Guided by host Bess Myerson, by then a fixture of daytime television and evening game shows, Americans were introduced to Miss California, Miss Florida, Miss Michigan, Miss Pennsylvania, and Miss South Carolina, and they watched rapt as each gave their answers to three questions—How would she use her scholarship winnings? What would be her "most vivid" memory of the pageant? What did she understand to be the essential responsibilities of Miss America?—before Miss California, Lee Meriwether, was crowned, a sight previously beheld live only by those in attendance in Atlantic City.* The telecast was hugely successful and it broke records for viewership, reaching about 39 percent of everyone who watched TV that night, or nearly 27 million people.

As the numbers rolled in, the Miss America organization turned their attention to creating a live television event produced with home viewers in mind. The broadcast in 1955 would amplify the many layers of commercial sales, product placement, and promotion that the pageant had come to view as its ideological and economic lifeblood. Longtime sponsor Philco directed their efforts in the months leading up to the broadcast to selling the event—and the televisions on which to view it, promising consumers that their sets would make them feel as though "you're right on the stage of Convention Hall," a line meant to evoke both the experience of having a front-row seat, and the aspiration of walking the stage as a contestant. Advertisements also highlighted the scope of the excitement to come: "Millions of television viewers from coast to coast will be able to share the thrills of the Convention Hall audience, and see a new Miss America begin her reign."

On September 10, 1955, at 7:30 p.m. on the West Coast and 10:30 on the East Coast, those millions did indeed turn their dials to ABC to watch the pageant in its entirety. Bess Myerson continued in her role as "television hostess," joined by Bert Parks in his debut as the master of ceremonies, a job that would catapult him to celebrity.

Born Bertram Jacobson in Atlanta, Georgia, in 1914, Parks got his start in radio as a teenager. By the time he turned twenty, he had a new name and a job in New York City as a staff announcer for CBS Radio; when the game shows and variety programs he hosted moved to television, Parks went with them. A workaday fixture of daytime and evening programing in 1955, Parks found a place among the pantheon of television legends as the voice of the iconic Miss America theme, "There She Is," which also debuted during the 1955 telecast. He crooned the song as the newly crowned Miss America took her first steps

* It is fitting that Lee Meriwether, the first woman crowned Miss America on national television, went on herself to be an Emmy-nominated actor in television comedy, soap opera, and drama.

The Miss America Pageant featuring Bert Parks as Master of Ceremonies, September 7, 1957

in the role, smiling, crying, and waving to the crowd. The song and its lyrics—including "There she is, your ideal," and celebrating "her all-American face and form"—were received as a warm tribute to the American (white) feminine aesthetic, as well as an exhortation to appreciate that aesthetic.

The song, Bert Parks, and the new telecast were all hits. Just days earlier, much of the country had been focused elsewhere on Chicago, and the open-casket funeral of Emmett Till, the fourteen-year-old Black boy who'd been tortured and murdered in Mississippi after supposedly whistling at a white woman.

There was nothing coincidental in the adjacence of these two events in American history. The nation's witness of Till's brutal killing and the debut of "There She Is, Miss America" in the critical moment of the pageant's expansion via national television comingled in the ways that dominant notions of feminine beauty, desire, and white supremacy fed on and fueled one another. It made horrifically evident their capacity to define the nation—its best and its worst, and who belonged and who could be violently expelled. The pageant song celebrated idealized womanhood and national beauty by encouraging looking, assessing, and wanting—or wanting to be. But Till's murder, and the long line of American lynchings it joined, served as a reminder of the deadly consequences of the "wrong" person's admiration. The near simultaneity of these events heightened the focus not only on national investments in white women's beauty but also on who was allowed to look, assess, and comment, on who could judge and desire, and who could be put to death for it.

16

BLACK IS BEAUTIFUL

Emmett Till's mother, Mamie Till-Mobley, demanded an open casket for her son's service, "so all the world can see what they did to my boy." Long lines wove past the casket for hours at the public viewing in Chicago, people showing their respect and support for Till's family, as well as their collective horror and resistance. Many thousands more saw pictures in *Jet Magazine* of what had been done to the boy, also thanks to his mother. The college students who started the sit-in movement in 1960 had been exactly Till's age when he was murdered, and none would ever forget seeing those pictures five years earlier.

As the civil rights movement coalesced around legal challenges and nonviolent direct action in the 1950s and early 1960s, activists harnessed the power of the media, particularly visual culture, to rattle the moral conscience of the nation and to call the country to task for its failures to uphold its own oft professed values of equality, freedom, and democracy. This action included the visual power of integrating white-dominated beauty pageants. After several years of young Black women competing in local pageants that fed state-level contests that led to the Miss America finals, the first Black woman competed in a state pageant for the title of Miss Michigan in 1955.

The following year, a parade float of Black beauty queens moved along the Atlantic City boardwalk, the first time Black women appeared in the popular Miss America event as an object of beauty rather than as one of the laborers supporting white people. The float was sponsored by the Black-owned Apex Hair and News Company, and it featured the winner of its Miss Apex Pageant, Nancy Miller, as well as her court, which was made up of Black beauty queens from various contests: Miss Afro-American; Newark, New Jersey's Miss Board of Trade; and Miss Negro Press among them. The Black business owners and civil rights advocates who sponsored the contests saw the float as a meaningful victory, showcasing the beauty of Black women at the premier beauty pageant in the country, in front of more than 200,000 spectators.

The year 1956 was also the first time the wider public recognized Margaret Taliaferro, wardrobe mistress for the Miss America Pageant, as a skilled professional who was integral to its success. Taliaferro designed and led the team of women of color who made the costumes and matching contestants' gowns and parade gear. She was a prominent NAACP activist and club woman in southern New Jersey when the pageant hired her in 1951, and was well known in regional Black communities. As the pageant garnered greater national attention through the final's live telecast—a transition Taliaferro and her team made with the organization—she gained national prominence after *Ebony* magazine published a celebratory photo spread and article about her and her work. If Taliaferro's role in the country's premier segregated pageant wasn't enough to remind Black readers of their complex relationships with beauty and national representation, a full-page advertisement running opposite the photos of her at work in Atlantic City reinforced the point; the ad featured a light-skinned young woman urging them to "Share my secret to a Lighter lovelier skin / use Mercolized Wax Cream."

However, *Ebony*'s limited ability to uplift the meaning of Margaret Taliaferro's work for the pageant and its contestants was made clear in 1958, when an Associated Press image appeared in newspapers across the country, showing Taliaferro backstage, ironing a contestant's evening gown. While the image itself was not that different from several that appeared in *Ebony* two years earlier, its framing was diametrically opposed. The contestant in the photo is identified as Miss Illinois Anita Ruth Olson; Taliaferro is not named at all, referenced only as "a wardrobe mistress." She looks down at her ironing, while Olson gazes up and out at the viewer; the placement of the women's arms are mirrored, but while Olson's bare upper arm looks soft and disappears into an elbow-length glove, Taliaferro's forearm looks muscled as she moves the clearly visible iron across the gown's skirts. It's a stark illustration of America's ideal of female beauty: white femininity, maintained but never shared by Black women.

In the battle for integration, beauty was a powerful tool. It had been crucial to the success of the *Brown v. Board of Education* case when married psychologists Kenneth and Mamie Clark captured the consciences of Supreme Court Justices and the nation with the findings of their "doll test," which showed most Black children, when asked to identify the "nice" or "pretty" one, selected the white doll.

When Central High School, in Little Rock, Arkansas, became the first major test of the *Brown* decision in 1957, the nation (and world) was introduced to Daisy Bates, president of the state's NAACP Conference of Branches. She shepherded the "Little Rock Nine" through their attempts to attend school, confronting white harassment and violence that ultimately compelled President Eisenhower to mobilize the National Guard. Famously beautiful and glamorous herself, Bates counseled the students on their appearance, poise, and clothing choices, ever attentive to the critical importance of image to the struggle. She understood this better than many. Along with the Black newspaper she and her husband ran, Bates built a base of influence and power that was rare for women of her day in the NAACP. Her job with the Cotton Makers' Jubilee beauty pageant—an event founded in Memphis, Tennessee, in the 1930s—celebrated and promoted Black contributions to cotton production and manufacturing, in direct response to the city's famed whites-only Cotton Carnival. From 1950 to 1954, Bates served as chaperone to the annual pageant winner as she traveled to New Orleans, Washington, D.C., Haiti, and Cuba, not only as an "emissary of Cotton fashions and good will" but also as a symbol of Black expertise in the industry.

Every year, Black women in greater numbers entered local pageants in the Miss America system, each seeking to breach the beauty color line. With greater numbers also came greater success, publicity, and escalating pressure on the Miss America organization. The June 1959 issue of *Jet* featured three "bronze lassies" who had won local preliminary pageants and were on their way to state finals in California, Indiana, and Illinois—the last critical contests for reaching

Atlantic City. The cover depicted one of them, Nancy Streets, Miss Indiana University, in her crown and sash, looking every inch the standard beauty queen, including her very "white" features and light skin.

When Pat Williams, also featured in the *Jet* piece, won the Miss Sacramento pageant the month before, Lenora Slaughter tried to minimize the significance of her victory by spinning an alternate version of the pageant's postwar history, describing an inclusive pageant that well represented a diverse nation. Slaughter said the success of a Black woman in the pageant wasn't so unusual and should not be treated with "undue fuss." After all, the Miss America organization staged

> 3,500 preliminary local and state contests every year, and the only rules laid down by national headquarters require that contestants be American citizens, between the ages of 18 and 28, who have earned high school diplomas. There are no restrictions as to race, color, creed, or national origin. Since World War Two there have been national finalists competing who were full blooded Indians, Mexicans, Puerto Ricans, and Orientals, and every religion and national origin has been represented.

Slaughter's *Nothing to see here, people,* was perhaps the best indication of the effectiveness of the Black women's challenge.

Diane Nash, a student at Fisk University originally from Chicago, emerged early as one of the most visible leaders of the sit-in movement and Freedom Riders in Nashville, Tennessee, a group that included future SNCC chairman and later U.S. Representative from Georgia John Lewis, and a future mayor of Washington, D.C., Marion Barry. In August 1960, Nash was the only woman in a SNCC delegation sent to the Republican National Convention to urge the party to include an endorsement of the group's aims in their platform. As her public role in the movement grew, most press coverage of Nash inevitably began by pointing out her good looks and her history as an aspiring Miss America in the Chicago pageant system. To this day, Diane Nash remains one of the few women recognized among the icons of the 1960s Black Freedom Movement.

"The first thing you have to say about Diane—the first thing anyone who encountered her noticed, and there was no way not to notice," explained John

Lewis, "is that she is one of God's beautiful creatures, just about the most gorgeous woman any of us had ever seen." She was "small and shapely," he added, "with honey brown skin and bright green eyes." Nash was also smart, a brilliant public speaker who was quick on her feet, self-possessed, and fiercely brave. Lewis and others recognized and respected all these things about Nash, but "the first thing you had to say" about her was that she was beautiful.

In subtle ways, Diane Nash's beauty remained the "first thing" acknowledged throughout her activism and leadership in the movement. *Jet* magazine's announcement of Nash's marriage in 1962 to a fellow leader of the Freedom Riders, Rev. James Bevel, read: "Miss Nash, a former Chicago 'Miss America' contestant who quit Fisk University to join the sit-in movement, has been arrested several times for her leadership in the Nashville boycotts, South Carolina sit-ins and the Mississippi Freedom Ride." (By the end of the announcement, she was referred to as "Mrs. Bevel" and pictures of the pair were captioned, "The

Musician and actor Harry Belafonte (left), with Freedom Riders Diane Nash and Charles Jones (center and right), July 14, 1961

James Bevels.") For Nash, gravitas and authority were facilitated and amplified by her beauty, which remained defined by idealized white femininity. Being perceived as beautiful was useful, a power to be wielded, but it could undermine one's sense of confidence and ability as much as build it.

This impacted not only Diane Nash and others like her but also every woman in SNCC or who worked alongside the group; it affected every girl and woman who contemplated joining SNCC, read or watched news about the group, or even paid its actions only the barest attention. What they all saw was that the powerful, popular women who commanded attention at meetings, achieved national notice, or drew photographers' lenses were conventionally attractive and, more often than not, strikingly so. Time and again, they learned that women's value seemed to rest on beauty and sex appeal, and that it was just as true in the movement as it was in the world they were working to transform.

Living in New York City in 1960, former Miss America Yolande Betbeze Fox mobilized the authority of her beauty and the pageant to amplify support for SNCC and the sit-ins, including being pictured in the *New York Times* picketing the Woolworths store in Midtown Manhattan with a group from CORE. She reminded journalists that she had been Miss Alabama when she won in Atlantic City, and she quipped, "I'm a Southern girl but I'm a thinking girl."

Uptown in Harlem, the annual Miss Natural Standard of Beauty pageant celebrated a very different kind of Black aesthetic. The event was sponsored by a Black nationalist organization with roots dating to the 1920s and to Marcus Garvey's Universal Negro Improvement Association (UNIA). Contestants were required to compete without makeup or processed hair in a pageant that was structured with recognizable similarity to the Miss America contest with the eveningwear, swimsuit, and interview portions all dedicated to demonstrating Pan-African consciousness, culture, and fashion.

As strong as white supremacy's pull on beauty was—and remains—it was matched by a long tradition of Black resistance to conformity and conflicts among activists and wider communities about the meaning and appearance of Black women's beauty. Calls to de-center the white standards and mainstream acceptance hit multiple political registers, at once challenging both the assimilationist aims of integrationists in the civil rights movement and the racism and structural inequities of the dominant culture. The phrase "Black is Beautiful" was first popularized in 1962, and it leapt quickly into common usage, but the idea had much deeper historical roots in Black nationalism and the Pan-African movements. Inspired by the Miss Natural Standard of Beauty pageant, a group connected to New York's jazz recording industry called the Grandassa Models and photographer Kwame Brathwaite staged their own fashion show in 1962, under the banner of "Black is Beautiful." Their assertion was not that Black *could be* beautiful, à la Black women competing for Miss America feeder pageants, but that Black *was fundamentally* beautiful on its own terms and in the context of global movements for liberation and decolonization. Notably, while Grandassa Models wearing natural hair and African-inspired fashions graced the covers of several jazz albums in 1962, the Beach Boys' released their debut album, *Surfin' Safari*, which included the song, "Little Girl (You're My Miss America)," with the refrain:

Blue eyes, blond hair,
Lips like a movie star.

In 1965, a new NAACP poster for its voter registration campaign made clear that the organization's leadership felt they could not ignore the popularity of "Black is Beautiful," but refused to leave open the question of whether they endorsed the nationalist politics associated with the phrase. The poster depicted a photograph of a young Black girl, bundled up for a chilly day and waving an American flag. The lines "Protect Her Future" and "REGISTER AND VOTE" are printed in white text around the girl in the photo itself, while beneath the photo, appearing in black text against a white background, is the line: "BLACK IS BEAUTIFUL—BUT YOU LOOK PRETTIER WHEN YOU ARE REGISTERED."

The NAACP's incorporation of the radical phrase was at once a nod to both its growing popularity among activists, particularly younger ones, and its greater purchase on the wider culture, while the quick rejoinder, "But you look prettier when you are registered" to vote made a counterargument for liberal integration through electoral politics.

Newly amplified calls to celebrate Black beauty reverberated throughout

NAACP poster for voter registration, 1965

the culture, including the popular pageantry of campus life at one of the country's most elite HBCUs, Howard University. Located in the nation's capital and named for the Union general who'd led the Freedmen's Bureau after the Civil War, the university had been a path to upward mobility and status for generations of Black Americans, a path that was fraught with beauty politics. In 1966, the same year Howard alum Stokely Carmichael first called for Black Power, homecoming celebrations came with the crowning of honor student, SNCC activist, and D.C. native Robin Gregory—the first Miss Howard to wear an afro. The stadium rung with cries of "Black Power!" when Gregory and her court were presented. Of the reactions by returning alums to the new homecoming queen, the student newspaper reported that "the thought of a girl who does not straighten her hair being the 'bearer of the crown,'" had appealed to many, while "the product of white brainwashing [were] ever more chagrined because the 'natural look' [had] won the sacred crown." Robin Gregory said that, to her, winning meant "that we as a people began to accept ourselves, you know, just as who we were. Because over the years there was a tremendous amount of shame.

You know, we were made to feel ugly, essentially because of media images and things people told us; and we did everything we could do so that we wouldn't look like who we were, which was, you know, descendants of African people."

Speaking to a crowd of about five hundred Atlantic City residents and officials in 1965, Phillip H. Savage could feel the group's energy building as he neared the crescendo of his remarks. Although based in Philadelphia, he was a familiar face to the resort communities of the shore that were part of his responsibilities as the NAACP's tri-state director, which included Pennsylvania and Delaware along with New Jersey. He was there to help with the group's voter registration drive and membership rally, held in front of City Hall and sponsored by the city's local chapter. Most of the crowd was with him, save for the city commissioner sitting just a few feet away from where Savage stood, who was looking, wrote one journalist later, "expressionless throughout."

You know, Savage told the crowd, dropping the heat to a simmer before firing them back up again, he had been in Atlantic City the week before, to see the Miss America boardwalk parade.

"I watched it very, very carefully," he reported, and "I counted the Negroes involved in it, and I was angry. I saw one pretty black girl on a float and that was it and I say to all those responsible for the Miss White America Pageant: You better find some black faces next year or you may not have" a pageant. The crowd roared with applause and cheers for Savage.

Once they had quieted down again, he continued, "I saw floats from some of your major corporations and major stores on the Boardwalk and not one black face was to be found." Strange, since Black folks in Atlantic City were customers of the electric, water, and gas companies, and they did their banking in town, he mused, "Well, God darn, make sure you get some black faces on those floats next year!"

He'd also noted that only one of the cars pulling the individual contestant floats had been driven by a Black man (he was driving Miss Florida). What an excellent example of the "typical white hypocrisy" of the North, quipped Savage. "In the South, whites know they're wrong and are going to have to change, but in the North?" White Northerners liked to pretend that racism wasn't an issue.

"I say to Atlantic City now, a Boardwalk there won't be next year with so much ease and luxury and economy and comfort if we don't find a different kind of Miss America contest from the one you've been holding," Savage said. "It's time for Miss America to BE Miss America, not Miss White America!" Again, the crowd roared while the city councilman sat there, showing no expression.

Back in his Philadelphia office the following week, where a copy of the new "Protect Her Future . . . Register And Vote" poster hung on the wall behind his desk, Savage related that the rally—and his speech—had been a success, in his monthly report to Gloster Current, national director of branches and Savage's immediate boss. His references to the Miss America Pageant had been especially effective, Savage wrote to Current, explaining they had been given "wide circulation" in area newspapers. Overall, the Atlantic City drive had yielded about 1,000 new voter registrations.

Often in this period, Phillip Savage and the leadership of the Atlantic City

Miss Sepia float in the Miss America Pageant Parade, September 5, 1967

branch invoked direct threats to the Miss America Pageant and the regional economy it anchored. The Miss America Pageant had long been one of the activists' strongest points for exerting pressure on local politicians and businesses, threatening disruptions to the pageant, which simultaneously meant significant threats to local businesses and sponsors. The greater reach of the pageant and of Miss America as national icons meant greater, often national amplification of their political claims. This was the case the following year, in September 1966, when Savage returned to the issue of increasing Black women's presence on the parade floats. A UPI wire service story appeared in newspapers around the country, reporting that while Savage and the NAACP had extracted pledges from a number of regional businesses to feature Black women on their sponsored floats, the Miss America parade would still reflect the glaring absence of any Black woman on any state finalist contestant floats because, just like every year of the pageant preceding 1966, there were no Black women among the finalists.

In the summer of 1967, the Afro-American Unity Movement appeared on the scene in Atlantic City to challenge the primacy of the NAACP in the resort community, shaking up the Black activist ecosystem there. Inspired by the similarly named Black nationalist Organization for Afro-American Unity—the latter founded by Malcolm X in 1964, after his break with the Nation of Islam—the organization presented the city with a long list of demands in August. They called for greater Black representation in the political, social, and economic life of the community and immediate remedies to correct systemic inequities across these areas. With the pageant finals just weeks away, their demands included an end to the racial exclusions of the Miss America Pageant. The group gave the pageant organization a year to produce a Black finalist, and it promised to picket the finals in 1968 if this demand was not met. *Jet* magazine amplified the new organization's challenge by reporting their call for protesting the pageant to its national readership in a January issue.

The spotlight on racism in Atlantic City would be bright in the summer of 1968, given that the NAACP was set to hold its large annual meeting there in Convention Hall. Thousands of activists and organization leaders would pour into the city from all over the country during the last week of June, along with many journalists. In keeping with their convention venue, the NAACP began in February to promote a new facet of the event to be held at its closing gala: a Miss NAACP Pageant. This led to stories and headlines in the Black press, like the *Chicago Defender*'s "NAACP To Crown Its First Queen." Calling her a "queen" was new, but Miss NAACP contests had long been a feature of chapter activities, usually connected to membership drives and special events. In 1968, national leadership capitalized on the fact they would be naming those winners in Atlantic City, and added another (albeit subtle) layer to criticisms of the Miss America Pageant's racial exclusions. While it would resemble a pageant with a "parade" of twenty-five young women competing for the Miss NAACP title and scholarship money, the event was not a beauty contest. The winner and her "court" of three runners-up would be the four young women who had sold the largest numbers of new memberships for their chapters in the annual drive.

With the convention set to open officially the following day, NAACP Executive Director Roy Wilkins joined Edgar Harris, president of the Atlantic City Chapter, in a press conference at the Ritz-Carlton, just up the boardwalk from Convention Hall. Harris denounced the Miss America Pageant's continued racial discrimination, as evidenced not only by the absence of any Black finalists but also the fact that no Black person had ever sat on the organization's board of directors or a judges' panel. In a clear warning to pageant leaders, Harris told the gathered journalists that his chapter was seeking national support in "whatever action was necessary to integrate the Pageant." His chapter would be meeting with other branches at the convention to "decide upon whatever direct action is called for." Wilkins made clear that Harris and the Atlantic City Chapter had the full support of the NAACP, to the top of the national leadership. He called the Miss America Pageant an "anachronism in that it forgot more than 22 million black Americans" and demanded that the pageant "shed its lily-whiteness and stop living in the past."

The Youth Council of the Atlantic City branch announced its submission of a resolution to the executive board of the NAACP Youth Council to be considered by its full membership of 5,000 young people.

> We, the members of the Atlantic City Branch NAACP Youth Council feel that the Miss America Pageant held in Atlantic City is a segregated and

pretentious affair and is a detriment to the black Americans who have helped to make this country what it is today.

We hereby resolve that we will take definite action to absolve this farce that has taken place in Atlantic City for a number of years, unless:

a. the board of directors of the pageant is integrated
b. the panel of judges is desegregated
c. the contestants truly represent America and not a lily-white society

Wilkins spent most of Sunday's press conference fielding questions from journalists about the likelihood of a revolt by members, demanding more radical, liberationist aims and greater representation for those perspectives in the leadership, including the "Young Turks" (officially the National Committee to Revitalize the NAACP) and proponents of Black Power, many of whom were clustered in the youth and college divisions. Understood by most as a generational conflict within the organization that was approaching schismatic rupture, this focus on the Miss NAACP contest and other Youth Council activities had been fueled in part by these concerns. Ultimately, the biggest story to emerge from the convention would be the mass walkout by dissident delegates after their efforts were blocked by Wilkins and others in the "Old Guard." This would be followed a few days later by a similar walkout over the same concerns at CORE's annual convention in Columbus, Ohio.

The executive director of the pageant, Albert "Al" Marks Jr., was quick to defend the Miss America Pageant in the press, saying that he "definitely disagreed" with Roy Wilkins and pointedly refusing to acknowledge Harris or the Atlantic City Chapter directly. Concerning Black judges, Marks said they had asked singer and actress Diahann Carroll to be on that year's panel, but she had declined, owing to schedule conflicts. (Carroll was about to make television history in September 1968, as the eponymous lead in the new sitcom *Julia,* which was the first show to feature a major Black female character who wasn't a domestic worker or enslaved.) While there was no denying that a Black woman had never competed for the crown in Atlantic City, Marks noted that "we have had Negro contestants in 60 or 70 percent of the state contests." It wasn't that Black women were excluded, he claimed, but that none had been successful in making it to the finals. "We have no control over who wins those state contests," he stated. Marks responded as the pageant had for several years: the national organization relied upon local and state pageants for finalists, and if they did not send Black women, then there was nothing Atlantic City could do.

While the assertion that they had no control was true on its face, the argument was specious, not least because it implied such independence on the part of state pageant organizations, but mostly in that it sidestepped altogether the core issue of structural racism. The Miss America Pageant was "always willing to look at those who are qualified to serve in any capacity," Marks continued, as "color is no factor and never has been." He did not take this as an opportunity to publicly pressure local and state pageants to be more inclusive or to take a stand on racism as others, including some former Miss Americas, had done themselves; instead, he hauled out the same old discriminatory rationale: Black women had not been able personally—individually—to win because they weren't ready, weren't talented, or weren't sophisticated or pretty enough, and until some of them made it through the system, the pageant organization's hands were tied.

An investment banker by profession, Al Marks loved hard-ball negotiations, cigarettes, and the Miss America Pageant. A business leader in Atlantic City and a member of the pageant's board of directors since the mid-1950s, Marks was best known as the man responsible for putting Miss America on national television. When Lenora Slaughter retired in November 1967, after holding the executive director role for more than twenty-five years, Marks was her obvious successor. The 1968 pageant was the first to happen without Slaughter at the helm, and its new executive, who enjoyed being known as "Mr. Miss America," wanted everything to be perfect. Highly publicized accusations of racism from the NAACP and the Afro-American Unity Movement, and promises of protests at the pageant itself, threatened not only Miss America in Marks's view but his personal reputation as well.

Wilkins's and Harris's press conference had come in the midst of another unfolding controversy that had caught Marks by surprise. Two weeks earlier, the country had learned that Bert Parks would not be singing "There She Is, Miss America" when the next newly crowned winner took her first steps down the runway in September. This was thanks to an interview given by the song's writer, Bernie Wayne, which was not at all how Marks had planned to reveal the change.

Once it was made public, Marks's decision to drop the song was met with nothing but horror and escalating complaints. These reactions came from the general public, but even more concerning to Marks at the time were those from state pageant organizations, which were entering the busiest weeks of the year, when their contests crowned the state queens who would go on to Atlantic City to compete for the Miss America title.

The *Chicago Tribune* marveled that news of the axed song had even reached the battlefront in Vietnam, prompting one soldier to write an emotional letter of protest. Al Marks claimed he'd been brought to tears by the young serviceman's letter, adding, "I'm amazed at the reaction to our decision," but "to some people this song is in the same category as 'The Star-Spangled Banner.'" To a different journalist, Marks confided that he just "couldn't believe that one single song, a minor element, is that important."

Marks had underestimated the song's value to many Americans—or at least had set its estimation below the $1,500 Bernie Wayne was asking for its use in the 1968 telecast. Since writing "There She Is, Miss America" for the show thirteen years earlier, Wayne reportedly had never received royalties for its annual performance. Pageant officials may have assumed that, like so many other contributions to their events, the song would be volunteered in perpetuity. Shortly after the previous year's telecast (and Lenora Slaughter's announced retirement), Wayne made it known that he would be seeking payment in the future for its use. Subsequently, his contract was not renewed. Marks insisted that this was only because the board of directors had decided it was time for some changes to bring the pageant up to date, to give its music more of a contemporary "rock beat." Wayne cried foul in the press, but Marks stuck to his story.

It is possible that Al Marks's professed surprise about the public's reaction to dropping "There She Is, Miss America" was a negotiating strategy, designed to shame Bernie Wayne into continuing to volunteer his song's use in the annual broadcast. In fact, the crowning of Debra Barnes in 1967 had reminded everyone of the song's iconic status, right before Wayne suggested the pageant should pay him royalties. As Barnes had begun her first walk down the runway as Miss

America, Bert Parks started to sing but couldn't be heard. His microphone was dead. "His face of despair in full color was beamed into millions of homes," the *New York Times* reported, and queried jokingly whether the transformation of Miss Kansas 1967 into Miss America 1968 was truly complete in the song's and, perhaps more to the point, Parks's vocal absence. "The question remains whether Miss America of 1968 has been legitimately crowned: What gaineth beauty if Bert is mute?"

In mid-1968, the sudden change to the Miss America theme song seemed to many of a piece with the generally disturbing unpredictability of the times. Readers of the June 13 evening *Standard-Examiner* in Ogden, Utah, encountered front-page reports of impending rocket attacks by "reds" in Saigon, efforts by the United Nations to slow the global spread of nuclear weapons, and plans by "campus radicals" in SDS to infiltrate factory jobs in order to spread their "gospel of revolution to America's working classes." Boxed off, in the lower left-hand corner of the page, under the heading, "Names in the News," was an update on the condition of Andy Warhol (just removed from the critical list) and the ongoing psychiatric testing of the woman who shot him, Valerie Solanas (misidentified as "Valeria Solanis")—a news item that bled directly into news of the new song for Miss America.

In some ways, this was more fitting than it might appear. The first big story published in 1965 about Andy Warhol and the scene developing around his foil-covered Factory that had catapulted him to national and global celebrity beyond New York's contemporary art scene—and which made Warhol someone whom readers in Ogden, Utah, would know about three years later—had included the journalist's observation that stuck to one of the loft's shiny columns was a copy of the complete lyrics to "There She Is, Miss America."

With the next Miss America Pageant only two months away, Al Marks added heading off civil rights demonstrations and combating charges of racism in the press to the tasks of finding a new signature song and convincing the public that the change was a good one. He and the other men running the Miss America Pageant had no idea that protests by women's liberation were on the horizon.

PART III

NO MORE MISS AMERICA!

17

THE SYMBOL OF EVERYTHING

AUGUST 5, 1968

There was no time to waste. If the New York Radical Women (NYRW) were going to stage a major protest at the Miss America Pageant in less than five weeks, they had to get started. But first, Carol Hanisch and Kathie Amatniek had to convince the rest of the group that it was a good idea to do it at all. This, they'd agreed in the car on the way home from Maryland, would not be easy. The Sandy Spring meeting had made that clear enough. It had also shown Hanisch and Amatniek that if women's liberation was ever going to get beyond its circles of radical women—beyond the SCEF offices and Sandy Spring meetings—to become a true movement for revolutionary change in the lives of all women, they needed to connect with those women. The action had to be big and attention grabbing, and it had to make sense to everyone, not just the activists. "Protesting the pageant in Atlantic City just might be a way to bring the fledgling Women's Liberation Movement into the public arena," Hanisch explained later, "to reach out to other women with our ideas and our dreams of a better life."

Decades later, Amatniek recalled being electrified by her friend's suggestion. "My gosh! That's the symbol of everything! The Miss America Pageant!" She couldn't believe how perfect it was. "That should be our first symbol of everything—protesting the Miss America Pageant."

With the New York City outline in sight, Hanisch and Amatniek decided to present the idea to the group four days later, at the Thursday meeting. The next morning, they borrowed a car (that wasn't having steering problems) and headed out to Jones Beach State Park, a popular spot for New Yorkers on the southern coast of Long Island, to strategize and refine their pitch. It seemed fitting to plan a protest in Atlantic City while looking at the ocean, surrounded by sunbathers and hit by sea spray; plus, the public beach had just made its own feminist history earlier that summer by hiring women to be lifeguards for the first time since it opened thirty-nine years earlier.

Going into the Republican Convention as the clear frontrunner for the presidential nomination, Richard Nixon was the only candidate not yet in Miami Beach when the first gavel sounded on Monday morning. Two of his most popular surrogates, daughters Tricia and Julie, had arrived during the weekend, however, along with Julie's fiancé, David Eisenhower, grandson of the former president. Nixon's daughters got to work as soon as their feet hit the tarmac, assuring reporters that their father would win the nomination on the first ballot. David played his part, too, announcing that he and Julie had set their wedding date for shortly after the election.

At twenty-two and twenty, respectively, Tricia and Julie Nixon blended elements of wholesome college student and sophisticated woman with girlish delight, fame, and a political acumen borne of lifetimes in politics. When the girls were younger, Nixon had famously quipped that the Miss America Pageant telecast was the only show he allowed them to stay up late for. Julie was just four years old when Nixon became vice president and almost as young, many loved to point out, when she first met David. Wrapping appeals to steady continuity and warm nostalgia in fresh possibility, the sisters were perfect faces for the much-ballyhooed "New Nixon" of 1968.

Young women and teenage girls were similarly stationed all over Miami Beach and mainland airport tarmacs, representing the political ambitions of the men seeking the Republican presidential nomination. Organized in teams like pep squads or drill corps, they traveled in coordinated packs, wore matching uniforms for their candidates, and often broke out in short kick lines or cheer routines. "Everywhere one turned there were girls," noted a political reporter for the U.K.'s London *Daily Express,* adding that this quality of the convention represented the most significant difference between political conferences in the United States and his own country.

Girls and young women interested in politics had been widely encouraged to participate in these groups. Back during the 1964 presidential race, for instance, *Seventeen* magazine told readers, "Your Help is Wanted in Politics." The article detailed the work of the official party youth organizations: Teen Dems and the Teen-Age Republicans. Aimed at cultivating lifetimes of party loyalty and volunteerism, the groups also looked forward to the near-term likelihood of the national voting age being lowered from twenty-one to eighteen (which happened in 1971, with the ratification of the 26th Amendment to the U.S. Constitution). Among the various ways one could contribute, "if you are a girl," was "participating in cheerleader groups such as the Nixonettes for Richard Nixon in 1960 and the Goldwater Girls this year." No comparable option was listed for young men and boys.

The Nixonettes were back in 1968. The group working the convention were all college-aged women from New Orleans, who, reported one journalist, "showed inexhaustible energy in Miami's heat." Another observer noted that there only ever seemed to be one Black woman among the otherwise white faces when they showed up, and he was fairly certain it was the same Black woman. They had different costumes for various occasions, but always appeared wearing the same outfits, making the women recognizable in any crowd. The same was true of the cheer squads fielded by Nixon's chief rivals for the nomination, Nelson Rockefeller's "Go-Go Rocky Girls" and Ronald Reagan's "Reagan Girls." Miniskirts were de rigueur for everyone except the Reagan Girls, who tended to be older and costumed to project a nostalgic, more conservative sensibility. Straw boaters with candidate's names, headbands, and beauty queen sashes were common.

Journalists reported the unique ways each squad represented their candidates beyond their beauty, bodies, and energy. The Nixonettes were well organized and seemed more like professionals than volunteers; they never wilted in the heat, and they high-kicked like Rockettes all over Miami Beach. The Rocky Girls blended bubbly enthusiasm with Northeast cool and were said to be mostly students from elite Seven Sisters women's colleges. And the Reagan Girls were old-fashioned. In addition to representing the men, showing lots of leg, and energizing the crowds, the cheer squads were expected to keep up the candidates' spirits. It seemed that whenever Rockefeller emerged from an elevator or appeared in a hotel lobby, pre-positioned Rocky Girls crowded around him and chanted, "We want Rocky! We want Rocky!"

The Nixon campaign upped the ante at the 1968 convention with the late addition of a second group, the "Nixonaires." A few days before the official convention opener, the Nixon for President Committee circulated a press release announcing that 100 Florida-based stewardesses* would "not only give up their free time" for the candidate but also had "agreed to pay $10 each for the slick new uniforms" they'd wear while working the convention. These were similar to new mod-look uniforms recently introduced by United Airlines, complete with gold-wing pins spelling out "Nixonaire" adorning their chests. While the EEOC continued to delay claims from flight attendants and NOW pushed the body to act and petitioned the Federal Aviation Administration, the Nixon campaign put the women—and the glamour, availability, and sex appeal they represented—into service for the candidate, and Republican conventioneers and the mainstream press ate them up.

Whether they were presented as moral matrons, cute college students, or swinging stewardesses, none of these women were expected to talk policy or know anything substantial about their candidate's positions. On the narrow continuum of roles officially available to women at the convention, the various cheer squads registered far from Mary Brooks and the National Federation of Republican Women (NFRW) and closer to the women dancing at a popular go-go bar next door to the Fontainebleau Hotel, one of the event's official headquarters, which was featured in the opening scenes of the 1964 James Bond film *Goldfinger*. One of the hotel's oceanfront competitors borrowed the Bond associations for its own popular 007½ Lounge featuring go-go dancers—the "Goldswinger Girls"—who performed atop the tables, as boasted in advertisements, rather than "in the usual cages." During the convention, they, too, were

* "Flight attendant" as a term wouldn't come into use as a common referent of professional respect until the later 1970s, when more men had joined their ranks.

made gyrating human billboards for the candidates and the democratic process as they danced with bikinis and go-go boots covered in campaign stickers.

What did this look like to other women and girls moving through convention spaces and along the streets of Miami Beach? How did it feel to the female delegates and alternates as they pursued their work, enjoyed the Florida sunshine, and decided whether to attend the fashion shows and luncheons featuring slimming "Keep in Shape for '68" menus? They had been schooled to dress subtly so they wouldn't stand out on camera, dotted among the sea of men in suits and ties. How many girls, like Phyllis Schlafly's young daughters, imagined one day becoming cheerleaders for Republican candidates as they padded to hotel swimming pools through lobbies dotted with squads of high-kicking political cheerleaders? And what of the college-aged women who had managed to find their ways into campaign jobs, and who sought careers for themselves in and around politics?

Hillary Rodham was one of these young women in Miami Beach in 1968. When she arrived at the convention as part of Rockefeller's campaign operation, she was conflicted; four years earlier as a high school senior, she'd been wearing a "Goldwater Girl" sash and campaigning for the Republican candidate in her hometown of Park Ridge, a suburb of Chicago. When Rodham started at Wellesley College in the fall, she became president of the school's College Republicans chapter. As a political science major, her studies were entwined with the examination of her own political views and values, which were also shaped by the persistent escalation of the war in Vietnam, which she came to oppose. In 1968, Rodham spent cold late-winter weekends in New Hampshire, campaigning for Eugene McCarthy in the Democratic presidential primary, and then went to Washington, D.C., for most of the summer to serve as an intern with the House Republican Conference, led by Minority Leader Gerald Ford. She suspected that she was in her last days with the Republican Party, which also meant the last days of sharing a political identity with her parents.*

By the time Rodham got to Miami Beach, she was also nearly certain that

* In recounting this story in her 2003 memoir, *Living History*, Hillary Rodham Clinton notes that her father still had the picture of her as a young intern in 1968, standing beside Gerald Ford and other House Republican leaders, hanging in his bedroom when he died in 1993, about three months into her tenure as first lady alongside Democratic President Bill Clinton.

the candidate she was there to work for didn't stand a chance. *The party was already set on Nixon,* she thought, and the place for moderates like Rockefeller or herself was disappearing. Hillary Rodham was twenty years old and a month away from starting her senior year at one of the Seven Sisters colleges located in the suburbs of Boston. She was the same age and shared a basic profile with many of the "Rockefeller Girls" roaming the city. As an anti-war moderate and a feminist, she also shared toe-in-the-water connections in the Republican Party with at least two important figures of the emergent women's liberation movement: Donna Allen and Ti-Grace Atkinson. Allen had run for (and lost) election to be a Republican delegate from Washington, D.C., with the express purpose of bringing anti-war voices to the convention. Ti-Grace Atkinson came from a Republican family—uncommon in Louisiana—and actively campaigned for New York Mayor John Lindsay to seek the party's nomination while leading the city's NOW chapter. The war made Independents of many in 1968; Charlotte Curtis had written to her mother in March, "this was the week in which Governor Rockefeller decided not to run (so I sent a check to Eugene McCarthy.)" Now she was covering Rockefeller's campaign in Miami Beach.

Rodham had never stayed in a hotel before, much less at a glamourous place like the Fontainebleau. Decades later, she would still remember ordering room service for the first time, and the plump fresh peach wrapped in a cloth napkin on the tray when it arrived. She and a few other campaign workers got to meet Frank Sinatra at a party in the hotel's penthouse. Heading down to her own floor afterward, Rodham ended up standing next to the actor John Wayne. He didn't look good, like he was about to be sick. When their eyes caught, "Duke" complained to the nameless young woman next to him about the crummy food at Sinatra's place.

Wayne was the star of the most anticipated moment of the opening morning, when he took the stage to give a short inspirational talk called "Why I Am Proud to Be an American." The sixty-one-year-old actor invoked his daughter Marisa, who was not yet three: "I'd like her to know some of the values that we knew as kids," he said, "some of those values that too many people these days are thinking are old fashioned." Like Wayne, most of the delegates' childhoods dated to the 1910s and 1920s, a time before the New Deal's expansion of the federal state and the dramatic social changes that followed World War II, new immigration policies, civil rights, resurgent feminism, and the sexual revolution. Wayne's widely shared belief was that the Republican Party could be a vehicle for unwinding these changes and building a cleansed future of order and authority, restoring traditional hierarchies of age, race, gender, ethnicity, religion, and social class. (This version of America sat nicely with Wayne's pro-war, anti-communist Vietnam film *The Green Berets*, which went into wide release in 1968, on the Fourth of July, and became a summer box office hit.)

Simultaneous with the first day of the convention, the National Organization for Women (NOW) scored its first major victory when the EEOC finally ruled that sex-segregated want ads in newspapers were in violation of Title VII of the 1964 Civil Rights Act. This reversed the commission's November 1965 interpretive guidelines that had provided a qualification on the issue of sex to Title VII's clear and plain language making it unlawful "to print . . . any notice or advertisement relating to employment . . . indicating any preference, limitation, specification, or discrimination based on race, color, religion, sex, or national origin."

In New York City, Ti-Grace Atkinson issued a press release hailing the victory and highlighting the role of her chapter in organizing to bring the change to fruition. The "Commission's action appeared to be the result of 1½ years' work by members of NOW," she announced, "particularly the recent picketing (July 23 thru 26) of the *New York Times* Classified Ad offices at 1457 Broadway." Direct action in the streets (a week before the decision was released) had been crucial to NOW's success, argued Atkinson, adding to the general sentiment of the summer that demonstrations, not just lobbying and legal challenges, were key to the success of the women's movement.

Betty Friedan agreed, if cautiously, and celebrated NOW's EEOC victory while making the rounds for her convention story in Miami Beach. An end to jobs identified as belonging to one sex or the other brought women one step closer to workplace equality by making all positions at least conceptually open to them. That future still seemed far away, however, when everywhere she looked Friedan saw scantily clad women in cheer squads promoting the all-male field of candidates and party leaders. Drafting her *Mademoiselle* piece, Friedan described Miami Beach as crowded with "official hostesses who were a cross between old-time chorus girls or high school cheerleaders and Playboy bunnies. . . . There was even a group of former Goldwater Girls, calling themselves GOP girls, who were willing [to use] their sexual charms for any candidate." It was a "denigration of women," she lamented, that only perpetuated more, including "our own self-denigration of women which won't let us run for Senate or vote for other women." It was enough to give a feminist whiplash.

18

FEAR OF A LILY-WHITE PARTY

AUGUST 5, 1968

Other than the appearance of John Wayne, Monday morning's Republican Party Convention opener was uneventful and mostly ignored by delegates and national viewing audiences alike. One newspaper reported its most noteworthy aspect being that the session started and finished exactly on time, a first in convention history, but hardly breaking news or riveting television. Planners hoped the fireworks would come later, during prime time when the Republican Party presented its spectacle of unity, inclusion, and law-and-order policies to the nation. Before then, the real action was in and around the press conferences held in hotel meeting rooms or just outside the convention center, where local protesters began to gather.

Black Republicans and civil rights leaders had come to Miami Beach to sound a warning about the burgeoning leadership of Southern segregationists in the GOP, and the shifting allegiance of Southern Democrats that it portended. Thus, 1968 might to be the last chance for preserving and possibly growing a Black membership and holding on to the Republicans' legacy as the "Party of Lincoln." The picture was already bleak. The number of Black delegates was at a historic low in 1968, standing at just 26 out of 1,333. The *Los Angeles Sentinel* noted that there were more Black journalists in town covering the convention than there were Black delegates participating in it, which wasn't intended as a celebration of Black representation among members of the press. The *Sentinel's* reporter in Miami Beach, A. "Doc" Young, recounted an incident when an irate John Wayne—again on a Fontainebleau elevator—complained loudly about the management of ticketed events at the convention and was overheard grumbling, "This would be a helluva story if the newspapers got ahold of it." That Wayne and his companion weren't alone did not seem to faze the actor, if it even registered. "It never crossed his mind," wrote Young, "that the two Negroes riding the elevator [with him] were newspaper writers."

In the weeks leading up to the convention, a new organization called the National Council of Concerned Afro-Americans launched with about two hundred and fifty members from thirty-six states to coordinate Black Republican efforts. Representatives gave testimony before the committee seeking rule changes so that all-white state delegations could not be seated in 1972 and encouraging the dedication of ten seats for Black members on the Republican National Committee. Comprising committed party members, the council never threatened to leave the GOP. Their spokesman, Washington, D.C., lawyer Thurmond Dodson, told reporters, "We're going to stay with them, but we are going to demand that they straighten out and fly right."

While the council caucused and lobbied for these changes from their base at the Montmartre Hotel, and John Wayne took the stage, local Black Republicans picketed outside the convention center. They similarly decried the lack of Black representation among the delegates and the party's leadership, but they focused primarily on Florida's all-white delegation. The men—no Black women appear to have participated in the demonstration—carried signs like: "The Florida Republican Party Is a Lily White Party" and "Florida Republican Party Excludes Negroes from Delegation."

In a different Ocean Drive hotel, civil rights leader James Farmer, former director of CORE and current candidate for the U.S. House of Representatives, co-hosted a press conference, urging delegates to turn away from Nixon and the segregationists who supported him to embrace Black Republicans and to court new voters among urban communities of color. He himself was running for a new district seat in Brooklyn, New York, on a joint Independent–Republican ticket. (His opponent was Democratic New York State Congresswoman and

NOW member Shirley Chisholm.) Roy Wilkins, in town to give testimony before the Platform Committee on behalf of the NAACP, echoed these concerns. In his role as head of the bipartisan Leadership Conference of Civil Rights Organizations, Wilkins published open letters to both the Republican and the Democratic parties, urging them to reject the credentials of all-white Southern state delegations and forbid them in the future. Reverend Ralph Abernathy, who'd brought the Poor People's Campaign to Miami Beach, weighed in to argue that the Republicans should select Rockefeller for the nomination, not Nixon, if they wished to save the GOP from the violent hatred that had murdered Martin Luther King Jr. just five months earlier. When questioned about his organization's new politicization, Abernathy said SCLC was still bipartisan, but not *non-partisan*.

In a bit of heavily orchestrated political theater, Ronald Reagan pretended to be surprised when the California delegation voted to support their favorite son for the nomination if he would enter the race. At a press conference not long after, he ended the speculation and announced that he would heed their call. Just that morning, the "For and About Women" section of the *Miami Herald* had run a full-color glamour shot of Nancy Reagan above a short piece reporting, "Some Reagan watchers say the petite and pretty former actress is more than [her husband's "greatest fan"]: She is a great influence on her husband and interested in exchanging her role as first lady of California for first lady of the United States. But it is an interest the brown-haired Mrs. Reagan denies. 'All I'm concerned about is being Ronald Reagan's wife.'" The coy denials were over by Monday afternoon. Ronald Reagan was in the race.

Nixon's first ballot victory suddenly appeared far less inevitable. Alone, it was unlikely that Reagan or Rockefeller would garner enough delegates to deny Nixon the nomination outright. Together, however, the men could act as a pincer, carving votes from both the further right and the more moderate wings of the GOP, thus forcing more rounds of balloting and opening the convention up to a range of possible outcomes. At that point, it would be every man for himself.

Reagan's candidacy raised another issue for the Nixon campaign by threatening the candidate's hold on Southern state delegations that Strom Thurmond had brokered a few months earlier, in Atlanta. There was great love for Reagan in the South, which in the absence of his declared candidacy had been guided to Nixon (and, Republicans hoped, away from the third-party challenger, former Alabama Governor George Wallace).

Just a few miles from Convention Hall and the glittering resorts of Miami Beach, a chasm far wider than Biscayne Bay—"and a drawbridge!" many were so quick to remind GOP conventioneers—separated the South Florida tourist playground from Liberty City, Miami's segregated Black neighborhood. Taxis and limos ferrying people from Miami International Airport drove past Liberty City along the expressway and directly through the uncreatively monikered "Central Negro District." By 1968, the district was already colloquially known by its official name today, Overtown, a reference that came from residents who had sought their own suburban dreams almost two decades earlier, but still went "over town" to the old neighborhood to patronize the Black businesses they relied upon.

The Liberty City Model Community had been established in the late-1940s to provide opportunities for Black suburban homeownership and economic mobility, without disrupting Miami's stark residential segregation. Since then, a lack of zoning and the mass displacements created by interstate construction and urban "renewal" policies had swelled and strained the community. What had been a thriving area of single-family homes with yards and plentiful green spaces changed radically in the 1960s, when thousands of Black Miamians were forced to relocate to hastily built concrete apartment buildings owned and managed by predominantly white landlords. The I-95 path through Overtown displaced not only residents but also many of the Black-owned businesses it would eventually be named after, which were replaced by white-owned stores. By 1968, most Black consumer dollars and rent payments were flowing out of the neighborhood and the community.

In their campaign to draw the conventions to Miami Beach, boosters had touted South Florida as a comparatively progressive Southern community in terms of "race relations." They pointed to the absence of riots in Miami as evidence of its contented Black population; "Burn, Baby, Burn" was just something the pale delegates would have to worry about while on the beach, not the urge to Black rebellion it had been elsewhere since the Watts uprising in 1965. This same line was still being fed to the Democratic National Committee in early August when, with their own convention just weeks away, they were encouraged to move it to Miami Beach to avoid the unrest sure to greet them in Chicago.

Black Miamians were furious at this framing. Not only was it a misrepresentation of the area's civil rights history, they charged, but it also flew in the face of the grim realities of Black life in the eight months since Miami Police Chief Walter Headley had announced he was "declaring war" on crime in the city's Black neighborhoods. On the day after Christmas in 1967, Headley had staged a press conference about his new "get tough" policy of aggressive policing by increased numbers of officers armed with shotguns, dogs, and orders that allowed everything up to and including the use of deadly force in felony cases. "Felons will learn," Headley crowed, "that they can't be bonded out from the morgue." The chief stated bluntly that the policy was aimed at young Black men (and boys) from the ages of fifteen to twenty-one, whom he also described as "hoodlums who have taken advantage of the civil rights campaign" to avoid prosecution. Before the press conference had ended, Headley made a statement that would turn him into a national figure: "We haven't had any serious problems with civil uprisings and looting because I've let the word filter down that when the looting starts, the shooting starts."* In the months that followed, Black Miamians suffered a relentless, violent pacification campaign on the streets of Liberty City, parts of Coconut Grove, and what was left of the original segregated neighborhood downtown.

Many of the same Republicans who gathered in Miami Beach in August celebrated Headley and his methods as part of their law-and-order campaign. This included Phyllis Schlafly, who heralded the Florida police chief in her May 1968 issue of *The Schlafly Report*. "The only solution to the present rise in crime

* Walter Headley's 1967 statement made national news again in 2020, when it was seemingly invoked by President Donald Trump in tweets responding to protests that erupted in Minneapolis, Minnesota, after the May 25 murder of George Floyd by police. "These THUGS are dishonoring the memory of George Floyd, and I won't let that happen. Just spoke to Governor Tim Walz and told him that the Military is with him all the way. Any difficulty and we will assume control but, when the looting starts, the shooting starts. Thank you!" (see @realDonald Trump, 12:53 a.m., May 29, 2020).

and riots," she wrote, was "*to elect to office this November public officials who will enforce the law.*" The American people needed and wanted tough policing, she said. "Tell your candidates that courageous law enforcement will be supported by the public. The 'get tough' policy of Miami's police chief, with use of shotguns and police dogs, has caused crime in that city to drop by two-thirds and is fully supported by Negroes there." Neither of Schlafly's broad statements about the outcomes of Headley's policy or Black support were wholly true.

Flyers announcing a "mass rally of concerned Black people" to be held on Wednesday, August 7, in Liberty City began to appear around the convention early in the week. They described a rally for "Black control of Black ghetto—politically, economically and educationally," and called for Black policemen and firemen working in their communities, and poverty programs run by poor people, among other priorities.

The rally was organized by the Vote Power League, which operated out of a storefront on 62nd Street in Liberty City, in coalition with local representatives from SNCC, CORE, SCLC, the Black Panthers, and the United Black Students. They planned to denounce GOP racism and show the city, state, and country how bad things really were for Black Miamians, as well as how determined they were to be heard and enact change. The event would be long, from 1:00 in the afternoon to 1:00 a.m., to accommodate those who would be over at the convention center for the roll call and nomination that night. This included professional basketball superstar Wilt "the Stilt" Chamberlain, who was at the convention with the Nixon campaign to promote the candidate's "Black Capitalism" initiative deployed to counter criticism of his "Southern Strategy." Massachusetts Senator Ed Brooke might have been the proffered face of Republican racial inclusion for the convention's televised spectacle, but Chamberlain was the most prominent Black Republican in attendance. The protest flyer listed him first in its list of promised speakers.

Early Monday evening, Richard Nixon's plane circled above Miami International Airport for nearly half an hour, waiting for the sun to set enough to produce a perfect, golden shot of his arrival for the news cameras. The campaign was aiming for an air of relaxed certainty, steadiness, and their (new) man's easy vitality. Nixon had been holed up in a Hamptons vacation home in the small town of Montauk, New York, preparing his acceptance speech for the nomination and trying to stay relaxed. He'd gotten a tan. Perched at the farthest tip of Long Island, the wealthy beachfront community was quite different from Miami Beach, and despite its geographic proximity, was galaxies away from Jones Beach, where Carol Hanisch and Kathie Amatniek spent the day working on their Miss America protest pitch. Once on the ground in Miami, Nixon worked hard to appear unfazed by Reagan's announcement, while his campaign went into overdrive to shore up delegate commitments, especially from Southern states.

Convention prime time kicked off later that night at 8:00, with the presentation of the colors by U.S. Marines; the crowd's booming recitation of the Pledge of Allegiance, led by the Mayor of Birmingham, Alabama; and a rousing rendition of the national anthem sung by former Miss Oklahoma and current face of the Florida Citrus Commission Anita Bryant. Once the convention was called to order in a series of remarks by GOP convention officials, the gathered party faithful and the national viewing audience were addressed by Dwight Eisenhower via closed-circuit television from Walter Reed Army Hospital, in Washington, D.C., where he had been for several weeks following a heart attack. Nixon had finally gotten an endorsement from the former president a few months earlier.

Mary Brooks took the stage to give her speech on "The Challenge to American Woman," after the first intermission (and commercial break) following Eisenhower's message. Charlotte Curtis thought she looked nervous, noting that Brooks was "clutching her glasses" and that her orange dress and low-heeled white shoes looked bright "against [the] baby blue of the stage." It was a historic moment for women in the Republican Party, and with the presentation of the gavel and address to come from temporary chairman Ed Brooke, was the start of a clear, if understated, argument for the party's diversity.

"I have listened to thousands of women in the cities and in the towns during this past year," Mary Brooks opened, "and I have found a new unhappy mood among them. In fact, I have never known the women of this country to be as concerned—as frightened—and as aroused as we are today."

Women's fear would be the theme of Brooks's call to vote Republican in

November. American women were afraid for the "security of our families, and for ourselves"; each faced "constant daily worry about her husband, her brother, her son, or her grandson going off to war"; they feared rising food and housing costs, worried about the family budget not covering all the bills. "Many a woman is becoming inhibited in her daily life by fear," Brooks lamented. "She is virtually a prisoner in her own home. She is afraid to go out alone at night."

Curtis struggled to hear Brooks and wondered if the woman's mic was poorly positioned. She noted that most of the delegates weren't listening anyway, and she jotted multiple iterations of "no one listening" in her notebook.

As Brooks began to close, she promised that in their peril, American women could gain strength of conviction to take action in the voting booth and choose the right Republicans—the right men—to protect them and their families. "We can be effective—we can be decisive," urged Brooks, and meet the challenge of making the "all important choice" of the country's next president.

Brooks did not know then that neither network offering live "gavel-to-gavel" coverage of the convention had shown her on the air. CBS carried an interview with Ronald Reagan instead, while NBC had kept their feed on evening news co-anchor Chet Huntley doing commentary. (ABC had opted not to feature extended convention coverage in 1968, but aired a nightly post-show devoted largely to now legendary battling partisan takes from Gore Vidal and William F. Buckley.) "It took her nearly a week to write the speech & then no one would listen—& they couldn't hear," observed Curtis, and "not much applause" when it was over.

Curtis did not include Brooks or the speech in her convention coverage for Tuesday morning's *New York Times*. She chose to file instead a tart but generally atmospheric piece on the different yachts festooned with campaign banners that cruised the Indian Creek waterway, running the length of Miami Beach. Betty Friedan did not include the speech in her own story for *Mademoiselle*, but quoted a steelier, if tired Mary Brooks sighing, "I'm so tired of fashion shows."

19

THE HARD WORK OF BECOMING THE IDEAL GIRL

AUGUST 5, 1968

Glory, glory, hallelujah! Anita Bryant's heart swelled as she hit the soaring chorus in her signature arrangement of the "Battle Hymn of the Republic," while making her third appearance in twenty-four hours at the convention. *Glory, glory, hallelujah.* She felt so full of joy and God's grace—not from the politics or the audience of Republican delegates and operatives (Bryant was a Democrat) but because of the sweet, new knowledge that she was pregnant. Earlier that day, backstage at the convention hall, she had found a phone to call her doctor's office and held her breath. "Good news, Mrs. Green. Your tests are positive." She'd rushed to tell Bob, her husband and manager, and then for a moment, both "forgot the hustle and bustle, the confusion and din of the great banner-hung convention hall," and "simply rejoiced." *Glory, glory, hallelujah!* They had been trying and praying for this baby, through months of wrenching disappointments and experimental fertility treatments, and now their prayers had been answered. *His truth is marching on.* In that convention hall, carrying their miracle, she was fueled by the truth of God's many blessings and the certainty that He had a plan for her—a plan that had begun taking shape ten years before when, just out of high school, Bryant had been crowned Miss Oklahoma and traveled on to the Atlantic City finals. God's plan for Anita Bryant had started with the Miss America Pageant.

"I never felt I 'lost' the Miss America contest," Bryant explained when looking back on 1958. "Instead, I never asked God to let me win." But from the time she was a little girl, Anita had been asking God to make her a star. She was born in 1940, in a town nestled between the Osage Indian Reservation and land that had been the Cherokee Nation until Oklahoma became a state in 1907. Bryant's young years were spent in various company-owned camps of temporary housing that dotted the landscape of what she described as "raw, rugged Oklahoma oil country." At three years old, in a little town called Seminole, in the central part of the state, she got her first taste of the stage when the local high school recruited her to play a part in their musical. Anita had one line and one song, and after opening night, she promptly informed her family, "I'm going to be a star someday."

Not long after, the peripatetic Bryants moved south to the oil fields near the Texas border in what had been the Chickasaw Nation. By the time she was nine, Anita was making weekly appearances on local television variety shows broadcast by Oklahoma City's WKY-TV. The music director for WKY radio became Bryant's manager, and at twelve, she got her own fifteen-minute television spot that aired every Friday night; not yet a teenager, she juggled a professional singing career with being a student and an active member of her church. (Bryant was eight years old when she was "born again," and was nine when she embraced the Southern Baptist faith that would come to define her.) By graduation day at Will Rogers High in 1958, right before Bryant was named Miss Tulsa and then went on to win the Miss Oklahoma Pageant, she'd already made appearances on a nationally televised talent showcase and had toured regionally with the child actor turned teen-idol pop star, Ricky Nelson.

As an adult, Anita Bryant was always careful to note that her youthful ambitions had been all her own, not spurred on by a "stage mother" or pressure from other adults. Instead, Bryant told a story of parental support and sacrifice that softened some of the more complicated aspects of her family history. Performing and church were the constants in Bryant's life, while her family was often in upheaval and on the move. Her parents married and divorced one another twice before Bryant started high school, with both marrying again to other people after the second divorce. Whatever troubles her parents faced, Bryant explained, their willingness never flagged to do whatever it took to support her dreams of fame and singing stardom.

After high school graduation, Bryant was set on having more time to perform, tour, and produce a record. But a local radio station wanted to sponsor her for the Miss Tulsa contest, and Bryant couldn't refuse. When she won and proceeded to the Miss Oklahoma Pageant, the Tulsa Jaycees assumed the sponsorship role and brought in a former pageant winner, Toni Spencer, to act as her coach. Bryant won the state crown, making her, at eighteen, one of the youngest contestants at the 1958 Miss America Pageant, as well as one of the few without at least some college or a completed degree. Bryant had only six weeks to prepare; it was a time the seasoned professional described later as "some of the hardest work I ever did."

Anita Bryant was far from the pageant's "ideal American girl." When one of the judges of the Miss Oklahoma Pageant asked if Bryant liked sack dresses, she replied that she did but never wore one because "men don't usually like them." When Bryant spoke to journalists after her victory, she admitted she hadn't made up her mind about what to do with the $1,000 prize money, but was considering using it for voice and theater training in New York or California. In addition to her professional achievements and career aspirations, the *Daily Oklahoman* reported the state pageant winner's professed hobby to be "people" and quoted Bryant saying that she liked anything "that pleases men," which the journalist described as "a formula that is usually pretty successful." These would not be persuasive answers in Atlantic City. "You're going to need a lot more this time than just your good looks, talent, and winning personality," Toni Spencer advised her contestant. "Anita, the judges also will be interested in your mind," she said, and expect her to know "something about world affairs, and to have some opinions" of her own.

Anita Bryant was much more like a Miss America contestant from the early days of the pageant than she was the average crown-seeker of the 1950s, especially before Toni Spencer got hold of her. She was a young, professional entertainer with no real plans for college, who hoped the accolades and publicity that came with winning the Miss America title would catapult her to national fame and celebrity. By 1958, Lenora Slaughter and the Miss America Organization had spent several years attempting to distance the pageant from just this kind of contestant.

After World War II, the Miss America scholarship programs had become the cornerstone of the pageant's claims to respectability, refinement, and a literal investment in the totality of the young women seeking to represent the American ideal, not just their outward beauty. As Anita Bryant labored to make herself fit this mold in 1958, newspapers across the country ran a syndicated Associated Press story detailing the range of qualities and talents pageant contestants needed to be competitive and all they stood to gain, including a chance to win the $10,000 college scholarship that came with the crown. "While most other contests mainly use the tape measure as a basis for judging, the Miss America pageant believes beauty is not just skin deep," the story explained, and "this year there is more emphasis on talent, personality, and brains than ever before." It also described the efforts of Lenora Slaughter, who had spent the months leading up to the finals attending as many state contests as she could to encourage compliance with these stated values and the offer of scholarship prizes at the local and state levels. "We don't offer movie contracts," she noted. "We are looking for the ambitious girl with sufficient intelligence to know that success comes through work and training." Slaughter offered a simple if not uncontentious equation for making Miss America: add a third each of talent, intellect, and beauty. "We are trying to select the ideal American girl," she concluded, "not the most beautiful."

The Anita Bryant who arrived in Atlantic City for Pageant Week was very different from the young woman who had won the Miss Tulsa pageant earlier that year. Gone were the noncommittal descriptions of her plans for using the scholarship money and seeming disinterest in higher education; Bryant now explained to reporters and judges that while she had deferred school for a year, she was excited to start classes the next fall.

Though she was only named second runner-up, Bryant's prayers for stardom were answered. As a top-ten finalist, her performance for the talent portion was televised. And while it wasn't the first time she'd sung for a national broadcast, this was her largest audience. After the pageant, she moved to Chicago, where she began making daily appearances on ABC radio's popular "Don McNeill's Breakfast Show" and used her scholarship money to enroll at Northwestern University, where she planned to major in speech. In the meantime, Bryant's eponymously titled first album of popular Broadway hits reached the million-records-sold mark after she charted with a pop rendition of "Till There Was You," from the popular musical *The Music Man*. She toured, made an appearance on Dick Clark's American Bandstand TV program, and quickly recorded another album, resulting in a relentless schedule that prompted her to leave Northwestern. None of these things would have been possible had Bryant won the title of Miss America in 1958—she would have been under exclusive contract for the year with the pageant organization, traveling the country making appearances, performing, and doing commercial endorsements.

From his post with Miami's WINZ radio, Bob Green was one of the powerful disk jockeys who helped to catapult Bryant's first single onto and up the charts. Bryant was nineteen when she first met him at a record-label showcase, where she'd shared the stage with the likes of Frank Sinatra, Connie Francis, Pat Boone, and Peggy Lee. Green pursued her from the start, and though Bryant had planned to delay marriage to focus on her career, the two wed in the summer of 1960. The wedding of Miss Oklahoma was a big deal in her home state; the radio station that had sponsored her for the Miss Tulsa contest declared her wedding day, June 25, to be "Anita Bryant Day"—until after the ceremony at noon, when they switched it to "Mrs. Bob Green Day." The couple left their reception to catch a flight to New York City so Bryant could appear on a television variety special sponsored by Coca-Cola.

While Anita Bryant would come to see their hasty departure to make a performance date as a portent of what her marriage to Bob Green would become, at the time neither believed she would continue her career after meeting obligations set before the wedding. After a delayed honeymoon in Puerto Rico, the Greens settled in Miami; Bob went back to his job at the radio station, and Anita set about becoming a housewife. Meanwhile, two songs from her sophomore effort, *Hear Anita Bryant in Your Home Tonight*, an album released earlier that year, were climbing the charts. "Paper Roses" and "My Little Corner of the World" would go on to be two of the biggest hits of Bryant's career. But as they rocketed into *Billboard*'s top 100 singles of 1960, Bryant was keeping house as a newlywed and was utterly miserable. She was vacuuming the carpets and learning to cook while watching everything she'd worked for since childhood be "ground to a dead halt." "I felt guilty for having such thoughts," she confessed to her fans later in her first memoir, *Mine Eyes Have Seen the Glory*. "A new bride should be content with home and husband," she castigated herself, "what was wrong with me?" When he could take his unhappy home no longer, Bob Green encouraged his wife to make some concert dates. It wasn't long before Bryant was back to touring and album promotion.

Anita Bryant's childhood proclamation came true: she was a star. Bob Hope invited her to join his famed USO show, and she became a regular fixture of his tours alongside other pageant winners and model-entertainers. She got major endorsement deals with Coca-Cola and later the Orange Growers' Association. Bryant was popular enough by 1962 to be included in that year's Miss America Pageant official program—along with Cloris Leachman (Miss Chicago 1946) and Vera Miles (Miss Kansas 1948)—in a feature titled "As Bernie Wayne Says in his New Pageant Song, 'Everybody Can't Be a Winner,'" which celebrated "the many girls who never wore the crown but, through the years, have reached fame and success in the entertainment spotlight." She became synonymous with the pageant and always identified as one of America's favorite beauty queens.

The end to one half of the couple's misery brought new unhappiness for the other, as the length and frequency of their separations grew. Green wanted it to end, but Bryant wasn't prepared to give everything up again. At the suggestion of his best man at the wedding, Green quit the disk jockey business to become Bryant's manager; rather than splitting over her work, the pair could work together (with him in the driver's seat).

Three years into their marriage, Bryant learned she might never be able to have children. Doctors were hopeful about surgical intervention, but were far from certain it would work. The Greens decided to adopt while continuing to pursue medical options, and their adopted son, Bobby, was born in September. Shortly after, Bryant learned she was pregnant and Bobby's younger sister, Gloria Lynn, was born eight months later. Continued fertility problems after the birth of their daughter tore at Anita's and Bob's dreams of having a large family, until August 1968, when Bryant learned she was pregnant before taking the stage at the convention in Miami Beach.

Anita Bryant had always identified—and voted—as a Democrat (and was booked for the convention in Chicago). A favorite of President Lyndon Johnson, Bryant performed at the White House several times, including at a State Dinner for the prime minister of Somalia in March, just two weeks before the president announced he would not seek reelection. (Bryant and her husband had stayed at the White House as Johnson's guests that night, after the dinner and her forty-minute performance that had closed out the evening.) Once her pregnancy was known to the public, Bryant would joke that it was the reason she had looked so much happier singing for the Republicans.

20

NIXON'S THE ONE

AUGUST 6–8, 1968

In the newspaper's analysis of Ronald Reagan's late confirmation of his presidential ambitions, Tuesday morning's *Washington Post* featured another well-known Democrat from the world of Miss America: Bess Myerson. She recounted her experiences as television co-host with Reagan for the annual broadcasts of the Rose Bowl Parade in 1964 and 1965, in a story that identified her as "Miss Bess Myerson, former Miss America, now Mrs. Arnold Grant of New York." As co-hosts, Myerson and Reagan had alternated announcing floats as they passed before the grandstand and ABC's cameras. In two different instances, Myerson revealed, Reagan's social and political views had prompted him to request that she take his turn so he would not have to announce a float with which he didn't want to be associated.

In 1964, Reagan asked her to name the U.S. Savings Bonds float in his stead, explaining, "I just don't believe in the Savings Bonds." The following year, the story continued, he "asked Miss Myerson to announce a Negro float. It was the first time Negroes had entered a float in the Rose Bowl parade, and he grumbled about having to identify it publicly." The article did not identify Myerson's longtime affiliation with the Democratic Party, nor did it note her role as one of three co-chairs for the national Women for Humphrey operation in 1968. (One of Myerson's fellow co-chairs was Margaret Truman Daniel, daughter of President Harry S. Truman and wife of Clifton Daniel, of the *New York Times*.)

One had to get much deeper into Tuesday's *Washington Post* to find coverage of Mary Brooks's address from the night before. It appeared in Section D's "For and About Women" pages, the location for most accounts of the speech published in morning editions around the country. The *Chicago Tribune* stood out with a story about Brooks's remarks printed alongside other national news in the first section of the paper; its headline: "G.O.P. Told Feminine Gripes."

The Republicans' parade of smiling beauty queens—those very opposites of "griping" females—continued. Tuesday night prime-time coverage kicked off with Miss America 1966, Deborah Bryant Wilson, leading the convention in the Pledge of Allegiance.

Nixon continued projecting the studied nonchalance of a frontrunner, while behind the scenes his campaign was in a frenzy to hold on to promised delegates for the next day's roll call. Their first line of defense was to go back to Strom Thurmond. The South Carolina senator had already extracted a number of promises from Nixon while in Atlanta, including conservative justices on the Supreme Court; a commitment that as president he wouldn't support withholding federal education funds from communities that still had no plans for desegregating public schools; and that Nixon would consider carefully the Southerners' preference for a conservative vice president, among other things. Thurmond now saw the opportunity to ask for more.

On Tuesday, the senator sent one of his closest advisors, Harry Dent, to find Phyllis Schlafly. Nixon was panicking, Dent told her, and ready to give the party's hard-right flank just about anything to hold the South, including their choice for VP. He asked Schlafly to draw up a list of acceptable and no-go candidates that Thurmond could use when he met with Nixon's people. This was a very different conversation from the one Schlafly had had with the senator himself just days earlier, when she had approached him about supporting her own scheme to keep a moderate VP off the ballot with Nixon. Thurmond had declined then, claiming to stay clear of such unseemly backroom negotiating. "Oh, I don't play that way," he'd told her—which was rich coming from the man who'd just brokered Southern delegation support for Nixon in May. What a difference a couple of days made. Schlafly composed her list and passed it along to Dent.

• • •

Like most of the journalists in town, Charlotte Curtis was looking to find out what was happening behind all those "Nixon's the One!" banners, as the campaign reacted to Reagan's challenge. Unlike those other journalists, however, she went to Nixon's wife and daughters to get the fuller picture. Curtis spent much of Wednesday with Pat Nixon, Tricia, and Julie, or watching them from the edges of receiving lines, head tables, and receptions. "In the tense hours before" Nixon was nominated, her story for the next morning's paper would begin, "Mrs. Nixon and their daughters were still enthusiastically shaking hands, signing autographs and generally endearing themselves not just to the party faithful but also to thousands of total strangers." The theme of Curtis's story came with the next line, "It was a long, hard day, and it started early."

When Curtis arrived at the Nixons' suite in the Hilton Plaza Hotel at 8:00 in the morning, the sisters were having a breakfast of juice, toast, and Danishes from a tray their father had brought them. It would be the last time they saw him before Convention Hall and the start of the delegation roll call later that evening. All three Nixon women were scheduled to appear at the "Leading Ladies Brunch" to honor over a thousand wives of delegates and alternates hosted by Mary Brooks at the Fontainebleau, before attending a large afternoon reception in their honor held jointly by the Florida Nixon Committee and Women for Nixon. Richard Nixon had at least six meetings with different delegations on his schedule. During brunch, Charlotte Curtis never saw Pat Nixon eat anything, as the smiling woman made small talk with the other candidates' wives, Happy Rockefeller and Nancy Reagan, and the waves of women who approached their table. Similarly inundated by well-wishers and autograph seekers, Tricia and Julie managed a few bites from the low-cholesterol "Keep in Shape for '68" menu sponsored by the Standard Brands corporation, which featured cold, jellied tomato soup; chicken à la orange; a "continental rice" blend; broccoli with Fleischmann's margarine; lightly dressed mixed greens; and a dessert of ladyfingers and Pistachio Royal Instant Pudding with skim milk. "I'm still starving," Tricia whispered to Curtis after the plates were cleared and the program had begun.

After a quick stop by the suite to change outfits, it was time for the reception and another receiving line. Watching and listening, Curtis couldn't help but be impressed by the women's skills and endurance. She clocked Pat Nixon artfully wielding "that handshake," clasping her left hand over the other person's right, still in her own, and gently squeezing. And then there was "the wink," which she only gave to certain people, instantly wrapping the recipient in a gently conspiratorial circle of two. Julie laughed brightly and always looked people in the eye as she talked to them, including, Curtis recorded, when she spoke smartly and with conviction about her father's campaign and policies. When the reception was over, they had about twenty minutes to complete another costume change, this time into gowns for the convention's crucial night. Curtis asked if either sister was wearing a good luck charm. "We don't need anything like that," replied Tricia with obvious pride. "We're *in* luck. We're already there."

Wednesday's session began early to accommodate the length of the roll call, which was well underway when national television audiences first learned that something was happening in one of Miami's Black neighborhoods. At 7:15 p.m., NBC's Chet Huntley reported a "disturbance" in Liberty City but gave no details. When a floor reporter for the network interviewed Governor Kirk and other members of the Florida delegation not long after, he made no reference to the unfolding event, nor did he ask Kirk for a comment.

About a hundred people, mostly teenagers hoping to meet Wilt Chamberlain, had gathered outside the Vote Power League's office-turned-meeting-hall at the corner of 62nd Street and 17th Avenue earlier that afternoon. Inside, despite posted notices that only Black reporters would be admitted, two white men from a local paper entered the meeting and refused multiple requests to leave, at which point they were thrown out. Throughout this time, the crowd outside continued to grow—and grow increasingly bored and restless. Some teens began to hassle drivers and throw things at passing cars on 62nd Street, which was a major throughfare for northwest Miami. Wilt Chamberlain and Ralph Abernathy weren't expected at the rally for hours—after the nomination was made about seven miles away, at the Miami Beach Convention Center.

Someone called the police about "white media rejected" from inside the rally hall, prompting a dramatic response from authorities. While a surveillance team had been on site all day, the arrival of more police cars and heavily armed officers amplified the tensions and swelled the size of the crowd in the street. More trash and rocks were hurled into traffic as Liberty City residents increased the direct confrontations with passersby and police. But by 6:00 p.m., after road barriers stopped the vehicular traffic on that stretch of NW 62nd Street, the group began to thin out and the general atmosphere appeared to calm. Police removed their barriers and allowed regular traffic to resume about an hour later.

Within minutes of 62nd Street's reopening, a white man in a yellow Mercury, boasting a prominent "Wallace for President" sticker, cruised past the Vote Power League office. The remaining rally goers jeered at the driver and began pelting his car with rocks and bottles. The driver swerved, hit another car, and came to an abrupt stop near the intersection. He looked up to see a crowd running toward his car. Patrons from a corner bar on the other side of the intersection yelled at the driver to run, beckoning him to the bar. The driver leapt out of the car and sprinted into the bar, where the manager guided him out the back door and away from the scene. (Later reports would make much of the fact that everyone in the bar who helped the driver had been Black.) The white man was unharmed, while his car, with its sticker calling for a segregationist Southern president, was turned over and set on fire. This was the moment, wrote one reporter, when the Liberty City "riot had begun."

It was hard to miss a "Wallace for President" bumper sticker in 1968, with its stark design of neon orange all-caps block print against a dark blue background. As the former governor of the neighboring state of Alabama, Wallace was popular in Florida, and the number of his stickers around the state had grown considerably after a recent four-city campaign tour. He had just rallied thousands of supporters in Miami on Sunday, July 28, right before the start of the GOP convention. His last stop on the trip was in Tampa, where a journalist described Wallace's arrival at a rally of more than 8,000 people: "A Dixieland band warmed the large rally crowd, which in turn welcomed Wallace with a roar and the waving of rebel flags." The candidate razzed Governor Kirk for his recent tour of Alabama promoting Republicans and encouraging people not to vote for Wallace (who was running as an Independent), and promised the crowd that he would be on the ballot in every state. "If we can't get them to love us," he said, "we're going to get them to respect us."

As noticeable as the Confederate rebel flags was the army of Wallace Girls, who fanned out at every rally and campaign appearance. Unlike other candidates' cheer squads, they worked the crowds, soliciting change and small bills, which they collected in yellow buckets. Many scoffed at the small-donor fund-raising tactic, including Betty Friedan, who reported in *Mademoiselle* that Wallace's "'girls' went around selling their kisses, or whatever, for $20 for the campaign," simultaneously depicting them as cheap and tacky while highlighting the commodification of women at the heart of the scheme. Despite the express designs of the campaign to present the Wallace Girls as sophisticated and modern, many observers saw them the same way as they pictured their candidate: backward, Southern rednecks with no class, but at least in the women's case, pretty faces, or as one young man put it, "honey-faced somewhat-stupid 'Wallace Girls.'"

George Wallace had made his first run for the presidency as a Democrat in 1964, while he was still a sitting governor. Four years later, he no longer held the seat officially and was the presidential nominee of the American Independent Party. He was also the recently widowed "first gentleman" to the governorship of his late wife, Lurleen Wallace. The state's constitution barred consecutive terms in office, so in 1966, Lurleen ran for the top job with a campaign that made it clear a vote for her was a vote for her husband continuing in his role as governor. She won and served from January 1967 to May 7, 1968, when she died from cancer.*

Lurleen Wallace may have been holding the chair for her husband and acting on his behalf, but she was no cipher. Alabama's first lady turned governor was outspoken, had always been active in her husband's campaigns, and shared his values. She was an avowed white supremacist who worked hard in and out of the governor's office to maintain racial segregation in all aspects of Alabama life, but particularly in its public schools. She had also been a vocal advocate for herself throughout their marriage, despite the pair's differences in age, education, and power. They married in 1943, when Lurleen was sixteen years old and George was twenty-four. He was already a politician when the couple wed and

* Of the forty-nine women to date who have been elected governor of a U.S. state and the three who have served as governors of U.S. territories, Lurleen Wallace was the third in history. Her two predecessors, also Democrats, similarly entered office as surrogates for their term-limited or deceased husbands.

he campaigned relentlessly for the duration of their sometimes-volatile union. Lurleen left George twice because of his infidelities, going so far as to file for divorce at one point, but then extracted promises from her husband and stayed.

When the Wallaces' fourth child was born in 1961, Lurleen's OB-GYN discovered cancer. He informed George, not her, and her husband chose to stay silent, ordering the doctor not to say anything, either. Nearly four years later, in 1965, Lurleen visited a gynecologist for abnormal bleeding and was diagnosed with advanced uterine cancer. Shortly after, a staffer told Lurleen that the governor had been discussing her diagnosis with campaign people since 1962.

Lurleen had a hysterectomy, which was kept secret from voters. She campaigned through it all, won the governorship, and then, after the election, began radiation treatments in December 1965. Shortly after her inauguration, her condition worsened, until her death the following year. As the public watched her get sicker and sicker, knowing something was seriously wrong, she and her husband, and everyone around them, continued to claim she was fine. Finally, when it became impossible to hold to that narrative in the face of such obvious evidence to the contrary, the governor announced her cancer and treatment.

George insisted until the end, when Lurleen Wallace barely weighed eighty pounds, that she was in remission. He had been on the road campaigning for president since February. At Lurleen's request, he canceled a scheduled trip to Michigan to be at her side with their family when she died on May 7, 1968, at the age of forty-one. After three weeks of public mourning and private grief, George Wallace resumed his campaign.

As Liberty City burned, the state delegation roll call—and nominating and seconding speeches—creeped on, with delegates seeming largely unfazed by the events unfolding nearby. Reporting from the scene at about 9:45 p.m., Mel Goode, a popular Black reporter for Miami's local ABC affiliate, drew the connection for viewers: "To be sure, this might have been triggered by the lily-white climate of the Republican convention, which is in progress right now just a few miles from here."

Seven and a half hours after the roll call started, just after 1:00 a.m., Wisconsin's thirty delegate votes gave Nixon his first ballot victory. Then the struggle to nominate a candidate for vice president got started.

Strom Thurmond rang Phyllis Schlafly's hotel room phone at about 4:00 a.m. on Thursday morning to tell her that, after a long VP fight, they had gotten their way. The nominee would be Maryland Governor Spiro T. Agnew, whom Schlafly described on her list as "doubtful, but acceptable." Agnew had cemented his appeal with the hard-right law-and-order wing of the GOP with his response to the Baltimore uprising that had erupted four months earlier, in the aftermath of Martin Luther King Jr.'s assassination, in which he'd mobilized most of the Maryland Nation Guard before requesting federal military intervention. Agnew blamed the violence on a recent visit from Stokely Carmichael, and he berated Black leaders in the city for caving to radicals. He dismissed the Kerner Commission findings that identified structural racism as the root cause of urban unrest, and he argued instead that, "If one wants to pinpoint the cause of riots, it would be this permissive climate and the misguided compassion of public opinion. . . . It is not evil conditions that cause riots, but evil men."

While the Right applauded him and liberal-to-moderate GOP delegates fumed, Agnew, less than two years in the governor's seat, was relatively unknown outside his own state. The "What's a Spiro Agnew?" jokes started before the convention ended. Once again, Charlotte Curtis turned her gimlet eye toward the governor's wife, Judy Agnew, to find answers. "Mrs. Spiro Agnew?" her story opened, "The Maryland Governor's wife, whose face, ample figure and personality are virtually unknown even in Republican circles, has a name that was on virtually every lip here today." What followed was a less than flattering story about "a stocky brunette with big brown eyes and a round face," wearing a "waistless yellow and white silk dress," who "appeared only slightly nervous" in her initial outing before the press. The woman Curtis described was even more unprepared than she realized for the role she had just been thrust into. As the convention and country learned of Nixon's "choice" for running mate, the uprising in northwest Miami continued and spread to other Black neighborhoods. When Richard Nixon delivered his acceptance speech that night, and he clasped Spiro Agnew's shoulder to thundering applause in Convention Hall, the air in Liberty City, Coconut Grove, and Overtown was still heavy with tear gas and smoke from the burning buildings. Three Black men were dead, all of them unarmed, after being shot by police.

21

GET THIS . . . WE ARE GOING TO DISRUPT THE MISS AMERICA PAGEANT

AUGUST 8, 1968

Carol Hanisch listened more than she spoke in most situations. So, the fact that she was the one to propose protesting the Miss America Pageant was meaningful to the women at Thursday's meeting. "One of the things I remember about Carol," recalled one who was there, "[s]he didn't speak often, but when she did it was strong and important."

Hanisch began her pitch in a somber tone, describing her own relationship to Miss America, her history watching the pageant every year, and its impacts. "I cried with the winner!" She talked about how it had dawned on her only recently how much the Miss America ideal and beauty standards had shaped her own choices, options, and behaviors; how something so seemingly superficial had seeped into her consciousness and sense of self—and how she believed it was doing this to all women and girls.

Hanisch underscored the importance of building a mass women's liberation movement. To unite women, they must take on issues that speak to the oppression they all experience in daily life, she said. And here's "this American icon—the Miss America Pageant—telling women what to look like, what to wear, how to wear it, how to walk, how to speak, what to say (and what not to say) to be considered attractive. In short: look beautiful (no matter the cost in time and money), smile (no matter what you're feeling), and don't rock the boat."

This is just the boat to start rocking, thought Hanisch. She ended with a simple appeal: "Let's do a Miss America action."

The room was reluctant. While a few were as enthusiastic from the start as Kathie Amatniek had been when she'd first heard the idea, most were not. The hesitancy stemmed less from outright rejection of the idea and more from concerns about how such an action would be perceived.

People will think of the action as "frivolous and petty," they worried, just like they dismiss the Miss America Pageant. The demonstration wouldn't be taken seriously, they said, but just seen "as a silly women's action." A few of the women at the meeting were indeed opposed to the concept itself, arguing that the Miss America Pageant just wasn't that big a deal. Who really cared about a beauty pageant? (Hanisch would later observe, "If more than half the television viewers in the country watch the pageant, somebody cares!")

Hanisch and Amatniek responded by suggesting that the group do a consciousness-raising session about Miss America. Then they could take up the question of whether New York Radical Women (NYRW) should stage a protest.

They began to go around the room, each woman sharing her experience of the pageant and how she felt about it. As they did, a more complex picture of Miss America's overt and more insidious effects began to emerge. Some who denigrated or professed not to care nevertheless had to admit they still watched it. Others explained that, like Hanisch, they had identified with the women competing for the Miss America crown. Amatniek said that she'd never actually watched the pageant, but knew its messages about femininity and beauty had still affected her deeply and negatively. Other members echoed the sentiment.

The thought of taking NYRW's consciousness-raising practice into direct action was a powerful motivator. Recalling that meeting and her own commitment to the protest, Bev Grant explained:

> The pageant, to me, added to my feelings of inferiority as far as having what it takes to be a beautiful woman, as presented by the pageant. I could never be that. I never had big tits, you know? And all of those things that were being emphasized. I thought the action was perfect. It would be a great way to get some of those feelings out and relate to many more women because it was personal, but it was really deeply political. . . . I liked what we talked about in consciousness-raising groups because it was personal. That whole concept of the personal being political was very clear to me. So the Miss America thing really appealed to me. It was: *Let's go make some noise!*

By the time they finished, the reluctance was largely gone. Instead, ideas for what the protest should look like and how they would organize flew around the room. Women's liberation was going to make some serious noise in Atlantic City.

The next day, Amatniek went up to the MetroMedia Television Center in Midtown, home of New York's Channel 5, to join Kate Millet and a few other NYRW members at a meeting with producers from the *David Susskind Show*. The nationally syndicated talk show, which tilted heavily toward politics and contemporary social issues, had since the start of summer been considering a program about women's liberation. Now, they wanted to get a sense of which women might be good on TV in a group conversation with the host. They were looking for guests who were well-spoken and dynamic, but it became clear to Amatniek that the producers were also looking for young feminists who were pretty. Where, they'd asked, was Roz Baxandall? If they were going to do the show, she had to be on it. Amatniek was hurt, and she couldn't help but think about everything they'd discussed at the meeting the night before.

Amatniek was one of the few in her NYRW circle who didn't live on the East Side. She was still ruminating about the *Susskind* meeting when she got to her building, a six-story walk-up at the corner of Sullivan and Houston Streets, distinguished by the intricate scrolled ironwork on the fire escapes that hung from the building's front. Back in her "little apartment" she'd come to miss so much during her trip to California, Amatniek decided to write to Baxandall, who was still in Massachusetts, on Cape Cod. There was so much to tell her about—not just the Susskind meeting but also everything that had happened over the last week, starting with Sandy Spring. She grabbed a red ballpoint pen and began to cover both sides of thin typing paper. The meeting in Maryland had been "pretty indecisive," she wrote. The "best thing was meeting two women from Gainesville, Florida who wrote a fabulous position paper which brilliantly puts down the SDS line (& Chicago-Women radical line) on Women's Liberation and came up with an analysis which is very similar to ours." It had been so good, she told Baxandall, to see Carol Hanisch and have the chance to talk and spend time together. (Hanisch was already headed back to Louisville, Kentucky, to finish out the month at SCEF headquarters.)

Speaking of Carol, Amatniek continued, she "came up with an idea which what's left of our group has already decided to do as our 1st mass-consciousness-raising action. Get this . . . we are going to disrupt the Miss America Pageant."

Amatniek didn't go into details about the CR work it had taken to get to the group's decision, but instead jumped right into the initial plans. "The idea so far is for us to go in chains . . . wearing big blue county fair-type prize winning ribbons . . . the whole thing being something on the order of we, as women, are enslaved by beauty standards." She would explain more to Baxandall when she visited soon. "The action is for the weekend after Labor Day . . . so start working out ideas because we've got lots of work to do, fast."

Amatniek no longer thought of NYRW as one group, if she ever really had, and she shared her fears that the divisions of Sandy Spring would bedevil the Miss America protest, too. Referring to the politico-leaning left women in NYRW, like Florika Remetier, who met on their own most weeks in addition to attending the Thursday nights, Amatniek warned that "people in other groups are really turned on by the idea & may want to join . . . but I think we have to be careful that they don't interject the consumer slant so strongly that the really important issues get clouded."

Amatniek turned to the *David Susskind Show* at the close of her letter to Baxandall, after first noting that Baxandall's picture, taken at a recent abortion-rights protest, was in the current issue of *Time* magazine. *Susskind* was "still up in the air," Amatniek said, "but if they decide to do the show they still want you (they hear that in addition to being very articulate, you're also a knock-out . . . I had the feeling that Kate [Millet] and I didn't quite fit the total bill and got mad at the whole emphasis on having to have really good looking feminists."

22

OUR VIETNAM GIRLS

AUGUST 11, 1968

As women's liberationists were debating whether to protest the pageant in Atlantic City, the second Miss America USO Show Troupe was on its way to a sixteen-day tour of U.S. military installations in Japan and South Korea. Miss America 1968, Debbie Barnes, and the six other pageant winners (mostly state finalists Barnes had beaten for the crown), would perform a variety show called "It's Today," made up, as Barnes told a reporter, of contemporary hits from different genres, "all the up tunes—folk, rock, blues, love songs."

The Miss America Pageant, its state and local preliminaries, and individual contestants had long been associated with patriotic spectacle and the military. In 1967, the organization made this relationship more formal with the creation of the first USO Miss America Troupe Tour. The program took Miss America and several state finalists to the frontlines in Vietnam and to bases throughout Southeast Asia and the Pacific, with the aim of representing home, showing support for the troops, and boosting morale. The war—and the organization's express support for it—was back into the pageant.

The year before, the Armed Forces Radio and Television Service agreed to air the 1966 pageant telecast—the first to be broadcast in color—to U.S. military installations around the world. Notably, the year had also opened with a two-week tour of Vietnam bases in January, given by Jo Collins, who was *Playboy*'s 1965 Playmate of the Year; the trip was organized by the magazine and made possible with the help of the U.S. Department of Defense. Whether or not the pageant organization's leadership had Collins's tour in mind or that they understood Miss America to be her wholesome counterpoint, both tours shared a certain logic in seeking to boost servicemen's morale by letting them engage with a parade of beautiful American women, authenticated in their representative physical attributes by their appearances in *Playboy* or on the Miss America stage.

While the 1967 show may have represented the first Miss America Pageant–sponsored travel and entertainment dispatched to the front, pageant winners from the Miss USA and Miss World pageants were already regular features in USO entertainments, usually as part of Bob Hope's shows. Miss America had already been there, too, in the person of Anita Bryant.

Anita Bryant on USO tour, circa 1970

In 1966, the same year the pageant was first broadcast globally on Armed Forces television, the USO celebrated its 25th anniversary and awarded Bryant its highest honor: the Silver Medallion. Her receipt of the award was the concluding segment of an hour-long television special called *Whatever Happened to Miss Oklahoma?* The program featured clips from several of Bryant's performances over the years, including visits to Cuba, Japan, Thailand, and Vietnam. While now she was a famous singer and entertainer, it was Bryant's former beauty queen status that featured most prominently in promotions for the special. "Chances are you can't name the lovely hunk of pulchritude who became Miss America of 1959," opened one story in the *Chicago Tribune*. "Neither can we. But odds are that the third runner-up in that contest—Miss Oklahoma—is familiar to millions of television viewers and thousands of servicemen in Viet Nam. Her name? Anita Bryant!" A picture of Bryant in an insignia-covered campaign hat, holding a set of Vietnam Jump Wings to her chest, ran above the headline, "Beauty Queen Goes to War."

In 1967, the pageant organization nevertheless promoted its new USO show as the first time a Miss America had "entered a war zone to entertain." Then serving in the role of pageant executive committee chairman, Al Marks explained, "we are enormously pleased to be able to send this troupe to Vietnam. It adds a full measure to the meaning of the Miss America Pageant, and we hope it can contribute in however small a degree to the wellbeing of our servicemen there."

The announcement of the tour couldn't have come at a better time for its headliner, Miss America 1967, Jane Jayroe, who found in it a renewed purpose. After months wearing the crown, her Miss America spark was dimming. While making appearances throughout South Carolina, a weary Jayroe paused to write in her diary about her frustrations that she would never dare say out loud. "I've lost all enthusiasm for these things. I'm not a person to these people—and when I get off a Piedmont puddle jumper at 7:30 after starting at 11:00 that morning, I don't look like the person they expect to see." She had felt ready to be done with Miss America, to go home to Oklahoma and "accomplish something" and "do something besides smile!" Jayroe found that "something" sooner than she thought, however, when she learned that the pageant was sending their own "troupe" on a seventeen-day tour in Vietnam.

Upon the group's return, Jayroe was invited to the White House, along with wounded veterans from a D.C.-area military hospital, to meet President Johnson. When asked by a reporter about her position on the war and her own recent experience "in country," Jayroe held to the pageant's prohibitions against Miss America winners or contestants addressing controversial topics or voicing political opinions in public. Her answers were typically vague, but far from apolitical. Asked what she thought of the war, Jayroe replied, "We went over there just to entertain and see the boys." As for the boys, "they were great, and their morale was fine," adding that she left believing that most Americans "definitely aren't aware of the good we're doing over there." Jayroe and the rest of the Miss America troupe had only just returned from Vietnam the day before her White House visit. By the time her comments were published, she was en route to Atlantic City for the start of Pageant Week. This timing would be the standard for subsequent tours, making the USO tour the last major event of Miss America's reign before she passed the crown to the next winner.

There was no rest for the troupe in Atlantic City. The USO show was featured prominently in performances at various events throughout Pageant Week and during the finale telecast, billed as "The 1967 Miss America Sisters Vietnam Troupe." Pageant president Jack Rowe bragged to journalists, "We're very proud of our Miss America girls as you well know. We think they're the greatest girls in the country." He praised their abilities and strength, boasting that "These girls are adaptable; they're flexible; they're talented; they're intelligent. They can do just about anything they have to do. When we put the USO unit together, it didn't faze them in the least."

During the pageant finale, Bert Parks brought the troupe to the pageant stage after the swimsuit competition and a commercial break, while the judges conferred to select five finalists from the ten semifinalists who had just finished walking the runway in their one-pieces and high heels. "On August 14, a big jet airliner took off from New York City, the destination was Vietnam, and among the passengers were six excited young ladies, Miss America, Jane Jayroe, and five of her Alpha Sigma pageant sorority sisters," announced Parks, stumbling a bit over the last part of the sentence. "This was the beginning of a special USO Vietnam tour for these girls, who played to more than 85,000 of our servicemen at camps and at hospitals. They just arrived back in the States this past week and I know you're anxious to meet them." After introductions, the women performed a version of "If They Could See Me Now," from the 1966 hit Broadway musical *Sweet Charity*. New lyrics included "We're eating Army chow and keeping crazy hours," and "Wow, so this is Vietnam" (pronounced to rhyme with "jam"). The crowd cheered as the women left the stage, waved off by Parks. "There they go, our Vietnam girls. They really did marvelously well."

Debbie Barnes hailed from Moran, Kansas, a small community of less than six hundred people in the eastern part of the state. Majoring in music at Kansas State College, where she played the piano, organ, trumpet, and French horn, Barnes planned to pursue a graduate degree and become a professor of music. When she became Miss America in 1967, a number of news outlets simply reported her professional goals as "teacher." Like many other contestants, Barnes explained that it was the scholarship money that prompted her to enter the pageant. She wrapped this in a wider narrative of self-sufficiency and hard work from a young age, necessitated by her mother's multiple sclerosis (MS) diagnosis when Debbie was around nine years old.

During her reign as Miss America, Barnes described her childhood and her mother's illness in a personal essay entitled "A Lesson I Learned from Life" for the nationally syndicated weekend insert in *Parade* magazine. In the piece, she encouraged parents to be open with their children about family hardships and to give them greater responsibilities. Describing the degenerative qualities of MS, Barnes wrote that her mother explained she "would be able to do less and less around the house," and that the girls, Debbie and her then five-year-old sister Barbara, "would have to do more for ourselves and for our father, too—that we would all have to be self-reliant." While help came from her grandmother and another woman hired by the family, Debbie described taking on more housework and cooking as a young teen. Her mother had been a piano teacher in their home—Debbie learned to play the instrument and gained her love of music from her mom—and at twelve, she took over teaching the lessons. In addition to all this, Barnes managed to find time to be an active high school student and a cheerleader. She was selected homecoming queen in her junior year.

Barnes turned twenty while in Atlantic City, in 1967. The pageant organization surprised her with a birthday cake and impromptu party with all the contestants during the day's television rehearsals. An Associated Press photographer captured Miss Georgia, Sandra McRee, offering Debbie a dollop of icing at the end of her finger. Though it was a cute bit of wholesome cheesecake, the image winked at potentially darker competitive impulses, given the pageant's upcoming swimsuit competition, which Barnes would, in fact, go on to win.

Barnes said that her best birthday present that year came from her hometown, which had raised enough money to pay for her father and sister to go with her to Atlantic City for Pageant Week. Her mother had by that time been hospitalized in a long-term care facility for nearly three years. Nurses had turned the pageant telecast on in her room, but they could not be sure if Debbie's mother understood that her daughter had won, as she was no longer able to communicate. "She is a beautiful woman, smiles when we visit her, but we do not know if she realizes what we say since there is no sign of recognition other than her smile," Barnes told a journalist during an appearance in Ohio a month after her win. "I will get to see her within a few weeks when I travel to Kansas" for her college homecoming weekend, at which she would appear as Miss America. During and after her reign, and long before contestants had platforms or were required to show a record of community service, Barnes worked as a national advocate for MS research and awareness.

Now it was Debbie Barnes who was departing for the USO tour. Shortly before she left, her father told a reporter how excited she was for the opportunity, and he noted that of all the people his daughter had met while being Miss America, President Johnson had been the most exciting for her. That was really saying something, he added, because Debbie had always been a Republican.

The original tour was planned for sites in Vietnam, visiting troops in the field as well as in hospitals. A week before the group's departure, however, the organizers announced a changed itinerary, citing transportation logistics. Much later, one of the show's members said that concern for their safety had been the primary cause for the shift, after a group of USO performers were killed not long before the tour was to start. They would now be headed for military hospitals and installations in Japan and Korea. The troupe would be joined there by Irene Bryant, an official chaperone employed by the Miss America Organization (a woman from tour sponsor Pepsi Co. had served as chaperone in 1967).

Whether she was opening a car show in Texas or visiting wounded soldiers at a military hospital in Asia, Miss America never traveled or made an appearance without a chaperone. Among chaperones, Irene Bryant had a unique relationship to the pageant, in that her own daughter had been Miss America 1966. She was Deborah Bryant—the same former Miss America who had just led the Republican National Convention in reciting the Pledge of Allegiance on national television a few days before. Irene got her start as an alternate chaperone for her daughter; she became one of Jane Jayroe's official companions the following year, and then started traveling with Debbie Barnes in 1967.

As the mother of a very popular recent Miss America and a regular presence at Barnes's appearances around the country, Irene Bryant was often featured in the press in her own right (described as "herself an extremely beautiful woman"). She was with Barnes at many of her first official engagements, helping the young woman acclimate to her new place in the public spotlight. A month after Debbie won the crown, the Hudson County *Jersey Journal*, serving the densely populated part of New Jersey just across the river from New York City, ran a long story on the front page of its "Home and Family" section, entitled "Miss America '68 Chaperone Veteran at Job." It was accompanied by a photo of a smiling Bryant standing above a seated Debbie Barnes, who smiles up at the older woman as she pats Debbie's sculpted updo into place. After noting Bryant's role during her daughter's reign, the story continued, "Now she is 'mothering' Debra Dene Barnes, the current Miss America, who coincidentally also represented the state of Kansas. The two Debbies had a chance to meet during the pageant, but were able to chat only briefly, due to the tight schedule of the contestants." The women's meeting may have been brief, but the "Two Debbies" moniker and her predecessor's mother would be a constant presence throughout Barnes's time as Miss America. If Barnes ever wished she didn't have to spend her year being chaperoned by another Miss America's mother, when her own was hospitalized and could not communicate with her, she never let on. Shortly before the USO show left for Japan, several papers around the country ran a picture of Irene Bryant and Debbie Barnes standing side by side, with the caption, "Beauties to Vietnam."

In addition to Irene Bryant, Barnes was joined on the USO tour by state finalists from Georgia, Minnesota, New Hampshire, New Mexico, and Wyoming, as well as Texan Betty Buckley, Miss Fort Worth 1966. The inclusion of the winner of a feeder pageant who did not take the state title was unusual; it was the work of the pageant telecast director who was so impressed by Buckley in 1966 that he thought she was a shoo-in for Miss Texas and on her way to becoming Miss America. When that didn't happen, he continued to promote Buckley's career and hired her as part of the professional ensemble for the pageant finals in 1967 (the year Barnes won) and then brought her on for the 1968 USO show. Buckley credits the Miss America Pageant with helping to launch her career, but has described struggling with the experience as a young feminist in the 1960s:

> It was uncomfortable for me, because I never thought of myself as a pretty girl. I thought of myself as a good performer, a good singer, but I didn't identify myself as a great beauty. I didn't like the swimsuit competition. I loathed the idea of standing on a stage and having people compare me to other girls. It was horrible. . . . The legacy they hand you as an all-American girl is tough and rather phony.

Not unlike for Anita Bryant, the Miss America stage became a showcase for Buckley's talents. In 1969, she made her Broadway debut as Martha Jefferson in the original cast of the award-winning musical *1776*; she went on to become a fixture of stage, television, and film to the present day. Among Buckley's many credits and awards was her early role as the kind gym teacher to Sissy Spacek's *Carrie*, in the 1976 film adaptation of Stephen King's novel; that role secured her a place among the pantheon of American pop culture icons.

The 1968 Miss America USO Show Troupe tour started with a performance at the Marine Corps Air Station in Iwakuni, Japan. Located near Hiroshima Bay, the station provided air support for infantry in Vietnam. Aside from an impromptu concert the women had given in the USO club in the San Francisco airport, Iwakuni was their first show. Debbie Barnes had never traveled outside the United States, but there wouldn't be much time for sightseeing.

The women arrived in Tokyo on Saturday and flew to Iwakuni, after getting about three hours' sleep. Marines had been milling around outside the venue for more than two hours, waiting for the show; when they were allowed inside, they charged the auditorium and smashed through the glass doors in a rush to see the beauty queens. Inside, they whistled and cheered, especially when the women left the stage to move through the audience, selecting men to bring up for a dance lesson. An AP reporter framed the destruction caused by the "eager" and "over-enthusiastic" Marines as humorous, which was in keeping with the generally wholesome and controlled environment projected by the pageant organization.

Reviewing a performance at the Army's 121st Evacuation Hospital at the Yongsan Garrison in Seoul, South Korea, a reporter for the Pacific edition of *Stars & Stripes* described a good show despite malfunctioning microphones and an out-of-tune upright piano. "Their success," he noted, "was due in large measure to the booming Broadway voice of Betty Lynn Buckley, the multi-talented Miss Ft. Worth 1966." The women performed for over an hour before plunging "into the audience to be mobbed for smiles and autographs." Two days later, they became the first USO show performed for "frontline GIs north of the Imjin River," in the demilitarized zone between North and South Korea.

23

A CERTAIN IMAGE AND PUBLICITY VALUE

AUGUST 12–15, 1968

Roy Wilkins was deeply irritated when he saw the offer from the Miss America Pageant while he was working through the correspondence that had piled up during the Republican Convention. In a letter dated July 30, 1968, Al Marks and the new president of the board, Adrian Phillips, said the pageant wished to fund an annual scholarship of $1,000, to be administered by the NAACP for the support of young Black women's development into "qualified contestants" for the Miss America pipeline of local pageants. This, the men explained, would enable a Black woman to one day win a state title and thus go on to compete for the Miss America crown in Atlantic City.

It was clear that Wilkins's statements in June about the "lily-white," un-American pageant—and the national press they garnered—had struck a nerve. Marks sought to end the cycle of terrible publicity and perennial threats of protest. That Marks wanted to see a Black finalist compete in Atlantic City was undeniable; that he and other pageant leaders believed the Miss America Pageant to be responsible for Black women's exclusion since Rule No. 7 was struck—that was questionable.

Marks's overriding, fundamental aim was to protect the pageant's reputation and ability to draw advertiser-sponsors. Adrian Phillips, who had ascended to the board's presidency when it was vacated by Marks, shared these goals. An Atlantic City hotelier, Phillips joined the board in 1922 after falling in love with the pageant during its inaugural year. No one had a longer history with the pageant's operations than did Phillips, not even Lenora Slaughter, whom he'd helped hire. The "solution" he and Marks devised was a new spin on the same old response to charges of Miss America's racism: we don't control what happens at the franchise levels, and the failure of Black women to win there is wholly their own, based on their lack of qualification; recent Black competitors had not been polished enough, talented enough, or beautiful enough to win at the local and state levels. Any systemic problem could be remedied by providing better paths to preparation and by encouraging the right kind of Black women to compete. It was a Miss America Pageant gradual integration scheme.

As Roy Wilkins saw it, the pageant was trying to make addressing its racism and exclusion of Black women the NAACP's problem. He shared the offer with the national director of public relations, Henry Moon, and he sought guidance about how to proceed while venting his frustrations. This is the role of the chapters, an issue of "purely local terms," Wilkins complained to Moon. Instead, the pageant sought "to get us involved as a national organization and to place certain responsibilities on our shoulders."

The day after Marks and Phillips posted their offer to Wilkins, the men announced the other part of their plan to head off Black criticism, bad press, and potential protests in Atlantic City during Pageant Week. They were pleased to report the selection of the first Black member of the pageant board, Reverend Kenneth E. MacDonald, the rector of St. Augustine's Episcopal Parish, which served historically Black congregations in Asbury Park and Atlantic City. The *New York Times* reported the announcement, noting that MacDonald, one of twenty-seven board members, was "the first Negro named to any official position in the 47-year history of the pageant, the nation's oldest beauty contest."

Responding to Wilkins on August 14, Henry Moon argued that the benefits of accepting the pageant's scholarship offer generally outweighed the problems. "We do not regard the 'Miss America' stunt as an important issue, but it does have a certain image and publicity value," he said, which the Publicity Department thinks "we should take advantage of." It could also present an opportunity to negotiate for more significant efforts from the pageant, including granting local franchises to Black-owned businesses and community organizations. It was hardly lost on either man that this "stunt" was about managing the press and getting ahead of persistent criticism about the lack of Black contestants, but Moon believed it could be used to the NAACP's advantage.

With the start of Pageant Week looming, Al Marks had tired of waiting for a response from Wilkins and the NAACP to the board's offer. If they were going to head off accusations of Miss America's racism and coverage focused on the contest's segregation, he figured they needed to get the story out there.

With no word from Wilkins, and no knowledge of the NAACP's internal conversations that seemed very near to giving him exactly what he wanted, Marks shifted tactics and called a press conference for August 15. Marks had decided to announce the offer itself, rather than what he had assumed would be the NAACP's prompt acceptance and its implied partnership with the civil rights organization (albeit on Miss America's terms). In the absence of the photo op Marks had wanted with the national director, he staged a local version by inviting Edgar Harris, head of the Atlantic City branch, to join.

Harris and Marks sat next to one another at a boardroom table, on either side of a corner, with copies of the original letter and notes spread before them. Both men wore light, summer-weight sport coats and skinny ties. Al Marks's ever-present cigarette hung from his right hand while he made an opening statement to the journalists gathered around the table, each with their own copy of the letter.

The Miss America Pageant was neither racist nor "lily-white," Marks began, despite the accusations made by Roy Wilkins at the NAACP's convention in late June. It was true, he conceded, a Black woman had never competed in the national finals, but that was not by design. Local pageant pipelines just weren't producing Black finalists, and the situation, with its *appearance* of discrimination, Marks argued, had resulted in misunderstandings that the Miss America organization wished to correct. With this, he turned to the July 30 letter and the pageant's offer to the NAACP of an annual scholarship fund.

Wilkins's highly publicized charges against the pageant, made with Edgar Harris standing at his side, had prompted Marks, Phillips, and others in its leadership to sit down with the local NAACP leader for the first time earlier that summer. "Our discussion denoted a complete lack of communication between the Black community and the pageant," said Marks with an air of surprise. The absence of communication fueled misunderstandings that were amplified in the media; the resulting letter was both a corrective and proposal aimed at shaping a different future, eventually.

Edgar Harris knew well what Al Marks hoped to achieve by having him at the press conference, including the implication of the optics that the civil rights activist—newly informed of the offer—accepted the pageant's explanations and professed commitment to "non-discrimination." Harris deftly complicated that picture in his responses to journalists' questions. When asked if the meeting and subsequent letter had "brought the pageant closer to the Black community," Harris gave no comment.

Pressed on the matter, he paused and considered for a long time before answering, "I'd rather not say at this point. These things have just been implemented. We'll have to wait until later to get the pulse of the people."

At which point, Marks cut in, blurting, "Two colored hostesses have been named for this year's pageant." (In its coverage of the press conference, the *New York Times* noted that the women were "both Negroes and wives of local physicians" and had been named as "chaperones to the 50 girls during Pageant Week.")

With this, Al Marks went on to offer the pageant officials' usual refrain: the national organization doesn't control local or state contests; we get the finalists they send to Atlantic City. But in mid-August 1968, it came with a new caveat. "We can't tell them what to do," Marks claimed. "However, if there is discrimination and it can be proved, the [local] organization will be immediately disenfranchised." What constituted discrimination or proof that it had occurred was never clarified. (The obvious limits of this approach would be highlighted by sports journalist Frank Deford in his 1971 book, *There She Is: The Life and Times of Miss America,* in which he summarized the responses of local Jaycees: "Why, we'd love to have some colored girls in our Pageant, but none ever applies [*sic*].")

The national Miss America organization could name Black judges, and Marks assured the press that the pageant's board was making every effort to integrate the panel, reminding them that Diahann Carroll had been invited but had declined. Around the time of the press conference, Marks and his board had learned that one of the judges would have to drop out. Finding a replacement on short notice was a problem, but it was also an opportunity—one the men did not take to impanel a Black judge. Instead, they asked Charlotte Curtis, and she accepted their invitation.

Coverage resulting from the press conference went largely as Marks hoped. An Associated Press story appeared in papers around the country, including the *Washington Post,* which reported the Miss America Pageant's scholarship offer and details under the headline, "Negro Girls Are Sought for Pageant." It appeared that the plan devised by Marks and Phillips was working. Less than twenty-four hours later, however, news broke that a Miss Black America Pageant would be held in Atlantic City on the same weekend as the Miss America finals.

24

A BEVY OF "BLACK AND BEAUTIFUL" YOUNG WOMEN

AUGUST 17, 1968

The first word of a Miss Black America Pageant happening in Atlantic City came with the announcement of the pageant's preliminaries to be held in Philadelphia on August 17. It appeared in a Black-owned paper, the *Philadelphia Tribune,* which had been in continuous publication since 1884, serving Black readerships in and around the city, as well as the wider Mid-Atlantic. "Fashionable Productions of Philadelphia is really going to have this nation talking, come Sept. 6, 7, and 8, when they present in Atlantic City . . . the Miss Black America Beauty Pageant." The language was unmistakably that of the company's founder and Black entertainment impresario, J. Morris Anderson, and the weekend dates were immediately recognizable as coinciding with the Miss America Pageant finals.

While the Miss Black America Pageant would soon be promoted as a direct protest to Miss America's racism, this first incarnation was more of a piece, with a long line of Anderson's genre-blending entertainments: part fashion parade, part scripted theater and Black Arts variety show, and part beauty contest. It seems that Anderson had ambitions to create an annual event from the start, but at this point it is unclear the extent to which he wanted to craft a national pageant organization with a network of state franchises feeding into a national final.

John Morris Anderson spent his formative years in Greenville, South Carolina, where he was known as John Burton. When John was a baby, his father, Herbert L. Burton, worked as a presser at a laundry and earned a bachelor's degree by correspondence from Lane College, a historically Black institution founded by the Colored Methodist Episcopal Church (CME) in Tennessee. Upon graduating, Burton began work as a teacher and principal in the Greenville public school system and served as a circuit preacher for the church. In 1945, when John was eight years old, his father was named pastor of the Israel Metropolitan CME Church in Washington, D.C., and the family moved to the capital. They moved again nine years later, when Burton was appointed pastor to Phillips Temple CME Church in Indianapolis, where he would serve for twenty-four years.

At some point, either before the move from Washington or shortly after, John changed his last name to Anderson. His father and mother, Grace Burton, were active community leaders within and beyond the church. Herbert was president of the Indianapolis chapter of the NAACP and a member of the Urban League; in addition to working with her husband in these civil rights organizations, Grace was a celebrated advocate for the blind. As the founder of the Miss Black America Pageant, J. Morris Anderson would point to his parents as major influences, not only in shaping his values and sense of race pride but also in his creativity: "I was reared in the home of a minister, and I was exposed to church music at an early age."

In 1959, John Anderson started a record company with business partner John Daniels called Fabulous Records. The pair became most well known as "John and John Productions" for the themed parties they hosted in various Indianapolis Black communities. In the summer of 1959, the men staged an event called "Le Cabaret Francaise," featuring cocktails, dancing, chorus girls, and live music in a fully themed "authentic French setting" (a transformed Indiana State Teachers Association building). John and John described it as the second in a series of "globe-trotting nights away from Naptown," following their inaugural event in February, called the "Latin-American Fiesta." One of the live acts at Le Cabaret Francaise was "The Playboys," singing two original songs that would soon be available from the Fabulous label. The night culminated in a Miss Fabulous Productions beauty contest, featuring fifteen women vying for the title and a trip to Washington, D.C. The *Indianapolis Recorder* raved that "hundreds of young adults enjoyed a night in Paris" at the party.

John Anderson left not long after and went back to D.C. to attend American University for graduate training in business. Upon completion of his degree, he started his own stock brokerage firm and assumed his professional moniker, J. Morris Anderson—"Jay" to friends and associates. The firm was short-lived, however, and Anderson soon returned to entertainment. During this time, he married Lana Turner and the couple moved to Los Angeles and started a family. On the West Coast, Anderson founded a publishing business with two flagship magazines aimed at Black readers, *Elegant* and *Fashionation*. Like his Indianapolis record label, the publishing company was also a vehicle for hosting live events and promotions.

In the summer of 1964, ads in the *California Sentinel* for "Elegant Magazine's 'Vogue for Judgement Day'" described a "new twist in fashion presentations" and a "two-act fashion play presenting exquisite fashions in a new and different manner." Co-sponsored by the Church of the Advent, advance tickets were made available for purchase at two local Black-owned businesses, a record store and a clothing shop. "Superb is the word," opened the *Sentinel*'s review a week later. The paper described the show as a "unique" event that "brought a fresh approach to the presentation of fashions. It also brought out a moral study, a lot of humor, and much food for thought." With its drama of St. Peter and Satan bringing the models and other characters into heaven or hell, the review urged repeat performances "so that more people could enjoy the style show and the drama showing the eternal struggle of the forces of good and evil." If that weren't tantalizing enough, the paper added, "Church people could readily recognize themselves and their neighbors in the characters portrayed. The styles worn by the glamour models were something else again. All were in excellent taste and worn with a professional air which hinted of Paris. The presentation of the topless bathing suit was effective." One of the featured models, Barbara Tennell, was identified in promotions as a "former Miss Bronze of California." That fall, the *California Eagle* reported a "Vogue for Judgement Day Party" to raise money for the Los Angeles chapter of the NAACP.

Three years later, the Andersons put on a longer, revised version of the show in Indianapolis, where Jay was greeted as a favorite son. It was sponsored by the Dramatic Guild of the Ohio Conference of the CME Church and was staged in the auditorium of the Christian Theological Seminary; proceeds went to the conference's Youth Department and scholarship funds. Advance promotion in the *Indianapolis Recorder* described the play's presentation of "the beautiful woman of color in all her walks of life and the garments she wears are all indicative of such." Community leaders would serve as "Judges for the Fashions," and the best-dressed lady in the audience would be awarded a "luscious mink stole." The paper promised audiences "Spicy, elegant fashions to be seen in [the] production" that had already been staged in Los Angeles, Washington, D.C., Atlantic City, and Philadelphia. As prominent figures in the community and CME Church, Anderson's family got involved at many levels of the production. His little sister, Jacqui Burton, a recent graduate of Crispus Attucks High School and a new student at her father's alma mater, Lane College, worked on production. Their mother chaired the Dramatic Guild committee that would go on to award a scholarship to a senior at the Indiana School for the Blind.

The origins of the Miss Black America Pageant lay in Anderson's community-based entertainment business and his affinity for beauty contests and fashion. With Fashionable Productions, J. Morris Anderson created events for Black people, grounded in churches and mainstream civil rights organizations like the NAACP, Urban League, and National Association of Colored Women (NACW), each of which had their own long histories of support for Black girls' and women's pageantry. Helpfully, Fashionable Productions was the publisher of the NACW's magazine, *National Notes*, which became an invaluable early national platform for advertising the new pageant.

The preliminary Miss Black American contest would be held in the Philadelphia Civic Center's Gold Ballroom, in partnership with the city's Department of Recreation. Referencing the bigger event to come in Atlantic City, the announcement promised "a bevy of 'Black and Beautiful' young women" at the preliminaries competing "for the prestigious title of Miss Black America of 1968. At that time spectators will bear witness to the beauty and talent of these contestants. They will be able to witness the new 'voice' and 'awareness' of the 'Black and Beautiful' women of America." Twenty-four young women, all from Philadelphia and surrounding communities, were slated to compete. Published on the *Philadelphia Tribune*'s youth page, the article ran alongside a report on another Recreation Department initiative that summer, offered to young women as part of Philadelphia's Action Summer '68, which provided activities for youth with the aim of keeping them busy and out of trouble. One of these was a six-week Model Teen Beauty and Charm course, in which "more than two thousand Philadelphia teenagers" were "learning how to 'enjoy being a girl' through the city's unique" offering.

Other than extolling their general virtues as symbols of pride and talent, very little was said about the competitors themselves or how they ended up in the pageant. While never explaining the process, Anderson made it known that the original group of contestants for the "Miss Black America Beauty Pageant–1968—Black and Beautiful!" were *selected* rather than rising through a preliminary system of pageants or via newspaper and radio contests. They had been carefully chosen, he said, to demonstrate the range of Black women's skin tones and to ensure that all forms of Black beauty, including the dark-skinned, were recognized and celebrated, "projected in all her charm, poise, and beauty. She is crowned to reign as our queen, be she black, bronze, sepia or in between." The Miss Black America Pageant would provide a long-denied national stage for celebrating "Black Beauty and parad[ing] the Women of Color as a Universal Symbol of Pride." Less clear, however, was where individual Black women competing for the crown were to be found—or find themselves—in the transformation to universal symbol.

25

THEY GOT TO ME BEFORE I GOT TO ME

Robin Morgan was ready to protest the Miss America Pageant from the moment Carol Hanisch suggested it at the early August meeting. As a self-described New Left "heavy" and fierce politico, Morgan rarely found herself in easy agreement with Hanisch, Amatniek, or the other radical feminists in New York Radical Women (NYRW). She didn't spend much time with them outside gatherings at the SCEF office, and she considered her smaller regular group that met most Tuesdays to be her true home in women's liberation.

Morgan's memory of the moment she first learned that radical women in New York City were organizing for themselves would remain vivid, even decades later. It was an evening in late autumn of 1967; Morgan was alone in the apartment she shared with her husband and was listening to the radio. As usual, it was tuned to WBAI, a community station that provided an ever-present soundtrack to the lives of activists, leftists, and fellow travelers in the city, many of whom populated its talk-heavy lineup of news, politics, and arts and culture shows as guests. That night, a group of New Left women were discussing the meaning and impacts of the Mary King and Casey Hayden memo. Morgan was rapt, surprised to hear that one of the guests, Judith Duffet, was someone she knew from the non-student SDS-affiliate Movement for a Democratic Society.

Like Morgan, Duffett attended meetings with her husband. The two women had never really talked much, but Robin liked and had come to quietly rely on Judith. She recalled how they would "raise eyebrows at each other when the men said stupid things," which was often in their shared estimations. Now, Morgan was listening to Duffett talk about organizing women to change the "stupid things" rather than just quietly commiserate about them. At the end of the show, Duffett said a group of women were meeting weekly and gave a number to call if listeners were interested.

Oh my God, thought Morgan, *I need this.*

She telephoned Duffett and joined the group at the next meeting.

Robin Morgan might have needed that group, but she didn't think of herself as a *feminist*. In fact, she believed feminism to be part of the liberal problem that she and others on the revolutionary left were fighting. She had argued as much to Shulamith Firestone during the Jeannette Rankin Brigade protest back in January. Not only was feminism "stupid," Morgan had reasoned to Firestone, but it was bad for organizing because it "turned people off."*

In time, Morgan would view her anti-feminist stance as being driven by her desire for affirmation from and leadership roles in the male-dominated New Left. She drew energy and a powerful sense of authority from being the only woman in the room, which led her to qualify her initial interest in women's liberation. Morgan's "subconscious agenda" may have been *Oh my God, I need this,* but her "conscious agenda was, 'I'm a good leftist revolutionary woman, I'm going in there to give these women some real politics.'" She thought her access to and influence on male leaders of the Yippies, the National Mobilization Committee to End the War in Vietnam (known simply as MOBE), and Students for a Democratic Society (SDS), made her the best person to educate the nascent women's liberation movement. "I'm dealing over here with Abbie [Hoffman] and with Jerry [Rubin] and with Rennie [Davis] and with Tom [Hayden]. And I'm the one woman they'll listen to. . . . I'm real heavy." So, Morgan believed, "these women *need* me."

"And of course, thank God, they got to me before I got to me."

* In 1994, Robin Morgan referenced feeling "everlasting feminist shame" as she described her own rejection of feminism in the late-1960s to journalist and fellow veteran of women's liberation Susan Brownmiller. Regarding her argument that just the term "feminism" turned people off, Morgan added ruefully, "Unfortunately, I was right. But for the wrong reasons."

• • •

While Robin Morgan's origin story in women's liberation would be echoed in the epiphanic relief described by many other radical women, her path to the movement through childhood celebrity as a star of radio and television was unique. Morgan's mother, Malkah Teitelbaum, called "Faith," was the youngest and only child born in the United States to Jewish parents from "The Pale," at the western border of Imperial Russia. Morgan's father, Mates Morgenstern, was a physician from an elite Jewish family in Vienna, Austria, who immigrated to the United States as an adult around the time of the Anschluss, when Nazi Germany annexed his country. After Robin was born in January 1941, and Morgenstern left her and Faith, they moved in with her mother's widowed older sister, Sally, in New York. Never married to Robin's father, Faith changed both her and her daughter's last name to "Morgan."

Morgan began working as a child performer on radio at the age of three, landing her own nationally syndicated program, *The Little Robin Morgan Show*, in 1945, when she was only four. As with other popular radio personalities of the time, her roles migrated to the live dramas and variety programs of television's dawning Golden Age. Before the age of ten, Morgan was a national celebrity, thanks to her role as youngest daughter Dagmar on CBS's comedy-drama series *I Remember Mama*, about a Norwegian-American family in early twentieth-century San Francisco, which aired from 1949 to 1957. Morgan's career was managed by her mother and aunt; her paychecks supported all three of them. By the time she was a teenager, Morgan had long been a household name; she was being sent on staged dates with young actors like Sal Mineo for pictures in fan magazines, and she desperately wanted out of the business.

When Morgan was accepted to the University of Chicago with the help of her tutor, her mother forbade her to go and fired the tutor. By gaining thirty-five pounds in six months, and making herself unemployable, Morgan eventually managed her industry escape. It would be nearly four more years, however, before she could slip from her mother's control, secure her own apartment and a job as an executive assistant at the Curtis Brown literary agency, and get on with making her life as the writer she hoped to become. Her older boyfriend, the poet Kenneth Pitchford, still lived with his partner, a composer and musician named Bob with whom Morgan was also close. She and her mother had met the two men at a party a few years earlier, and Morgan had found appealing their easy public acknowledgment of being gay and together. Robin's and Kenneth's relationship was electric, but never conventional or easy.

Pitchford had just learned that Bob was in love with another man and was leaving their shared home and open relationship when he proposed to Morgan. The pair married in 1962, and after Bob moved out, Robin moved into the enviably spacious, if perpetually in disrepair, apartment that spanned two floors of a four-story, 1830s federal-style townhouse at 109 Third Avenue, between 13th and 14th Streets in the East Village. Dwarfed by tenements of later construction on both sides, the building's ground floor was—and remains today—the site of the original Kiehl's Pharmacy, progenitor of the contemporary global skin-care company. Morgan would come to host many a women's liberation meeting there; none who entered could believe or forget that apartment, including the author of photo captions for a *New York Times Sunday Magazine* piece on "women in the revolution" that identified Morgan (in characteristically understated style) seated "in her comfortable apartment with a friend from The Movement."

Morgan and Pitchford lived the early days of their marriage in the heady atmospheres of the New York literary establishment, downtown arts scene, and radical activism. Morgan was becoming known as a poet in her own right, and was active in the civil rights movement, including working for CORE during Freedom Summer. In 1965, she began devoting her organizing energies to the anti-war movement. She and Pitchford would be part of just about every major protest in the city against the Vietnam War, and some beyond it. In late 1966, they read poetry and distributed leaflets from the back of a flatbed truck, roving the streets of Manhattan during Angry Arts Week; in 1967, they demonstrated for peace at the United Nations, marched on the Pentagon, confronted Secretary of State Dean Rusk at the New York Hilton, and protested the busiest Army induction center in the city. When the student strike and occupation at Columbia University began in April 1968, Morgan and Pitchford provided aid through the Movement for a Democratic Society (where Morgan met Judith Duffett). A few months after calling for an anti-war countercultural invasion of Chicago, during the 1968 Democratic National Convention, the Yippies formed a coalition with SDS and MOBE, which also planned to demonstrate there, and the couple became part of the organizers' inner circle.

The Yippies, which was short for Youth International Party, looked to merge anti-war activism, direct action, and the Free Speech Movement with the counterculture, expressed mostly through guerilla theater and spectacles of the ridiculous that carried sincere critiques of society. With roots in Jerry Rubin's infamous promise to levitate the Pentagon during the October 1967 March on the Pentagon against the Vietnam War, the group had been active since January 1968. They staged direct "zap" actions, such as showering fake dollars onto the floor of the New York Stock Exchange, laughing as traders scrambled to gather the "money." Their two most visible and intentionally outrageous leaders were Jerry Rubin and Abbie Hoffman. After announcing their plans to go to Chicago, the Yippies began issuing a steady stream of statements publicizing their intentions—a Festival of Life conceived as an alternative to the Democratic Party's war-drenched convention of death—and threatening shocking tactics of disruption, like dosing the city's water supply with LSD.

Morgan was drawn to the artistry, theatrics, and humor of the Yippies, as much as she resonated with their politics. They were a breath of fresh air in a movement that often felt over-serious and ideologically rigid to her. Explaining this to a reporter, Morgan said, "I just walked into the Yippie office one day. There was this hysterical loft with groovy posters and people sitting around rapping and coffee spilled on the floor, and whenever the phone would ring whoever picked it up would yell, 'Yippie!' It seemed life-affirming, myth-making, just beautiful!" What Morgan didn't tell the male journalist was how it felt to be a Yippie woman when the group's leaders celebrated their ideal world of "free grass, free food, free shelter, free chicks" and stabbed at middle-class mores with "humorous" slogans like "Shake a chick's tit instead of her hand!"

What she did explain, however, was the movement's sexism that led her to women's liberation. "A lot of women came [into the movement] expecting a radically new scene," she said. "[H]ere was a group of young people with a new politics, a new lifestyle, a new sexual honesty and freedom. And still, the notion of a liberated woman was someone who is indiscriminate about whom she sleeps with, not a realization that women don't want to be objects." This was just the dominant suburban culture and *Playboy* made over in love beads, calls for revolution, and dope. "A lot of Movement women might just as well have gone to Scarsdale."

• • •

When Kathie Amatniek expressed concerns to Ros Baxandall that the enthusiasm of "people in other groups" risked skewing any Miss America demonstration toward leftist economics and "the consumer slant," and away from the "really important issues," she was referring mostly to Robin Morgan and the Tuesday night group. Amatniek recognized the power of the demonstration's ability to bridge intensifying ideological differences among members of NYRW, but she worried about the dilution of what she saw as the *real* message of women's liberation.

There was genius in identifying the Miss America Pageant as both a target for action and a public platform for broadcasting women's liberation. No matter a woman's perspective or specific experience, it was nearly impossible to avoid the Miss America Pageant and its proscriptions for ideal American femininity and beauty. For the activists themselves, "as mixed feminists and lefties," said Morgan, "it was a perfect combination." The pageant "objectified women, but it also touched the base of capitalism, militarism, racism, and sexism." It was as if it had been "made to order" for a massive "public zap action" where they could take everything on "in one fell swoop."

Amatniek's concerns would prove prescient. Carol Hanisch left shortly after the meeting to finish her summer work in Louisville, Kentucky, at SCEF headquarters, and she could only be involved with planning from a distance. In her absence, along with that of so many others, the Tuesday night group's leftist action orientation and Yippie-inspired membership moved to the center of planning, with Robin Morgan taking the lead.

26

THE TEN POINTS, WE PROTEST

AUGUST 8–22, 1968

Once the group agreed on doing a Miss America Pageant protest, the brainstorming came in a torrent. By the end of the meeting that had opened with Carol Hanisch making her case, the favorite idea was for women to show up at Convention Hall in chains, wearing "big blue county fair-type prize winning ribbons" like animals raised to slaughter, judged to be the best of a parade of living and lovely animals, already just meat for consumption—so delicious you could almost taste them. Early suggestions ran toward the theme of women's enslavement to beauty standards, which would be symbolized by the chains.

The more the activists thought about the ranging power of the Miss America Pageant's ability to represent so much that held women down in American society, the more their plans for the protest grew. In the coming days, they planned for theatrical demonstrations throughout the action on the boardwalk: women would dance around a Miss America maypole to which they were chained; there would be an "Animal Parade" comprising only female creatures like sheep, hens, cats, and "bitch dogs"; and a bonfire or large garbage can in which participants would be encouraged to trash the tools of their oppression, including bras, wigs, girdles, false eyelashes and makeup, hot rollers, women's magazines, and aprons. Groups of women would fan out across Atlantic City to lobby pageant contestants and judges to enlist in the protest, "Join US!" They would urge a national boycott of all products sponsoring and promoted by Miss America.

Original plans included inviting popular leftist figures and celebrities to raise the profile of the protest and lend it radical recognizability and star power. Among those on the wish list were guerilla theater groups like the Vermont-based Bread and Puppet Theatre (excluding male actors), and dream speakers for a closing rally that would include authors Grace Paley, Marge Piercy, and Susan Sontag; singer-songwriters Buffy St. Marie, Judy Collins, and Janis Ian; civil rights activists Flo Kennedy, Fannie Lou Hamer, and Paule Marshall (Black Panther women were notably absent). Public statements of support would be requested from the likes of Simone de Beauvoir, Coretta Scott King, and Margaret Mead. In the annotations Robin Morgan jotted next to the typed list, she identified herself as the person responsible for extending all the invitations.

There would be so much to the protest, most believed they would have to extend it over two days. And while all this was happening outside Convention Hall, a small "secret tactics" group was planning something more disruptive, to be executed inside during the pageant itself.

Over the next two weeks, the women narrowed the scope of the protest to a demonstration on the day of the pageant finals and the work of the "secret tactics" group. Instead of celebrity speakers and endorsements, they wanted to fill the boardwalk with as many women they could persuade to join them, including those from other women's liberation groups. On August 22, the group readied a long press release outlining ten points of explanation for the protest for circulation and leafleting.

WE PROTEST:

1. **THE DEGRADING MINDLESS-BOOB-GIRLIE SYMBOL.** The Pageant contestants epitomize the roles we are all forced to play as women. The parade down the runway blares the metaphor of the 4-H Club county fair, where the nervous animals are judged for teeth, fleece, etc., and where the best "specimen" gets the blue ribbon. So are women in our society forced

daily to compete for male approval, enslaved by ludicrous "beauty" standards we ourselves are conditioned to take seriously.

2. **RACISM WITH ROSES.** Since its inception in 1921, the Pageant has not had one Black finalist, and this has not been for lack of test-case contestants. There has never been a Puerto Rican, Alaskan, Hawaiian, or Mexican-American winner. Nor has there been a true Miss America—an American Indian.
3. **MISS AMERICA AS MILITARY DEATH MASCOT.** The highlight of her reign each year is a cheer-leader tour of American troops abroad—last year she went to Vietnam to pep-talk our husbands, fathers, sons and boyfriends into dying and killing with a better spirit. She personifies the "unstained patriotic American womanhood our boys are fighting for." The Living Bra and the Dead Soldier. We refuse to be used as Mascots for Murder.
4. **THE CONSUMER CON-GAME.** The Pageant is sponsored by Pepsi-Cola, Toni, and Oldsmobile—Miss America is a walking commercial. Wind her up and she plugs your product on promotion tours and TV—all in an "honest, objective" endorsement. What a shill.
5. **COMPETITION RIGGED AND UNRIGGED.** We deplore the encouragement of an American myth that oppresses men as well as women: the win-or-you're-worthless competitive disease. The "beauty contest" creates only one winner to be "used" and forty-nine losers who are "useless."
6. **THE WOMAN AS POP CULTURE OBSOLESCENT THEME.** Spindle, mutilate, and then discard tomorrow. What is so ignored as last year's Miss America? This only reflects the gospel of our society, according to Saint Male: women must be young, juicy, malleable—hence age discrimination and the cult of youth. And we women are brain-washed into believing it ourselves!
7. **THE UNBEATABLE MADONNA-WHORE COMBINATION.** Miss America and Playboy's centerfold are sisters over the skin. To win approval, we must be both sexy and wholesome, delicate but able to cope, demure yet titillatingly bitchy. Deviation of any sort brings, we are told, disaster; "You won't get a man!"
8. **THE IRRELEVANT CROWN ON THE THRONE OF MEDIOCRITY.** Miss America

Members of the New York Radical Women at a planning meeting for the Miss America protest at the Southern Conference Educational Fund (SCEF) office in New York City, August 1968. Some are holding copies of the group's *10 Points* press release.

Kathie Amatniek (right), holding a pencil

represents what women are supposed to be: unoffensive, bland, apolitical. If you are tall, short, over or under what weight the Man prescribes you to be, forget it. Personality, articulateness, intelligence, commitment—unwise. Conformity is key to the crown—and by extension to success in our society.

9. **MISS AMERICA AS DREAM EQUIVALENT TO—?** In this reputedly democratic society, where every little boy can supposedly grow up to be President, what can every little girl hope to grow to be? Miss America. That's where it's at. Real power to control our own lives is restricted to men, while women get patronizing pseudo-power, an ermine cloak, and a bunch of flowers; men are judged by their actions, women by their appearance.
10. **MISS AMERICA AS BIG SISTER WATCHING YOU.** The Pageant exercises Thought Control, attempts to sear the Image onto our minds, to further make women oppressed and men oppressors; to enslave us all the more in high-heeled, low-status roles; to inculcate false values in little girls; to use women as beasts of buying, to seduce us to prostitute ourselves before our own oppression.

Several people involved in organizing the Miss America protest were simultaneously in the midst of planning for NOW-NYC's series of demonstrations outside the Manhattan headquarters of Colgate-Palmolive. The chapter's August 22 meeting was opened to the public in order to share information about the demonstration, as well as give Shirley Chisholm a chance to address attendees about her race for Congress. When she finished, Flo Kennedy headed to the front of the room to rousing applause, and she encouraged the audience of mostly women to embrace participating in direct-action protest and to join them in September. Picketing, she said, was "exciting . . . sexy . . . dangerous: you can make it anything you want!" Demonstrations were fun and effective, she said, especially when peopled by diverse crowds that included average middle-class women who looked respectable and, in a consumer action like the one against Colgate-Palmolive, like good customers. "Bring kids—kids love to picket. Let your mother come down—old ladies love to picket even if they only do it for half an hour. Make it exciting; make it swing!"

Kennedy acknowledged that doing an action could make a person self-conscious or afraid. "The first two minutes are the worst," she said, which was why you stayed in a group. Before long somebody would get "a little rowdy, you sing and you yell and this sport really gets to you." Lisa Hammel, one of Charlotte Curtis's Women's News reporters, covered the meeting for the *New York Times*. She described an exuberant, funny Kennedy and a crowd that was clearly inspired by her, but also nervous, noting people's questions about arrest or the possibility of violence.

Four days later, NOW received a letter from the Overseas Press Club (OPC), informing them that the organization was henceforth "persona non grata," and that "NOW's use of our facilities for protesting (re Colgate-Palmolive products) during your last meeting here has forced us to come to this decision." The ouster received more coverage in the New York–area press, including radio and television spots, than did the offending meeting itself, and almost uniformly leaned toward NOW by arguing that the OPC was absurdly heavy-handed in its reaction.

Located in the historic Webster Hotel on West 45th Street, the Overseas Press Club was, and remains, next door to the city's Harvard Club and around the corner from the likes of the New York Yacht Club, the Century Club, and several other elite, members-only facilities. The difference between the site of NOW-NYC uptown meetings and NYRW's SCEF office downtown could not have been starker, but several women were moving regularly between both during the summer of 1968. One of these was founding chapter member Anselma Dell'Olio.

Dell'Olio moved to New York City from Rome after college in 1966 to take a job with Avon International, the direct-sales cosmetics company. She never forgot how cold it was that night when she and Ti-Grace Atkinson met at the address for the NOW-NYC chapter, only to realize they were on the right street but the wrong side of Central Park. The pair grabbed a cab to the East Side and arrived at Muriel Fox's apartment a little late, which is why so many would later recall Atkinson's sweeping into the meeting in her fox coat. Everyone in the gorgeously appointed apartment seemed so "elegant and substantial" and very American to Dell'Olio. She was impressed, overwhelmed, and felt "ignorant as a goat on the subject" of feminism, but when the form to join NOW went around the room, and "Ti-Grace signed with a flourish, and handed it to me, taking for granted I would do the same," she did. During the next year, she read feminist texts, attended meetings, and worked on several committees for the chapter. When Dell'Olio heard about NYRW, she joined and attended religiously the weekly meetings and CR sessions. "Feminism allowed me to make the leap from rumbling volcano, always threatening to explode, to rebel with a cause."

Five months after that meeting, when Betty Friedan had announced that NOW would not be endorsing candidates until they responded to the organization's questionnaire about the men's stances on issues related to equality for women, she also promised a slate of what she called more "militant" actions to come during the summer. These included the boycott of the Colgate-Palmolive corporation and pickets at their national headquarters to protest alleged "extreme employment discrimination against women workers" at the company. (After a federal court found in favor of Colgate-Palmolive, NOW filed an appeal in 1967, which was ongoing at the time, but which later affirmed the judgment in favor of Colgate-Palmolive.) The same women who'd once cringed at Flo Kennedy's suggestion of consumer boycotts were now organizing them in 1968.

In the case of the Colgate-Palmolive action, the boycotts were largely organized by Anselma Dell'Olio. She was miserable in her job at Avon, but relied on it for "photocopies, stationery, stamps, and even printing privileges with the collusion of the mail-room guys." She was grateful and a little surprised that the men "were so sweet and cooperative about helping me produce feminist documents"—until she discovered that they all knew her from a photograph passed around the department of her in a bikini, which was taken at an Avon picnic during her first year with the company. In August, Dell'Olio added working on the Miss America protest to her organizing activities.

Robin Morgan had been similarly pulled in multiple directions, working with the core group of New Left activists and Yippies organizing protests in Chicago. But right before the Democratic Convention, Morgan stunned everyone by announcing that she couldn't go to Chicago because she was in the midst of organizing for the women's liberation protest in Atlantic City.

Morgan revealed her decision at one of the Yippie/MOBE organizers' usual meeting spots—Jerry Rubin's apartment in the East Village, on St. Mark's Street. Rubin, Abbie Hoffman, and Tom Hayden were dumbfounded.

"You don't want to miss *Chicago*!" Hayden cried. How could Robin not get, he implored, that the "second American *revolution*" would be happening there!?

From the corner of the pot-hazed room, Morgan's husband, Kenneth, said, "It's *you* guys, I think, who don't get it." He gestured for someone to pass him the joint. "My money's on the second American revolution taking place in Atlantic City."

27

WELCOME TO WOMEN DEMOCRATS

It would have been hard for the Democrats to select a convention location in 1968 that was more different from Miami Beach. The left, including MOBE and the Yippies, but also the civil rights and anti-war wings of the Democratic Party, had been organizing and publicizing their plans for Chicago for months. In more recent weeks, the press covered consistent denials of march and rally permits and the dramatic escalation of police and military in Chicago and its suburbs. Indeed, in the days leading up to the Democratic Convention, the city became known as "Fortress Chicago." The police presence alone would be nearly doubled during the convention, from 6,000 to 11,900, all working twelve-hour shifts rather than the usual eight. None were being coached on their best Miss America smiles and congeniality; they were preparing for battle.

Many in the party had wanted to move the event, and Miami Beach officials made clear throughout the Republican Convention two weeks earlier that they would be happy and ready to accommodate the Democrats, too. The sentiment was strong enough that some in the press had been loath to dismantle and move their equipment from Miami Beach. It may have been more wishful thinking on their part, once the networks learned that live coverage of anything in Chicago outside the International Amphitheater would be impossible, owing to Mayor

Daley's negotiations to end a telephone strike. The agreement limited press contracts to lines at the amphitheater and included none of the necessary wiring for live coverage in the streets or outside hotels and other venues. Journalists suspected this was by design, like so many other aspects of the Chicago convention. Vice President Hubert Humphrey, the party's presumptive nominee, wanted to move the convention, but President Johnson remained adamant that it would stay in Chicago and under the thumb of Mayor Daley.

Whereas the Republicans' 1964 convention site near San Francisco—the Daly City Cow Palace—was named in homage to earlier livestock shows and a building of the same name featured at the Pan-American World's Fair, the Democrats' International Amphitheater in Chicago was an active commercial center for the beef and pork industries in 1968. The building fronted blocks of corrals butted up against freight train tracks, and the stench of livestock hovered over everything. Add to this the August heat and an enormous pile of manure being converted into commercial fertilizer nearby—the convention literally smelled like shit.

From their hotels downtown, the delegates, alternates, and press had to be bused, flown by helicopter, or find other transportation to the amphitheater, about five miles away. Many roads connecting the two parts of the city were lined with temporary wattle fencing, erected to shield people from the area's blighted state. Made from plywood strips in a tight, basket-weave pattern, the obtrusive fencing mostly called attention to the attempt at concealment. Upon arrival at the International Amphitheater, the conventioneers were met with perimeter walls topped by several feet of strung barbed wire, visible snipers on the rooftops, and constant patrols by police and military vehicles, all of which only added to the sense of a convention under siege.

Surfaces free of barbed wire were plastered with images of Mayor Daley's face and "Welcome Delegates!" or "Welcome to Chicago!" signage in jarringly friendly juxtaposition. Once inside, there were still layers of security to negotiate, including an electronic identification checkpoint using new swipe-card technology that created bottlenecks and slowed the comings and goings considerably, especially once the convention officially began on August 26.

It was an obstinate show of state force in the face of promised dissent that cast protesters (and anti-LBJ/Humphrey Democrats) as invading enemies bent on destruction. Protesters began arriving at the same time as the delegates, the press, and people giving testimony at committee meetings the week before the convention opener, with the Yippies and MOBE coalescing in Lincoln Park, a few miles north of the hotels in the Loop. In addition to coverage in the national press, alternative publications like Northern California's *Berkeley Barb* had for weeks been publicizing information and calls to converge on Chicago. The August 16 issue had included a widely circulated Yippie map of Lincoln Park, site of the Festival of Life counter-convention and free concerts (starting with a promised opener by Country Joe and the Fish). The map depicted a suggestive, if satirical, planned environment that included "Grub Town," "Free Store," "Music Area," "Church of the Free Spirit," and a "Hog Farm," along with various encampment sites with names like "Free City" and "Biker Park." The Communications and Hospital, Out House, and a Yippie Pentagon made up a centralized infrastructure more aspirational than achievable, none of which was yet permitted. "But permit, or no, Chicago is a pretty up-tight town," warned the *Berkeley Barb*, "and the local hip community cannot offer the shelter and support that Hashbury or Berkeley could. Anything could happen in Chicago. Yippies will need to be a tough breed indeed."

A federal district court denied protest permits to the Coalition for an Open Convention at the start of the week, which prompted MOBE and the Yippies to file their own lawsuits. No one planned to leave Lincoln Park if (when) the permits were denied. On Tuesday, August 20, as Credentials Committee hearings were underway, the governor of Illinois deployed the National Guard to Chicago and the *New York Times* reported that Army units had been undergoing special training in Texas and were standing by to address "civil disturbance" in Chicago. When the Soviet Union invaded Czechoslovakia later that night, ending the Prague Spring through force, it was all too easy to draw parallels.

While Chicago readied for battle in streets, the Democratic National Committee prepared for conflict inside the amphitheater. There were challenges to the seating of all-white or almost entirely white delegations from Southern states, challenges to delegate distribution for some states by the McCarthy campaign, and conflicts over individual versus delegate-at-large voting. Entwined with credentials challenges, another fight loomed: Would the party's platform make room for anti-war Democrats or hold the Johnson administration's line on

Vietnam? This was of particular concern to Humphrey, who supported a peace plank but had not been allowed to distance himself from the president. Both issues dominated the work of the committees in the week before the official start of the convention, and were all but guaranteed to define the convention itself.

The Democrats had their own problems from 1964 to address in Chicago—namely, continued fallout from their failure to seat the Mississippi Freedom Democratic Party delegation in Atlantic City. This time, the Credentials Committee reversed course and voted to seat the "Loyal Democrats" of the state's racially integrated, demographically proportional challengers, rather than the segregationist official delegation. The committee then took a different tack with the Georgia delegation, deciding to give half its votes to the "regulars" sent by the state and half to the challenge delegates from the Georgia Loyal National Democrats. Implementation of this compromise was another matter, of course. Mississippi's was the only challenge to win the committee vote by a margin significant enough to avoid a minority report at the convention itself. Georgia would be decided along with challenges to the segregated Texas, Alabama, and North Carolina delegations on the amphitheater floor, which also meant on national television.

Betty Friedan testified before the Platform Committee on behalf of NOW, late on the afternoon of Thursday, August 22. With a presentation similar to her statement in Miami Beach, Friedan urged Democrats to include the Bill of Rights for Women in the platform. As an active campaigner for McCarthy, her work in Chicago was different from her role at the Republican Convention—something signaled by her inclusion, alongside Harry Belafonte, as a notable sighting at one of the official opening parties in Charlotte Curtis's first Democratic Convention piece of the week.

Friedan remained officially at the convention as a member of the press covering Chicago for *Mademoiselle*. To make the magazine's October issue, she was in the odd position of having to file her story comparing both conventions right before the Democrats' event got fully underway; Friedan hit the opening weekend's parties having just submitted her article on Friday. During committee meetings that week, she'd drafted some of her thoughts on the state of women in the Democratic Party on pages from her packet of McCarthy credentials challenge materials. Scrawled on the back of the Michigan challenge brief was "The Democratic Convention seems to have a view—or non-view of women—which is dangerously behind the times, is almost, but not quite, as obsolete as the Republicans'. There is a kind of . . . split between its view of women . . . and the reality of the women here . . . the women delegates and attendees and . . . to the reality of the young women out in the streets."

As the work of the committees had given way to the start of the convention proper, Friedan received a letter at her hotel from Clairol, addressed to "Miss Reporter." It informed her that the company's Courtesy Lounge for Ladies of the Press had been so popular in Miami Beach that it would be open again in Chicago, starting on Saturday, for everything a lady journalist might need: technicians would be "on hand with our Kindness Instant Hairsetters to give you a hair re-do in just five to ten minutes. Our cosmetic consultant will give you complimentary makeups or just the analysis if you are short on time. We'll still have that quiet corner and typewriter so you can turn out a story, if you desire. However, if all you care to do is just relax and chat, stop by too." Clairol's marketing tactic of high-profile courtesy treatments underscored the costs (and potential profits) in time and expense of the unspoken "beauty work" requirement for professional women. At the same time, the promise of a "quiet corner" and equipment, as well as friendly chatter, was a reminder of the many other functions these spaces served, including being places of retreat and sociality among women.

Both aspects of women's beauty work had been highlighted on the floor of Congress the previous December, when it appeared that the House Beauty Shop would close permanently. Located in the basement of the Longworth Office Building, the small shop had been serving secretaries, staff members, and growing numbers of congresswomen since 1932, when it was established by an entrepreneurial beautician. As a private enterprise relying on public resources, the shop came under greater scrutiny by House members in the mid-1960s as part of a wider slate of reforms. Before that work could be completed, though, the business's owner abruptly left, taking all the equipment and her employees with her. Congresswoman Edith Green, a Democrat from Oregon, showed up for an appointment at 7:30 the next Monday morning, to find the place empty. Scheduled to speak on the House floor a few hours later, Green recalled that she'd "had no choice" but to rush home to pick up a wig. Three years after she deftly maneuvered the inclusion of sex as a protected category under the Civil Rights Act of 1964, Minnesota congresswoman Martha Griffiths saved the day, moving quickly to secure a small loan and get the shop running again under the oversight of a new House Select Committee on the Beauty Shop, which she chaired. More than speaker-ready hair was at stake in maintaining the Beauty Shop; it was also about holding on to a rare space for women at the House. Along with the small talk and moments to close one's eyes while under the hair dryer, a great deal of politicking and information sharing must have happened in the House Beauty Shop.

Like Clairol's "beauty retreat," located at the Essex Inn, across the street from convention headquarters at the Conrad Hilton Hotel, every event or facility dedicated to women, official and otherwise, was presented in relation to accommodations provided by the Republicans in Florida. Recommendations from the DNC's Office of Women's Activities on what to pack for Chicago told convention-goers not to worry about it, as the Republicans had. "The Democratic Party, the majority one, is big enough to accommodate all styles, all ages, all imbued with one idea," assured the press release, leading the *Los Angeles Times* to headline their report, "Looks Don't Count at Chicago" for Democratic women. Some practical advice was offered, however, including to bring a sweater or wrap, and "since the convention will be televised in color, it is advisable to wear solid colors or prints—but not white. Hats are in the way, unless they are small and head-hugging."

Three women's luncheon events were scheduled throughout convention week, generally billed by the Office of Women's Activities as "Food for Thought—A Smorgasbord of Political Ideas to Take Home." Writing for the syndicated Women's News Service, Vera Glaser noted, "Unlike their Republican sisters, whose fun and games in Miami Beach centered on yachts and low-cholesterol menus, Democratic gals will be served a diet of issues." While the DNC was at pains to draw these kinds of distinctions, Glaser added, they shared with Republicans an under-representation of women among delegates and alternates. "Meanwhile, although women do 90% of the grassroots political chores, relatively few make it to party conventions as delegates or alternates. This year both Republicans and Democrats have announced that women comprise about 16 per cent of the delegate-and-alternate strength at their nominating conclaves."

A notable exception to the "diet of ideas" on offer to women at the convention was a luncheon fashion show sponsored by the Chicago Women's Host Committee and Mayor Daley's office. Held in the International Ballroom of the Conrad Hilton, with capacity for two thousand, the models' runway fronted a wall of gold and light blue, with letters spelling "Welcome to Women Democrats" nestled among laurel leaves. The runway was flanked by two "very feminine" versions of the traditional donkeys with "oversized jeweled eyes with glitter eyelashes . . . mounted on white glittery platforms and made of white petals with halos of gold laurel leaves," standing six feet across and nearly five feet high.

There was significant concern in Daley's camp about attendance for this event. Double booking necessitated canceling that day's women's "Food for Thought" luncheon—events that were already seeing low attendance. Betty Friedan would note, "In Chicago, things were a little different" from how they had been in Miami Beach. "The luncheons and brunches given as usual by the Democratic Ladies' Auxiliary—called 'Smorgasbord for Thought' this year—didn't even attract many of the wives, much less the 16 percent of the Democratic delegates who were women," she explained. In the end, leading organizers were forced to offer free lunches to vendors in order to fill seats for the speakers.

Democratic women in Chicago viewed these events for women that the DNC insisted on scheduling as superfluous to the work at hand and out of touch with the real stakes of the convention. Those sparsely populated banquet halls spoke volumes about the changing expectations of Democratic women and how far the party establishment lagged behind them.

As the courts dismissed or ruled against the last options for Yippies and MOBE to get permits for remaining in the park after 11:00 p.m. or marching on Friday, August 23—by which time they were already ensconced in Lincoln Park a few miles north of the Conrad Hilton and over ten miles from the amphitheater—the Festival of Life began with the nomination of their own presidential candidate, a female pig called "Pigasus," its sex central to the gag. "The five-day Yippie festival in Chicago's Lincoln Park will also feature a Miss Yippie contest, a swimming party 'with bathing suits optional,' a birth-control-pill hunt and bonfires of underwear and money," reported that morning's *Wall Street Journal,* and one had to wonder if the inclusion of Miss Yippie wasn't directed at Robin Morgan. Paul Krassner explained to the *Journal* reporter that contestants would represent astrological signs, not states. "It's one of the aspects of the cultural revolution," he explained. "We're satirizing the mainstream, the Miss America" contest. The peace march to the Amphitheater by a thousand "bare-breasted women volunteers" was canceled, but "incidents of female nudity" might still occur. That night, police arrested seven people and seized the pig.

Confrontations with police continued throughout the weekend and grew notably more violent on Sunday night, the eve of the convention's official start, when helmeted police wielding billy clubs stormed Lincoln Park after the 11:00 curfew. They fanned out, indiscriminately clubbing anyone they came across, including journalists, photographers, and members of television film crews. Several more protesters, including Tom Hayden, were arrested. Many "Welcome to Chicago!" signs were graffitied by demonstrators to read, "Welcome to Prague!"

While the Yippies promised beauty queens (along with public nudity and open sexuality) outside, most observers remarked on their absence inside Democratic Convention spaces, another notable contrast with Miami Beach's ever-present Nixonaires and candidate cheer squads. "The atmosphere was completely different from that at the Republican convention," said a British journalist. "The organizers had already decided there would be no girls, no brass bands, no balloons, not even demonstrations." The conventions had one celebrated beauty in common, though—former Miss Oklahoma Anita Bryant. In 1968, she and Billy Graham were the only two people to appear at both conventions in an official capacity. Where Bryant had performed in Miami Beach as a professional entertainer, her role in Chicago would be a labor of love and political passion, as well as a gig. She would be there for President Johnson.

When the convention kicked off in prime time on Monday, August 26, the general sentiment across the networks was that all was fairly bleak in Chicago and probably only going to get worse. On CBS, Walter Cronkite told viewers, "Overall, the security around this International Amphitheater has been worthy of an armed camp, a military installation," while the anchorman's colleague, correspondent Roger Mudd, remarked that "the dominant mood here in Chicago is one of gloom." Over on ABC, Frank Reynolds concluded that the "gathering of Democrats in the stockyards has about it an air of doom that seems unhappily appropriate to surroundings," suggesting they were marching toward their gruesome ends. The night that followed did nothing to contradict those statements.

As part of the DNC's efforts to promote their civil rights bona fides, and to show public support for Black voters, the convention's prime-time opening lineup included the national anthem performed by twenty-six-year-old gospel and soul singer Aretha Franklin, whose star was on the rise. Her song "Respect" had topped both the R&B and the pop charts in 1967, and had earned the singer her first Grammy award in February 1968. Two months later, she performed a wrenching version of the hymn "Precious Lord, Take My Hand" at Martin Luther King Jr.'s funeral in Atlanta, cementing her association with the movement. Convention organizers sought her star power and moral gravitas for their stage to demonstrate that the Democrats were the party of racial inclusion and progress. (King's funeral had been treated like a command performance by presidential hopefuls from both parties. Among them, Vice President Humphrey attended on behalf of the administration and as quasi-incumbent, while Richard Nixon showed up with Wilt Chamberlain. Towering above the others, the basketball star had been a kind of beacon in the crowd that also put Nixon in front of photographers' lenses.)

Standing behind the speaker's podium during the convention's televised opener, Franklin performed an arrangement of the anthem that was slowed down and soulful, more yearning than triumphal. Most of the predominantly white Democratic Party faithful in the amphitheater seemed to hate it. From the start of Franklin's performance, the standing crowd of delegates singing along, hands over hearts, were ahead of her in the lyrics, unable or unwilling to match her slower tempo. With that many voices, it was impossible to miss the disconnect inside the amphitheater or even while viewing from home, as was the growing discontent and pockets of visibly disgruntled people in the crowd. Clearly unsettled by her audience's reactions and insistent off-pace singing,

Franklin briefly stumbled over a lyric, drawing specious charges that she didn't know the words to the national anthem.*

Criticism of the performance filled the next day's news, particularly in the Southern papers, and continued throughout the week, often via the Letters to the Editors sections: "It was a travesty—a shame, and a disgrace to our national anthem, and an insult to every citizen regardless of his color or party affiliation"; "I have never felt any more grieved than I was when I heard Aretha Franklin on television from the Democratic Convention yelling the National Anthem in a jazz-like way in broken black and blue notes.... [W]hat is to become of us if everything we hold dear is allowed to be cheapened with such dishonor"; and Franklin's "color does not disturb me, but her offensive version of 'The Star-Spangled Banner' at the opening of the Democratic National Convention made me see red."

Reactions to Franklin's performance in the moment and afterward threw in sharp relief the disconnect and suspicion that characterized the Democratic Party's relationship to Black Americans. Rather than showcase the party's diverse coalition and its liberal values, Franklin's treatment suggested that the Democratic Party's embrace of Black people and its commitments to their civil and political rights were limited and conditional upon total assimilation to the dominant culture. The fights over delegate seating that took up the rest of that long opening night made clear to many that it might never be enough. If the Republican Convention in Miami Beach signaled the ascendence of the Southern strategy and mass coalition shift, Chicago showed the ugly depths to which the party could sink while trying to hold on to Southern Democrats.

The fight over Georgia's delegation took center stage and dominated prime-time coverage. Over the weekend, the "regulars," led by the state's Wallace-esque, avowed segregationist Governor Lester Maddox, had refused to accept the committee's compromise plan to split votes between the two delegations.

* This was the first of three performances of the national anthem Aretha Franklin would give at a Democratic convention; others followed in 1992 and 1996. At the 2009 inaugural for Barack Obama, she sang "My Country, Tis of Thee," honoring the new president as well as renowned Black opera singer Marian Anderson, who once performed the song on the steps of the Lincoln Memorial after being denied access to Constitution Hall by the DAR because she was Black. Franklin's interpretation of the anthem in 1968 echoed Anderson's slight but powerful change of the lyrics in the 1930s, singing "to" the possibility of a "sweet land of liberty," rather than "of" its existence.

When the convention opened on Monday, the full delegation of "regulars" was seated in Georgia's designated spot on the floor. The Loyalist delegation was directed to sit in the upper-tier spectators' area, where there were no microphones and little access to journalists and network cameras.

The challengers were led by Julian Bond, the founding member of SNCC and its director of communications, whom Mary King had worked with earlier in the decade. Bond had resigned from the organization in the wake of its embrace of Black Power, and in 1965 had won a seat in the Georgia State Legislature. State representatives refused to seat Bond in January 1966, citing his history with SNCC and the organization's position against the Vietnam War as the reasons, and called a special election to fill the seat—which Bond also won. It would ultimately take a ruling of the U.S. Supreme Court for Bond to assume the office he had been elected to twice.

After protesting their delegation's relegation to the upper tier and getting floor passes from New Jersey Governor Richard Hughes, the Credentials Committee chair, Julian Bond led the delegation onto the floor to confront the "regulars" and take their rightful seats. The dramatic moment was aired on national television, and Bond became the convention's righteous face of moral bravery and justice—its very handsome face. Since the earliest days of SNCC, Bond had been at the forefront as a spokesperson and leader. The light-skinned son of college professors, he was known for his eloquence, cool, and striking good looks, which were invariably referenced by comrades and press alike. In this, he was treated more like Diane Nash than other men in the organization's leadership. In his account of the Chicago convention, Norman Mailer said that among convention-goers, Bond was "adored for his magically good looks," and so popular by the end that "people cheered hysterically" at just the mention of his name.

At 1:00 in the morning, when network anchors began reporting clashes between police and protesters in Lincoln Park, the credentials fight had reached only the halfway point. It was another thirty minutes before CBS became the first to get footage on the air, since live reporting had been made impossible from locations outside the amphitheater. What the anchors and their viewers saw was horrifying, including police beating a CBS reporter filming the violence. The night ended without resolution on all the delegation challenges, which would have to be taken up again the next evening.

. . .

"I want everyone in the world to know what's happening in Alabama," Zecozy Williams told Charlotte Curtis on Tuesday. "The regulars stole our seats. I should have been seated." A challenge delegate from Montgomery, Williams explained that before she became a cook for Project Head Start, she'd worked for a white family. She left when her employer cornered her about the civil rights movement and said, "You Negroes are always getting into trouble, you Negroes never get things right."

After the floor fight of Monday night, Curtis spent the day interviewing Black women who were at the convention as delegates or were working in other capacities. Her aim was to write a story showcasing the diversity of Black women's opinions on the party and the issues through compelling individuals. While it carried some characteristic Curtis touches, her third convention piece, "At Chicago, Black Women Speak Their Mind," was mostly devoted to providing space for them to do so. "Black women are having their say at the Democratic National Convention, but aside from an abiding concern for minority rights and a strong antipathy to Gov. Lester Maddox's Presidential candidacy, no two of them seem to agree on anything. Whether they are cooks from the South, union leaders from the North, highly trained professionals, students or just plain housewives, they have all battled to achieve what status they have attained, and they are determined to be heard." With an ugly fight underway about which man would lead the Democratic Party, and possibly the nation, a fraternity that now included Monday night's star, Julian Bond, Curtis was just as determined to provide the women with a platform.

Unlike Zecozy Williams, who was furious with New Jersey Governor Richard Hughes, chair of the Credentials Committee ("I wouldn't support him if he were the last man on earth"), Johnnie Johnson, a delegate from the state, told Curtis, "He's all right. He's been a good governor." A supervisor and former shop steward at a textiles factory, Johnson was the first Black woman to serve as a ward chairman in Newark. An unwavering labor-movement Democrat, she had been a delegate to the first Black Power Convention, held in the summer of 1967, just days after the bloody Newark uprising. Johnson recalled moving through the streets during the "riot," devastated and tearful: "The thing that bothered me was the looting. But when I saw the conditions they live in, I understood. It could have been beautiful, really beautiful, if they hadn't looted. I believe in non-violence, but if I was provoked, I'm not sure I could turn the other cheek." After casting an obligatory first-ballot vote for favorite son Governor Hughes, Johnson would be for Hubert Humphrey.

The other delegate Curtis featured was Gail McHenry from Kentucky, who at nineteen years old was also the youngest delegate at the convention. (Kentucky was one of the states that had a voting age of eighteen in 1968.) As a sociology major at Indiana University, McHenry was active in the Afro-American Student Association. She had supported Robert Kennedy for president until his murder, when she switched to McCarthy. Curtis described McHenry as "an attractive girl with short, straightened hair and an affection for up-to-the-minute dresses, [who] also is adamant about the use of the word Negro."

"It doesn't mean anything," explained McHenry. "Negro" was not a personal identification, but a label; "The whites gave it to us."

A different term was on the lips of the women in Curtis's story, one that could mean everything. They were all, she explained, "struggling for a workable definition of black power." A voting-rights activist weeks from the start of graduate school in education at Harvard University, Velma Hill provided Curtis with a jumping-off point. Black Power is "a slogan that combines a movement for economic and political control over black communities with the fostering of cultural nationalism," explained Hill. "It's a concentration on black pride and an awareness of black historical contributions." Hill was adamant that this did not mean retreating from electoral politics but, rather, crafting a pragmatic approach through the process that addressed the immediate needs of Black working people. Johnnie Johnson shared a similar perspective.

When Curtis asked for a definition from Dr. Dorothy L. Brown, a Tennessee state representative and chief of surgery at Nashville's Riverside Hospital, she got a very different reply. "I can't define black power because it changes everyday," said Brown. "In Nashville, it can mean impatient, irrational violence. We have a group trying to make it rational in the sense of green power—economics, academic and social power." Curtis interviewed the representative after Tuesday's luncheon for women, at which Brown had been honored for her contributions to the party.

Dorothy Brown had a powerful story to tell. Originally from Troy, New

York, Brown had grown up in an orphanage from the time she was a baby, where she was one of six Black children among a group of three hundred. The institution was across the street from the Emma Willard School. Brown told Curtis about a formative moment in her youth when she and the other Black children were not allowed by their orphanage to participate in an event held at the elite private girls' school. "It was the first time I knew I was different," she said, and "I have never got over the hurt."

From the moment Brown had her tonsils removed as a child, she knew she wanted to be a doctor. Brown was an excellent student, supported by the orphanage and trained on her dream of studying medicine—a dream that was threatened when Brown was thirteen and her mother appeared to take her "home." Home was a crumbling tenement apartment building in an impoverished neighborhood, with a struggling mother she did not know; Brown subsequently ran away. "The physician, a gregarious, handsome, well-dressed woman, said she quit school at fourteen to become a maid," wrote Curtis. Over the next few years, Brown would also work in a mill and at a commercial laundry while going to school as much and whenever she could. She remained a terrific and driven student, and came to the attention of a Methodist women's group that sponsored a Black education project. Through them she earned a scholarship to Bennett College in Greensboro, North Carolina, and money for medical school.

Charlotte Curtis was charmed by Brown's daughter, Lola, who was celebrating her twelfth birthday with a trip to Chicago to watch her mother receive honors for her achievements at the convention luncheon. Brown had been one of the first single women allowed to adopt a child in the state of Tennessee, when Lola came into her life as a baby. Now the girl was a bright, energetic seventh grader. Did she wish to become a doctor like her mom? "I might study surgery," she told Curtis. "But mother has to stay up too long. I think I'll be a housewife. Maybe I'll try modeling. I think I'm a good modeler." No matter what she decided to do, Lola would have great preparation, bringing her mother's story full circle and Curtis's article to a close by announcing excitedly that she would be attending the Emma Willard School. "That's right," Dr. Brown said, beaming at the child. "She's going there two years from now. She's already been accepted."

Illustrated with several photos of the women—and Lola—Curtis painted a visual and textual picture of viewpoint diversity and general excellence among

Black Democratic women who rarely drew the same kind of attention as their male counterparts. Curtis's impulse to seek them out on Tuesday, and not Julian Bond, was a pointed one.

Tuesday was "Lyndon Johnson Day" at the convention in honor of the president's birthday, which offered a bit of tantalizing poetry for those still holding out for a successful "Draft Johnson" campaign. At various points, that push had included the president himself, but Johnson would not be going to Chicago. Instead, he left Washington to spend the day at his ranch in Texas. With Senator Edward "Teddy" Kennedy firmly declining a VP spot, after rejecting Daley's very public entreaties to run for the nomination, Humphrey's path to first-ballot victory was clearer. But it had to get through the Alabama credentials contest and the floor fight over the Vietnam War plank of the platform. Everyone knew another long, brutal slog of a night lay in front of them.

Prime time began with a benediction from Billy Graham and a set by Anita Bryant, the president's favorite singer, to celebrate his birthday. When she stepped up to the podium to start with the National Anthem, Bryant was greeted by thunderous applause. Once again, the delegates stood, placed hundreds of boater hats and many more hands over hearts, and began to sing along as the familiar face of the USO and godly patriotism belted out a familiar version of "The Star-Spangled Banner." Bryant followed with a reprise of her original "Happy Birthday" to the president, and the amphitheater continued to sing with her, saluting the incumbent who wasn't there, as he watched from home like the rest of America. The set ended with Bryant's signature arrangement of the "Battle Hymn of the Republic," and the amphitheater went wild. The standing ovation went on for several minutes, as conventioneers cheered and called the singer back to the stage for another bow and more applause.

Eyes and cameras followed as Bryant collected her husband and son to go sit with Governor Connally at the head of the Texas delegation. It was a show of support not only for the president but also for the "regular" delegation led by the state's governor, who had threatened to nominate Johnson on the first ballot to embarrass Humphrey if challenger delegations were seated and the "unit rule" that protected Southern Democrats' control was not maintained. Not long after, the family headed to the airport for a flight to Salem, Oregon, where the next day Bryant would be giving the first of three performances at the Oregon State Fair. Wednesday's papers described Bryant's performance as heroic, under headlines like the *Daily Oklahoman*'s "Anita Gives Democrats a Big Lift." They inevitably drew comparisons to Aretha Franklin's performance from the night before, while newspaper opinion pages and letters to the editor sections still teemed with criticism for Aretha Franklin and her "un-American" anthem.

An hour after Bryant and her family arrived in Oregon, she sat down with the Women's News editor of Salem's *Capitol Journal*. Marian Lowry Fischer described her as a "stunning brunette" who was "relaxed and ready to engage in a visit without any outward sign of weariness—but it had been a tiring trip from Chicago." While the Tuesday night session ground on at the convention, Bryant told Fischer that the United States was fighting godless communism in Vietnam and would—must—win the war.

The platform plank had yet to be discussed in Chicago at that point; most of the night had been spent on whether to seat the Loyal Democrats from Alabama (including Zecozy Williams) and dealing with continued fallout from the Georgia compromise. Fannie Lou Hamer was back, this time to testify on behalf of the Alabama challengers to the regular delegation, which included the notorious former police chief of Birmingham, Bull Connor. The night also dragged on owing to a procedural slowdown managed by Daley to push the Vietnam debate into the early morning hours, when no one would be watching television. The delegates were allowed to leave at around 2:00 in the morning, having finally thwarted the mayor's plan, although the discussion and vote were scheduled for a special session at noon the next day, well before the start of prime time.

As delegates debated the "peace plank," which included calling for a halt to bombing in North Vietnam, on Wednesday afternoon, protesters gathered in Grant Park, across Michigan Avenue from the convention hotels. Given its proximity to the delegate lodgings, candidate headquarters, and downtown press operations, the park had become the common scene of demonstrators yelling across the avenue, "Join Us! Join Us," and the ever popular, "Dump the Hump!" Now, around fifteen thousand people gathered for a sanctioned rally, some with plans to march to the amphitheater, despite having been denied a permit.

The only authorized action was a procession by Reverend Abernathy and the Poor People's Campaign mule train, going from downtown to the convention for the night's nominating roll call. Thousands of demonstrators followed, falling in behind Abernathy's procession and filling the road. Police allowed the mule train to pass before blocking Michigan Avenue at a cross street with a wide formation of helmeted, billy club–wielding officers, stopping the protesters in front of the Conrad Hilton while more poured into the intersection behind them. With National Guard troops already stationed in the park blocking another way out, the demonstrators tried to move back the way they had come, only to meet more police. They were trapped in the intersection, and then the police descended.

What followed is still most commonly referred to as a "police riot," a misnomer suggesting a spontaneous, unplanned eruption of violence, when this was anything but. Police waving clubs waded into the crowds smashing anything and anyone in their path, while tear gas ripped through the air. Upstairs at the Hilton, in Hubert Humphrey's suite on the twenty-ninth floor, journalist and historian Theodore H. White was at work on the next installment of his *Making of the President* series. Standing to the side, he was surveying the room as the vice president prepared to watch the roll call on television with family, friends, and campaign staffers. This was when White and others began to smell the faint but unmistakable odor of tear gas; it was coming in through the hotel's air-conditioning system.

When White left a few minutes later, and took the elevator down, the doors opened onto a scene of chaos soon blurred by his own streaming eyes. The lobby was full of tear gas billowing in from Michigan Avenue, as people rushed through the doors trying to get away from police and their chemical crowd control. The police not only followed them into the lobby but also injured many who were not protesters in their indiscriminate violence. McCarthy's headquarters on the fifteenth floor was turned into a makeshift infirmary. Before it was all over, rampaging officers would smash through the enormous plate-glass window where the hotel's bar looked out over Michigan Avenue.

After spending the afternoon going through her page proofs from *Mademoiselle*, Betty Friedan was composing four short additions about the events in Chicago to phone in right before the last deadline to go to press. She struggled to focus, knowing that her oldest, Daniel, a rising senior at Princeton University, was somewhere down on the street among the protesters, possibly injured or arrested, or both. (He was, in fact, hurt but not badly, she would later write.)

Out at the amphitheater, news of what was happening downtown trickled in, but did not disrupt the roll call or the platform speeches. The networks reported the violent events, but it was another hour before they had any footage to air. By this time, it was 8:00 p.m., and the mayhem was reaching its terrible violent crescendo. That mayhem wouldn't be shown until around 9:00, when the bloodiest images of the night were broadcast. Rising above the sounds of clubs, scuffling, and cries was the rhythmic chanting of demonstrators: "The whole world is watching. The whole world is watching."

In New York City to visit Valerie Solanas, Roxanne Dunbar watched the violence unfold in Chicago, on the television in Flo Kennedy's apartment. While she couldn't look away, it still "seemed removed from the world of the women's liberation movement. Not for a minute did it cross my mind that what was happening in Chicago might be more important than women's liberation or helping Valerie. I didn't deny that the Chicago phenomenon was important, but in my view, it contained the seeds of the movement's destruction because it reinforced male supremacy rather than questioning it."

Hillary Rodham also watched on television from her parents' house in Park Ridge, where she'd returned after the Republican convention. She was closer to the action, but not close enough. Rodham told her parents that she and her best friend from childhood were going to a movie. They drove instead to Chicago and Grant Park so they could witness the carnage for themselves.

"The allegedly beautiful people of the Democratic National Convention were playing with Hugh M. Hefner's waterfall button early this morning," described Charlotte Curtis in the opening lines of a story to the *New York Times* about how celebrities, conventioneers, and Democratic operatives had been partying nonstop at Hugh Hefner's *Playboy* mansion. "The party, which is five days older than the convention itself, began last Wednesday when the *Playboy* magazine publisher casually invited everyone who is anyone to drop by, and it has been going ever since." While the party was usually busiest between 11:00 p.m. and

3:00 a.m., "at 6:00 a.m. today guests were still hashing and rehashing politics and the brutality that has marked the police treatment of student demonstrators." Referring to 6:00 a.m. on Wednesday morning, this line carried new resonance in the aftermath of the convention's most brutal police violence in the "Battle of Michigan Avenue."

The Democratic Party was no stranger to *Playboy* and Hugh Hefner's support. Eugene McCarthy may not have had any "McCarthy Girls"—although he did have an army of freshly shorn "Clean for Gene" college-aged men volunteering—he did have Bunnies for McCarthy. In the heat of the California primaries in June, a Playboy Bunny–staffed fund-raiser had garnered significant publicity. Now they were part of the scene in Chicago.

Playboy Bunnies posing at a McCarthy fundraiser in Santa Monica, California, June 2, 1968

The convention was "a good show—a lot better than Miami Beach," said Broadway producer David Merrick, lounging in the mansion where Curtis found him in the wee hours. He compared Chicago to Vietnam: "Those checkpoints. The barricades. The soldiers. Everything at gunpoint."

Curtis painted a damning picture of a political party establishment failing to meet the moment, instead fiddling away at the Playboy Mansion while the city, country, and world burned. Her closing line was the last push of the dagger, "Guests sign somebody else's name now and then so there will be no record of them having ever been inside what in some quarters is still considered Mr. Hefner's Bunny Hutch."

The story was a smash, and would ultimately be the most popular piece from Curtis's coverage of both conventions. Steve Conn referenced it in his response to his friend and former boss's news that she'd been asked to judge the Miss America Pageant. "Are you a Bunny yet or does that come after the Miss America bit? Are you entered or merely a judge? Did Hugh Hefner get you the job or did [t]he *Times* medical department recommend it as rest and recuperation from Chicago?" Conn closed his letter, "Pick us a winner in Atlantic City, Charlotte. Better yet, enter yourself. Then write about it for *Esquire*."

While the Republicans had clearly staged and embraced their politics of beauty in Miami Beach, the Democratic Convention was a muddle. Traditional expectations for women's roles and representations in the party were giving way, but were far from gone. The quotidian sexism and demands on women's appearance, behavior, and maintenance of beauty standards were evident. Some things weren't changing.

Charlotte Curtis's last story of the convention focused on the nominees' wives and their joint press conference to highlight the many layers of disconnection at work in the Democratic Party. In her piece "Mrs. Humphrey Looks Back at Chicago," the Conrad Hilton Beverly Suite, where the press conference was taking place, was "still smelling of stink bombs." "It was a long, exciting week full of emotions and many events," said Mrs. Humphrey. "A very fulfilling week." Like everyone else she was upset about the violence—"I was saddened, of course. I wish it hadn't happened." But she believed it and the protesters were receiving too much attention in the press. They are "noisy and rude," not representative. The Humphreys have been talking to young people, and they knew the score: "Our youngsters [the Humphreys' children and their spouses] are all over talking with the young executives and young Jaycees." Finally, of Chicago, she was "proud things have come off as well as they did . . . things could have been a lot worse."

Mrs. Edmund Muskie said little throughout the press conference, but her comments said it all—and Curtis gave her the last word. Mrs. Muskie described her husband as unusually nervous about the VP spot. "He said, 'Mummy, I think we're stuck,' Mrs. Muskie said. And my answer was 'That's too bad.' I know it sounds strange, but that's what I said."

28

NAACP TO HOLD "BLACK PAGEANT"

AUGUST 28 – SEPTEMBER 1, 1968

In the week and a half since the first stories had appeared about a new Miss Black America Pageant slated to coincide with the Miss America finals, its profile and stated aims had changed considerably. This was due to the addition of organizing partner Phillip H. Savage, tri-state director of the NAACP and long-time Miss America contest critic. As exhausted delegates reconvened in Chicago to vote on the contested Vietnam plank of their party platform, Savage and J. Morris Anderson appeared before journalists in Philadelphia (where both men lived and worked) to announce the Miss Black America Pageant and debut their collaboration.

"We want to be in Atlantic City at the same time that the hypocritical Miss America contest is being held," Savage told reporters, adding that while the upcoming Miss America Pageant "will be lily white . . . ours will be Black."

Twelve young women would arrive in Atlantic City on Friday, September 6, for contest semifinals; after a midday boardwalk parade, the finals would be held late Saturday night, scheduled to start as the Miss America Pageant was ending. The Miss Black America Pageant had been established "to provide Black young ladies with an open and fair contest," in which they would "be judged by Black judges on the basis of beauty, talent, and charm," explained Savage as he covered the logistics. This was in sharp contrast to the Miss America Pageant, he continued, "which remains an all white affair, reinforcing a false and hypocritical sense of racial awareness in its viewers."

Much was new here. The contestants now hailed from a wider range of locations and regions of the country, including Georgia, Alabama, Mississippi, South Carolina, Pennsylvania, Illinois, and California. There would be more events across a two-day schedule that mirrored a truncated version of Pageant Week, including the parade and parties, and the winner would now receive a week-long, all-expenses-paid trip to Puerto Rico, a new wardrobe, and a trophy along with the crown.

Thanks to the AP and UPI reporters in attendance, next-day newspapers around the country, dominated by coverage of the previous night's events in Chicago, also reported the emergence of a Black challenger to the Miss America contest. To a one, the articles centered on Savage and the NAACP; most failed to mention Fashionable Productions at all, and none appeared to have named J. Morris Anderson. The purpose of the stories was to report directly or by association that the NAACP was sponsoring the Miss Black America Pageant as a protest against the racism of the Miss America organization, or as one New Jersey paper put it, "NAACP to Hold 'Black Pageant.'"

That Anderson and Savage knew one another and would see common cause in the Miss Black America Pageant were not surprising, even if the length and exact nature of their partnership were unclear. They lived and worked in the same networks of Black business and religious leaders, civic associations, civil rights organizations, and municipal agency partnerships in Philadelphia and surrounding areas. In his role as tri-state director, Phillip Savage had spent years working with Black communities and NAACP chapters all along the Jersey Shore, including in Atlantic City, where he had a history of denouncing the racism of the Miss America Pageant while using threats to its far-reaching impacts on the economy of the region to gain concessions for Black workers. National publicity for the Miss Black America Pageant challenge would make his profile and platform that much stronger and would raise the stakes of any challenge to Miss America Pageant operations in the future. And, as J. Morrison Anderson would have well understood, the involvement of the NAACP would bring greater publicity and lend authority and respectability to the new pageant.

Still, no one had seen this partnership coming—not the national leadership of the NAACP, not the activists in Atlantic City from the local chapter and the Afro-American Unity Movement, not the director of the Miss Sepia America Beauty Pageant, and certainly not the men who ran the Miss America Pageant.

Savage had worked for years with NAACP chapters in southern New Jersey, but his unexpected appearance with a Black beauty pageant, suddenly on the scene in Atlantic City and aimed in direct protest to the Miss America Pageant, threatened to swamp the complex activist ecosystem and Black economic interests that had developed around the pageant. This included not only the Afro-American Unity Movement's months-long work and NAACP protests but also the Black business and community leaders who had partnered with the Miss America Pageant in recent years to make gradual inroads into parade representation and advertising, not to mention Kentucky Avenue's Black-owned restaurants and nightclubs whose fortunes similarly rose with the influx of pageant people at the end of the summer season.

Perhaps no one was more furious, however, than Savage's and Anderson's fellow Philadelphian Robert Duke Morgan, who had owned and directed the Miss Sepia America Pageant for almost three decades. It was Morgan who had spent years working with Lenora Slaughter and the Miss America organization to build a pageant for Black women that would, he said later, lead eventually to integration. And it was to Morgan and his Miss Sepia America Pageant that Slaughter had long gestured in providing her rationale for beauty's ongoing racial segregation.

Now, speaking to a journalist from the *Philadelphia Inquirer*, Morgan lambasted the Miss Black America Pageant as a huge mistake that would "only make it harder to integrate" Miss America. It was no longer "right to have an all-black pageant," in 1968; "It's just another separation." He had "been trying to integrate the Miss America Pageant for twenty-five years, and although there was discrimination in the past," Morgan admitted, "I don't think it exists today." That no Black woman had ever appeared in the national pageant was not due to continued racism and systemic exclusion, he continued, echoing the arguments of Slaughter's successor, Al Marks. "I've been placing black girls in these contests, but they are not ready yet. They still have to be developed. If we could find a young black girl with beauty and talent, she would definitely have a fair chance in Atlantic City."

When asked for comment, J. Morris Anderson response was blunt. "Anytime a black man says that a black woman is not ready, he is speaking like an Uncle Tom," and Robert Duke Morgan's primary concern was holding on to the "support of the white power structure with whom he aligns himself." Black women were beautiful and were born ready, but they had no chance to truly compete because they were being judged by white supremacist beauty standards. To enter these contests, a Black woman had to "wear a wig or have her hair processed and put lotion on her skin to make it lighter. The black woman is beautiful for what she is."

Anderson never went so far as to describe the Miss Black America Pageant as a protest explicitly, however, but he left that to the suggestive timing and juxtaposition of the two pageants—or to be voiced by Phillip Savage. Why make this "an either-or," Anderson averred; the men were just "giving the black woman the chance to be judged by black judges and by black standards."

Since first learning of the NAACP's endorsement of the Miss Black America Pageant, Marilyn Parker had grown increasingly alarmed—so much so that she decided to write Gloster Current. The whole thing was just "so unbelievable," she told the national director of branches. After outlining her work with the Women's Auxiliary and her success in soliciting new members for the Pittsburgh Branch, Parker noted that her daughter had been the previous year's "Pittsburgh Youth Queen," and now she felt betrayed and angry. "I have always believed that the philosophy upon which NAACP was founded, grew and continues to stress, is that of total integration—one America. This pageant certainly would oppose that philosophy." She not only thought it antithetical to the mission of the organization that Parker and her family had given so much to but also worried that the contestants had been selected mysteriously, the winner would earn prizes but no scholarship, and that hastily produced, the pageant would prove a slapdash affair and an embarrassment in Atlantic City that would only fuel more discrimination.

While Anderson and Savage celebrated a platform for the demonstration of Black beauty, which they believed all Black women wanted and that they wanted for Black women, Parker found the entire "separatist, segregated program" to be misguided. "How can NAACP support a project so limited in scope as a beauty pageant when both sexes of our youth need our efforts to relieve their frustrations today?" Ultimately, Parker worried about what the women drawn to compete in the contest would actually represent, or how they would reflect upon the NAACP. "How many attractive, intelligent, talented Negro young women" would prioritize a beauty competition over other pressing concerns?

29

BRA BURNERS PLAN MISS AMERICA PROTEST

SEPTEMBER 1–3, 1968

"The Miss America action looks as if it might turn out to be a real mind blower if we get the least little bit of mass media coverage," wrote Kathie Amatniek in a letter to Ros Baxandall at the end of the long Labor Day weekend. By the same time on Saturday—just five days away—Amatniek and the others would be in Atlantic City, blowing minds.

Kathie and her boyfriend, Ted (who was back in New York and back in the picture), were supposed to have spent the holiday with Baxandall and her family out on Cape Cod, but a last-minute change to Amatniek's work schedule had thrown a wrench into those plans. She'd been wavering a little already, admittedly. "A very important planning meeting for the Miss America action [is] scheduled for today," so she'd decided she had "better stick it out in the city."

Amatniek felt like she needed to be at every planning meeting she could, so as to hold the feminist line on the protest. Carol Hanisch wouldn't return from Kentucky until the following day, Tuesday, September 3, and so she had missed all of them, and so few women from their core group had been around, including Baxandall. Still, things had gone better than Amatniek had hoped, she wrote. The women she saw as Judith Duffett's group—the politicos—had "carried almost the entire burden of work and planning." She added:

> Fortunately, they are a very good group. Though don't think they are as militant feminists as our group's core, they are militant enough to grove [*sic*] on destroying the beauty contest idea, though I had to constantly fight to keep the consumer line from taking over the entire action. Judith, fortunately, kept plugging for a strong woman's oppression theme and also a very good woman named Robin Morgan who wrote most of the enclosed press release (actually Judith's version of the original press release was better, more simple and straight forward. Robin's style runs a little too heavily toward the camp for my taste. Maybe her being a poet and married to an ex-homosexual has something to do with that).

It may not have been to her taste, but, as she wrote, the press release had already brought "free publicity in the *Village Voice*, the *Guardian*, the *New York Free Press* and WBAI" so far. "Anyway," she concluded, "I think it's going to be an HISTORIC action and I wish you could be there."

The publicity may have been free, but it was not all kind. The *Village Voice* had run a piece in its "Scenes" section the week before, making it one of the earliest public notices the protest got in New York City. The story opened with lines taken out of context from Anne Koedt's essay in *Notes from the First Year* about the myth of vaginal orgasms, before noting, "these angry young women are now planning a larger action than a magazine: they're gathering forces for a big demonstration at the Miss America Pageant, September 7." The story explained the aims of the protest with some lines taken from the press release itself, before closing with the comment: "They don't want any sympathetic male demonstrators and will refuse to talk to any male reporters, but they will gladly accept male money and male cars to get down to Atlantic City. Interested?" The article was laced with mockery, but it included contact information so (female) readers could join the action. Like the *Ramparts* story at the beginning of the year, the article's tone probably motivated more women's participation than it discouraged.

The first notice in a mainstream daily paper in the city appeared in Leonard Lyons's column for the *New York Post*, at the start of the Labor Day weekend. It was the last item in his regular punchy round-up of notable happenings in the

New York scene. "Rap Brown's lawyer and Robin Morgan, the poet and ex-child actress, are organizing a mass picketing in Atlantic City to end the Miss America pageant."

The *New York Post* wasn't through with the protest planners yet. During the Tuesday morning City Desk meeting after Labor Day, an editor tossed a copy of the press release at one of his new reporters, a woman in her early twenties, named Lindsy Van Gelder. "Why don't you see what you can do with this one."

He said it in a way that Van Gelder knew meant her editor wanted something funny. Like it was all a big joke. *Makes sense,* she thought, *anyone protesting Miss America had to be a kook.* The release had been sent with a cover letter from Robin Morgan that included her phone number and reiterated that only female reporters need make contact. Van Gelder recognized the name right away; she'd watched *I Remember Mama* as a kid. Soon, she was headed downtown to interview Morgan in her apartment above Kiehl's.

Lindsy Van Gelder was no stranger to the workplace inequities facing women. Shortly after graduating from Sarah Lawrence College in 1966, the newly married Van Gelder began looking for jobs in print journalism, where she ran into the same barriers confronted by Carol Hanisch, Charlotte Curtis, and so many others. Van Gelder eventually landed a job with the UPI, which she had just left for the *New York Post* earlier in the summer of 1968.

Now, she was sitting in Robin Morgan's absurdly large apartment, listening to a grown-up Dagmar explain women's liberation and the upcoming Miss America protest. Van Gelder had been turned off by the press release—*strident, rhetoric filled, and anti-intellectual,* she'd thought, just like other Yippie-inspired texts she'd come across. But the woman in front of her was far from being any of these things, much less a kook. *She's so much more interesting and intelligent than that press release,* Van Gelder decided, as she warmed up to what Morgan was saying. She could have been describing Van Gelder's life and the experiences of every woman she knew, and nothing about it was very funny.

Soon, Van Gelder was thinking, *Women's liberation? Sign me up!* She would worry about maintaining her journalistic objectivity later.

In person, Van Gelder found Morgan to be especially good at drawing connections between women's liberation and other political movements, which the journalist wanted to get across in her story. Morgan had talked about the lack of Black contestants and the Vietnam War, and how "Miss Americas were made mascots, and had to entertain the troops," all of which cast the radical women and their protest as so much more understandable and, Van Gelder believed, would help to "legitimize feminism" for her readers. More than this, she knew that like her friends, other women "of the same generation were going to respond emotionally" to women's liberation "now that it was out there." *They knew about NOW*, she thought, *but this was different.*

When Morgan mentioned NYRW's plans to dump and perhaps burn symbols of women's oppression in a "freedom trash can" on the Atlantic City boardwalk, Van Gelder knew she had the opening hook for a serious story about the politics of this new movement and their protest: "Lighting a match to a draft card or a flag has been a standing gambit of protest groups in recent years, but something new is due to go up in flames this Saturday. Would you believe a bra burning?"

Uptown and on the other side of Manhattan later that evening, an AP reporter attended a planning meeting of about forty women who ranged in age from thirteen to fifty-two. Peggy Dobbins, identified as twenty-nine and married, answered the woman's questions as the spokesperson for the meeting. Dobbins described the protest's organizers as an "informal" group that was part of a larger movement for women's liberation. When asked how many people they expected to show up in Atlantic City, she replied that it was impossible to know, but could be anywhere from a hundred to a thousand. While describing various plans for protest events, Dobbins said they were considering burning bras along with other symbols of women's oppression and confinement. This immediately piqued the reporter's interest, just as it had Van Gelder's, and her story's opening lines included a "'bra burning' as a possible attention-getter" on Saturday.

When Ros Baxandall penned a reply to Kathie Amatniek's letter, it was to say that, alas, she wouldn't be leaving Cape Cod until the 8th and so would have to miss the protest. Baxandall was sorely tempted to return earlier, but felt, she explained to Kathie, that being in Atlantic City would be wrong and a "cop out" on her part, since she hadn't done any of "the hard planning thinking sweating grueling work" for the protest. She wished she'd been a part of the organizing.

"God, I hope it goes well—are other groups joining? I'd love to see groups of spunky aged women joining—did anyone contact the welfare women[?]—most of them are black & militant & might go along, WSP, PFP, NOW—It's a good idea." She thought the *10 Points* leaflet was "okay—a bit cute & coy for my taste, women have to learn to be strong, tell it like it is, analytical hard rather than peppy & cute. Maybe I'm just convincing myself but I would have loved to work on the shaping planning."

Bra burning was all the news in Wednesday's papers, particularly if one scanned only the headlines. For Van Gelder's piece, the *New York Post* went with "Bra Burners Plan Miss America Protest." Of the many newspapers around the country that published some version of the AP story, several ran under titles like the *Corpus Christie Caller*'s "Bra Burning Considered as Protest" or the "Bra Bonfire" promised by the *Daily Reporter* in Wellsville, New York.

The *Ithaca Journal* ran the Miss America protest story as a sort of continuation of another syndicated piece from the AP, this one with a byline credited to Robert A. Dobkin, about what different Miss America contestants were looking for in a man. (Miss Colorado sought a mate who only wanted to be himself but still prioritized family; Miss Arkansas wanted an ambitious husband who "loved life"; and Miss Alabama, "a statuesque brunette who measures 37-24-37 on a 5-foot-6 frame," sought a devout man she described as one "'who really puts God first in all areas.'") To the left of both stories was a feature about a new luxury commuter bus line in Flint, Michigan, that periodically carried young, female "bus bunnies" to serve coffee and doughnuts to passengers headed to work; the accompanying photo showed a woman barely in her twenties standing in the aisle of a bus, surrounded by several older men in suits, all seated and grinning.

The UK's *Daily Mirror* ran the story the next day with the headline "Burn Your Bras for Freedom." The article was short and devoted almost entirely to flaming female undergarments. "Women are to strike a new blow for freedom—by burning their bras. Girdles, too, will go up in smoke in the big bon fire planned by forty American wives."

The Miss America Pageant finals and the protest were still four days away, but women's liberation had been branded as a bunch of "bra burners" before the women ever set foot in Atlantic City.

30

WALKING AND SMILING

AUGUST 30, 1968 – SEPTEMBER 4, 1968

The 1968 Labor Day Weekend in Atlantic City proved the power of the pageant's original alchemy to transform the summer season. The long weekend marked no ending but, rather, the start of the resort's most exciting, glamorous, and lucrative event of the year: Miss America Pageant Week. Tradition held that everything was kicked off whenever the first contestant arrived in town, and that she would carry special luck into the contest. Described by the local press as "tiny and tantalizing," deeply suntanned, and, at 5'3", the shortest of the fifty contenders for the crown, Miss New Mexico claimed the spot by arriving at noon on Friday, followed not long after by others, who were disappointed to lose the storied advantage of earliest arrival.

On Saturday morning, a discarded cigarette butt left smoldering beneath the creosote-treated boards of the city's boardwalk almost derailed everything. By the time a teenage boy saw smoke and sounded the alarm, at around 9:15, the fire was gaining strength and spreading. With flames reaching as high as fifty feet and with thick black smoke billowing along the beachfront, the blaze had consumed fourteen businesses and had come perilously close to the entertainments on one of the piers before firefighters could put it out. The city rallied a crew of men to repair the damage, who had the entire stretch of burned boardwalk patched in just hours. By that afternoon, holiday crowds were moving up and down the boardwalk unimpeded and thirty more contestants had arrived.

Debbie Barnes was in town, too, having returned to the United States from her USO tour just two days earlier, as the Democratic National Convention was coming to its violent conclusion amid news from Prague and foundering peace talks in Paris. In light of the circumstances, Barnes had not stopped first in Washington, D.C., to make an appearance at the White House, as her predecessor had the year before, but instead went straight to Atlantic City. A long week of public appearances stretched before Barnes: smiling, schmoozing pageant sponsors and civic elites, smiling, television rehearsals, press interviews, smiling, the nonstop fishbowl intensity of the countdown to no longer wearing the crown, and always, more smiling. Just behind her lay a sixteen-day tour in Japan and Korea that had often included two shows a day interspersed with visits to staff and wounded servicemen at military hospitals. Barnes had seen Mount Fuji and the Tokyo Tower from the air, through the window of a military transport helicopter. *It would be nice to come back to Japan so I could see Japan*, she'd thought.

Barnes and her fellow troupe members had seen the human devastation of war at every military hospital they'd been to. Betty Buckley returned to the United States shattered by all they had witnessed. She and Debbie Barnes were the oldest "girls" on the tour, at twenty-one (or almost twenty-one, in Barnes's case), Buckley explained later, "taken into all of the intensive-care units to meet these young soldiers. It was an eye-opening and sobering and life-forming experience for me." Buckley "didn't want to pursue anything" when she got back to the United States, "because I was depressed by what I had seen." Barnes did not have that option, and so she arrived in Atlantic City for the start of Pageant Week jetlagged and physically and emotionally exhausted.

Official pageant events began on Monday, with registration. As with every other event that would follow throughout the week, news reporters and photographers were there to capture each moment for the national outlets and hungry hometown papers. So, too, were the pageant's official photographers, some of whom would record behind-the-scenes images and major events for a set of slides that would be made available for purchase by pre-order. Other official Miss America–branded items filled the businesses along the boardwalk and popular food and entertainment outlets; one of the more popular items was a city guide produced annually that featured the current Miss America on the cover. Inside the guide were maps and other sorts of information deemed useful to tourists, including where most Protestants, Catholics, and Jews could find a place of worship, as well as several pages of advertising. A black-and-white image of Debra Dene

Barnes in crown, sash, and holding her scepter, all of which were highlighted in bright yellow, beamed from a vibrant orange cover all along the boardwalk.

Registration was the first time contestants, spectators, and the press got a look at all the year's contenders for the crown, gathered together in one location. Each young woman wore an outfit carefully selected for making the right impression; it had to be in the current fashion, seasonally appropriate but not casual, and absolutely no beachwear (the women would don their official coordinated swimsuits for group photos around the city and on the beach later that day). Most of the women had received a new Atlantic City–ready wardrobe as part of their state crown winnings, some by a sponsoring local retail outlet or designer. Intense public scrutiny and semi-official judging had begun the moment each woman set foot in town. At registration, each received her sash, as well as hotel and fellow-contestant roommate assignments; they also met the chaperones, and most vitally, got their group appointments (Alpha, Sigma, or Mu) and accompanying preliminary contest schedules. These events were ticketed, open to the public, and held on Wednesday, Thursday, and Friday nights. Known popularly as "the bible," this guidebook also contained the day-by-day, hour-by-hour schedule of rehearsals, interviews with judges, photo sessions, fittings, meals, and a list of all the rules the women were expected to live by for the week, at the risk of being excluded from the competition. These rules included no nightclubs, drinking, smoking, and no men.

Elizabeth Alton, who had compiled the rules for inclusion in "the bible" some years earlier, directed the chaperones and local hostess programs, and was the only woman with a seat on the pageant's board. She had been close to Lenora Slaughter, and like the rest of the leadership, was facing the first Pageant Week and finals without her. Unlike them, she was now doing so as the only woman with a formal position of authority—authority that was itself limited to responsibilities considered feminine. When registration was completed, the contestants and press gathered for introductions and an overview of the week's events and expectations, given by Alton and then Debbie Barnes. When Barnes took the podium and began to speak, she was visibly emotional; one UPI reporter would describe her voice as shaking as she told the gathered contestants, in his words, to "shape up or ship out." In Debbie's words, "If you don't like doing your hair every day, putting on makeup, meeting people, and traveling, you don't belong here."

• • •

On Tuesday, a hundred thousand visitors—about twice the regular population of the community—poured into Atlantic City for the annual parade along the boardwalk that afternoon. Some held pre-sale tickets for a two-tiered grandstand erected on one side and a long, continuous row of the city's historic "rolling chairs" turned VIP-seating on the other side, where the boardwalk met the sand; the vast majority of watchers would line the entire route of several blocks, standing as much as ten people deep in places where the parade began. The year's co-marshals for the parade were James Antell, the national president of the Jaycees who had also served as one of Lyndon Johnson's appointed poll watchers for the 1967 South Vietnamese elections, and none other than the "other Debbie"—Miss America 1966, Deborah Bryant, almost a month to the day after her appearance at the Republican Convention. It still seemed that wherever Miss America 1968 was appearing, so also was at least one of the Bryant women. For Pageant Week, it was both of them; Irene Bryant had gone straight from the USO tour to acting as Barnes's chaperone in Atlantic City.

The contestants spent much of Wednesday's first rehearsal for the Saturday night telecast in Convention Hall learning to walk the 120-foot runway that jutted into the orchestra seats from the middle of the stage. The women were run through their paces by the show's directors before an audience of pageant officials, journalists, and Bert Parks, who showed off his tanned legs in yellow shorts and was wearing a white polo, looking, remarked Barbara Carlson of the *Hartford Courant*, like "an All-American boy." As the contestants practiced their walks, waves, and smiles (for both live audience and TV cameras), someone handed Al Marks a copy of the *10 Points* press release and protest call. The boardwalk was buzzing about it by the time the preliminaries got underway that evening (Evening Gown for the Mu group, Talent for the Alphas, and Swimsuit for Sigmas). Al Marks was seen carrying a copy of the "manifesto," but "didn't seem especially disturbed by the protest threat," reported Carlson.

Charlotte Curtis had received a copy of the press release, too. It promised something more important to her than being a judge for the pageant: an important story. So, right before the preliminaries started, Curtis withdrew from the judges panel in order to report on the pageant and its protesters instead.

31

THEY SOUND LIKE US

SEPTEMBER 5–6, 1968

As bellmen at the Waldorf-Astoria moved through a usual busy Thursday in New York City, they could see women with protest signs and journalists gathered in front of the Colgate-Palmolive Building, directly across Park Avenue from the hotel's gilded main entrance. It wasn't the bellmen's first protest of the week, but this one wasn't their problem. On Sunday night, five hundred protesters had been on their side of the avenue to challenge Vice President Hubert Humphrey's official campaign launch at the hotel. Protesters and signs ("With Humphrey and Fascist Daley—Who Needs Enemies?") filled the sidewalk and spilled into the street, hemmed in by police and a large Secret Service detail. Voices chanting "What do we want?" were followed by responses of "Peace!," filling the air and rising above the usual din of Midtown traffic at night. To avoid confrontation, Humphrey had been taken in through a side door on East 50th Street.

Now, the Colgate-Palmolive protest that Betty Friedan had been promising for months, and that had gotten the NOW-NYC chapter kicked out of their regular meeting place at the Overseas Press Club, was kicking off. Thursday opened a series of demonstrations in New York and a national consumer boycott against the Colgate-Palmolive Company for its alleged discrimination against women workers while relying on the spending of predominantly female shoppers. Around twenty-five women marched along the sidewalk in an oblong circle with placards reading "Colgate Breaks the Law," "Ultra Bright Blights Women's Rights," "Down the Drain with AJAX," "The White Night is a Dirty Old Man," and "Cold Power Versus Woman Power!" (A court eventually ruled in favor of Colgate-Palmolive, dismissing the discrimination case.)

Several of the protest's organizers, including Flo Kennedy, Cindy Cisler, Kate Millet, and Anselma Dell'Olio, were affiliated with NYRW, as well as members of NOW. While Ti-Grace Atkinson was friends with many in NYRW and had attended at least one meeting, she never joined NYRW. Cindy Cisler, the former Yale architecture student who had attended the Sandy Spring meeting and who had been in the car when Carol Hanisch first declared they should protest the pageant, was also active in NOW. A week before the picketing started on Park Avenue, Cisler had penned a request to Atkinson for NOW's assistance, prepared in her distinctive architect's lettering that immediately announced her presence in a fellow feminist's mailbox (or her later archived papers). NYRW was looking for two things for the Miss America action, she told Atkinson: additional attorneys, besides Flo Kennedy, who could be on standby in New Jersey on September 7, and "Money: leaflets, posters, other visual stuff is really costing. Do you know people who (NOW or not) would like to go with us in $pirit? The people in our group seem to be quite poor, almost by definition, & you might know of a few names we could approach to help us make up our deficit. (I figure there may be N.O.W. people who may want to go, can't, but would like to participate vicariously!)" Cisler closed her letter by encouraging Atkinson to attend their final big planning meeting on Labor Day. Both women were at the start of the Colgate-Palmolive action on Thursday.

Cisler had a stack of flyers for the Miss America protest on Saturday that she handed out to passersby and NOW members on Park Avenue. One woman she handed a flyer to that day would miss the action in Atlantic City but join NYRW soon after. Recalling that day on Park Avenue, she'd later say, "All I remember was Cindy was having a ball, absolutely," and the image of Atkinson marching in pedal pushers and "looking like an Episcopalian."

Thursday's national news continued to feature stories on the impending Miss America protest, almost all of which included quotes from a new AP interview with Robin Morgan. "The protesters have no formal organization," she was quoted saying, but were part of a "growing women's underground—a women's liberation movement." When asked to describe those who would be protesting in Atlantic City, she responded that they are "pretty much in their 20s, a young, groovy bunch." Many papers printed the syndicated story alongside other pageant coverage, often in their "women's news" sections, like one daily in St. Joseph, Missouri, that flanked it with pictures of the previous night's winners of the Swimsuit and Talent preliminary.

Morgan's role as a spokesperson, and the woman most popularly associated with organizing the demonstration, grew with every interview and syndicated article that appeared in the weeks leading up to the protest. She served as the leader and representative women's liberationist in a story published, on the day before the pageant finals, in the *Wall Street Journal*. "They've protested napalm, marched against the draft and picketed the conventions," the story opened. "Tomorrow the forces of dissent will try to bring down the beauty monarchy." The article described Morgan as a "27-year-old poetess" and *the* "organizer of the protest." Morgan made no mention of bra burning, given the parameters of the protest's newly acquired permit, which had cited Saturday's fire and generally dry conditions as the reason nothing could be burned, along with proscriptions against loud amplification. As she had in her permit request to the mayor's office, Morgan assured that nothing like the recent events in Chicago would happen in Atlantic City at the activists' instigation.

"We don't plan heavy disruptive tactics," she told Pauline Tai, the author of the piece. "Many of us have been too wounded in Chicago. It's going to be a light-hearted demonstration. We neither invite nor provoke arrest, nor will we be intimidated. But we are prepared. We have lots of women lawyers."

By all indications, wrote Tai, the civic and commercial sponsors of the pageant appeared unconcerned about the protest, quoting the response from Mall Dodson, director of promotion and advertising for Atlantic City, "We're dying to see what these women look like." Dodson was given the last line of the Tai article with a question: "What kind of women would want to burn their bras?"

Despite Morgan's public assertions that there would be no "heavy disruptive tactics" on Saturday, the protest's "secret operations" team had readied plans to disrupt the telecast itself, which would dramatically extend the reach of their demonstration. Knowledge of the plan was kept to a small core of NYRW members, never shared widely. Executing the plot meant purchasing tickets to get inside Convention Hall, which presented a significant cost to the women Cindy Cisler had described as "quite poor." When the issue came up during a planning session as a potentially insurmountable hurdle, Alix Kates Shulman decided on the spot that she would take care of it. "I'll buy the tickets," she said, and then wrote out a check for $70 for a block of seats in the balcony from the joint account she shared with her husband. The amount was significant—equivalent to about $635 in 2025 dollars*—but Shulman didn't consult him first, nor did she have plans to tell him after the fact. He made most of the family income, she explained in an interview later, adding that her freelancer's earnings "barely paid the babysitter." So, the act was "such a moment for me," to which the interviewer, a fellow former women's liberation activist, quipped, "Revolutionary," and chuckled. "It was," responded Shulman.

The first women's liberation meeting Shulman attended had been in Robin Morgan's apartment. A friend had heard about the group on WBAI and had called her: "They're having a meeting, they sound like us. Let's go." They arrived to find themselves the oldest women in the room and the only ones with school-aged kids. Everyone was delighted with their presence, thrilled to have attracted to a meeting two strangers who were "housewives." "We were older than the others . . . and we had children, so we were this wonderful thing, you know. The genuine article."

Peggy Dobbins had also been at the first meeting Shulman attended. Now, they were planning a disruption of the Miss America Pageant telecast together and making final preparations. Dobbins's husband had knowingly contributed to the protest by constructing the large pieces for an enormous Miss America puppet—originally conceived as a maypole—that would be at the center of the satirical political theater planned for the boardwalk demonstration.

It had been four weeks of furious planning, organizing, and promoting the Miss America protest, and now the day was finally upon them. Tomorrow the women would liberate Atlantic City.

* To put this number into perspective, the average salary for a new teacher in the New York City public schools in 1967 was $5,400 per year, equivalent to about $36,803 in 2025.

32

WHY WE'RE HERE

SEPTEMBER 6, 1968

The Miss Black America Pageant was the first protest to get underway in Atlantic City, when J. Morris Anderson and Phillip Savage announced to the gathered press that they were not in town to stage a protest. The Friday afternoon press conference was held at the Ritz-Carlton Hotel, where Roy Wilkins had stood beside the local chapter president and decried the Miss America Pageant's racism in June, and where the Miss Black America Pageant would begin with its semifinal contest that night, scheduled to start after the last of the Miss America semifinals. For the Miss Black America contestants, the preliminary marked the start of their events, to be followed on Saturday afternoon by a boardwalk parade and a beach party that was also ticketed for guests. Anderson and Savage had squeezed a truncated version of Pageant Week into less than thirty-six hours.

Anderson took the lead at the press conference, making a statement that put more distance between his contest and the Miss America Pageant. He claimed it wasn't about protesting an individual pageant but, rather, about challenging "a particular standard of beauty—the white standard of beauty." He went on to say, "We don't condemn the white man for saying white is beautiful, but we are saying Black is beautiful." Phillip Savage's remarks on the matter resonated more with statements made by local and national NAACP leaders. "We want it clearly understood," he said, "that this is simply an expression of Black beauty, and is held at the same time as the Miss America Pageant only by coincidence.

And that is the truth." He added that the Miss America Pageant had "moved ahead aggressively" in seeking to remedy the problem, and had "come a long way since original charges of discrimination two years ago." Gloster Current, to whom Savage reported, had shared the surprise and outrage expressed by Marilyn Parker in her letter, when he learned from the press along with the rest of the national leadership about the NAACP's presumed connection to the pageant. It was too late to counter that perception, so Current had demanded a change in the framing.

"This is a pageant city," declared Anderson, "and there's no reason [Miss Black America] shouldn't be held here. We just want to show what is beautiful in Black America here. We didn't come down here angry or to prove a point." Of the late start times for the preliminaries and finals that ensured no overlap with the Miss America events and allow the press to be at both, Anderson introduced an alternative explanation. That night's preliminaries and Saturday's finals were scheduled for midnight, he said, to accommodate the work schedules of their audience. "This is basically a beauty pageant for Black people. Black people are basically working people, and it is easier for them to get there at that time." The *Hartford Courant*'s Barbara Carlson followed Anderson's remark in her own story by noting that the Miss Black America Pageant was "not a bourgeois thing where people can take a week for a pageant."

After the press conference, Anderson sat down in the hotel's coffee shop with *Atlantic City Press* reporter John Katz to share more about why he was staging the pageant. "Pride is the basic thing," he said. "Somebody has to take the first step—make the first investment. . . . Somebody has to stand up and say, 'I am proud, I am beautiful.'" And that somebody was Anderson and the women he'd brought to Atlantic City. "That's why we're here. Not to protest or compete with the Miss America Pageant, but to make black women feel that they, too, are beautiful." Like the women Charlotte Curtis had interviewed the week before in Chicago, Anderson was promoting a definition of Black Power that was about economic power and pride, which was another layer in his argument that Miss Black America was less a protest and more about Black enterprise.

Anderson continued, "Why should I cry or riot because you have a nice business, and I don't? I should start my own business, and that's just the type of thinking we're trying to bring about here. We don't need to stop the Miss

America Pageant to have one of our own, just like I don't need to burn your business down to start one of my own."

Anderson wove a subtle argument for law-and-order through economic development as an explanation for starting the pageant that was not dissimilar from Nixon's promotion of Black capitalism or the positions of Republicans like Wilt Chamberlain. Beyond easy partisan definitions, similar arguments ran through the Philadelphia summer programs for Black youth that were part of Miss Black America's foundations. This included Phillip Savage's involvement. Just the previous summer he had urged the NAACP to adopt a plan for "riot prevention" that he called "TOPS: Teenagers' Organization for a Productive Summer." Where Dr. King had famously argued in 1966 that "a riot is the language of the unheard" by a system that oppresses them, Savage's program put the onus largely at the feet of kids on the corner who had nothing to do. What was important about the pageant, Anderson told John Katz, was that it meant "a black woman could look in the mirror and say, I, too, am beautiful. Then she'll feel like a person. Once you feel like a person, you start acting like a person." This included ultimately (and perhaps primarily) the personhood, pride, and actions of Black men. The pageant meant that "the male black can be proud of his woman," Anderson explained, for how could he "be proud of her if she feels inferior because she's ignored?"

While the *Atlantic City Press*'s photographer got a shot of Anderson with three contestants as they signed in on Friday afternoon, none of the women were featured or quoted in any of the paper's several stories. At least one reporter for another news outlet was discouraged by the pageant's director and choreographer when he sought to interview contestants during rehearsal, which he implied was a nefarious move to keep him from learning how the women were chosen to compete, but could have been about the tight schedule and not allowing interruption of the rehearsal itself. In any case, the absence of contestants' voices in the coverage of the Miss Black America Pageant leading up to its start is notable (and frustrating). Anderson's, and to a lesser degree Savage's, versions of the contest's meanings—of the meanings of Black women's beauty itself—dominated. Once the preliminaries got underway Friday night, however, it would become clear that the women competing for the crown did not necessarily share the men's perspectives.

• • •

While Anderson and Savage were speaking to the press in Atlantic City, one of their contestants was still at home in Washington, D.C., trying to decide if she was going to participate at all. Theresa Claytor, a twenty-year-old model and dancer, and Washington's current Miss NAACP, would be headed to the Pratt Institute, in New York City, to study fashion design in a few weeks. She had already rejected a modeling agent's suggestion that she try for the Miss America Pageant that year. "I didn't have the time or the money," she explained, "and I didn't think I had a chance because I'm Black."

Claytor was, in fact, there when the semifinal contest started at midnight in the auditorium of the Ritz-Carlton Hotel. She'd made her decision to go at about 5:00 p.m., explaining that she knew that "the beginning of the Miss Black America Beauty Pageant [would] make history," and "bring out the love of one Black man for another and in time it [would] bring out the love of one man for another, of whatever color."

Nine other women joined Claytor on the red-carpeted stage to compete in the categories of Evening Gown, Swimsuit, Talent, and Extemporaneous Speech (sometimes referenced by reporters as "Projection" or "Intelligence"). They did so in front of an audience of seventy-five and a panel of seven judges. A pair of local television personalities served as co-hosts, providing introductions and entertaining commentary from a substantial podium at the front of the stage, near the start of a forty-foot runway reaching out into the audience. Like Anderson and Savage, they hailed from Philadelphia, as did most of the judges. Among the panel's members were the city's deputy mayor, Charles W. Bowser, and the coordinator of Project Human Renewal and the Department of Recreation youth programs, Ulysses Young, as well as fashion model Mae Madrid and representatives from local businesses and education.

Saundra Williams won the Talent portion with her spoken word about a young girl becoming aware of her own distinctive Black beauty and thus rejecting the dominant white standard that had diminished her. This was the path to pride. It was a different version of beauty's power to lift the self than Anderson's celebration of beautiful Black women as universal symbols of pride. Williams emerged as a clear front-runner going into the finals on Saturday night.

Of the women not chosen to continue on, one had to wonder if in Ernestine

Banks's case, the Extemporaneous Speech portion had something to do with it. When asked, "How would you react if a riot suddenly broke out in your neighborhood?," the nineteen-year-old Philadelphian responded, "There would have to be a cause. If it did—beautiful." Along with the slate of Philadelphia judges, Phillip Savage must have cringed.

33

COME LIBERATE ATLANTIC CITY

SEPTEMBER 7, 1968

Was she really already a has-been at twenty-one?

That's exactly how Debbie Barnes had described herself a few days earlier. An Associated Press reporter doing a story on the last days of her reign as Miss America 1968 had asked her about what came next. He'd wondered, as he put it in his article later, about the shape of her life after "spending a year as a real-life Cinderella." She'd replied, "I'm a has-been at twenty-one, but I don't have any regrets."

She'd been joking, of course, demonstrating the self-deprecating humor she'd honed throughout a year of making appearances around the country and internationally, a year of smiling, waving, shaking hands, and talking to reporters. Debbie had a natural talent for getting along with people, and as most women then and now know, there's no better weapon in the beautiful woman's arsenal—and no stronger armor—than the ability to laugh at oneself.

But there was some niggling truth to that label "has-been."

Alone in the rare quiet of the morning, Barnes knew that before the day was over, she'd be crowning her successor in front of a packed hall and a television audience of millions. Like everyone else, she would watch as a new Miss America gave her first wave while the beloved host, Bert Parks, crooned, "There

She Is. . . ." In that moment, Debbie Barnes would become a member of the small sorority of former Miss Americas. The camera lenses and flashbulbs of the past year would now be aimed elsewhere. She'd have to chart a course for what came after the crown, a path through "there she *was*."

It would include the new diamond ring on her left hand.

Her boyfriend, Mitch, had surprised Barnes the day before, coming to the door of her hotel room and asking if she could spare a little time between appointments. Then, as her chaperone, Irene Bryant, looked on, he proposed. Mitch and Debbie were both music majors at Kansas State Teachers College, in Pittsburg, not far from the small towns where they'd grown up. They had been dating for six months when she became Miss America, but she hadn't been allowed to speak about Mitch publicly. Officially, Miss America doesn't have a boyfriend. Her response to that same AP reporter's question about whether she might get married soon had been "No comment." But with only five days left before she crowned her successor at that point, she had added that "someone special" was waiting for her back at school. Barnes thought Mitch might be the one, but she hadn't expected a proposal on her birthday in Atlantic City.

It had been a wonderful present, and the party that night, which was originally planned for her twenty-first birthday, had become a celebration of their engagement as well. Barnes had really wanted to share the news only with her friends, but word spread quickly along Pageant Week's boardwalk grapevine. They'd ended the evening by making an official announcement and doing press interviews. When a reporter asked if Mitch had minded the pageant chaperone's presence in the couple's special moment, Barnes replied, "He's used to it by now."

Used to it, perhaps, but neither of them would miss the constant scrutiny that came with her celebrity. It would be nice to go back to being just Debbie Barnes—Debbie Miles in a few months—rather than Miss America 1968, Debra Dene Barnes. She would regain some of the anonymity she had lost in Atlantic City exactly one year before. She looked forward to it.

As Robin Morgan made her way to the north side of Union Square, in New York—the designated meeting spot for those riding "down the shore" together—she hoped she would find many women waiting. Optimistically,

Morgan had reserved two buses, and she hoped enough women would show up to fill at least one of them.

When she arrived at Union Square, Morgan found what seemed like a hundred women milling around East 18th Street. Flooded with relief and joy, she snapped into organizer mode. Morgan had to find a phone booth. They were going to need another bus.

Later, Morgan would recall the day in sensory terms, trying to capture the enormity of the experience and the way it had touched everything and made even the awful, exhausting parts good. There was "the acid taste of coffee from paper containers and of cigarettes from crumpled packs" in her mouth. "My eyes were bloodshot," she remembered, "and my glasses kept slipping down my nose, my feet hurt, and my neck ached, and my voice had gone hoarse—and I was deliriously happy."

Among the waiting women was Flo Kennedy, wearing dark sunglasses and an outfit entirely of white: ankle-length pants over mod boots, topped with a light jacket over a high-necked shirt, both white, and a white short-billed hat resembling a Greek fisherman's cap. The ensemble made her long colorful necklaces—one with a large women's symbol pendant and the other with a round medallion—really pop. Bev Grant moved through the crowd, camera always at the ready, capturing the event and moods of the moment, as she would throughout the day. Charlotte Curtis was there, too, in but not of the crowd, in a summer-weight black sheath dress and pearls, hair carefully coiffed to start a long day of interviews and observation, and to soak in the scene on the bus trip down to Atlantic City.

Some of the women who had been involved in the planning would not be able to attend the protest itself ("I had to work that day," explained one). Anne Forer walked to Union Square with several women getting on the bus, but decided not to go on with them to the demonstration. It was a decision she would regret, responding to an interviewer's question many years later: "Well, that's not such a happy story. You know I was terrible at cleaning my house, and I always thought I should clean my house, and for some reason I walked them all . . . to get onto the buses to go to Miss America and I said, 'but I'm going to go home and clean my house.' Of course, I did not go home and clean my house, I didn't clean my house for ten years. But I made a bad choice, I didn't go to Miss America, no. I walked them all to the buses."

Others were traveling separately. A group of husbands, including Morgan's, drove down together because no men were allowed on the buses (an exception was made for the drivers). Alix Kates Shulman's husband, Martin, drove her and a few more down, still unaware he'd helped pay for a block of tickets to the pageant finals that night. They went by Union Square on their way out of the city to pick up a group that included an eighteen-year-old man that Shulman later described as a friend who "was passing through and he got this opportunity to see the revolution."

In the end, about sixty-five women rode down on the buses. As they pulled away from Union Square and drove through the Holland Tunnel to New Jersey, the protesters talked excitedly across the two-person banquette seats, anticipation and nervous energy fizzing through the thickening summer heat of late morning. As she had for the Jeanette Rankin Brigade protest in January, Bev Grant had composed several songs to popular tunes for the Miss America demonstration. Lyric sheets printed on blue paper were passed among the travelers, and everyone sang the songs that harkened to the years of the first Miss America bathing beauty contests and would become part of the day's soundtrack of resistance.

It was the sound of Tin Pan Alley and "Down by the Riverside," an African American spiritual popular among activists protesting the Vietnam War. Grant's new lyrics of the latter included asking their "sisters" to join the protest, and "Don't be no Miss America no more." To the tune of "Ain't She Sweet?," they sang, "Ain't she cute? Walking in her bathing suit" to sell beauty products. This was rounded out with a version of Irving Berlin's "A Pretty Girl Is Like a Melody," made popular as the theme to the Ziegfeld Follies, that focused on judging the girl "by looks alone"—looks that were augmented by makeup created from chemicals originally developed for military purposes.

If DC Women's Liberation accepted NYRW's invitation to join the Miss America protest, argued one member, "You know what will happen." They would show up in Atlantic City, and "then they'll attack us." It would just be Sandy Spring all over again.

As they passed the *10 Points* press release around the meeting, the emerging consensus on whether to join NYRW at the Miss America protest appeared to be against it. That was, until Donna Allen intervened. The fight was precisely the reason they *had to go* to Atlantic City, she insisted.

"You know it's coming so you can just face it. You've got to go and find out that attack is not the end of the world. Of course they're going to attack, that's why you're doing this because you're against it." Allen's own daughter, Dana Densmore, had "attacked" the women from D.C. in Sandy Spring, too. The substance of the argument wasn't the point for Allen; it was the idea that the Washington, D.C., group would let the fear of a conflict stop them from acting that she couldn't abide. (Allen wasn't a member of the D.C. group, but often worked with them; had she not been at the meeting, things probably would have gone differently.)

As it was, on Saturday morning, a car full of women from Washington, D.C., headed up to Atlantic City. As one of them explained it, they thought of their group as "more Left and a little less strident" than New York's, and they "wanted to present a little more Leftist analysis of what the Miss America thing was about." So, taking the *10 Points* press release as a foundation, they made their own flyer.

The D.C. women's flyer was more visually arresting and succinct than Morgan's text-heavy, more narrative *10 Points*. The press release had been boiled down to eight points framed by chant-like exclamations that were printed in decorative fonts of various sizes: "SLAVERY EXISTS! MISS AMERICA IS A SLAVE TO: . . ." The theme of women's enslavement—by beauty, capitalism, militarism, and patriarchy—was echoed below the newly worded list in statements likening the pageant to an auction: "Keep Women Off the Block!" "Boycott the Pageant!" That the women so objectified were white was made clear by a border formed with a repeating clip-art image of a pair of buxom white women with shoulder-length hair in a 1940s style, wearing what could be the bustiers of sleeveless evening gowns or swimsuits. The cookie-cutter uniformity of the repeating image was amplified by the fact that the two women already appeared almost identical.

It was a good flyer, advancing a specious message. The fight against slavery and structural racism had brought generations of white women to greater understandings of their own oppression. What it hadn't brought them was meaningful understandings of the specific oppressions experienced by women of color

SLAVERY EXISTS!

MISS AMERICA IS A SLAVE TO:

THE IMAGE OF SEX	The best specimen gets the blue ribbon. She is an object not a person.
A VIRGINAL PRETTINESS	To win approval she must be both sexy and wholesome.
THE GLORY OF WAR	The highlight of her reign each year is a cheerleader for American troops abroad.
A MINDLESS CONFORMITY	Miss America represents what women are supposed to be: unoffensive, bland, apolitical.
ACCEPTANCE OF RACISM!	There has never been a Black, Puerto Rican, Alaskan, Hawaiian or Mexican-American winner. Nor has there ever been a true Miss America -- an American Indian.
THE CULT OF YOUTH	Women must be young, juicy, malleable—thus age discrimination.
THE COMPETITIVE SPIRIT	She perpetuates the American myth of having to get ahead in order to have any worth.
THE CAPITALISTIC SYSTEM	She is a walking commercial, wind her up and she plugs your product on promotion tours and TV.

Keep Women Off The Block!

Boycott the Pageant!

Washington Women's Liberation / Further information, call: 483-1647 or 667-8305

Washington (D.C.) Women's Liberation flyer
for Miss America Pageant protest, 1968

that were unlike their own—and that, more often than not, white women had a significant hand in. The "SLAVERY EXISTS!" flyer marshaled the analogy to race that Western feminism had relied upon since at least Wollstonecraft to make (white) women's oppression recognizable as a condition forced upon them, rather than an expression of their natures, all the while challenging the racism of the Miss America Pageant as it pushed Black women and other women of color out of the frame.

From Gainesville, Florida, Carol Giardina was the first demonstrator at the boardwalk protest site. Dressed in a short brown miniskirt and toting signs, she was obvious to the journalists milling around and the police already in place. In addition to the rule that no one should speak to a male journalist, Giardina understood that only designated spokespeople should engage with the press, and she was not a designated spokesperson. Of course, that didn't stop reporters from approaching her—descending on her, it felt like. As Giardina attempted to fend off questions, her agitation rose—and that's when she heard it.

"This huge clopping" sound, as if hundreds were marching toward her, their feet like thunder. It was the crowd from the buses, walking up from where they had parked. "I looked down the boardwalk, and here they come with their signs, and they were chanting," she said. "It really was quite a feeling." Giardina was not alone.

34

CAN MAKEUP COVER THE WOUNDS OF OUR OPPRESSION?

SEPTEMBER 7, 1968

The city had cordoned off a large area of the John F. Kennedy Plaza that fronted Convention Hall with police barricades, blocking the protesters from the hall's entrances. A long colonnaded path to the beach bordered the other side of the boardwalk and served as a place to congregate in the shade; Saturday was a scorcher.

Kathie Amatniek took in the scene around her. Protesters continued to arrive from New York and elsewhere, while women made more signs, prepared the Freedom Trash Can, and got other props and costumes together for their guerilla theater piece featuring the large Miss America puppet. Carol Hanisch was busy wrangling a sheep they had rented from a nearby farm to crown as the demonstration's Miss America, in another bit of political theater that echoed the Yippie's Pigasus from Chicago. (The job fell mostly to Hanisch as the only woman there with a background in agriculture.) But when Amatniek spotted a woman sitting in the shade of the colonnade, lettering a large sign that read, "There's No Good Man but a Dead Man," she felt a pang of horrified disbelief.

Amatniek grabbed some of the women around her, and they rushed over to where the woman was sitting on the boardwalk. Surrounding her, Kathie prayed that the press photographers hadn't already gotten a shot of the offending sign. She explained to the woman that the protest could not feature a sign like that—that it was pointlessly antagonistic and might alienate women they hoped to bring to the cause. Neither Amatniek nor Hanisch had been persuaded by Roxanne Dunbar's and Dana Densmore's promotion of Valerie Solanas at Sandy Spring; also, the sign's sentiment surely contradicted the connections the demonstration was making elsewhere about Miss America's role in promoting the war in Southeast Asia and the needless deaths of thousands of men there.

That sign did not make it to the picket line. As a growing crowd of spectators pressed against the police barricades, a long line of women marched toward the center of the cordoned-off area to begin picketing in a long oval. Their slogans included: "Miss America, Mayor Daley loves you," "Women Are Enslaved by Beauty Standards," "No More Miss America," "Women's Liberation," "Miss America Is a Big Falsie," "Women Not Things," "Women Are People, Not Livestock," "ALL Women Are Beautiful," "Can Makeup Cover the Wounds of Our Oppression?"

The oldest protester there, sixty-eight-year-old Clara DeMiha, held a sign that read, "Girls Crowned, Boys Killed." A proud Jeanette Rankin Brigade member, she also carried a large shopping tote printed with "Mothers Say: Stop the War in Vietnam, Women Strike for Peace." Asked about her sign and her reasons for being at the protest by a reporter from WNYC radio, DiMiha replied, "Okay, darling, first of all . . . I told the girls to make this sign [because] I feel that in the midst of crowning the girls they're killing their own boys, the boys that would be their future husbands or future sweethearts." She went on to explain that the pageant was designed to sell people things "to distract their attention from the real issues of this country and of the world," and that she was on the boardwalk participating in the women's liberation action "to point out that the older people or the middle-aged people must be along with the young people if they want to avoid the gap of generations . . . if you want to be with the young people you've got to help them in their struggle."

The activists sang Bev Grant's songs and chanted as they marched. "Atlantic City is a town with class. They raise your morals while they judge your ass!" Other women moved along the barricades, handing out flyers and attempting to

Left: Policeman viewing Alix Kates Shulman, holding "All Women Are Beautiful" poster at the Miss America protest

Right: Carol Giardina (left) holding "Can Make-Up Cover the Wounds of Our Oppression?" sign in the Miss America protest

engage willing spectators. When the women from Washington, D.C., began to pass around their own flyers, they got a version of the conflict they'd expected. Robin Morgan told them to stop handing them out, arguing that they would muddle the message, and that the NYRW flyer was to be the only one. When Charlotte Bunch recalled the argument later, she explained, "I think we probably said, 'Oh, what the fuck. It's not that big of a deal, we'll put our fliers back. We're here for the demonstration, let's not spend the whole time fighting over our fliers.'"

If any of the protesters took special notice of the Miss Black America Pageant motorcade when it drove by near the start of the picketing, they didn't share their reactions. If they had been following news of the pageant after it was announced, it wasn't reflected in their last days of organizing. Charlotte Curtis asked one of the few Black women among the women's liberation demonstrators, Bonnie Allen, about it, but reported her response as largely one of confusion at the contradictions: "I'm for beauty contests, but then again, maybe I'm against them. I think Black people have a right to protest." She also posed the question to Robin Morgan, who said, "Basically we're against all beauty contests. We deplore Miss Black America as much as Miss White America, but we understand the black issue involved." Curtis reported that the Miss Black America contestants were "cheered everywhere" their parade went, in contrast to reactions received by the women's liberationists. "The predominantly white strollers along the boardwalk waved and applauded," she wrote, "but nowhere was the reception more enthusiastic than along the main streets within the Negro community."

White spectators cheered easily for the Miss Black America Pageant contestants in the same way they had celebrated the Black women who appeared on floats in Tuesday night's Miss America Parade. While some were no doubt sincere in their desire to applaud the inclusion of Black women where they could find it, others saw no challenge to the pageant's exclusions in the parades. These women could be folded into Miss America's longstanding commitment to keeping beauty segregated where the pageant was concerned.

This would be the closest the two protests came to one another in person—parallel actions passing each other by. That was a trait reiterated in the behind-the-scenes organization of the women's liberation demonstration, too. Nearly twelve hours of protesting stretched before the women's liberationists. In addition to having all-female medical and legal teams on standby, Flo Kennedy had made arrangements with a local family to use their house as a place to rest, meet with press, and get dinner in shifts, outlined in a Demonstration Information Sheet distributed to participants. "We have an Atlantic City headquarters, in the Black community," on North New Hampshire Avenue, it read, to "be used for press conferences, parking of private cars, and film showings, and there will be room available for people to rest and change clothes. A telephone will be womaned at all times. Starting around 4 p.m., demonstrators can go there in shifts for a soul food dinner." The result was a complicated picture. Black residents of Atlantic City were providing shelter and sustenance to the protesters, almost all of whom were white, but did not appear to join them on the boardwalk as comrades in arms.

Spectators along the boardwalk. The Black spectator wears a "Black is Beautiful" button and holds a Miss Black America pageant flyer.

Bev Grant took several pictures of the women, men, girls, and boys who watched and often jeered the women's liberation protesters on the boardwalk. While she did not photograph the Miss Black America motorcade, she did capture the intersections of the two protests in the crowd. The photo depicts three teenage boys, laughing and heckling. One boy squeezes beyond his friend's shoulder to push an arm across the police barricade, with a thumbs-down for the protesters. The biggest boy, muscled to the front of the crowd, seems caught in the act of speaking or yelling, his football jersey stained from what looks like melted ice cream or greasy fingers. All three look as if they've been on the boardwalk for a while. Next to them, striking in his sunglasses, madras shirt, and three-button sport coat, a Black man leans forward to watch the demonstration, seeming intent on ignoring the boys. Even more striking is the prominent "Black is Beautiful" pin on his jacket and the carefully rolled-up Miss Black America flyer in his left hand.

• • •

As the protest hit its stride, the women laughed and sang and chanted, and tried to ignore the hecklers, which proved increasingly difficult as the crowd at the barricades grew in size—and grew rowdier. One demonstrator described the crude remarks hurled by men in the crowd at the protesting women whom they deemed attractive, while those they found ugly were told so just as loudly. "The men acted as if we were conducting a beauty contest," she said. "I'd never felt such humiliation. The experience was worth a hundred consciousness-raising sessions."

At times, it appeared that no one in Atlantic City wanted to hear what the women's liberationists had to say—most times, perhaps. But there were also points of connection: speaking with a woman who seemed to get it, watching a man thoughtfully read the flyer he'd just been handed, or catching on film, as Bev Grant did, the moment when a policeman leaned over to scratch the head and ears of the sheep before sharing a smile with the woman holding its leash.

While some behind the police barriers yelled out to the protesters and to one another, others spoke to journalists. Like a man from Philadelphia, who complained to Charlotte Curtis that the women's liberationists were "vulgar." He pointed to a sign reading "Miss America Sells It" and another, "Up Against the Wall, Miss America," and said, "They're protesting the pageant and yet they have signs like that."

WNYC radio's Eleanor Fischer talked to a different clutch of people. It was unclear if they'd known one another before they came to watch. "They just have to have something to cry about," said one man, before another chimed in, angrily, "They're just a disgrace for Americans. I'm on total disability from the Service and to see something like this is a disgrace to me."

Other voices from the crowd floated into the interview. A woman said, "I don't know, I'm shocked." A man laughed, and added simply, "Miss America is beautiful," to which another added, "They're all smart girls, too. Most of them are. They're not all looks like a dumb broad like Marilyn Monroe or Raquel Welch or somebody. They're talented and intelligent. And they're good looking."

Someone agreed, "They're nice looking!"

Had Lenora Slaughter been present for this exchange, she would have been pleased. Her vision for the pageant as a demonstration of what ideal American beauty entailed—not sex appeal or mere attractiveness—had become the view of the average man on the boardwalk. And it was this man to whom the women's liberation protesters now turned.

"Yessiree, boys, step right up! How much am I offered for this number one piece of prime American property?"

The picketers left the plaza and were replaced by Peggy Dobbins wearing an oversized three-piece suit and men's dress shoes, her long hair pulled back into a ponytail and tucked into a bowler hat. It was her stockbroker-auctioneer's costume. "She sings in the kitchen, hums at the typewriter, and purrs in bed. She walks, she talks, she even weds."

Behind Dobbins loomed the Miss America puppet, several heads taller than most of the demonstrators and wearing a stars-and-stripes swimsuit that barely covered her prominent breasts. These breasts were made of large, perfect circles of wood and were attached to a tiny-waisted torso with curvaceous hips. Above the breasts, the puppet wore a permanent red-lipsticked smile and bouffant; on her feet, a pair of high heels.

"And thanks to the research of Toni and Revlon, you can get this standard quality model wherever you go. The perfect model. She doesn't talk back. In fact, she doesn't talk at all unless you want her to! And then she only says what you programmed her to say." Four women, including Bonnie Allen, Florika Remetier, and Flo Kennedy, were chained to the puppet and made slow swooping motions, turning in circles around her, while Dobbins played the auctioneer.

"Yessiree," Dobbins cried, "you can use her to push your product, push your politics, or push your war. She's the girl back home every man is fighting for!"

Morgan may have rejected the flyers brought by DC Women's Liberation, but the boardwalk remained drenched in metaphors of slavery, from slogans on signs, chants, and song lyrics to this parody of a slave auction. That two of the only Black women in the protest constituted half the group chained to Miss America made these connections all the more stark.

They named the sheep their new Miss America. Festooned with a prize blue ribbon and a Miss America sash, it was paraded around the boardwalk. *There she is, Miss America.*

Later, Robin Morgan helped another woman carry the Freedom Trash Can to the center of the plaza, and protesters gathered around with their symbolic "instruments of women's torture" to throw away. Girdles, eyelash curlers, hair-spray, makeup, and *Playboy*, *Good Housekeeping*, and *Cosmopolitan* magazines, along with bras, were thrown into the can.

Clara DeMiha danced forward with a pair of high heels. "Down with these shoes!" she cried as she threw them away, while a chorus from the crowd yelled "And down with bound feet!" and "Tell it like it is!"

"Why don't you throw yourselves in there?" yelled a man. "It would be a lot more useful."

"Go home and wash your bras!" cried another.

In went more pages from magazines, shoes, bras, and makeup, as the activists' cheers ran into the exclamations and cruelties from women on the sidelines: "Oh, look at that bra they are throwing away, look!" "Honey, you need all

The Freedom Trash Can

the help you can get, don't give any away!" The last taunt, from a young woman, drew gales of laughter from the people around her.

Bev Grant's pictures of the men and women in the crowd captured their interests and sentiments in ways that direct quotes could not. Like the image of an angry, middle-aged white man gesticulating with a handful of "George Wallace for President" flyers, prominently displaying the Alabama segregationist's face and insurgent campaign slogan, "Stand Up for America." The man had paused his own political work on the boardwalk to rail against the feminists, thrusting at them Wallace and all he represented.

That man was not the only Wallace supporter working the crowd and poking at the activists. Later in the afternoon, a "nice-looking young man" described as a new "jeer-leader" by a reporter for *The Guardian*, joined the crowd and began handing out Wallace literature. He then "proudly introduced his pretty young wife (who was not observed to open her mouth for any purpose all afternoon)," as a member of the hard-right John Birch Society—"a Bircher" at the age of twenty. "She joined of her own accord, too," added the woman's husband, and then he patted her on the head.

Man with George Wallace flyers

While they had more in common with the "jeer-leader" and his wife than they did the women's liberationists, Terry Meeuwsen, with her "Nixon for President" button and pro–Miss America sign, presented a very different picture of the politics of conservative womanhood. She and her small group of counter-protesting friends assertively spoke for themselves and their pride in traditional gender roles and feminine beauty.

While the demonstration carried on outside, Al Marks spent part of his afternoon inside Convention Hall, watching the last rehearsals before the pageant finals and telecast. When he paused to speak with a journalist, the sounds of fifty women rehearsing the night's stage and runway choreography could be heard in the background.

"We sharply differentiate between what it is that we do and the type of individual that we attract as a contestant vis-a-vis what happened in Chicago last week . . . where an entirely different type, that I think many of us in the great American middle class don't regard as representative at all, put on a show that I think none of us are proud of anywhere in America except for a few far-out people who go for that sort of thing!"

The woman prompted him further, asking if Marks believed that the pageant offered a "healthy contrast" to events at the Democratic Convention.

"I should say that this is a distinctly healthy contrast," Marks replied. "And *I'm* enough of an American to think that these girls are truly representative of what we would look for and want in our daughters, and our son's wives or fiancés or what have you, rather than some of the other things we see from time to time lately!'"

The journalist ended her interview by asking Marks directly what he thought of the women protesting. They were, he replied, "a bunch of *nuts*! I can't call them anything else. . . . This to me is a rather cheap publicity stunt, which I prefer to ignore. Being a male 100%, I wonder how many of these females out on the boardwalk, if they had a man, would have the time to do what it is they're doing. Maybe there is an omission here that leads to frustration."

Elsewhere in the hall, Elizabeth Alton decided to step out of the rehearsal for a moment to go see the women's liberation protest for herself. When she mentioned to the police captain on the doors to the boardwalk where she was headed, he said, "Don't go, Mrs. Alton. It's a disgusting show out there and not worth your time to see." She took his advice and headed back inside.

As the time for ticket holders to enter Convention Hall drew near, the fifteen women planning to disrupt the pageant itself headed to Hampshire House to eat and rest, before changing into their evening clothes and doing their hair and makeup. They "had to look like ladies," explained Alix Kates Shulman, if they were going to get past security and the police, some of whom may have been watching the women on the boardwalk all afternoon. Shulman had been part of the "secret operations" planning and had purchased the tickets but would not be among the infiltrators. She had two kids at home, ages four and six, and did not want to risk getting arrested—a very real threat, given the colossal disruption they were about to attempt on national television.

35

ONCE UPON A SOMEDAY

How did one spot a women's liberationist in a crowd of thousands? There had been a great deal of talk about the type of woman who would protest the Miss America Pageant—about what a feminist looked like—in the days leading up to the finals. The "secret operations" group hoped security and police at Convention Hall were on the lookout for braless, underdressed, scraggily haired women with unattractive, makeup-free faces that bore obvious markers of their bitter spinsterhood. The small clutch of infiltrators, including Kathie Amatniek, Peggy Dobbins, Bev Grant, and Carol Hanish, were effective "ladies" impersonators; no one noticed the rolled-up "Women's Liberation" banner under one woman's evening gown or the squeeze bottles of Toni home permanent hair solution smuggled in by Dobbins and Grant.

The pageant finals began at 8:30 p.m. for the live audience, while the telecast would not start until 10:00 p.m. Some of the first hour and a half was spent presenting awards for Tuesday night's parade and other items of local interest, but it mostly served as a preview of the show to come after intermission, when Glenn Osser and The Miss America Orchestra played the "Television Overture" and NBC began its live program. The audience would see the big song-and-dance numbers, learn who the ten semifinalists were, and watch each one present herself in the Evening Gown and Swimsuit competitions, and then get to see them all over again at 10 p.m. The Talent and Q&A portions were only staged for the telecast.

As the NYRW demonstrators went upstairs to find their balcony seats, Dobbins, Grant, and another woman peeled off and headed onto the main floor of the hall. As they split up and moved through different parts of the orchestra section, opening their bottles of permanent solution, Bev Grant took a moment to get some close-up photos of the stage and candid shots of the denizens of the expensive seats. Trying to remain inconspicuous, the women walked along the aisle seats, squirting the strong-smelling hair treatment into the carpet. An acrid, chemical smell rose from the floor. *Sponsoring Miss America stinks and makes us stink.*

Unbeknownst to Peggy Dobbins, she had been spotted by two Convention Hall security guards, who thought she was behaving suspiciously. The guards pointed her out to the two closest police officers from the large pageant security detail, a captain and patrolman from the nearby community of Margate. They arrested Dobbins before she made it to the end of her aisle. As the policemen began dragging her away, Dobbins yelled to the audience members nearby, "Is this your America?" They took her out the back of Convention Hall to their squad car and drove her to headquarters, where she was booked on charges of disorderly conduct. Dobbins refused to say if she was part of the group demonstrating on the boardwalk, admitting only that she was sympathetic to their cause. She would end up watching the pageant's finale from a holding cell, talking about women's liberation with others who'd been arrested that evening, mostly for prostitution. When Atlantic City Chief of Police Mario Floriani spoke to the press, he described a "stink bomb" incident occurring less than ten feet from where the mayor of Atlantic City and his wife were seated, and he said they were investigating possible connections to the demonstrators on the boardwalk.

The telecast opened with sweeping aerial shots inside Convention Hall, a picture of glamour, action, and intermission mingling—the candidness of the scene its biggest reminder that viewers at home were watching it *live.* The orchestra's playing swelled as the shot cut to the title credits, including the show's three sponsors: Toni, Oldsmobile, and Pepsi-Cola. Every advertisement aired during the telecast would come from these three companies.

The show itself began with Bess Myerson in an evening gown, seated in an elevated press box overlooking the stage. As television hostess, she provided commentary and guided the audience through the contest in a setup that was not that different from the ones used by network anchors during the conventions in the previous month. She introduced the show by reminding audiences that the Miss America Pageant sat at the top of a vast national operation of local and state preliminary pageants run entirely by civic-minded volunteers, amounting to "over 200,000 civic leaders staging more than 3,500 preliminary pageants featuring 17,000 hopeful young women to get to" the final group of contestants.

"There's no doubt that tonight each of our fifty girls feels as if she were living in character in one of the happiest and most exciting of all storybooks," Myerson concluded, setting up the show's theme, which she announced by bringing a large book to the camera's lens that read, "Once Upon a Someday." The show cut to a shot of the stage, and a giant version of the same book, and then followed a little white girl in white, patent-leather Mary Janes and a short, enormous puff of a pink dress, skipping toward the book, up the runway. After investigating the book, the girl pulled back the cover to reveal Miss Wisconsin 1967, waiting to take her by the hand onto a stage-set path leading to a distant castle through a vista of pink-on-pink glitter, as the first musical number, "Somewhere Out There," got underway (for the second time of the night). All fifty contestants entered the stage wearing complementary costumes of pert hats and travel attire—a jacket and smart skirt—and carrying matching round suitcases bearing the names of their states. Bert Parks glided in behind them, finishing the song and getting "our 1968 royal state ambassadors" started on their journey up the "somewhere road." In about two hours, the country would have a new Miss America.

After some statistics from Myerson (there were 38 brunettes, 11 blondes, and one redhead; the shortest was 5'3" and the tallest, 5'10"; for the first time in pageant history, every contestant was a current college student or recent graduate) and an explanation of the preliminary contests, interviews, and scoring, Parks announced the ten semifinalists, chosen by the "Royal Panel of Selectors," in no apparent order to heighten the suspense for television viewers. Everyone on stage and in the audience already knew who would be going on in the competition. While the semifinalists went backstage to change for the Evening Gown portion, another musical number began, featuring the girl, now identified as "Little Miss Someday," looking into a mirror to see her future, behind which stood a smiling Debbie Barnes wearing a pink, tiered gown created by longtime pageant sponsor Banlon, her hair piled high beneath her crown. Barnes walked the runway, careful to look and wave to the crowd in Convention Hall and at home, while Bert Parks sang, "Oh, look at her! Look at her! She's our Miss America, the one we waited for. . . ." Those who had followed the summer's song controversy would know this as the new anthem originally intended to replace "There She Is."

With a charming blown kiss to the television audience from the end of the runway, Barnes turned and walked back to the stage, where she sat down at a grand piano to finish the number with a solo. Then it was on to Evening Gowns, cued by Myerson's explanation that the judges' task was to find in the women "those intangibles: poise and personality. These you know are vital for the selection of the girl who for the next year, both at home and abroad, will be the personification of the fine qualities which can be found in the young American girl."

Next came the Talent competition, during which each of the ten women presented the same talent she had performed in the previous three-nights' preliminary contests. Miss Tennessee went first, singing a ballad of lost love. Miss Oregon danced "The Dying Swan" from the ballet *Swan Lake*, followed by opera singer Miss New York performing a selection from *The Marriage of Figaro*, and a commercial for Oldsmobile that featured a smirking George Plimpton praising the car manufacturer's new test protocols: "The truth is Oldsmobile has pounded these 1969s unmercifully so they'll behave beautifully for you."

The break was followed by Miss Iowa on the grand piano, playing the "Warsaw Concerto," and Miss Virginia singing part of the titular female role in the opera *Samson and Delilah*. Between these two came Miss Florida, with a decidedly more lowbrow crowd-pleaser. Dressed in a pink flapper costume, she performed a comedic dance while theatrically chewing gum and blowing bubbles on musical cue, before concluding with a series of moves about as risqué as the Miss America stage got: blowing an enormous bubble until it popped, shooting her pink garter into the audience, and turning to exit the stage with a light tap of her own bottom. Later, Elizabeth Alton would reference this performance as an example of how far a chaperone would go to help "her girl," recalling that Miss Florida's chaperone was backstage that night chewing frantically on a huge wad of bubblegum so it would be at optimal bubble-blowing consistency when she took the stage.

In addition to a pianist performing a piece by Debussy and a singer doing a Broadway number, rounding out the Talent portion were two pageant firsts. Miss Illinois, Judith Anne "Judi" Ford, wowed the crowd and Bert Parks with a high-flying trampoline routine, making her the first contestant in Miss America history to showcase athleticism as her talent. (Having just completed her first year of college, Ford was the first woman in her school's history to earn a varsity letter; she was the only woman on the men's trampoline team and was a Junior National Champion in the sport.) Miss Massachusetts, Katherine Monroe, did a spoken-word and sign-language version of the song "What the World Needs Now Is Love," making her the first person to bring American Sign Language to the Miss America stage.

When Bess Myerson introduced the Swimsuit competition as the last contest for the ten semifinalists, she first cut to a commercial: "In the meantime, here's another brand of girl watching." The commercial opened with Diet Pepsi's signature trumpet jingle, "Music to Watch Girls By," as a young woman in a tight-knit shirt and white pedal pushers walked happily through a marina, seemingly oblivious to the men staring at her and distractedly fumbling their various nautical activities as she passed them. The camera angles matched the gazes of the men, focusing on the woman's bustline or bottom, as a male voice-over cut in, "Girl watching is the top spectator sport in America today. And the girls girl watchers watch drink Diet Pepsi Cola." The commercial closed with another upward shot that centered on the watched woman's butt in her tight white pants as the disembodied male voice gave the diet soda's slogan: "Diet Pepsi, try it—someone will be watching."*

* This was one of a series of commercials for Diet Pepsi using the same jingle, setup, and slogan, but featuring different settings for "girl watching." A version set in Washington, D.C., won a Clio Award—the advertising industry's top honor—in 1969; it featured an oblivious blonde walking through iconic sites along the mall to the voice-over: "We're a nation of sightseers and this is one of the nation's most beautiful sights." It ended with a male figure, presumed to be the president, peeping at her from behind a curtained window in the White House.

After a song about rainbows and some of Parks's characteristic patter—"Girls never seem more colorful than when they are in swimsuits"—the competition got underway. Each of the ten semifinalists, wearing a one-piece swimsuit and heels, came from backstage to the top of a riser made to look like a large flower. After a pause, they descended a few stairs to the stage, walking across it one way, turning, and then walking back.

During the presentation of awards like Miss Congeniality and a big music-and-parade number that brought all fifty contestants and Debbie Barnes back onto the stage, the judges conferred to select five finalists, who were then announced by Bert Parks: Miss Oregon, Miss Iowa, Miss Indiana, Miss Massachusetts, and finally Miss Illinois. (Though he had announced he would be "calling the girls alphabetically by state," the list was anything but.)

The crowd was still clapping for Miss Illinois's selection when Parks transitioned to the final interview event, and he called Miss Oregon to the mic to start the questioning. The stage direction was tight, requiring the contestant being interviewed and Parks to use the same standing mic; the television camera shot was also tight, focusing in on the pair of their closely pressed heads and shoulders. It made for many awkward moments of exchange, as contestants tried not to visibly pull away from Parks. The questions, based on the contestants' answers to questionnaires given earlier in the week, were brief. All five contestants were interviewed in as many minutes.

After that, it was on to more awards and special scholarships, while the judges held their last conference to pick the winner and order of runners-up. It seemed that the fumbled list of finalists had been only the beginning of a series of gaffes. When Bert Parks began to announce the women who earned special notice and awards from the judges despite not being selected as semifinalists, the names were all wrong. It took a minute for someone from the pageant organization to realize that Parks had been given a list of names from the previous year. The states were correct, apparently, but the names were from 1967. Parks continued distributing the awards by announcing only the state of the winners; the women's names went entirely unsaid.

Second to the announcement of the winner, everyone was waiting for the farewell address from Debbie Barnes. As she approached the mic, standing alone near the front of the stage, her hooped gown moved a little stiffly. Barnes looked out at the audience of eighteen thousand and into the cameras at the tens of millions of people watching on television, and she began her goodbye.

"A year ago tonight my somewhere road was miraculously extended to include all of the highways and airways of America, and my love of America and its people has deepened with every mile. With the help of USO, my somewhere road led to Japan and Korea, where the appreciation of thousands of servicemen gave me the satisfaction to know that I was doing just something to alleviate the loneliness."

Barnes was hitting her marks, enunciating clearly and calmly, pausing to smile, sweeping her eyes slowly across the entire auditorium, and looking into the cameras.

"As any worthwhile experience, my road hasn't always been easy, but the rough places taught me a lesson that I will never forget as I walk this last time up the somewhere road. I will make way for Miss America 1969 to search for her special someday. . . ."

Suddenly, she heard a loud noise coming from somewhere out in the auditorium. The energy and attention of the live audience shifted away from the stage, and Barnes slowed her speech for an unnatural beat.

"But . . ."

The sound . . . was it yelling? Someone—no, several people—were yelling. Barnes was very alone at the front of the stage. The lights were hot and nearly blinding. Then she realized it was women chanting.

"Freedom for women!"

"No more Miss America!"

If Barnes noticed the white banner reading "Women's Liberation" spill over the side of the balcony, she didn't show it. She didn't turn her head toward the disturbance, or even cut her eyes in that direction in any noticeable way. She continued speaking.

"Even though I will be sad to see or to leave all these precious friends that I have made here in Atlantic City, my heart will contain only 1 percent sadness and 99 percent gratitude."

The chanting continued mostly unmuffled by Barnes's speaking until she finished and the orchestra began to play. Bert Parks boomed, "Here's a special song for our departing Miss America!," and he sang as Miss America 1968,

Debra Dene Barnes, walked down the runway for the last time. Television audiences heard Bess Myerson's voice-over: "Debbie's plans for the future include returning to Kansas State College of Pittsburg, where she'll be a junior. She's majoring in classical piano, working for her bachelor of music. After graduation, she hopes to teach."

The show would go on.

To watch the pageant live on a home television, as opposed to watching it as one of thousands of audience members in the convention hall, were never identical experiences, but in 1968 the two diverged more than ever before. Everyone in the auditorium knew of the disturbance, and many could see the "Women's Liberation" banner that Hanisch, Amatniek, and the others had dropped over the edge of the balcony. Those with seats nearby watched as police physically removed the activists and their banner. Yet, other than the moment Debbie

View of outgoing Miss America 1968, Debra Barnes, as she walks the runway for the last time

Barnes made a conspicuous pause in her farewell address, while sounds of something else could be heard, viewers at home had no idea what was happening. The NBC crew did not allow it. Not one cameraman swung his lens toward the disturbance or the banner. Instead, the live feed remained trained on the stage and the carefully schooled face of Debbie Barnes. Television audiences were given no explanation for what they could hear, if not see, and the pageant carried on as usual.

As Barnes spoke and the police apprehended the women's liberationists, the pageant officials tabulated the scores. When it was time for Parks to announce the four runners-up and winner, the forty-five other contestants stood arrayed behind the five finalists. As he called their names, each woman rose, hugged Debbie Barnes, and walked across the stage. After the first three names—Miss Indiana, Miss Oregon, and then Miss Iowa—it was down to two: Miss Illinois and Miss Massachusetts. Seated side by side, the women clasped hands, looked at one another, and smiled. One of them was about to be named the new Miss America, which would essentially occur when the other was announced as the first runner-up. A drum roll was started, and Bert Parks took his time. "The first runner-up . . . Katherine Monroe, Miss Massachusetts!" Monroe sat completely still, absorbing her loss, while millions watched Judith Anne Ford look momentarily stunned, her jaw dropping open before she burst into tears. Parks boomed over a celebratory peel of horns, "Miss America, Miss Illinois!"

Ford stood and cried while a new sash was draped over her shoulder and Debbie Barnes fixed the crown onto her heavily sprayed updo. Someone handed Ford a scepter decorated with flowers that she clutched in both hands, as she began walking down the runway to Parks's serenade. "There she is, Miss America! There she is, our ideal. . . ."

Shortly after the pageant, Judi Ford sat resplendent on her gilded throne, not a little overwhelmed as she met with reporters for the first time as Miss America. Tears ran down her cheeks intermittently. A pageant chaperone, described by one journalist as "stern-faced," stood at Ford's shoulder ready to assist or intervene if she thought a question unfair or too controversial. A man working as the pageant's press coordinator moved among the crowd of journalists, managing the order as they posed their questions.

View of newly crowned Miss America 1969,
Judith Anne Ford, as she walks the runway for the first time

"What's your thoughts about what happened in Chicago, since you're from Illinois?"

"Well," started Ford, laughing nervously yet knowingly, "that's a very controversial subject. They've had a lot of discussion about this, about whether the police overreacted or whether the demonstrators were in the wrong, and I think maybe, I don't really know where the blame lies. I imagine it would be a little bit on both sides."

The same reporter had a follow-up question: "Well, would you say the citizens of Illinois are very indignant over what happened?"

"Yes, uh, I can't say for all the citizens of Illinois, but some are and some aren't." Ford laughed half-heartedly again, adding, "I hate to make my opinion on this because it is so controversial."

When asked about whether the voting age should be lowered from twenty-one to eighteen, Ford consulted the chaperone. After a bit of back and forth, the woman said it was fine for Ford to offer her opinion. "Personally, I think they should [allow eighteen-year-olds to vote] because if, well, a boy's old enough to go over in a war and give his life for his country, then he should be old enough to have a say in who runs it." More questions followed, querying Ford on her thoughts about hippies and Yippies—"to each his own . . . but I wouldn't want to be one"—and the disruption of the pageant by women's liberation activists: "It was just too bad, I'm sorry it happened."

Before Ford could answer a question about the Miss Black America Pageant, the press coordinator shouted from the back of the crowd, "Don't answer that!" When another reporter tried later to get the question in again, the man interrupted once more. "No questions about the Miss Black America Pageant because Miss America is in our own Miss America Pageant, and she has nothing to do with that." He did, however, allow Ford to respond to a general question about whether a Black woman could ever be Miss America. "As long as she's the prettiest," Ford replied. "I don't think a girl should become Miss America just because she's a Negro."

36

THIS IS BETTER THAN BEING MISS AMERICA

Journalists peeled away from the crowd around Judi Ford to make their way down the boardwalk to the Ritz-Carlton's auditorium for the start of the Miss Black America Pageant, entering a scene at once familiar yet radically different from what they had just experienced. The ballroom-style space was set up in banquet format, with white cloth–draped tables placed throughout, each with a pitcher of ice water, drinking glasses, and small stack of individual ashtrays at their centers. A stage had been installed at the front of the room with a forty-foot runway extending from the center into the room.

The room hummed with anticipatory energy, as about two hundred people got settled in their seats; it was after midnight, but no one seemed tired, and all looked fresh in their evening clothes. People chatted excitedly, flipped through programs, looked for activity on stage, and checked out the rest of the audience, which ranged in age from teenagers to seniors. Whereas the crowd in Convention Hall had been almost as white as the group of contestants and entertainers on stage, just about everyone in the Ritz-Carlton auditorium was Black—and those who were not tended to be members of the press.

Backstage, the eight contestants made last touches to their hair and makeup, prepped their costumes and gowns for smooth changes between competitions, and reviewed dance steps, song lyrics, or monologues. While a few had previous pageant experience, more had backgrounds in dance, theater, and modeling; they all had expectations for what winning the Miss Black America crown would entail. There were the prizes, of course, the list of which had grown since the preliminary contest held in Philadelphia, including the new promise of a scholarship. They looked forward to the possibility of travel and public appearances, based on plans J. Morris Anderson had described, but also by the precedent Miss America had set. More than all of this, perhaps, was the feeling that would come from being named the ideal Black American woman, of being the chosen symbol of race pride and face of resistant Black beauty. It was this last part that had convinced Theresa Claytor to participate, to "make history."

Vivian Whitted, the contestant from New York City, knew what this felt like. Two weeks earlier, she had been crowned Miss Harlem in front of a crowd of nine thousand at the Harlem Cultural Festival. She prevailed over twenty-five other contestants in the pageant, held in Mount Morris Park, that was a capstone event for the summer-long festival. The man who crowned her was New York Assemblyman Charles Rangel, who was then in his first term as an elected official. (Rangel would go on to serve in the U.S. House of Representatives from 1971, after defeating incumbent Adam Clayton Powell Jr., until his retirement in 2017.)

Miss Black America's color scheme was a muted red, white, and blue. The red-carpeted stage and runway were edged by decorative arrangements of white tissue and blue chiffon, with a white drape to the floor. At rear center stage, swooping red material accented by blue chiffon framed a large white backdrop cut to look like the entrance to a tented pavilion. It shielded one of the auditorium's doors through which contestants would enter and exit the stage during the pageant. The event began with introductions by the night's pair of MCs from Philadelphia's WFIL-TV (home of *American Bandstand*), who stood behind a significant speakers' podium near the top of the runway, stage right.

As expected, the run of show was similar in organization to the Miss America Pageant, starting with an opening number that included all the contestants, followed by competitions in Talent, Swimsuit, Evening Gown, and the Q & A, before the judges conferred and a winner and runners-up were declared. The show itself was very different, however. Whereas the Miss America Pageant always opened with a spectacle that featured all the contestants identified by state, often wearing their own outfits keyed to a common theme, the Miss Black America Pageant finale began with a dance performance representing the women's unity. They entered the stage in a tight cluster, wearing identical long-sleeved black leotards; the women's legs and feet remained bare, and they wore no jewelry. Arranged in four pairs, they held hands and were pressed front to back, moving down the runway as a single undulating mass before separating slightly to face one another and continue the slow, rippling choreography in mirrored movements.

Several of the contestants were dancers, including Theresa Claytor and Saundra Williams, who both performed pieces of their own for the Talent portion of the pageant. Claytor's was a modern interpretive dance set to funk and R&B saxophonist Jimmy Castor's "Ham Hocks Espanol," from his 1967 debut album. Wearing bells at her ankles and a lemon-yellow jumpsuit with a high neck and close-set shoulder straps, Williams wowed with an "African-inspired" dance of her own choreography that earned her another win for the Talent competition. In addition to being a skilled performer and creator, Williams taught modern ballet, tap, interpretive, and African dance in Philadelphia and at Maryland State University, the HBCU where she studied sociology and belonged to the NAACP and Alpha Kappa Alpha (AKA) sorority.

Like many student activists of the period, Saundra Williams described going away to college in 1967 as an awakening. In her case, it came from the experience of leaving Philadelphia to go to college in Princess Anne, a small town on Maryland's Eastern Shore with the dubious distinction of being the site of that state's last recorded lynching, in 1933. "I was accustomed to big city life with its freedom," she explained, and Princess Anne "was an entirely new experience." Williams described confronting racism and her own Blackness in unfamiliar ways. "We couldn't eat in a restaurant because they wouldn't serve blacks. There was no such thing as 'your friend the policeman,'" she explained, referring to a community relations comic book produced by police departments in the 1960s. She helped organize students in a group called the Black Awareness Movement, which demonstrated against segregated businesses in the community. (Judy Klemesrud, from the *New York Times,* described Williams beaming as she told her, "That restaurant is integrated now.")

After winning the talent competition, Williams charmed judges and audience alike during the interview portion of the contest. The paillettes of her long white gown winked under the stage lights, just as she'd knew they would.

"Should husbands and wives share domestic responsibilities?"

"Yes, day-to-day responsibilities should be shared equally," Williams replied, before adding slyly, "But I'll tell you, the man is getting awfully lazy these days."

It was 2:45 in the morning when the judges decided upon their winner for the first Miss Black America title. The finalists lined up shoulder to shoulder in their evening gowns and elbow-length white gloves for the last nerve-wracking minutes of the pageant, when any outcome was still possible.

From the podium, one MC announced the runners-up—Linda Johnson of Philadelphia as second runner-up and Washington, D.C.'s Theresa Claytor as the first. The other MC congratulated the women while handing them their trophies.

When Saundra Williams was named Miss Black America, she smiled with eyes alight, but did not cry. As she made her first victorious turn on the runway, a throne was placed in front of the line of contestants. The pageant's director, who ran a modeling school for Fabulous Productions, met Williams on her return and placed the crown on her head. Another woman helped the winner into a beaded, rich cream-colored cape and handed her a scepter wrapped in red velvet. As Williams walked the runway again, this time in full royal splendor, a camera person zoomed in on Johnson and Claytor individually, capturing their grace in disappointment, wobbling smiles, and wet eyes. Accustomed to the newly announced Miss America bursting into tears, as Judi Ford had just done a few hours earlier, journalists remarked upon their absence when Williams took her throne and proclaimed, "This is better than being Miss America."

After the pageant ended at around 3:00 in the morning, Williams still had to speak with journalists. Like Ford, she sat on her throne in the first flush of winning, still holding her scepter, while members of the press stood at the edge of the stage and lobbed questions.

One of the first people to speak asked about the purpose of the Miss Black America Pageant, to which Williams replied that it demonstrated "that Black

The first Miss Black America, Saundra Williams (center), flanked by first runner-up Theresa Claytor (right) and second runner-up Linda Johnson (left)

beauty is equal to the beauty of the white woman and that it can be represented and that we as a race should be proud."

Then Eleanor Fischer from WNYC radio followed up, asking if Williams thought the Miss America Pageant truly represented the nation. No, Williams responded, because Black women were excluded.

Was it discrimination?

Yes, Williams concluded, but discrimination that was born out of a lack of self-awareness.

Later, when Fischer asked Williams what advice she had for all young women, the pageant winner replied that they should try to be ladies, and to educate themselves so they might be true partners to their husbands in bearing the heavy burden of a life together.

And what did Williams think of the protesters? This is a country of free speech and the freedom to assemble, Williams said. The demonstrators were exercising their constitutional rights.

Judy Klemesrud would later write that Williams "looked bored when asked about the 100 women demonstrators, mostly white, who had picketed the Miss America Pageant on the grounds that women are enslaved by 'ludicrous standards of beauty.'" There were many possibilities in that "bored" look—if that was, in fact, what Williams was feeling. It could have been the slavery analogy or a critique of pageants she did not share; it could have been that the new Miss Black America was simply exhausted by being asked about white people.

The women's liberation buses were long gone by the time Saundra Williams was crowned. Earlier, after the women who'd been ejected from Convention Hall by police, but not arrested, joined up with remaining protesters on the boardwalk, a large group descended upon the precinct station where five of their compatriots were being held. Bail had been set high, making it impossible for the demonstrators to come up with enough cash among them to pay for the release of their friends. Someone suggested they occupy the station's waiting area until the five women were let go. The police weighed their options and tolerance for the women's disruptions, and started lowering the bail amount until they decided no amount was worth it. They let the women go on the condition that they leave town immediately and escorted them to their buses to make sure. "More than anything," surmised Susan Sutheim in *The Guardian* a week later, "they [did] not want these crazy women to stay in Atlantic City." She didn't note how different this outcome was from the police's treatment of protesters in Chicago two weeks earlier, or the brutality Black women had experienced time and again when arrested for civil rights activism.

Out of the fifteen women who had been inside Convention Hall, Peggy Dobbins and one other were still not accounted for. Robin Morgan stayed behind in Atlantic City, and spent the next two hours frantically trying to locate them and calling around to raise bail money. It was impossible to get clear information on their whereabouts from Atlantic City police, so Morgan started searching other stations in the area. At around 3:00 a.m., she finally landed on the right place. The cop at the desk confirmed that Peggy Dobbins and another woman had been there, but they'd been released earlier on cash bail—paid, he said, by "some older woman" named Charlotte Curtis.

• • •

On Sunday morning, at 9:00 a.m., Judi Ford held her first official press conference, prepped and flanked by pageant officials. She was operating on about two hours of sleep.

"How did you feel about the title after getting up this morning?"

Judi replied, "When I awoke this morning, I expected it to be yesterday. I was sure that last night never happened, that it was all just a dream."

"Do blondes really have more fun?"

"I don't know. I've never been a brunette to compare it with," she quipped.

Asked what she thought the ideal Miss America was, she responded: "Pretty and talented—and everything—and poised and lots of personality." Concerning the USO tour, Ford said that she would "love" to go to Vietnam.

Once again, Ford was told not to answer any questions about the Miss Black America Pageant. Of the women's liberation disruption during the show, Ford said that she hadn't understood what was happening from where she stood on the stage, but that the whole situation had made her nervous.

After the news conference, Ford joined the rest of the contestants for their last pageant event—an awards breakfast in the ballroom of the Traymore Hotel. Bowls of red roses graced the center of every table and live trees strung with paper butterflies and flowers were positioned throughout. The television cameras were gone, but several reporters continued to work the room, getting last comments and one more interview. Several contestants took roses with them as they left, observed Barbara Carlson at the *Courant*. She also noted that no one on the program of pageant officials and community leaders had referenced either the Miss Black America Pageant or the women's liberation demonstration and arrests.

The demonstrators from New York who were also members of NOW, like Flo Kennedy, Kate Millett, Cindy Cisler, and Anselma Dell'Olio, were similarly running on very little sleep Sunday morning as they arrived at 300 Park Avenue for another day of picketing in front of the Colgate-Palmolive headquarters. Millett showed up carrying a full-size ceramic toilet that the demonstrators used to stage a "Flush-In." With echoes of the previous day's Freedom Trash Can, protesters ceremonially poured iconic Colgate-Palmolive products into the toilet bowl to show just what they thought of them and the company that exploited the women who made, promoted, and purchased them.

The *New York Times* ran a pair of stories on Monday beneath a single headline: "Along with Miss America, There's Now Miss Black America." The bylines belonged to Charlotte Curtis and Judy Klemesrud, respectively. The layout, which set the two stories in unavoidable relation to one another, was Curtis's work as the section's editor.

The juxtaposition of the articles' opening lines provided a clear journalistic perspective on the value of the two pageants. Klemesrud's feature on Saundra Williams began by describing her as "a 19-year-old Philadelphian who wears her hair natural, does African dances and helped lead a student strike at her college last spring. She's what the new black woman is all about." Curtis's piece, by comparison, began with the declaration, "What matters about 18-year-old Judith Anne Ford, aside from her becoming Miss America of 1969 early today, is the color of her hair. The Illinois gymnast is the first blonde to win the title in 11 years. 'I'm so glad,' she said. 'I feel like it's a breakthrough.'"

Later that day, Curtis received a note from Clifton Daniels through the *Times'* interoffice message system: "I like the play on the two Misses America on your page this morning. The Miss Black America story, however, left me hungry for more information. Who financed it? What awards did Miss Black America win? What will she be doing for the next year, as compared with what Miss White America will be doing?"

Daniels's hunger for information about the Miss Black America, Saundra Williams, and the new pageant organization would be little remedied in the days and weeks to come. While reports of Williams's victory were woven through most accounts of Saturday's events in news outlets throughout the country, the details were largely drawn from the same two syndicated news service articles. The resulting stories shared the same set of details, the same images, and the same flat silences.

The AP and UPI similarly influenced the picture of Judi Ford that took hold in the national press in the immediate wake of her crowning, drawing on well-worn tropes of Miss America's effortless all-American beauty, talent, and humble, good nature. Ford was "a bouncy, natural blonde trampoline artist who spiraled her way to the crown Saturday night with an amazing acrobatic display . . . radiant as she appeared at a 9 a.m. news conference after only two hours sleep," wrote the AP's reporter. Ford was, added the UPI, an "admitted tomboy who prefers blue jeans and sweatshirts to dresses." The inherent racial specificity of these tropes was highlighted by their notable absence in stories about Saundra Williams.

37

THERE ARE NO UGLIES—ONLY UGLY BEAUTY STANDARDS

"What right have you to disrupt the Miss America Pageant?" asked the author of an angry letter to Robin Morgan. "Just because you are a frustrated female who, because of her homely face, can never have a chance doesn't give you the right to cause trouble. Only an insane person would do a thing like this." Morgan's name was never used; instead the letter opened, "Dear Ugly." (Notably, this letter was used to introduce Morgan in a *New York Times Sunday Magazine* profile of activist women in 1969, as the setup for describing her as very attractive, married, and a former child star.)

The Miss America protest hit a nerve. In the days and weeks to follow, it was covered widely in the press, including in major national publications like *Life* and *Time* magazines. Reactions ranged from sympathetic or agnostic to dismissive and outraged. Descriptions from the latter part of that continuum were heavily populated with "bra burners" and ugly, humorless women in comfortable shoes who either could not land a man or were lesbians. Some explanations suggested a certain inability on the part of the journalists to conceptualize the women's concerns, such as in an AP story that appeared shortly after, including the line, "A group called 'Women's Liberation' also protested the Miss America pageant, claiming it denied young women their suffrage."

The *New York Post*'s Harriet Van Horne combined several tropes in the September 9, 1968, installment of her syndicated column. "While I'm prepared to defend anybody's right to protest, even in Chicago," she opened, "I find myself embarrassed by those sturdy lasses in their sensible shoes who picketed the Miss America contest in Atlantic City Saturday night." The highlight of the event, Van Horne reported, was a bra burning. Noting her receipt of the press release and invitation to cover the protest, "Well, this lady of the press usually has something nicer to do on Saturday night than burn her undergarments on the boardwalk in Atlantic City. And I suspect the deep-down, aching trouble with these lassies is that they haven't. One ought to feel a surge of sympathy. But in the face of such tasteless, idiotic behavior, it's hard." Notably, Van Horne admitted, "I didn't happen to see a photograph of these Amazons in action but they're there, fully formed, in my mind's eye."

Van Horne's fellow *Post* columnist, Art Buchwald, followed a few days later with "The Bra Burners." He wrote, "It is one thing to protest a system or an institution, but it [*sic*] another to take the law in your own hands and burn your bra. . . . If the women in Atlantic City wanted to picket the Miss America Beauty Pageant because it is lily white, that is one thing, and if they wanted to picket because it is a bore, that is also a legitimate excuse." But burning bras and telling women not to make themselves beautiful were not. Buchwald's column employed a common sentiment among liberals and those to the left: fighting racism and agitating to end the war in Vietnam were meaningful aims, while calling for the liberation of women was frivolous, unseemly, and just the sort of thing a silly woman would do.

Time published a short piece the week after the demonstration. "'No more Miss America,' announced the flyer from the Women's Liberation Force. The protest came from a group of angry ladies led by Robin Morgan, 27, poetess and housewife." While the framing minimized the actions of "angry ladies" led by a "housewife" who wrote poetry, what followed was a direct summary of the *10 Points* news release and a brief description of the Freedom Trash Can.

Life's piece came the next week, with a two-page photo spread covering both pageants and the women's liberation protest. "The winner, a rival in black, and some ribroast ribbing." In addition to a photo of Judi Ford crying as Debbie Barnes affixed the crown to her hairspray-hardened updo, the magazine included a photo of Ford soaring above her trampoline, arching into a flip (the short text marveled at the fact that Ford's hair did not move at all throughout the high-flying routine). Saundra Williams, flanked by Linda Johnson and Theresa Claytor, smiled from the same AP image that appeared in most publications across the country. *Life* stood out, however, with its choice of photo illustrating the women's liberation demonstration: a seven- or eight-year-old girl holds a poster almost as tall as she is. Her grinning face pops over the top, leaving otherwise visible only her feet and small fingers curling around each side of the mounted image. A few adult women can be seen picketing in the background across an expanse of boardwalk. The poster itself is a popular advertisement for Cattle Baron that depicts a nude, white woman on her knees, back to the camera, looking over her shoulder at the viewer from beneath a cowboy hat pulled low over her eyes. The *Playboy*-style pinup shot is transformed by lines drawn on her body and labeled in the style of a butcher's chart, showing cuts of meat (rib, loin, round, rump, etc.) and the tagline, "Break the Dull Steak Habit." The poster-turned-protest-sign was just that; there were no slogans scrawled across the offending advertisement because it spoke for itself.

The Miss America protest made the Cattle Baron advertisement iconic, as well as notorious; it continues to be one of the most common illustrations of the Miss America protest today. The sexual objectification of idealized female beauty in the service of selling meat, and a place where (male) customers could buy and consume it, was—and is—impossible to miss. The ad's inclusion in the protest, sometimes alongside a sign reading "Welcome to the Miss America Cattle Auction," reiterated one of the demonstration's animating themes, likening the pageant to an auction, peddling women for consumption.

While *Life* magazine's photo spread was no doubt aligned with both demonstrations' challenges to the pageant, writer Shana Alexander used the platform of her regular column, "The Feminine Eye," to strike at the very foundations of the Miss America Pageant and its meanings, before concluding, "my own sympathies were closer to the bra-burners', and I began to wish they'd gone further." In a delicious twist of history, Alexander's father and Tin Pan Alley legend, Martin Ager, composed the music for "Ain't She Sweet," which had rung out on the buses and across the boardwalk with Bev Grant's new lyrics, throughout the demonstration.

Perhaps even more important than setting one of the nation's leading mainstream publications squarely on the side of the protesters in Atlantic City was the several column inches Alexander devoted to dismantling the pageant's place as an arbiter of ideal American beauty and tradition. Her column opened with a typical scene of settling down in front of the television to watch the Miss America Pageant, expectations heightened in the aftermath of Chicago, hungrier for the pageant's familiar marshmallow pleasures:

> Sound came up first—that rich, remembered schmaltz of soggy strings, brass ooze and Disney choir. Then the Easter-egg colors brightened into lights, runways, gowns, gloves and girls—those same dear striding girls in bathing suits and high-heels wearing the same special smiles, each girl so alike with her hard-edge face of blue eyelids, apricot cheeks and cotton-candy hair you wondered if they all had the same makeup man or perhaps the same mother.

The pageant telecast's well-worn scenes and rhythms were not comforting, Alexander wrote, even as something to enjoy laughing at or dismissing; it was distressing. Watching the parade of hollowed-out young women glide carefully on their high heels across her screen was itself hollowing, she said, even harrowing. "Where *are* the girls inside these living Barbie dolls with the Styrofoam smiles? Behind every Miss is there really a miss? And what is behind that smile?"

So much was wrong with the pageant, surmised Alexander, that it was hard to know where to begin. "It is dull and pretentious and racist and exploitative and icky and sad. It is fake in everything from wigs to talents to sentiments. It does not worship beauty, but beauty products. Though the girls are not fakes, they themselves are treated as products. Beauty contests are not so much anti-female as they are antihuman. The complication of the so-called 'talent contest' obliges them to conspire in their own humiliation. And despite all the schmaltz and sanitizing, there clings to the proceedings a strong taint of the auction block."

Like her fellow Vassar alum, Charlotte Curtis, Shana Alexander was a ceiling-breaker, turning her years spent as a freelancer and then researcher for *Life* in the 1950s into a top spot among its featured writers. Both women fell in love with journalism thanks to a summer job, and Alexander graduated five years before Curtis, in 1945, meaning the women just missed overlapping at their alma mater. Alexander almost didn't finish college at all, however, dropping out briefly before her father, who did not have a college degree, insisted she return. "After interviewing Gypsy Rose Lee as a cub reporter in the summer, who wanted to go to school?" she told a reporter. Alexander married at nineteen, thinking it would give her independence (and, she told the same interviewer, because her mother told her not to) only to find misery and soon divorced. Her second marriage was longer but had ended, too, by the time she was at the precipice of becoming one of the country's most prominent feminist voices of print and television.

In 1969, Alexander was named managing editor of *McCalls,* the country's largest circulation magazine for women at the time, which had not had a female editor since 1920. Alexander resigned two years later, saying she could no longer stand the entrenched sexism at the magazine, and she became a columnist at *Newsweek.* In 1975, she joined CBS's *60 Minutes* as the feminist, liberal counterpoint to conservative James Kilpatrick in the weekly debate segments.

Life's treatment of Miss America and its protesters was unusual for the mainstream press, which tended to celebrate the former while qualifying that support with reference to the pageant's racism via coverage of the Miss Black America Pageant. Tone and sentiment ranged widely where the women's liberation protest was concerned, including in alternative publications and counterculture outlets. Notably consistent, however, were the women's names on the bylines—the result of the activists' insistence that they would give interviews only to female journalists.

The *New York Free Press* published two long stories about the protest written by Suzanne Giddens, who had ridden the bus down and back from Atlantic City with the protesters. The first article, which ran with a title that incorporated a chant from the boardwalk, "No More Miss America: Atlantic City Is a Town with Class. They Raid Your Morals and Sell Your Ass," was published a few days after the demonstration and disruptions by infiltrators. The story was illustrated with a closeup shot of the Cattle Baron poster and gave a sweeping picture of the entire day, including the actions of hecklers, Terry Ann Meeuwsen's counterprotest, and details about the police forcibly removing the activists and their banner from the balcony, as well as the arrests of Dobbins and others. Giddens's brief mention of Saundra Williams's victory in the Miss Black America Pageant made clear that she had not attended the pageant or interviewed Williams herself, but borrowed a quote from an earlier publication, most likely Judy Klemesrud's article from the *New York Times*.

Susan Sutheim's "Radical Women Protest Ugly Pageant," which appeared two days later in *The Guardian*, did not reference the Miss Black America Pageant or race at all, but focused on negative reactions to the women's liberation demonstrators by onlookers, including the George Wallace supporters among them, the arrests inside Convention Hall, and NBC's refusal to show the pageant's disruption on air. "What to make of it all?" she asked in closing. "The most obvious conclusion was that in spite of the political diversity among the demonstrators (Betty Friedan 'women's rights' types to sophisticated Marxists), and in spite of hasty, last-minute planning, a very small group of women—because they were women—had quite an impact. Second, it was clear that the reservations some of the women had about such an action (fear that it would be dismissed as 'cute,' fear that it would be misunderstood) were irrelevant." (The latter was not because the protesters weren't misunderstood, but because they had left a notable impression, nonetheless.) "Political education has to begin somewhere," after all, wrote Sutheim, and this was a pretty good start, all things considered.

In the wake of these early stories about the protest and its impacts, Robin Morgan worked tirelessly to manage the narrative in the mainstream and alternative presses, which contributed to popular perceptions that she was the leader or primary organizer of the demonstration. She gave interviews, wrote to editors seeking corrections, and published her own accounts of "zapping" the Miss America Pageant, which she had begun drafting almost as soon as it was over, flipping one of Bev Grant's song sheets over to write in blue ballpoint, "We have attended the Pageant itself, and exercised our rights of free speech and dissent against it." She restated now-familiar points about why they protested the pageant before moving into what they had intended to achieve, editing lightly as she went. "We wanted our sisters across the country, isolated in their kitchen ghettos to see that women were militant & together enough to declare freedom during the live telecast." Pageant officials were "running scared of us," Morgan crowed, fearing they would have to tape the finals and air with a delay in the future for fear of more disruptions, or maybe even "cease completely" with the broadcast.

Robin Morgan wrote and spoke in powerful strokes, full of superlatives and hyperbole with an eye toward legacy. There was nothing hesitant in her writing about the protest in its near aftermath (or later, for that matter). Like Cindy Cisler's architect handwriting, a piece of Robin Morgan's writing was unmistakable.

Not long after her first story appeared in the *New York Free Press,* Morgan and Flo Kennedy sat down with Suzanne Giddens to talk about the demonstration and what would be coming next from women's liberation. "We caused more havoc than we thought," boasted Morgan (whom Giddens would go on to describe as an "ex-Yippie and co-ordinator of the Miss America Protest"). "The mayor seems to think Atlantic City will never be the same." Women's liberation wouldn't be the same either, she added. "This thing has completely mushroomed now. . . . The energy is tremendous."

"Women's Liberation is the cutting-edge, the movement to push the revolution over the edge," Kennedy told Giddens. "Black people, no matter how militant, are still a minority. Peace people, no matter how committed, are still a minority. But women are a *majority*. This is really the first attempt to mobilize an oppressed majority; empathy for other oppressed groups is magnified when it's your own thing."

In October, Morgan published her own accounts of the demonstration in two key alternative publications on the left: "Miss America Goes Down" in *Rat* and "On Freedom for Women" in *Liberation*. Both drew upon her initial ideas from the back of the song sheet and reflected her desire to counter some of the perceptions of the protest circulating in the press. They also reveal Morgan's sense of who her readers would be. In the case of *Rat,* she imagined young leftist men drawn as much to the paper's often misogynist underground humor and pornographic cartoons as to its radical politics. Her piece opened with a direct case for the importance of the protest: "The Miss America Pageant—a seemingly ludicrous target for an action—is actually one of the more dangerous rituals going. It neatly combines all the good old America values: racism, capitalism, militarism (the winner tours Vietnam), competition, vulgarity, puritanism, male chauvinism AND light heartedness, a protection from anyone taking it seriously and maybe doing something about it." She reiterated the point with a quote from Flo Kennedy, "Chicago is comparable to throwing a brick through the window of a police station. The Atlantic City action is comparable to peeing on an expensive rug at a polite cocktail party. The Man never expects the second kind of protest, and very often that's the one that really gets him uptight."

As a way to make clear the demonstration's importance, Chicago loomed large in Morgan's account. In her description of the arrest of Peggy Dobbins (which included the address for the defense fund to cover her expenses), Morgan noted that the Toni hair solution she'd used in Convention Hall "smells like what was put into the ventilation system of Humphrey's hotel in Chicago, and Toni is, what's more, a sponsor of the Pageant." Emphasizing arrests and police behavior in Atlantic City, Morgan not only filled a gap in the narrative but also reinforced her argument to presumed skeptic readers. Near the article's midpoint, she writes, "I can see the smiles of some male-chauvinist readers of RAT, self-styled revolutionaries"— that the Miss America demonstration had been dangerous and for real.

Morgan further underscored this aspect in the article for *Liberation*. Founded in New York in the 1950s by a group that included MOBE's David Dellinger, the magazine supported the New Left in 1968, but was not of it. Its readership was older on average and reflected a wider swath of the American left. Morgan's article was similar in content to her piece for *Rat*, but adjusted to this different readership. Flo Kennedy's comment to Suzanne Giddens about mobilizing an oppressed majority served as an epigraph; her comment that the demonstration in Atlantic City was like a bunch of women taking a piss on the rug at a fancy cocktail party was not included. In the article, Morgan provided a history of the emergence of women's liberation, including the Jeannette Rankin Brigade protest, before turning to the Miss America protest itself:

> Where else could one find such a perfect combination of American values—racism, militarism, capitalism—all packaged in one "ideal" symbol, a woman. This was, of course, the basic reason why the protesters

> disrupted the Pageant—the contestants epitomize the role all women are forced to play in this society, one way or the other: apolitical, unoffending, passive, sex-object-drudge, delicate mindless thing. The crowning of a live sheep as Miss America (part of the boardwalk guerilla theatre that went on all day) was relevant to where this society is at; the crowning of Miss Illinois as the "real" Miss America, her smile still blood-flecked from Mayor Daley's kiss, was also relevant.

While referencing the pageant's racism in both articles, Morgan did not mention the simultaneous Miss Black America Pageant in either piece. This silence would become a consistent trend in the months and years to come.

38

I'M HERE BECAUSE I'M ANGRY

"I guess I'm here because I'm angry and I want some company in my anger or I'll go crazy," explained a student from Bryn Mawr College. It was a Thursday night at the SCEF office not long after the pageant protest, and as with every meeting since Atlantic City, there were many new faces. The group was going around the room responding to the question, "Why are you here?" As was her habit, Kathie Amatniek jotted light notes as the women spoke.

One of that night's new faces was well known to every person in the room. When it was Betty Friedan's turn to speak, she said, "I'm here because I think the historic moment has come, to use it politically, not just to rap." Drawn to the energy and possibilities presented by the successes of the Miss America Pageant protest, as well as suspicious of the radical women, Friedan was clear that she had not come downtown just to participate in a consciousness-raising session.

One of the women who reached out to SCEF shortly after Atlantic City was none other than Miss America 1951 Yolande Betbeze, now Yolande Fox. When her husband, Matthew Fox, died of a heart attack at fifty-three, leaving Yolande a young widow with a daughter not yet two years old, she bought the house in Georgetown that Jackie Kennedy had moved into with her kids when they left the White House after JFK's assassination. Fox became a fixture of the political scene as the girlfriend of the striking young ambassador from Algeria, Cherif Guellal. His diplomatic appointment ended when he was called home in 1967, in the aftermath of the Six-Day War. (Although Betbeze remained in the United States, their partnership lasted until his death in 2009.) After the Miss America protest, Betbeze began to identify herself as a women's liberationist. She talked about it in interviews at the time and throughout the decades that followed—interviews that inevitably identified her as a former Miss America, focused on her unchanged measurements and weight since her crowning, and set her beauty in contrast to her feminism.

Women's liberation emerged from the Miss America protest with national publicity and momentum, just as Carol Hanisch had known it would when she'd suggested the demonstration two months earlier. The debates over what constituted liberation for women and how to achieve it—debates that had motivated Hanisch in the first place—still very much remained. So, too, did the summer's trend toward more meetings of small groups with increasingly distinct identities.

While she wasn't involved in the Miss America protest, Roxanne Dunbar and other activists in Cambridge and Boston capitalized upon it in a fund-raiser for their group, then known as the Boston Women's Revolutionary Liberation Front (BWRLF), which was putting together a journal for women's liberation theory, called *No More Fun and Games* (the group would soon change their name to Cell 16). The bulk of the money to publish the first issue came from a benefit screening of a feature documentary released earlier that year, called *The Queen*. The film was a behind-the-scenes picture of the Miss All-America Camp Beauty Contest, a drag event modeled after the Miss America Pageant. Andy Warhol and George Plimpton served as judges alongside several others. Both the original contest, staged off-Broadway at New York's Town Hall in February 1967, and the film released in the summer of 1968 brought mainstream visibility to a vibrant national subculture. The *New York Times*'s Renata Adler described the documentary as "extraordinary" in its portrayal of twenty-eight contestants who "were transvestites from all over the country—some of them winners in regional contests—judged for walking, talking, bathing suit, makeup, hairdo, and, of course, beauty." The pageant was the creation of Frank Doroshow, whose stage name was Flawless Sabrina, and his Nationals Academy company that had, since 1959, run about forty-six contests a year all over the country, culminating in the annual national finals.

A pair of reviews from *Women's Wear Daily* (*WWD*) and the *Chicago Sun-Times*'s Roger Ebert, also published in June, when the film premiered in New York City, made clear the reasons for the Boston activists' affinity for the film. The leading fashion industry publication noted that the drag contest was "itself a camp phenomenon, mocking the dumbness and the anti-sex of the Miss America contests." The filmmaker revealed the "contestants from as many points of view as possible—as foolish, as pathetic, as victims, as freaks, as comic objects, as people. He watches them alone and in groups, rehearsing in men's clothes and moving through the weird and wretched complications of assuming a female look. Do women really go through all of this to look beautiful and is that beautiful? Are these men grotesque or are they only emphasizing a grotesque thing that women have become?" Roger Ebert also loved the film but understood its commentary on the labors of femininity and dominant beauty standards very differently. "Any dumb broad can be beautiful," he said, "but it takes a bit of thought, an ounce of imagination, and even a certain sense of humor to put oneself on the line in a transvestite contest."

Like the reviewer for *WWD*, Dunbar and others in the BWRLF saw the film as an illustration of the oppression, objectification, and commodification wrought by dominant beauty standards. Flyers for the movie screening posted around Boston and Cambridge described it as a "Benefit Showing for Women's Liberation," and noted that the cost would be "$2.00 for Women and Homosexuals, $3.00 for others." The flyers also included the lines:

The Drag Queen is Every Woman
To please "the Man" wear a mask
The Queen <u>chooses</u> the slavery of a female
we are born slaves
We are whores ~ a hot water bottle for your bed
We are dolls ~ to be dressed in pretties for each new occasion
The Queen is Every Woman.

While likening the condition of womanhood to slavery invoked the common racial analogy to mark (white) women's oppression, nothing was said on the flyer—or in most contemporaneous reviews of the film—about *The Queen*'s examination of racism in the Miss All-America Camp Beauty contest; that was another element it shared with Miss America.

At the end of the film, the selection of Harlow, a young, white Miss Philadelphia with very little competition experience as the Miss All-America Queen, prompted the Black contestant, Miss Manhattan Crystal LaBeija, to challenge the racism of the event and its standards for judgment. LaBeija's friends had encouraged her to skip the pageant altogether that year, after rumors that the contest "was rigged for white women and wasn't worth the pain." LaBeija was one of the few Black contestants to have made it through New York's white drag contest scene in the 1960s, which one recent observer attributed partly to her lighter skin. "True," he writes, "she was fair in complexion and beat to high heavens with powder—but so what?"*

Everyone knew they were making a movie about the drag pageant in 1967, which fueled rumors that the contest was fixed. Many believed that Harlow, described by Renata Adler as "a frail, blond, pouting young man," had been selected as the winner before anyone set foot on the finals stage. In the last ten minutes of the film, after Harlow has indeed been crowned Miss All-America Camp Beauty, LaBeija and another contestant of color break down the racism on display that night. The scene includes LaBeija furiously declaring to the camera, "I have the *right* to show my color, Darling. . . . I *am* beautiful, and I *know* I'm beautiful!"

Twenty-first century readers may be startled to see radical feminists aligning themselves with *The Queen*'s politics, given their association with transphobia since the early 2000s, an association solidified by the popularization of the term "TERF" for trans-exclusionary radical feminist, in 2008. The accusation is well-earned, particularly when one considers that Kathie Sarachild (formerly Amatniek), Carol Hanisch, Ti-Grace Atkinson, and Robin Morgan, along with many other founders of the women's liberation movement, have been counted among their numbers or expressed trans-exclusionary sentiments. The association is also far too sweeping. It glosses over a history—and contemporary political terrain—that is more complex. While TERF narrowed the category initially

* Crystal LaBeija would transform Harlem's Black and Latinx drag ball culture as the founding Mother of the House of LaBeija in the late 1970s. By the time Jennie Livingston chronicled the scene in her 1990 documentary *Paris Is Burning*, the house system was its defining feature.

to a specific set of transatlantic radical feminists, its use became generalized over time to frame radical feminism itself as inherently and inevitably transphobic. The benefit showing of *The Queen* to raise funds for the inaugural issue of one of the period's most radical feminist journals suggests this was not the case.

Peggy Dobbins appeared before a grand jury on September 27, 1968, and was charged with possession and use of an "offensive smelling substance." Her bail was set at $1,000. In her article about the Miss America protest for *Voice of the Women's Liberation Movement*, Judith Duffett, one of the NYRW members in the balcony during the pageant, expressed surprise at the indictment, which carried "a possible sentence of two to three years."

The general thrust of Duffett's piece celebrated the action's successes and the visibility it had brought women's liberation. Without identifying either woman, she closed with references to Yolande Betbeze, a former Miss America "who is on our side," and Charlotte Curtis, whom she described as "a woman who was asked to be a judge but declined, partly because she heard of our plans." In the same issue with Duffett's story, *Voice of a Women's Liberation Movement* ran a notice encouraging readers to support NOW's Colgate-Palmolive boycott. For their part, the October issue of the newsletter *NOW in the News* included congratulations for the Miss America Pageant protest and advertised a fund-raiser for Peggy Dobbins's legal costs.

NOW-NYC's publicity newsletter also advertised the *David Susskind Show* that had been in the works all summer, but was now a post–Miss America protest episode. Guests were Kate Millet, Anselma Dell'Olio, Jacqui Ceballos, and the person Susskind had been so insistent upon including, Ros Baxandall. Susskind planned on doing a segment of only twenty minutes, but Baxandall argued him into a full hour. When he finally said, *fine, fine, we'll do the hour*, Baxandall made him write out an IOU. Susskind grabbed an oversized index card and scrawled "I promise to put on the Women's Liberation Movement at 6:30 p.m. for a minimum of 1 hour on Oct. 14, 1968," and signed it. Baxandall folded it over three times into a small square and slipped it into her pocket. When the show aired, Susskind introduced it with, "There are some women here tonight and they're very angry." Another NYRW member watching at home was thrilled when Baxandall replied, "We're New York Radical Women, but we're also called Women's

Liberation." Throughout the hour, Susskind's preference for good-looking feminists remained clear to viewers and participants alike. (It made Baxandall wonder at the host's obvious dislike for Dell'Olio: "So odd . . . [she was] very pretty and you think he would have liked her but then he didn't.")

The nationally syndicated show added to the momentum, further amplifying not only the Miss America protest but also the wider movement for women's liberation. It sparked "enormous appeal all over America," recalled Baxandall, and prompted a new wave of letters and requests for information. "I mean we had some movement at the beginning. . . . We were really talking to everyone. I mean it was a real rapport." When the Ukrainian woman on the building's cleaning staff began stopping to attend parts of their meetings at the SCEF office, Baxandall thought the group was "really here, you know? We could talk to anyone." The sense that they were at the cusp of a truly mass movement was both palpable and energizing. It also made the stakes that much higher.

Carol Hanisch grew disappointed in the Miss America protest as her doubts mounted about what they'd really achieved. She wished it had been more impactful, more clearly understood, more inspiring, more instigating—just *more*—and she spent hours talking through the events with Amatniek and others, reflecting on how they might have done things differently. The national women's liberation conference in November (which had been on the agenda at Sandy Spring) gave Hanisch the opportunity to share her concerns more widely, in the form of the missive "What Can Be Learned: A Critique of the Miss America Protest" for circulation. "No action taken in the Women's Liberation Struggle will be all good or all bad," she wrote. "It is necessary that we analyze each step to see what we did that was effective, what was not and what was downright destructive." This was necessary to achieve the two "primary immediate goals" of the struggle: "(1) Awakening the latent consciousness of women about their own oppression, and (2) building sisterhood."

The paper largely focused on what Hanisch had identified as ineffective or destructive, and mostly attributed them to people like Robin Morgan, Peggy Dobbins, and others of similar mind. One of the "biggest mistakes" was allowing an individualistic "spirit of every woman 'do her own thing'" (even if the group had already decided against that thing), that led to a strain of "anti-womanism" in the protest. Slogans like "Up Against the Wall," "Miss America or Miss America is a Big Falsie" undercut sisterhood. "Miss America and all beautiful women came off as our enemy instead of our sisters who suffer with us." This was reinforced in the guerilla-theater tactics, which Hanisch thought too open to misinterpretation. "Crowning a live sheep Miss America sort of said that beautiful women are sheep."

The *10 Points* press release and its subsequent use as the protest flyer was also a root source of the problem. It was, "too long, too wordy, too complex, too hippy-yippie-campy," argued Hanisch. In other words: *too Robin Morgan*. "If we are going to reach masses of women, we must give up all the 'in-talk' of the New Left/Hippie movements. . . . We can use simple language (real language) that everyone from Queens to Iowa will understand and not misunderstand." Hanisch's frustration was heavily freighted with enduring conflicts between *feminists* and *politicos*. It was also fueled by Hanisch's formative experience as a white civil rights activist in Mississippi in the aftermath of Freedom Summer. Cadres of leaders speaking only to one another would never build a mass movement. "Unfortunately," she concluded, "the best slogan for the action came up about a month after when Roz [*sic*] Baxandall came out on the David Susskind show with 'Every day in a woman's life is a walking Miss America Contest.'"

While popular coverage of the Miss America demonstration often misidentified the women's liberationists as a group that had broken away from NOW, the organization's New York City chapter actually did go through a very public split along these lines in the fall of 1968. The tensions between liberal feminist members committed to women's equality (like Betty Friedan) and radical women increasingly identified with women's liberation and Black Power (like Flo Kennedy and Ti-Grace Atkinson), which had been amplified by the Valerie Solanas controversy, had grown unmanageable. The blending and mutual support of NOW and women's liberation that was evident in their respective October periodicals were not welcomed by all—indeed, far from it.

A protracted battle at the chapter and national board levels over by-law changes related to organization leadership positions led Ti-Grace Atkinson to resign as president of NOW-NYC in October. She promptly founded a new group, called the October 17th Movement, commemorating the date of her resignation. Memorably heralded by her (and repeated in the press) as a movement of the "Young, Black, and Beautiful," Atkinson's new group and the conflict within NOW was covered as emblematic of divisions between liberals and radicals across the left and civil rights movement.

It was in this context that Betty Friedan became more outspoken in her criticism of women's liberation. Less than a week after Atkinson's resignation, Friedan was quoted in the *Washington Post* as telling a meeting of the D.C. chapter that, "She hoped they would not through pseudo-radicalism become 'infantile deviates,' reacting to sex discrimination by advocating abolition of marriage and family." Friedan worried that "our brightest and most spirited young women [were] turning their backs on society."

Flo Kennedy had known from her first NOW chapter meeting on that frigid night the previous February that they were not really her people. A year and a half later, the benefits she had seen then to staying—and becoming a leader—in the chapter were no longer enough. In November, she submitted her letter of resignation to the "Officialdom of NOW: National and New York," in which she made clear the host of longstanding reasons for her departure. There had been several "last straws," wrote Kennedy, which she had endured for the sake of the bigger, intwined projects of race and gender justice and radical change. She added:

> The first straw was the negative reaction at the very first organizational meeting of New York NOW when I suggested that we take a position against the war in Viet Nam. And the "last straw" which resulted in my assuming an informally inactive status was a racist remark of National president Betty Friedan at an Executive Committee meeting at the home of Shep and Muriel Fox Aronson demanding that I focus my attention on matters of black power and not dare to interfere with the public relations of NOW.

A "second 'last straw'" had been the "paranoid" reactions by national and chapter officers to the *New York Times* article about her legal work for Valerie Solanas. "The interference with my clientele and law practice by national and local officers was, to say the least, oppressive."

Ti-Grace Atkinson's spectacular departure from NOW was not Flo Kennedy's reason for resigning, but it was part of her sense that the work she'd been able to do from within the organization was over. She would take her Black feminism and activist vision elsewhere.

39

BEAUTY QUEEN STUMPS

Less than a week before the election, the *New York Times* ran a story about strong support for Nixon—not Wallace—among the monied elite, old and new, of Macon, Georgia. It featured Miss America 1953, Neva Langley (now Mrs. William A. Fickling Jr.) as a "Nixon supporter," a "glowing beauty," and "typical of Macon's suburban young-marrieds in the new-money set." After noting the many attributes of Nixon (and his wife) that she liked, and how strongly she disliked Humphrey's liberalism, the article continued, "She finds all three Presidential candidates physically unattractive, and as for Mr. Wallace, Mrs. Fickling can hardly bear to watch him on television."

It was a rare turning of the tables in the usual accounting of beauty's political currency in the 1968 election. Teams of Nixonettes, Nixonaires, and bucket-toting Wallace Girls had been all over the country since the summer, decorating campaign events, cheering, and selling their candidates. Hubert Humphrey fielded no cheer teams, but did have his own campaign beauty queen in the person of his daughter-in-law, Donna Humphrey. Reporting a campaign stop in New York City shortly before the start of the Democratic Convention, the *New York Daily News* made the case bluntly, in a story headlined, "Beauty Queen Stumps for Dad-in-Law Hubie," which opened, "In the escalating battle to win the glamour vote away from Julie and Tricia Nixon, Hubert Humphrey deployed his platinum-haired daughter-in-law, a former beauty queen, in the streets of

Manhattan yesterday." Convention coverage then ran pictures of Donna dancing with celebrities in the "Hubaret" disco and hospitality suite sponsored by Young Citizens for Humphrey, at the Conrad Hilton Hotel, and she became a constant presence on the campaign after his nomination, usually in the service of reaching young voters.

A month before Donna Humphrey became a campaign fixture, though, she had served as one of the judges for the Miss Illinois Pageant who crowned Judi Ford and set her on the path to Atlantic City. When the mayor of Aurora, Illinois, host city to the state's pageant, declared the last week of October 1968 to be "Miss America Week," in honor of Ford's arrival for a two-day extravaganza planned by the Aurora Jaycees, Hubert Humphrey sent a telegram to be read at the opening banquet. "Dear Judi—Donna told me when you were selected Miss Illinois and that your beauty, charm and poise were a credit to Illinois and that you would go on to be Miss America. I want to add my welcome to what I know must be a warm and great homecoming for you tonight." In her own account of her daughter's time as Miss America, *Sharing the Crown*, Marjorie Ford would recall a Republican congressman sputtering afterward that he knew Richard Nixon was very excited for Judi Ford's Miss America victory, too, as well as for the good people of Illinois with whom she shared it.

It was unusual for the Nixon campaign to pass up an opportunity to associate themselves with the Miss America Pageant, but they had been working very hard to keep one connection out of the public eye since the Republican convention in August. Strom Thurmond was in a relationship with Miss South Carolina 1965, Nancy Moore, who was forty-four years younger than the senator. The couple's courtship had been suspected by some for at least a year, and it was known to Thurmond's closest advisors, most of whom begged him to step away from Moore. While official versions of their story tend to start with Thurmond's making a routine call of congratulations to the new Miss South Carolina in the summer of 1965, they'd first met the previous summer, a few weeks before Moore began her freshman year at Duke University. In 1967, she had spent a month interning in Thurmond's office, and she returned for the entire summer in 1968, after graduating with honors. She was planning to attend the University of South Carolina Law School in the fall.

Harry Dent, who had brokered getting the list of VP candidates from Phyllis Schlafly at the convention, had learned of the romance—and the gossip about it—when he got back to South Carolina from Miami Beach. "People were aghast at the idea that Senator Thurmond (then approaching his sixty-sixth birthday) was considering marriage with this girl," Dent shared with one of the senator's biographers later. He and another staffer convinced Thurmond to distance himself from Moore until after the election, to avoid a scandal that might hurt Nixon. They hoped the relationship would wither before November.

Betty Friedan's article about the August Republican and Democratic conventions was published in the October issue of *Mademoiselle,* making it a commentary on the status of women in both major parties on the eve of the election. A few weeks later, Norman Mailer's account of his time in Miami Beach and Chicago was published in *Harper's* magazine's November issue, as well as a Signet paperback. Fresh on the heels of his success with *The Armies of the Night,* about the October 1967 March on the Pentagon against the Vietnam War, *Miami and the Siege of Chicago* was Mailer's follow-up experiment in New Journalism. Ultimately, the opening lines of his still-much-celebrated book suggested the tone and perspective of both the author and his imagined audience. Describing the South Florida heat and humidity in August, Mailer wrote, "The sensation of breathing, then living, was not unlike being obliged to make love to a 300-pound woman who has decided to get on top. Got it?" Got it.

Otherwise, it seemed that the Nixonettes, Nixonaires, and Nixon's daughters were the only women Norman Mailer actually saw in Miami Beach. He devoted several lines to the various uniforms and leatherette details of the "bevy of good-looking chicks with sharp noses and tight mouths" who kicked, cheered, and stumped for Nixon around the convention. Mailer spent nearly two pages pondering the beauty and demeanors of Nixon's daughters: "both lovely looking girls." The only statement from either that he quoted directly, attributed simply to "one of Nixon's daughters," was that their father "had never spanked them." They'd never given him cause, the interchangeable daughter explained in a way made lascivious by Mailer, "'We never wanted to displease him. We wanted to be good.'" Even as objects of desire in tasteless innuendo, Julie and Tricia were only representations of their father. Mailer wrote that he was discomfited by having to reappraise Nixon, but "a man who could produce daughters like that could not be all bad." The Nixon campaign banked on such sentiments until the end.

On Monday, November 4, 1968, Richard Nixon and Hubert Humphrey both held election-eve telethons, billed as four hours of prime-time television during which the candidates would answer questions phoned in by the American people. Nixon aired his telethon from the NBC Studios in Burbank, California, in the large studio for the *Bob Hope Show*. There, 125 telephones were installed for the operators, who were all young women, including Tricia and Julie. It was the last and biggest in a campaign-long series of local and national television programs for Nixon produced by the Nixon campaign's special television advisor Roger Ailes, who was twenty-eight years old and formerly a producer for the *Mike Douglas Show.* George Wallace kept himself on television that night with a much cheaper (but still costly) half-hour, pre-taped program that aired on the three networks at different times. NBC executives proclaimed the Nixon election-eve telethon to be "the most complicated production ever mounted" at the Burbank studios. Coverage of the program before and after the election in the industry press was significant, earning Roger Ailes kudos and publicity. The Nixon campaign and its success in 1968 would secure Ailes's reputation in the industry and set him on the path that would lead to his creation of Fox News.

But on the weekend before the election, everyone with the campaign was amped up and anxious. After coaching Nixon through an appearance on NBC's *Meet the Press* on Sunday morning, Roger Ailes met a friend at a small airstrip outside of LA and took his first parachute jump. On his second jump, he tore the ligaments in an ankle while landing.

On Monday morning, Ailes limped around the studio on crutches. He and others for Nixon were frank about the fact that they had pre-written questions at the ready, claiming they were only trying to plan ahead for likely subjects with clear and concise versions of the phoned-in queries. Ailes's idea was that the callers would show the campaign where they needed to go, but the format would allow them to tailor the versions of their questions to keep Nixon comfortably on message. The term Ailes used to describe the plan was a "semi-forgery" of spontaneous live TV.

When Ailes was staging the show with other members of the team, he worried about how best to use Nixon's daughters. "If we put Julie and Tricia over there, answering phones," he said, "we have to be careful about who we put around them." Ailes then told his assistant, "Dolores, make a note of that. Make sure we get good-looking girls around Julie and Tricia."

With all the lights and people in the studio, it was bound to get hot, and everyone was worried about Nixon's sweating. The team decided to cancel the 5:00 p.m. dress rehearsal so they could turn out all the lights and crank up the air-conditioning. Nixon would be on live television for a total of four hours, and part of Ailes's direction was to create opportunities—shots of the phone banks or Tricia and Julie—to mop Nixon's face with witch hazel and touch up his makeup.

During the studio cooling break, Ailes stretched out on a couch to elevate his ankle and talk with Roger McGinnis, who was at work on what would become his book, *The Selling of the President*. "This is the beginning of a whole new concept," Ailes told the reporter. "This is it. This is the way they will be elected forevermore. The next guys up will have to be performers."

When the women chosen to answer the phones—later called "young girl volunteers" and "Nixonaires" in the press—were brought into the studio and shown to their places, Nixon's campaign communications director, Frank Shakespeare, was horrified that they all appeared to be white. "This is terrible," he erupted. "Where are the Black faces? Where are the Black faces?"

"We're going live across the country on Election Eve in an hour and a half and there's not one Black face up there," Shakespeare continued. "We can't do that. It looks terrible."

Then someone noticed a lone Black woman near the back of the phone bank. "I could ask her to come down front, so you'd be sure to get her in the picture," offered the volunteer coordinator.

"Yes," said Shakespeare, "yes, do that. Terrific."

The morning after Nixon was elected, Clifton Daniels dropped a note to Charlotte Curtis through the *New York Times*'s interoffice mail. He joked about a lost ambassadorship and expressed regret that Curtis would now not have the opportunity to cover his "first ball at Winfield House."

A few weeks later, Curtis received a letter from the office of President-elect Richard Nixon, a sure sign of the cultural and political power she wielded by 1968. It was addressed to "Mr. Curtis," identifying "him" as a leader in "his" field and asking that if "he" had any ideas about people the new administration should hire, to please forward them to Nixon's office.

Curtis was by this time preparing to cover the wedding of Julie Nixon and David Eisenhower on December 22, in New York, officiated by Norman Vincent Peale, at the Marble Collegiate Church on Fifth Avenue. Ladybird Johnson had been surprised that the Nixons would pass up the opportunity for a White House wedding; had it been up to the president-elect, they might not have. But Julie had insisted on keeping the date before the inauguration and for "limiting" the guest list to five hundred; the Agnews and a few new cabinet members would be the only figures from the new administration in attendance. She and David already knew it would be "the last major event we could keep private before the omnivorous publicity" of the next several years.

Charlotte Curtis's story about the wedding would appear on the front page of the *Times*, wedged between the headlines: "Astronauts Give Television Show on Way to Moon" and "82 In Pueblo Crew Freed; US Gives North Koreans 'Confession,' Disavows It." Inside the paper, nestled among announcements of the nuptials for a young couple from Montclair, New Jersey, and the engagement of the son of the former ambassador and Harvard professor, John Kenneth Galbraith, was the news that "Senator Strom Thurmond, 66 years old and a man who seldom shuns publicity, married twenty-two-year-old Nancy Moore, a former Miss South Carolina, in secrecy today."

40

GIVE BACK THE VOTE

Driving home to New York from the women's liberation conference in Lake Villa, Illinois, a car full of women from NYRW decided the group should participate in MOBE's counter-inaugural protest on the day before Nixon's inauguration on January 20, 1969. Driving through the night, freezing in a rental car with a broken heater, the women talked about staging a "Give Back the Vote" guerilla-theater action during which they would burn voter registration forms (like draft cards). The action would demonstrate the futilities of liberal democracy by rejecting the signature success of the first-wave feminists. Symbolically rejecting the vote would say that women didn't want equal participation in an oppressive system; they wanted something radically new that could never be built through electoral politics.

The idea appealed to others in the group who wanted a women's liberation presence at the Counter-Inaugural, despite reservations about how much the rest of the coalition wanted them there. The "Give Back the Vote" action would lend presence and specificity to their involvement and the aims of women's liberation, they felt, keeping them from getting lost amid the inevitable spectacle of New Left patriarchy. It was never clear in the weeks leading up to the event that MOBE was much invested in the women's participation—something made more obvious when the national call for the protest did not include a women's liberation group among the other sponsoring organizations of the coalition.

Planning the action necessitated collaborative organizing between women's liberationists in New York and Washington, which was mostly carried off by Ros Baxandall and Marilyn Webb. The women had developed a strong working relationship since Lake Villa, which was rare in the atmosphere of distrust that persisted between the two groups. When the New Yorkers arrived in Washington for the Counter-Inauguration, conflict erupted at once with the announcement that Webb had already been selected by MOBE as the spokesperson for women's liberation. With only hours before the next day's action to come to a resolution, the women compromised: Shulamith Firestone would speak for New York and the "Give Back the Vote" action, and Webb would speak for Washington, D.C.

Early on Sunday morning, Barbara Mehrhof went to visit Alice Paul at her home in Washington, D.C. Mehrof was one of the original road trippers who had come up with the "Give Back the Vote" idea on that long night in the frigid rental car. She wanted to tell Paul about their action and find out what she thought of women's liberation. She wanted her support, and for Paul to agree that the vote had not been the panacea for women's equality that the elder generation had thought it would be (forgetting, perhaps, that Alice Paul and the National Woman's Party had never planned to stop at suffrage, and had promptly originated the ERA after the 19th Amendment's ratification). Paul was horrified at the idea of "giving back the vote" and argued to Mehrof that women's freedom was and remained fundamentally premised upon unfettered access to participation in elections.

It was an astonishing moment when the most radical parts of first- and second-wave feminism met and confronted one another. That Alice Paul was still alive and active in Washington, D.C., brings home how very little time had passed since ratification of the 19th Amendment, and how fraught was the ongoing struggle for the ERA.

The center of MOBE's operations in the course of the three days of inaugural events was a huge striped tent erected on the National Mall, just south of the Washington Monument. Thousands of protesters gathered at the tent on Sunday, January 19, for a rally at which speeches from counter-inaugural coalition members would be interspersed with musical acts. On Monday, Nixon would take the oath of office, and MOBE would lead a massive protest march.

January in the capital was rainy and cold, and the ground beneath the tent was slick with mud. It was almost a year to the day since Shulamith Firestone had been in Washington in similarly slushy conditions with Kathie Amatniek, Peggy Dobbins, Bev Grant, Carol Hanisch, and others from New York to stage their funeral for traditional womanhood and protest the Jeannette Rankin Brigade's woman-power march. It had been one year since they had joined new radical women's groups from around the country to put the women's movement on notice: women's liberation had arrived. So much had changed in the twelve months and four days since then; so much had stayed infuriatingly the same or had gotten worse.

When Firestone and Webb were finally given the stage—the last to address the crowd—nothing about their arguments cohered. Webb spoke about the place of women in the New Left and the role of women's liberation in the larger movement represented at the counter-inaugural, while Firestone denounced the male chauvinism of the left and declared the need for independent women's liberation. While Firestone burned voter registration forms and the two women continued to speak at odds with one another, the crowd became increasingly agitated. Verbal and then physical fights erupted between men who were taking different sides of the women's liberation issue, while many wanted both women and their ideas about liberation to go away.

Suddenly, as Webb was speaking, a clear male voice rose above the pandemonium: "Take her off the stage and fuck her!" Other men joined in, making similar jeers about assaulting and silencing the women.

Firestone, continuing to burn voter registration forms, shouted back. The men's urge to sexual violence was evidence that she was correct: women could never achieve their own liberation from within the New Left. Indeed, she yelled, "Let's start talking about where *we live*, baby!"

MOBE director Dave Dellinger turned to other men from his organization who were posted near the speakers and yelled, "Shut Shulie up!" They jumped to hustle Firestone and Webb off the stage and away from the seething crowd.

This scene was a turning point for Marilyn Webb and many movement women who had been holding fast to the idea that they could organize for their own liberation from within the left. But their male comrades would not recognize their own oppression by the patriarchy; they could not see that they were women's natural allies, not their enemies. It was a terrible, clarifying bookend to Webb's concluding assurance—"We love you!"—to her SDS brothers, after having presented the women's liberation resolution to the national conference in July 1967. Now, in the shadow of the Washington Monument, at the counter-inaugural in 1969, they responded with a violent "Fuck you!"

Later, when Webb was home in her apartment, still shaken by what had happened, her phone rang. When she put the receiver to her ear, a women spat out, "If you ever make a speech like that again, and continue to push Women's Liberation on the Movement, we will kill you." The woman on the phone didn't identify herself, but Webb was convinced (incorrectly) that it was SDS leader Cathy Wilkerson.

Marilyn Webb would tell the story of this call often as the time Cathy Wilkerson threatened her after the counter-inaugural. Wilkerson never stopped denying that it was her, but Webb was unpersuaded. Several years later, after the FBI's COINTELPRO operations against women's liberation and other radical groups in the late 1960s and 1970s were revealed, Webb came to believe that the call must have come from an FBI agent as part of their project to undermine activist organizations by creating internal conflicts—or by fueling them.

When Nixon took his oath of office the following day, both recent Miss Americas from Kansas, Deborah Bryant and Debbie Barnes, were among the honored guests. So was the new Miss Indian America XV, Thomasine Hill, a Crow-Pawnee woman from Crow Agency, Montana, near the site of the historic 1876 Battle of the Little Big Horn. Hill had been crowned Miss Indian America a month after the American Indian Movement (AIM) was founded in Minneapolis. With a platform of challenging stereotypes and Native American self-determination, she had far more in common with the cultural nationalists of AIM than with the founding ethos of the pageant she represented. Before going to Washington for the inauguration, she made clear to journalists that she had not voted for Nixon and that she was a registered Democrat.

The following Saturday was Debbie Barnes's much-anticipated wedding day after which, as the *Iola Register* put it, "Debra is not Miss America anymore, she's Mrs. Mitchell Miles." Press photographers and television crews were on the scene but were barred from entering the church, left waiting "in sub-freezing weather for nothing," as one photographer complained to a journalist. The wedding devolved into a public relations nightmare when groomsmen forcibly repelled the news crews as they attempted to get shots of the couple leaving the church. A steady stream of articles and op-eds lambasting Barnes followed. The *St. Joseph Herald-Press* opined, "A beauty queen who has lived for 12 months on publicity should not deny her fans knowledge of the most romantic event of all—her marriage." She may not have been Miss America anymore, but she still belonged to the American people and the media that fed them.

PART IV

POSITIVELY BEAUTIFUL

41

LET'S HEAR FROM SOME *REAL* EXPERTS

It had become a familiar scene on the streets of Manhattan: smartly dressed women and a smattering of men picketing in an elongated loop in front of a government building or corporate headquarters. On February 13, 1969, picketers assembled outside the city's Health Department to protest hearings on the reform of New York State's restrictive abortion law, which allowed abortion only in cases of the mother's imminent death. The Joint Legislative Committee on the Problems of Public Health was readying to hear testimony from experts about other conditions under which abortion could be legal, including in cases of rape or incest, if the mother was very young, if her physical or mental health was "gravely imperiled," or if the child would have a significant disability that made it impossible for them to care for themselves. This was the most recent instance of a reform movement that had been active in the state for several years and more recently among its legislators. Throughout this time, other voices, including those from NOW and women's liberation, had called for an outright repeal of the law and the legalization of abortion.

When women from the New York chapter of NOW learned about the scheduled hearings from a story in the *New York Times*, they contacted the committee chair, asking to be included among those offering testimony. The chair declined the request, saying that there would be no public comment period, only testimony from invited experts—a group of fifteen comprising fourteen men and a Catholic nun. Pivoting, they joined a coalition of repeal activists in protest, including many from women's liberation. The picket was the first action by the Redstockings, a group founded by Shulamith Firestone and Ellen Willis (the first rock/pop music critic for the *New Yorker*) in reaction to the events at the counter-inaugural. The group was for radical feminists only, as opposed to the mixed collective that NYRW had once been. Robin Morgan, Peggy Dobbins, Florika Remetier, and others were already much more ensconced in their new guerrilla theater, zap action group, WITCH. As was her way, Ros Baxandall was part of both.

The women's liberationists walked the line and moved through the crowd distributing flyers that read: "The only real experts on abortions are women. Women who have known the pain, fear, and socially imposed guilt of an illegal abortion. Women who have seen their friends dead or in agony from post-abortion infection. Women who have had children by the wrong man, at the wrong time, because no doctor would help them." They were joined by Flo Kennedy, who stood out among the picketers as she sauntered the line, not just because she was one of the only Black people there but also because she was dressed in her usual striking style. On this cold February morning, Kennedy wore a tall fur hat and sunglasses, and a shiny leather trench coat topped by a large fur stole—impossible to miss in the sea of wool coats.

As the protesters marched and chanted, journalists peeled different women off the picket line to ask for comments. City Councilwoman Carol Greitzer responded to one television news man's question with, "I'm here because I'm in favor of abortion law repeal, rather than just simple reform of the abortion laws, and this group is protesting the fact that none of us were invited to testify, and they are only allowing invited speakers to speak today and there's only one woman representing a religious organization." The very idea was "outrageous," she continued. "Most women are in favor of repeal, they don't think there should be any restrictions on a woman's basic civil rights, which is not to bear an unwanted child." Throughout the interview, Greitzer held a sign in front of her reading, "Reform is the Enemy of Meaningful Change—Repeal Abortion Laws."

The protest outside lasted until 10 a.m., when the hearings got underway in the Health Department's first-floor auditorium, which was quickly filled with women. The eight members of the Joint Committee, all men, sat in a line on a dais at the front of the room, looking wary as the chair opened the session by stating that it would be a hearing for testimony from "experts familiar with the psychological and sociological facts" of abortion, and would not be opened to the floor for public comment. He then invited the first person, a representative from the governor's commission, to speak.

Kathie Amatniek, looking somewhat prim with her longish pixie cut, small earrings, and sweater set topped by a single strand of pearls, jumped up near the front of the room and yelled, "Okay, folks, now it's time to hear from the real experts! I don't mean the public opinion you're so uninterested in. I mean concrete evidence from the people who really know—women. I can tell you the psychological and sociological effect the law has had on *me*—it's made me *angry*! It's made me think about things like forcing doctors to operate at gunpoint."

The auditorium erupted, as more women cheered and spoke, assemblymen sputtered, and journalists got excited.

"What about the American Revolution?" asked one woman who had moved up to the dais to confront the men directly. "Taxation without representation? Abortion laws without representation!"

The committee chair tried to get order, finally offering, "If you girls can organize yourselves and elect a spokesman. . . ." He was cut off by a woman saying "We want to testify, not have a spokesperson," while others booed and jeered, prompting him to blurt out: "We will let you talk if you keep quiet!" Not long after, he moved to adjourn the hearing and shifted the proceedings to a closed executive meeting in an upstairs room.

Women's liberationists filled the hall outside the new location. Barred from entry by several police officers posted at the door, they chanted, "We are the experts!"

In order to continue with the hearing, the committee struck a compromise that allowed four women from the group to speak. One of the assemblymen, Senator Seymour R. Thaler, who was himself pro-repeal, confronted the women with exasperation. "Why were they doing this? Why be so disruptive when several were on their side, including four of the men scheduled to testify that day? Couldn't they see," he implored, "that their actions were not advancing their cause?"

To this, one of the activists replied that they did not want to rely on others, on men, to speak for them—they wanted to speak for themselves. "Even if we accepted your definition of expert—and we don't," she added, "couldn't you find any female doctors or lawyers?"

"I agree with you about the law," Thaler responded, "but you're just acting out of your personal pique against men."

"Not personal pique—*political grievance*!"

"All I can say," he growled, "is that you're the rudest bunch of people I've ever met."

The next day's headline in the *New York Daily News* read, "Gals Squeal for Repeal, Abort State Hearing," and featured a picture of Amatniek shouting, while a woman next to her jabbed her finger forward as she addressed the assemblymen. The paper misidentified Kathie as being from NOW. This was the last time she would give her last name to the press or anyone else as "Amatniek." She stopped using her stepfather's name and began to go by the name Sarachild, after her mother. From this point on, she was Kathie, child of Sara.

On March 21, 1969, the Redstockings held an "Abortion Speak Out," during which twelve members of the group openly talked about their own abortions. The public testimony action blended a consciousness-raising session with the hearing from which they had been barred. Journalist Susan Brownmiller described for the *Village Voice* a scene of three hundred women and men filling the sanctuary of the Washington Square Methodist Church in the West Village to receive the women's stories, and in some cases, to share their own experiences. She wrote:

> The panelists prepared no speeches for the Friday night open meeting. They set up an unobtrusive tape recorder, kept the lights comfortably dim to encourage conversation, and protected their anonymity by using first names only. The result, which could have been exhibitionistic or melodramatic, was neither—it was an honest rap. And it worked.

The women spoke truth to oppression, narrating their real, female experiences to advance the cause of repeal and to let other women hear and see that they were not alone.

Ros Baxandall was one of the twelve who that night shared her story of having had an illegal abortion. Many years later, she revisited the story in an interview with Brownmiller. Baxandall had the abortion in Milwaukee, Wisconsin, during which she had been provided no anesthetic. When she yelled out in pain, the doctor told her to hush. "There's no reason to scream," he barked, "you're no n—ger." His racism seemed so disconnected from what was happening to her, and his callousness so unnecessary. It was a trauma she shared publicly for the first time in 1969—one that she would carry for a lifetime.

Sitting in the audience, Flo Kennedy was moved and inspired. She would take this experience into her pro-bono work with four other attorneys to file a class action lawsuit against the State of New York on behalf of women harmed by not having access to safe, legal abortions. *Abramowicz v. Lefkowitz* would be the first case of its kind in the country to focus on the experiences and testimony of women who had had abortions, rather than testimony by medical "experts"—a premise based on Kennedy's powerful witness at the "Abortion Speak Out." The attorneys would hinge the case's argument on these harms and the equal protection clause of the 15th Amendment (not the "right to privacy" arguments used in earlier access to birth control cases, which would become the basis of *Roe v. Wade*—and then part of its repeal with the *Dodd* decision in 2022). Kennedy and the other lawyers assumed they were facing an inevitable loss in New York, but they were focused on starting an appeals process that could take the case and the issue to the U.S. Supreme Court.

Susan Brownmiller was at the "Abortion Speak Out" to report on it, but also as a member of women's liberation in support of her activist community. She had attended her first NYRW meeting two weeks after the Miss America protest; this attendance was at the prompting of a close friend with whom she had gone to Mississippi as part of Freedom Summer in 1964. Brownmiller's next four years were devoted to building her career as a journalist; in addition to pieces in the *Village Voice* and regular freelance gigs for national magazines, she landed a full-time job as a television news writer for ABC. Although Brownmiller was already friends with women in NYRW, including Carol Hanisch, she had not been drawn to join earlier, in part because she had no time. "Slightly put off by my careerist incarnation, Carol hadn't thought I'd get the idea of women's oppression," Brownmiller wrote later. But she "got it smack in the face that very first night" when during the consciousness-raising session she had been moved to speak openly for the first time about her own illegal abortions.

Gloria Steinem covered the February 1969 abortion hearing and its disruption by the Redstockings as a political columnist for *New York* magazine. Moved, she attended the "Abortion Speak Out" in the same capacity the following month. It was there that the penny dropped for Steinem—in movement speak, things *clicked*—and she realized she was a feminist. She explained:

> I didn't begin my active life as a feminist until I went to an abortion speak-out in a church basement in the Village in 1969, when I was already in my mid-thirties. I was there covering it, and I was sitting there on the window-sill on the side, still being a reporter. . . . There was something about seeing women tell the truth about their lives in public . . . It made sense of my own experience—I had had an abortion and had never told anyone.

Steinem published her first column about feminism on April 7, 1969. Titled "After Black Power, Women's Liberation," it presented a picture of radical feminist foment in the city with the potential of "becoming sort of a revolutionary vanguard." Writing from the perspective of an observer, rather than a participant or new convert, she took readers on a quick tour of women's liberation groups and their activities, including WITCH and the Redstockings. "If the 'consciousness-raising' programs of the WLM work, they'll see them as rallying points for women *qua* women," she concluded. "And that might forge the final revolutionary link. Rumblings are already being heard inside the Democratic party in New York. It's the women who staff and win elections, and they may finally balk at working for only men—not very qualified men at that—in the mayoral primary."

Steinem was by this time already a New York celebrity journalist with a growing national profile—not unlike Charlotte Curtis in some ways, to whom she looked for mentoring at least once. Like Betty Friedan, a fellow Smith College alum, she had been working and writing for years and burst onto the public scene in 1963, not with a bombshell feminist bestseller but as a Playboy Bunny. Steinem had spent eleven days undercover in Chicago's Playboy Club for *Show* magazine. The editors explained at the start of the article that Steinem was chosen for the assignment because she "combines the hidden qualities of a Phi Beta Kappa, *magnum cum laude* graduate of Smith College with the more obvious ones of an ex-dancer and beauty queen."

As Steinem's profile as a journalist grew, so did her popularity as a subject for others. Society pages noted her presence at political and cultural events, tracked her social life, and reported on famous boyfriends; profiles in national media outlets proliferated. And not one of those accounts went by without remarking upon her style, her hair, and how beautiful she was. The headlines often said it all, from *Newsday*'s "The World's Most Beautiful Byline" in 1965 to "Easy on the Eyes" in *Ladies Home Journal* the next year and "Writer's Life Can be Glorious and Beautiful" in the *Washington Post* in 1967.

Steinem's *New York* magazine column about women's liberation was received within this context. It positioned her as a go-to commentator on women's liberation and feminism; she got several media requests and speaking invitations, and quickly built a reputation as more than an observer—as a feminist spokesperson. Notably, before the spring of 1969, Steinem had never been involved in a feminist action, gone to a women's liberation meeting, or identified herself as a feminist in the vein of NOW. Nevertheless, her ascent in and centrality to the movement was staggeringly fast, and today she remains not only an icon but also often the only feminist many people can name. But Gloria Steinem didn't come from the organizing ferment, and this fact would generate an enormous amount of suspicion, frustration, and anger about her prominence—her media "darling-ness"—among the activists she initially wrote about.

Steinem became the beautiful face of a movement she did not come from, and her face, her beauty, and her glamorous life were key to all of it.

42

A POSITIVE PROTEST

"What a night! It was like a dream come true," enthused Saundra Williams about becoming the first Miss Black America. "For years I'd been brainwashed into thinking that beauty consisted of straight hair, a thin straight nose, and thin lips. The contest proved what I'd recently learned—black *is* beautiful." The quote was part of a long feature in the March 1969 issue of *Seventeen* magazine that gave Williams the largest national platform of her reign since the night she was crowned in Atlantic City. In it, she described her life as a high school student in Philadelphia, where she had taken for granted the segregation of her neighborhood despite her integrated public school and diverse group of friends at Overbrook High. The story traced how her move to Maryland for college sparked a new racial awareness and Black cultural and historical education, leading her to activism and to Miss Black America.

Pageant winners had to be quick studies in managing press interviews and their public images, and Williams was no exception. As the first Miss Black America, she bore the additional burden of being asked to not only represent collective Black pride, womanhood, and beauty but also speak to "race relations" and racism. The *Seventeen* interview demonstrated this aspect of her experience and the code-switching it demanded. Everything about Williams's account of her path to the crown seemed carefully narrated to educate, but not alienate, the magazine's majority-white readership of teenaged girls.

Williams also addressed Black Power in that *Seventeen* article, explaining that to her it meant "brain power and green power," or education, good jobs, and economic development. The statement distanced Williams from possible association with radicalism, including the Black Panthers, while locating her within the moment's wider political terrain. The integrationist wing of the Black Freedom Movement had been making similar arguments for years, but the stakes heightened in 1968, as organizations like the NAACP and CORE struggled to hold on to the more radical, generally younger parts of their memberships.

The "Black Power is green power" argument was part of the organizing ethos of the Miss Black America Pageant, but by 1969, it also carried clear echoes of Nixon's "Black Capitalism" campaign promises to Black voters, personified in Wilt Chamberlain and the self-empowerment and economic uplift agenda of the Black Republicans he would bring into the administration, soon to become known as Nixon's "Black Cabinet."

The *Seventeen* story was covered extensively by the Black press as a major achievement and a high-water mark for Williams's visibility. In the *Omaha Star*, the story with her comments about consciousness was run next to a column entitled "Black is Beautiful" that resonated with Williams's points about empowering hair styles and clothing. By contrast, the *Pittsburgh Courier* ran a similar story with the same picture from *Seventeen* next to an advertisement for a Skin Success Cream that promised to tone "the shades of your skin for a fairer, clearer, natural-looking loveliness" and was pointedly described as "creamy white." The difference highlighted the divided visions of Black beauty within Black communities and the media that Williams and the Miss Black America Pageant had encountered.

By the time that magazine hit newsstands, Saundra Williams was angry. Outside of the *Seventeen* feature, her time as Miss Black America had lacked many of the expected high-profile appearances or coordination from the pageant organization in the months following her victory. Williams shared her frustrations during an early March appearance on a popular morning show on Philadelphia's ABC affiliate, WFIL-TV (the same station that the pageant's MCs and one judge had come from). *On Camera* was hosted by John S. "Jack" Saunders, a prominent Black journalist and editor of the city's leading Black paper, the *Philadelphia Tribune*. What had Williams earned as Miss Black America, "the first of her race to be so honored?" he asked.

"Very little," she replied. "I was promised a scholarship, but I'm still waiting to get it. . . . I was promised several personal appearance tours, and I'm still waiting for them to start."

This is not the sort of issue Williams would have raised when speaking to a white journalist or for a predominantly white audience. She certainly hadn't brought it up for *Seventeen* magazine. But going on a Philadelphia television station with close connections to the city's Black communities meant challenging J. Morris Anderson directly, and creating a public relations problem in the place where the Miss Black America Pageant lived.

Williams spoke with similar candor about her problems with the leadership of Maryland State College, and how that had informed her own activist journey and political views. "They are too entrenched in their complacency and outmoded thinking," she said, noting that many students thought of them and some professors as "Uncle Toms." When Saunders asked her to clarify what she meant by the term, Williams explained: "A Negro whose existence depends upon the white man; one who does only what the white man dictates; one who smiles to gain favor; one who will take advantage of his fellow Black brothers and sisters in order to gain for himself; one who is ashamed of Blackness and tried to be white; one who is a traitor to his heritage." She added that direct action protest and demonstrations were "necessary in order to dramatize legitimate demands," but that she and her fellow activists at the college did "not believe in the burn, baby, burn bit. That is self-destruction."

Saunders asked Williams if she thought there would be another Miss Black America Pageant in 1969. "Oh, yes, I think the contest caught on big," she responded immediately. "I believe, however, that this year's winner will receive a great deal more than I received."

Saundra Williams was right. The following week, Madison Square Garden announced that it would host the 1969 Miss Black America Pageant, acting as a co-sponsor with Miss Black America Beauty Pageant, Inc. The move out of Atlantic City was significant. Miss Black America "is not only a protest against the white Miss America Pageant, held in Atlantic City. It protests that the Black woman in America hasn't been credited for being beautiful, talented and cultured," said J. Morris Anderson, explaining the pageant's new home in New York City. The pageant had to "stand on its own because Black beauty stands on its own [which was] one reason we moved physically away from Atlantic City."

Phillip Savage was gone from Miss Black America, along with the implied NAACP sponsorship that his involvement had initiated in 1968. Gloster Current made Savage sever the connection after an investigation the previous fall. The agreement with Madison Square Garden brought an infusion of capital that made pageant expansion possible, and Anderson set about rapidly establishing preliminary contests around the country. This was often accomplished by partnering with already extant local pageant groups and Black-owned modeling agencies, all with an eye toward developing Miss Black America Pageant franchises in the future. The National Association of Colored Women's Clubs sponsored this effort, which lent the authority and respectability of the historic organization and made official the association suggested by the Miss Black America Pageant's prominence in the pages of their magazine, *National Notes,* which Anderson's company still published. Over the next several months, Saundra Williams appeared at new state-level Miss Black America pageants around the country.

The move out of Atlantic City and away from Miss America was part of refocusing the Miss Black America Pageant as a "positive protest," a description J. Morris Anderson had begun to use the summer before but now employed regularly. It was about promoting the message of Black beauty, pride, and excellence, he said, rather than spotlighting the racism and exclusions of the Miss America Pageant. It was about rejecting the forces of "negativism."

Anderson had always centered the race and gendered pride Black men gained by recognizing "their" women's beauty as a primary achievement of his pageant. In 1969, he published a short book, *Recipes for Black Togetherness,* that elaborated upon his position and provided insight as to why he founded Miss Black America. Anderson gave his reasons for writing the book in an epigraph: "to point out, reiterate and call to the attention of Black America the need for Black men to work for solidarity, togetherness and liberation for all Brothers in order to effectively tear down the walls of injustice, racism and oppression FOREVER." Along with the titular formula for Black togetherness, what followed was a set of politically pointed and at times funny recipes for things like: "How to Get Rid of House N---ers," "How to Keep Your Black Woman," and "How to Make a Black Panther" or "Nasty White Cracker," "Soul Sister," and "Uncle Tom." The natural beauty of Black women and the love and leadership of the Black men who desired, cared for, and protected them were common ingredients. The ruinous qualities of feminism and women's liberation were also regular features.

This was most obvious with Anderson's method for "How to Liberate a Black Woman." The long list of ingredients began with "5 million Black men, 5 million Black Housewives, 25 million Black Babies," and went on to itemize various things like diapers, dishes, makeup, wigs, bras, and tampons. It included "2 million dependent Black women, ½ million equal employment opportunities," and many thousands each of women in jobs understood to be men's work (from corporate leaders to wardens to truck drivers) and it ended with "50,000 Lesbians."

The list was illustrated with two images of nude Black women depicting the before and after of liberation. The first is a female silhouette in chains, her head bowed, while the second figure's pretty face is revealed. She wears an Afro and large hoop earrings, and sits on one hip, resting her weight on her right hand, glancing to the side. The cuffs attaching the chains to the first figure have become jewelry for the liberated woman, whose left arm drapes across the tipped-up knee of her left leg, leaving her bare breasts and vulva open to the viewer. The recipe itself begins on the next page, with various combinations of the ingredients going into mixing bowls and pans, cooked in various ways at very hot temperatures, before concluding: "Drain off all Lesbians, roll them out with a rolling pin, place on cutting board and chop with meat cleaver. Take all the ingredients and pour into garbage disposal and press button. Place remaining Black women together with Black men—Black men will give Black women a good fucking—all Black women will say in unison—ahh—we have been liberated."

The negativist legions of feminism could not liberate Black women in Anderson's estimation, nor could their own ambition and striving. The agent of their liberation was Black men drawn to and publicly affirming their Black beauty and desirable bodies; their objectification *was* liberation. Considered in this light, Anderson's understanding of himself and his pageant was as liberators of Black women, freeing them from negative self-image and the tyranny of dominant white beauty standards, if not from the beauty imperative itself.

On the last day of May, Senator Edward Brooke stepped up to a podium under the shade of a tent to address Wellesley College's graduating class of 1969. His usual late-spring politician's uniform was concealed beneath the billowing red-and-black regalia of the senator's law school alma mater, Boston University, topped by a tasseled velvet tam with a jaunty tip to the left. After a tin-eared opener ("Wellesley has even more admirers than its girls have beaux, and I am pleased to be among this college's most enthusiastic boosters"), Brooke devoted most of his commencement address to urging a politics of positive action rather than negative protests. He expanded on what he saw as the "line between productive dissent and counter-productive disruption," with the sprawling New Left squarely among the latter.

For the first time in the college's history, Wellesley followed their commencement speaker with an address from a student selected by the graduating class in response to student activism and demands. When the college's president, Ruth M. Adams, introduced their chosen speaker, she explained that the Class of 1969 had "expressed a desire" for a student to "speak to them and for them" at the morning's commencement. "There was no debate as far as I could ascertain as to who their spokesperson was to be," she continued: "Miss Hillary Rodham."

Rodham removed her mortar board before approaching the podium, revealing long hair pinned in a loose updo with a single tendril pulled artfully in front of each ear. She carried a copy of her speech that she'd begun rewriting in her head as Brooke spoke. Rodham had worked for his senatorial campaign in 1966 when she was a sophomore still active in College Republicans, and had watched him negotiate a complex role at the convention in Miami Beach the previous summer. On this day, she'd listened to his address with a frustration that tipped into outrage. Why wasn't he talking to the women about the important issues that awaited them—needed them—after graduation? Why was Brooke just parroting empty Nixon administration talking points at them?

Looking out to the audience through her octagonal, wire-rimmed glasses, Rodham began:

> I am very glad that Miss Adams made it clear that what I am speaking for today is all of us—the 400 of us—and I find myself in a familiar position, that of reacting, something that our generation has been doing for quite a while now. We're not in the positions yet of leadership and power, but we do have that indispensable element of criticizing and constructive protest, and I find myself reacting just briefly to some of the things that Senator Brooke said.

Rodham deftly blended her pointed responses to Brooke with the themes of her planned remarks. "We've had lots of empathy; we've had lots of sympathy, but we feel that for too long our leaders have viewed politics as the art of the possible." Did the eyes of four hundred students and their two thousand gathered families and friends all look toward Brooke at once? "The challenge now," Rodham continued, was to reject this small aim and "to practice politics as the art of making what appears to be impossible possible."

This was where the Wellesley Class of '69 came in. They had arrived at college four years earlier, having come of age in years "dominated by men with dreams, men in the civil rights movement, the Peace Corps, the space program—so we arrived at Wellesley and we found, as all of us have found, that there was a gap between expectation and realities." But they didn't let that stop them from acting. When Rodham finished speaking about her fellow graduates' "art of making possible," in spite of politics like Brooke's, the standing ovation lasted for seven minutes.

"Senator Brooke Upstaged at Wellesley Commencement," blared the front page of the next day's *Boston Globe*.

"Park Ridge Girl Raps Brooke," crowed the *Chicago Tribune* for Rodham's hometown readers.

Both papers published longer articles about Rodham and her speech two days later, as the story of the college "girl" who took on, and took down, a senator gathered momentum. The *Des Moines Tribune* framed their own take on the story through its quick cultural saturation:

> Five years ago, blond Hillary Rodham was a 'Goldwater Girl' in suburban Park Ridge with, as she says now, 'a very limited social perspective.' Five days ago, she was just another uncommonly pretty girl in the ranks of this year's

legion of college graduates. Her enthusiasms had veered from Barry Goldwater to the likes of Senator Eugene McCarthy, Gov. Nelson Rockefeller and that sociological hell raiser Saul Alinsky. But hardly anyone, beyond her campus at Wellesley and her parents, had noticed. Today she is a celebrity who is being quoted from coast to coast and on network television. To her great amusement, she has been editorially spanked.

At the Rodham's home in Park Ridge, where Hillary had returned shortly after graduation, the phone rang off the hook with requests for interviews. One of them came from *Life* magazine, which dispatched photographer Lee Balterman to Illinois to get a photo of Rodham for inclusion in their feature on "The Class of '69: With eloquent defiance, top students protest right through commencement." Taken in the den of her family home, Rodham is pictured near full bookshelves, an upright piano, and an elaborately decorated outlet cover. She wears striking vertically striped pants with flat sandals and a white, button-front blouse with slightly puffed sleeves cuffed at her wrists. Rodham gesticulates in many of the pictures and often leans forward, as if she is pressing a point; in others, she looks softly into the camera's lens without glasses, her long hair falling over her shoulders. Balterman noted to his editor, "Had to go for nothing more than informal portraits, but should be some good expressions & hand gestures, etc.," before concluding, "Her glasses helped."

The photo *Life* chose to publish appears to capture a gently smiling Rodham who is just about to say something. She sits on an ottoman, its companion chair and a bookshelf just visible behind her, and she looks directly into the camera (through her glasses), leaning forward with her elbows on her knees and her fingers tented. All the other photos of students included in the article were taken at graduations or featured male subjects as they spoke; one woman's formal yearbook photo was used. Rodham's photo stands out as the only one taken in an informal, non-college setting.

Hillary Rodham was everywhere in June of 1969. Had John Wayne found himself sharing an elevator with her then, he might have recognized her.

On the evening of August 22, 1969, a bigger, glitzier Miss Black America Pageant opened before a near-capacity crowd in the 6,000-seat Felt Forum of Madison

Square Garden (known today as The Theater at Madison Square Garden). The master of ceremonies was pioneering Black New York City radio DJ Hal Jackson. He led the audience through a night of pageantry punctuated by performances from Stevie Wonder and other artists from Motown, a pageant sponsor, as seventeen women competed for the Miss Black America crown. This included the national stage debut of the Jackson 5, during which Michael Jackson, one week shy of his eleventh birthday, thrilled the audience as he danced down the pageant's white flower-lined runway, singing a cover of "It's Your Thing."

That night, the Impressions debuted the pageant's new theme, "Miss Black America." Written by Curtis Mayfield, the song would be included on the B-side of his first solo album, *Curtis*, released the following year. The official track begins with a spoken exchange between Mayfield and a young girl over piano and light percussion that concludes:

> *What most do you hope to be when you become a big girl?*
> Daddy, I would like to be Miss Black America.

Then, layered strings and a horn section swell over the rhythm of a bass guitar as Mayfield begins to sing of saluting natural Black beauty, racial equality, and blessing and watching over Miss Black America.

The pageant's judges were a cultural and political who's who of Black America, including Congresswoman Shirley Chisholm; Betty Shabazz, the widow of Malcolm X; novelist John O. Killens; Willis Reed, team captain for the New York Knicks; and civil rights leader and active Republican Floyd McKissick, who had led CORE from 1966 to 1968, endorsed Nixon for president, and was at work on Soul City, a planned community experiment in Black capitalism located in North Carolina. They chose Miss Black New York, Gloria O. Smith, as the second Miss Black America. Smith, who grew up in New Bern, North Carolina, arrived in New York City at the age of eighteen to attend City College. After two years, she left to focus on her singing career, which she hoped would be advanced by winning the Miss Black America crown. This included the exposure that would come when Metromedia aired an edited version of the pageant on many of its stations around the country in the weeks that followed.

Publicity for the Miss Black America Pageant prompted journalists to seek comment about the lack of Black contestants in the Miss America contest. Al Marks responded with his usual line, "Nothing would give me more pleasure than to have a number of Black girls among the 50 finalists," he claimed. "I suppose we'll have epithets hurled at us that we're still lily white, but we have no influence on the judges—some of them Black—of the 3,500 pageants."

The Miss Black America Pageant did not return to Atlantic City in 1969, but women's liberation did. "Last year's demonstration was good," in that it promised an open invitation to activists, "but this year's will be DYNAMITE." The statement captured women's liberationists' nostalgia for that first demonstration, already iconic within the movement and to the wider public, as well as the desire to create something new. It reflected some of the processing that Hanisch had encouraged, as well as the more expansive geography of women's liberation that had emerged in the wake of the 1968 protest. "Since last year our movement has grown in many creative, revolutionary ways, we will demonstrate this at Atlantic City," explained the statement. "This is a chance for all of us to act together—cutting across age, class, race, political or geographical barriers." It went to some pains to support this assertion by noting that no one group was claiming ownership of the protest. The organizers described themselves as "a few of us" from New York City who had come together in an "ad-hoc committee" to handle logistics and communications. They weren't leading the demonstration, nor were they "setting policies or limiting tactics," they promised.

This August 28, 1969, call to protest was also more bombastic. It carried a new emblem designed for the protest that would become a common motif across the women's movement in the 1970s. It was a women's symbol—a circle resting on a cross—transformed by the addition of a Black Power fist thrust into the circle as if the bottom were a woman's arm. The design came from Robin Morgan, who was a member of the release's authoring group, the Ad-hoc Committee for the Miss America Demonstration.

The statement bore other Morgan markers, including the resistant spelling of America with a "k": Amerika. "Last year, the women's liberation movement picketed outside the Miss Amerika Pageant and disrupted the live telecast of the Plastic Auction Sale inside. This year, women from all over the country will be returning to Atlantic City to confront the sexist, racist Pageant—and this year, the sky's the limit." It went on to note how much the movement had grown "in numbers and in militance," and its impacts since '68, citing NOW's victory over sex-segregated want ads, the Redstockings' disruption of the New York State hearings on abortion laws, and the spread of WITCH covens around the country "zapping" everything from "beauty parlors to burlesque houses."

While absent from the ad hoc group and still living in Gainesville, Carol Hanisch's lasting influence was also evident in the length and style of the announcement. Demonstrators were headed to Atlantic City to achieve five aims:

1. **EXPRESS** solidarity with the sister-contestants who are pressured into epitomizing the roles all women are forced to play in this society. Free the sisters! Free all women!
2. **REJECT** the degrading image of women as propagandized by the Pageant concept: brainless, smiling, sex-object pieces of meat.
3. **PROTEST** the blatant racism of a Pageant that has never had one non-white finalist.
3. **BOYCOTT** the products pushed by the Pageant sponsors, and demand an end to the symbolic use of a woman to sell those products and the attempt to manipulate us all as consumers.
4. **DENOUNCE** the Pageant's collaboration with the bloody Vietnam War and the practice of sending Miss America overseas each year to urge our men to kill and die "in defense of American womanhood."

In addition to being addressed only to female journalists, the release noted that in case of arrests, demonstrators would only recognize the authority of policewomen to arrest them. This would be hard in Atlantic City where, the release highlighted, female police were restricted from making arrests. It ended: "THE BOARDWALK BELONGS TO THE WOMEN! FREE THE SISTERS! DON'T MISS AMERICA!"

On the day of the Miss America motorcade, with Pageant Week in full swing, a registered letter arrived at the Atlantic City mayor's office, seeking a permit to protest on the boardwalk on Saturday. Despite a general sense of outrage from pageant officials and fans, whose numbers were growing throughout the day as the parade kick-off time neared, the mayor issued a permit for John F.

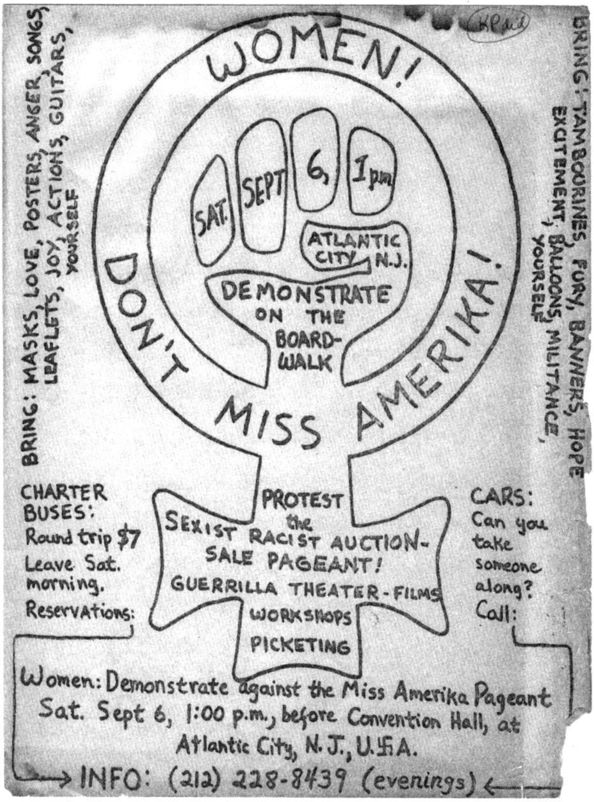

"Women! Don't Miss Amerika!" flyer advertising the second Miss America protest in Atlantic City, September 6, 1969

Kennedy Plaza, the same location as the previous year. It was "their legal right" to protest, he explained to journalists, but they would be doing so within clear and tight parameters. But this wasn't enough for Al Marks, who promised that he would be pursuing "every legal means at my command not to subject the Miss America Pageant to any ridicule."

"At last year's pageant," explained the *Atlantic City Press* in reporting on the imminent return of women's liberation to the city, protesters "burned their bras in a symbolic protest and also set off an odor inside Convention Hall. Police said it was a stink bomb, but movement leaders claimed it was a can of hair-spray." While not a single bra or other object had been burned during the 1968 protest, in less than a year it had become the common wisdom that they had been, even among city and pageant officials, journalists, and community members who had witnessed the protests. Factual accounts of the Freedom Trash Can shared space in paragraphs that exaggerated and repeated the false narrative, entrenching it deeper into the dominant psyche.

Some of this was the direct outcome of misrepresentation by pageant officials and police, who insisted on describing the squeeze bottle of permanent hair solution found on Peggy Dobbins as a "stink bomb," never referencing in public that it was in fact a chemical produced by pageant sponsor Toni Hair Care Products. This was particularly evident in court filings for a restraining order, made the day after the Atlantic City mayor had granted the protest permit requested by pageant attorney and board member Leonard Horn. Al Marks gave an affidavit that presented the previous year's demonstrations in the direst of terms, describing the women "dropping a bomb or using some other device" to distribute a "noxious odor" inside Convention Hall, while "displaying certain signs and by being generally noisy and abusive did interfere with and disrupt the speech of Miss America during the final minutes of the television cast." He claimed that earlier in the day protesters "did use loud and offensive language to passersby and to persons entering into and exiting from the Convention Hall; they did display signs such as 'Miss America is a Whore,' 'Miss America is Six Months Pregnant,' and "Miss America is a Virgin'; they did spit on passersby and did incite people in the area to violence . . . and did burn girdles, bras, and other articles of women's clothing and underwear." The pageant was granted a ranging restraining order by a judge from the Atlantic County Superior Court.

"It appears that once again we will be visited by the 'ban the bra' girls. For some reason these people seem bent upon making women less attractive through the questionable process of doing away with underwear," crowed Marks to a journalist after winning the restraining order. "Being opposed to beauty and constructive accomplishment, I suppose it is natural for them to single out the Miss America Pageant as the epitome of these qualities." The pageant had sought the order not to limit free speech but to protect decency and the safety of pageant fans and contestants. "The Miss America pageant is fully appreciative of the importance of freedom of speech in this country, even if the ideas expressed may seem ridiculous to most of us," he said. "However, we do most emphatically object to any activities on the part of this or any group which offend or insult good taste and decency and threaten public safety."

On Saturday afternoon, Atlantic City police were waiting when the demonstrators marched onto John F. Kennedy Plaza at around 2 p.m. Police read the order to the group and began checking signs and placards for "offensive" language. Among those placards were several large images of first-wave feminists, including Susan B. Anthony, Elizabeth Cady Stanton, Sojourner Truth, Lucy Stone, and Frances Harper, each labeled "Our Heroine." Police barricades pushed the demonstration nearly onto the beach and far from entrances to the hall. Once the pageant's start drew near, more and more police appeared and encircled the building; by 7 p.m., they numbered 350. This uniformed force was joined by about 20 plainclothes officers, a sheriff's detachment, and a group from the county prosecutor's office on hand, should there be arrests. Ultimately, there were none.

That night's telecast was the first one not hosted by Bess Myerson; Deborah Bryant Wilson did the television commentary. The show was designed with an eye toward the contemporary, which meant psychedelic colors and hippie costumes, as well as rock and folk-themed musical numbers. The *Hartford Courant* called it a pageant "with a facelift—a modern now-generation format on the theme of 'The Sound of Young.'" Noting "Bess Replaced," the paper added that Myerson was "now New York City's Consumer Affairs consultant."

When the new Miss America, Pamela Eldred, of Michigan, faced journalists for the first time, she was so politic in her answers that her ability to handle the press became a part of the story. Her answers were also conservative, which reflected the general positions of the pageant organization. The Miss Black America Pageant was "very nice," and she thought a Black woman would be crowned Miss America someday. "When a girl deserves to win it, she will win it," she said, implying that the absence of Black finalists had been a lack of deserving competitors. "It's not just a beauty pageant—a girl has to be ambitious, want to help herself and help other people." Of women's liberation and the demonstrations, Eldred said simply that she had not seen them and could not comment, but added that she did know the pageant was terrific and the contestants all wonderful, hardworking, and talented people. "I love my country," she added, "and I'd like to do something for it."

Eldred signaled a change for Miss America contestants and winners, who would go from being symbols of a particular mom, country, and apple pie patriotism useful to others to being vocal political voices in their own rights—voices that narrowed quickly to conservative, usually evangelical Christian, and explicitly Republican. This was partially due to the need winners felt to defend themselves and the pageant after 1968, as well as the fact that most were being drawn from predominantly white, largely conservative suburban and rural communities.

The sense that the pageant was under threat escalated when rumors picked up in the press that a women's liberation activist had infiltrated the contest and was among the finalists, ready to disrupt the pageant from within during the telecast. When Bert Parks was asked by a journalist how he would handle the situation should it happen, he replied, "I'd grab her by the throat and keep on singing."

A week after the pageant, three women, one of whom was the novelist and freelancer Jeannie Sakol, and another the former lobbyist and editor of the Women's News Service of the United Features Syndicate, Lucianne Goldberg,* had lunch in Manhattan. When the conversation turned to the recent demonstration at the Miss America finals, they denounced the protests and women's liberation in general. Laughing, the friends decided they should start their own group for professional, fun, urbane women like themselves to oppose inequality *and* the feminists.

Goldberg and Sakol transformed what began as a joke shared among well-connected friends into the shell of an organization—the Pussycat League—that both women would ride to some fame and notoriety over the next several years. Describing their new group as "feminine, not feminist," Jeannie Sakol told the *Washington Post*'s Myra McPherson that her group of "lusty ladies" organized because "we felt the shenanigans or techniques of militant women were giving other women—who believe in femininity—a bad name." In fact, their aims

* Lucianne Goldberg is best known today for her pivotal role in exposing Bill Clinton's affair with Monica Lewinsky in 1998, leading to his impeachment. It was Goldberg who encouraged Linda Tripp to record her conversations with Lewinsky.

were similar, Sakol argued, including accessible daycare for working women, repeal of abortion restrictions, and equal pay for equal work. It was in their approach and demeanors, she explained, that they were radically different, not the least of which was having a sense of humor.

Sakol's arguments on behalf of "forgotten women," or the "Silent Femajority" as another journalist put it, were resonating even more than they expected. "We would use our femininity rather than deny it. We will represent the millions of American women who believe that the way to achieve a better society is by working with men, not against them. By being sweet, soft and smelling good and using our attributes to persuade, not force men to work for women's rights, we'll wind up with more than equal rights." By 1971, the Pussycat League was incorporated and claimed seven thousand members who had paid $7 each for a pin and membership card.

As Sakol and Goldberg were founding the Pussycat League, all nineteen Playboy Clubs dotted throughout North America, the Caribbean, and the U.K. held beauty contests to select the most beautiful "Bunnies" from their "Hutches" to compete in the first Playboy Bunny Beauty Pageant on November 16, 1969. Held at the Playboy Club Hotel in Lake Geneva, Wisconsin, the pageant celebrated the 10th anniversary of club operations by way of this explicit response to the women's liberation protests of Miss America Pageant, while simultaneously aiming to promote a sexier, more contemporary counter-pageant to the iconic beauty contest. The five judges were celebrity model Jean Shrimpton and four men: actor and comedian Bill Cosby, the lieutenant governor of Wisconsin, the director of Chicago's Museum of Contemporary Art, and an attorney from Cleveland.

The winner was Gina Byrams, who was from the Baltimore Playboy Club and the only Black woman in the final contest—another obvious counterpoint to the Miss America Pageant. As Byrams was "crowned" by Hugh Hefner (who replaced her silver bunny ears with gold ones), one of the pageant organizers excitedly quipped to a journalist, "What could be more Now than a Black bunny queen?" (The ease with which this comment was made suggested a big change from 1962, when the first clubs were opening and the magazine's editorial policy was to exclude non-white models because they were "not the generally accepted idea of the all-American beauty.")

By the end of 1969, Kansas was poised to pass women's rights legislation aimed mostly at addressing pay inequality. While press coverage dwelled on what it framed as the East Coast inspirations for heartland feminists' actions, the underlying assumption that change was in the air signaled certain successes for liberal feminism. Asked for a comment on the legislation and its proponents, Debbie Barnes Miles replied that she was "in sympathy with the idea that a woman who works at the same job as a man—and does as good a job—should be paid equally," but that she would never carry a picket sign for women's liberation. "Taking care of our house and keeping my husband happy is what I consider the goal of my life. That's where my rewards will be," she concluded. "Others are beginning to feel differently, but I'm not."

43

WOMEN IN REVOLT

"Women's liberation is hot stuff this season, in media terms," proclaimed journalist Susan Brownmiller in a March 1970 piece for the *New York Times Sunday Magazine* that billed her as "a member of the Women's Liberation Movement," explaining "what it's all about." The year 1970 was, indeed, a watershed in popular media coverage and engagement with feminism and the women's movement in the United States. From television news and talk shows to mass-circulation magazines like *Newsweek* and *Time*, and a stream of new books from major publishers hitting store shelves, feminists appeared to be everywhere—certain versions of them, at least. Of the publicity onslaught, Robin Morgan would later quip, "The year 1970 hit like a meteor."

Morgan was part of a group that took over *Rat*, a popular alternative paper, at the start of the year when she found she could no longer sustain her position as a women's liberationist within the New Left. Where she had once believed that liberation was impossible unless it was harnessed to radical economic change, Morgan had concluded that only an independent, feminist liberation movement could ever be successful. In an essay titled "Goodbye to All That," the once proud movement "heavy" announced that she was done with "the good guys who think they know what 'Women's Lib,' as they so chummily call it, is all about—who then proceed to degrade and destroy women by almost everything they say and do. . . . No more, brothers. No more well-meaning ignorance, no more cooptation, no more assuming that this thing we're all fighting for is the same; one revolution under *man*, with liberty and justice for all. No more."

Morgan was also done with being cowed by the caricature of the ugly, bitter man-hater, and she encouraged other radical women among *Rat*'s readership to do the same. "Let it all hang out," she cheered. "Let it seem bitchy, catty, dykey, Solanasesque, frustrated, crazy, nutty, frigid, ridiculous, bitter, embarrassing, man-hating, libelous, pure, unfair, envious, intuitive, low-down, stupid, petty, liberating. We are the women that men have warned us about."

In March, Atkinson, Dunbar, and Freeman were featured in a *Newsweek* cover story: "Women's Lib: The War on 'Sexism.'" The magazine's design was impossible to miss, but unclear in its intentions. Centered in a field of mustard yellow was a photo-like illustration of a nude white woman with long hair cascading around her shoulders, her face tilted up and back in apparent ecstasy as her right fist punched up, Black Power–style. Why was she naked? The woman was punching through a royal blue women's symbol, broken in three places and into the magazine's title, printed in the same color. The only other text on the cover, in black and all caps, read: "WOMEN IN REVOLT."

The ambivalent messaging of the cover characterized the entire feature. The story itself was prefaced with an editors' note, explaining their decision to go outside the magazine's regular group of writers for its author: "In the age of social protest, the old cause of U.S. feminism has flared into new and angry life in the women's liberation movement. It is a phenomenon difficult to cover; most of the feminists won't even talk to male journalists, who are hard put in turn to tell the story with the kind of insight a woman can bring to it. For this week's coverage *Newsweek* sought out Helen Dudar, a topflight journalist who is also a woman." Between the lines was a more complex story already infamous among women in journalism. The piece had originally been assigned to an assistant editor, one of the few women in such a role at the magazine, but the finished work was rejected by editors, all men, who cited the author's lack of objectivity. After several failed attempts at rewriting the story, it was assigned to Dudar, a freelancer who was married to one of *Newsweek*'s senior editors.

The saga of this women's movement story was the final straw for women working at *Newsweek*, most of whom had found themselves stalled at the level of researcher, never promoted to writer or editor. A group reached out to the

EEOC about filing a sex-discrimination complaint. They held a press conference on March 16 to make their charges public, the same day the "Women in Revolt" issue hit the newsstands. The numbers told the story, they explained: out of thirty-five researchers at *Newsweek*, one was a man, while only one woman worked among the fifty-two writers employed there. (The claim was settled in 1973 without admission of wrongdoing.)

Dudar's article was a sweeping overview of the central aims of women's liberation and some of the individuals and groups working toward them, drawn mostly from New York City. She contextualized the "New Feminism" in relation to its nineteenth-century forebears and drew a clear distinction between liberationists and the liberal feminists of NOW. Most notable, perhaps, was Dudar's discussion of her own relationship to the subject and how it changed as she reported the story. "I have spent years rejecting feminists without bothering to look too closely at their charges," she wrote. "Stridency numbs me, and, in common with a lot of people, it has always been easy to dismiss substance out of dislike for style."

Talking to women's liberationists and reading their work had changed Dudar's mind, however. So, too, had a conversation she recounted with friend and fellow journalist Lindsy Van Gelder, who told her that professional women "established in male-dominated fields resented the liberation movement because their solitude gave them a sense of superiority." Seeing herself in that unflattering description, Dudar was transformed. "Women's lib questions everything; and while intellectually I approve of that," she wrote, "emotionally I am unstrung by a lot of it." Of the liberationists asking those questions, Dudar concluded in the last line of her article, "I thank them, and so, I think, will a lot of other women."

Framing Dudar's article were two other pieces: a set of short profiles of "representative" liberationists with photos, including Ti-Grace Atkinson, Roxanne Dunbar, and Jo Freeman; and an article about "expert" reactions from medicine, psychiatry, and academia; it was titled "Other Voices: How Social Scientists See Women's Lib." The latter piece tilted toward rejection of liberationists' "extremism," and offered an extended argument for the innate differences between men and women that shaped their societal roles. Of the four activists profiled, the first two, Leslye Russell and Ti-Grace Atkinson, were introduced as "pretty, blond," and "tall, elegantly feline," respectively, while nothing was said of Dunbar's or Freeman's looks—which by comparison said quite a lot.

Susan Brownmiller's *New York Times* story was published the day before the *Newsweek* issue came out, and the magazine's female staffers held their press conference. Both added extra punch to Brownmiller's account of mainstream media attention and its limitations, including her anecdote about how she should frame the piece: "'Get the bra burning and the karate up front,' an editor I know told a writer I know." (Robin Morgan was one of the women featured in a photo of karate class in the *Newsweek* story.) Brownmiller's piece was largely an account of NYRW's founding, internal conflicts over whether men or capitalism was the enemy, and the split after the Miss America Pageant protest (when Brownmiller became involved) into WITCH, Redstockings, and other groups that formed after Atkinson's departure from NOW-NYC. She described the feeling of being caricatured and "met with laughter and hostility," adding, "Each time a man sloughs off the women's movement with the comment, 'They're nothing but a bunch of lesbians and frustrated bitches,' we quiver with collective rage." This led Brownmiller to an aside about Betty Friedan's fears that the presence of out lesbians within the women's movement, or any official embrace of lesbian concerns by feminists, would ruin the movement's image and threaten its ability to attract the masses. Friedan had called lesbians "the lavender menace," reported Brownmiller, who concluded they were more "lavender *herring*" than serious threat—which was not a repudiation of Friedan's position but a minimization of it. Of everything covered in the article, it was Friedan's "lavender menace" comment, offered by Brownmiller as a parenthetical aside, that readers—and history—would remember.

Five days later, Betty Friedan stood before a crowd at NOW's annual convention in Chicago and gave her last presidential address before Aileen Hernandez assumed the organization's national leadership. It was a major transition for Friedan, for whom leading NOW had become a core aspect of her identity as well as a mission. There had been so many significant life changes for Friedan over the last year: Friedan had divorced Carl the previous May, and as part of the settlement, the apartment in the Dakota and the Fire Island house that had been so important to her had to be sold. By the time she went to Chicago to hand off leadership of NOW, Betty and the couple's two teenagers who still lived at home were in a new place farther uptown.

Friedan spoke for two hours that afternoon, making the case for NOW to spearhead organizing a nationwide general strike of women for Wednesday, August 26, to mark the 50th anniversary of the ratification of the 19th Amendment. While many, including Hernandez, did not support it, largely because of the short lead time to organize something so big, as well as the attention, resources, and labor it would draw away from other initiatives, NOW's board approved the proposal the following day.

Friedan talked of history, momentum, and ingenuity—including the new energy she saw in women's liberation despite her concerns—and the need for American women to realize their collective power by channeling it into something undeniable and unifying, like the strike. That momentum included recent progress in the push to pass the Equal Rights Amendment. In February, women from the Pittsburgh chapter of NOW had quietly disrupted the Senate Judiciary Committee hearings on the proposed 26th Amendment to lower the national voting age; they did this by holding up signs demanding hearings for the ERA. The subcommittee chair for Constitutional amendments, Senator Birch Bayh (D-IN), met with the women and agreed to hold hearings, which were scheduled for May. One of the people invited to give testimony in support of the ERA was Gloria Steinem.

Since the publication of her 1969 *New York* magazine article about women's liberation, Steinem had been a popular guest on talk shows to speak about the subject, and she had consistently booked engagements with fellow feminist activist Dorothy Pittman Hughes (and later Flo Kennedy) to talk to college communities and civic groups around the country. The person who invited her to testify for the ERA had seen her on the *David Susskind Show*, and she might have also seen a full-page profile on Steinem with several photos by AP reporter Lynn Sherr that appeared in papers across the country throughout April. It described the thirty-five-year-old Steinem as a "writer-activist-antiwar-gorgeous bachelor girl" who came from modest means to build her own career and public profile. "It has been said of her that she is the ideal woman—beautiful, involved, and free to choose whatever she wants. She has chosen: what Gloria Steinem wants to do is write on the things she cares about—politics, urban sociology and women's liberation."

Gloria Steinem, April 1970

In one of the images, Steinem leans back in a comfortable chair and looks over her shoulder into the camera, unsmiling and with a gentle smolder to her eyes. She is holding her cat. Books, papers, and ashtrays vie with a purse, basket of flowers, and candles covering every surface, while presidential campaign Robert F. Kennedy smiles out from behind an anti-war poster amid other images of liberal and leftist men layered like pin-ups from fan magazines. It's more Pussycat League than "cat lady," but really a rebuke to both.

At the Senate hearings for the ERA on May 6, Steinem spoke powerfully of the professional, social, and political barriers she faced as a woman, while noting how they nevertheless paled in comparison to those with less privilege than herself. When Betty Friedan asked her to co-host an East Hampton benefit for the Women's Strike for Equality in early August, it was not only for Steinem's connections to potential donors, high profile among the city's cultural elite, and glamour quotient, but also her as a nationally visible advocate for the women's movement and ERA.

Two days after the benefit, on August 10, Congresswoman Martha Griffiths succeeded in getting the ERA out of the House Judiciary Committee, where it had been trapped for fifteen years by the committee's powerful chair, Representative Emanuel Celler (in his forty-eighth year in office). In early June, Griffiths had filed a discharge petition, which meant that if she could marshal the support of two-thirds of her colleagues, 218 members, the ERA would bypass Celler and go directly to the floor for exactly one hour of debate and a vote. This meant convincing enough people from both parties to sign the petition, while also preparing for that pivotal hour should the petition succeed. When it did on July 20, the debate was set for August 10. The ERA won by an enormous margin that day, 350 to 15, with 64 members not voting. It went on to the Senate, where opponents first worked to slow it through committee and then, once it reached the Senate floor, began amending it into oblivion. By that point, their aim was running out the clock; the 91st Congress would end in December and take the ERA with it. The whole process would have to start again with the next Congress. But August 10 was still a day of great victory for the feminists and their political allies who'd managed to get the bill onto the House floor for a vote, and that energy carried into the national women's strike on August 26.

In 1970, Charlotte Curtis began doing five-minute opinion pieces on the news of the day for WQXR radio, New York City's leading classical music station, which was owned by the *New York Times*. Her short radio essays were punchy, often funny, and gave Curtis the opportunity to make some of her most direct comments about contemporary politics and America culture, and they provided a much clearer window into her thoughts about feminism than other public outlets.

"Women are out waging the Women's Strike for Equality today, demanding childcare centers, equal employment and abortion. And, amid all these observations of this—the 50th anniversary of women's suffrage—I am reminded of Alice Paul. Wherever that incredible 85-year-old lady is today, she is still fighting for women's rights." Curtis described Paul and her National Woman's Party as the radical front edge of the suffrage movement in the early twentieth century, which often drew the ire of others in the movement. "When I hear people criticize the women who burned their bras at the Miss America Pageant in Atlantic City or attempted to liberate the Statue of Liberty, I want to remind those critics of Miss Paul. While it may well be true that the hard, boring, dull and unpublicized work behind the scenes is what gets laws changed in this country, I wonder how much of that work would actually be done if it weren't for the radicals up front?" Nevertheless, Curtis warned that the medium could kill the message, when "the attention-grabbing activities of the radicals obscures the importance of the cause itself." Curtis concluded, sounding a bit like Carol Hanisch, "Perhaps what I'm saying on this anniversary of women's suffrage is that if women want to be taken as seriously as they deserve, they will have to get their message across not just loud and clear but logically and simply. Otherwise, nobody's really going to understand how important this movement is."

As a day of demonstrations, the Women's Strike for Equality was a success. Protestors rallied around the country in communities large and small. The biggest event, which also garnered the greatest media coverage, was in New York City, where an estimated 50,000 women paraded down Fifth Avenue behind Betty Friedan and others, filling the street for block after long block. Images of the march ran above the fold on the *New York Times*'s front page the next day. The publicity was generally positive; NOW's national membership nearly doubled in the months that followed.

Much of the coverage focused with palpable relief on the idea that more reasonable, liberal feminists were setting the agenda within a coalition of organizations. *New York Times* reporter Judy Klemesrud argued that the strength of the women's movement was well measured by the vociferousness of its opposition, among whom she included the Pussycat League, "whose slogan is 'Purr, Baby, Purr.'" This would also be the title of a book by Jeannie Sakol and Lucianne Goldberg, published in 1971, that promised, "You can be feminine and liberated." The cover of the paperback edition added to this description, "The long-overdue answer to the Women's Lib and Anti-Man campaigns . . . a realistic antidote to bra-burning and other inanities of the WITCH, BITCH and NOW marching societies." To the authors, "feminine" and feminist were mutually exclusive.

As the Miss America Pageant drew near, it was protests from within the organization that drew the most attention. The first came in June, when a Black woman named Cheryl Browne won the Miss Iowa Pageant. Browne was a student at a small Lutheran college in Decorah, Iowa, a community of about seven thousand people in the northeast corner of the state. Her home was New York City, however, in the Jamaica neighborhood of Queens. Charlotte Curtis talked about Browne in a radio spot in early July, after the Miss Black America Pageant date had been announced. That "contest officially began last year, although the first Miss Black America was named two years ago, in Atlantic City—in the same city and on the same night as that year's Miss America—Miss White America—got her crown," said Curtis. "Unlike its competitors, the Miss Black America Contest was as much a protest against the lily-white character of the Miss America contest as a confirmation that black is beautiful." But this year would be different, because "for the first time in its showy, campy, perfumed and lily-white history, at least one of the 50 states will be represented by a Black woman—a New Yorker who comes to the contest via Iowa, of all places. . . . Miss Iowa says her crown proves that in America you can be accepted for what you are rather than the color of your skin, which may or may not be true everywhere. But it certainly seems to be the way Iowa is going at the moment."

Her race had been "a delicate subject for some Iowans at first," Browne told journalists after her state pageant victory. She described people's awkward attempts to locate the young woman racially, ethnically, and nationally, often avoiding the most obvious answer. "'Now let's see,' someone asked, 'your father is West Indian, and your mother is half American Indian. How do you consider yourself?'" Browne recalled, before grinning at the journalist and replying, "I say I'm either Negro or Black."

Instead of going home, Browne would live for the summer in the family home of her college roommate not far from Decorah, so she could prepare for the pageant in the state she'd be representing. "I thought I would be going back to New York Monday," she said right after the Miss Iowa contest. "Guess I'm the girl who came to dinner."

Stories about Browne in the mainstream press, which appeared throughout the summer in the leadup to the pageant, dwelled on two central themes: how recognizable Browne was to white suburbanites who consumed Miss America news, and how unthreatening she was as a Black woman. The stories never failed to mention that Browne's father, Carl, was a narcotics officer for the Port Authority at JFK Airport—sure to please law-and-order readers—and almost never referenced her mother's work as an office manager for a medical clinic. Their home was always described as being on Long Island, rather than in Queens.

The stories continually found a way to make clear that Cheryl Browne was not an activist seeking to integrate the Miss America Pageant, but just an average American girl who dreamed of winning the crown. While Browne sometimes appealed to that narrative herself, and never rejected it outright, she highlighted her own awareness of its existence with winking asides about being "the girl who came to dinner" or loving descriptions of her West Indian neighborhood, culture, and large, diasporic family stretching from the Caribbean to New York City. "We cook in the West Indian style, too," she said, "with a lot of spices." She joked, "I may look familiar to you, despite my skin color, just like any other candidate for Miss America, but I'm not."

"To a certain extent, I'm a little scared about being the first Black in the 'Miss America' finals," Browne admitted. "I'm used to being the only Black or one of only a few blacks in various situations I've been in. I'm sure if I just be myself and have fun, everything will turn out all right. With all the racial problems there are today, I hope my winning the 'Miss Iowa' title will show the radicals in the Black Power movement that things aren't so bad, and you can be accepted for what you are, rather than the color of your skin."

On behalf of the Miss America Pageant, Al Marks gave a characteristic response to the news of a Black finalist. "I couldn't be more delighted," he said. "Finally, the color line is broken."

The day before Cheryl Browne was crowned Miss Iowa, a recent graduate of Helena Senior High School, Katherine Huppe, won the Miss Montana Pageant. She joined Browne at the top of the Miss America news a few weeks later, when she shocked the pageant community by resigning her title rather than agree to limits on her public opinions. The Jaycees of Billings, Montana, who sponsored the state pageant, required winners to sign a contract that prohibited comments about politics, current events, or controversial issues (as defined by the Jaycees), and required advance approval for any speech or writing. Handed the contract while still in the flush of winning the night she was crowned, Huppe realized only then the degree to which her speech would be limited. "They can't have a girl who is going to do anything controversial," she explained, but "I'm not a middle of the road person and I'm not willing to become a middle of the road person." Huppe had been involved in politics in high school, including joining fellow students in rewriting the state's constitution as a form of protest. She was an editor of *The Paper Tiger*, an alternative paper for high school students, and was an active participant in demonstrations against the war in Southeast Asia. "If there were moratoriums next year, I would participate, because that's something I really believe in," said Huppe, adding that she had told the Jaycees that she "would put my beliefs above the pageant." The pageant director accepted her resignation and told the press of plans to make the restrictions clear to the next winners before they signed anything.

Huppe's resignation garnered significant national press coverage. The sentiments slid between a sense of surprise at an outspokenly left-leaning beauty queen from the Mountain West who prioritized her political voice and the derision directed at the pageant for requiring her to make such a choice. The following week, Al Marks announced that the national Miss America Pageant organization would remove restrictions on contestants' speech. He had taken "a good long look at the whole picture," and decided that "today's youths are smart enough to answer for themselves"—as long as it wasn't about sex. Not surprisingly, Marks added that this did not apply to state pageant organizers, who set their own rules.

Huppe's experience contrasted sharply with that of Miss Black America 1969, Gloria Smith, who had returned from her USO tour critical of the war and what she had seen at the front. At a March ceremony to recognize her contributions to the organization, Noble Sissle, fellow (retired) Black performer and USO board member, presented Smith with the award. "I am proud of the US because it saw fit to place Miss Smith on a pedestal," he said during the event. "Not only is Gloria talented and beautiful, she is cultured. This is a great step forward. No race can rise above its womanhood." When asked by reporters at the ceremony about the general morale of Black troops, Smith replied frankly that their attitude was "negative, about as negative as one can be towards a war. Especially if you don't know why you are even there." This, she added, was true of the white soldiers she'd met, as well. Smith was similarly direct with a reporter for the military newspaper, *Stars & Stripes*, apparently feeling no need to soften or paint a positive light around her statements. Nor did she appear to be censured for them.

The *Des Moines Register* reported that Iowa was making history twice in 1970 where Black beauty pageant contestants were concerned. Cheryl Browne was headed to Atlantic City, and Bonnie Jean Franks had just arrived in New York City as the first woman from Iowa to represent the state in the Miss Black America Pageant. The paper ran a picture of Franks waving from the top of the airstairs, after stepping out of the plane wearing white gloves, a travel suit, and her hair styled in a medium Afro. She would join thirty other women competing once again at Madison Square Garden, with Hal Jackson hosting once again. Another impressive panel of Black public figures served as the judging panel, including U.S. Representative John Conyers from Detroit, plus Fannie Lou Hamer, Jackie Robinson, Rev. Jesse Jackson, and Ellis Haizlip, producer of *Soul!* for NET TV.

The winner of Miss Black America was Stephanie Clark, a nineteen-year-old college sophomore from Washington, D.C. Speaking to a journalist for the *Washington Post* a few months later, Clark said for her, the importance of the Black beauty queen was that she "speaks for Black women, helps uplift the Black man's pride, doesn't compete against him and reminds him how much he has in the Black woman." She said she was proud to be dark-skinned like fellow singer Nina Simone, and never smiled unless she meant it. Since winning the crown, she explained her duties as promoting the pageant's magazine and cosmetics line, visiting schools, making a record, and doing guest spots on television. She took care with her schedule, adding, "I'm not a machine." Of her upcoming thirty-five-day USO tour in Vietnam and the Philippines, Clark said she opposed war, but hoped to "bring a little inspiration to the lives of some soldiers—to show them someone does care."

From the moment her plane touched down at the Atlantic City airport on Sunday, September 6, 1970, it seemed that all eyes were on Cheryl Browne. Speaking to journalists at registration, Browne said that while being the first Black finalist to compete in the Miss America Pageant added "a little more pride and an awful lot of responsibility," she didn't consider herself any different from the other contestants and hoped no one else would either. "As for women's

Miss Black America 1970, Stephanie Clark

liberation, Miss Iowa doesn't feel like she's being degraded by the contest," reported the *Atlantic City Press*. "Miss Browne said the lib women have some valid arguments, but the pageant isn't one of them."

Miss New York, Katherine Karlsrud, caused a stir upon her arrival in Atlantic City, when she said the swimsuit competition was, in fact, degrading to contestants and should be dropped from the competition. In a radio piece she ultimately decided to scrap, Charlotte Curtis explained the pageant's response to this statement:

> Essentially, Mr. Marks seems to agree with the contestants. He said he wouldn't want to walk around a runway in a bathing suit, either. But he didn't promise to make any immediate changes in the contest procedure.... Which still leaves us with Bert Parks, baton twirlers, gooey production numbers, rhinestone crowns, super-slicked-up hairdos with ringlets, fussy evening dresses, false eyelashes, high-heeled shoes on bare feet, and all those

girls in bathing suits. Let's face it. Miss America is a skin show, and a skin show it's apparently going to be.

Cheryl Browne was the ideal person to break the color line, in the eyes of the pageant organization. She looked "right," with her long, straightened hair and prim, tailored outfits; she was from a recognizably religious college, and her talent was classical ballet; and she was not an outspoken civil rights activist. Also, she was used to being the only Black woman in a predominantly white environment, and managed the pressure and scrutiny well. "Iowa could not have selected a better young girl to make the Miss America breakthrough, in the opinion of veteran observers," reported a journalist from Atlantic City. One paper included a photo that showed Lenora Slaughter, in town for the pageant's golden anniversary celebrations, cheering from the audience at one of the preliminary contests; she was sporting a prominent button featuring Cheryl Browne's face.

Many were surprised when Browne was not among the ten semifinalists (neither was the first runner-up, who rose to the title of Miss Montana when

Miss Iowa 1970, Cheryl Browne (left), and Miss Maryland 1970, Sharon Anne Cannon (right)

Huppe resigned). The winner was an aspiring television broadcaster from Texas Christian University, Phyllis George.

The *Atlantic City Press* asserted, "The racial barrier fell at the Pageant, and we are pleased to report that no one seemed to notice it. The other 49 contestants treated Cheryl as they treated one another: with jolly-good warmth and enthusiasm, but also with the usual undercurrent of coldblooded feminine cattiness aroused by the rivalry and competition for the high stakes. Miss Iowa, beautiful and black, blended into this normal Establishment scene."

Blended, perhaps, but Browne left pageant fans and organizers wondering. The same journalist reported the incredible frustration of press photographers at the boardwalk motorcade who failed to capture a suggestive moment. "Miss Iowa rode by a large group of black young men wearing afros and dashikis," he noted. "As she waved in Establishment fashion, they let out a tremendous roar. The façade broke. Miss Iowa stopped waving, clenched her fist, and raised her arm in the Black Panther salute. Then the moment was over, and Miss Iowa resumed her waving, in proper Establishment fashion. Peek-a-boo, Miss Iowa." The only image of a contestant raising her fist would be Huppe's awkward, thumb-out salute from the pages of *Life* magazine.

The reality of a 1970 pageant being disrupted by women's liberationists would come only later in November, when a group of demonstrators stood outside the Chicago Playboy Club in frigid temperatures to protest the Second International Bunny of the Year Beauty Pageant. When the nineteen-year-old winner, "Bunny Cheryl of Chicago," was asked about the activists' charge that the contest was insulting to women, she replied, "You can take a good thing and push it too far. I think that's what they're doing. Some of their ideas are really good, and some of their ideas, if you really look at them and study them, are some of the same ideas *Playboy* has."

"What are those?" asked the AP *Roving Report* interviewer as he directed his mic back toward Cheryl Lee, who stood next to him in a tiara and gold bunny ears, holding a golden bunny statue, and still wearing the silver-sequined strapless one-piece swimsuit all the contestants had worn for the pageant finale.

"The idea of letting a woman be herself. *Playboy* doesn't make a woman, you know, follow a set of rules. She can be herself and she can express herself; she doesn't have to do anything she doesn't want to do."

The man, clearly having reached the limits of his interest in feminism and the self-determination of a "bunny," followed Lee's statement with, "Another criticism that's been leveled over the years is the fact that *Playboy* bunnies are very attractive and they're nice to look at, but you can't touch, and some people say that this runs contrary to the *Playboy* philosophy." It was a stark reminder that what made the "bunny" beautiful was her body, not her mind.

Phyllis Schlafly spent much of 1970 running for Congress for the second time. She had not sought an appointment with the Nixon administration after campaigning for him throughout the fall of 1968, and serving as a key line of communication with hard-right Republicans—or she hadn't been offered one (unlike Mary Brooks, who was named director of the U.S. Mint, in 1969). Schlafly had wanted a spot on the Foreign Intelligence Advisory Board, and had strong support from others to Nixon's right—all men—but the president ultimately chose one of Schlafly's moderate Republican nemeses, Nelson Rockefeller.

As the midterm elections approached, the RNC encouraged Schlafly to run in her home district in Illinois against longtime Democratic congressman George Shipley, who looked ripe for picking off, in their efforts to carve away at the Democratic majority in the House. It would be a very different race from her first run in 1952, not least because of the national influence she'd gained since that time, but also because the full resources and support of the party would be behind her now. Schlafly would run on Nixon's central issues: law and order, the economy, and against college campus revolts and the legacies of Johnson's Great Society—to which she added her particular focus on military preparedness and foreign relations. The RNC provided her with a sizable war chest, and James Brady* signed on as her campaign manager. They blanketed the district with high-profile advertising, including a radio spot featuring John Wayne's endorsement and a direct-mail appeal from Barry Goldwater, as well as thousands of mostly women volunteers who knocked on doors for Schlafly. National fundraising appeals kept the campaign going, including an event in Los Angeles organized by the leadership of the California Federation of Republican Women.

* James Brady would go on to become Ronald Reagan's first press secretary in 1980. He survived being shot during the attempted assassination of Reagan on March 30, 1981.

It was the members' "duty as responsible women leaders and volunteers to help elect women to public office," urged the invitation. "It's a man's world only because women permit it to be. We are the majority." It was an argument that could easily have been penned by Betty Friedan; in fact, a version of it had been, just two years earlier.

Shipley defended his seat by framing Schlafly as an urbane, college-educated, know-it-all outsider, in part by pointing to her high-profile endorsements, national popularity, and use of a professional campaign public relations firm. She might live in the district, he suggested, but Schlafly wasn't of the place and didn't share local values, including about women's roles in the family and public life. He pointed to the fact that she had six kids at home and he questioned her expertise—any woman's expertise—in military affairs and national security.

As with her first run for office, Schlafly never yielded overtly to gendered attacks, while also looking to capitalize on her role as a woman to frame herself as the better candidate. "Women do the family spending," she said in a live television spot. "They are more careful with other people's money and better at getting a dollar's value for every dollar spent. If we can stop runaway spending by Congress, we can stop inflation." In an interesting turn on the uniformed cheer squads of the 1968 presidential race, women who volunteered for Schlafly wore red and blue aprons emblazoned with her name and decorated with elephants and eagles, celebrating traditional womanhood in order to challenge it. Some may have recognized it as a callback to a famous press photo taken the morning after Schlafly won the Republican primary in 1952, in which she posed at the stove in a frilled, polka-dot apron, spatula in hand, preparing breakfast for her husband and toddler.

Schlafly lost in November by a definitive margin, and she blamed the outcome on statewide voter anger about the Republican governor's tax policy. She had gone into the midterms wary of the directions Nixon had taken since his inauguration, questioning his commitment to the Right and frustrated by what she and others saw as his catering to liberals in an attempt to shrink the Democrats' legislative majorities. After the midterms, she joined the steady march to the open revolt of the GOP's right wing.

When the 92nd Congress opened on January 3, 1971, passing the ERA was a priority for many. So was defeating it. As proponents got to work on freeing the bill from the House and Senate Judiciary Committees, there was a sense of momentum and possibility that change was coming, even if the fights continued in the near term. On newsstands, the year's first issue of *New York* magazine was dedicated to the ten most powerful men in the city. Asked to give her list of ten, Charlotte Curtis offered the names of thirteen individuals, two of whom were women: U.S. Representative Shirley Chisholm and the socialite and philanthropist Mary Lasker. Betty Friedan was also asked for a list, and she named mostly women, including Charlotte Curtis and Bess Myerson.

Myerson had proven enormously effective in her consumer protection role, and was by this time one of the city's favorite public officials. She had closed 1969 with the greatest of many victories in her inaugural year in government: passage of the New York City Consumer Protection Law. It was the strongest consumer protection act in the nation at the time, widely covered in the press and soon modeled in other communities. Beyond her significant popularity in New York, people started putting Myerson in league with other national consumer advocates like Ralph Nader. Still, she remained in the public's thinking as a beauty queen first, and her success was that much more amplified because of it. Every story and event introduced Myerson first as a former Miss America, noted her continued beauty and slim figure, and then went on to her (implied unlikely) success as an advocate and policymaker. The crown gave Myerson a unique platform, but it also felt to her like a caricature that challenged her intelligence and seriousness, and undermined her efficacy. In an interview with Studs Terkel in 1974, Myerson recalled that images of herself in a swimsuit in 1945 popped up continuously in the press during her first year in the job, including industry periodicals for businesses she was challenging or seeking to regulate. It felt like it would always be the first thing fans, foes, and the largely indifferent thought of when they heard her name.

The ratification of the 26th Amendment, lowering the national voting age to eighteen, meant that the 1972 elections would include 11 million newly enfranchised young voters. A moment of possibility for both major parties, it coincided with a major overhaul of the nominating process by Democrats after the debacles of Chicago. Shirley Chisholm began exploring a run. She joined Gloria Steinem, Betty Friedan, and Bella Abzug in founding the National Women's Political Caucus (NWPC) to increase the presence of women in electoral politics by drawing more attention to their issues and lobbying for changes to the processes of delegate and candidate selection.

With an eye toward those younger voters, Nixon's reelection strategists began thinking about how best to mobilize the president's daughters. On September 20, 1971, Patrick Buchanan, now special assistant to the president, sat down at his typewriter to compose a "Briefing Paper" memo to White House Chief of Staff H. R. Haldeman about Julie Nixon Eisenhower's value to the upcoming campaign. He opened it by noting that it would be a "serious mistake" to over program her, since one of her "most attractive features [was] her ebullience and spontaneity and freshness; we don't want to lose that." He could not recall a time Julie had really "muffed the ball" with the press—she has always been "a tremendous asset to the President"—but the "hostile press" would surely try to draw her into "controversial social issues," "generational conflicts," and "sex-related issues," so they should prepare her. This included an extensive outline on "Women's Lib: The Butch Brigade," which "will be after Julie to come off one hundred percent for the movement." Buchanan counseled on keeping the focus of any comments to Nixon's policy of "Equal Pay for Equal Work," with emphasis on:

> the dignity in the role of housewife, the necessity of "freedom of choice" [to be a homemaker] and the President's opposition to having women in social roles such as bearing arms in the nation's defense. She will probably have to finesse the women's rights amendment. Some in here think RN ought to push it—my view is that it is not good for the country; although we have endorsed it in the past. . . . As for the extremists in the movement, they are a target of opportunity as far as I am concerned. A defense of femininity and the woman's role in American life would be well-received. Female militants are more an object of ridicule and a pain in the butt than the black chauvinists.

The long memo ended with a final suggestion, "Why not have Julie call up Miss America, invite her to the White House for lunch, drop in on her father and then march her over to the Press Gallery for a light press conference—the newsies would enjoy it." Miss Ohio, Laurie Lea Schaefer, an outspoken Nixon supporter and conservative Christian, had just been crowned on September 11.

• • •

By her own admission, Phyllis Schlafly was ambivalent about the ERA, and even vaguely supportive of the amendment when the House passed it in October by a massive majority of 354 to 23. This would change dramatically by the end of the year. "I figured ERA was something between innocuous and mildly helpful," she told journalist Carol Felsenthal for her biography, *Sweetheart of the Silent Majority*, published in 1981. Schlafly would become more dismissive and pricklier about it over time, claiming in later interviews that feminists had been simply too absurd to pay attention to, so she hadn't followed the ERA until after it had already passed the House and was on a clear path to passage in the Senate. This was her recollection—and common spin—on the other side of several decades as the nation's leading antifeminist voice, but the December 1971 chronology never changed.

When a friend and fellow conservative activist in Connecticut asked Schlafly to come speak against the ERA in a debate with a feminist proponent, Schlafly told her that she wasn't interested in the ERA, offering instead, "How about a debate on national defense?"

The woman pressed until Schlafly finally revealed that she wasn't even sure what side of the issue she was on. Convinced that she would be against the ERA once she understood it, the woman sent Schlafly some material—and she was right. It was too late to stop the bill in Congress, so Schlafly set her sights on the states and the ratification process.

Up to this point, while her faith, understandings of sex and gender, and political location on the Far Right had put Schlafly squarely at odds with radical women's liberation, she rarely commented on it and claimed not to think much about it (albeit in a they-aren't-worth-thinking-about sort of way). Initially, Schlafly didn't think the ERA was a problem—maybe it was even a good thing. Perhaps the amendment would address the barriers she continually ran into but hated to acknowledge directly.

Republican and conservative women generally were not automatically hostile to liberal feminist appeals, particularly concerning equal pay, education, and access to political leadership roles. It took a lot of work to create a politics that pit conservative women against their feminist counterparts; it was work that ran counter to the women's experiences—work that Phyllis Schlafly was about to pursue with unparalleled vehemence.

44

THE POWER OF THE POSITIVE WOMAN

Phyllis Schlafly hit the new year laser-focused on defeating the ERA, which meant mobilizing her monthly newsletter readers into a coordinated opposition. She knew the fight would have to be taken to state legislatures and the ratification process; the U.S. Senate was poised to pass the legislation with a large majority, just as the House had done in October. With subscribers all over the country, Schlafly's monthly newsletter provided a powerful organ for rallying conservative women to her new cause. The February 1972 issue, "What's Wrong with Equal Rights for Women?," outlined her arguments against the amendment in familiar terms: "fraud" and epic stakes of nothing less than an existential threat to the family, womanhood, and Western civilization. And the enemy? "Women's Lib" and "Libbers."

The newsletter was dense with arguments against the amendment and it covered no other topic. One biographer would later describe it as an anti-feminist manifesto: "The last couple of years, a noisy movement has sprung up agitating for 'women's right.' Suddenly, everywhere we are afflicted with aggressive females on television talk shows yapping about how mistreated American women are, suggesting that marriage has put us in some kind of 'slavery,' that housework is menial and degrading, and—perish the thought—that women are discriminated against." Schlafly urged her readers not to be fooled. "The claim that American women are downtrodden and unfairly treated is the fraud of the century. The truth is that American women never had it so good. Why should we lower ourselves to 'equal rights' when we already have the status of special privilege?"

She continued, "The great heroes of women's liberation are not the straggly-haired women on television talk shows and picket lines," but Thomas Edison, Elias Howe, Clarence Birdseye, and Henry Ford, whose inventions of electricity, the sewing machine, the industrial process of freezing food, and the automobile, respectively, liberated women from the drudgery of their labor, which she added, was all due to the system of "American free enterprise."

Schlafly deployed "women's lib" as an umbrella term that included everything from NOW, Gloria Steinem, and politicians like Bella Abzug and Martha Griffiths, to radical groups like the Redstockings and WITCH, the diminutive "lib" designed to do just that—diminish. It also served to draw "reasonable" concerns like equal pay and access to professional schools out of the realm of feminism altogether. "Many women are under the mistaken impression that 'women's lib' means more job employment opportunities for women, equal pay for equal work, appointments of women to high positions, admitting more women to medical schools, and other desirable objectives that all women favor," Schlafly wrote. "We all support these purposes as well as any necessary legislation which would bring them about." But that's not what pro-ERA forces want, she claimed. Instead, that was just the "sweet syrup which covers the deadly poison" of feminists' "total assault on the family, on marriage, and on children."

Ultimately, Schlafly argued, "libbers" were unattractive, bitter, lonely, loud women who just wanted everyone to be as miserable as they were. "The women's libbers don't understand that most women want to be wife, mother and homemaker—and are happy in that role. The women's libbers actively resent the mother who stays at home with her children and likes it that way. The principal purpose of *Ms.*'s shrill tirade is to sow seeds of discontent among happy married women so that *all* women can be unhappy in a new sisterhood of frustrated togetherness."

As Schlafly assumed, when the ERA finally made it to the floor of the Senate for a vote on Wednesday, March 22, 1972, it passed by a huge margin of 84 to 8. Hawai'i became the first state to ratify on the same day. Before the week was over, New Hampshire, Delaware, Iowa, and Idaho had joined them; fifteen more states ratified by the end of June. While it did not match the speed with which the 26th Amendment had been ratified the year before (March 23, 1971, to June 30, 1971), the ERA seemed on track to reach the thirty-eight-state threshold. In the fall, it ran into Schlafly's organization, STOP ERA (STOP being an acronym for Stop Taking Our Privileges).

That March, Loretta Lynn released a new single called "One's on the Way" about the plight of women left to do all the work of housekeeping and childrearing in Middle America. The song resonated with popular calls for changes to women's lives and greater equality that simultaneously rejected women's liberation and feminism, which it framed as a world apart from the average American woman: "The girls in New York City, they all march for Women's Lib." Magazines like *Better Homes and Gardens* depicted homes and modern furnishings that normal women—women from Topeka, Kansas, in the song's story—had no access to. "And the pill may change the world tomorrow but, meanwhile, today," in the rain and gloom, with a kitchen full of dirty dishes and crying children and a husband out carousing with his friends, life remained relentlessly difficult and unsatisfying. Loretta Lynn sang about inequality that was real and about women's lives that were hard and unfair that women's liberation wasn't addressing and seemed not to really see.

Activists like Carol Hanisch and Kathie Sarachild had been concerned about alienating average women from the start. In 1972, this worry merged with their anger at what they variously saw as a co-option, a watering down, a theft, and the commercializing of women's liberation by its mainstreaming. They pulled together several members of the Redstockings to begin work on a book to contest this, particularly as they saw it being done by Gloria Steinem and her new magazine *Ms.*, which had launched in December 1971. Hanisch and Sarachild also wanted to assert their roles as founders of the women's liberation movement and the creators of many of its key ideas, such as consciousness raising, the original Miss America Pageant protest, and slogans like "The Personal is Political" and "Sisterhood is Powerful." They were far from alone among the long-term activists in their sense that they were losing *their* women's liberation—the one they'd worked so hard and sacrificed so much to develop.

As Loretta Lynn's song climbed the country charts, a far more critical depiction of women's liberation, one that accused the movement of being out of touch, emerged from a very different place in the culture: the films of Andy Warhol. *Women in Revolt,* an Andy Warhol production written and directed by Paul Morrissey, was playing in art house theaters, on college campuses, and in art museums that spring. It depicted the entwined lives of three unhappy women made unhappier by their involvement in a women's liberation group called "Politically Involved Girls," or PIGs. Framed as a parody of feminists, the film finds nothing important or redeeming in women's liberation, which it depicts as absurd, exploitive, and misguided in equal measure. As most reviewers understood it, the heart of the parody was in the fact that the film's three main characters—"Candy," "Holly," and "Jackie"—were played by transgender Warhol superstars Candy Darling, Holly Woodlawn, and Jackie Curtis. "What better put-down of Gloria Steinem and her ilk could Warhol have dreamed up than to cast three female impersonators?" queried one generally positive review. Another critic who panned the film described it as a "grotesque parody of women's lib in which the three main female roles are played by male homosexuals dressed as women."

It is likely that more people read the coverage of the film than actually saw it, but it had real pop culture sticking power. This was perhaps best demonstrated by a piece that appeared in *Vogue* several months later, entitled "Warhol's Women Who Are Men," accompanied by a full-page photo of Curtis, Darling, and Woodlawn taken by Richard Avedon. It described *Women in Revolt* as a "sudsy topical 'woman's picture' with scenery-chewing roles that forty years ago might have been acted by Joan Crawford, Bette Davis, and Miriam Hopkins, instead of by men dressed as women." Far from seeing the film as parody or an insult to women's liberation, *Vogue* positioned it as a timely and trenchant commentary on "an accelerating American phenomenon, with its origins perhaps in Women's Lib, that views sexual identity solely in terms of arbitrary roles assigned by society. . . . Closely linked with the avalanche of cross-dressing men on the screen and stage, transexuals make the most radical challenge to traditional sexual roles—asserting on one level that to them being women is the only ethical, justifiable mode of living. Behind the laughs, there is a provocative, knowing gesture of truth."

• • •

Beyond the regular readership of the *Phyllis Schlafly Report,* STOP ERA's message resonated with a number of women who identified as evangelical Christians. The early 1970s saw the rapid expansion of an evangelical consumer market that included its own publishing boom, at the center of which stood established Christian authors like Norman Vincent Peale and those new to writing books, like Anita Bryant. After her first memoir, *Mine Eyes Have Seen the Glory,* was published in 1970, Bryant released a book a year for much of the decade—each one increasingly more overtly evangelical and more political than the last. In February 1971, a South Florida journalist described Bryant as "more than a beautiful smile circling even white teeth, more than a stunning woman with long, deep red hair and darkly expressive brown eyes. She's involved and committed and knows where the action is in this 'now' generation. And she comes on strong for the things in which she believes." As described, one of the things Bryant felt strongly about was "Women's Lib":

> I think the best thing would be if they could be liberated, then they'd find out it wasn't what they wanted in the first place. It seems to me that these women really want to be liberated from themselves. They are interested in self rather than how they are told to be women in the Bible. . . . I used to be a very ambitious, forward, bold, brash person. I had this need to please and to be accepted. Now these needs have been channeled in a different direction. It hasn't been easy, but we have let the Lord lead our lives and we have found an inner peace and happiness.

Bryant's movement from "I" to "we" was a reference to her husband and manager Bob Green, their new ministry, and their commitments to daily professions of faith. The article bolstered Bryant's Christian celebrity by reminding readers that she and Billy Graham were the only people invited to appear at both conventions in 1968, and that Bryant had been included as a subject in one of Norman Vincent Peale's books, thereby putting her in relation to the two most famous and politically connected Christian leaders of the day.

Early Cold War America was marked by growing church attendance, a more visible role for Christianity in government and civic life, and the expansive popularization of clinical psychology and psychiatry. At the confluence of all three trends stood Norman Vincent Peale, who emerged in this period as a major voice in American public life, ministering to souls and psyches from his pulpit in New York City and developing media empire. In 1937, Peale and psychiatrist Dr. Smiley Blanton had founded the Religio-Psychiatric Clinic (later the American Foundation of Religion and Psychiatry) at Marble Collegiate Church, which was a forerunner of the pastoral counseling movement. In 1945, Peale produced the first issue of *Guideposts,* a devotional magazine of daily prayer, affirmations, and Bible study, aimed initially at new veterans and their families. Subscriptions grew, along with a regular radio program and syndicated newspaper column, with the publication of Peale's first bestseller, *A Guide to Confident Living,* in 1948. They surged with *The Power of Positive Thinking* four years later, in which Peale offered a blend of faith in oneself and in Christianity as "the greatest secret for eliminating the inferiority complex." This could be achieved through a formula of positive thinking and "prayer power," which he described in 1952 as: "(1) PRAYERIZE, (2) PICTURIZE, (3) ACTUALIZE."

In his book, Peale demonstrated his formula's ability to address "all manner of negativism," with the example of a woman who'd discovered that her husband was cheating. Devastated, she sought counsel from her minister, and upon questioning from him, "admitted being a careless homemaker and that she had also become self-centered, sharp-tongued, and nagging." With the source of her husband's wandering-eye problem identified, the minister guided her through Peale's steps. She should picture herself as attractive and capable, he said, adding, "'God runs a beauty parlor,' and that faith techniques could put beauty on a person's face and charm and ease in her manor." With her new abilities to "prayerize" and "picturize"—including, Peale seemed delighted to note, adapting her minister's instructions to *picturize* her husband drying the dishes—the woman drew his attention back to her and the couple did not divorce.

Like Billy Graham, with whom he sometimes collaborated, Norman Vincent Peale was closely associated with conservative business groups like the National Association of Manufacturers and the U.S. Chamber of Commerce. The men helped forge a particular blend of anti-communism based in Christianity and free enterprise that put them at the center of national politics. In Peale's case, his political affiliation was mostly limited to Republican administrations, a relationship later enhanced by his early association with Richard Nixon, who first attended services at Marble Collegiate Church while stationed with the Navy in New York City in the 1940s. When the Nixons moved to New York in the 1960s, they attended church there regularly. This included Julie, who came with David Eisenhower after the two began dating; Peale officiated the couple's wedding in 1968. As ties between the Republican Party and Miss America grew, so, too, did the pageant contestants' and winners' connections to Peale and the "power of positive thinking."

In 1971, the Christian publishing house Revel released Bryant's second memoir, *Amazing Grace,* and a new book by Miss America 1965, Vonda Kay Van Dyke, called *Reach Up.* A former Miss Arizona (Goldwater country), Van Dyke was an early outspoken Christian Miss America, notable for her many appearances at churches and Christian youth groups. She had already written two books with another publisher: a Christian self-help for girls, *That Girl in Your Mirror* (1966), and a follow-up the next year, *Dear Vonda Kay* (1967), comprising letters from readers of her first book seeking advice and Van Dyke's replies. She was also breaking into the rapidly growing Christian music market, which put her on the radar of Anita Bryant.

Van Dyke's book outlined her philosophy for happiness and success: "plan, prepare and pray," to which she had added, after winning the Miss America crown, "hold your goals in mind in a positive picture." This "positive picture" stretched from personal mindset to social mission. "From what I've seen, despite the negative protesters who make news with their demonstrations, ours is an affirmative generation," she wrote. In addition to promoting this Peale-esque approach, Van Dyke's book offered a response to women's liberation as a young, newly married Christian woman who wanted a career, but did not want their vision of womanhood. "If, in the name of women's lib, they're asking for equal pay for women doing equal jobs equally as well as men, then I'm all for them," she wrote. "But some of the fringe benefits they seem to be demanding don't seem like benefits to me. I don't think the right to look unattractive, to assume a man's role, to let him take over my apron or my kitchen, is either a great privilege or progress."

In *Sharing the Crown,* published the same year, Judi Ford's mother, Marjorie, echoed Van Dyke's focus on faith and positivity in her own book:

> The positive approach of these girls [Miss America contestants] is a particularly refreshing contrast to the seemingly negative philosophy which is so prevalent in America today. Almost everything one sees or hears today emphasizes moral degeneracy, permissiveness, free love, sexual perversion, pornography, luridness in movies and books, drug addiction, college demonstrations, strikes, racial riots, destruction of property, radical dissent movements, and a complete disregard for authority, law, and order. . . . By spending our time accentuating the positive elements in our society, there will be very little time to dwell at length on its negative aspects, and our adoption of this philosophy should help us become more successful as we strive to make America better.

Miss America's victory over the forces of negativity seemed aptly demonstrated in Atlantic City in September 1972. Held the same month as Phyllis Schlafly officially founded STOP ERA, the pageant's theme was "Keeping America Beautiful . . . Our Way!" It assumed a defensive posture that resonated with the conservative activist's warnings about the threats to traditional womanhood posed by the ERA. This Miss America "way" included assurances in the collectible program that outgoing Miss America Laurie Lea Schaefer had "not lost the feminine touch" despite her busy schedule that had culminated in the USO tour. Similar to Schlafly and Vonda Kay Van Dyke before her, the narrative continued: "Laurie is a determined young woman who believes in women's rights. She is an advocate, however, of the philosophy that a woman need not lose her sense of feminity [*sic*] to achieve her goals and take her rightful place in society."

Terry Anne Meeuwsen became the first woman from Wisconsin to win the Miss America title. Last seen in Atlantic City protesting women's liberation demonstrators while wearing her "Nixon for President" button in 1968, Meeuwsen described the intervening years as a dark whirlpool of celebrity, drugs, and disaffection as a member of the popular folk ensemble the New Christy Minstrels. She had experienced the literal hellscape of bleak immorality and negativity that Marjorie Ford described, until she was saved by an insistent young evangelical at a McDonald's in Texas, where she was born again. Meeuwsen left the road and the group, and returned to pageant competition newly motivated, with a desire to profess her faith in Jesus Christ. A reporter for the *Memphis Commercial Appeal* would later write, "Terry Anne Meeuwsen is the All-American girl who says clearly and proudly, 'I'm one of God's reborn children.'"

In addition to noting her relative old age—she was twenty-three years old when she became Miss America—Meeuwsen's Christianity and conservative politics were consistently referenced in accounts of her win, along with her measurements and victory in the Swimsuit competition. Also commonly noted was the silver POW bracelet she wore for Army Major Theodore Gostas, who had been missing in action since the Tet Offensive, in 1968. During the traditional press conference the morning after her win, Meeuwsen explained to reporters that she had been introduced to Gostas's wife through the organization that produced the bracelets, Voices in Vital America (VIVA). When asked if she felt exploited by the pageant, Meeuwsen listed her scholarship and prizes and said, "If this is being exploited, exploit me every day." On a more serious note, she added, "Not all women need to be liberated."

"On Women's Lib, Miss Meeuwsen said she favored equal pay for women who did an equal amount of work," wrote one journalist. "But she didn't go along with demonstrations. 'If a person feels the need to be liberated, she should work on an individual level, not in a group.'"

A week into her reign as the new Miss America, Meeuwsen joined her predecessor and fellow Nixon-supporter, Laurie Lee Schaefer, in a visit to the White House to meet the president. Amid the congratulations, small talk, and laughter captured by the then-secret Oval Office recording system, Nixon can be heard telling Meeuwsen, "I like what you said about the POWs. It's a good cause."

Like Schaefer, Terry Anne Meeuwsen made an impression on Nixon and his advisors with her support. Earlier that summer, White House Chief of Staff H. R. Haldeman had expressed frustration that they hadn't been using Schaefer and others on the campaign for reelection. "What in the world has happened to the Miss Americas? Why aren't we working them in somewhere? We've got the support of the present, past, and practically all the ones going back to 1903. We at least ought to get the ones who can still walk lined up for us and the latest ones on our shows." That would change after the women's visit to the White House in September. Not only would they campaign formally and informally for Nixon, but Meeuwsen would also co-host the inaugural concert with Happy Rockefeller, the first lady of New York; she also sang the national anthem at the concert.

Meeuwsen would be widely celebrated within the pageant organization and beyond it for making more money through bookings and appearances than any winner before her. And though Albert Marks would chalk this up to her having "more personality and charisma than our former winners," it was largely due to her popularity in the growing evangelical movement of non-denominational "mega-churches" and in the Protestant entertainment and consumer cultures. She participated in several ministries for young singles, offering lectures on topics such as How to be a Winner and How to be a Woman. Particularly important to Meeuwsen's later career* in Christian broadcasting was her early connection to televangelist Robert Schuller, who had begun broadcasting the *Hour of Power* television show in 1970 from his Crystal Cathedral, in Garden Grove, California. Schuller trained with Norman Vincent Peale before founding his ministry of "possibility thinking" in Southern California in the 1950s. Many women in Schuller's California congregation and his national television audiences later would become members of STOP ERA or similar organizations.

By 1972, Anita Bryant was consistently challenging "women's lib" in her books, like that year's *Bless this House,* and in just about every interview she gave promoting them or during her heavy concert schedule. *Bless This House* was based on the couple's own marriage and struggles to manage busy careers and family through the teachings of fundamentalist Christianity. It was about, explained Bryant, "What we need in America today—children respecting parents, the father as the boss of the home, family praying." This all coincided with the couple's building new Christian businesses (including a talent agency and summer camp in Boca Raton, called Bibletown), their deepening commitments to evangelical witnessing, and Bob Green's promotion to deacon in their church.

The place of women as wives, mothers, and in the workplace was taken up through the question of 'How much freedom women should have?," which

* In 1981, Meeuwsen began hosting a morning show for CBN, the Christian Broadcasting Network founded by Pat Robertson in 1960. She joined Robertson as co-host on his flagship program *The 700 Club,* becoming the show's host after his death in 2023.

Bryant discussed with a journalist in Austin, Texas. "Miss Bryant firmly believes women should be second in command in the household and that men and women should not compete for positions in society," he wrote. "When *Cosmopolitan* magazine called to ask her if a woman should be president, Miss Bryant said no, because 'God meant there to be a vast difference between men and women. Man should be president, woman vice president.'"

"As far as I'm concerned," explained Bryant, "I was truly liberated when I accepted Jesus Christ as my Savior at age eight. That's what you must have to really be fulfilled as a total woman. This animosity and hatred some women have generated for men is completely contrary to the way God intended it to be."

No one could deny that Anita Bryant loved her work and was enormously successful in her career, which had long been the family business. Nevertheless, the contradictions between her work and celebrity and her religious beliefs and conservative politics were becoming far harder to square. The year before, when she was working on *Bless This House,* Bryant had tried to explain it. "Writing this book, I'm much more Anita Green than Anita Bryant. Not that there is any role conflict. . . . [T]he best role I could play is Anita Green, Bob's wife and our children's mommy."

She was often more revealing in interviews than she may have intended, such as when she told the *Austin American,* "I do think that women should get equal pay if they have the same job as a man and I can understand why some women who are unhappy with their husbands will grasp at anything, like women's liberation, but women need other outlets sometimes besides their families. My career has been an outlet and therapy to me." The same interview noted, "Miss Bryant says she wants to take care of her children and cook the family meals, so she no longer has 'live-in help.'"

"It's a difficult life sometimes," she said. "I never dreamed I would be an author of three best-selling books and sing for so many people." It's clear that Bryant felt pressure to live what she (and her husband) preached, just like any other traditional mother and housewife—but she had never really been those things. It took a great deal of work to play the role, which is where fellow South Floridian Marabel Morgan came in.

In 1973, Morgan took the country by storm with her Christian self-help best seller, *The Total Woman,* based on classes she'd been giving around Dade

County, Florida, to teach women how to be happy in their roles as wives and mothers, presented through her program of "4 A's"—Accept, Admire, Adapt, and Appreciate (your husband). Anita Bryant was an early student of Morgan's and was so impressed with the program and its creator that she brought Morgan to her Christian publisher, Revel, which released the initial edition of *The Total Woman*. "Do you know that your personal happiness depends on the attitude you decide you will have?" her book asked. "It does. Norman Vincent Peale said that attitudes are more important than facts." Morgan's program featured several hot sex tips for the Christian wife and a solution to her discontent other than "women's lib."

Terry Anne Meeuwsen, Anita Bryant, Marabel Morgan, and Phyllis Schlafly pursued intersecting agendas in the 1970s that forged a new path for conservative women in politics—a path made by traditional femininity, attention to beauty and appearance, and heterosexuality defined by a particular kind of acceptance and positive attitude in public and at home.

By early 1973, thirty states had ratified the ERA, with just eight more needed to amend the Constitution. But STOP ERA was making significant gains. In 1974, three more states ratified, but four others voted to rescind their previous ratifications—actions that would have to be decided in the courts.

STOP ERA's demonstrations aimed at capturing press coverage and the imaginations, stomachs, and "no" votes of legislators were not dissimilar from the guerilla theater of women's liberation. Espousing the motto "I am for Mom and Apple Pie," Schlafly and her comrades distributed fresh-baked pies in state houses around the country, with notes attached reading, "My heart and hands went into this dough. For the sake of the family, please say no," or "I enjoy being a girl." (The latter was a reference to the song of the same title from the 1958 Rodgers and Hammerstein musical *Flower Drum Song*, which became Phyllis Schlafly's semi-official theme song in the 1970s.) "Operation Mom's Apple Pie" begat other actions featuring homemade jams, bread, and signs like "To the Breadwinners from the Bread Makers" and "Preserve Us From a Congressional Jam; Vote Against the ERA Sham."

Schlafly called these their "femininity tactics," and said they were by far their best. How the women looked while performing them was key; Schlafly stressed the importance of general prettiness, good grooming, and always presenting oneself as a lady—all in stark contrast to "straggly haired" feminists. She ran workshops for STOP ERA chapters on how to testify at public hearings, respond to questions and counterpoints, and stay poised and smiling while being attacked; these were offered alongside tips about grooming, makeup, and how to choose colors that would be good on television. The STOP ERA activists never showed up at demonstrations wearing pants. When the women were lobbying individual legislators, Schlafly actively chose good-looking young moms, and encouraged chapter leaders to do the same. Schlafly would later boast, "It was pretty easy to tell the difference between the two sides by looking at them."

The Great American Beauty Contest, an ABC-TV movie that aired in February 1973, demonstrated the power of "femininity tactics" in a different way . It told the story of a women's liberation infiltrator of a Miss America–style beauty pageant who becomes enchanted with the pageant and its people, decides not to disrupt it, and, so converted, goes on to win the contest. Eleanor Parker, perhaps best known for her role as the Baroness Elsa von Schraeder in *The Sound of Music*, plays the Slaughter-esque pageant director, but with a twist—she's a former Great American Beauty winner dealing with aging in the industry as a now older, "less beautiful" woman. The film also featured an early supporting role for Farrah Fawcett, who played a fellow contestant.

Later that year, the Pussycat League and founder Lucianne Goldberg became a brief flashpoint in the rapidly unspooling Watergate scandal. In a top-of-the-fold, front-page *New York Times* story, "Writer Declares She was GOP Spy in McGovern Camp," Lucianne Goldberg claimed that as a journalist covering the McGovern campaign, she was paid $1,000 a week by Nixon associate Murray Chotiner to report any schedule changes, internal polling data, plans and "'sexy' details—'who is sleeping with whom and things like that,'" as part of a dirty tricks operation. Goldberg thought Nixon was aware of her activities, but said she was always paid with a private check and had no connection to the Committee for the Reelection of the President. (Investigations would later show that Chotiner had been reimbursed by the committee.) The story referenced *Purr, Baby, Purr* and ended by noting, "Several years ago, she and another women founded the Pussycat League, an organization designed to counteract the message of women's liberation."

• • •

In 1974, Charlotte Curtis was promoted to editor of the Op-Ed page and associate editor of the *New York Times*, making her the first woman ever to appear on the paper's masthead. Her success was bittersweet. In early 1972, Curtis had received a breast cancer diagnosis and was told she would need a mastectomy. Not wanting to take leave from work or undergo the surgery in New York City, she delayed it a few months with her oncologist's okay.* She told no one at work of her diagnosis. When Curtis got her mastectomy in Ohio in July, they discovered her cancer was far worse than they thought and very aggressive. She was told there was a 95 percent chance the cancer would return, and that when it did, it would be terminal. Charlotte Curtis was given five years to live. She went back to work and told no one, in part because she was sure she would never get another promotion at the paper if they knew she'd had breast cancer, let alone her prognosis. Two years later, she was on the masthead.

Not long after Curtis's promotion, women at the *Times* filed a class-action lawsuit for employment discrimination. Many of the women had worked with and for Curtis, had been mentored by her, and looked to her as a friend. Now they lobbied her to join them, to bring the power of her name and experience to the cause. To their immense disappointment, Curtis did not join the suit, stating her new role as an associate editor of the paper, and thus management, made her ineligible, nor did she ever publicly support the women. It was, to many, an unforgivable betrayal. (The paper settled the case without any admission of liability in 1978.)

Bess Myerson confronted similar fears that an illness—her troubled female body—would undo the authority she'd built. Myerson left the term-limited and lame-duck John Lindsay mayoral administration in 1973 as one of the most popular public figures in New York City, certainly as far as government was concerned. Soon after, buttons reading "Bess Myerson for Mayor" mysteriously began to appear all over the city, and journalists constantly asked her if she planned to run. Meanwhile, Governor Rockefeller conducted a secret poll

* Since the late 1960s, Curtis had been in a relationship with a professor of surgery at Ohio State University Medical School; they married on June 15, 1972, moving between homes in Columbus and New York.

concerning six possible candidates for mayor of New York City, including Myerson; she was far and away the people's favorite, garnering 49 percent of those polled (the next candidate got 39 percent). Rockefeller approached her about running on a Liberal-Republican ticket, and although she had ambitions for higher office, Myerson declined. In November of that same year, Myerson was diagnosed with ovarian cancer and began eighteen months of chemotherapy, before getting a hysterectomy. Like Charlotte Curtis, she kept her diagnosis a secret and continued with her consulting work and television appearances.

In May 1975, on the eve of the publication of their new book, *Feminist Revolution,* Carol Hanisch, Kathie Sarachild, and other members of the Redstockings held a press conference announcing they had evidence linking Gloria Steinem to the CIA. Their press release opened:

> Redstockings has called this press conference to release information we have uncovered showing that Gloria Steinem has a ten-year association with the CIA stretching from 1959 to 1969 which she has misrepresented and covered up. Further we have become convinced that *Ms.* magazine, founded and edited by her, is hurting the women's liberation movement.

The *New York Times* had, in 1967, first exposed Steinem's role in an organization called the Independent Research Service, shortly after it was revealed to have been funded by the CIA. The Independent Research Service was founded to facilitate the participation of American students in World Youth Festivals in Vienna, Austria, in 1957, and in Helsinki, Finland, in 1962. The festivals' sponsoring organizations were believed by U.S. officials to be fronts for Soviet propaganda, and the festivals themselves dominated by communists. Steinem confirmed the funding connection, reported the *Times,* "but insisted that the CIA had never tried to alter the policy of the foundation," and that she "'was never asked to report on other Americans or assess foreign nationals I had met.'"

At their press conference, the Redstockings announced their discovery of documentation showing that Steinem's role was bigger and had lasted for longer than she had admitted, and that political dossiers on individual activists had been created by the Independent Research Service under Steinem's direction.

They connected this history to Steinem's founding of *Ms.* magazine, suggesting a conspiracy to destroy the women's liberation movement from within:

> To many people, *Ms.* appears to be the voice of the women's liberation movement. But in actuality it has substituted itself for the movement, blocking knowledge of the authentic activists and ideas. *Ms.* outgrowths proliferate into many other areas—women's studies programs, television shows, feminist organizations—duplicating and many times substituting for the original, authentic activists and groups that sparked the movement. It is widely recognized that one major strategy is to create or support "parallel" organizations which provide an alternative to radicalism.

The release, which was attached to a section of their forthcoming book specifying these connections, ended: "Women's liberation's popularity and groundbreaking successes preceded the installation of Gloria Steinem as the movement's 'leader' by the rich and powerful. Today all the trappings of the radical upsurge remain, but the content and style have been watered down. We have reached a point when the movement must have a revival of the radical ideas and leadership which marked its early growth and success."

Random House refused to publish the book *Feminist Revolution* with the chapter on Steinem and the CIA; they excised the material and added mention of "an abridged edition" to the cover, prompting the Redstockings to distribute an insert called "The Censored Section of Feminist Revolution."

The charges against Steinem resonated. Many remained skeptical of Steinem's sudden appearance on the feminist scene, her celebrity, and the uses—by herself and others—of her beauty. It wasn't hard to make the leap from thinking Steinem an opportunistic interloper to believing she had infiltrated the movement in order to destroy it right under their noses. It only got easier when the extent of the FBI's Internal Security Counterintelligence Program (COINTELPRO), including surveillance of and informants in women's liberation groups, was revealed in 1976. (Suspicion about the extent of Steinem's work for the CIA has followed her throughout the decades, particularly among radicals who are critical of liberal feminists' quest for simple inclusion. Curiosity spiked more generally with the publication in 2015 of her memoir, *My*

Life on the Road, and her explanation to critics that the intelligence organization was, in her experience, "liberal, nonviolent and honorable." She drew a distinction between blanket perceptions of the CIA's activities in the 1950s and early 1960s and the aims and tactics of the sort of work she did. "It's so interesting now, because the initials C.I.A. will make people believe anything," she told the *New York Times* in 2016. "It just wasn't like that.")

With the Democrats back in the White House, 1977 was a big year for American feminists and their opponents. The federally funded National Women's Conference in Houston, Texas, in November, gave Betty Friedan, Gloria Steinem, Bella Abzug, and other feminist leaders from around the country a huge platform in conjunction with International Women's Year. It also gave Phyllis Schlafly and her compatriots on the Right an enormous target representing everything from anti-family and anti-woman policies to federal overreach and fiscal irresponsibility.

Schlafly had come within a single vote of successfully convincing enough members of the Platform Committee to remove support for the ERA from the party platform at the Republican Convention the year before. A Ronald Reagan supporter, Schlafly accused President Ford and the first lady of "intimate involvement with the radical women's lib movement" in her testimony. Her fury at Betty Ford stemmed from the latter's support for the *Roe* decision and "statements tolerating fornicating and illegal pot smoking." But the "intimacy" Schlafly was most concerned with was what she saw as Ford's sanction of illegal use of federal funds from the International Women's Year Commission for pro-ERA activities.

The August 1977 *Phyllis Schlafly Report* was devoted almost entirely to the International Women's Year as a "Front for Radicals and Lesbians." Schlafly argued, "IWY Conferences (at state level) serve as a front to give media exposure to and respectability to radicals, lesbians, and MSfits who want to agitate for their anti-family goals at the taxpayers' expense." Conservative women headed to Houston as well, some as delegates (wearing STOP ERA badges) to the National Women's Conference, but most joined Schlafly at the pro-life, pro-family counter-rally in the Astrodome. That rally gave various constituencies on the Right a national stage from which to challenge the women's movement and

Phyllis Schlafly and members of STOP ERA, seated in a hearing of the Platform Committee at the Republican National Convention, Kansas City, Missouri, August 10, 1976

demonstrate the strength of anti-feminist forces and the power of what Schlafly was calling "Positive Women."

That summer, Schlafly published *The Power of the Positive Woman,* a book that combined aspects of Norman Vincent Peale, Marabel Morgan, and other self-help guides aimed at conservative women with the politics and femininity tactics of STOP ERA and her Eagle Forum organization. Its thesis was clear: "The Positive Woman in America today has a near-infinite opportunity to control her own destiny, to reach new heights of achievement, and to motivate and influence others. Her potential is limited only by the artificial barriers erected by a negative view of herself or by the stultifying myths of the women's liberation movement."

This was the crux of Peale's positive thinking engineered to denounce feminism as not only dangerous and unnatural but also as the real barrier to women's power and success. Individual mindset, not systems of oppression, were the problem for women, Schlafly argued, but the ugly negativism of "radical women's lib" poisoned women's perceptions of men and senses of self with constant complaining, bitterness, selfish behavior, and the constant pointing out of slights and problems (that were only "problems" if you hated men, the family, God, and yourself).

The year 1977 also marked Anita Bryant's turn to direct political activism as an evangelical. First in South Florida, where she successfully campaigned against an amendment to the Dade County anti-discrimination code to include housing and workplace protections for gays and lesbians, and then around the country. Bryant focused on the specter of gay teachers as likely sexual abusers and agents for normalizing their unnatural "lifestyles," and is often credited with some variation of the remark, "Since homosexuals can't reproduce, they must recruit." Phyllis Schlafly lent her support to Bryant's movement by way of appearances in Miami, as did conservative televangelist Jerry Fallwell, who would go on to cofound the Moral Majority less than two years later.

Schlafly and Bryant were also united in 1977 through the shared experience of being "pied" by political opponents. In April, while attending a reception for the Women's National Republican Club at the Waldorf-Astoria, in New York, Schlafly was hit in the face with an apple pie by well-known Yippie "pie man" Aron Kay. He chose the fruit pie over his usual lighter and more explosive cream pies, Kay said, because "it was in the tradition of motherhood and apple pie." Six months later, at a press conference in Des Moines, Iowa, Anita Bryant got a cream pie to the face on television from a local gay liberation activist. Still images and film footage of the event went national; the latter remains enormously popular on YouTube.

Bryant and Schlafly were not the only political figures "pied" in the 1970s. Aron Kay's list alone was long and included William F. Buckley, Senator Daniel Patrick Moynihan, and Watergate break-in planner Howard Hunt. But the relish with which Schlafly's and Bryant's experiences were reported, and the images reproduced, suggested that their femininity and much-acknowledged beauty made them different kinds of targets.

The Miss Black America Pageant reached its largest audience yet in 1977, when it was telecast in prime time by NBC. When J. Morris Anderson announced the deal, he said, "The Miss Black America Pageant has been sowing the seeds of positivity for ten years, and now it is reaping the flowers of success. When the 10th Anniversary celebration of the pageant unfolds, thanks to the NBC television network, the greatest tribute in the history of America will be paid to black people in general and to the black woman in particular." The theme of positivity shaped every aspect of the pageant and its promotions, including Anderson's accounts of its history. In response to descriptions of the pageant's origins in protest, Anderson told the *Washington Post* that the contest was "a positive protest initially, but it stands on its own. It has never been a negative situation." In 1968, Anderson told another journalist that "he didn't look to support from the civil rights groups of the day, though some congratulated him on the undertaking." He added that using the term "Black" carried a militant edge then, but that Miss Black America was "fighting a different sort of battle" than civil rights groups; it was a "cultural program . . . of positive physical and mental development." Anderson's vision of positivity, like Schlafly's, stood in direct counterpoint to the activist legacies of 1968, as well as the contemporary activists of 1977. The *Chicago Tribune*'s Charitey Simmons sought a comment about the pageant from another figure of 1968, Robin Morgan, who concluded, "I think that if there is a message in terms of racial progress it is a message between men and men. . . . [W]hat it boils down to is separate but equal sexism."

On the eve of the telecast, Miss Black California, Ronalda Ay Nicholas, her hair long and straight, pulled into a high bun, with a looping tendril of hair on either side of her face, explained the philosophy of life that would guide her in the contest: "I believe that positive attitudes and ideas inspire positive reactions, which produce positive situations and opportunities." The convergence of conservative beauty politics was signaled before the first Miss Black America Pageant in 1968 was complete.

The pageant was a star-studded event, beginning with its host, actor Billy Dee Williams. The panel of eleven judges brought many of the country's biggest Black celebrities together, including Diahann Carroll, LeVar Burton, and Louis Gossett Jr., the latter two both Emmy Award nominees for their roles in the television epic *Roots*. Andrew Young, a historic civil rights leader who would go on to be the first Black congressman from Georgia since Reconstruction, and was at the time President Carter's new ambassador to the United Nations, was the only political figure on the panel. There was significant promotion of the three white judges on the panel: popular radio and television psychologist Dr. Joyce Brothers; Frank Price, president of Universal Television; and supermodel Margaux Hemingway.

During the telecast, Pearl Bailey brought legendary Black glamour and celebrity to the stage as she administered the Miss Black America Pageant's new "Oath of Positivity" to the contestants. They pledged their commitment to demonstrating positive mindsets and attitudes through their appearance, bearing, manners, and speech: "The positive look in my eyes will always indicate the self-confidence and positive spirits inside me."

After getting her start in Philadelphia's Black nightclub scene as a singer and dancer, Bailey toured with the USO during World War II and as part of ensembles with Cab Calloway and Duke Ellington. After making her Broadway debut in 1946, Bailey became a fixture of the American stage, radio, film, and television. In 1967, she and Calloway led an all-Black cast of *Hello, Dolly!*, which earned her a Tony Award; in 1968, she published *The Raw Pearl*, which was the first of several books. During the 1970s, she had her own variety series on ABC, *The Pearl Bailey Show*, and was a common guest star on programs like *The Carol Burnett Show*, *The Love Boat*, and *The Muppet Show*.

Pearl Bailey also brought to the Miss Black America stage her newer role as one of the highest profile Black Republicans in the country. In November 1970, Nixon had named her the U.S.'s official "Ambassador of Love," coming through on an impromptu promise he'd made at a White House dinner earlier that year. Speaking to journalists, Bailey declined to specify her party affiliation at that time. "Nobody knows how I vote. Mr. Nixon asked me to be his ambassador as a human being, not as a Republican or Democrat." Gerald Ford expanded Bailey's role when he assumed the presidency, by making Bailey a Goodwill Ambassador for the United Nations. By 1976, she was well-known as a Republican and she appeared in a campaign commercial for Ford, in which she made a direct appeal to Americans to vote for him, just as she had planned to do. (Bailey would later be a vocal supporter of Ronald Reagan and a frequent guest at his White House; in 1988, Reagan awarded her the Presidential Medal of Freedom.)

When Claire D. Ford, an eighteen-year-old, new high school graduate from Memphis, Tennessee, was crowned the new Miss Black America 1977, she committed to the pageant's new ethos. It fit neatly with her evangelical Christianity, which infused Ford's work as the pageant winner. When she was asked for advice on approaching the new year a few months later, Ford replied, "Pray more, and believe in your prayers. God has an answer to all problems, so pray about anything that bothers you." She described everything she had done since winning, which included visiting churches, military installations, secondary schools, and colleges, where she delivered "inspirational talks on her favorite topics, praying and positive thinking"; she also made a guest appearance on television's *Fantasy Island.* "I pray every day to become a better person physically, mentally, and spiritually. And I owe everything I've ever accomplished to the powers of prayer and positive thinking."

Phyllis Schlafly's book *The Power of the Positive Woman* brought the antifeminist political trajectory of positivity to its apex. J. Morris Anderson joined her in publishing his own book, *Seeds of Positivity,* written, he said, "To help Miss Black America contestants act and think like winners" and serving as the basis for classes for the public the following year. For the next Miss Black America Pageant, held in Philadelphia on August 18, 1978, he declared the day as National Black Woman's Day. "After 400 years," Anderson announced, "it's about time somebody launched a campaign to praise and applaud the Black woman for the positive contributions she has made to society in her role as mother, sister, wife, friend, and propagator of the species. For this reason, the Miss Black America Pageant has instituted National Black Woman's Day as an annual event." The defining characteristics of the Black women's positive contributions in Anderson's list were notably limited to traditional roles in the family and among friends—all based in private, personal relationships, not on public positions of authority or leadership—as well as their capacities to give birth.

To mark the day, he encouraged every Black American to wear their finest clothes, adding that audience members at the pageant would be expected to participate, and that no one would be admitted to the Philadelphia Civic Center who did not comply. In some senses, it was a return to Anderson's earliest days as an event promoter. "To encourage them to dress up for Black Woman's Day, I will present cash prizes to the best-dressed members of the audience at the Miss Black America Pageant," he said. "I will award $500 each to the best-dressed male, female, and couple in the formal wear category; and $500 each to the best-dressed male, female, and couple in the high fashion category." Anderson promised that the winners, along with the rest of the audience, would be featured throughout the ninety-minute national telecast.

A week after the 1977 Miss Black America Pageant, Terry Anne Meeuwsen and Phyllis George co-hosted that year's Miss America telecast. The two women had been friends since 1971, when George encouraged Meeuwsen in her return to pageant competition. Since then, George had become the most prominent woman in sports broadcasting, after joining CBS's *The NFL Today* in 1975. The following year, she became the first woman to host a Super Bowl telecast; now, she was using her play-by-play skills for Miss America. Of her status as a historic first, George assured her audiences, "I'm not a feminist in any way."

By that same September, it was clear to the leadership of NOW and others that the ERA was unlikely to be ratified by the deadline of March 22, 1979. Indiana had become the thirty-fifth state to ratify the ERA earlier that year, but the path to gaining three more states was unclear, as was the status of those attempting to rescind their earlier votes in the affirmative. After intense lobbying, Congress voted to extend the deadline, but only until June 30, 1982.

Phyllis George became a devoted student of Norman Vincent Peale, describing him as her spiritual advisor. In 1979, she married John Y. Brown, who had made his fortune creating the Kentucky Fried Chicken fast-food chain and was running for governor of Kentucky. The pair were wed in New York, at Marble Collegiate Church, with Rev. Peale officiating. Brown won the governor's race several months later, making Phyllis George the first lady of the Commonwealth of Kentucky. Referring to herself as "Phyllis George Brown" on the campaign trail had not come easy, but it had proved necessary. This was illustrated at a campaign stop in eastern Kentucky a few weeks after the wedding (described by one journalist as the scene of a glamorous, well-dressed alien dropping from a helicopter with her candidate husband into the rural, Appalachian community to shake hands with suspicious mountaineers).

"I'm Phyllis George. My husband's John Y. Brown, and he's running for governor. I'd like to ask you to vote for him."

"Lady," replied a grizzled man, taking his hand back, "in these parts, we happen to believe that when a women marries a man, she ought to take his name, too."

For Anita Bryant, not taking her husband's name had always been a professional necessity that neither spouse liked, but had accommodated themselves to. The situation became more awkward in 1977, with Bryant's growing public evangelicalism, conservative politics, and anti-gay activism, at the center of which had always been her own marriage, children, and Christian family values.

On May 22, 1980, Anita Bryant shocked the nation—and her husband, Bob Green, and their minister—by filing for divorce in a Dade County courthouse, citing a struggle for her name and what it meant as a major cause. Bryant made a public statement that Green had "violated my most precious asset: my very conscience," and joined "with certain hired staff members [of Anita Bryant Ministries, Inc.] who conspired to control me and to use my name and reputation to build their personal careers instead of my ministry." There had been the opposing forces of a family's wealth, a church's mission, and a conservative Christian political organization reliant upon Anita Bryant's talents, career, and celebrity, on the one hand, and her compulsory, faith-based submission to her husband and the authority of male church leaders, on the other; it had finally become impossible to hold the two together.

Many of the same newspapers that reported on Bryant's divorce filing, and her departure from the family home with the couple's four children, carried "an open letter to my wife" from Green the next day, appealing for her return. "Dear Anita," it read. "I love you with all my heart and I am awaiting your return as my wife and the mother of our children. God's love and forgiveness is open to both of us if we will but seek it." In a few short lines, Green had painted himself as a wronged patriarch, humble before God and millions of American newspaper readers, seeking only to repair what was broken. "Let us both put aside all other earthly considerations and reunite our lives in Christian love," Green concluded, deftly summoning the specter of the selfish feminist as a counterpoint to Bryant's assertions that the men in her life were trying to control her and using her name for their own gain. The public back and forth continued throughout the summer, until the divorce was granted in August, during which Bryant highlighted her financial struggles (despite having been the family's breadwinner) and explained in an interview with *Good Housekeeping* that her marriage had been troubled from the start. In addition, Bryant's anti-gay crusading and evangelicalism had alienated her from much of the secular entertainment industry that had made her a star, including lost endorsement deals because she had become "too controversial." In 1980, the divorce, and her role in instigating it, drove a wedge between Bryant and the Florida Citrus Commission, which canceled her contract, and alienated many evangelical followers—the ones she'd counseled in the ways of submission and sanctity of the family, above all.

Anita Bryant's divorce and declining fortunes drew a range of reactions, from the powerful satisfaction of the gays and lesbians she had demonized—whose rights and very humanity she'd sought to destroy in the name of family values—to not a little schadenfreude across American popular culture. This turn in Bryant's story elicited complex sympathies, as well as the anger and certain satisfaction among feminists all along the continuum, from liberal journalists like Ellen Goodman to radical women's liberationists like Andrea Dworkin. "Spare me the Saturday night snide jokes" about Bryant's divorce and comeuppance, wrote Goodman a week after the news broke. The journalist wanted it made clear that she was "no fan of Anita Bryant's politics," but that like others before her who had found power in being "a public defender of the family and traditional female role, [she] was pushed or grew out of submission." She was "hardly a feminist" but had nevertheless "chosen her individual conscience over her role. The lady tried to be a leader in the world and an obedient follower in the marriage. But these are the two ways you can't have it anymore."

In her 1982 book *Right-Wing Women*, Dworkin noted how different Bryant's relationship to feminism had become in the wake of her divorce. The basis for the book was a story Dworkin published in *Ms.* magazine in 1979, "Safety, Shelter, Rules, Form, Love: The Promise of the Ultra-Right." The story analyzed the appeal of women like Bryant, Schlafly, and Marabel Morgan to the same people feminists and women's liberationists had been trying to reach. Dworkin quoted an interview Bryant gave a month after she left Bob Green, in which she said:

> What has happened to me makes me understand why there are angry women who want to pass ERA. That still is not the answer. But the church doesn't deal with the problems of women as it should. There's been some really bad teachings , and I think that's why I'm really concerned for my own

> children—particularly the girls. You have to recognize that there has been discrimination against women, that women have not had the teaching of the fullness and uniqueness of their abilities.

To which Dworkin added, "*Pace* [*sic*], sister."

Bryant's divorce saga was treated as a soapy backdrop to the wider politics of conservative Christianity and anti-feminism in the run-up to the 1980 presidential race. After coming close to winning in 1976, the Republican Party finally nominated Ronald Reagan, a vocal opponent of the ERA, for president, and voted to remove support for ERA from the party's platform, which had been there since 1940 (the Democrats had added it to their platform in 1944). What had seemed to most Republican officials an obvious benefit to society (and their own political futures) less than a decade earlier was now believed to be in fundamental contradiction to their world views and party values. Conservative women, including those who wore the Miss America crown, drove this transformation. Ronald Reagan won the presidency, but Phyllis Schlafly characteristically took much of the credit. She wasn't too far off.

Vanessa Williams didn't grow up dreaming of becoming Miss America, but the day she was born in 1963 hinted at her destiny. Her mother Helen Williams announced Vanessa's birth on a bright pink card with a white-and-gold banner across the top that read: "Here She Is—Miss America!" Beneath it was an illustration of a cheeky baby girl in a diaper and large crown, holding a scepter and trailing an ermine cloak. Notably, the baby was white. Twenty years later, Vanessa Williams became the first Black woman to win the Miss America Pageant in 1983.

Williams was a sophomore with a musical theater major at Syracuse University when she was recruited by a Miss Greater Syracuse Pageant board member, who saw her perform in the students' Fall Review. It took some convincing after Williams's initial reaction: "Me—a beauty queen? I don't think so!" In the end, the scholarship money convinced her. When Williams arrived in Atlantic City as Miss New York in early September, she had participated in only two other pageants—the ones she had won to get there. And, as the first contestant to

Vanessa Williams becomes the first Black Miss America in history in 1983 as first runner-up Suzette Charles (left) looks on

arrive on Friday morning, she carried that storied extra bit of luck into Pageant Week, which saw her win the preliminary competitions in Swimsuit and Talent.

With three other Black women among the year's competitors—the highest number ever to appear together on the Miss America stage—there was significant buzz that 1983 could be the year for a Black winner. Deneen Graham had already made history as not only the first Black woman to win Miss North Carolina but also the first Black finalist ever from the Deep South. As Pageant Week got underway, the *Atlantic City Press* published a long front-page story, "Many Believe Black May Win," which explored the recent history of race and the pageant. Staff writer Barton Jones had interviewed Cheryl Browne about her experience as the first Black finalist in 1970, who had told him that she had learned later it had been "said to members of the [Iowa] state pageant board at the time that the national pageant didn't feel the country was ready for a black Miss America," and that "to a certain extent" the remarks made her feel "cheated." When asked to comment about this, Al Marks, still the organization's executive director, responded, "Anybody who said that, and I knew about it, would have been fired on the spot." Marks also told Jones, "We've been accused in the past by the NAACP of being lily-white, racist and everything else, which is absolutely not true," once again parroting his refrain about the national organization's lack of control over what happened at the state level. Marks's assertion, however, was belied by his next remark, "I've always had the feeling Miss America is open to anyone morally qualified."

On that Saturday night in 1983, no one was surprised when Vanessa Williams was announced as one of the ten semifinalists to move forward in the contest. She was joined by another of the four closely watched Black contestants—Miss New Jersey, Suzette Charles. A biracial woman from nearby Mays Landing who had won her first pageant at age seven, Charles was described by Barton Jones as being "relatively light skinned" and having "appeared on television programs portraying characters of Spanish, Italian and black origin." Like Williams, who performed a crowd-pleasing version of "Happy Days Are Here Again" for her talent, Charles was a singer. She opened the night's competition with a sweeping rendition of Barbra Streisand's "Kiss Me in the Rain."

Charles was followed by Miss Texas, Dana Rogers, who performed "An American Trilogy," a signature song for Elvis Presley later in his career in the 1970s. A medley invoking the history of the Civil War, the song's arrangement moved from "Dixie" to "Battle Hymn of the Republic," representing the South and the North, before weaving in part of the popular Black gospel song "All My Trials."

In the pageant's lineup, this meant that the night's first performance by one of two Black semifinalists was followed immediately by a blonde, white woman from Texas belting, "Oh, I wish I was in the land of cotton, old times there are not forgotten, look away, look away, look away, Dixieland." Vanessa Williams closed out the Talent portion with her performance, creating a kind of racialized bookend.

When Suzette Charles was announced later as the first runner-up, six women remained, five who had not placed, and the new Miss America. Master of Ceremonies Gary Collins, who was married to 1959 Miss America, Mary

Ann Mobley, seemed less inclined than his predecessor, Bert Parks, to stoke the drama by drawing things out. He moved on to the big announcement with little preamble, "And, our new Miss America is Vanessa Williams! Miss New York!"

The next day, Ronald Reagan called Williams to offer his congratulations, saying that her victory was a "wonderful thing for our nation." The sentiment rested uneasily with the president's history and contemporary policy agenda. Since his run for the nomination in 1976, Reagan had built a case against welfare and "big government"—and his rightness for office to address them—by demonizing Black women as lazy, recalcitrant drains on the resources of good, hard-working (white) American taxpayers, thereby enshrining the toxic caricature of the "welfare queen" in American political discourse. After kicking off his 1980 campaign with a speech about state's rights in Philadelphia, Mississippi, on August 3—where the bodies of murdered civil rights workers Chaney, Goodman, and Schwerner had been finally located fourteen years earlier, on August 4, 1964—the Reagan administration had set about dismantling federal civil rights protections and the agencies that managed them, including tapping the Black, anti–affirmative-action conservative Clarence Thomas to lead the EEOC (a position that set him on the path toward his nomination to the U.S. Supreme Court in 1991). When Williams broke the Miss America color barrier in 1983, Reagan was in the midst of fighting the establishment of a federal holiday to honor Martin Luther King Jr. The president was, however, also sincere in his congratulations to Vanessa Williams, no doubt seeing her in that moment as evidence of the individual accomplishments he believed possible for any American, no matter their race, as long as one had the initiative, discipline, talent, and drive to succeed.

The varied expectations for and experience of being the first Black Miss America did not often make Williams feel seen as an individual. After her win, she told reporters, "At times I get annoyed because people and the press aren't focusing on me as a person and my achievements but are focusing on my being Black. I believe I can be a good representation of what can happen to ambitious young women who work hard, not just Black women. I hope it encourages more Blacks to enter and realize the things that can happen in America."

But many Black Americans did not see Williams as an example of what could happen for *them* in America—because they did not see in her a very Black person. They saw a woman of color who epitomized the dominant standards of white beauty and had been rewarded for it. They saw in Williams a woman too light-skinned, with eyes that were too blue, features too small, and hair that was too feathered to move through the world and meet its judgments in the same ways as they did.

Williams never shied away from questions about race and politics, but as a registered Independent who described herself as liberal in some areas and conservative in others, tended to tack toward the middle. "People aren't getting used to change, but I think it has to happen. I don't think I'm going to be torn over that. I'm an individual. Just because I'm Black doesn't mean I'm going to support every Black cause," she said, following up with a statement of support for the King holiday. Williams was for the ERA, and when asked about her feelings on abortion replied, "It is a right women should have. I think it should be there for women to use, but I don't think every woman should use it." In October, she spoke at the National Press Club in Washington, D.C., where she specified, "I am very much in favor of the ERA," but that she was "not a feminist, [not] an activist. I believe in it. If a woman can do a job the same way as a man can, she should get equal pay."

Everything changed about Vanessa Williams's Miss America story on Friday, July 13, 1984. She was in Watertown, New York, to appear at that weekend's state pageant, where she would crown her successor as Miss New York—the first of a string of benchmark moments in her final passage of the title to the next Miss America. That Friday was a busy day, like so many others had been over the last year, and it started with an official breakfast appearance, rehearsals, and several press interviews, one of which a reporter from the *New York Post* conducted over the phone.

From her room in the Ramada Inn, Williams answered the reporter's questions, the bulk of their conversation focusing on her fellow New Yorker, Congresswoman Geraldine Ferraro. After weeks of talk, the presumptive Democratic choice for president, Walter Mondale, had announced that he would be choosing Ferraro as his running mate, making her the first woman in history to be nominated for vice president by a major party. (By 1984, national political conventions were looking more like the versions we know today, with most of the decision-making happening during the primaries.) "I think it's fantastic,"

Williams said, when asked to comment. "She'll do a wonderful job. I think it's a great thing for our country."

Just before Williams hung up the phone, the reporter stopped her and asked: "Oh, by the way, I heard from a very reliable source that there are nude photos of you coming out in September's *Penthouse*. Is it true?"

"Excuse me?" she croaked. Williams felt like she couldn't breathe.

Two years earlier, during the summer after her freshman year at Syracuse, Williams had worked as a receptionist and makeup artist for a photographer, Tom Chiapel, in Mount Kisco, New York. Chiapel specialized in portfolios for aspiring models. Williams had gotten the job after responding to a "Models Wanted" ad. It wasn't the modeling work the ad had implied, but Chiapel promised to do Williams's portfolio for free as a bonus if she took the job. One afternoon, he asked her if she would pose with a friend of his who was coming over to shoot some stylized, black-and-white nudes; they were for his art practice and nothing else, Chiapel promised, adding that neither woman's face would be recognizable because he was merely capturing form and line through silhouette. It took some convincing—Williams had never posed nude before and had never planned to—but eventually she agreed. "After he felt we had loosened up" with lots of white wine and solo shots, Williams recalled much later, Chiapel "asked us to pose together. He positioned us and told us what to do. It felt silly, stupid, and not very artistic." It was all awkwardness and giggles, but also exciting, carrying a sense of daring and adventure; being a little bad felt good, even freeing. Looking back, Williams said, "We were two young women giving the man behind the lens all the power in the room."

The day Geraldine Ferraro took the stage at the Democratic Convention in San Francisco, to accept her historic nomination for vice president—July 19, 1984—was also the day the story broke that *Penthouse* would publish nude photos of Miss America in sexually suggestive poses with another woman in its September issue, which was being rushed to publish in time for the next pageant. Williams had met with Al Marks (who brought his wife) earlier in the week in Atlantic City and was still awaiting the pageant organization's decision about next steps. On Friday, a week after she had first learned of the magazine's plans, Al Marks and a special committee of the pageant's board demanded Vanessa Williams's resignation. She was in Little Rock, Arkansas, making an official appearance at the time. Her only comment was that she would hold a press conference on Monday, July 23, to address the situation.

"For 10 months, Vanessa Williams has served the pageant and the title of Miss America well," Marks had said with attorney Leonard Horn standing by his side. "But we must make it clear that we cannot and do not condone her actions." It wasn't his place to judge Williams's character, Marks said, but he believed that she "had violated the spirit of the pageant" and threatened its wholesome image—an image the organization thought that sponsors, advertisers, and the American public relied upon.

On Monday, three hundred television, radio, and print journalists filled a Manhattan hotel function room for the press conference, after a weekend of nonstop should-she-or-shouldn't-she-resign coverage. The photographers crushed against the short dais where Williams stood at a lectern with family and an advisor nearby. The men shouldered one another, jostling for position, holding their cameras aloft, their flash bulbs right at Williams's eye level. Other cameramen and reporters farther back yelled at the men in front to stop blocking their sightlines (every photographer at the front, captured by ABC's television camera, was a man). The flashes and sounds of shutters—and men yelling—would be constants throughout Williams's ten-minute reading of a prepared statement. She seemed a beacon of calm, easy poise, and strength—remarkable, given the circumstances and unruly scene in front of her.

After explaining the context of the photographs, and making clear that she had never consented to their use, Williams said, "Last Friday, I heard on the news that the pictures were going to be published. I also learned that the pageant had asked me to resign my title and that I would have 72 hours to make my decision. I was shocked, surprised, and deeply hurt." At several points, she attempted to impress the situation's emotional toll.

"I felt a deep sense of personal embarrassment. . . ."

"Hey!" shouted a man from somewhere in the back of the room. "Get that camera down!"

Without acknowledging the interruption, she continued, "It is one thing to face up to a mistake that one makes in youth, but it is almost totally devastating to have to share it with the American public and the world at large as both a human being and as Miss America."

Williams then turned to "the question everyone has been pondering, including myself . . . should I try to retain my title as Miss America in spite of the circumstances?" While Marks and the board had cited a morals clause and had argued that Williams had been obligated to declare the images' existence before competing, they had requested her resignation instead of firing Williams outright—because there was no clear legal justification for them to do so. Reactions to the controversy throughout the weekend seemed divided, with a tilt in favor of Williams fighting to retain her title.

Before she gave her answer, Williams explained what being Miss America had meant, reminding everyone of the stakes in the decision that Marks, Leonard, and the rest of the pageant leadership had foisted on her. "Over the past ten months it has been both an honor and a great privilege for me to serve the American people and the pageant as Miss America. It is an honor which has been shared and brought lots of happiness to me, my family, my community, and the world." Williams praised the opportunities the Miss America system had given her and "millions of aspiring young women" over the years, and she noted how much she had given the pageant in return. "I feel that I have, to the best of my abilities, tried to maintain all those positive qualities that have encompassed my duties and responsibility to the title of Miss America."

Williams "was not a person who gives up when the going gets rough," she said, but her experience of the last week had made clear the obstacles the controversy presented to doing the job of Miss America, to how disruptive it would be. Throughout this part of Williams's statement, a chorus of grumbling and urgent conversation grew in the room; the men thought they knew where this was going.

"It has never been and is not my desire in any way to injure the Miss America title or pageant. I feel at this time I should expend my energies in landing what I hope will be a successful career in the entertainment business." Williams explained that she was excited about taking on her next professional challenge. "Therefore, I do officially relinquish my title as Miss America 1984 to the Miss America Pageant." The moment "relinquish" was out of Williams's mouth, several men in the room started yelling, "No!" As she moved toward concluding, a crush of photographers in the squeeze at the front of the room turned and pushed their way out, having gotten what they came for.

Everyone coming and going from that press conference met a group of women outside the hotel, protesting in support of Williams and against *Penthouse,* although the latter was their primary focus. The protesters distributed copies of a statement identifying themselves as members of Women Against Pornography (WAP) and charging that, "By promoting these pornographic photos without Ms. Williams' consent, against her will, *Penthouse* is violating her civil rights and subjecting her to photographic rape." (Claims that resonated with the controversy surrounding Williams but were not formalized as legal allegations by her or others.) WAP was part of the feminist anti-pornography campaign that coalesced in the mid-1970s around the movement to eradicate violence against women. They argued that sexual assault was fundamentally about power, and the domination of women by men in the maintenance of patriarchy through "rape culture." Pornography not only normalized and encouraged violence against women, in this framework, but was itself also violence and thus a violation of women's rights. In New York City, Susan Brownmiller, Robin Morgan, and Andrea Dworkin were key figures in WAP as organizers; as writers with national and international audiences, they helped broadcast this cultural analysis, summed up by Robin Morgan in 1977 as "Pornography is the theory, and rape the practice."

For anti-pornography feminists, the events prompting Vanessa Williams's resignation provided a powerful example of the pornographic and violent ends of any objectification of women, including the Miss America Pageant. Ellen Goodman made similar connections for readers of her syndicated column, most of whom did not identify as radical feminists. "Last fall, Miss Williams told a reporter fervently, 'I am more than a piece of good-looking meat on a stage.' But pageants and *Penthouses* are both in the flesh biz," Goodman wrote. "A beauty contest displays a woman solely as a body; a pornographer subdivides that body into its parts. Both make their subject into an object, both offer her up for the pleasure of the devouring public." Two weeks later, Flo Kennedy and Ti-Grace Atkinson announced the creation of an "Ad Hoc Committee Against *Penthouse* Magazine and the Miss America Pageant," with plans to seek a legal injunction to stop *Penthouse* from publishing more pictures of Vanessa Williams and "stop the 1984 Miss America Pageant in Atlantic City."

The same week Goodman's piece appeared, fellow syndicated columnist Patrick Buchanan published "In Defense of the Miss America Contest." In several papers across the country, the two columns appeared on the same page. Since his time in the Nixon administration, Buchanan had become a popular conservative voice providing regular political commentary in print and on radio, and on television with *The McLaughlin Group* and *Crossfire*. These outlets provided the foundation for his increasing promotion of an American "culture war" demanding Republican action. In his defense of the pageant, Buchanan argued, "To describe the Miss America pageant as sexist and exploitive 'on a continuum' with what [Bob Guccione, founder of *Penthouse*] does for a living is a comment rooted in feminist ideology, not common sense." Pageants and porn were not a part of the same systemic oppression of women, he claimed, because, well, they just weren't. "The Miss America contest celebrates physical beauty, of face and form. *Penthouse* publishes hardcore pornography."

To Buchanan, the difference between appreciating female beauty on the pageant stage and ogling women in sexual acts was self-evident, and to suggest otherwise was to denigrate beauty itself. "The feminist ideal of the young American woman may be the undergraduate at Radcliffe who eschews makeup and personal appearances so as to devote more time for important matters like the nuclear freeze. Fine. To each her own. But there is nothing inherently degrading about the ideal of Miss America as championed by the Atlantic City pageant. And there is much that is positive about it."

Minutes after Williams announced her resignation in Manhattan, Al Marks addressed the gathered press in Atlantic City at the offices of the Miss America organization with Suzette Charles by his side. The circumstances were regrettable, said Marks, and he urged the "American public to support Miss Williams in her future endeavors," before introducing Charles as Miss America.

With her proud parents and grandparents looking on, Charles answered a few questions about becoming Miss America. "It feels wonderful," she replied, but added, "It's a very unfortunate situation. I have mixed emotions. But we move on and I will try to uplift the image of Miss America, which is my number one priority." Speaking of the events in Manhattan, she told reporters that Williams "had left with class."

These comments about Williams and the controversy were more measured than the ones Charles had made over the weekend, when all was still unclear.

She had been more critical then, saying she had no skeletons in her closet because she would never have put herself in such a situation. She also told reporters that she would not be political if she became Miss America; she would keep her vote to herself and explain to kids that "they can reach their goals" because "there are no racist barriers holding you up."

Charles had been put in a fairly impossible situation. None of this was how she wanted to become Miss America—something she had wanted for a very long time. The first title winner from New Jersey in the pageant's history, Charles had grown up not far from Atlantic City and had been around the pageant her entire life. At seven, she won her first title, Little Miss New Jersey, the same year Cheryl Brown broke the Miss America color line as Miss Iowa. She wanted to be the first Black Miss America; now, she had about six weeks to be the second Black Miss America, known mostly for not being Vanessa Williams.

The pageant proceeded to spend the next six weeks attempting to erase Williams's existence from the upcoming pageant. There would be no pictures of her time in the crown, no references to her or her absence in the program or other souvenir materials, no expression of thanks for her ten months of, by their own accounts, excellent service. This process began at the press conference with the removal of Williams's formal portrait from the wall in the pageant's office. In its place they hung the previous winner's portrait, as if the crown had never been transferred to Vanessa Williams at all.

Vanessa Williams's Blackness had everything to do with how this controversy unfolded, although its principal subjects, including Williams herself, rarely acknowledged it directly at the time. The reference to her "community" in the middle of the statement was the only moment that hinted at Williams's historic role as the first Black Miss America, and the unique pride and particular representational burdens that came with it. Whenever Marks was asked if racism was a factor in the organization's actions, or to comment about the pageant's history of racial exclusion in relation to the controversy, he gave a side-stepping version of the same answer: nothing about the pageant's actions was racially motivated; the woman who would replace Williams if she resigned, Suzette Charles, was also Black. It was hardly a persuasive argument, and one had to wonder what his response would have been if the first runner-up had been one of the other eight semifinalists, all of whom were white.

Would the pageant have stood by a different Miss America in the same situation, or at least not have been so quick to believe the worst of her? It had all occurred in a ten-day period, from the moment Williams learned about *Penthouse*'s plans to publish and notified Al Marks of her decision to resign as pageant leadership. Might the pageant have taken more time to consider their options, if only to get a better read on the general public reaction than the one they presumed?

The answers were to be found in the history of white supremacy and anti-Blackness, particularly as they were expressed by dominant standards of beauty. The treatment of Vanessa Williams made clear how tenuous the gains of being "accepted" as a representation of ideal American femininity were when the ideal itself had been created through the exclusion of Black women. The pictures of Williams in sexually suggestive poses with a white woman pulled on worn caricatures of Black women's hypersexuality that were produced in the era of slavery to explain away their abuse by white men—of painting enslaved women as insistent sexual aggressors who lured the men. In the political discourse of the 1980s, though, that caricature was twisted through the "welfare queen" image into a version of Black women's excessive sexuality leading to high rates of out-of-wedlock births, all with the supposed aim of having more babies to get bigger welfare checks. This was amplified by the images' lesbian erotics, which were highlighted throughout the controversy via cropped photos reprinted in the press or shown on television news, and by reports like those from the first weekend after the story broke, noting the appearance in Williams's hometown of "Vanessa is a lesbian nudie!" spraypainted on the pavement.

Was there ever a professional success so sweet as the one Vanessa Williams built after Miss America? While she took roles on stage and in film and television, Williams primarily devoted the rest of the 1980s to her singing career. Her first studio album, *The Right Stuff*, released in 1988, put her on the R&B, pop, and dance charts, and earned Williams a Grammy nomination for "Best Female R&B Vocal Performance." Her 1991 follow-up, *The Comfort Zone*, featuring number one single, "Save the Best for Last," made her a star.

In 1992, Vanessa Williams sat down for a long interview with Oprah Winfrey that was featured in a prime-time television special called *Oprah: Behind the Scenes*—proof in itself of Williams's stardom. It was a meeting of two of the most famous Black women in American popular culture, who were also famously adored by white audiences, recognizing that Winfrey was already in a sphere of celebrity all her own on both counts.

It was also a meeting of two women whose careers had been jumpstarted by their pageant victories—Winfrey as Miss Black Tennessee 1972 and a competitor in that year's Miss Black America Pageant, and Williams as the first Black Miss America. Sitting right across from one another in tall director's chairs, they were a picture of beauty's history, power, costs, and compromises.

Of course, Winfrey asked Williams about her experience with Miss America and the resignation. "I wonder what it was that made you—I don't know if it was believe in yourself—but to withstand, because I think what you went through was about the worst anybody would have to go through publicly."

"Maybe it is being a Black woman," Williams responded, "because we've had to withstand so many obstacles and barriers. I think that's one of the kinships that we all, you know, we've been surviving for hundreds of years." Gone were the days of avoiding direct discussions of race relating to the resignation, although the charge of racism on the part of the Miss America organization was still implied rather than asserted.

Oprah Winfrey was nineteen years old when she won the Miss Black Nashville competition that earned her a place in the Miss Black Tennessee Pageant. She was a speech and communications and performing arts major at HBCU Tennessee State University, seeking a career in broadcasting. Winfrey was already working for a radio station serving Black communities in the area when she competed in the pageant, and was spotted as a talent for television. In 1973, she became the first Black woman to anchor network television news in the Nashville market. From there she began her career climb to larger and larger media markets, first to Baltimore and then, in 1984, to Chicago to take over its last-place morning news program *A.M. Chicago*.

Winfrey turned the show into a leader in a year, and in 1986, it became the nationally syndicated *Oprah Winfrey Show*. Winfrey's mainstream success was driven by her large audience of white female fans, to whom she was simply "Oprah." These women who saw in Winfrey someone who was both relatable to and affirming of their concerns and interests, a Black woman who embraced them—for many, the only Black woman they had "intimate" contact with—but made no demands of them. These were dynamics already scripted for audiences by depictions of the faithful enslaved "Mammies" who loved the white people who enslaved them, mothered them and their children, and identified with their interests—and the interests of white supremacy—rather than those of their own families and other Black people.

When she interviewed Vanessa Williams in 1992, Winfrey shared with her the constant scrutiny of her appearance that came with being a female celebrity. The more popular she became, the more intense the interest in her body, hair, and clothes, and the attendant speculation about her romantic life. Winfrey's weight and her status as unmarried were top of the list. (This, too, was contoured through associations with the "Mammy" figure, whose large size and supposed undesirability, paired with her own asexuality, stood in direct counterpoint to stereotypes of Black hypersexuality.) On November 15, 1988, after more than four months on a strict liquid diet, Winfrey made a dramatic reveal of her new 145-pound, size 10 body on her talk show. Wearing a body-hugging black turtleneck tucked into skin-tight Calvin Kleins, Winfrey took the stage pulling a red Radio Flyer wagon filled with 67 pounds—the amount of weight she'd lost—of animal fat that the show had obtained from a local meat wholesaler. It would be the most highly watched episode of her show in its twenty-five-year run, and later, something Winfrey regretted airing.

Now, sitting across from Williams four years later, Winfrey was no longer a size 10, having regained the weight she'd lost and feeling that scrutiny even more acutely. She would recall later hoping not to win an Emmy that year because she couldn't face everyone in the audience watching her and her larger body approach the stage.

As she walked Williams through the Miss America story, Winfrey described it as a "fluke" that she'd entered that first contest at all—"to get scholarship money," Williams interjected—and asked, so then what had it meant to her when she won?

"I didn't know what it meant," said Williams. "That's what was, I think, my biggest problem. I had no idea what an impact it would make that the first Black Miss America would be chosen in 1983." When the edit cut to Winfrey's reaction, she kept nodding, but her smile faltered and she squinted.

Williams continued, "You know it was the first time I had been in competition, so my beauty was never something that I marketed or targeted or used."

Before she finished the comment, the camera had moved back to Winfrey, unsmiling and thoughtful, an index finger resting beneath her lower lip. "Or, thought about?" she interjected.

Williams nodded. "Yeah," and then nodded some more, "yeah."

"Vanessa," Winfrey replied, drawing out her name with a look and tone that said, unmistakably, *get real.*

"Vanessa. When you look in the mirror, though, Miss Blue Eyes, Miss Green Eyes, Miss—you are a beautiful, you, you, you're one of the greats! I mean, really, I was looking at you on the monitor, I said the girl is just one of the prettiest people in the world."

Winfrey seemed as amazed by Williams's failure to acknowledge knowing the power of her own beauty, as she was of that beauty itself. It was a signature Oprah Winfrey moment, with its mix of keeping her subject honest while showing some of her own vulnerability, even a little envy. What remained unquestioned—or did not make the program's final edit as anything other than the quick squint of Winfrey's eyes and slip of her smile—was Williams's claim she hadn't understood when going into the pageant the impact of breaking the Miss America color line.

While she had focused on the lightness of Williams's eyes as the central feature of her beauty, Winfrey would go on to express dismay at the criticism Williams received from some Black people when she won the Miss America crown—that she "wasn't Black enough" for it to amount to a significant breakthrough. "I've heard that a lot in my life," Winfrey shared, before returning to that mirror. "I mean, I look in the mirror—you look in the mirror and there's this Black face staring back at you, so, who the hell are you if you're not Black?"

Williams punctuated the point with a story from the summer. In June, she had performed for President George H. W. Bush at an event held at Ford's Theater, and at the dinner afterward, while still in the designer gown she had worn on stage, Williams was mistaken for a server by a white woman on the buffet line. "She didn't even take the time to look up to see who it was," Williams said. "She just assumed I was a Black girl, and I was there to serve her."

The story came near the interview's conclusion, like a terrible coda to the women's conversation and all that it had implied about Black women's struggles with societal expectations, professional success and setbacks, beauty culture, and the perpetual struggle to be seen and to see themselves as individuals. It was a stark reminder to viewers of the racism that conditioned all of it, including Black women's relationships to white women.

Oprah: Behind the Scenes aired in the midst of renewed national attention to the effects of dominant standards of beauty on the lives of women, thanks to the previous year's publication of Naomi Wolf's bestselling *The Beauty Myth: How Images of Beauty Are Used Against Women.* "We are in the midst of a violent backlash against feminism," Wolf argued, one "that uses images of female beauty as a political weapon against women's advancement: the beauty myth." With a structure and cultural impact that shared much with Friedan's *The Feminine Mystique,* Wolf's book posited that successful, highly educated professional women who had been able to capitalize on the gains of feminism since the 1960s remained mired in constant quests to achieve ideal beauty and the attendant negative self-images and lack of confidence that came with it. She argued that the last true bastion of patriarchal power was the "beauty myth" marshaled against them through magazines, cosmetics companies, surgeons, and advertising agencies hocking diet plans, gym memberships, and more products—leaving women psychologically, financially, and socially stalled before they could break through the remaining glass ceilings. Wolf also shared the racial and class blinders of Friedan's earlier work, never addressing the impacts of the "beauty myth" on women of color, working-class women, or the poor. Neither Vanessa Williams nor Oprah Winfrey could find themselves in the pages of Wolf's text, let alone the millions of Black women and girls who would never have their celebrity.

More immediately, Winfrey's interview with Williams aired the day after Bill Clinton defeated George H. W. Bush for the presidency, the day after Hillary Rodham Clinton became the country's next first lady. At the Republican National Convention in Houston, Patrick Buchanan had given a fiery opening night address that declared a "culture war" in America. The conservative pundit had challenged Bush in the primaries, making the first of what would be three runs for the presidency. Now, he aimed his warning cry at bringing his supporters into the fold behind Bush:

Elect me, and you get "two for the price of one," Mr. Clinton says of his lawyer-spouse. And what does Hillary believe? Well, Hillary believes that 12-year-olds should have the right to sue their parents. And Hillary has compared marriage and the family, as institutions, to slavery and life on an Indian reservation. Well, speak for yourself, Hillary.

This, my friends, is radical feminism. The agenda that Clinton & Clinton would impose on America: abortion on demand, a litmus test for the Supreme Court, homosexual rights, discrimination against religious schools, women in combat units. That's change, all right. But that's not the kind of change America needs.

EPILOGUE

THE NASTY, THE FIERCE, AND THE FACES OF MAR-A-LAGO

In 2015, Vanessa Williams returned to the Miss America Pageant stage for the first time since her resignation, as a judge and guest performer, offering some of her star power to the pageant now struggling to regain a portion of its annual television share and cultural relevance. After her performance of "Oh, How the Years Go By" as part of the show's opener, Williams was surprised to be joined on stage by Sam Haskell, CEO of the Miss America Organization. Holding a mic in one hand while wrapping his arm around her back and resting his other on her hip, Haskell looked into Williams's eyes on live television and began speaking. "You have lived your life in grace and dignity, and never was it more evident than during the events of 1984 when you resigned. Though none of us currently in the organization were involved then, on behalf of today's organization, I want to apologize to you. And, to your mother, Ms. Helen Williams. I want to apologize for anything that was said or done that made you feel less than the Miss America you are and the Miss America you always will be." Williams accepted the apology graciously, Haskell beamed, and the audience went wild.

In late December 2017, as much of the country was winding down for the holidays, *HuffPost* broke a story about a cache of emails written and received by Haskell over a three-year period—including when he had made his apology to Williams—that appeared to objectify and denigrate several winners and contestants, thereby casting the CEO and the pageant in a very different light. In addition to wishing one former Miss America dead and speculating about another's high number of sexual partners, the exchange most commonly referenced, in the deluge of coverage that followed, was prompted by Haskell's 2014 request to the telecast's head writer, Lewis Friedman. His request was to drop the practice of calling previous pageant winners "Forever Miss Americas," and instead refer to them in the script as "Former Miss Americas." Friedman replied, "I'd already changed 'Forevers' to 'Cunts.' Does that work for you?" This prompted Haskell to write, "Perfect . . . bahahaha." (Friedman and Haskell did not publicly deny writing this email exchange, which was published in *HuffPost*; Haskell and others did issue formal apologies.)

Facing scandal and public anger, and demands for accountability from forty-nine former Miss Americas, Haskell and other senior leadership resigned within days of the initial story. In January 2018, journalist and Miss America 1989, Gretchen Carlson, was announced as the new leader of the organization, making her the first former winner (or contestant) to run the national pageant.

Events moved quickly. The pageant was getting more media attention than it had received in a long time, but for all the wrong reasons. The story of the Miss America Pageant in the twenty-first century is one of declining national significance and increasingly niche presence in a glutted cultural terrain of cable television and digital platforms. At the same time, its power to evoke a set of popularly understood tropes about femininity and beauty—images of ditzy bubbleheads in swimsuits painfully pontificating about world peace perhaps chief among them—has not dimmed. In late 2017, it made for a perfect atmosphere to brew a scandal, as well as produce a feminist-adjacent beauty queen hero.

Thus, while historic, Carlson's appointment was not surprising. Beyond her own experience as a former Miss America, Carlson had served as a board member for several years, was a successful broadcast journalist, and had a significant national profile. What she was best known for in 2017, however, was being the woman who sued her employer, Roger Ailes—the founding chairman and

CEO of Fox News Corp.—for sexual harassment. This had paved the way for other women at Fox to come forward with their own stories, leading to Ailes's resignation, a large settlement for Carlson, and her signature on a nondisclosure agreement for Fox. While Ailes and Fox News denied all allegations of sexual harassment, Fox News offered an apology as part of the settlement, saying "We sincerely regret and apologize for the fact that Gretchen was not treated with the respect and dignity that she and all of our colleagues deserve."

Since filing the suit in July 2016, Carlson had become a powerful advocate for workplace justice and equity for women, amid a surge in national attention to the matter. In October of that year, just weeks before he was elected to his first term in the White House, the audio recording was released of Donald Trump boasting to *Access Hollywood*'s Billy Bush about his access to beautiful women—including his now infamous claim: "Grab 'em by the pussy. You can do anything" when you're a "star." This had come on the heels of controversy concerning Trump's alleged treatment of Miss Venezuela, Alicia Machado, who was crowned Miss Universe in 1996, which occurred during his first year as owner of the pageant franchise.

Hillary Clinton had raised the issue during their first presidential debate on September 26, 2016, as an example of her opponent's long history of demeaning and allegedly harassing women. "He called this woman 'Miss Piggy,'" she said as the split-screen caught Trump's reactions, and "then he called her 'Miss Housekeeping,' because she was Latina." The next day, Trump took to social media and appeared on the show that had made Carlson famous, *Fox & Friends*, where he continued to attack Machado: "She gained a massive amount of weight, and it was a real problem. Not only that, her attitude. And we had a real problem with her."

As a contest between two baby boomers (Trump was born in 1946 and Clinton in 1947), the 2016 election pitted an iconic liberal second-wave feminist against a man many perceived as an unrepentant misogynist. Trump's comment that Clinton was "such a nasty woman" while she was still speaking came to represent this story of the race—a story that made the election a referendum on the successes and failures of the women's movement that had emerged from the foment of 1968.

• • •

Gretchen Carlson published her second book during Trump's first year in office. *Be Fierce: Stop Sexual Harassment and Take Your Power Back* was released in September 2017; a month later, the *New York Times* and the *New Yorker* reported the many accusations of rape, sexual assault, and abuse against Harvey Weinstein that catalyzed the #MeToo movement. This atmosphere fueled the Miss America scandal and prompted the speedy resignations, while Gretchen Carlson's place within it as a heroic figure made her seem an ideal solution.

It was an awkward thing for Carlson, though, being heralded as a feminist. She'd spent so many years as a self-proclaimed "culture warrior" and conservative opponent of feminism, particularly while building her reputation and brand at Fox News. Carlson wielded the power and broadcast the grievances of the "Positive Woman" for the twenty-first century, built on foundations established by the Miss America Pageant and Phyllis Schlafly and her compatriots forty years earlier.

Born in 1966, Gretchen Carlson was raised in Anoka, Minnesota, a small town on the Mississippi River, north of Minneapolis-St. Paul. Her father co-owned the family car dealership started by his father, while her mother was a homemaker and active volunteer in the community; Gretchen was the second of four children. The family was a picture of the mid-century American suburban ideal, but was more prominent than most in her predominantly Swedish American Lutheran community, owing to her maternal grandfather's regional celebrity as a minister and founding leader of an early precursor of the "megachurch." At five years old, she discovered the violin; a prodigy, Carlson began intensive study of the instrument a year later. From this point, lessons, practice, and competitions defined much of her life, as did becoming a high-achieving student. By the time she was a teenager, Carlson was competing and winning at the highest national levels for young musicians; at fifteen, she was taking second place to her contemporary from Indiana, Joshua Bell (today, one of the most famous and celebrated classical musicians in the world). Gretchen Carlson was the valedictorian at her high school graduation in 1984, and she went on to Stanford University, where she decided to pull back from her study of the violin, much to her parents' dismay.

It was the machinations of Carlson's mother to get her daughter playing the violin again that led to the Miss America Pageant in 1988. During Carlson's junior year studying abroad at Oxford University, her mom began urging her to enter the pageant competition when she came home (instead of staying in the UK for the summer). Her talent would, of course, be the violin. "I was definitely not a pageant person," Carlson explained, "and I never watched pageants on TV. But my mom showed me some literature about how it was *definitely* not a beauty contest" but, rather, about scholarships and showcasing excellence. Carlson was hooked.

With only two months to prepare for an open contest (no residency required) in Cottage Grove, Minnesota, Carlson attacked the process in her usual manner—a pageant coach, strategy, and constant work. She also had to attack another part of her life that had commanded her time and attention since childhood: her weight. A self-described "chubby" girl, Carlson spent most of her youth on a diet under her mom's watchful eye, but had little success losing weight. This changed in the tenth grade, when Carlson did not get a role in the school's production of *Oklahoma!* because, her mother said, she was too "jiggly." This disappointment was followed by the "real turning point": overhearing her crush, a baseball player, tell someone, "Gretchen has a great personality, but she's too fat to date." Three months later, Carlson was thirty pounds lighter.

After enjoying pints and pub food at Oxford, Carlson now added exercise and weight loss to her pageant preparations. In August 1987, she was named Miss Cottage Grove, winning the first pageant she'd entered and starting on her path to becoming Miss Minnesota and then Miss America the following summer.

The general take on the 1988 pageant and Gretchen Carlson's victory was that Stanford had won it for her. She was the "smart Miss America"—not a favorite, definitely not the prettiest, and too chubby, all of which were made clear to her before she even made it home from Atlantic City. In the first pages of her 2015 memoir, *Getting Real*, Carlson recounts a story of seeing the cover of *Star* magazine as she walked through the airport, its eye-catching teaser: "Blimpo Becomes Miss America." A year later, one of the judges from her pageant—screen writer William Goldman (whose credits include the film adaptations of *The Stepford Wives* [1975] and *All the President's Men* [1976])—published a book about his experience in the role. While noting her intelligence and self-possession, Goldman also described Carlson as "chunky," a "God-clutcher," and gave credence to claims that the pageant organizers had wanted her Stanford credentials more than her. Goldman summed up that part of his book in the line, "Miss Piggy won the crown."

This was all compounded by Carlson's sense that winning the pageant made her just another "dumb blonde" in the eyes of most people, that it was their first and, too often, last impression, no matter who Carlson actually was or what she was capable of (echoing Bess Myerson's remark to Studs Turkel that even as a successful public servant, the title of Miss America would always enter a room before she did). The first story Carlson relates in *Getting Real* is of being humiliated during a press conference in New York City by a female reporter bent on disproving the new pageant winner's intelligence and deriding her Middle American Christian values. After a decade of rising through the ranks of broadcast news at network affiliates in Richmond, Virginia; Cincinnati and Cleveland, Ohio; and Dallas-Fort Worth, Texas, Carlson was back in New York City in 2000, with a new job as national correspondent for *CBS News*. She got the opportunity to reintroduce herself to that journalist, she writes in her book, telling her, "I'm the Miss America you demoralized in 1989—and I'd like to let you know that I still made it. I'm a CBS News correspondent . . . and you're not." Revenge-seeking was out of character, Carlson assured readers, "but I went for it. I did it for myself and for all the other women who've been made fun of, called names, put down—just because."

Like several Miss America winners before her, Gretchen Carlson has always been quick to note that the pageant gave her the public notice and opportunity to build a career in broadcasting. After three years anchoring CBS's Saturday *Early Show,* Carlson moved to Fox News in 2005, where she co-anchored the popular morning show *Fox & Friends* with Steve Doocy and Brian Kilmeade until 2013, when she got her own afternoon program, *The Real Story.*

Carlson also shared with these earlier Miss Americas her political and social conservatism, evangelical Christianity, and the vocal rejection of feminism—all of which were amplified at Fox. "I like to joke that when I joined Fox News, I hit the 'bimbo trifecta': *Former Miss America. Blonde. Fox News Host.* . . . I've learned that sometimes when people don't like what you have to say, and don't want to debate you on ideas, it's just easier to call you a dumb blonde from Fox News." Carlson was no pushover, including where her treatment as a woman was concerned. She famously walked off the set during a broadcast after one of her co-hosts made an anti-woman "joke" on air, and revealed to a reporter in 2013 that women anchors at Fox News were not allowed to wear pants.

As her 2015 memoir demonstrated, Carlson exemplified the dominant mode of the powerful conservative woman's address and authority: righteous grievance. She was proud to be called a culture warrior, Carlson wrote, which for her included being a warrior for women's equality, but not feminism. "The National Organization for Women has never invited me to play on their team, and that's okay with me. I don't like boxes or labels. But no one feels as strongly as I do about equality for women," she writes on the first page of *Getting Real*. The statement had a familiar ring to it; many Miss Americas and other "Positive Women" had been saying for years that they were for certain kinds of equality in the workplace and believed in empowering women but rejected feminism or being called "feminists." Carlson's assertion grounded these sentiments in the claim that feminists had rejected *her* and her values, and those who shared them.

Carlson's 2016 sexual harassment suit against Ailes and Fox News unsettled this picture. Aside from the fact that it was the work of feminists, particularly the legal and legislative efforts of those in and around NOW, as well as the courage of Anita Hill's transformative public testimony about her own harassment in 1992, that made her lawsuit possible, Carlson was celebrated (or pilloried) as a feminist for her actions. She didn't actively discourage the descriptor, but she didn't apply it to herself, either—opting instead for a different *f*-word: *fierce*. It was the titular encouragement of her book, and the label she gave to women who, like herself, spoke up for themselves and against harassment and workplace inequity. (It was a label stolen from Black and Latinx trans women and ballroom drag culture, mainstreamed through pop music, film, and television, including RuPaul's *Drag Race*.)

As the new board chair, Carlson set about making Miss America "fierce," too. All was kept under wraps until June 2018, when Carlson unveiled "Miss America 2.0" during an appearance on ABC's *Good Morning America* (the network set to air the pageant three months later).

"We are no longer a pageant, we are a competition," she said. "[W]e will no longer judge our candidates on their outward physical appearance."

Here, she was interrupted by her interviewer, "That's huge!"

"And that means we will no longer have a swimsuit competition."

In a statement released after her appearance on the popular morning show, Carlson said, "Miss America will represent a new generation of female leaders focused on scholarship, social impact, talent, and empowerment." It was a job interview, she explained, not a beauty pageant. "We're experiencing a cultural revolution in our country with women finding the courage to stand up and have their voices heard on many issues. Miss America is proud to evolve as an organization and join this empowerment movement."

The announcement caught fans and the wider organization by surprise. While the demise of the swimsuit competition, which many had been urging for decades, seemed more welcome than not, resistance to Carlson's revolution was significant. It was aimed at her leadership style and consolidation of power, as much as at the reforms and new messaging. Within a month, twenty-two state pageant directors had signed a petition calling for the resignations of Carlson and the new board of directors. Carlson and her detractors both took the fight to the popular news outlets and social media, with former Miss Americas weighing in on both sides.

It was a historic year across the worlds of pageantry. When Miss New York, Nia Amani Franklin, an African American woman from North Carolina, was crowned the first Miss America 2.0, she became part of the year that saw every major pageant—Miss America, Miss Teen USA, Miss USA, Miss World, and Miss Universe—won by Black women.

It is no coincidence that Donald Trump's path to the presidency included a long association with beauty pageants and that it intersected with Gretchen Carlson's journey to the running of the Miss America organization. The ascendance of both owed much to the Positive Women of the New Right coalition that came together in the 1970s and to the politics of beauty they proliferated.

Trump also owed a great deal to Norman Vincent Peale. Trump's father led the family to Marble Collegiate Church in the 1960s, when Peale was at the peak of his influence with conservative business leaders and politicians, including fellow parishioner Richard Nixon. Peale officiated at the wedding of Donald and Ivana Trump in 1977, the same year Phyllis Schlafly began celebrating the "Positive Woman." The last book Schlafly published in March 2016 (it was released the day after her death) was *The Conservative Case for Trump,* in which

Casino owner Donald Trump entertains 22 Miss America Pageant contestants on his yacht *Trump Princess,* 1988. Miss Minnesota Gretchen Carlson sits in the front row, second woman from the right.

she argued: "Critics can, and will, go on and on about Trump having been married three times, and about how, in the past, he boasted about his indiscretions. But anyone who meets him today will meet an old-fashioned man grounded in his two great priorities—hard work and family—and a man who in other respects has led a remarkably clean life." She also described Trump as a man with strong Christian foundations, including having "learned a lot about spirituality and the inner strength that comes from it by getting to know Norman Vincent Peale and attending his church."

Trump's pageant connections go back almost as far to the early 1980s, when the real estate developer set his sights on casinos and Atlantic City. His first property on the boardwalk, Trump Plaza, opened in 1983, followed by Trump Castle in 1985 and Trump Taj Mahal in 1990. The Miss America Pageant was entwined from the start with the resort city's turn to casino gaming in the late 1970s. Not only did casinos come to provide the hotel accommodations, meeting spaces, and event venues for the pageant, but they also offered co-branding opportunities. It made for some eyebrow-raising partnerships, such as when the Atlantic City Women's Chamber of Commerce held their annual Miss Atlantic City Pageant at the Playboy Hotel and Casino in 1982 (the year before Vanessa Williams won the crown).

A tradition since the very first Miss America contest, the woman chosen to be Miss Atlantic City served as honorary host to Miss America contestants in Atlantic City. The pageant program's back cover featured *Playboy*'s iconic bunny logo, while inside was a message of gratitude: "The Atlantic City Women's Chamber of Commerce expresses sincere thanks to the executives and staff of Playboy Hotel and Casino for the total cooperation and warm hospitality that made this evening possible," an evening that had featured a production called "Playboy Fantasy."

Donald Trump became a fixture at the pageant, while Trump Plaza, Trump Marina (formerly Trump Castle), and Trump Taj Mahal all became popular venues and accommodations for the contest. In 1988, Gretchen Carlson was among a group of twenty-two finalists Trump hosted on his yacht. The photo commemorating the event depicts a smiling Trump surrounded by the women; Carlson sits with five others at his feet. The following year, Trump was one of the judges who selected the woman Carlson crowned as her successor.

In 1996, Donald Trump purchased the Miss Universe Pageant group that included Miss America's number-one competitor, the Miss USA contest, as well as the Miss Teen USA. In addition to his alleged treatment of Alicia Machado, which included demonstrations for the press of Trump's overseeing her exercise in a gym to lose weight, word of the pageant owner making frequent unannounced appearances in dressing rooms during costume changes, and other kinds of arguable harassment, circulated from the start. After he became a high-demand guest for late-night television and shock radio, with the success of *The Apprentice* in 2004, Trump gleefully told these stories himself. In 2005, he bragged to Howard Stern about the "perks" of owning a beauty pageant. "Well, I'll tell you the funniest is that before a show, I'll go backstage and everyone's getting dressed, and everything else, and you know, no men are anywhere, and I'm allowed to go in because I'm the owner of the pageant and therefore I'm inspecting it," Trump said. "You know, the dresses. 'Is everyone okay?' You know, they're standing there with no clothes. 'Is everybody okay?' And you see these incredible looking women, and so, I sort of get away with things like that."

Later in the episode, Stern asked Trump to confirm that "the chicks" would "be almost naked" in his pageants. Absolutely, assured Trump. He noted that before his purchase of the Miss Universe group, they had started "to take women who were educated over women who were hot." And he added in disbelief, "They had a person who was extremely proud that a number of the women had become doctors. . . . I wasn't interested." Five years later, Trump boasted to David Letterman that he'd "made the heels higher and bathing suits smaller," after purchasing the pageant.

Trump never concealed the fact that he seemingly prioritized women's looks over other attributes and that he saw the women he was associated with largely as extensions of his own image. When he entered national politics as a candidate in 2015, this aspect of his public life ran headlong into the warm embrace of decades of conservative beauty politics—and into the arms of "Positive Women" steeped in the culture of beauty—as a platform for conservative family values and traditional femininity, demonstrated not by being born beautiful so much as by doing the *work to appear beautiful* by conforming to a set of dominant standards.

I finished this book during the first year of Trump's second administration, which began in January 2025. His opponent (after incumbent President Joe Biden dropped out of the race) had been Kamala Harris, another woman from the Democratic Party's liberal center, and the first woman in history to serve as vice president. She was also the first person of South Asian descent and the second Black person in the executive position. Born in 1964 to immigrant parents (her father is from Jamaica and her mother is from India), Harris came of age in the country that feminism and the Black civil rights movement had already transformed, but with the work unfinished and the radical promises of liberation growing more distant from the conversation. Harris came of age with the ascendance of the New Right, including the defeat of the ERA and the politics of beauty that fueled it.

On the eve of the Biden-Harris victory, one of her former Howard University classmates, and Alpha Kappa Alpha sorority sister, published a reminiscence about their time together in both institutions and what that meant for Harris's success. She singled out the moment when she was a freshman and Harris was a sophomore and they joined others to watch Vanessa Williams compete for Miss America and win: "We watched, crowded around small televisions in the Tubman Quadrangle. I remember a classmate saying through tears 'she won it for all of us.'"

Whereas Trump had constantly attempted to belittle Hillary Rodham Clinton as unattractive, old, and a real turn-off, piling onto decades of derision about her feminism, her looks, her clothes (the pantsuits!), her voice, and her laugh, in Harris, Trump confronted a younger candidate whose attractiveness was generally unquestioned, and that he himself had attested to. Her looks and style, including those cheeky Converse chucks, were central to her campaign's social media arm and merch shop, including "Brat Kamala" and a picture from her college days—short hair and all '80s glamour.

In a preview of the attacks on federal employees to come, Trump and his surrogates called Harris a "DEI hire," based on the fact of her very presence as a nonwhite (and female) person in a position of professional authority. These claims were often comingled with assertions that Harris's good looks and sexuality were the reasons for her success, seemingly implying that she'd slept her way up the career ladder. Trump's misogynist vitriol for his female opponents, present and past, came together when a meme was reposted by Trump's Truth Social account with a candid photo of Kamala Harris and Hillary Rodham Clinton smiling for the camera, beneath which was written "Funny how blowjobs impacted both their careers differently."

As Trump began announcing his nominees for leadership roles in his second administration, a number of women were among them, including Susie Wiles, as his chief of staff—the first woman in history to serve in the role—and the youngest press secretary ever, Karoline Leavitt. Ultimately, about one-third of Trump's cabinet would be women in 2025.

While some of these women were skilled political operatives, few had expertise in the areas they were nominated to oversee—a quality they shared with many of their male counterparts. Strikingly, the women looked remarkably similar to one another, beyond their nearly uniform whiteness. They had a common aesthetic, particularly those who would be fronting agencies or speaking for the administration from a podium. Their features tend to be exaggerated by heavy makeup and/or noticeable plastic surgery and fillers; most wear their hair long, parted down the middle and wavy, some achieving the look with extensions. Most of them are slender and favor sheath dresses and pencil skirts for work. (Department of Homeland Security Secretary Kristi Noem augmented this with a dressed-down uniform of skinny jeans, tight T-shirt, and baseball cap when "in the field.") The look extends to women supporting Trump as national and state elected officials, members of right-wing media, and MAGA activists and adherents, including the worlds of tradwives and Turning Point USA, a conservative nonprofit founded by Charlie Kirk. It is a version of female beauty that is, above everything else, extremely artificial, because unnatural beauty is the point.

Content creators and journalists began referring to this MAGA beauty formation as "conservative girl makeup," "Mar-a-Lago Face," or "brutal aesthetics." Writing for *Mother Jones* in March 2025, Inae Oh explored the look as a declaration of loyalty to Trump and his agenda, arguing that it seems "intended to signal membership with Trump, a man notoriously obsessed with the literal pageantry of beauty, and his broader efforts to force strict gender norms onto the electorate." They argue the reality of two distinct sexes by highlighting the artificiality of their femininity—by drawing attention to its labors, steep time tax, and expense. It is the hyper-representation of their efforts that demonstrates their commitments to traditional femininity, rather than signal the inherent unreality and instability of the gender binary.

There is terrible irony in the undeniably drag-ish quality of MAGA beauty, which sits neatly with the co-opting of "fierce" from queer Black and Latinx drag cultures and transpeople. There are ghosts of the Nixonaires, Nixonettes, and Rocky Girls here, too, but they are historical traces rather than the substance of what's happening. A team of women with a uniform set of looks has been deployed to represent, as well as implement, the power and ambitions of the president, including his intention to dismantle the gains made in transgender people's rights, force them from public life, and enforce a stark gender binary, as well as his administration's pro-natalism and traditional family policies.

It is wrong to tie this right-wing aesthetic phenomenon solely to the desire to show fealty to Donald Trump, however. This is not the story of one man's influence and ability to bend others—literally bend and shape their faces—to his will. Trump is as much a *product* of the politics of beauty that emerged from the events and figures surrounding the Miss America Pageant in 1968 as are the women in his cabinet. This is much bigger than Donald Trump, Mar-a-Lago, or MAGA. It is the historical outcome of decades of denigrating feminists not only as ugly but also as selfish and lazy in their supposed refusals to do anything about it: the outcome of the Positive Woman's path to political power and public authority in the New Right through the explicit rejection of feminism and glorification of traditional gender hierarchies and attendant heterosexuality, all made visible through the woman's labored striving to be beautiful. What results is the villainization of any woman for her failure to perform the necessary beauty work and pleasantries of womanhood. Ultimately, "brutal aesthetics," with its architectural resonances, gets closest to describing what we saw in 2025: the barricades of patriarchy and white supremacy manned by women whose bodies and faces made clear the place of beauty at their very foundations.

ACKNOWLEDGMENTS AND NOTE ON SOURCES

At the core of the conflicts among "second-wave" feminists was a debate about history and its importance to contemporary women's activism. Was it a cautionary tale, playbook, inspiration, or some combination of these things? Liberals and liberationists alike agreed that women and girls had been excised from the story, and thus part of feminism's (unfinished) project was the necessary rectifying of this absence and a reckoning with the consequences. They disagreed about the lessons and legacies of that barely told story, but never the fact that it did, indeed, need to be told. It is perhaps not surprising, then, that so many foundational figures of the movement became professional historians (and history-adjacent scholars and writers), including Ros Baxandall, Susan Brownmiller, Peggy Dobbins, Roxanne Dunbar-Ortiz, Alice Echols, Sara Evans, Jo Freeman, Carol Giardina, Paula Giddings, Linda Gordon, Beverly Guy-Sheftall, Amy Kesselman, Ruth Rosen, Alix Kates Shulman, Hortense Spillers, Barbara Smith, and Marilyn Webb, to name only a few.

Many of this cohort have worked on the subjects and period explored in *Liberation Summer.* Writing the history you had a direct hand in making is a complex endeavor, requiring a constant set of negotiations with one's ego and memories. Who better to tell the story than one who lived it—and who worse? I am indebted to their work, not only because it would have been impossible to write this book without it, but also because my career as a feminist academic and historian of women, gender, race, and sexuality in the United States would not have been possible without them. Here, I wish to note my debts and thanks to one woman in particular: I was a graduate student of Linda Gordon's at New York University, and I am honored to call her a mentor and friend and to be among the legion of the many who've been lucky enough to train with her.

The following books were crucial to this project and outstanding resources for anyone interested in the subject: Rosalyn Baxandall and Linda Gordon's *Dear Sisters: Dispatches from the Women's Liberation Movement*; Dorothy Sue

Cobble, Linda Gordon, and Astrid Henry's *Feminism Unfinished: A Short, Surprising History of American Women's Movements*; Alice Echols's *Daring to Be Bad: Radical Feminism in America, 1967–1975*; Sara Evans's *Personal Politics: The Roots of Women's Liberation in the Civil Rights Movement & New Left* and *Tidal Wave: How Women Changed America at Century's End*; Carol Giardina's *Freedom for Women: Forging the Women's Liberation Movement, 1953–1970*; and Ruth Rosen's *The World Split Open: How the Modern Women's Movement Changed America.*

I am not an oral historian and did no original interviews for this book, but I benefited enormously from the many interviews done with *Liberation Summer*'s principal figures by other historians and journalists over the years. I am especially indebted to journalist and women's liberationist Susan Brownmiller, who deposited with her papers in the Schlesinger Library of Harvard's Radcliffe Institute a vast archive of interviews with feminist activists, journalists, and academics done in the 1990s while she was working on her memoir and history of the movement, *In Our Time: Memoir of a Revolution.* I also heavily relied upon the *Voices of Feminism Oral History Project* in the Sophia Smith Collection of Women's History of Smith College Special Collections and the interviews archived online by the Veteran Feminists of America, as well as the published works: Rachel Blau DuPlessis and Ann Snitow's *The Feminist Memoir Project: Voices from Women's Liberation*; Constance Curry's *Deep in Our Hearts: Nine White Women in the Freedom Movement*; Breanne Fahs's *Firebrand Feminism: The Radical Lives of Ti-Grace Atkinson, Kathie Sarachild, Roxanne Dunbar-Ortiz, and Dana Densmore*; and Keeanga-Yamahtta Taylor's *How We Get Free: Black Feminism and the Combahee River Collective.*

Among the many memoirs and other personal narratives published by individuals represented in these pages that I consulted, in addition to Brownmiller's, I wish to note three from Anita Bryant: *Mine Eyes Have Seen the Glory*; *Amazing Grace*; and *The Anita Bryant Story: The Survival of Our Nation's Families and the Threat of Militant Homosexuality*; Roxanne Dunbar-Ortiz's *Outlaw Woman: A Memoir of the War Years, 1960–1975*; three from Betty Friedan: *"It Changed My Life": Writings on the Women's Movement*; *The Second Stage*; and *Life So Far: A Memoir*; Flo Kennedy's *Color Me Flo: My Hard Life and Good* Times; Mary King's *Freedom Song: A Personal Story of the 1960s Civil Rights Movement*; Robin

Morgan's *Saturday's Child: A Memoir*; Alix Kates Shulman's novels, *Memoirs of an Ex-Prom Queen* and *Burning Questions: A Novel*; and Gloria Steinem's *Revolution from Within: A Book of Self-Esteem* and *My Life on the Road.*

Many outstanding biographies served as guides to the principal figures in this book and the histories that surrounded them. Especially important to me were: Donald T. Critchlow's *Phyllis Schlafly and Grassroots Conservatism: A Woman's Crusade*; Susan Dworkin's *Miss America, 1945: Bess Myerson's Own Story;* Carol Felsenthal's *Phyllis Schlafly: The Sweetheart of the Silent Majority*; Marilyn S. Greenwald's *A Woman of the Times: Journalism, Feminism, and the Career of Charlotte Curtis*; Daniel Horowitz's *Betty Friedan and the Making of "The Feminine Mystique": The American Left, the Cold War, and Modern Feminism*; Jennifer Preston's *Queen Bess: An Unauthorized Biography of Bess Myerson;* Sherie M. Randolph's *Florynce "Flo" Kennedy: The Life of a Black Feminist Radical*; and Rachel Shtier's *Betty Friedan: Magnificent Disruptor.*

Among the texts shaping the ways I've thought about beauty, politics, and subjectivity, some of the most important to this project were: Kathleen M. Barry's *Femininity in Flight: A History of Flight Attendants*; Elspeth H. Brown's *Work! A Queer History of Modeling*; Anne Anlin Cheng's "Wounded Beauty: An Exploratory Essay on Race, Feminism, and the Aesthetic Question"; Tressie McMillan Cottom's *THICK and Other Essays*; Tanisha C. Ford's *Liberated Threads: Black Women, Style, and the Global Politics of Soul*; Tiffany M. Gill's *Beauty Shop Politics: African American Women's Activism in the Beauty Industry*; and Kathy Peiss's *Hope in a Jar: The Making of America's Beauty Culture.*

In addition to the texts listed above, several other histories of feminism, women's liberation, Black feminism, and intersectionality are required reading, including: Bonnie J. Dow's *Watching Women's Liberation, 1970: Feminism's Pivotal Year on the Network News;* Flora Davis's *Moving the Mountain: The Women's Movement in America Since 1960;* Ashley D. Farmer's *Remaking Black Power: How Black Women Transformed an Era*; Stephanie Gilmore's *Groundswell: Grassroots Feminist Activism in Postwar America;* Victoria Hesford's *Feeling Women's Liberation*; Sophie Lewis's *Enemy Feminisms: TERFS, Policewomen, and Girlbosses Against Liberation*; Kimberly Springer's *Living for the Revolution: Black Feminist Organizations, 1968–1980*; Marjorie J. Spruill's *Divided We Stand: The Battle Over Women's Rights and Family Values That Polarized American Politics*;

Rebecca Traister's *Big Girls Don't Cry: The Election That Changed Everything for American Women* and *Good and Mad: The Revolutionary Power of Women's Anger*; and Judy Tzu-Chun Wu's *Radicals on the Road: Internationalism, Orientalism, and Feminism During the Vietnam Era.*

Similarly crucial to understanding this history is the growing body of work on conservative women, the Republican Party, and the New Right, including: Kristin Kobes Du Mez's *Jesus and John Wayne: How White Evangelicals Corrupted a Faith and Fractured a Nation;* Emily Suzanne Johnson's *This Is Our Message: Women's Leadership in the New Christian Right;* Elizabeth Gillespie McRae's *Mothers of Massive Resistance: White Women and the Politics of White Supremacy;* Michelle M. Nickerson's *Mothers of Conservatism: Women and the Postwar Right;* Leah Wright Rigueur's *The Loneliness of the Black Republican: Pragmatic Politics and the Pursuit of Power;* and Catherine E. Rymph's *Republican Women: Feminism and Conservatism from Suffrage through the Rise of the New Right.*

On the history of beauty pageants, see: Sarah Banet-Weiser's *The Most Beautiful Girl in the World: Beauty Pageants and National Identity*; Genevieve Alva Clutario's *Beauty Regimes: A History of Power and Modern Empire in the Philippines, 1898–1941*; Maxine Leeds Craig's *Ain't I a Beauty Queen? Black Women, Beauty, and the Politics of Race*; Hilary Levey Friedman's *Here She Is: The Complicated Reign of the Beauty Pageant in America;* Kimberly Brown Pellam's *Black Beauties: African American Pageant Queens in the Segregated South*; Blain Roberts's *Pageants, Parlors, and Pretty Women: Race and Beauty in the Twentieth Century South*; and Judy Tzu-Chun Wu's "Loveliest Daughter of our Ancient Cathay!: Representations of Ethnic and Gender Identity in the Miss Chinatown USA Beauty Pageant."

Finally, this work draws from a number of books on the specific histories of the Miss America Pageant, including: Amy Argetsinger's *There She Was: The Secret History of Miss America;* Frank Deford's *There She Is: The Life and Times of Miss America*; Mandy McMichael's *Miss America's God: Faith and Identity in America's Oldest Pageant*; Margot Mifflin's *Looking for Miss America: A Pageant's 100-Year Quest to Define Womanhood*; and A. R. Riverol's *Live From Atlantic City: A History of the Miss America Pageant.* One cannot understand the local or national history of the Miss America Pageant without the benefit of Bryant Simon's *Boardwalk of Dreams: Atlantic City and the Fate of Urban America.*

• • •

Every published work is a manifestation of more instances of care, secular grace, assistance, guidance, and companionship than one can enumerate, some more than others. *Liberation Summer* falls into that latter category and I have many people and institutions to thank.

Making the transition from writing for university presses and "academic trade" audiences to writing for general readers is exciting, deeply rewarding, and even more difficult than I thought it would be. I am beyond grateful to my agent, Lauren Sharp, for guiding me through it all with kindness, patience, and good humor, for her fierce advocacy, and to the entire team at Aevitas Creative Management.

To my editors, Julianna Haubner and Amy Guay, and everyone at Avid Reader Press and Simon and Schuster, how many ways are there to say thank you? Definitely not enough. I have learned so much about story craft, narrative, and myself as a writer from Julianna and Amy, and I feel incredibly lucky to have the benefit of their combined insights and ranging knowledge. They have been great champions of this book and its author, for which I am eternally grateful. My thanks also to Carolyn Levin, Amy Medeiros, and Carole Berglie.

Research and writing were made possible by a Public Scholar Award from the National Endowment for the Humanities (2022–2023) and a fellowship at the University of Connecticut Humanities Institute (UCHI, 2021–2022). Additional funding was provided by the Felberbaum Family Faculty Fund Award (UCHI), the Scholarship Facilitation Fund Award (UConn), and a Fund for Interdisciplinary Research Award (CLAS, UConn).

Thanks to the incredible archivists and librarians at the Atlantic City Free Public Library, the Archives Center of the Smithsonian National Museum of American History, Archives and Special Collections of the University of Connecticut Library, the Sallie Bingham Center for Women's History and Culture at the David M. Rubenstein Rare Book & Manuscript Library of Duke University, Special Collections at the Leonard H. Axe Library of Pittsburg State University, and the Schlesinger Library of the Harvard Radcliffe Institute.

I presented parts of this work at Carlton College, Marist College, the Massachusetts Historical Society (MHS), and Northern Arizona University, and benefited enormously from the comments and questions of audiences there. Special thanks to Genevieve Clutario for her formal comment on my paper at the MHS.

There are a number of friends, colleagues, and others whose support was crucial to the work of this book: Emma Amador, Viola Augustin, Fakhreddin Azimi, Peter Baldwin, Kristin Bayer, Kornel Chang, Laura Chang, Chris Clark, Leah Stephens Clark, Dierdre Cooper Owens, Marla Cummins, Nina Dayton, Elizabeth Della Zazzera, Anna Mae Duane, Alexis Dudden, Jonathan Entis, Rachel Fish, Dexter Gabriel, Linda Gordon, Adele Haber, Merrily Harris, Kate Haulman, Susan Herbst, Victoria Hindley, Kathy Knapp, Sergio Luzzatto, Michael Lynch, Bill McCarty, Adam McGee, Gabriella Mira, Kevin Murphy, Alain Nineberg, Melina Pappademos, Jeff Ogbar, Alyssa Rautenberg, Evelyn Simien, Bryant Simon, Brad Simpson, Martina Tanga, Uwe Wenzel, Sarah Willen, the late Edvin Yegir, Serena Zabin, Peter Zarrow, and Victor Zatsepine.

Special thanks to the head of the History Department, Mark Healey, for facilitating fellowship leaves, among other things. Thanks are also due to the department's administrative staff, past and present, for facilitating everything: Rachel Bobadilla, Ted Burmiester, the late Nancy Comarella, Kathy Erickson, Kathy O'Dea, Jessica Muirhead, Heather A. Parker, and Kira Svirskiy.

Many undergraduate and graduate students at the University of Connecticut have lived the writing of this book along with me—I am grateful for their inspiration, engagement, epic patience, and enthusiasm for this project and the work we do together in the classroom. There is little better than the opportunity to teach and learn from all of them.

My love and gratitude to my family, who have lived even more closely—and at times less than comfortably—with this book and its author: My parents, Cindy and Mike McElya; my brother and his wife, Jim and Kara McElya; my in-laws, Llyena Boylan Spieth and the late Donald Spieth, Jim and Jo Ann Boylan, Gabe Boylan and Christine Smallwood, and Nicko Boylan. In the time I was writing this book, my family grew by several nephews and a niece, who each in their own ways have shown me a whole new kind of beauty. Talulah, Boone, and Skeeter McElya and Lonnie and Damon Boylan, I am so glad you're here.

For my wife, Alexis Boylan, words fail to capture the level and variety of thanks I have every day that she exists in the world and in my life. While its limitations are all mine, this book would not exist without her and was made so much better by her contributions, support, and sharp eye. Our dog, Busy, came to us in this book's early stages, and we have spent many a walk working through this project together. Nearly every day, we traverse our neighborhood's historical geography of women's liberation along Pleasant Street, past the Cambridge Women's Center founded in 1971 by activists who occupied a building owned by Harvard University for over a week in demand of women's spaces, and the small apartment building a couple of blocks away where Roxanne Dunbar-Ortiz and other future members of the group that became Cell 16 lived in the late 1960s.

Micki McElya
Cambridge, MA
March 2026

NOTES

SHORTENED REFERENCES FOR MANUSCRIPT COLLECTIONS

The following archives have been helpful in the preparation of this book. References to these archives have been shortened to the following:

Betty Friedan Papers: Papers of Betty Friedan, 1933–1985, Schlesinger Library, Radcliffe Institute, Harvard University

Charlotte Curtis Papers: Papers of Charlotte Curtis, 1928–1987, Schlesinger Library, Radcliffe Institute, Harvard University

Debra Barnes Papers: Debra Dene Barnes Collection, 1965–2008, Scrapbook Series, vol. 1, folder 5, Special Collection, Leonard H. Axe Library, Pittsburgh State University

Florynce Kennedy Papers: Papers of Florynce Kennedy, 1915–2004, Schlesinger Library, Radcliffe Institute, Harvard University

Lenora Slaughter Papers: Lenora Slaughter Papers (unprocessed), Box 3, Smithsonian National Museum of American History, Archives Center, Washington, D.C.

Marilyn Webb Papers: Papers of Marilynn Webb, 1968–2006, Schlesinger Library, Radcliffe Institute, Harvard University

Rosalyn Baxandall Papers: Papers of Rosalyn Baxandall, 1933–2015, Schlesinger Library, Radcliffe Institute, Harvard University

Susan Brownmiller Papers: Susan Brownmiller Papers, 1935–2000, Schlesinger Library, Radcliffe Institute, Harvard University

Ti-Grace Atkinson Papers: Papers of Ti-Grace Atkinson, 1938–2013, Schlesinger Library, Radcliffe Institute, Harvard University

Additionally, the following collections have been helpful; references to these also have been shortened, as follows:

NAACP Papers: National Association for the Advancement of Colored People, Papers of the NAACP (microform), Library of Congress, Washington, D.C.

Redstockings Action Archives: Redstockings of the Women's Liberation Movement, New York, New York.

Women's Print Culture Collection: Women's Liberation Movement Print Culture Collection (digital), David M. Rubenstein Rare Book & Manuscript Library, Duke University

PROLOGUE: BOARDWALK REVOLUTIONS

1 *celebrants and the curious*: "Black America Contestants Ride on Boardwalk," *Atlantic City Bulletin,* September 8, 1968, n.p.

2 *her own poem*: "'Men Getting Awfully Lazy,' Asserts Miss Black America," *Philadelphia Tribune,* September 10, 1968, 1.

2 *She had stopped straightening*: "Face to Face with Miss Black America," *Seventeen* l 28, no. 3 (March 1969): 151.

3 *"They're expressing freedom"*: Judy Klemesrud, "Along with Miss America, There's Now Miss Black America," *New York Times*, September 8, 1968, 54.

3 *"Miss America is Still"*: Charlotte Curtis, Miss America Pageant Is Picketed by 100 Women," *New York Times*, September 8, 1968, 8D.

4 *"You're too ugly"*: Susan Sutheim, "Radical Women Protest Ugly Pageant," *The Guardian*, September 14, 1968, n.p., Women's Print Culture Collection.

4 *"Go back to Russia"*: Susan Brownmiller, *In Our Time: Memoir of a Revolution* (Dial Press, 1999), 39.

1. NEW FEMINIST EYES

11 *It was all so beautiful*: Roxanne Dunbar-Ortiz, *Outlaw Woman: A Memoir of the War Years, 1960–1975* (City Lights Books, 2001), 115–118.

12 *"Super Woman-Power Advocate Shoots"*: Dunbar-Ortiz, *Outlaw Woman*, 118–119.

13 *A sickening feeling of déjà vu*: Cay Sophie Rabinowitz, ed., *Bev Grant Photography 1968–1972* (Osmos Books, 2021), 65.

13 *"It was a life-changing experience"*: Bev Grant, VFA Pioneer Histories Project, November 2021, https://veteranfeministsofamerica.org/interview-bev-grant/.

15 *the CR session Hanisch wanted*: Ariel Dougherty, "Feminist Film, A 'First Foray' as Change Agent," in Bryan Konefsky, David Camarena, and Angela Beauchamp, eds., *Experiments in She-ness: Women and Undependent Cinema* (Basement Films, 2016), 6–15.

16 *Schmeerguntz*: *Schmeerguntz*, directed by Gunvor Nelson and Dorothy Wiley (Canyon Cinema, 1965), 15 min.

17 *The images transported Hanisch back*: Carol Hanisch, "What Can Be Learned: A Critique of the Miss America Protest," November 27, 1968, Women's Print Culture Collection.

17 *"new feminist eyes"*: "In Our Time": Transcript of Interview with Carol Hanisch, 1994, box 27, folder 1, p. 21, Susan Brownmiller Papers.

2. WOMEN'S NEWS

19 *"Use of this stationary"*: Stephen R. Conn to Charlotte Curtis, April 25, 1968, box 7, folder 7, Charlotte Curtis Papers.

19 *"Where's the goddamn telephone?"*: Charlotte Curtis to Lucile Atcherson Curtis, June 18, 1968, box 6, folder 12, Charlotte Curtis Papers.

20 *"performance rating was"*: Edward R. Kennedy to Whom It May Concern, August 14, 1947, box 11, folder 9, Charlotte Curtis Papers.

21 *"a story on the women of the big top"*: Kennedy letter, Charlotte Curtis Papers.

22 *Overall employment numbers*: U.S. Department of Labor & Women's Bureau, *Women as Workers, A Statistical Guide*, vol. D–65 of Special Bulletin (U.S. Government Printing Office, 1953); and Mitra Toossi, "A Century of Change: The U.S. Labor Force, 1950–2050," *Monthly Labor Review*, May 2002, 15–28.

23 *"Just because Emily Post"*: Anonymous postcard, 1950, box 11, folder 10, Charlotte Curtis Papers (emphasis in original).

23 *"He assumed I'd be Mrs. Lawyer"*: Marilyn S. Greenwald, *A Woman of the* Times: *Journalism, Feminism, and the Career of Charlotte Curtis* (Ohio University Press, 1999), 44.

24 *a kind of "sociology"*: Greenwald, *A Woman of the* Times, chap. 5.

24 *"a suit in which I can sit"*: Nan Robertson, *The Girls in the Balcony: Women, Men, and the New York Times* (Random House, 1992), 84–85.

25 *"a metaphor for what working women"*: Robertson, *The Girls in the Balcony*, 99.

25 *"If you could forget"*: Charlotte Curtis to Staff, June 17, 1966, box 7, folder 14, Charlotte Curtis Papers.

25 *"five-foot fast-stepping Vassar alumna"*: Gay Talese, *The Kingdom and the Power* (World Publishing, 1969), 149–150.

26 *"one of the most powerful men"*: Talese, *The Kingdom and the Power*, 556.

26 *"[b]right, tough little broad"*: Talese, *The Kingdom and the Power*, 557.

26 *"Miss Curtis is rarely flattering"*: Talese, *The Kingdom and the Power*, 149–150.

26 *Addressed to "Charlotte Chere"*: Marylin Bender to Charlotte Curtis, n.d. (1965), box 7, folder 13, Charlotte Curtis Papers.

27 *"I think marriage is insurance"*: Helen Gurley Brown, *Sex and the Single Girl* (Pocket Books, 1963), 2.

28 *"To get into a position"*: Brown, *Sex and the Single Girl*, 187–188.

28 *The "fabulous face"*: Brown, *Sex and the Single Girl*, 187–188.

28 *"You're intelligent as well"*: Robert Lipsyte to Charlotte Curtis, October 8, 1967, box 7, folder 7, Charlotte Curtis Papers.

28 *"as lovely as I remember"*: Joe [indecipherable] to Charlotte Curtis, January 24, 1969, box 7, folder 7, Charlotte Curtis Papers.

29 *The "delinquents"*: Charlotte Curtis, "White House Candidates Let the Women Down," *New York Times*, May 7, 1968, 40.

30 *"should have been treated"*: Betty Friedan to Editor of *New York Times*, May 8, 1968, box 124, folder 1514, Betty Friedan Papers.

30 *Charlotte Curtis would find this story*: Charlotte Curtis, "On Train, Kennedy Elan," *New York Times*, June 9, 1968, 1.

3. TRULY EQUAL PARTNERSHIP

32 *"woman's world was confined"*: Betty Friedan, *The Feminine Mystique* (W.W. Norton, 1963), 31.

34 *Friedan became even more concerned*: Rachel Shteir, *Betty Friedan: Magnificent Disrupter* (Yale University Press, 2023), chaps. 6 and 7.

34 *The wording was short and direct*: H.J. Res. 75, Proposing an Equal Rights Amendment to the Constitution, 12/13/1923 (HR68A-D18), Bill Files, 1903–1968; Records of the U.S. House of Representatives, Record Group 233, National Archives, https://docsteach.org/document/equal-rights-amendment-1923/, March 9, 2026.

35 *"present troublesome and futile"*: Flora Davis, *Moving the Mountain: The Women's Movement in America since 1960* (Simon & Schuster, 1991), 34.

37 *"A beautiful University of Texas coed"*: Lynne Olson, *Freedom's Daughters: The Unsung Heroines of the Civil Rights Movement from 1830–1970* (Simon & Schuster, 2002), 170.

38 *"We face," he said*: John F. Kennedy, Radio and Television Report to the American People on Civil Rights, American Presidency Project, founded by Gerhard Peters and John T. Woolley, University of California, Santa Barbara, https://www.presidency.ucsb.edu/node/236675.

39 *"not intended to exclude"*: Davis, *Moving the Mountain*, 59–60.

40 *"The purpose of NOW"*: National Organization for Women (NOW), Statement of Purpose (adopted at the Organizing Conference in Washington, D.C., October 29, 1966), box 46, folder 6, Ti-Grace Atkinson Papers.

4. FREEDOM SUMMER

42 *when she picked up the phone*: Mary King, *Freedom Song: A Personal Story of the 1960s Civil Rights Movement* (William Morrow, 1987), chap. 10.

43 *She "fascinated me"*: King, *Freedom Song*, 36.

44 *"The aftermath of nonviolence"*: "The Beloved Community," King Center, Atlanta, Georgia, https://thekingcenter.org/about-tkc/the-king-philosophy/.

44 *"underlined, creased, marked up"*: King, *Freedom Song*, 76.

44 *"irrelevant and marginal"*: King, *Freedom Song*, 78.

44 *Lyndon Johnson got word*: Conversation with Lee White, August 4, 1964, Secret White House Tapes, Miller Center, University of Virginia, https://millercenter.org/the-presidency/secret-white-house-tapes/conversation-lee-white-august-4-1964.

46 *"not the number of persons"*: SNCC Position Paper (name withheld by request), 1964, SNCC Digital Gateway, (emphasis in original), https://snccdigital.org/events/snccs-waveland-conference/.

46 *overheard "strong females"*: Harold L. Smith, "Casey Hayden: Gender and the Origins of SNCC, SDS, and the Women's Liberation Movement," in Elizabeth Hayes Turner, Stephanie Cole, and Rebecca Sharpless, eds., *Texas Women: Their Histories, Their Lives* (University of Georgia Press, 2015), 378.

47 *"quiet isolation"*: Casey Hayden, "Fields of Blue," in Constance Curry et al., *Deep in Our Hearts: Nine White Women in the Freedom Movement* (University of Georgia Press, 2000), 370.

47 *"we could start a movement"*: Casey Hayden and Mary King, "A Kind of Memo," November 18, 1965, SNCC Digital Gateway, https://snccdigital.org/events/snccs-waveland-conference/.

47 *"The caste system perspective"*: "Sex and Caste: A Kind of Memo from Casey Hayden and Mary King to a Number of Other Women in the Peace and Freedom Movements," *Liberation* 11, no. 2 (April 1966): 35.

49 *"Girls Say Yes"*: Alice Echols, *Daring to Be Bad: Radical Feminism in America, 1967–1975* (University of Minnesota Press, 1989), 38.

49 *"Woman Question"*: National Convention Schedule, *New Left Notes* 2, no. 25 (1967): 2.

49 *"[T]here is a certain kind of woman"*: Containment and Change, advertisement in *New Left Notes*, 18.

50 *a resolution on the "liberation of women"*: "Liberation of Women," *New Left Notes* 2, no. 26 (1967): 4.

51 *"The most disturbing session"*: Donald McKelvey, "Thoughts on the Convention," *New Left Notes* 2, no. 29 (1967): 5.

51 *"We want our Rights"*: "Liberation of Women," *New Left Notes*, 4.

5. WE NEVER TOOK ANY SHIT

52 *"NOW should be for Black Power"*: Florynce Kennedy, *Color Me Flo: My Life and Good Times* (Prentice-Hall, 1976), 62.

53 *"was no place for [her] to spend"*: Kennedy, *Color Me Flo*, 62.

53 *"very snobbish about color"*: Kennedy, *Color Me Flo*, 24.

53 *"Black people always described"*: Kennedy, *Color Me Flo*, 24.

54 *"hair was longer"*: Kennedy, *Color Me Flo*, 25.

54 *"We were political in the sense"*: Sherie M. Randolph, *Florynce "Flo" Kennedy: The Life of a Black Feminist Radical* (University of North Carolina Press, 2015), 13.

54 *Kennedy would later say*: Randolph, *Florynce "Flo" Kennedy*, 41.

54 *"were better off than others"*: Randolph, *Florynce "Flo" Kennedy*, 37.

55 *"A Comparative Study Accentuating"*: Kennedy, *Color Me Flo*, 120.

55 *characterizes the relationship:* Randolph, *Florynce "Flo" Kennedy*, 60.
56 *"The white men she trusted"*: Randolph, *Florynce "Flo" Kennedy*, 70.
56 *"police pounced"*: "Lady Lawyer Cries Police Brutality," *Amsterdam News*, August 14, 1965, 1.
56 *"getting loud"*: Randolph, *Florynce "Flo" Kennedy*, 95–96.
57 *"Flo was different"*: Randolph, *Florynce "Flo" Kennedy*, 97.

6. MOVE ON, LITTLE GIRL

59 *When Allen protested*: "In Our Time": Transcript of Interview with Donna Allen, 1995, box 27, folder 1, p. 5, Susan Brownmiller Papers.
59 *"If you want to know how"*: "In Our Time": Allen Interview, Susan Brownmiller Papers.
60 *"already had a woman"*: Jo Freeman (Joreen), "On the Origins of the Women's Liberation Movement from a Strictly Personal Perspective," in Rachel Blau Duplessis and Ann Snitow, eds., *The Feminist Memoir Project: Voices from Women's Liberation* (Rutgers University Press, 2007), 180.
61 *"Move on, little girl"*: Alice Echols, *Daring to Be Bad: Radical Feminism in America, 1967–1975* (University of Minnesota Press, 1989), 49.
61 *"That was the genesis"*: Echols, *Daring to Be Bad*, 49.

7. DOING WOMEN'S LIBERATION

62 *"I met this wonderful woman"*: "In Our Time": Transcript of Interview with Carol Hanisch, 1994, box 27, folder 1, p. 7, Susan Brownmiller Papers.
63 *"very energetic, forceful"*: "In Our Time": Hanisch Interview, pp. 6–8, Susan Brownmiller Papers.
64 *"Carol Hanisch demonstrated"*: "Seneca Stars," *Fenton Reporter*, March 1, 1960, 14.
65 *"Let Children Assist"*: Carol Hanisch, "Let Children Assist with the Decorations," *Cedar Rapids Gazette*, December 13, 1964, 14C.
65 *"For Your Party Favors"*: Carol Hanisch, "For Your Party Favors: Popcorn Christmas Trees," *Cedar Rapids Gazette*, December 22, 1964, 14C.
65 *"large information gap"*: Proposal for the Freedom Information Service, November 15, 1965, p. 2, Civil Rights Movement Archive (emphasis in original), https://www.crmvet.org/docs/dochome.htm.
66 *Kathie's feminist awakening*: "In Our Time": Transcript of Interview with Kathie Amatniek, box 29, folder 1, pp. 4–5, Susan Brownmiller Papers.
67 *were similarly harassed*: Report re: Police Harassment—Traffic Violations, June 28, 1964, Civil Rights Movement Archive, https://www.crmvet.org/lets/640628_bates_traffic-rpt.pdf.
67 *"These two women are starting"*: "In Our Time": Amatniek Interview, p. 2, Susan Brownmiller Papers.
68 This is me, *she thought*: "In Our Time": Amatniek Interview, Susan Brownmiller Papers.
68 *"Doing women's liberation these days"*: "In Our Time": Transcript of Interview with Anne Forer, 1995, box 26, folder 13, p. 3, Susan Brownmiller Papers.
68 *"always looking to meet boys"*: "In Our Time": Forer Interview, Susan Brownmiller Papers.
68 Not a great place for: "In Our Time": Forer Interview, Susan Brownmiller Papers.
68 *"I showed up and"*: "In Our Time": Forer Interview, Susan Brownmiller Papers.
69 *"I have no idea how"*: "In Our Time": Forer Interview, box 26, folder 13, p. 4, Susan Brownmiller Papers.
69 *She suspected that*: "In Our Time": Forer Interview, Susan Brownmiller Papers.

8. DON'T CRY, RESIST

71 *Women "have a special power"*: "Women's Brigade Sets Goal: Bring Boys Back from Viet," *Wichita Beacon*, December 15, 1967, 4A.

71 *"sweet-faced, gentle-voiced"*: "Women's Brigade Sets Goal."

71 *"[T]here is no reason why"*: Marjorie Hunter, "5,000 Women Rally in Capital Against War," *New York Times*, January 16, 1968, 3.

72 *You are joyfully invited*: Ruth Rosen, "The Day They Buried 'Traditional Womanhood': Women and the Politics of Peace Protest," *Vietnam Generation* 1, no. 3 (1989), article 18, http://digitalcommons.lasalle.edu/vietnamgeneration/vol1/iss3/18.

73 *Allen felt "just as much"*: "In Our Time": Transcript of Interview with Donna Allen, 1995, box 27, folder 1, p. 3, Susan Brownmiller Papers.

73 *"larger-than-life dummy"*: Shulamith Firestone, "The Jeanette [*sic*] Rankin Brigade: Woman Power?," *Notes from the First Year*, June 1968, 18.

74 *"ARE AMERICAN WOMEN TRULY"*: "Are American Women Truly Beautiful?," Jeannette Rankin Brigade Action, January 15, 1968, series II:B, no. 1968.03, Redstockings Action Archives.

74 *TRADITIONAL WOMANHOOD IS DEAD!*: Firestone, "The Jeanette [*sic*] Rankin Brigade."

75 *"A Funeral Oration for"*: Kathie Amatniek, "A Funeral Oration for Traditional Womanhood," *Notes from the First Year*, June 1968, 20–22.

75 *"Women's Liberation! It's happening!"*: "In Our Time": Allen Interview. Susan Brownmiller Papers.

75 *Baxandall knew she wanted*: "In Our Time": Transcript of Interview with Rosalyn Baxandall, 1994, box 25, folder 10, p. 21, Susan Brownmiller Papers.

76 *"mother found herself"*: Rosalyn Baxandall and Harriet Fraad, "Red Sisters of the Bourgeoise," in Judy Kaplan and Linn Shapiro, eds., *Red Diapers: Growing Up in the Communist Left* (University of Illinois Press, 1998), 95.

76 *"I read and reread"*: Rosalyn Fraad Baxandall, "Catching the Fire," in Rachel Blau Duplessis and Ann Snitow, eds., *The Feminist Memoir Project: Voices from Women's Liberation* (Rutgers University Press, 1998), 210.

76 *"What are you doing next?"*: "In Our Time": Baxandall Interview, box 25, folder 10, p. 25, Susan Brownmiller Papers.

9. THE MINISKIRT CAUCUS

77 *"Come to the first"*: Postcard, New York Radical Women, box 17, folder 12, Rosalyn Baxandall Papers.

77 *divvied up by region:* Radical Women's Caucus at Jeannette Rankin Brigade Coordinating Committee: Contact List, 1968, series II:B, no. 1968.02, Redstockings Action Archives.

79 *"You won't mind twisting"*: Warren Hinckle and Marianne Hinckle, "A History of the Rise of the Unusual Movement for Women Power in the United States 1961–1968," *Ramparts*, February 1968, 31.

80 *Jo Freeman captured this*: Joreen [Jo Freeman] Letter to Editor, *Ramparts*, May 1968, 4.

80 *"though one really needed"*: Jeannette Rankin Letter to Editor, *Ramparts*, May 1968, 8.

81 *"Beyond a . . . Feminist Stance"*: Pamela Allen, "Beyond a . . . Feminist Stance," *Guardian*, January 27, 1968, 2.

81 *"Our enemy is not men"*: Marilyn Salzman Webb, "Call for a Spring Conference," *Voice of the Women's Liberation Movement* 1, no. 1 (March 1968): 4.

81 *"We have developed our"*: Marilyn Salzman Webb, "Women: We Have a Common Enemy," *New Left Notes* 3, no. 20 (June 10, 1968): 15.

10. WHAT ARE YOU DOING NEXT?

82 *"faction . . . won out"*: Carol Hanisch, "Struggles over Leadership in the Women's Liberation Movement," 2001, https://www.carolhanisch.org/CHwritings/Leadership.html.

83 *the topics included*: "Women as Child," *Notes from the First Year*, June 1968, 18.

83 *Speak Pains to Recall Pains*: Carol Hanisch, "Impact of the Chinese Cultural Revolution on the Women's Liberation Movement," paper delivered at the New School for Social Research, 30th Anniversary Symposium on "China's Great Proletarian Cultural Revolution," December 14, 1996, https://www.carolhanisch.org/Speeches/ChinaWLMSpeech/ChinaWLspeech.html.

83 *"Packed an intellectual and"*: Anselma Dell'Olio, "Home Before Sundown," in Rachel Blau Duplessis and Ann Snitow, eds., *The Feminist Memoir Project: Voices from Women's Liberation* (Rutgers University Press, 2007), 150.

83 *"Early consciousness-raising groups"*: Rosalyn Fraad Baxandall, "Catching the Fire," in Rachel Blau Duplessis and Ann Snitow, eds., *The Feminist Memoir Project: Voices from Women's Liberation* (Rutgers University Press, 2007), 211.

84 *"We were, we believed"*: Baxandall, "Catching the Fire," 210.

85 *"This is not an opportune"*: Minutes from the Second National Conference of NOW, November 19, 1967, National Organization for Women, https:/350fem.blogs.brynmawr.edu/1967/11/19/national-conference-of-now-minutes/.

85 *"it was time"*: "In Our Time": Transcript of Interview with Carol Hanisch, 1994, box 27, folder 1, p. 6, Susan Brownmiller Papers.

86 *"What does the word 'feminism'"*: Shulamith Firestone, "The Women's Rights Movement in the United States: A New View," *Notes from the First Year*, June 1968, 1.

86 *a "new view" of feminism:* Firestone, "The Women's Rights Movement in the United States."

87 *"There are several important"*: Firestone, "The Women's Rights Movement in the United States," 7.

87 *"give the reader some sense"*: Firestone, "The Women's Rights Movement in the United States."

87 *"Males who continue to say"*: Firestone, "The Women's Rights Movement in the United States," 28.

88 *communities "very open"*: Roxanne Dunbar-Ortiz, *Outlaw Woman: A Memoir of the War Years, 1960–1975* (City Lights Books, 2001), 124.

88 *"I think you are wrong"*: Dunbar-Ortiz, *Outlaw Woman*, 123.

88 *"Female Liberation Front for Human"*: Dunbar-Ortiz, *Outlaw Woman*, 126.

89 *"I hope I did not disrupt"*: Roxanne Dunbar to Ros Baxandall, July 5, 1968, box 16, folder 6, Rosalyn Baxandall Papers.

89 *seeing "both Annes"*: Shulamith Firestone to Ros Baxandall, July 17, 1968, box 16, folder 6, Rosalyn Baxandall Papers.

89 *"It is strange that"*: Anne Forer to Ros Baxandall, June 1, 1968, box 16, folder 6, Rosalyn Baxandall Papers (emphasis in original).

90 *"I really miss you and the group"*: Kathie Amatniek to Carol Hanisch (undated, early June 1968), box 22, folder 11, Susan Brownmiller Papers.

11. A BUNCH OF MAN-HATING NUTS

91 *"Well, your honor, you"*: Sherie M. Randolph, *Florynce "Flo" Kennedy: The Life of a Black Feminist Radical* (University of North Carolina Press, 2015), 146.

92 *"he had too much control"*: Breanne Fahs, "Ti-Grace Atkinson and the Legacy of Radical Feminism," *Feminist Studies* 37, no. 3 (Fall 2011): 576.

92 *"finally some woman had done"*: Fahs, "Ti-Grace Atkinson."

92 *"one of the most important"*: Marylin Bender, "Valeria Solanis [*sic*] a Heroine to Feminists," *New York Times*, June 14, 1968, 14.
92 *"She has been called"*: Bender, "Valeria Solanis."
93 *"was cast yesterday"*: Bender, "Valeria Solanis."
93 *"Beautiful!" she exclaimed*: Ti-Grace Atkinson to Marylin Bender (copy), June 14, 1968, box 59, folder 2, Ti-Grace Atkinson Papers (emphasis in original).
93 *"I was most disturbed"*: Cynthia to Betty, June 13, 1968, box 128, folder 1569, Betty Friedan Papers.
93 *"mannishly dressed brunette"*: "Actress Shoots Andy Warhol," *New York Daily News*, June 4, 1968, 3.
94 *"DESIST IMMEDIATELY"*: In memo by Muriel Fox (copy), box 128, folder 1569, Betty Friedan Papers.
94 *"was always a beautiful"*: "In Our Time": Transcript of Interview with Delores Alexander, 1994, box 25, folder 2, p. 15, Susan Brownmiller Papers.
94 *"was a fabulously good-looking"*: "In Our Time": Alexander Interview, box 25, folder 2, p. 19, Susan Brownmiller Papers.
95 *"When I prepared to do"*: Martha Weinman Lear, "The Second Feminist Wave," *New York Times Sunday Magazine*, March 10, 1968, 25.
95 *"37, married, attractive"*: Lear, "The Second Feminist Wave," 50.
95 *"You're a married woman"*: Lear, "The Second Feminist Wave," 50.
95 *"small group called [New York] Radical Women"*: Lear, "The Second Feminist Wave," 50–51.
96 *To say that you can be*: Lear, "The Second Feminist Wave," 54.
96 *"Her social connections"*: Lear, "The Second Feminist Wave," 53.
96 *"as an individual, not as"*: Lear, "The Second Feminist Wave," 56.
96 *"I wanted to give you one"*: Ti-Grace Atkinson to Mrs. Cummins (cc. Betty Friedan), March 27, 1968, box 124, folder 1514, Betty Friedan Papers (emphasis in original).
97 *"would just go and do"*: "In Our Time": Alexander Interview, box 25, folder 2, pp. 17–18, Susan Brownmiller Papers.

12. A NEW WOMAN POWER

98 *"Mrs. Richard M. Nixon still"*: Charlotte Curtis, "Pat Nixon: 'Creature Comforts Don't Matter,'" *New York Times*, July 3, 1968, 30.
98 *"You don't have Nixon to kick"*: "Transcript of Nixon's News Conference on His Defeat by Brown in Race for Governor of California," *New York Times*, November 8, 1962, 18.
99 *"Well, that's about it"*: Richard Nixon, "Checkers Speech," September 23, 1952, Presidential Speeches, Miller Center, University of Virginia, https://millercenter.org/the-presidency/presidential-speeches/september-23-1952-checkers-speech.
99 *"Our little girl Tricia"*: Nixon, "Checkers Speech."
99 *"a volunteer for Nixon"*: Curtis, "Pat Nixon," 30.
100 *"Pat Nixon's Rewards"*: Charlotte Curtis, "Pat Nixon's Rewards: A Mink, Woman Power," *Chicago Tribune*, July 5, 1968, B1.
100 *"The only thing holding"*: Charlotte Curtis, "A Folksy Fulbright Shuns 'Braying Contest' with Hawkish Democratic Rival in Arkansas," *New York Times*, July 22, 1968, 40.
101 *"very fine piece"*: Bob Whalen to Charlotte Curtis, July 23, 1968, box 9, folder 4, Charlotte Curtis Papers.
101 *"I write to pay her"*: Frank Trippett to James Reston, August 14, 1968, box 9, folder 4, Charlotte Curtis Papers.

101 *"I assume that by now"*: Steve Conn to Charlotte Curtis, July 28, 1968, box 7, folder 7, Charlotte Curtis Papers.

101 *"a battle cry for the election"*: Betty Friedan to NOW Executive Board, July 16, 1968, and Betty Friedan to Eliza King Paschall, July 25, 1968, box 124, folder 1516, Betty Friedan Papers.

13. TARGET: REPUBLICAN WOMEN

104 *"being urged to smile"*: Rodney Gibson, "Miami Beach Spruces Up for Invasion," *Chicago Tribune,* August 4, 1968, 44.

104 *"ODDS AND ENDS: Flak jackets"*: Charlotte Curtis, "ODDS AND ENDS," box 32, folder 12, Charlotte Curtis Papers.

104 *"nine-mile-long sandbar"*: 1968 newscast, quoted in *Best of Enemies: Buckley vs. Vidal,* written and directed by Robert Gordon and Morgan Nevelle (Magnolia Pictures, Participant Media, 2015), 88 min.

106 *"I have been related to"*: George Dixon, "Would Transmute GOP into 'Fun Party'; Lady Politico Comes Up with Jolly Idea," *The* (Santa Fe) *New Mexican,* April 29, 1957, 4.

107 *she announced four regional*: "GOP Women Leaders Schedule Meetings," *Great Bend Western Kansas Press,* May 18, 1967, 2.

108 *"Eighteen States Increase Number"*: "Eighteen States Increase Number of Women Delegates to GOP Convention," Republican National Committee press release, July 29, 1968, box 102, folder 1173, Betty Friedan Papers.

108 *"Brunches, lunches, fashion shows"*: Charlotte Curtis, "ODDS AND ENDS," box 32, folder 12, Charlotte Curtis Papers.

108 *"advised women delegates"*: Curtis, "ODDS AND ENDS."

108 *"now holds, or has held"*: Mary Wiegers, "Meet Mrs. Delegate," *Boston Globe,* August 6, 1968, 30.

108 *"Average Woman Delegate Is"*: Mary Wiegers, "Average Woman Delegate Is," *Miami Herald,* clipping, box 102, folder 1173, Betty Friedan Papers.

109 *"great workers, but they're"*: Jules Witcover, "Nixon for President in '68?," *Saturday Evening Post* 240, no. 4 (February 25, 1967): 95–96.

110 *"For many years," she explained*: Phyllis Schlafly, "Women in Politics," *Phi Gamma Nu,* September 1960, quoted in Donald T. Critchlow, *Phyllis Schlafly and Grassroots Conservatism: A Woman's Crusade* (Princeton University Press, 2005), 139.

110 *"The time is past"*: Phyllis Schlafly, "Each Member a Leader," Report to the Illinois Federation of Republican Women, November, 1960, quoted in Critchlow, *Phyllis Schlafly and Grassroots Conservatism,* 140.

110 *Schlafly's book,* A Choice, Not an Echo: Phyllis Schlafly, *A Choice, Not an Echo* (Pere Marquette Press, 1964).

111 *her obvious "edge on"*: "Mrs. Schlafly, Price Answer Voter Queries," *Alton Evening Telegraph,* September 26, 1952, quoted in Critchlow, *Phyllis Schlafly and Grassroots Conservatism,* 58.

111 *"This lady has everything"*: George Tagge, "Political Lookout," *Chicago Tribune,* October 5, 1963, N18.

111 *"youth, beauty, and grace"*: Bob Jackson, "Women's Federation Aspirant Gets Warm Welcome Here," *Los Angeles Times,* March 14, 1967, 3.

112 *"charm and graciousness"*: Critchlow, *Phyllis Schlafly and Grassroots Conservatism,* 152.

112 *"Finally, Phyllis appeared"*: Irene Peshel, account of the 14th Biennial Convention of the NFRW, June 1967, quoted in Critchlow, *Phyllis Schlafly and Grassroots Conservatism,* 158.

112 *"strong pro-American viewpoint"*: Phyllis Schlafly to "Dear and Loyal Friend," May 10, 1967, quoted in Critchlow, *Phyllis Schlafly and Grassroots Conservatism,* 161.

112 *"liberals and their allies"*: Phyllis Schlafly, *Safe, Not Sorry* (Pere Marquette Press, 1967), 150.

114 *"I ask with some urgency"*: Betty Friedan, A Bill of Rights for Women in 1968: Testimony presented to the Platform Committee of the Republican National Convention in Miami, box 43, folder 10, Ti-Grace Atkinson Papers.

114 *"Everyone looked so shocked"*: Carolyn Jay, "Betty Friedan: The New Feminist," *Miami News*, clipping, box 102, folder 1173, Betty Friedan Papers.

115 *"All I've got to say"*: Jay, "Betty Friedan: The New Feminist."

116 *"very simple," she explained*: Charlotte Curtis, "Politics: Notebook #4," box 37, folder 14, p. 18, Charlotte Curtis Papers (emphasis in original).

116 *"a very unique year"*: Curtis, "Politics: Notebook #4" (emphasis in original).

116 *"I wouldn't want to"*: Curtis, "Politics: Notebook #4."

116 *"no doubt that women"* Curtis, "Politics: Notebook #4."

14. WHO IS THE ENEMY?

117 *"Some of us in Radical"*: Marilynn Webb to Ros Baxandall, June 5, 1968, box 17, folder 12, Rosalyn Baxandall Papers.

117 *Marilyn Webb's conference list*: Conference List, 1968, box 6, folder 2, Marilyn Webb Papers.

118 *It would be hot*: Marilyn Webb to All, July 27, 1968, box 6, folder 2, Marilyn Webb Papers.

118 *"This meeting should not be seen"*: Marilynn Webb to All, July 27, 1968.

118 *The Tentative Agenda*: Tentative Agenda, 1968, box 6, folder 2, Marilyn Webb Papers.

119 *"Oh," she stuttered*: "In Our Time": Transcript of Interview with Jo Freeman, 1994, box 26, folder 16, p. 57, Susan Brownmiller Papers.

120 *"the* Notes *people"*: "In Our Time": Transcript of Interview with Kathie Amatniek, 1995, box 29, folder 1, p. 28, Susan Brownmiller Papers.

120 *"The first of the Lower East Side"*: Meeting, Friday, August 2, 1968, partial transcript, box 21, folder 6, p. 1, Susan Brownmiller Papers.

120 *"Our group did not know"*: Meeting, Friday, August 2, 1968, partial transcript.

121 *she wrote to Brown*: "In Our Time": Transcript of Interview with Carol Hanisch, 1994, box 27, folder 1, p. 23, Susan Brownmiller Papers.

122 *"I am just so convinced"*: Sandy Spring Conference, tape 1, 1968, side 1, Marilyn Webb Papers.

122 *"No one's going to understand"*: Kathie Amatniek notes, Sandy Spring meeting, Redstockings Action Archives.

123 *"These SDS women"*: "In Our Time": Transcript of Interview with Roxanne Dunbar, 1994, box 26, folder 9, p. 7, Susan Brownmiller Papers.

123 *"You said that none"*: Sandy Spring Conference, tape 1, 1968, side 1.

123 *"just when it gets interesting"*: Sandy Spring Conference, tape 1, 1968, side 2, Marilyn Webb Papers.

124 *"Why don't we bring the peanut"*: Sandy Spring Conference, tape 1, 1968, side 2.

124 *"We've been waiting"*: Sandy Spring Conference, tape 1, 1968, side 2.

124 *"We fall into the man-is-the-enemy"*: The following exchange, to end of this section, is drawn from Sandy Spring Conference, tape 1, 1968, side 2.

127 *"What happened yesterday"*: Sandy Spring meeting, August 24, 1968, partial transcript, box 21, folder 6, pp. 29–32, Susan Brownmiller Papers.

128 *"I'm glad I don't have"*: Chude Pamela Allen to Susan Brownmiller, January 17, 1995, box 19, folder 14, Susan Brownmiller Papers.

128 *discussion as it was represented*: This lengthy discussion, to the end of this section, is drawn from Sandy Spring meeting, partial transcript, August 24, 1968, in "In Our Time": Hanisch Interview, box 21, folder 6, pp. 33–38, Susan Brownmiller Papers.

132 *"We should protest the Miss America Pageant"*: Susan Brownmiller, *In Our Time: Memoir of a Revolution* (Dial Press, 1999), 35.

15. THERE SHE IS

136 *"tremendous honors"*: "Harding Greets Gorman Before Crowd of 10,000," *Washington Herald*, September 12, 1921, 9.

136 *"the type of womanhood"*: Lois Banner, *American Beauty* (Alfred A. Knopf, 1983), 268–269.

137 *"spectators gasped as they applauded"*: "1,000 Bathing Girls on View in Pageant," *New York Times*, September 9, 1921, 12.

137 *"typically American, an altogether"*: Frank Deford, *There She Is: The Life and Times of Miss America* (Viking, 1971), 248.

138 *"the difference that comes"*: Deford, *There She Is.*

138 *"ten thousand recollections"*: Thomas Jefferson, "Query XIV: Laws," *Notes on the State of Virginia* (1781–1787), https://www.monticello.org/notes-on-the-state-of-virginia/query-xiv.

138 *"difference fixed in nature"*: Jefferson, "Query XIV: Laws."

138 *"And is this difference"*: Jefferson, "Query XIV: Laws."

139 *"made to assume"*: Mary Wollstonecraft, *A Vindication of the Rights of Woman* (1792; repr. Penguin Books, 1992), 123–140.

140 *"Who is the Prettiest"*: Blain Roberts, *Pageants, Parlors & Pretty Women: Race and Beauty in the Twentieth Century South* (University of North Carolina Press, 2014), 173.

141 *"Many white people are under"*: Roberts, *Pageants, Parlors & Pretty Women*, 173.

142 *"Exemplifying the highest type"*: "Highest Type Indian Beauty Shown by Princess America," *Spokane Daily Chronicle*, July 26, 1926, 2.

143 *"With a seriousness"*: "New Miss America Gives Impress of Extreme Youth," *Boston Globe*, September 20, 1926, 14.

143 *"She has mystery"*: "Mona Lisa and Mystery Supplant Flapper," *The China Press*, November 7, 1926, C3.

144 *"thrown to the wind"*: Deford, *There She Is*, 247.

144 *"to wage a concerted"*: "Women Condemn Beauty Parades," *New York Times*, May 9, 1924, 16.

144 *"the young woman who deliberately"*: Deford, *There She Is*, 245.

144 *"the willingness of a few"*: A. R. Riverol, *Live from Atlantic City: The History of the Miss America Pageant Before, After, and In Spite of Television* (Bowling Green State University Popular Press, 1992), 24.

144 *"an exploitation of feminine"*: "Bishop Condemns Beauty Pageant," *New York Times*, November 30, 1927, 10.

144 *"American women are sleeping"*: Deford, *There She Is*, 247.

144 *"exploitation of young women"*: "Attack Beauty Pageant, Philadelphia Women Sign Protest to Atlantic City Authorities," *New York Times*, March 1, 1927, 3.

144 *"outlived its usefulness"*: "Ignores Pageant Protests, Atlantic City Chamber Minimizes Criticism of Beauty Contest," *New York Times*, March 2, 1927, 26.

145 *"She picked up the pageant"*: Deford, *There She Is*, 149.

146 *"the boardwalk witnesses daily"*: "Camp Boardwalk," *Saturday Evening Post*, February 27, 1943, 26.

147 *"I was* delighted *to talk"*: Lenora Slaughter, quoted in Ann-Marie Bivens, *Miss America: In Pursuit of the Crown* (Master Media Limited, 1991), 8 (emphasis in original).

147 *"I never went to college"*: Susan Dworkin, *Miss America, 1945: Bess Myerson's Own Story* (Newmarket Press, 1987), 98.

147 *"envy Miss America"*: Lenora S. Slaughter to the Board of Directors, November 10, 1944, box 3, Lenora Slaughter Papers.

149 *"as much splendor"*: Roberts, *Pageants, Parlors & Pretty Women,* 191.

151 *"I felt like Scarlett O'Hara"*: Dworkin, *Miss America, 1945,* 179.

151 *something more "attractive"*: Dworkin, *Miss America, 1945,* 92–93.

152 *"Hate is a corroding disease"*: "All Beauty Destroyed by Bias, 'Miss America' Warns Pupils," *Baltimore Afro-American,* March 30, 1946, 15.

152 *"political events" inappropriate*: Dworkin, *Miss America, 1945,* 202.

152 *"one of the most un-American*: "Local Indian Protests Beauty Contest Rules," *Rapid City Daily Journal,* April 15, 1948, 2.

153 *"be proud and happy"*: "National Beauty Pageant Okays Indian Entries," *Rapid City* (South Dakota) *Daily Journal,* April 24, 1948, 1.

154 *"Lovely Lassies"*: "Lovely Lassies in the Sepia Miss America Contest," *The Crisis,* July 1944, 221.

156 *"Naturally a contest"*: "'Miss America' Calls for End of Color Line," *Baltimore Afro-American,* May 31, 1952, 11.

156 *"cleared themselves"*: "'Miss America' Calls for End of Color Line," *Baltimore Afro-American.*

157 *"How could anyone ever"*: Gregory Nickerson, "All-American Indian Days and the Miss Indian America Pageant," *Montana: The Magazine of Western History,* Summer 2017, 12.

157 *"Miss Yellow Mule"*: William Henry Harrison, "From the Capitol Steps," *News Letter Journal* (Newcastle, Wyoming), October 23, 1952, 2.

158 *"outstanding achievement"*: Nickerson, "All-American Indian Days," 11.

160 *"you're right on the stage"*: Philco advertisement, *Official Yearbook of the Miss America Pageant,* 1956, 2.

16. BLACK IS BEAUTIFUL

163 *"so all the world can see"*: Ruth Feldstein, "'I Wanted the Whole World to See': Race, Gender, and Constructions of Motherhood in the Death of Emmett Till," in Joanne Meyerowitz, ed., *Not June Cleaver: Women and Gender in Postwar America, 1945–1960* (Temple University Press, 1994), 263–303.

164 *Margaret Taliaferro, wardrobe mistress*: "'Miss America' Wardrobe Mistress," *Ebony,* October 1956, 68 and 70.

164 *"a wardrobe mistress"*: "Crown-Seeking Beauties Told Fame Is Fleeting," *Hartford Courant,* September 5, 1958, 7.

165 *"emissary of Cotton fashions"*: Blain Roberts, *Pageants, Parlors & Pretty Women: Race and Beauty in the Twentieth Century South* (University of North Carolina Press, 2014), 154.

165 *"bronze lassies"*: "Negro Beauties from 3 States Seek 'Miss America' Crown," *Jet,* June 11, 1959, 60–61.

166 *treated with "undue fuss"*: "Tan 'Miss America' Entry Not Unusual," *Baltimore Afro American,* May 9, 1959, 15.

166 *"The first thing you have"*: John Lewis, quoted in Lynne Olson, *Freedom's Daughters: The Unsung Heroines of the Civil Rights Movement from 1830–1970* (Simon & Schuster, 2002), 152.

167 *"Miss Nash, a former"*: "Freedom Riders Marry, Settle in Mississippi," *Jet,* January 11, 1962, 23.

168 *"I'm a Southern girl"*: "Bias Foes Picket Woolworth Here," *New York Times,* June 16, 1960, 25.

170 *"the thought of a girl"*: Jennifer C. Thomas, "Pageantry and Politics: Miss Howard University from Civil Rights to Black Power," *Journal of Negro Education* 87, no. 1 (2018): 27.

170 *"that we as a people"*: Thomas, "Pageantry and Politics."

171 *"expressionless throughout"*: "'No Colored No Pageant,' Warns Savage," *Baltimore Afro-American*, September 18, 1965, 14.

171 *"I watched it very, very carefully"*: "NAACP Official Assails 'White' Beauty Pageant," *Philadelphia Inquirer*, September 16, 1965.

172 *Savage related that the*: "Phillip Savage, "Voter Registration & Branch Problems," Monthly Report to Gloster Current, September 29, 1965, p. 1, in part 29A, reel 9, NAACP Papers.

173 *Savage and the NAACP had extracted*: "Whites Only for Miss America," *Morning Call* (Paterson, New Jersey), September 7, 1966, 5.

174 *"NAACP To Crown"*: "NAACP To Crown First Queen," *Chicago Defender*, February 17, 1968, 31.

174 *"whatever action was necessary"*: John Katz, "Roy Wilkins Demands Negro Girls in 'Lily-White' Pageant," *Atlantic City Press*, June 24, 1968, 1.

174 *We, the members of the*: "Negro Youth Backs Pageant Resolution," *Atlantic City Press*, June 24, 1968, 3.

175 *he "definitely disagreed"*: "Pageant Bias Denied," *Atlantic City Press*, June 24, 1968, 1.

175 *"we have had Negro"*: "Pageant Bias Denied," *Atlantic City Press*.

176 *"always willing to look"*: "Pageant Bias Denied," *Atlantic City Press*.

177 *"I'm amazed at the reaction"*: UPI, "There She Goes: Miss America," *Buffalo* (New York) *Evening News*, June 13, 1968, 71.

177 *contemporary "rock beat"*: "Tradition Falls to 'Rock Beat,'" *Alexandria* (Louisiana) *Daily Town Talk*, June 13, 1968, B9.

178 *"His face of despair"*: "Bert Parks Suffers Crowning Indignity," *New York Times*, September 11, 1967, 54.

178 *"gospel of revolution"*: "Names in the News," *Standard Examiner* (Ogden, Utah), June 13, 1968, 1.

17. THE SYMBOL OF EVERYTHING

181 *"Protesting the pageant in Atlantic City"*: Carol Hanisch, "Two Letters from the Women's Liberation Movement," in Rachel Blau Duplessis and Ann Snitow, eds., *The Feminist Memoir Project: Voices from Women's Liberation* (Rutgers University Press, 2007), 197.

181 *"My gosh! That's"*: Ann Heppermann and Kara Oehler, "This Weekend in 1968: Miss America," American Public Radio broadcast, January 24, 2009, https://weekendamerica.publicradio.org/display/web/2008/09/06/1968_miss_america.html.

183 *"Everywhere one turned"*: David English, *Divided They Stand: The American Election 1968* (Prentice-Hall, 1969), 276.

183 *"if you are a girl"*: Raymond Hartley, "Your Help is Wanted in Politics," *Seventeen* 23, no. 9 (September 1964): 132–133, 204, 206–208.

183 *"showed inexhaustible energy"*: English, *Divided They Stand*, 274.

184 *"We want Rocky!"*: English, *Divided They Stand*, 273.

184 *"not only give up"*: Nixonaires, Nixon for President Committee, press release, July 31, 1968, New York, box 102, folder 1175, Betty Friedan Papers.

185 *"Keep in Shape for '68"*: "GOP Assistant National Chairman Briefs Press on Convention Events for Women," Republican National Committee, July 16, 1968, box 32, folder 12, Charlotte Curtis Papers.

185 *she was conflicted*: Hillary Rodham Clinton, *Living History* (Simon & Schuster, 2003), 35–36.

186 *"this was the week in which"*: Charlotte Curtis to Lucile Atcherson Curtis, March 22, 1968, box 6, folder 11, Charlotte Curtis Papers.

186 *"Duke" complained*: Clinton, *Living History*, 35–36.

186 *"I'd like her to know"*: "GOP 'Cares,' John Wayne Tells Conclave," *Los Angeles Times*, August 6, 1968, 4.

187 *"to print . . . any notice"*: Flora Davis, *Moving the Mountain: The Women's Movement in America since 1960* (Simon & Schuster, 1991), 60–61.

187 *"Commission's action appeared"*: "NOW Announces Victory," press release, July 31, 1968, box 43, folder 9, Ti-Grace Atkinson Papers.

187 *"official hostesses who"*: "An Opinion: The Conventions, *Mademoiselle*, 1968," box 102, folder 1177, Betty Friedan Papers (emphasis in original).

18. FEAR OF A LILY-WHITE PARTY

190 *"This would be a helluva"*: A. "Doc" Young, "Convention Notes," *Los Angeles Sentinel*, August 8, 1968, A3.

190 *"We're going to stay with"*: Ian Menzies, "2 Black Leaders Warn GOP," *Boston Globe*, August 6, 1968, 1.

191 *bipartisan, but not* non-partisan: "All-White Delegations Criticized—Negroes Seek 10 At-Large Seats," *Tampa Bay Times*, August 6, 1968, 9.

191 *"Some Reagan watchers"*: "Mrs. Reagan," *Miami Herald* clipping, box 102, folder 1173, Betty Friedan Papers.

193 *"get tough policy"*: Jim Savage, "Miami Police Open Up 'Get Tough Policy,'" *Miami Herald*, December 27, 1967, 67.

193 *"Felons will learn"*: Savage, "Miami Police Open Up."

193 *"The only solution"*: Phyllis Schlafly, "Crisis in Law and Order," *The Phyllis Schlafly Report*, May 1968, 2 (emphasis in original).

194 *"mass rally of concerned"*: Black Mass Rally flyer, National Commission on the Causes and Prevention of Violence, *Miami Report: The Report of the Miami Study Team on Civil Disturbances in Miami, Florida, During Week of August 5, 1968* (U.S. Government Printing Office, 1969), Appendix IV.

195 *"clutching her glasses"*: The description of Brooks's speech and reactions are drawn from "Notebook: Republican National Convention, 1968," box 37, folder 14, p. 47, Charlotte Curtis Papers.

196 *"I'm so tired of"*: "An Opinion: The Conventions, *Mademoiselle*, 1968," box 102, folder 1177, Betty Friedan Papers.

19. THE HARD WORK OF BECOMING THE IDEAL GIRL

197 *"Good news, Mrs. Green"*: Anita Bryant, *Mine Eyes Have Seen the Glory* (Fleming H. Revell Co., 1970), 96–97.

198 *"I never felt I 'lost'"*: Bryant, *Mine Eyes Have Seen the Glory*, 38.

198 *"raw, rugged Oklahoma"*: The following description of Bryant's early life is drawn from Bryant, *Mine Eyes Have Seen the Glory.*

199 *"some of the hardest"*: Bryant, *Mine Eyes Have Seen the Glory*, 36.

199 *"men don't usually like"*: Jack Jones, "Beauty Title Brings Dream of Singing Career," *Daily Oklahoman*, July 20, 1958, 28A.

199 *hobby to be "people"*: Jones, "Beauty Title Brings Dream."

199 *"You're going to need"*: Bryant, *Mine Eyes Have Seen the Glory*, 36.

200 *"While most other contests"*: "It Takes Brains Plus Beauty," *Daily Oklahoman*, August 31, 1958, 3.

202 *"ground to a dead halt"*: Further details in this section and the next about Bryant's life are drawn from Bryant, *Mine Eyes Have Seen the Glory.*

202 *"the many girls who"*: "As Bernie Wayne Says in His Pageant Song, 'Everybody Can't Be a Winner,'" *Official Yearbook of the Miss America Pageant*, 1962, p. 4, box 1, Lenora Slaughter Papers.

20. NIXON'S THE ONE

204 *"Miss Bess Myerson, former"*: Drew Pearson, "Reagan's Political Switches Traced," *Washington Post*, August 6, 1968, B11.

204 *"I just don't believe"*: "Leader Says GOP Would Banish Viet Fears," *Washington Post*, August 6, 1968, D1.

205 *"G.O.P. Told Feminine Gripes"*: "GOP Told Feminine Gripes," *Chicago Tribune*, August 6, 1968, 5.

205 *"Oh, I don't play"*: Donald T. Critchlow, *Phyllis Schlafly and Grassroots Conservatism: A Woman's Crusade* (Princeton University Press, 2005), 191.

206 *"In the tense hours"*: Charlotte Curtis, "Nixon Family Keeps Smiling and Working," *New York Times*, August 8, 1968, 23.

206 *"Keep in Shape for '68"*: "GOP Assistant National Chairman Briefs Press on Convention Events for Women," Republican National Committee, press release, July 16, 1968, box 32, folder 12, Charlotte Curtis Papers.

206 *"I'm still starving"*: Curtis, "Nixon Family Keeps Smiling."

207 *"disturbance" in Liberty City*: "'68 RNC, Night 3, Part 1," *NBC Evening News*, August 7, 1968, https://www.youtube.com/watch?v=wNkzHWWw6SM.

207 *About a hundred people*: National Commission on the Causes and Prevention of Violence, *Miami Report: The Report of the Miami Study Team on Civil Disturbances in Miami, Florida, During Week of August 5, 1968* (U.S. Government Printing Office, 1969), 1–10.

208 *"riot had begun"*: National Commission, *Miami Report*, 11.

208 *"A Dixieland band"*: "Wallace Pledges to Revamp Nation's Spending Programs," *Panama City Herald*, July 30, 1968, 2.

209 *"'girls' went around selling"*: "An Opinion: The Conventions, *Mademoiselle*, 1968," box 102, folder 1177, Betty Friedan Papers.

209 *"honey-faced"*: Dan Carter, *The Politics of Rage: George Wallace, the Origins of the New Conservatism, and the Transformation of American Politics* (Simon & Schuster, 1995), 341.

209 *Lurleen Wallace may have been*: Carter, *The Politics of Rage*, chap. 9.

210 *"To be sure, this"*: "Miami Race Riots," 1968 Special Report, ABC News Video Source, Hezakya Newz & Films, YouTube, https://www.youtube.com/watch?app=desktop&v=z7WILArRWyA.

211 *"doubtful, but acceptable"*: Critchlow, *Phyllis Schlafly and Grassroots Conservatism*, 191.

211 *"If one wants to pinpoint"*: "Nation: The Unlikely No. 2," *Time*, August 16, 1968, https://time.com/archive/6632632/nation-the-unlikely-no-2/.

211 *"Mrs. Spiro Agnew?"*: Charlotte Curtis, "Judy Agnew: From Obscurity to National Spotlight in Ten Minutes," *New York Times*, August 9, 1968, 24.

21. GET THIS . . . WE ARE GOING TO DISRUPT THE MISS AMERICA PAGEANT

212 *"One of the things I remember"*: "In Our Time": Transcript of Interview with Irene Peslikis, 1994, box 28, folder 11, p. 199, Susan Brownmiller Papers.

212 *"I cried with the winner"*: Carol Hanisch, "Two Letters from the Women's Liberation Movement," in Rachel Blau Duplessis and Ann Snitow, eds., *The Feminist Memoir Project: Voices from Women's Liberation* (Rutgers University Press, 2007), 198.

213 *"this American icon"*: Hanisch, "Two Letters from the Women's Liberation Movement."

213 *"Let's do a Miss America action"*: "In Our Time": Peslikis Interview, box 28, folder 11, p. 197, Susan Brownmiller Papers.

213 *"frivolous and petty"*: "In Our Time": Peslikis Interview.

213 *"If more than half"*: Carol Hanisch, "What Can Be Learned: A Critique of the Miss America Protest," November 27, 1968, 3, Women's Print Culture Collection.

214 *The pageant, to me*: Bev Grant, "No More Miss America: A Collective Memory of Liberatory Action," *Dissent*, September 7, 2018 (emphasis in original), https://dissentmagazine.org/online_articles/no-more-miss-america-1968-pageant-protest-oral-history-women-liberation/.

214 *it became clear to*: Kathie Amatniek to Rosalyn Baxandall, August 9, 1968, box 16, folder 10, Rosalyn Baxandall Papers.

215 *"pretty indecisive"*: Amatniek to Baxandall, August 9, 1968 (emphasis in original).

22. OUR VIETNAM GIRLS

216 *"all the up tunes"*: *Topeka Daily Capital,* August 12, 1968, clipping, Scrapbook Series, vol. 1, folder 5, Debra Barnes Papers.

218 *"Chances are you can't"*: Marion Purcelli, "Beauty Queen Goes to War," *Chicago Tribune,* May 21, 1966, D13.

218 *"we are enormously"*: "Miss America to Deliver Resort's Regards to GIs," *Atlantic City Press,* August 12, 1967, 16.

218 *"I've lost all enthusiasm"*: Jane Jayroe with Bob Burke, *More Grace than Glamour: My Life as Miss America and Beyond* (Oklahoma Heritage Association, 2006), 110.

219 *"We went over there"*: "Miss America Visits Johnson," *Atlantic City Press,* September 1, 1967, 17.

219 *"We're very proud of"*: David Williams, "Six Beauties Given Awards," *Atlantic City Press,* September 9, 1967, 17.

219 *"On August 14, a big jet"*: Miss America Pageant 1968, telecast, September 9, 1967, Pageants HeyDay, YouTube, https://www.youtube.com/watch?v=vrDVBJHIOFw.

220 *"would be able to do less"*: Details here of Barnes's life are drawn from Debra Barnes, "A lesson I Learned from Life," *Boston Globe,* March 10, 1968, G4.

221 *offering Debbie a dollop*: "A Piece of Cake," *Hartford Courant,* September 8, 1967, 14.

221 *"She is a beautiful"*: Min Grimes, "Ironton Provides 'Miss America' with Hospitality and Two Firsts," *Ironton Tribune* (Ohio), October 12, 1967, 1.

221 *one of the show's members*: Evan Smith, "Betty Buckley, On Singing for her Supper," *Texas Monthly,* September 2006, https://www.texasmonthly.com/arts-entertainment/betty-buckley/.

222 *"Now she is 'mothering'"*: Dianne Kenny, "Miss America '68 Chaperone Veteran at the Job," *Jersey Journal,* October 10, 1967, 15.

222 *"Beauties to Vietnam"*: "Beauties to Vietnam," *Trenton* (New Jersey) *Times,* August 4, 1968, 24.

223 *It was uncomfortable for me*: Smith, "Betty Buckley."

224 *"eager" and "over-enthusiastic"*: "Leathernecks Are Wowed by Miss America," *Chicago Tribune,* August 12, 1968, 22.

224 *"Their success," he noted*: "No One Would Miss Six Hits?" *Pacific Stars and Stripes,* August 20, 1968, 24.

23. A CERTAIN IMAGE AND PUBLICITY VALUE

225 *In a letter dated July 30*: Georgia Paige Welch, "'Up Against the Wall Miss America': Women's Liberation and Miss Black America in Atlantic City, 1968," *Feminist Formations* 27, no. 2 (Summer 2015): 75–76.

226 *"purely local terms"*: Welch, "'Up Against the Wall Miss America.'"
226 *"the first Negro named"*: "Miss America Pageant Names Negro to Its Board," *New York Times,* August 1, 1968, 17.
226 *"We do not regard"*: Welch, "'Up Against the Wall Miss America,'" 75–76.
227 *neither racist nor "lily-white"*: "Pageant Officials Will Drive Hard for Negro Participation," *Atlantic City Press,* August 15, 1968, 1.
228 *"brought the pageant closer"*: "Pageant Officials Will Drive Hard,"*Atlantic City Press,* 14.
228 *In its coverage of the press conference*: "Negroes Sought to Enter Contests for Miss America," *New York Times,* August 15, 1968, 20.
228 *"Why, we'd love to have"*: Frank Deford, *There She Is: The Life and Times of Miss America* (Viking, 1971), 252.
229 *"Negro Girls Are Sought"*: "Negro Girls Are Sought for Pageant," *Washington Post,* August 16, 1968, C4.

24. A BEVY OF "BLACK AND BEAUTIFUL" YOUNG WOMEN

230 *"Fashionable Productions of Philadelphia"*: "Fashionable Productions Hold Miss Black American Beauty Preliminaries," *Philadelphia Tribune,* August 17, 1968, 15.
231 *Anderson spent his formative years*: U.S. Bureau of the Census, *Sixteenth Census of the United States, 1940,* Greenville City, Greenville, South Carolina, S.D. No. 4, E.D. No. 23–50, Sheet 4; U.S. Bureau of the Census, *Seventeenth Census of the United States, 1950,* District of Columbia, Washington, E.D. No. 1–71, Sheet 3; "Certificate Given to Pastor's Wife for Service to the Blind," *Indianapolis Recorder,* April 1, 1961, 5; John Katz, "Pageant Director Seeks to Instill Black Pride," *Atlantic City Press,* September 7, 1968, 22.
231 *"I was reared in"*: John Katz, "Pageant Director Seeks to Instill Pride," *Atlantic City Press,* September 7, 1968, 22.
231 *"Le Cabaret Francaise"*: "John and John Offer City Authentic 'Night in Paris,'" *Indianapolis Recorder,* June 13, 1959, 1.
232 *"hundreds of young adults"*: Richard Henderson, "Social Scene . . . ," *Indianapolis Recorder,* June 20, 1959, 4.
232 *"new twist in fashion"*: "Elegant Magazine's 'Vogue for Judgement Day,'" advertisement, *California Sentinel* (Los Angeles), July 23, 1964, C2; "Vogue for Judgement Day Style Review Set at Center," *California Eagle* (Los Angeles), July 23, 1964, 33.
232 *"Superb is the word"*: "Vogue for Judgement Fashions Thrill Crowd," *California Sentinel* (Los Angeles), July 30, 1964, 34.
233 *"the beautiful woman of*: "'Vogue for Judgement Day' Play by Ex-Local Writer to Be Presented at C.T.S. Nov. 25," *Indianapolis Recorder,* October 14, 1967, 2.
233 *"a bevy of 'Black'"*: "Fashionable Productions Hold Miss Black American Beauty Preliminaries," *Philadelphia Tribune,* August 17, 1968, 15.
234 *"Miss Black America Beauty Pageant–1968"*: Advertisement in *National Notes,* September-October 1968, 21.

25. THEY GOT TO ME BEFORE I GOT TO ME

236 *"raise eyebrows"*: "In Our Time": Transcript of Interview with Robin Morgan, 1994, box 28, folder 4, p. 7, Susan Brownmiller Papers.
236 Oh my God, *thought Morgan*: "In Our Time": Morgan Interview, Susan Brownmiller Papers.
236 *"subconscious agenda"*: "In Our Time": Morgan Interview, box 28, folder 4, p. 8, Susan Brownmiller Papers.
236 *"I'm dealing over here"*: "In Our Time": Morgan Interview, Susan Brownmiller Papers.

237 *While Robin Morgan's origin story*: Robin Morgan, *Saturday's Child: A Memoir* (Norton, 2001).
238 *"women in the revolution"*: Peter Babcock, "Meet the Women of the Revolution, 1969," *New York Times Sunday Magazine,* February 9, 1969, 34.
239 *"I just walked into"*: Babcock, "Meet the Women of the Revolution."
239 *"free grass, free food"*: Morgan, *Saturday's Child,* 237.
239 *"A lot of women came"*: Babcock, "Meet the Women of the Revolution."
240 *"as mixed feminists and lefties"*: Morgan, *Saturday's Child.*

26. THE TEN POINTS, WE PROTEST

241 *"big blue county fair-type"*: Kathie Amatniek to Rosalyn Baxandall, August 9, 1968, box 16, folder 10, Rosalyn Baxandall Papers.
241 *"Animal Parade"*: Robin Morgan, annotated planning notes for the Miss America protest, August 1968, Women's Print Culture Collection.
242 *Original plans included*: Morgan, annotated planning notes.
242 *a small "secret tactics" group*: Morgan, annotated planning notes.
242 *WE PROTEST*: New York Radical Women, press release, August 22, 1968, Women's Print Culture Collection.
245 *"exciting . . . sexy . . . dangerous"*: Lisa Hammel, "A Class of Fledgling Pickets Gets the Word: Make it Exciting! Make it Swing!," *New York Times,* August 24, 1968, 33.
246 *"persona non grata"*: "Colgate Palmolive Picket," *NOW in the News,* October 1968, box 42, folder 3, Rosalyn Baxandall Papers.
246 *"elegant and substantial"*: Anselma Dell'Olio, "Home Before Sundown," in Rachel Blau Duplessis and Ann Snitow, eds., *The Feminist Memoir Project: Voices from Women's Liberation* (Rutgers University Press, 2007), 149.
247 *"Feminism allowed me"*: Dell'Olio, "Home Before Sundown," 150.
247 *"extreme employment discrimination"*: Charlotte Curtis, "White House Candidates Let the Women Down," *New York Times,* May 7, 1968, 40.
247 *"photocopies, stationery, stamps"*: Dell'Olio, "Home Before Sundown."
248 *"You don't want to miss"*: Robin Morgan, *Saturday's Child: A Memoir* (Norton, 2001), 246.

27. WELCOME TO WOMEN DEMOCRATS

249 *sentiment was strong*: Heather Hendershot, *When the News Broke: Chicago, 1968, and the Polarizing of America* (University of Chicago Press, 2022), 36–37.
251 *widely circulated Yippie map*: "All Set to Surge Festival of Life," *Berkeley Barb,* August 16–22, 1968, 5.
252 *signaled by her inclusion*: Charlotte Curtis, "There's Hubaret, the Abigail, and Parties, Parties, Parties," *New York Times,* August 26, 1968, 43.
253 *"The Democratic Convention seems"*: Thoughts on Women and the Democratic Party, drafted on reverse of McCarthy for President Michigan Challenge, August 19, 1968, box 102, folder 1172, Betty Friedan Papers.
253 *addressed to "Miss Reporter"*: Norma A. Lee, Clairol Public Relations to Miss Reporter, August 1968, box 81, folder 10, Betty Friedan Papers.
254 *she'd "had no choice"*: "Wash, Rinse, and Equal Treatment," October 24, 2016, U.S. House of Representatives, *History, Art, Archives,* https://history.house.gov/Blog/Detail/15032439907.
254 *"Looks Don't Count"*: "Looks Don't Count at Chicago—Democrats," *Los Angeles Times,* August 19, 1968, F11.

254 *"Food for Thought"*: Vera Glaser, "Women Plan 'Issue' Diet," *Columbia* (South Carolina) *Record*, August 22, 1968, C1.

255 *"oversized jeweled eyes"*: "Chicago Welcomes Women Demos at Luncheon, Fashion Showing," *Chicago Daily Defender*, August 28, 1968, 18.

255 *"In Chicago, things were"*: "An Opinion: The Conventions, *Mademoiselle*, 1968," box 102, folder 1177, Betty Friedan Papers.

256 *"five-day Yippie festival*: Peter H. Prugh, "A Pig for President: Yippies to Burlesque the Political Process," *Wall Street Journal*, August 23, 1968, 1.

256 *"The atmosphere was completely"*: David English, *Divided They Stand: The American Election 1968* (Prentice-Hall, 1969), 303.

257 *"Overall, the security around"*: Heather Hendershot, *When the News Broke: Chicago, 1968, and the Polarizing of America* (University of Chicago Press, 2022), 64–65.

258 *"It was a travesty"*: Paul Jones, "'Soul' Anthem Hasn't a Ghost of a Chance," *Atlanta Constitution*, August 28, 1968, 20.

258 *"I have never felt"*: Sara Louise Eckert, "Grieved at Aretha Franklin's Rendition of the National Anthem," *Memphis Press*, August 28, 1968, 10.

258 *"color does not disturb"*: "Offensive, Says Marion Freelander," *Houston Post*, August 29, 1968, 35.

259 *"adored for his"*: Norman Mailer, *Miami and the Siege of Chicago: An Informal History of the Republican and Democratic Conventions in 1968* (World Publishing, 1968; repr. New York Review of Books, 2008), 207.

260 *"I want everyone in the world"*: Much of the following description is drawn from Charlotte Curtis, "At Chicago, Black Women Speak Their Mind," *New York Times*, August 28, 1968, 52.

264 *"Anita gives Democrats"*: "Anita Gives Democrats a Big Lift," *Daily Oklahoman*, August 28, 1968, 7.

264 *"stunning brunette"*: Marian Lowry Fischer, "Anita Bryant in Salem to Star at State Fair," *Capital Journal* (Salem, Oregon), August 29, 1968, 6.

265 *commonly referred to as a "police riot"*: David Farber, *Chicago '68* (University Chicago Press, 1988).

266 *hurt but not badly*: Betty Friedan, *Life So Far: A Memoir* (Simon & Schuster, 2000), xx.

266 *"seemed removed from"*: Roxanne Dunbar-Ortiz, *Outlaw Woman: A Memoir of the War Years, 1960–1975* (City Lights Books, 2001), 137.

266 *"allegedly beautiful people"*: Charlotte Curtis, "Guests Flock to Week-Long Party Given By Playboy's Publisher," *New York Times*, August 29, 1968, 27.

268 *"Are you a Bunny"*: Steve Conn to Charlotte Curtis, September 4, 1968, box 7, folder 7, Charlotte Curtis Papers.

268 *"still smelling of stink"*: Charlotte Curtis, "Mrs. Humphrey Looks Back at Chicago," *New York Times*, August, 31, 1968, 10.

28. NAACP TO HOLD "BLACK PAGEANT"

270 *"We want to be in Atlantic City"*: "Negroes Plan Show to Rival Contest for Miss America," *New York Times*, August 29, 1968, 38.

270 *"to provide Black young"*: "1st 'Miss Black America' Pageant to be Staged in Atlantic City," *Chicago Defender*, August 31, 1968, 18.

271 *"NAACP to Hold 'Black Pageant'"*: "NAACP to Hold 'Black Pageant,'" *Bridgewater* (New Jersey) *Courier-News*, August 29, 1968, 25.

272 *"only make it harder"*: "Creation of Miss Black America Pageant Assailed by Rival Contest," *Philadelphia Inquirer*, September 1, 1968, 14.

273 *"Anytime a black man says"*: "Creation of Miss Black America Pageant," *Philadelphia Inquirer.*

273 *just "so unbelievable"*: Mrs. Marilyn W. B. Parker to Mr. Gloster B. Current, September 4, 1968, part 29, series A: Field Staff Files, 1965–72, reel 18, NAACP Papers.

29. BRA BURNERS PLAN MISS AMERICA PROTEST

275 *"The Miss America action looks"*: Kathie Amatniek to Ros Baxandall, September 2, 1968, box 16, folder 10, Rosalyn Baxandall Papers.

276 *"these angry young women"*: "Scenes," *Village Voice,* August 29, 1968, 10.

277 *"Rap Brown's lawyer"*: Leonard Lyons, "The Lyons Den," *New York Post,* August 31, 1968, 27.

277 *"Why don't you see"*: "In Our Time": Transcript of Interview with Lindsy Van Gelder, 1994, box 29, folder 13, p. 3, Susan Brownmiller Papers.

278 *"of the same generation"*: "In Our Time": Van Gelder Interview, box 29, folder 13, p. 6, Susan Brownmiller Papers.

278 *"Lighting a match"*: Lindsy Van Gelder, "Bra Burners Plan Miss America Protest," *New York Post,* September 4, 1968, n.p.

278 *"'bra burning' as a possible"*: "Bra Burning Considered as Protest," *Corpus Christie Caller,* September 4, 1986, 4A.

278 *a "cop out"*: Ros Baxandall to Kathie Amatniek, September 2, 1968, box 16, folder 10, Rosalyn Baxandall Papers.

279 *Bra burning was all the news*: "Bra Burning Considered as Protest," *Corpus Christie Caller;* "'Bra Bonfire' Bids Lack of Support for Pageant Ideals," *Daily Reporter* (Wellsville, New York), September 4, 1968.

279 *Miss Colorado sought a mate*: Robert A. Dobkin, "Contestants Know What They Want," *Ithaca Journal,* September 4, 1968, 10.

279 *"Women are to strike"*: "Burn Your Bras for Freedom," *Daily Mirror* (UK), September 5, 1968, 3.

30. WALKING AND SMILING

280 *"tiny and tantalizing"*: Frank Prendergast, "First Pageant Girl Arrives," *Atlantic City Press,* August 31, 1968, 1.

281 *"taken into all of the"*: Evan Smith, "Betty Buckley, On Singing for Her Supper," *Texas Monthly,* September 2006, https://www.texasmonthly.com/arts-entertainment/betty-buckley/.

282 *"shape up or ship out"*: "Miss America Advises Contestants to Work," *Boston Globe,* September 3, 1968, 16.

283 *"an All-American boy"*: Barbara Carlson, "Feminist Liberators Would Make Miss America Honest Women," *Hartford Courant,* September 5, 1968, 24.

31. THEY SOUND LIKE US

284 *"With Humphrey and Fascist"*: "Humphrey Enters Picketed Hotel, *New York Times,* September 2, 1968, 20.

285 *"Money: leaflets"*: Cindy Cisler to Ti-Grace Atkinson, August 30, 1968, box 32, folder 14, Ti-Grace Atkinson Papers (emphasis in original).

285 *"All I remember was Cindy"*: "In Our Time": Transcript of Interview with Barbara Mehrof, 1994, box 28, folder 1, p. 10, Susan Brownmiller Papers.

285 *"The protesters have no"*: "Against Beauty Show," *St. Joseph* (Missouri) *News-Press,* September 5, 1968, 1.

286 *"They've protested napalm"*: Pauline Tai, "Miss America Pageant Chosen as the Latest Target of Protesters," *Wall Street Journal,* September 6, 1968, 4.

287 *"I'll buy the tickets"*: "In Our Time": Transcript of Interview with Alix Kates Shulman, 1994, box 29, folder 3, pp. 23–24, Susan Brownmiller Papers.

287 *"They're having a meeting"*: "In Our Time": Shulman Interview, box 29, folder 3, pp. 1–2, Susan Brownmiller Papers.

32. WHY WE'RE HERE

288 *"a particular standard of"*: Barbara Carlson, "14 Gain Semi-Finals in Black Beauty Contest," *Hartford Courant,* September 7, 1968, 11.

289 *"not a bourgeois thing"*: Carlson, "14 Gain Semi-Finals."

289 *"Pride is the basic"*: John Katz, "Pageant Director Seeks to Instill Black Pride," *Atlantic City Press,* September 7, 1968, 1.

290 *for "riot prevention"*: "NAACP Eyes Preventative Riot Program," *Afro American,* July 1, 1967, 12.

290 *"a black woman could look"*: Katz, "Pageant Director Seeks to Instill Black Pride."

291 *"I didn't have the time"*: Sue Cronk, "DC Girl Is Runner-up to Miss Black America," *Washington Post,* September 9, 1968, B2.

291 *"the beginning of the Miss Black"*: Cronk, "DC Girl Is Runner-up."

292 *"How would you react"*: William White, "8 Girls Named Finalists in Black America Pageant," September 7, 1968, n.p.

33. COME LIBERATE ATLANTIC CITY

293 *"spending a year as"*: Robert Dobkin, "Has-Been at 21—But No Regrets," *Uniontown Morning Herald,* September 4, 1968, 28.

295 *"the acid taste of"*: Robin Morgan, *The Word of a Woman: Feminist Dispatches, 1968–1992* (W. W. Norton, 1992), 21–22.

295 *"I had to work"*: "In Our Time": Transcript of Interview with Irene Peslikis, 1994, box 28, folder 9, Susan Brownmiller Papers.

295 *"Well, that's not such a happy"*: "In Our Time": Transcript of Interview with Anne Forer, 1995, box 26, folder 13, p. 5, Susan Brownmiller Papers.

296 *"was passing through"*: "In Our Time": Transcript of Interview with Alix Kates Shulman, 1994, box 28, folder 9, p. 17, Susan Brownmiller Papers.

296 *It was the sound of Tin Pan Alley*: "Protest songs for the Miss America protest," September 7, 1968, Women's Print Culture Collection.

296 *"You know what will happen"*: "In Our Time": Transcript of Interview with Donna Allen, 1995, box 25, folder 5, p. 6, Susan Brownmiller Papers.

297 *"more Left and a little less"*: "In Our Time": Transcript of Interview with Charlotte Bunch, 1997, box 25, folder 17, p. 20, Susan Brownmiller Papers.

297 *"SLAVERY EXISTS"*: "Slavery Exists: Miss America Is a Slave," flyer, September 7, 1968, Women's Print Culture Collection.

299 *"This huge clopping" sound*: Carol Giardina, interview by Stuart Landers, November 11, 1992, p. 26, Samuel Proctor Oral History Program, George A. Smathers Libraries Digital Collections, University of Florida.

34. CAN MAKEUP COVER THE WOUNDS OF OUR OPPRESSION?

300 *when Amatniek spotted*: "In Our Time": Transcript of Interview with Alix Kates Shulman, 1994, box 28, folder 9, p. 20, Susan Brownmiller Papers.

301 *"Okay, darling"*: Eleanor Fischer, "First Protests at the Miss America Pageant," September 8, 1968, WNYC/WNPR Archives and Preservation, https://www.wnyc.org/story/first-protest-miss-america-pageant-1968/.

302 *"I think we probably"*: "In Our Time": Transcript of Interview with Charlotte Bunch, 1997, box 25, folder 17, p. 19, Susan Brownmiller Papers.

303 *"I'm for beauty contests"*: Charlotte Curtis, "Miss America Pageant Is Picketed by 100 Women," *New York Times,* September 8, 1968, 8D.

303 *Demonstration Information Sheet*: Demonstration Information Sheet, September 7, 1968, Women's Print Culture Collection.

305 *"The men acted as"*: Susan Brownmiller, *In Our Time: Memoir of a Revolution* (Dial Press, 1999), 39.

305 *liberationists were "vulgar"*: Curtis, "Miss America Pageant Is Picketed."

305 *"They just have to have something"*: Fischer, "First Protests at Miss America Pageant."

306 *"Yessiree, boys"*: The events described in this section are drawn from "Up Against the Wall Miss America," 1968, Newsreel (collective), Internet Archive, https://archive.org/details/upagainstthewallmissamerica.

307 *"Down with these shoes!"*: Curtis, "Miss America Pageant Is Picketed."

308 *"nice-looking young man"*: Susan Sutheim, "Radical Women Protest Ugly Pageant," *Guardian,* September 14, 1968, Women's Print Culture Collection.

309 *"We sharply differentiate"*: Comments here from Al Marks are drawn from Fischer, "First Protests at Miss America Pageant."

310 *"Don't go, Mrs. Alton"*: Elizabeth B. Alton and Heather Perez, *Beauty Is Never Enough* (South Jersey Culture & History Center, 2021), 325.

310 *"had to look like ladies"*: "In Our Time": Shulman interview, box 29, folder 3, p. 24, Susan Brownmiller Papers.

35. ONCE UPON A SOMEDAY

312 Sponsoring Miss America stinks: Peggy Dobbins, "Women in Time Change History," Peggy Dobbins website, n.d., https://peggydobbins.net/aboutpeggydobbins.html.

312 *"Is this your America?"*: John L. Boucher, "Unbeautiful Scent leads to 'Seizure,'" *Atlantic City Press,* September 8, 1968, 2.

313 *"over 200,000 civic"*: This description of pageant events is drawn from Miss America Pageant 1969, telecast, September 7, 1968 (commercials included), YouTube, https://youtu.be/KKmHdXkGLzM.

315 *help "her girl"*: Elizabeth B. Alton and Heather Perez, *Beauty Is Never Enough* (South Jersey Culture & History Center, 2021), 217.

319 *described by one journalist as*: Eleanor Fischer, "First Protests at the Miss America Pageant," September 8, 1968, WNYC/WNPR Archives and Preservation, https://www.wnyc.org/story/first-protest-miss-america-pageant-1968/.

36. THIS IS BETTER THAN BEING MISS AMERICA

322 *no one seemed tired*: "1968 Throwback: Miss Black America," September 7, 1968, partial film, Hezakya Newz & Films, YouTube, https://youtu.be/cA1vMoBzd3o?si=1wevMAbHmWCilhFK.

323 *Vivian Whitted, the contestant*: Delores Alexander, "A Midsummer Daydream in Harlem," *Newsday,* August 26, 1968, 1A.

324 *"I was accustomed to big"*: "Face to Face with Miss Black America," *Seventeen* 28, no. 3 (1969): 151.

324 *"That restaurant is integrated"*: Judy Klemesrud, "Along with Miss America, There's Now Miss Black America," *New York Times,* September 8, 1968, 54.

325 *"This is better than"*: Klemesrud, "Along with Miss America."

325 *"that Black beauty is equal"*: Interview with Saundra Williams by Eleanor Fischer, "First Protests at the Miss America Pageant," September 8, 1968, WNYC/WNPR Archives and Preservation, https://www.wnyc.org/story/first-protest-miss-america-pageant-1968/.

327 *"looked bored when asked"*: Klemesrud, "Along with Miss America."

327 *"More than anything"*: Susan Sutheim, "Radical Women Protest Ugly Pageant," *Guardian*, September 14, 1968, clipping, Women's Print Culture Collection.

327 *It was impossible to get*: Robin Morgan, *Saturday's Child: A Memoir* (W. W. Norton, 2001), 261.

328 *"How did you feel about"*: "Miss America Bounces Back from 2-Hour Sleep," *Springfield* (Massachusetts) *Union*, September 9, 1968, 8.

328 *several contestants took roses*: Barbara Carlson, "Rose Curtain Falls on 'Someday' Land," *Hartford Courant*, September 9, 1968, 1.

328 *similarly running on very little sleep*: NOW-NYC, *NOW in the News*, October 1968, box 42, folder 3, Rosalyn Baxandall Papers.

329 *"a 19-year old Philadelphian"*: Klemesrud, "Along with Miss America."

329 *"What matters about 18-year-old"*: Charlotte Curtis, "Along with Miss America, There's Now Miss Black America," *New York Times*, September 9, 1968, 54.

329 *"I like the play"*: E. Clifton Daniels to Charlotte Curtis, September 9, 1968, box 9, folder 4, Charlotte Curtis Papers.

330 *"a bouncy, natural blonde"*: "New Miss America Poised," *Lubbock* (Texas) *Avalanche-Journal*, September 9, 1968, 10.

330 *"admitted tomboy who"*: "Miss America Begins Reign," *Anderson* (Indiana) *Daily Bulletin*, September 9, 1968, 1.

37. THERE ARE NO UGLIES—ONLY UGLY BEAUTY STANDARDS

331 *"What right have you"*: Peter Babcock, "Meet the Women of the Revolution, 1969," *New York Times Sunday Magazine*, February 9, 1969, 34.

332 *"A group called 'Women's Liberation'"*: "Miss America '69 Begins Her Reign," *The Tennessean*, September 9, 1968, 5.

332 *"While I'm prepared to defend"*: Harriet Van Horne, "Female Firebrands," *New York Post*, September 9, 1968, clipping, Women's Print Culture Collection.

332 *"It is one thing to protest"*: Art Buchwald, "The Bra Burners," *New York Post*, September 12, 1968, clipping, Women's Print Culture Collection.

332 *"'No more Miss America'"*: "People: Sep 13, 1968," *Time*, September 13, 1968, https://content.time.com/time/subscriber/article/0,33009,838679-3,00.html.

332 *"The winner, a rival in black"*: "The Winner, a Rival in Black and Some Ribroast Ribbing," *Life* 65, no. 12 (September 20, 1968): 91–92.

333 *"my own sympathies were"*: Shana Alexander, "Hooray! Getting Back to Normal," *Life* 65, no.12 (September 20, 1968): 28.

334 *Sound came up first*: Alexander, "Hooray!"

334 *Like her fellow Vassar alum*: Leslie Hanscom, "Shana Alexander's Writing Follows Careful Research," *Huntsville* (Alabama) *Times*, December 22, 1976, 22.

335 *a title that incorporated a chant*: Susanne Giddens, "No More Miss America: Atlantic City Is a Town with Class, They Raid Your Morals and Sell Your Ass," *New York Free Press*, September 1968, clipping, Women's Print Culture Collection.

336 *"What to make of it all?"*: Susan Sutheim, "Radical Women Protest and Ugly Pageant," *Guardian*, September 14, 1968, clipping, Women's Print Culture Collection.

336 *"We have attended the Pageant itself"*: Robin Morgan, untitled post-pageant reflection, Women's Print Culture Collection.

337 *"We caused more havoc"*: Giddens, "No More Miss America."

337 *"The Miss America Pageant*: Robin Morgan's view of the demonstration's importance is drawn from Morgan, "Miss America Goes Down," *Rat*, October 3, 1968, clipping, Women's Print Culture Collection.

338 *Where else could one find*: Robin Morgan, "On Freedom for Women," *Liberation*, October 3, 1968, clipping, Women's Print Culture Collection.

38. I'M HERE BECAUSE I'M ANGRY

340 *"I guess I'm here because"*: The events described here, to end of section, are drawn from Meeting notes, undated, shortly after 1968 Miss America protest, series II:B, Redstockings Action Archives.

341 *she talked about it in interviews*: Barbara Raskin, "Miss America 1951: Rebel with a Cause," *Mansfield* (Ohio) *News Journal*, November 26, 1969.

341 *"were transvestites from all over"*: Renata Adler, "Screen 'Queen' of Drag Is Crowned," *New York Times*, June 18, 1968.

342 *"itself a camp phenomenon"*: Review of *The Queen*, *Women's Wear Daily*, June 18, 1968.

342 *"Any dumb broad"*: Roger Ebert, "The Queen," film review, August 5, 1969, Roger Ebert website, https://www.rogerebert.com/reviews/the-queen-1969.

342 *"Benefit Showing for Women's Liberation"*: Roxanne Dunbar-Ortiz, *Outlaw Woman: A Memoir of the War Years, 1960–1975* (City Lights Books, 2001), 126–127.

343 *"was rigged for white women"*: Ricky Tucker, *And the Category is . . . Inside New York's Vogue, House, and Ballroom Community* (Beacon Press, 2022), chap. 2.

343 *"I have the* right *to show"*: *The Queen*, documentary directed by Frank Simon (Grove Press, 1968), 68 min.

344 *carried "a possible sentence"*: Judith Duffett, "WLM vs. Miss America," *Voice of the Women's Liberation Movement*, vol. 1, no. 7, October 1968, 1.

344 NOW in the News *included*: NOW-NYC, *NOW in the News*, October 1968, box 42, folder 3, Rosalyn Baxandall Papers.

344 *"I promise to put on the"*: David Suskind's Promissory Card, box 18, folder 7, Rosalyn Baxandall Papers.

344 *"There are some women"*: "In Our Time": Transcript of Interview with Barbara Mehrhof, 1994, box 28, folder 11, Susan Brownmiller Papers.

345 *"So odd . . . [she was] very pretty"*: "In Our Time": Transcript of Interview with Rosalyn Baxandall, 1994, box 25, folder 10, Susan Brownmiller Papers.

345 *"No action taken in the"*: Carol Hanisch, "What Can Be Learned: A Critique of the Miss America Protest," November 27, 1968, Women's Print Culture Collection.

346 *"Young, Black, and Beautiful"*: "'Young, Black, and Beautiful' Organize," *LA Times*, October 31, 1968), C4.

347 *"She hoped they would not"*: Elizabeth Shelton, "Friedan: Feminism Faces a Backlash," *Washington Post*, October 23, 1968, C2.

347 *"Officialdom of NOW"*: Florynce Kennedy resignation letter, Florynce Kennedy Papers.

39. BEAUTY QUEEN STUMPS

348 *as a "Nixon supporter"*: Nan Robertson, "The Old Georgia Names and New Money in Macon Are Strongly Behind Nixon," *New York Times*, October 31, 1968, 38.

348 *"in the escalating battle"*: Joseph Modzelewski, "Beauty Queen Stumps for Dad-in-Law Hubie," *New York Daily News*, August 16, 1968, 20.

349 *"Dear Judi—Donna"*: Marjorie Ford, *Sharing the Crown* (Publication Investments, 1971): 57.

349 *The couple's courtship*: Jack Bass and Marilyn W. Thompson, *Ol' Strom: An Unauthorized Biography of Strom Thurmond* (Taylor Publishing, 2001), chap. 19.
350 *"People were aghast"*: Bass and Thompson, *Ol' Strom.*
350 *"The sensation of breathing"*: Norman Mailer, *Miami and the Siege of Chicago: An Informal History of the Republican and Democratic Conventions* (World Publishing, 1968; repr. New York Review of Books, 2008), 1.
351 *"the most complicated production"*: "Week's Profile," *Broadcasting*, November 11, 1968, 101.
351 *"semi-forgery" of spontaneous*: Joe McGinnis, *The Selling of the President* (Simon & Schuster, 1969), chap. 13.
352 *"This is terrible"*: McGinnis, *The Selling of the President*, chap. 13.
352 *Clifton Daniels dropped a note*: Clifton Daniels to Charlotte Curtis, November 6, 1968, box 8, folder 1, Charlotte Curtis Papers.
353 *addressed to "Mr. Curtis"*: President-elect Richard Nixon to Mr. Charlotte Curtis, December 2, 1968, box 8, folder 1, Charlotte Curtis Papers.
353 *She and David already knew*: Julie Nixon Eisenhower, *Pat Nixon: The Untold Story* (Simon & Schuster, 1986), 257.
353 *"Senator Strom Thurmond, 66"*: "Nancy Moore Becomes Bride of Senator Strom Thurmond," *New York Times*, December 23, 1968, 51.

40. GIVE BACK THE VOTE

355 *Mehrhof went to visit Alice Paul*: "In Our Time": Transcript of Interview with Barbara Mehrhof, 1997, box 28, folder 1, pp. 29–34, Susan Brownmiller Papers.
356 *"Take her off the stage"*: Alice Echols, *Daring to Be Bad: Radical Feminism in America, 1967–1975* (University of Minnesota Press, 1989), 113–117.
356 *"Let's start talking about where"*: Joyce Antler, *Jewish Radical Feminism: Voices from the Women's Liberation Movement* (New York University Press, 2018), 129.
356 *"Shut Shulie up!"*: "In Our Time": Transcript of Interview with Marilyn Webb, 1994, box 29, folder 19, pp. 63–65, 83, Susan Brownmiller Papers.
357 *"If you ever make a speech"*: Marilyn Salzman Webb, "The Feminist," in Jeff Kisseloff, ed., *Generation on Fire: Voices of Protest from the 1960s, an Oral History* (University of Kentucky Press, 2007), 178.
357 *Webb would tell the story*: Marilyn S. Webb, "OOB and the Feminist Dream," in Ken Wachsberger, ed., *Insider Histories of the Vietnam Era Underground Press*, part 1 (Michigan State University Press, 2011), 188.
357 *"Debra is not Miss America anymore"*: "She's Mrs. Miles Now," *Iola Register*, January 29, 1969, 4.
358 *"A beauty queen who"*: "Bad Advice Suspected," *St. Joseph Herald Press*, February 15, 1969, 2.

41. LET'S HEAR FROM SOME *REAL* EXPERTS

362 *"I'm here because I'm in favor"*: "New York: Women Disrupt Hearing on Legal Reform of Abortion Law Demanding Complete Repeal," AP Archive, YouTube, https://www.youtube.com/watch?v=S-Ql1-fsjMU&list=PPSV.
363 *"Okay, folks, now it's time"*: The description of the Department of Public Health meeting is drawn from Ellen Willis, "Hearing," Department of Public Health, *New Yorker*, February 15, 1969, https://www.newyorker.com/magazine/1969/02/22/hearing.
364 *"Gals Squeal for Repeal"*: "Gal's Squeal for Repeal, Abort State Hearing," *New York Daily News*, February 14, 1969, 5.
364 *The panelists prepared no*: Susan Brownmiller, "Everywoman's Abortions, The Oppressor Is Man," *Village Voice*, March 27, 1969, n.p.

365 *"There's no reason to scream"*: "In Our Time": Transcript of Interview with Rosalyn Baxandall, 1994, box 25, folder 10, Susan Brownmiller Papers.

366 *"Slightly put off by my"*: Susan Brownmiller, *In Our Time: Memoir of a Revolution* (Dial Press, 1999), 5.

366 *I didn't begin my active life*: "Gloria Steinem: First Feminist," *New York*, April 6, 1998, https://nymag.com/nymetro/news/people/features/2438/.

366 *"becoming sort of a revolutionary"*: Gloria Steinem, "After Black Power, Women's Liberation," *New York*, April 4, 1969, https://nymag.com/news/politics/46802/.

367 *"combines the hidden qualities"*: Gloria Steinem, "A Bunny Tale," *Show*, May 1963, 90, 92, 94, 118; Gloria Steinem, "Bunny Tale Part II," *Show*, June 1963, 66–68, 110, 112, 114–116, 129.

42. A POSITIVE PROTEST

368 *"What a night!"*: "Face to Face with Miss Black America," *Seventeen* 28, no. 3 (March 1969): 151.

369 *Williams shared her frustrations*: Peyton Gray Jr., "On Camera Review," *Philadelphia Tribune*, March 18, 1969, 6.

370 *"is not only a protest against"*: "City to Get Miss Black America Pageant," *Newsday*, March 19, 1969, 3A.

371 *"to point out"*: J. Morris Anderson, *Recipes for Black Togetherness* (Consolidated Black Press, 1969), 22–25.

373 *After a tin-eared opener*: Senator Edward W. Brooke, Commencement Address, Wellesley College, May 31, 1969, https://www1.wellesley.edu/events/commencement/archives/1969commencement/commencementaddress

373 *"speak to them and for them"*: Hillary Rodham, Commencement Address, Wellesley College, May 31, 1969, https://www1.wellesley.edu/events/commencement/archives/1969commencement/studentspeech.

374 *"Senator Brooke Upstaged"*: James Stack, "Senator Brooke Upstaged at Wellesley Commencement," *Boston Globe*, June 1, 1969, 1.

374 *"Park Ridge Girl Raps Brooke"*: "Park Ridge Girl Raps Brooke," *Chicago Tribune*, June 2, 1969, 5.

374 *Five years ago, blond Hillary*: Raymond R. Coffey, "One Coed Who Won't Give Up on World Gone Haywire," *Des Moines Tribune*, June 4, 1969, 4.

375 *"Had to go for nothing more"*: Ben Cosgrove, "Hillary Clinton's First National Splash, Life 1969," *Life*, June 1969, https://www.life.com/people/life-with-hillary-portraits-of-a-wellesley-grad-1969/.

377 *"Nothing would give me"*: "Television in Review," *Pampa Daily News*, August 15, 1969, 12.

377 *"Last year's demonstration was good"*: The description of the 1969 statement is drawn from Miss America demonstration press release, August 28, 1969, Women's Print Culture Collection.

379 *"At last year's pageant"*: Mark E. Heisler and Stephen Prisament, "Pageant Officials Vow to Ward off Picketing," *Atlantic City Press*, September 4, 1969, 17.

380 *Al Marks gave an affidavit*: Albert A. Marks, Civil Action Affidavit, *The Miss America Pageant, a Corporation of the State of New Jersey, Plaintiff, vs. Women's Liberation Movement et al. Defendants*, September 4, 1969, Women's Print Culture Collection.

380 *"It appears that once again"*: Heisler and Prisament, "Pageant Officials Vow to Ward off Picketing."

381 *pageant "with a facelift"*: Janet Staihar, "Beauty Pageant Gets a Facelift in Format," *Hartford Courant*, September 1, 1969, 21.

381 *"When a girl deserves to win it"*: "Pamela Eldred Is an Ideal Miss America," *Ironwood Daily Globe*, September 9, 1969, 12.

382 *"I'd grab her by the throat"*: "The Feminists vs. the Contestants," *Time*, January 24, 2009, https://content.time.com/time/specials/packages/printout/0,29239,1873790_1873792_1873787,00.html.

382 *"feminine, not feminist"*: Myra McPherson, "The League of Pussycats," *Washington Post*, November 30, 1969, 137.

383 *"Silent Femajority"*: Arleen Abrahams, "Feminist Group Wants to Accentuate the Positive," *Arizona Republic*, November 30, 1969, 16M.

383 *"What could be more Now"*: "Pageant Chooses Most Beautiful Bunny of All," *Lake Geneva Regional News*, November 20, 1969, 1.

383 *"not the generally accepted idea"*: Quoted in Elizabeth Fraterrigo, *Playboy and the Making of the Good Life in Modern America* (Oxford University Press, 2009), 143.

384 *that she was "in sympathy"*: Wayne Lee, "Kansas Women Ready to Fight for Three-Letter Word," *Hutchinson News*, December 20, 1969, 1.

43. WOMEN IN REVOLT

385 *"Women's Liberation is hot stuff"*: Susan Brownmiller, "'Sisterhood Is Powerful': A Member of the Women's Liberation Movement Explains What It's All About," *New York Times Sunday Magazine*, March 15, 1970, 27.

385 *Robin Morgan would later quip*: Robin Morgan, *Saturday's Child: A Memoir* (W. W. Norton, 2001), 289.

385 *"the good guys who think"*: Robin Morgan, "Goodbye to All That," *Rat*, February 6, 1970, 6–7.

386 *"Women's Lib: The War on 'Sexism'"*: Helen Dudar, *"Women's Lib: The War on 'Sexism,'" Newsweek*, March 23, 1970, 71–74, 78.

387 *"I have spent years rejecting"*: Dudar, "Women's Lib."

388 *Five days later, Betty Friedan*: Betty Friedan, *It Changed My Life: Writings on the Women's Movement* (Harvard University Press, 1998).

389 *Friedan talked of history*: Friedan, *It Changed My Life.*

389 *"writer-activist-antiwar-gorgeous bachelor girl"*: Lynn Sherr, "Gloria Steinem Is One of the Beautiful People She Writes about—and She Does Lead an Interesting and Exciting Life," *Rocky Mountain Telegram*, April 19, 1970, 29.

391 *"Women are out waging"*: Charlotte Curtis, WXQR commentary, August 26, 1970, box 18, folder 4, Charlotte Curtis Papers.

392 *"whose slogan is 'Purr, Baby, Purr'"*: Judy Klemesrud, "Women on the March," *New York Times*, August 39, 1970, 4.

392 *"You can be feminine and liberated"*: Lucianne Goldberg and Jeannie Sakol, *Purr, Baby, Purr* (Hawthorn Books, 1971).

392 *"The long-overdue answer"*: Goldberg and Sakol, *Purr, Baby, Purr*, paperback ed. (Pinnacle Books, 1972).

393 *"contest officially began last year"*: Curtis, WXQR commentary.

393 *"a delicate subject for"*: Chuck Noland, "Iowa Sending First Black to Atlantic City Contest," *Mason City* (Iowa) *Globe-Gazette*, June 15, 1970, 8.

394 *"I couldn't be more delighted"*: Paul Learn, "The Good Odds for Miss Iowa," *Des Moines Sunday Register*, September 6, 1970, 6.

394 *"They can't have a girl"*: "Miss Montana Renounces Throne," *Atlantic City Press*, July 18, 1970, 22.

395 *"a good long look at the whole picture"*: "All's Fair in Love, War Talks for Pageant," *Atlantic City Press*, July 23, 1970, n.d.

395 *"I am proud of the US because"*: Lesly Jones, "Back from Vietnan [*sic*]," *New York Amsterdam News,* March 21, 1970, 7.
396 *Iowa was making history twice*: Learn, "The Good Odds for Miss Iowa," 6.
396 *"speaks for Black women"*: Nicholas von Hoffman, "The Beauties," *Washington Post,* December 9, 1970, C1.
396 *"a little more pride"*: Jon Katz, "Pageant's First Black Shuns 'Special' Tag," *Atlantic City Press,* September 7, 1970, 1.
397 *Essentially, Mr. Marks seems to agree*: Curtis, WXQR commentary.
398 *"Iowa could not have selected"*: Paul Learn, "'Inside' the Miss America Pageant," *Atlantic City Press,* September 20, 1970, 2.
399 *"The racial barrier fell"*: Learn, "'Inside' the Miss America Pageant."
399 *"You can take a good thing"*: "US Playboy's 'Bunny of the Year 1971,'" AP Archive, YouTube, https://www.youtube.com/watch?v=JCu34ycLlWk.
403 *"serious mistake" to over*: Patrick J. Buchanan to H. R. Haldeman, Briefing Paper, September 20, 1971, in Bruce Oudes, ed., *From the President: Richard Nixon's Secret Files* (Harper & Row, 1989), 320–323.
404 *"I figured ERA was something"*: Carol Felsenthal, *Sweetheart of the Silent Majority: A Biography of Phyllis Schlafly* (Doubleday, 1981), 240.

44. THE POWER OF THE POSITIVE WOMAN

405 *outlined her arguments*: "What's Wrong with 'Equal Rights' for Women?," *Phyllis Schlafly Report* 5, no. 7 (February 1972).
408 *"What better put-down"*: Sharon Cohen, "Warhol Film a Mixed Bag," *Tampa Tribune,* May 6, 1972, 6D.
408 *"grotesque parody of women's lib"*: Roy M. Close, "Warhol's Grotesque 'Women in Revolt' Limited in Concept," *Minneapolis Star,* April 5, 1972, 23B.
408 *"sudsy topical"*: "Warhol's Women Are Men," *Vogue* 159, no. 10 (1972): 134–135.
409 *"more than a beautiful smile"*: Prudy Taylor, "Miss Anita Bryant Knows Just Where Today's Action Is," *Fort Myers News Press,* February 5, 1971, B1.
410 *"the greatest secret for"*: Norman Vincent Peale, *The Power of Positive Thinking* (Fawcett World Library, 1966), 55.
410 *"all manner of negativism"*: Peale, *The Power of Positive Thinking,* 45.
411 *"plan, prepare, and pray"*: Vonda Kay Van Dyke, *Reach Up* (Fleming H. Revell, 1971), 105–106.
412 *The positive approach of these*: Marjorie Ford, *Sharing the Crown* (Publication Investments, 1971), 132–134.
412 *"not lost the feminine touch"*: The Miss America Pageant Souvenir Program, September 4–10, 1972, n.p.
413 *"Terry Anne Meeuwsen is the All-American"*: Nickii Elrod, "No. 1 Beauty Proudly Proclaims Faith," *Memphis Commercial Appeal,* November 2, 1972, 24.
413 *"What in the world has happened to"*: H. R. Haldeman to Dwight Chapin, July 27, 1972, White House Special Files: Contested Materials Collection, box 46, folder 22, Richard Nixon Presidential Library and Museum, Yorba Linda, California.
414 *"more personality and charisma"*: "Miss America 1973 Cashing in Big," *Rockford* (Illinois) *Morning Star,* November 28, 1972, 9.
414 *"What we need in America today"*: Michael Couture, "Anita Bryant Tells of Her Life, Faith," *Boca Raton News,* July 25, 1972, 9.
415 *"Miss Bryant firmly believes"*: Crispin James, "Anita Bryant Expresses Faith in God's Guidance," *Austin American,* November 20, 1972, 2.

416 *Accept, Admire, Adapt, and Appreciate*: Marabel Morgan *The Total Woman* (Pocket Books, 1973).

416 *"femininity tactics"*: Judy Klemesrud, "Schlafly Tactics Served Warm from the Oven," *Chicago Tribune*, January 1, 1976, H3.

417 *"'sexy' details"*: "Writer Declares She Was GOP Spy in McGovern Camp," *New York Times*, August 19, 1973, 1, 44.

419 *Redstockings has called*: Redstockings, "The Censored Section of Feminist Revolution: Restore Your 'Abridged' Book: Insert This" (Redstockings, Inc., 1975).

419 *first exposed Steinem's role*: Neil Sheehan, "Foundations Linked to CIA Are Found to Subsidize Other Youth Organizations," *New York Times*, February 16, 1967, 26.

420 *To many people*: Redstockings, "The Censored Section of Feminist Revolution.

421 *"liberal, nonviolent and honorable"*: Michael Kazin, "Dancing to the CIA's Tune: The Secret Funding of American Artists and Intellectuals in the '50s and '60s," *Washington Post*, January 27, 2008, 5.

421 *"It's so interesting now"*: John Leland, "Showgirls, Pastrami, and Candor: Gloria Steinem's New York," *New York Times*, October 7, 2016, MB1.

421 *"intimate involvement with the radical"*: Craig Phelon, "Schlafly Attacks Betty, Nominated for Honor," *Galesburg* (Illinois) *Register-Mail*, August 26, 1976, 4.

421 *"Front for Radicals and Lesbians"*: "Front for Radicals and Lesbians," *Phyllis Schlafly Report*, August 1977, 1.

422 *"The Positive Woman in America"*: Phyllis Schlafly, *The Power of the Positive Woman* (Jove/Harcourt Brace Jovanovich, 1977), 29.

423 *it was in the tradition of motherhood*: "Foes Cook Up Pie for Schlafly," *Chicago Tribune*, April 17, 1977, 2.

423 *"sowing the seeds of positivity"*: "Miss Black America to Go on 'Live' TV Special," *Atlanta Daily World*, July 14, 1977, 6.

424 *"a positive protest initially"*: Katharine Conger Kane, "The Beautiful Ones Parade on TV," *Washington Post*, September 4, 1977, 257.

424 *"he didn't look to support"*: "Black Pageant Sparks Debate Among Lib, Ethnic Elements," *Hartford Courant*, September 24, 1977, 19.

424 *another figure of 1968, Robin Morgan*: Charitey Simmons, "Success, Dissent Crown Black Pageant," *Chicago Tribune*, September 15, 1977, A1.

424 *"I believe that positive attitudes"*: "Beauty Credits Her Simple Philosophy," *Los Angeles Times*, August 25, 1977, WS1.

425 *"Oath of Positivity"*: "Miss Black America Official Creed Ready," *New York Amsterdam News*, April 22, 1978, B7.

425 *"Nobody knows how I vote"*: Nick Thimmesch, "Pearl Bailey Is Nixon's 'Ambassador of Love,'" *Portland* (Maine) *Evening Express*, November 21, 1970, 6.

426 *"Pray more, and believe"*: "Miss Black America Tells World to Pray More in '78," *Atlanta Daily World*, January 27, 1978, 3.

426 *"To help Miss Black America"*: Stephen J. Morgan, "Miss Black America Reveals Her Secrets of Positivity," *Danville* (Pennsylvania) *News*, August 17, 1978, 11.

426 *"After 400 years"*: "Miss Black America Pageant Proclaims Black Woman's Day," *Atlanta Daily World*, July 27, 1978, 3.

427 *"I'm not a feminist in any way"*: Louise Montgomery, "Phyllis George," *Miami Herald*, January 15, 1976, 31.

427 *"I'm Phyllis George"*: "Glamour in Kentucky: Will Phyllis George Be First Lady?," *Sunday World Herald* (Omaha), May 20, 1979, 3A.

428 *"violated my most precious"*: Rebecca Pflugfelder, "Singer Anita Bryant Files for Divorce," *Longview* (Texas) *Daily News*, May 23, 1980, 4B.

429 *"Spare me the Saturday night"*: Ellen Goodman, "Anita Bryant Chose to Obey Conscience," *Ann Arbor News*, June 1, 1980, 14.

429 *What has happened*: Andrea Dworkin, *Right Wing Women* (TarcherPerigee, 1983).

430 *"Me—a beauty queen?"*: Vanessa Williams and Helen Williams with Irene Zutzell, *You Have No Idea: A Famous Daughter, Her No-Nonsense Mother, and How They Survived Pageants, Hollywood, Love, Loss, and Each Other* (Avery, 2012).

431 *"Many Believe Black May Win"*: Barton Jones, "Many Believe Black May Win," *Atlantic City Press*, September 13, 1983, 1.

433 *"our new Miss America is Vanessa Williams"*: "Vanessa Williams Says Focus Should Not Be on Her Race," *Atlantic City Press*, September 19, 1983, 10.

433 *"wonderful thing for our nation"*: Courtland Milloy, "Miss America: Is Her Beauty Black?" *Flint* (Michigan) *Journal*, September 25, 1983, 18.

433 *"At times I get annoyed"*: "Black Is Beautiful," *Appleton* (Wisconsin) *Post-Crescent*, September 24, 1983, 4.

434 *"People aren't getting used to"*: "Miss America Speaks Her Mind," *Westchester Reporter Dispatch*, September 19, 1983, 12.

434 *"I am very much in favor of the ERA"*: "Miss America Gives Ideas on Politics," *Alabama Journal*, October 19, 1983, 9.

434 *"I think it's fantastic"*: Vanessa Williams and Helen Williams with Irene Zutzell, *You Have No Idea*, xx.

436 *"For 10 months, Vanessa Williams"*: John Froonjian, "Three Days to Get out of Crown," *Atlantic City Press*, July 21, 1984, 1.

436 *"Last Friday, I heard"*: Rick Hampson, "Vanessa Williams Gives up Her Miss America Crown," *Gettysburg Times*, July 24, 1984, 4.

438 *"By promoting these pornographic"*: "Feminists Castigate Penthouse," *Atlantic City Press*, July 24, 1984, 16.

438 *"Last fall, Miss Williams"*: Ellen Goodman, "Vanessa Williams Made Two Mistakes," *Tampa Bay Times*, July 27, 1984, 28.

439 *"To describe the Miss America"*: Patrick J. Buchanan, "In Defense of the Miss America Pageant," *Phiadelphia Inquirer*, July 28, 1984, 7.

441 *"Vanessa is a lesbian nudie!"*: "She's Still Miss America Despite Photos in Hometown," *Evening Telegram*, July 21, 1984, 10.

442 *"I wonder what it was"*: The account of Winfrey's interview with Williams is drawn from *Oprah: Behind the Scenes*, featuring Vanessa Williams, November 5, 1992, YouTube, https://youtu.be/WjGMUkhspUs?si=AdSh4hs1dbeS0gUr.

443 *"I didn't know what it meant"*: Winfrey interview with Williams.

445 *"We are in the midst"*: Naomi Wolf, *The Beauty Myth: How Images of Beauty Are Used Against Women* (Anchor Books, 1991), 10.

446 *Elect me, and you get*: Patrick J. Buchanan, "Address to the Republican National Convention," August 17, 1992, Houston, Buchanan.org website, http://buchanan.org/blog/1992-republican-national-convention-speech-148.

EPILOGUE: THE NASTY, THE FIERCE, AND THE FACES OF MAR-A-LAGO

447 *"You have lived your life"*: "Miss America Organization's Public Apology to Vanessa Williams: Secrets of Miss America," A&E Network, July 25, 2023, YouTube, https://www.youtube.com/watch?v=Ul5WR09vE0c.

448 *"I'd already changed"*: Yashar Ali, "The Miss America Emails: How the Pageant's CEO Really Talks About The Winners," *HuffPost,* December 21, 2017, https://www.huffpost.com/entry/miss-america-ceo-emails_n_5a3bd266e4b025f99e153fdb.

449 *"We sincerely regret and apologize"*: Molly Redden, "Fox Settles with Gretchen Carlson over Roger Ailes Sexual Harassment Claims," *Guardian,* September 6, 2016, https://www.theguardian.com/media/2016/sep/06/fox-news-gretchen-carlson-settlement-roger-ailes.

449 *"He called this woman"*: Lucia Graves, "Alicia Maschado, Miss Universe, Weight-Shamed by Trump, Speaks for Clinton," *Guardian,* September 28, 2016, https://www.theguardian.com/us-news/2016/sep/27/alicia-machado-miss-universe-weight-shame-trump-speaks-out-clinton.

451 *"I was definitely not"*: Background information on Carlson is drawn from Gretchen Carlson, *Getting Real* (Viking, 2015).

451 *"chunky," a "God-clutcher"*: Wayne Goldman, *Hope & Glory* (Villard Books, 1990), 247, 287.

452 *"Miss Piggy won the crown"*: Goldman, *Hope & Glory,* 297.

452 *"I'm the Miss America you"*: Carlson, *Getting Real,* 2.

452 *"I like to joke that"*: Carlson, *Getting Real,* 215.

453 *"The National Organization for Women"*: Carlson, *Getting Real,* 6.

453 *"We are no longer"*: "Miss America Eliminates Swimsuits, Won't Judge on Looks," CBS News, June 5, 2018, https://www.cbsnews.com/news/miss-america-2018-pageant-swimsuit-competition-gretchen-carlson-today-2018-06-05./

454 *"Miss America will represent*: "Miss America Eliminates Swimsuits," CBS News.

455 *"Critics can, and will"*: Phyllis Schlafly, Ed Martin, and Brett M. Decker, *The Conservative Case for Donald Trump* (Regnery, 2016), chap. 6.

456 *The Atlantic City Women's Chamber of Commerce*: Miss Atlantic City Pageant, 1982, sponsored by the Atlantic City Women's Chamber of Commerce, October 4, 1982, Miss America Collection, Atlantic City Free Public Library, Atlantic City, New Jersey.

456 *"Well, I'll tell you the funniest"*: Caitlin Yilek, "Trump Told Stern He Walked Backstage When Beauty Queens Were Naked," *The Hill,* October 9, 2016, https://thehill.com/blogs/ballot-box/presidential-races/300093-trump-confirms-he-walked-backstage-when-beauty-queens/mlite/.

458 *"We watched, crowded around"*: Jill Louis, "The Sisters of Alpha Kappa Alpha Sorority Knew All Along That Kamala Harris Was a Winner," *Andscape,* November 7, 2020, https://andscape.com/features/the-sisters-of-alpha-kappa-alpha-sorority-knew-all-along-that-kamala-harris-was-a-winner/.

459 *"intended to signal"*: Inae Oh, "In Your Face: The Brutal Aesthetics of MAGA," *Mother Jones,* March, 17, 2025, https://www.motherjones.com/politics/2025/03/maralago-face-conservative-girl-makeup-brutal-aesthetics-of-maga-trump-gaetz-guilfoyle/.

ILLUSTRATION CREDITS

23 Ben Martin/Getty Images
33 David Gahr/Getty Images
57 Courtesy of *Denver Post* via Getty Images
64 Courtesy of Drake University Archives & Special Collections
67 The University of Southern Mississippi
86 Bev Grant/Getty Images
150 Courtesy of AP Photo/Sam Myers, File
161 CBS Photo Archive/Getty Images
167 Afro American Newspapers/Gado/Getty Images
170 Courtesy of the Library of Congress
172 © Press of Atlantic City
217 Michael Ochs Archives/Getty Images
244 Bev Grant/Getty Images
244 Bev Grant/Getty Images
267 Ron Galella/Ron Galella Collection via Getty Images
298 Robin Morgan Papers, David M. Rubenstein Rare Book & Manuscript Library, Duke University
302 Alix Kates Shulman Papers, David M. Rubenstein Rare Book & Manuscript Library, Duke University. Photograph copyright Alix Kates Shulman; used with permission.
302 Alix Kates Shulman Papers, David M. Rubenstein Rare Book & Manuscript Library, Duke University. Photograph copyright Alix Kates Shulman; used with permission.
304 Bev Grant/Getty Images
307 Bev Grant/Getty Images
308 Bev Grant/Getty Images
318 Bev Grant/Getty Images
320 Bev Grant/Getty Images
326 Courtesy of AP Photo/File
379 Robin Morgan Papers, David M. Rubenstein Rare Book & Manuscript Library, Duke University
390 Courtesy of AP Photo
397 Photo by Archive Photos/Getty Images
398 AP Photo
422 AP Photo/File
431 Photo courtesy of Bettmann/Getty Images
455 Courtesy of Bettmann/Getty Images

INDEX

Note: Page numbers in italics indicate figures. Page numbers followed by n refer to footnotes.

ABOUT THE AUTHOR

MICKI McELYA is a professor of history at the University of Connecticut, specializing in the histories of women, gender, race, and sexuality in the United States from the Civil War to the present, with an emphasis on political culture and memory. Her most recent book, *The Politics of Mourning: Death and Honor in Arlington National Cemetery,* was a finalist for the Pulitzer Prize and received a number of other accolades; her 2007 book, *Clinging to Mammy: The Faithful Slave in Twentieth-Century America,* was the co-winner of a 2007 Outstanding Book Award from the Gustavus Myers Center for the Study of Bigotry and Human Rights. McElya has written for *The Atlantic* and *Boston Review,* and her work has been featured in the *New York Times,* on NPR and MSNBC, in *The Nation* and *Elle,* and more. She is a graduate of Bryn Mawr College and New York University, and is a Distinguished Lecturer for the Organization of American histories. She lives in Cambridge, Massachusetts.

Avid Reader Press, an imprint of Simon & Schuster, is built on the idea that the most rewarding publishing has three common denominators: great books, published with intense focus, in true partnership. Thank you to the Avid Reader Press colleagues who collaborated on *Liberation Summer*, as well as to the hundreds of professionals in the Simon & Schuster advertising, audio, communications, design, ebook, finance, human resources, legal, marketing, operations, production, sales, supply chain, subsidiary rights, and warehouse departments whose invaluable support and expertise benefit every one of our titles.

Editorial
Amy Guay, *Associate Editor*

Jacket Design
Alison Forner, *Senior Art Director*
Clay Smith, *Senior Designer*
Sydney Newman, *Art Associate*

Marketing
Meredith Vilarello, *VP and Associate Publisher*
Emily Lewis, *Marketing Manager*
Kayla Dee, *Associate Marketing Manager*
Katya Wiegmann, *Marketing and Publishing Assistant*

Production
Allison Green, *Managing Editor*
Hana Handzija, *Managing Editorial Assistant*
Jessica Chin, *Senior Manager of Copyediting*
Amy Medeiros, *Production Editor*
Alicia Brancato, *Production Manager*
Ruth Lee-Mui, *Interior Text Designer*
Briana Skerpan, *Desktop Compositor*
Cait Lamborne, *Ebook Developer*

Publicity
Rhina Garcia, *Senior Publicist*
Eva Kerins, *Publicity Assistant*

Subsidiary Rights
Paul O'Halloran, *VP and Director of Subsidiary Rights*
Fiona Sharp, *Subsidiary Rights Coordinator*